MILES

0   10   20

PENNSYLVANIA

PICTORIAL RESEARCH BY BROMLEY C. PALAMOUNTAIN
"PARTNERS IN PROGRESS" BY
MARK H. DORFMAN, MARGARET O. KIRK,
AND JANET COURY SMITH

PRODUCED IN COOPERATION WITH THE
PENNSYLVANIA CHAMBER OF COMMERCE

WINDSOR PUBLICATIONS, INC.
NORTHRIDGE, CALIFORNIA

PENNSYLVANIA

KEYSTONE TO PROGRESS

An Illustrated History

By E. Willard Miller

Windsor Publications, Inc.—History Book Division
Publisher: John M. Phillips
Editorial Director: Teri Davis Greenberg
Design Director: Alexander D'Anca

Staff for *Pennsylvania: Keystone to Progress*
Senior Editor: Pamela Schroeder
Picture Editor/Researcher: Teri Davis Greenberg
Text Editor: Margaret Tropp
Editorial Development: Lynn Kronzek
Director, Corporate Biographies: Karen Story
Assistant Director, Corporate Biographies: Phyllis Gray
Editor, Corporate Biographies: Judith Hunter
Editorial Assistants: Kathy M. Brown, Laura Cordova,
   Marcie Goldstein, Marilyn Horn, Pat Pittman,
   Sharon L. Volz
Design and Layout: Ellen Ifrah
Sales Representatives, Corporate Biographies: Glen
   Edwards, Fred Smithco, Diane Murphy, Robert
   Ottenheimer, Marcia Cohen, Diana Garren, Evelyn
   Burian, Anita Toll, Marva Glazer

Library of Congress Cataloging-in-Publication Data

Miller, E. Willard (Eugene Willard), 1915-
   Pennsylvania, keystone to progress.

   "'Partners in progress' by Mark H. Dorfman,
Margaret O. Kirk, and Janet Coury Smith"
   "Produced in cooperation with the Pennsylvania
Chamber of Commerce.
   Bibliography: p. 624
   Includes index.
   1. Pennsylvania—Economic conditions. 2. Pennsyl-
vania—Industries—History. I. Pennsylvania Chamber of
Commerce. II. Title.
HC107.P4M55   1986   330.9768   86-9207

Frontispiece: *The Wakefield Manufacturing Company of Germantown produced hosiery. This lithograph by P.S. Duval dates from 1850. Courtesy, The Historical Society of Pennsylvania*

Endpapers: *A map showing all the counties in Pennsylvania was produced for this book by the Deasy Geographics Laboratory, Dept. of Geography, The Pennsylvania State University*

Page 7: *In 1800 canals seemed to be the answer to Pennsylvania's transportation needs. This depiction of a canal boat with some colorful characters aboard was made in 1828.*

CONTENTS

INTRODUCTION

The economy of Pennsylvania has been evolving for more than 300 years. During the Pioneer Era from the early settlements of the 1680s to about 1830, primary activities, especially agriculture, dominated the economy. Directly allied with agriculture was the exploitation of the forests and the early endeavors to extract the mineral wealth of the state.

From about 1830 to 1920, the great industrial expansion of Pennsylvania occurred. Manufacturing became the catalyst to provide the good life for Pennsylvanians. The state was endowed with power resources that provided the basis for a great industrial economy. Of these the massive bituminous coalfields of western Pennsylvania were a key element in the industrial expansion. Anthracite provided the home heating fuel for most of the northeastern United States and the modern oil industry began in western Pennsylvania in Titusville. This was the time when the immigrants flocked to the industrial cities of the state. Although it was a period of flamboyant industrial expansion accompanied by growing prosperity, it was also a time of great industrial strife. The factory worker gained his rights only after vigorous and sometimes bloody campaigns. Nonetheless, all cities and towns throughout Pennsylvania sought to establish the factory system, for the factory was the sign of prosperity. By the twentieth century Pennsylvania had become one of the great industrial centers of the world.

As an economy evolves it advances from the primary stage, where development of the virgin resources is fundamental, to the secondary stage where manufacturing is the major catalyst to growth, and finally to the tertiary stage where services become the dynamic forces in the economy.

As the economy has evolved each of these sectors has experienced changes in order to remain economically viable. Agriculture, for example, has evolved from subsistence farming during the Pioneer Era to a diversified agricultural system in the nineteenth century to one where specialized activities, such as dairying, dominates in the twentieth century. In the period of great manufactural growth, Pennsylvania's fuel resources and raw materials were major factors in localizing industry. In the modern period skilled labor and transportation facilities are major factors in key manufacturing areas, as are the amenities provided by a particular region.

In the nineteenth and early twentieth centuries the great growth industries were iron and steel, textiles, clay and glass products, and leather. Today these industries are in decline. If the manufactural economy of Pennsylvania is to prosper, these industries must be replaced by the growth industries of the late twentieth century. These include high-tech industries such as electronics and instruments. The image of the "smokestack" industries is gradually being replaced by the well landscaped plant in a modern industrial park.

Regions that developed in the past must adjust to new and continually changing economic factors. Only those regions that have the ability and will to adjust to modern economic conditions will survive and prosper.

As the economy has matured the tertiary industries have become the dynamic generators of employment. The state has been a leader in providing medical and health services. A prosperous population demands better services in wholesale and retail trade, banking and finance, transportation, and a wide variety of personal services including health and recreation, as well as social, legal, and educational services. Most of these service activities requires specialized training. These must be nurtured if Pennsylvania is to provide the way of life desired by a modern family.

Pennsylvania with its labor force of five million remains of major importance in the industrial system of the United States. Today Pennsylvania's educational system is providing well-trained individuals who understand the modern industrial system and how they can be part of it. The state has long been known for its industrial and financial leaders. This tradition continues to the present day.

Pennsylvania's economy has been built on change. Pennsylvanians have recognized this challenge in the past and look with confidence to the future.

PART I
The Pioneer Economy:
1682 to 1830

Fig. 9.

Agriculture provided the foundation for the pioneer economy of Pennsylvania. From the arrival of William Penn in 1682 until about 1830, from 80 to 90 percent of the population was engaged in agricultural pursuits. In its focus on agriculture, Pennsylvania resembled the Southern colonies, but the principal products were wheat, corn, and livestock, not tobacco, rice, and indigo. Moreover, Pennsylvania agriculture was based on the family farm, rather than the plantation, with family members—rather than indentured servants or slaves—providing most of the labor.

As Pennsylvania's economy evolved, manufacturing and commercial activities increased in importance. During the eighteenth century, Pennsylvania's manufacturing was the most diverse of all the colonies. In Philadelphia, the largest city and major center of manufacturing, at least sixty different

The making of iron was Pennsylvania's major industrial activity during the pioneer period, though preparing iron ore was hardly as neat and effortless as this 1760 engraving would lead one to believe.
From the collection of the Spruance Library of the Bucks County Historical Society

types of goods were produced by the middle of the eighteenth century. The rich agricultural hinterland provided the market for a large variety of manufactured goods, and at the same time produced the raw materials such as timber, iron, and farm produce for the processing industries of the city.

As the Industrial Revolution gained momentum early in the nineteenth century, a sound foundation had already been established in Pennsylvania for rapid progress. Natural resources were being developed, energy was available from wood and coal, capital was present to finance new endeavors, and a skilled and resourceful people were available to manage and operate the developing economy. Finally, the state's geographical location in the middle of the Atlantic seaboard, with access to both New England and the Midwest, provided an ideal market orientation.

Chapter One
Pioneer Agriculture

For more than a century, from the early 1700s to about 1820, Pennsylvania was the leading food producer of the British North American colonies and the new United States. The growth of an agricultural economy was favored not only by the natural endowment of the land, but also by the immigrants who brought from Europe a tradition of farming. Pennsylvania was long recognized as the "breadbasket" of the nation.

When William Penn was granted a charter to Pennsylvania in 1681, he became the sole owner of approximately twenty-eight million acres, thus acquiring the right to distribute the land in any way he saw fit. The disposition of this vast domain constituted the largest single economic activity of the pioneer period.

William Penn recognized the Indian claim to the land, so that the province first had to acquire the land from the Indians before putting it up for sale to individual settlers. No settler could obtain legal title to any land directly from an Indian, but this policy did little to discourage squatters. The purchase of land from the Indians by colonial and state authorities extended over a century, culminating in the New Purchase Treaty of 1768 and the Last Purchase Treaty in 1785, both signed at Fort Stanwix, embracing huge tracts of land in north-central and northwestern Pennsylvania.

The Pennsylvania government tried many methods of distributing land. Initially William Penn sold about 300,000 acres to persons in England known as the First Purchasers. From the death of William Penn in 1718 until 1732, however, no land titles were granted. Instead, the provincial government issued "tickets" that would be validated when a regular land office opened. In 1732 a land office was established, but the system of purchase was complicated and the land office did not have sufficient personnel to operate effectively. By the 1750s thousands of squatters were ignoring the land office. To lessen the irregularities, a new

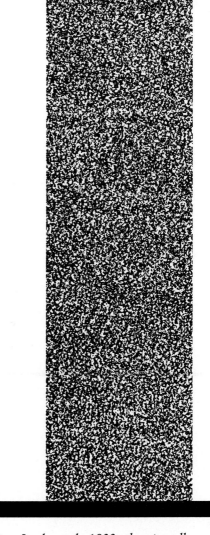
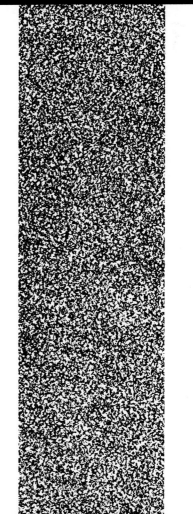

Opposite: *In the early 1800s the victuallers paraded through the streets of Philadelphia.*

Above: *In his frame of government for Pennsylvania, William Penn (1644-1718) provided for religious freedom and included an explicit clause permitting amendments. This 1797 engraving of Penn appeared in Robert Proud's* The History of Pennsylvania. *Courtesy, National Portrait Gallery, Smithsonian Institution, Washington, D.C.*

Above right: *Charles II (1630-1685), king of Great Britain from 1660-1685, granted a charter to William Penn giving him proprietary rights over the huge area of land that became part of Pennsylvania. Charles urged Penn to name the land Pennsylvania in honor of Sir William Penn, Penn's father. From Howard M. Jenkins,* Pennsylvania: Colonial and Federal, *vol. I, 1903*

"application system" was established in 1765. Under this system, an application was recorded and the land surveyed within a six months' period; full payment was to be made within an additional six months, at which time a deed would be issued. Again the system was largely ignored. As a consequence, there developed the widespread acceptance of the "law of improvements." Under this system, if a settler could prove that he actually lived on and had improved the land, he acquired the right to buy it, even though someone else might have applied for it at the county land office.

Land speculation was widespread during the pioneer era. The Holland Land Company, for example, purchased 1.5 million acres in western Pennsylvania between 1792 and 1794 at six cents per acre west of the Allegheny River and two cents per acre east of the Allegheny. In spite of the low cost of land, however, most speculators did not make a profit on land sales because of widespread squatting and long litigation of claims in the courts.

In addition to direct sales of land, the government also set aside areas of land for special

purposes. Between 1785 and 1792 the state established 112 tracts comprising 52,000 acres as "academy lands." These tracts were given to religious and educational groups; among the beneficiaries were Dickinson and Franklin and Marshall colleges and the Pittsburgh, Reading, and Washington academies. In addition, a large number of "state reservations" were set aside as townsites—among them, Beaver, Allegheny, Erie, Franklin, Waterford, and Warren.

Although Pennsylvania settlers could purchase land cheaply, a significant percentage never paid for the land they occupied from the state. In 1805 the state called for the foreclo-

William Penn, who advocated the fair treatment of Indians, tried to establish and preserve friendly and honorable relations with them. This engraving depicts Penn making a treaty with the Indians. At the time of Penn's arrival in 1682, the Delaware Indian population stood at about 4,000. From Edwin MacMinn, On the Frontier with Colonel Antes, *1900*

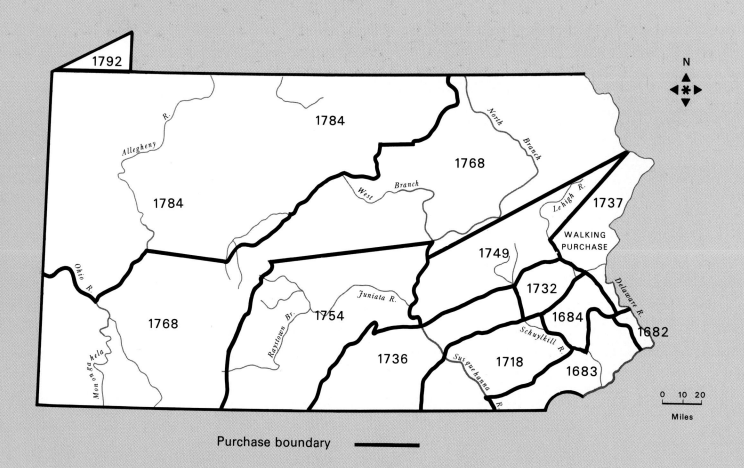

Purchase boundary ━━━━━

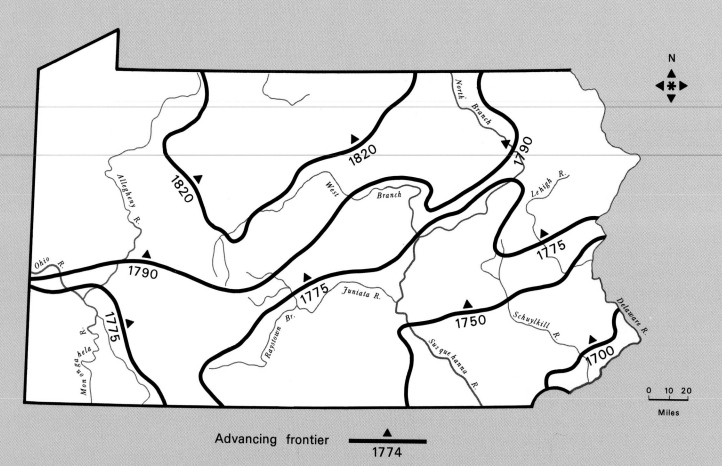

Advancing frontier ━━━▲━━━
1774

Above: *The state of Pennsylvania donated 52,000 acres of land from 1785-1792 to religious and educational groups. Dickinson College in Carlisle was one of the beneficiaries. This woodcut of Dickinson dates from about 1843. From Sherman Day,* Historical Collections of the State of Pennsylvania, *1843*

Opposite, top: *As settlement moved westward, the original tracts of land William Penn had purchased from the Indians were no longer adequate and additional lands were purchased by the Penn family. When Pennsylvania became a state in 1776, the colonial charter granted to the Penns ended, and the state bought their land. The final land purchase occurred in 1792 when Pennsylvania purchased the Erie Triangle from the Federal government. Prepared by the Deasy Laboratory of Geographics, Dept. of Geography, The Pennsylvania State University*

Opposite, bottom: *Settlement began in southeastern Pennsylvania and advanced westward and northward. The rugged topographic regions of the state were last to be populated. It required nearly 150 years before the pioneer frontier disappeared in north central Pennsylvania. Prepared by the Deasy Laboratory of Geographics, Dept. of Geography, The Pennsylvania State University*

sure of mortgages on unpaid-for land, but with almost no success. Similar laws were passed in 1820, 1835, 1858, and 1864—all equally ineffective for development of the land was more important than the money the state could collect. In 1874 the land office still recorded 2,365,000 acres for which no payment had been collected. Thus, the agricultural economy was largely established on land that was bought at a few cents per acre or on land acquired by squatters' rights.

ESTABLISHING THE FARM

The agricultural development of large areas of Pennsylvania was slow and difficult. Outside of the plains of southeastern Pennsylvania, the rugged Appalachian plateaus retarded agricultural penetration. These were densely wooded areas that required vast amounts of labor in clearing the land before crops could be planted and farms become productive. Most of the early settlers sought hardwood areas, for it was thought this land had the highest fertility. Much of northern Pennsylvania was covered by coniferous forests, and it required about 150 years before the farming frontier disappeared in the north-central part of the state.

Pennsylvania's settlers who came to the colony between 1681 and 1750 were from different

cultural backgrounds, and the method of clearing the land varied accordingly. Generally speaking, the English and Scotch-Irish in southeastern Pennsylvania did not clear the land initially, but adopted the Indian practice of girdling rather than felling the trees. The crops were then planted among the trees and the dead trees removed over a period of years. In contrast, the German settlers in southeastern Pennsylvania cleared the land by cutting down the trees, grubbing out the underbrush and all but the largest stumps, and burning the wood in the fields. Under this procedure the land was immediately ready for planting in crops and the wood ash from burning the logs provided the initial fertilizer. The major problem, of course, was the huge expenditure of labor required. The Swedish settlers usually followed a procedure midway between the English and German methods. They felled the trees but let them lie for a few years to dry. The useful logs were then removed, and grain crops were

sown among the stumps.

Whatever the method of clearing, the ground was usually not plowed for the first crop because roots made it impractical. For wheat or rye the surface was merely scratched by a harrow. The Indian practice of planting corn in hills was widely followed. During the first few years, the new farmland was generally planted in grain, with small patches of flax and tobacco and possibly a vegetable garden. At first, all of the cleared land was required to produce necessities for the family, and pastures and meadows were of little importance to the early farm economy.

THE CROPPING SYSTEM

The early European settlers brought with them not only their seeds and plants but also their methods of cultivation. Because it was a new environment, both physically and culturally, much of the pioneer era was a time of trial and error in establishing a sound agricultural sys-

Above: *Wheat was the principal crop of the eastern portion of the colony. Photo by John Collier. Courtesy, U.S. Office of War Information, Library of Congress*

Left: *Western Pennsylvania's pioneer farmers planted mostly corn. It was able to grow on newly cleared land, less vulnerable to destruction by insects and disease than were grains, and the excess could be made into whiskey and sold. From Gerald's* Herball, *1636*

Opposite page: *The colonial farmer harvested his wheat in early summer. From Uriah Hunt,* The Book of Commerce by Sea and Land, *1857*

tem. Further, the great physical diversity within Pennsylvania meant that many of the practices that were appropriate to eastern Pennsylvania were not applicable to western Pennsylvania. Thus, it was not until about 1800 that general patterns of crop and livestock husbandry were established.

The principal crop in eastern Pennsylvania was wheat. Not only was it well adapted to the physical environment but there was a good market for wheat, both in the other colonies and abroad. Wheat growing fit well into the seasonal chores of the farmers. It was common practice for wheat, as well as rye, to be sown in August and September and harvested in the early summer of the following year.

In western Pennsylvania the major crop was

*During Pennsylvania's pioneer period tobacco was grown
mostly for home consumption. After the plants ripened,
they were cut down and laid in a heap. The farmer
would then hang up the plants to dry, strip the leaves
from the stalks, and process them into plugs. From
Uriah Hunt,* The Book of Commerce by Sea and Land,
1857

corn. Corn culture had a number of advantages for the pioneer farmer. It could be grown on newly cleared land with a minimum of preparation. It was less vulnerable to destructive insects and disease than many grains, it required less labor in harvesting, and it could be harvested over a longer period of time. In western Pennsylvania, where there was little local market for excess production of grain and it was • too costly to ship grain to eastern markets, corn could be reduced in bulk by making it into whiskey, for which there was always a demand.

Besides wheat and corn, Pennsylvania farmers grew barley, rye, and oats. Barley became a major crop late in the eighteenth century when rust and the Hessian fly ravaged the wheat lands in southeastern Pennsylvania. Small acreage of rye was grown on most farms to produce straw for thatching roofs and making beehives and baskets. Rye was well adapted to infertile soils and newly cleared land. The yield per acre was usually higher than for wheat. At times when the price of wheat flour was high, rye, which was cheaper, became a major bread grain. Oats were of limited importance on the pioneer farms, being used mainly as a "nurse crop" in the development of grasslands. It was not a common practice to fatten cattle on grains, and oats were rarely used for human consumption except by the Scotch-Irish, who enjoyed oatmeal porridge.

Because labor was scarce and expensive and grassland was not as productive as grain farming, there was little development of cultivated grasslands. The early farmer relied largely on native grasses, and livestock were free to roam in the woods most of the year. There were few permanent pastures before 1750, and this use of land grew slowly until the early part of the nineteenth century.

The pioneer farmer made Pennsylvania a leader in the production of flax and hemp. Both of these fibers require high fertility, and in many areas newly cleared land was cropped in flax and hemp for a few years before being planted to produce wheat or corn when the fertility of the soil was lower. Nearly all farmers had a patch of flax for home consumption. One acre of flax provided sufficient yarn to produce summer clothes for a family of seven. Many farmers produced an excess of flax, providing the raw material for an early linen industry that was centered in Germantown. Hemp was used to produce rope for the pioneer farms.

The potato—now ranked second only to corn among America's contributions to the world's food supply—was little cultivated before the 1720s. The potato was generally considered to be poisonous, and many people believed the superstition that anyone who ate potatoes every day for several days would die within seven years. Such superstitions gradually disappeared, however, and by about 1770 a number of varieties had been introduced and cultivation was widely practiced. Nevertheless, many farmers considered the potato a poor crop. In 1811 John Lorain of Philipsburg wrote, "Potatoes cannot be grown extensively except for cattle, and it has been asserted by many who are well informed that they will not pay for cultivating."

Few vegetables were grown by the pioneer farmer. Fresh vegetables were not an important part of the eighteenth-century diet. Beans were grown and consumed, not as fresh green beans, but as dried beans. Peas were produced early, but by 1750 the weevil had become so destructive that most farmers abandoned cultivation. Turnips, carrots, mangel-wurzels, and rutabagas were grown to feed cattle.

Tobacco was grown on nearly every farm by the early colonists for home consumption. Although there were some expectations that the crop would develop commercially, this did not occur during the pioneer period. Within the home the farmer processed the tobacco into plugs, sometimes using the excess to pay debts in isolated areas where currency was scarce or nonexistent.

LIVESTOCK

The pioneer farmstead usually had a team of horses or oxen. Most farmers preferred oxen for plowing, as they required less feed, were dependable, and ultimately could be eaten. Horses were faster, however, and they were normally

Short-horn cattle such as this bull were brought to Pennsylvania by Colonel John Hare Powell of Philadelphia beginning in 1824. Most of Powell's cattle came from Yorkshire, England. At the beginning of the nineteenth century the area within a seventy-five mile radius west from Philadelphia became the beef-producing center of the United States. From Lewis F. Allen, American Cattle: Their History, Breeding, and Management, *1868*

used to pull wagons on the road.

The farmers from Great Britain, accustomed to the relatively mild English winters, provided only crude sheds and shelters for their animals. Unfortunately, the winters in Pennsylvania were much more severe, and animals suffered and even died. The German farmers, by contrast, coming from a colder continental climate, built tight barns as soon as they occupied the land. In many instances the logs cleared from the land provided the material for the first barns. By the end of the eighteenth century these German barns—many of them 60 to 120 feet in length—were famous throughout the nation. In 1799 John Beale Bradley wrote,

Farmers in Pennsylvania have a commendable spirit for building good barns, which are mostly of stone. On the ground floor are stalls in which their horses and oxen are fed with hay and cut straw and rye meal, but not always their other beasts . . . the second floor with the roof contains their sheaves of grain which are threshed on this floor. A part of their hay is also stored here.

The pioneer farmers grew grain for human consumption, not for animals. Livestock survived by foraging on natural grasses in the woodlands. These grasses, largely wild rye and broom straw, offered little nourishment and were soon exhausted, as cattle grazed them before they went to seed to produce the next year's crop. Permitted to roam unprotected in the forest, livestock frequently fell victim to wild predators. At the same time, the abundance of wild game gave little incentive at first for animal husbandry, as hunting provided meat for the family table. Milk was not an important food during the pioneer era.

By the last decade of the eighteenth century, however, so much land had been cleared in Pennsylvania that not all of it was needed to produce grain. Hay and pasture began to occupy some of the least desirable areas. The result was a transformation of animal husbandry in Pennsylvania after 1790. The central feature of this "new husbandry" was the introduction of red clover and grass into the previously all-grain rotation scheme. This fundamental change in agricultural practice made possible a marked increase not only in the number of cattle, but also in their quality. By 1800 the typical farm in southeastern Pennsylvania had about ninety acres in grass-grain rotation, another twenty-five acres in permanent pasture, and thirty acres in woodlands.

The growth of herds of livestock began in southeastern Pennsylvania, where the German farmers were the leaders in developing beef cattle. Although there was little domestic breeding, wealthy farmers improved their stock by importing animals, primarily from England. Domestic cattle raising was encouraged by the high price of imported beef caused by the Napoleonic Wars in Europe. Shortly after 1800 the area within a seventy-five-mile radius westward from Philadelphia became the beef-producing center of the nation. The beef-cattle industry became so profitable that by 1820 farms with good grazing lands near Philadelphia sold for $100 to $300 an acre.

During the period from 1790 to about 1830, it became the rage among wealthy amateur farmers to raise cattle of enormous size. At first the huge cattle were imported from England, but soon Pennsylvania farmers sought to excel by breeding domestic gargantuans, and a cattle show held in Philadelphia in March 1821, at the height of the craze, was billed as "Pennsylvania Against the World." These cattle were extremely expensive to produce, however, and the fad died out shortly after 1830.

By the early nineteenth century, a livestock industry was thriving in western Pennsylvania and the adjacent Ohio River valley. Because the local market was limited, farmers sought access to the larger and wealthier eastern market. Each spring and summer, from April to August, herds of 100 to 200 animals, both cattle and hogs, were driven slowly across the Alleghenies. The cattle were of two grades. A large number were grass-fed and sold to eastern farmers for fattening; however, many of the Ohio Valley cattle were fattened on local grains and slaughtered as soon as they reached the eastern market. These livestock drives reached a peak about 1830, but declined rapidly with the completion of the canals and railroads.

Swine were more important to the colonial farmer than cattle. The early Swedish, German, English, and Scotch-Irish settlers all brought swine with them. Swine did not need the care that cattle required. They could easily survive in the forests on roots, acorns, beechnuts, chestnuts, and other products from the wild. They were also better able to protect themselves from the predation of wild animals. Most farmers raised a few hogs. Not only did they provide meat for the family in the form of salt pork that could be kept for months, but the cured meat could be bartered at the local store for necessities or, if there was any left over, sold for cash.

Pennsylvania led the colonies in the export of salt pork, mainly to the New England fishing fleets and to the British West Indies. As demand increased after 1770 because of population growth and recognition of the quality of

Above: *This mechanical apparatus for shelling corn dates from about 1817. Most of the early corn shellers consisted of drums in a box with teeth on the drums. As the person operating the device turned a crank, the teeth would strip the corn off the cob.*

Above, right: *Among the agricultural implements made and sold by Adam Ekart of Philadelphia was this winnowing fan for cleaning wheat. This advertisement appeared in the* Virginia Gazette, *1774.*

Right: *Until the last twenty years of the eighteenth century, agricultural workers used a sickle to harvest grain. Then the grain cradle (pictured here) began to replace the sickle at harvest time. In a day the skillful operator of a cradle could cut more than twice as much grain as someone using a sickle or scythe. From Solon J. Buck and Elizabeth Hawthorne Buck,* The Planting of Civilization in Western Pennsylvania, *1939*

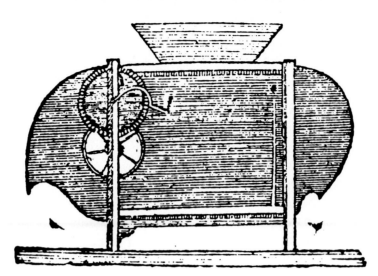

D U T C H F A N S,

FOR cleaning wheat or any other kind of grain, are made and fold by ADAM EKART, in Market ſtreet, Philadelphia. Likewiſe rolling fcreens, ſieves for ſitting iron ore, &c. warranted of the beſt make; alſo all ſorts of wire work, for cleaning wheat, barley, rye, flax ſeed, Indian corn, oats, or any other kind of grain. and wire ſhort-cloths for millers. The ſame to be had of captain Matthew Phripp, in Norfolk.

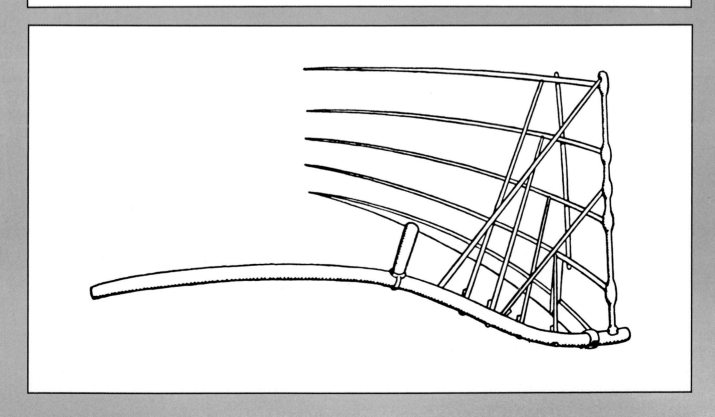

Pennsylvania pork, more swine were fattened on the farms than in the woods. The swine of the colonial period were razorbacks—narrow body, long snout, arched back, and long legs. As with cattle, improved swine herds were introduced from England after 1800.

The swine industry of Pennsylvania began to suffer after 1800, when corn-fed animals began to enter the eastern market from Ohio, Indiana, and Illinois. In 1810, when 40,000 swine were driven to the eastern market, most of them originated west of Pennsylvania.

The sheep industry was small in colonial Pennsylvania. Of all farm animals, sheep were the least capable of surviving in the woods. Most pioneer farmers, if they kept sheep at all, raised only enough sheep to clothe their families. Wool, not mutton, was the principal product. It was difficult to smoke or salt mutton, and the prejudice against its use resulted in the derogatory term "muttonheaded." Before and after the Revolution, Pennsylvania farmers depended largely on woolens imported from Britain.

FARM IMPLEMENTS

On the pioneer farms, implements were few and simple. Many had not changed in hundreds of years. The average farm had a plow, harrow, hoe, sickle, spade, axe, saw, grindstone, wheelbarrow, and reaping hook.

In the early colonial days, the plow and harrow were the only farm implements drawn by animal power. Until about 1750 the colonial harrow was made of a triangular, A-shaped homemade frame fitted with wooden pegs. After 1750 iron teeth produced by the local blacksmith gradually replaced the wooden pegs. On many farms a simple drag was substituted for the harrow to smooth the plowed field.

Until late in the eighteenth century, the Pennsylvania farmer used a wooden plow that was little better than the ones farmers had used in Eurasia thousands of years earlier. As the amount of land to be cultivated increased, it became evident that there was a need for a better plow.

A major improvement came in 1797 when Charles Newbold, a Philadelphia businessman, patented the first plow with the moldboard, share, and landside made of cast iron. In 1800 Robert Smith produced the first complete cast-iron plow. The Smith plow was widely used for half a century. After 1810 nearly every community had a blacksmith shop that could produce a cast-iron plow. Because each plow varied slightly in design, plowing contests were extremely popular to determine who produced the best plow.

Until about 1780 wheat, rye, and other small grains were harvested with a sickle that was little changed since the time of the Babylonians. After 1780 the cradle began to replace the sickle, but throughout the pioneer period many farmers continued to use the sickle.

Grain was threshed by hand using a flail or was trodden out by animals. The flail consisted of a wooden staff with strips of leather attached at the end. A strong worker could produce ten bushels of wheat or twenty bushels of oats in a long day's work. In the more settled farming areas, migrant workers went through the countryside threshing grain in return for a percentage of the crop. Most farmers did not favor the use of animals to tread out the grains because this process produced dirty grain. At the end of the pioneer era, the threshing machine was introduced and the age-old methods rapidly disappeared.

Grass was cut with a scythe until after 1840. Two different types of scythes were developed by the English and German farmers. The English blade was made of hard steel that was sharpened by a grindstone and whetstone. The broader German or "Dutch" scythe was made of soft metal and was sharpened by pounding the edge on an anvil. The mowing machine was not introduced until the 1840s.

During the pioneer era the hand tools of the farm were gradually improved. The most significant advance was the replacement of wooden forks, spades, scoops, and the like by the more durable and lighter steel blades and tines. The growth in demand for these tools was so great that Pittsburgh became the most important center in America for their production.

There was also a gradual evolution from the

predominance of hand labor on the farm to the increased use of animal power. At the beginning of the eighteenth century, horse or oxen power was used only to pull a plow, harrow, or two-wheeled cart. By the end of the pioneer agricultural era, heavy farm wagons were in general use and animal-powered machines were beginning to appear. To stimulate the production of farm equipment, the Tariff Act of 1828 placed a heavy duty on imported farm equipment. The threshold of the farm implement industry was in sight, signaling the decline of production of farm equipment in local blacksmith shops.

WHISKEY REBELLION

The so-called Whiskey Rebellion of western Pennsylvania was triggered by a tax on whiskey enacted by Congress in 1791. Under this act, all operators of stills under 400 gallons were required to pay a fifty-four-cent tax for each gallon of the still's capacity. Almost every farmer

Pages 26 and 27: *Pennsylvania, particularly in the west, was a hotbed of resistance to the government of the United States after the Revolution. President Washington and Pennsylvania authorities, however, were willing to use any force to stop the so-called Whiskey Rebellion. These records show the amount of money spent to move the most men in to pacify the countryside. Courtesy, Pennsylvania State Archives*

Below: *At a time when whiskey was used as a commodity of exchange in Pennsylvania, most farmers manufactured their own spirits from corn with a still such as this one. From Uriah Hunt,* The Book of Commerce by Sea and Land, *1857*

in western Pennsylvania operated a small still to convert corn to whiskey, and these farmers considered the tax exorbitant and unfair. They petitioned for repeal of the federal tax, claiming that it benefited the rich, that it invited fraud because the distillers certified the size of their own stills, that the tax was as much as 100 percent on cheap liquor, and that farmers could not transport their grain in bulk to the eastern markets. A final and particularly galling complaint was that all litigation arising from the tax had to be settled in Philadelphia.

The pioneer farmer of western Pennsylvania was a man of independence and, simply stated, he would not pay the tax. In 1792 and 1793 the local militia prevented the United States marshalls from collecting the tax. In July 1794 a federal marshall served scores of writs ordering trials in Philadelphia, and the rural countryside flew to arms. Some 500 angry men marched on a federal inspector's house near Pittsburgh, burned the house and farm, and wounded an army officer who tried to protect the residence. The western band vowed death to revenue collectors and withdrawal from the Union if President George Washington tried to enforce the law. To temper the federal role, Washington asked Governor Thomas Mifflin of Pennsylvania to enforce the law, but the governor refused to act.

Negotiations to settle the dispute continued during the summer and fall. When progress appeared minimal, an army was gradually assembled, and on October 4, 1794, President Washington joined the assembled troops at Carlisle. Before the army marched westward, word was received that the western Pennsylvanians would comply with the tax law. Washington dismissed the report, however, and 15,000 troops moved westward toward Parkinson's Ferry, where the rebels were meeting. When the army arrived there, the rebels had dispersed, and on November 8 General Henry Lee, the commander of the troops, issued a proclamation condemning the insurgents and asking all loyal citizens to take an oath supporting the federal Constitution.

The Whiskey Rebellion thus came quietly to an end. The troops rounded up several hundred men, of whom twenty were taken to Philadelphia for trial. The disproportionately large military force not only provided the basis for a bloodless victory, but carried with it long-range political implications by demonstrating in a concrete way the immense power of the federal government. At the subsequent trial in Philadelphia, most of the defendants were acquitted. Two of the twenty accused of treason were sentenced to death, but the President pardoned both. Only one man, David Bradford, did not receive amnesty, having fled to Spanish Louisiana.

Although the Whiskey Rebellion was a small popular uprising based on a single issue, its political repercussions were long lasting. Opposition to the Federalist party, considered antagonistic to western Pennsylvania's economic growth, persisted. In 1800 the region voted strongly for Jefferson, and it remained a Democratic stronghold for many years.

Frederick Longsdorf with his waggon and *four* horses is engaged in the service for the **Militia of Pennsylvania**, in the *2nd Brigade* from the *3d* day of *October* 1794, and is to draw forage and rations at any post or public magazine, on producing this certificate, provided the same is entered hereon.

Q. M. G. Pennsylvania.

Counterfigned

Wm W Biddle 2 M 2nd B'd

DATE	At what Post or Magazine.	Pounds of Hay.	Quarts of Grain	Rations of Provifions			
Oct. 15. 1794	Shippensburg Strasburg	41	3 bus. Rye 32 d°		0 =	15 .	0
						3 .	-
							6
17	Juniata	56				3	
18	Bedford	56	64 oats	2 Rations		3 5	
19	do	56			1 .	5 .	0
20	do	56	32 D°		. 3 :	0 .	6
30	South Creek		32 D°		. 8		
	Do		32 Choper		. 3.	8 ..	0
Nov. 17	Fort Hill	56					
T M°		56					
		377					

Chapter Two
Domestic Industry

The typical pioneer family not only had to build their own shelter but also had to produce most of what they needed to survive. The pioneer farmers of Pennsylvania had little opportunity to obtain manufactured goods. The frontier areas were isolated, and contact between settled areas was difficult. Money was extremely scarce, and only the absolute necessities were purchased. For all these reasons, domestic or home manufacture was universally practiced and was by far the dominant feature of colonial industrial enterprise.

Of home industry, the spinning of yarns and the making of clothing occupied a primary position. It is estimated that in eighteenth-century Pennsylvania more than 90 percent of the people wore clothing made from homespun cloth. Hemp, flax, wool, and rarely cotton were spun on a small, Saxon-type spinning wheel, then woven on a crude wooden loom. The cloth was dyed using indigo or other dyes prepared from natural substances such as goldenrod or black walnut. Curing leather to make boots or moccasins was another common domestic pursuit. Most of the household goods and the crude farm implements were also made on the homestead or at the local blacksmith shop. The production of goods was usually a part-time occupation. Much of the work was done during the long winter months, when farming activities were at their lowest ebb.

The eighteenth-century system of domestic manufacture provided the foundation on which the Industrial Revolution of the nineteenth century would be built. Out of this system came workers with the skills needed to perform industrial tasks. Remnants of this system persist today in activities such as home canning, knitting, and the making of clothes from manufactured cloth.

Alongside the domestic industry of the pioneer era, there arose a number of more specialized enterprises, providing processed goods that even pioneer families could not provide for themselves. Prominent among these were

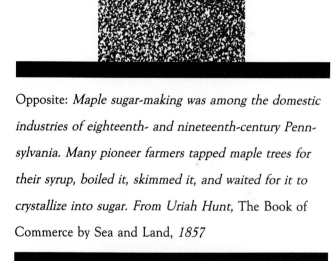

Opposite: *Maple sugar-making was among the domestic industries of eighteenth- and nineteenth-century Pennsylvania. Many pioneer farmers tapped maple trees for their syrup, boiled it, skimmed it, and waited for it to crystallize into sugar. From Uriah Hunt,* The Book of Commerce by Sea and Land, *1857*

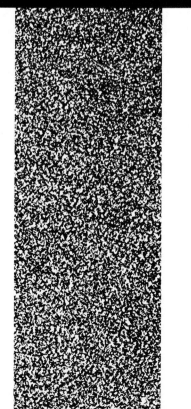

ironworks, sawmills, and gristmills, but as the eighteenth century wore on, a wide variety of goods came to be manufactured outside the home.

In the early nineteenth century, mechanical power began to play a great role in manufacturing. Water-powered mills became widespread, and the rudiments of the factory system were evident. The practice of making cloth at one place and sending it to another location to produce the finished product was well developed. Many of the workshop crafts had developed so effectively that they were in reality small factory production units. The production of flour, timber, iron, barrels, and ships constituted rudimentary factory procedures. A sound foundation was being laid for the Industrial Revolution of the nineteenth century.

PROCESSING RAW MATERIALS

The making of iron was the major industrial endeavor in Pennsylvania during the pioneer period. The industry came into existence in 1716 when Thomas Rutter, a blacksmith and Quaker minister, built a bloomery on Manatawny Creek, a tributary of the Schuylkill River. There the local iron ores were heated in low hearths and hammered into bars to supply the area's blacksmith shops. In 1720 Rutter built the first blast furnace in Chester County and named it Colebrookdale, after a famous English furnace.

The iron industry developed rapidly. The famous Durham Iron Works was established in the Delaware Valley in 1728, and the historic Cornwall furnace began producing iron about 1740. By 1750 Pennsylvania led the colonial world in iron production. In 1760 the Schuylkill Valley dominated production, with most of the furnaces situated in Chester and Berks counties, while the Delaware Valley was a secondary center. Between 1760 and 1776 the industry spread westward as furnaces were established west of the Susquehanna River. In the last two decades of the eighteenth century, iron furnaces spread throughout central and western Pennsylvania.

The significant growth of the iron industry was an important factor in the success of the colonists in their struggle for independence during the Revolutionary War. The iron industry produced cannon and shot, as well as the raw material for guns used in the campaigns. As early as 1770 the Provincial Assembly of Pennsylvania had encouraged steel making, thus defying a British edict that prohibited the erection of new furnaces. With the outbreak of war, the Provincial Convention encouraged the production of iron, steel, wire, and tin plate, while the Continental Congress contracted with firms to produce steel for the making of weapons.

The iron industry of Pennsylvania was the first large-scale manufacturing endeavor in the province. It required more capital and a higher level of technology than other pioneer industries. The amount of capital required, possibly $30,000 to $60,000, was so large that it was usually raised by creating partnerships. The industry was profitable, however, and the merchants of Philadelphia found it a sound investment.

The colonial blast furnaces and forges were oriented to local deposits of iron ore and large tracts of woods, needed to provide charcoal for the furnaces. As a consequence, many of the furnaces were far from the settled agricultural communities. This combination of circumstances created essentially self-sufficient com-

Opposite page: *Women and girls of colonial Pennsylvania spun hemp, flax, and wool on small spinning wheels like this one. At spinning frolics, neighbors would gather to eat and drink and sometimes sing "The Pennsylvania Spinner's Song." The last two lines read: "So let our wheels and reels go merrily round, while health, peace and virtue among us are found." From Edwin MacMinn,* On the Frontier with Colonel Antes, *1900*

Above: *In colonial Pennsylvania iron ore was separated from dirt, washed, and sorted. From the collection of the Spruance Library of the Bucks County Historical Society*

Above: *Though the Dove Mill is featured in this eighteenth-century poster, the artist has also incorporated the symbols of hard work (beehive), peace (dove), and the foundation of industry (books). Courtesy, The Library Company of Philadelphia*

Left: *Charcoal making in colonial America was possibly the single most wasteful enterprise in terms of time, labor, and raw material. Until coke was produced from bituminous coal, charcoal was the only fuel available to smelt iron ore. Thirty acres of forest might be needed to produce one ton of charcoal. From the collection of the Spruance Library of the Bucks County Historical Society*

munities known as "iron plantations." Many of these plantations encompassed several thousand acres of land, including the iron mines, forest land, the furnace and forge or forges, the charcoal house, the mansion house, the workers' houses, office, store, gristmill, sawmill, blacksmith shop, common bakery, barns, grain fields, and orchard. On smaller plantations the ironmaster was forced to buy wood for making charcoal from the owners of woodlands in neighboring districts.

In many ways the iron plantation resembled the feudal manor of medieval Europe. The typical ironmaster lived in a beautifully furnished mansion and had sufficient wealth to educate his children and to travel, not only in the colonies but to Europe. The workers, in contrast, had little money and enjoyed few of the amenities of the day. The plantation was essentially a self-contained economy in which workers were credited with the amount earned each day and debited for merchandise bought at the plantation store. In exchange for the iron sent to market, the ironmaster received goods and spirits for the plantation store. Many of the plantations were isolated, and the plantation community had little contact with other settlements.

The technology of the iron industry changed little during the pioneer period. It was the age of charcoal iron. The typical furnace, about twenty-five feet square at the bottom and the same in height, was built in the form of a pyramid. The iron ore, charcoal, and limestone were put in from the top, and the iron metal was drawn from the bottom once or twice a day. About 400 bushels of charcoal were needed to produce a ton of iron.

Many plantations had a refining forge built near the blast furnace. The process of heating and hammering produced bar iron that was sold to blacksmiths and merchants to produce a variety of tools and implements. Secondary ironworks were usually located in the larger towns. In a few places steel was produced, as well as tin plate and sheet metal.

In addition to iron making, sawmills and gristmills were among Pennsylvania's first industrial enterprises. Because the raw materials

Above: *Quarrying slate required fracturing the rock face by hand, without explosives, and following the geological path of Pennsylvania's northeastern rock tilt. Many of the slate miners had received their early training in coal mining. From the collection of the Spruance Library of the Bucks County Historical Society*

Opposite: *Gristmills, where grain was ground, were among Pennsylvania's first industrial structures. The one pictured here was built by Ludwig Derr about 1770 on the present site of Lewisburg. From Edwin MacMinn, On the Frontier with Colonel Antes, 1900*

for sawmills and gristmills were widely dispersed, waterpower readily accessible from small streams, and transportation difficult, the mills were situated to serve local markets. As settlement spread across Pennsylvania, the number of these mills increased until they were found in all parts of the colony. In 1760 there were eighty-three gristmills in Philadelphia County alone, and by 1770 there were mills along the Monongahela River and many other streams of western Pennsylvania. With the coming of the Conestoga wagon in about 1760 the excess flour and timber were transported to the larger towns, primarily Philadelphia. Philadelphia thus became the distribution point for these commodities to New England, the South, the West Indies, and Europe.

MANUFACTURING
By the end of the eighteenth century, a considerable number of manufacturing enterprises

were firmly established in Pennsylvania. Many factors contributed to this industrial development. Pennsylvania was particularly well endowed with natural resources including minerals, forests, and agricultural products. English, Scotch-Irish, German, Swedish, and Dutch settlers contributed a greater variety of crafts and skills than were found in any other colony. Rapid population growth provided a strong provincial market, and other markets were soon established in neighboring colonies, England, the West Indies, and southern Europe.

During the colonial period, industries that did not compete with those in the mother country were encouraged by favorable legislation in both the British Parliament and the colonial assembly. In the period immediately before the Revolution, local manufacturers were also stimulated by colonial nonimportation agreements designed to protect against British taxation. Although the motivation was primarily political, the agreements had the effect of promoting domestic production by limiting importation. Countering these stimulating factors were colonial laws restricting or prohibiting competition with British manufactures and, later, the chaotic conditions of the Revolutionary War period. Other limiting factors were a lack of capital, scarcity of labor (particularly skilled workers), and inadequate transportation.

The most important industrial development of the pioneer period, after iron and steel, was textile manufacturing. The provincial farms supplied the raw materials of wool, flax, and hemp for the small manufacturing establishments. The industry was centered in southeastern Pennsylvania, near Philadelphia. A principal center was Germantown, which was known especially for the production of stockings. One report states that in 1768 the area produced

Above: *Pennsylvania tanneries supplied leather to local shoemakers and saddlery shops. After the initial tanning process, the currier (pictured here) would scrape or shave the inside of the skin to reduce its substance and make it an even thickness all over. He would then rub it with oil or with tallow and oil to soften the leather.* From John Trussler, The Progress of Man in Society, 1790

Above, right: *This reconstructed central Pennsylvania rural shoe and leather shop may be seen in Bedford Village. During colonial times Pennsylvania supplied most of the tanned leather and shoes for the South. Photo by E. Willard Miller*

6,000 dozen pairs of woolen stockings. Much wool was also manufactured into clothing, and linsey-woolsey, a cloth of linen and wool, was much in demand for women's dresses. There were also small mills producing serges and laces.

Another noteworthy industry of the pioneer era was the manufacture of leather products. This industry thrived because of the availability of hides and bark for tanning coupled with a growing market not only in Pennsylvania but in other colonies. All of the large settlements had shoemaking, saddlery, and harness-making shops whose leather was secured from local tanneries. Pennsylvania assumed leadership among the colonies by the middle of the eighteenth century, producing a surplus of leather goods and supplying most of the tanned leather and shoes needed by the South. The leading center of leather manufacture was Philadelphia, which in 1789 had more than 600 shoemakers. Other important centers were Lancaster and York.

Because the rural Pennsylvanian had to protect his family and provide wild meat for the table, a gun was essential in every pioneer home. Of the various guns crafted in America during this period, the Pennsylvania long rifle, developed primarily in Lancaster County, was most famous. The developers were immigrant

German gunsmiths who previously had made short, heavy flintlock guns for hunters in central Europe. These German heavy rifles were superior to the smoothbore English guns. Over time the weapons were improved, producing a lighter and longer rifle that was more accurate over a longer range. The Pennsylvania rifle was copied in all of the colonies and came to be immortalized in song and legend as the Kentucky rifle. This rifle played no small role in the final outcome of the Revolutionary War. The Pennsylvania rifle remained the finest handcrafted gun well into the nineteenth century. Over time much attention was devoted to the artistic as well as the functional detail. The stocks were frequently carved into intricate patterns and inlaid with brass, silver, or even gold.

Also among the earliest industries were printing and publishing. Pennsylvania's first press was set up in 1686 in Philadelphia; its first publication was an almanac. By 1775 there were nine newspapers in Pennsylvania, of which seven were in Philadelphia, one in Germantown, and one in Lancaster. One of Pennsylvania's notable printers, of course, was Benjamin

Above: By the late eighteenth century Pennsylvania led the nation in the manufacturing of paper. The inset of this elaborate engraving shows a scene of papermaking in the early nineteenth century. From the collection of the Spruance Library of the Bucks County Historical Society

Above, left: Benjamin Franklin (1706-1790), one of Pennsylvania's most notable printers, was also an author, inventor, scientist, diplomat, and public official. In his scientific pursuits, Franklin constantly worked to combine natural research and discovery with practical applications. Engraving by Justus Chevillet. Courtesy, National Portrait Gallery, Smithsonian Institution, Washington, D.C.

Above: *As Philadelphia's export trade grew in the eighteenth and nineteenth centuries, shipbuilding became a growing and thriving business. This woodcut of ships under construction appeared as the frontispiece in* The Book of Commerce by Sea and Land, *first published by Uriah Hunt and Son of Philadelphia in 1836 and reprinted in 1850 and 1857.*

Opposite page: *Steam as a means of propulsion for ships was slowly accepted and not without great misgivings. Not until 1832 was the USS* Powhatan *built for the U.S. Navy as its first steam vessel. Philadelphia was the leading builder for the new steam navy. The Philadelphia Navy Yard is still active and specializes in refitting carriers and battleships. From the collection of the Spruance Library of the Bucks County Historical Society*

Franklin.

Closely associated with printing was the papermaking industry. The first paper mill was established in 1693. Philadelphia was the center of papermaking, as the city had the largest supply of raw material (rags), as well as the largest market. The number of paper mills in Philadelphia increased from six in 1769 to forty-eight in 1787, and Pennsylvania at this time led the new nation in paper manufacture.

The manufacture of beer and liquor was of major importance in Pennsylvania's economy. Brewing of beer began in the seventeenth century, and by 1721 Philadelphia beer was being shipped as far south as Charleston. The industry flourished in the eighteenth century, and by the 1780s the breweries of Philadelphia required more than 40,000 bushels of barley annually. The Scotch-Irish introduced the manufacture of whiskey in about 1720, and Pennsylvania assumed leadership in its production by 1740. Almost every farmer had a still, and whiskey became a principal commodity of exchange. Larger distilleries were established, and the surplus became a principal item of export.

Shipbuilding was established about 1700 and grew in importance. The growing eighteenth century export trade of Philadelphia encouraged the growth of this industry. There was also a demand for small boats for the fishing and whaling activities in the Delaware area. By 1721 Philadelphia was building double the tonnage of any other American port. The city became a leading center of naval architecture, and its vessels were known not only for their beauty but also for their speed.

A number of other, smaller industries contributed to the total variety of manufactures. A glass industry had developed by the middle of the eighteenth century. In 1762 one outstanding glassmaker, Heimrich Wilhelm Stiegel, laid out the village of Mannheim and established a large glass factory there. Securing glassworkers from Germany, he produced the finest glass products in the colonies, including window glass, bottles, jugs, dishes, plates, and specialty products. Other early manufactures included pewter ware, silver plate, and clocks, all of

Left: *Heimrich Wilhelm Stiegel (1729-1785) prospered as a Lancaster County ironmaster and developer of the town of Manheim before he became a highly successful glass manufacturer. Though his two glassworks made him a wealthy man, Stiegel's extravagant living and over-extended business ventures led to his downfall. He died in poverty in Berks County. From Cirker,* Dictionary of American Portraits, Dover, *1967*

Right: *As the leading cultural and economic city in America in the 1700s, Philadelphia soon became chief producer of luxury goods for the home, such as furniture, glassware, and silver. Pennsylvania products from this time may still be found in the finest homes in Europe.*

Below: *In Stiegel's glass factories in Manheim, workers turned out bottles, dishes, window glass, and other glass products. Dipping an iron tube into a pot of melted glass, the glassblower would blow into the tube, thereby swelling the glass. He would then repeatedly roll it on a flat piece of iron or marble to shape and polish it. From Uriah Hunt,* The Book of Commerce by Sea and Land, *1857*

them centered in Philadelphia. The city had a total of nineteen clockmakers in 1785, increasing to twenty-five in 1795.

DEVELOPMENT OF URBAN CENTERS

As early as 1750 Philadelphia was the principal manufacturing center of the United States. It possessed many advantages for manufacturing. It was the major transportation center for the flow of agricultural raw material from southeastern Pennsylvania. Many of the early immigrants from Europe were skilled craftsmen who practiced their trade in the New World. Not only the largest market for manufactured goods existed in Philadelphia, for it possessed the largest and wealthiest population of the colony, but it was the port for the export of finished products to other colonies and to Europe. The capital necessary to establish manufacturing was available from the wealthy merchants of the city.

Industry thrived from the time of the earliest settlement and grew steadily. By 1789, the city had, exclusive of carpenters, masons, and other skilled trades, 2,280 industrial workers, representing about 25 percent of the working population. Philadelphia was one of the first manufacturing centers to experience the change from the small craft shop to factory production. In 1790, when the factory system was still in its infancy, the city had thirty factories employing more than 300 workers. Manufacturing in Phil-

adelphia was highly diversified, including brewing, baking, brick making, shoemaking, printing and publishing, pewter making, saddlery, clock and watch making, textiles, clothes making, and shipbuilding.

Other centers of manufacturing were also developing in some of the larger settlements of southeastern Pennsylvania, the most notable of which were Bethlehem, Lancaster, and York. A visitor wrote of Bethlehem in 1751, "You can scarcely mention any trade which is in the largest city in this country, but what is at this place and carried on after the best manner." In 1760 a meeting of master artisans declared that more than 100 of the commodities sold in Bethlehem's stores could be produced in the community. York, founded in 1741, became the regional manufacturing center for a developing, prosperous agricultural region. By 1789 thirty-nine separate trades employed more than half of the town's 385 taxpayers, including shoemakers, tailors, blacksmiths, hatters, weavers, hosiers, locksmiths, dyers, silversmiths, potters, tinsmiths, and other artisans.

In western Pennsylvania manufacturing was centered in Pittsburgh. Much of the iron produced in the river valleys after 1800 was sent to Pittsburgh for manufacture into farm implements for the developing agricultural hinterland. Pittsburgh also supplied many of the essentials to people migrating westward, including tools, wagons, harnesses, and foodstuffs.

Chapter Three
Transportation and Trade

The importance of trade and commerce in Pennsylvania varied greatly from region to region during the pioneer period. People and commodities moved—slowly and often with difficulty—on natural waterways, trails, and crudely built roads. It was during this time, however, that the major patterns of land transportation in the state were conceived. Thus, for example, Route 30 and the Pennsylvania Turnpike today follow the same general route as the

first road built westward to Pittsburgh.

Forerunners of the pioneer farmers were the fur traders. The wilderness of Pennsylvania was a rich source of deer, beaver, bear, and other animal skins and, with the European demand for furs nearly insatiable, these became the first major exports from the colony. To obtain the furs, the Europeans developed a system of exchange with the Indians. Pennsylvania traders offered guns and powder, rum, cloth, and a variety of trinkets in exchange for the furs. Philadelphia merchants supplied the trade goods and received, stored, processed, and shipped the furs abroad, while frontier traders contacted the Indians in outposts of the interior. Lancaster was a site for one of the earliest posts. Shamokin and Sunbury on the Susquehanna filled the same role. In western Pennsylvania, Logstown (near Ambridge) on the Ohio was a major fur-trading post.

In the early decades of the eighteenth century, there were as many as 300 fur traders in Pennsylvania. Because the fur trade depended only on traversing Indian trails, geographical expansion of the trade was rapid, and by the 1750s it reached beyond the western borders of Pennsylvania. The fur trade was the greatest source of wealth in the early days of the colony and laid the foundation for the commercial and financial prominence of Philadelphia.

WATERWAYS AND TRAILS

The wooded land of southeastern Pennsylvania was so difficult to move across that early patterns of migration were determined by natural

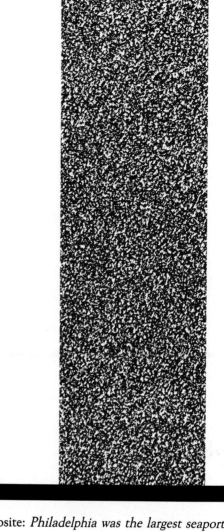

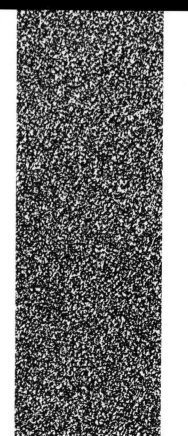

Opposite: *Philadelphia was the largest seaport in North America when John Birch made this view of the harbor around 1805. Marine archeologists continue to dredge up whole wooden ships from the Delaware River and its estuaries; many still contain valuable cargoes.*

A Trader's Camp.

Furs, Pennsylvania's first major exports, were obtained through trade with the Indians. This drawing depicts a mid-eighteenth-century trader's camp. From Edwin MacMinn, On the Frontier with Colonel Antes, *1900*

waterways. Thus, the first European settlements were established along the Delaware, Schuylkill, and Susquehanna rivers. The early settlers built no roads, but moved by dugout canoe on the streams. As late as 1749 Peter Kalm described the dugouts found on the Delaware River. "These canoes are boats made by one piece of wood and much in use among the farmers and other people along the Delaware and some little rivers." As agriculture flourished, the dugouts increased in size until the largest could carry up to 150 bushels of grain. The passage of these canoes was often hampered by dams, weirs, and baskets built by farmers to catch shad and other fish, resulting in frequent conflict between the "river men" and the "shore men."

As settlement spread inland from the rivers, Indian paths served as the first land routes of transportation. Movement along these trails was by foot or on horseback. These trails were often "blind" overgrown paths, difficult to follow. Sometimes alternate paths were used in different seasons. The pioneer farmers used these trails to send pelts and furs to market. Later, when agricultural products were produced in excess such items as poultry, meat, and butter were carried to towns in packs slung over the horse's back.

The packhorse trails were especially important in the movement of settlers to western Pennsylvania. After 1750 the route across the Allegheny Mountains was crowded with packhorse trains. At that time the wagon traffic terminated at Carlisle, where the goods to be moved westward were transferred to the backs of horses.

Packhorse transportation was expensive. In 1784 the cost of transporting a ton of goods from Philadelphia to Erie was $249. The movement of goods by packhorses to the western frontier reached its zenith about 1790. With the construction of roads and the use of wagons that carried larger loads, pack trains were rapidly replaced by the new and faster service.

EARLY ROADS
Pennsylvania's first roads were constructed in the more densely populated areas, their extent and direction influenced by settlement patterns and topographic conditions. As settlement spread from Philadelphia, it became the hub of transportation. With the growth of towns came the need to widen trails into roads. Most of the early roads were winding, following not only the contour of the land but also property lines and border fences. Many farmers had laid out their farms before roads existed and would not permit roads to cross their farmland, forcing them to circle around instead.

Gradually highways penetrated to the interior of the southeast. In 1706 the Queen's Path was established from Philadelphia to Chester. In 1711 the Old Yorke Road was constructed with a branch to Doylestown and Easton. The Old Conestoga Road from Philadelphia to Lancaster was begun in 1721, but not completed until 1733. These were earthen roads, with no firm base, and became virtually impassible during the wet seasons of the year.

For more than a century, the road-building

policy established by William Penn prevailed. This policy gave to local governments the responsibility for building and maintaining the roads within their respective boundaries. Further, it authorized local governments to require property owners to maintain the roads. Local governments lacked the capital resources, the manpower, and the ability to plan roads that connected distant settlements. Further, the county and township governments did not have the authority to levy or collect road taxes. The inadequate construction and poor maintenance of roads during the colonial period and for some years afterward was mainly due to this policy. Provincial government appropriations for roads were small and irregular and normally were only for military routes.

THE CONESTOGA WAGON
With the development of a demand for farm produce in Philadelphia and some of the larger settlements, combined with the production of surplus grain in the rural areas, there was a need for a vehicle to transport the farmers' output to distant markets. During the early 1700s English and German craftsmen—blacksmiths, wheelwrights, joiners, and turners—located in the Conestoga Valley of Lancaster County used the concepts of the road wagons of England and Germany to produce a sturdy freight-bearing vehicle.

The vehicle, known as the Conestoga wagon, was adapted to the poor roads of the day. Although the wagon was about sixteen feet in length, the wheels were only a few feet apart and the body was raised to a considerable height, enabling the wagon to negotiate narrow, deeply rutted tracks. The cloth top of linen or hemp bound over six or eight hoops, protected the load and offered shelter from the elements. Pulled by four to six horses, the Conestoga wagon could carry up to thirty barrels of flour or three tons of grain. Their use grew rapidly, and by 1750 it is estimated that there were 7,000 of them on the roads of Pennsylvania. In 1753 Lewis Evans wrote, "The economy of the Germans has taught us the method of bringing produce to Market from the remotest part at a small expense. Every German farmer in our province almost has a Waggon of his own."

In the second half of the eighteenth century, the Conestoga wagon became the most important vehicle of overland freighting, transporting not only agricultural products but iron ore, charcoal, and manufactured goods. It was also used for military purposes in the French and Indian Wars and the American Revolution, supplying Washington's troops at Valley Forge during the winter of 1777-1778.

The Conestoga wagon continued to expand its role as a freight carrier until about 1820, when it was finally replaced by new and better modes of transportation. The first inroads were made by canals, and these were soon followed by the railroads. As a consequence, not only wagoners but wheelwrights, blacksmiths, hostlers, and innkeepers had to seek a new means of livelihood. To many, it marked the end of an era.

THE ROAD WEST

Although rudimentary roads were fairly easily built across the plains of southeastern Pennsylvania, development of a western road network was long delayed by the rugged Appalachian Ridge and Valley and the Allegheny Plateau. The first road built between 1785 and 1810 crossing the ridge and valley from Lancaster through York and Cumberland counties to Bedford followed the low valleys and water and wind gaps through the mountains. From Bedford westward to Pittsburgh, the first road followed the military route cut through the forest by General John Forbes in 1758 in the British expedition to drive the French out of Fort Duquesne. Forbes, in turn, had followed an old Indian trail known as the Trading Path.

For many years after the "Western Road" was laid out, it could be used by wagons only during the summer season. The packhorse remained the dominant means of carrying commodities to the west until 1818. In the early years as many as 500 horses moved westward from Carlisle laden with salt, ironware, pewter plates, dishes, and other commodities in kegs and barrels. By 1785 this route had become the

major transportation artery to the west, and plans were initiated to improve the road.

As the road improved, the packhorse gradually disappeared and was replaced by the Conestoga wagon—or, as it was known regionally, the Pitt wagon. Between 1810 and 1820 there were 4,000 to 5,000 wagons leaving Philadelphia each year laden with goods for Pittsburgh. By 1820 fast mail went from Pittsburgh to Philadelphia in two and a half days, and passengers made the journey in four.

THE TURNPIKE ERA

In 1784 the burden of building and maintaining roads was removed from local governments, and the state took on the responsibility of developing long-distance roads. The first state appropriation in 1785 for the Western Road from Cumberland County to Pittsburgh was followed in 1786 by an authorization to build a road from the Lehigh Water Gap to the Susquehanna in Northumberland County. In 1794 the legislature authorized a highway from Reading to Erie. While some progress was thus made in the construction of roads to distant parts of the state, most of the existing roads, including state-owned roads, remained in a deplorable condition. To solve this problem, the Society for Promoting the Improvement of Roads and Inland Navigation was formed in 1789 in Philadelphia. This organization laid the foundation for the turnpike era that began on April 9, 1792, when the General Assembly passed an act incorporating the Philadelphia and Lancaster Turnpike Company.

The Lancaster Turnpike was financed by the sale of stock. The road, completed in 1794, had a solid stone base and was acclaimed a "masterpiece" of its kind. A toll was collected for use of the turnpike.

The Lancaster Turnpike was an immediate financial success, and other turnpike companies were rapidly organized. Although the building of turnpikes was concentrated in southeastern Pennsylvania, other areas of the state were also served. The major long-distance turnpikes included two turnpikes from Philadelphia to Pittsburgh; one from Philadelphia to Erie by

Lancaster County's Conestoga River valley was the birth-place of the Conestoga wagon. Developed in the early eighteenth century, the Conestoga wagon was first used to haul furs from Lancaster to Philadelphia. Later the wagons were used to carry farm produce and freight. Though mention was made of a "Conestogoe" wagon in 1717, use of the vehicle peaked between 1820 and 1850 and declined when the railroad crossed the Appalachians. Painting by William A. Falkler

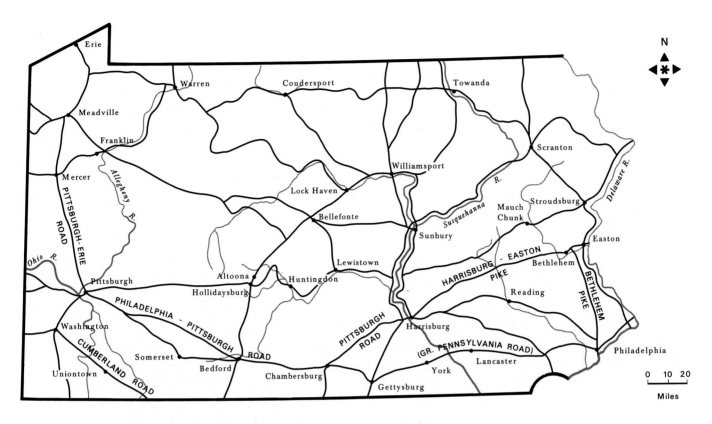

Major turnpike roads ━━━━━

Above: The economic development of the state depended upon the development of a transportation system, and by 1830 Pennsylvania had a network of turnpikes. Prepared by the Deasy Laboratory of Geographics, Dept. of Geography, The Pennsylvania State University

Opposite page: Isaac Jones of Philadelphia used this cartoon to advertise his Front Street tobacco establishment in 1760. Courtesy, The Library Company of Philadelphia

way of Sunbury, Bellefonte, Franklin, and Meadville; two roads from Philadelphia to the New York border, one through Berwick and the other through Bethlehem; and a stone road from Pittsburgh to Erie via Butler, Mercer, and Meadville.

By 1832, when the turnpike era reached its zenith, there were 220 companies. The turnpike system consisted of about 2,400 miles of completed highways, with another 600 miles projected. After 1832, however, more miles of turnpike roads were abandoned than newly constructed. Except for the Lancaster Turnpike and a few others, most of the turnpikes were financial failures. The tolls, frequently exorbitant, limited turnpike use. Two other factors also contributed to their decline. First, as the economy developed, state and local governments increasingly assumed the burden of maintaining toll-free roads through public funding. Second, the development of canals resulted in cheaper transportation, followed soon after by the greater speed and efficiency of railroads.

PHILADELPHIA: COMMERCIAL AND FINANCIAL CENTER

Although Philadelphia was settled much later than Boston or New York, it soon became the largest commercial center on the Atlantic coast. The city possessed a number of advantages. It served the largest and most prosperous farming area in the colonies. The collection of the farm produce was facilitated by two river systems, the Delaware and the Susquehanna. By 1800 the city shipped more than one-third of the exports of the United States, handling twice as much shipping as Baltimore and 25 percent more than New York.

The fur trade initiated the trade with England. As the economy of the colony developed, a variety of commodities became available for export, and trade grew dramatically in the eighteenth century. Between 1720 and 1750 the number of vessels clearing the port of Philadelphia rose from 140 to 358. Pennsylvania's exports were largely the products of farm and forest—products not greatly in demand in

England. Consequently, a triangular trading pattern evolved. The largest market for Pennsylvania products was the British West Indies. Here the ships picked up other cargoes, such as rum, sugar, and spices, that were much sought after in England, ultimately returning to Philadelphia laden with English goods that provided the necessities and some luxuries desired by the Pennsylvanians.

COLONIAL MONEY AND FINANCE

In addition to the problem of transportation, trade and commerce in colonial Pennsylvania were inhibited by a continual shortage of currency. Because each colony had different monetary policies, a uniform currency for trade did not exist. Specie—gold and silver—was the accepted monetary standard, but neither of these metals was mined in the English colonies. Some specie was obtained from the West Indies and other countries, but it was normally sent to England to pay for imported goods. This situation worsened when the British prohibited the ex-

49

port of coins to the colonies and refused to permit the colonies to mint foreign bullion.

Because there was little or no money available, a barter system developed in which storekeepers took in exchange for their goods all types of products from the local forests and farms. The local storekeeper, in turn, sent these goods to a nearby settlement, bartering the country goods for merchandise—hardware, sugar, molasses, thread, tools, glass, pottery, and other essentials—to restock the shelves of his store. As the needs of the community expanded, the variety of the merchandise increased. A major item in the country store was whiskey, normally delivered in a barrel and sold to customers by the gallon. The country store was more than a business center; it was a social center where people gathered to hear the news and discuss politics, religion, local affairs, and other issues of importance to the community.

Because of the shortage of currency, commodities became acceptable for payment of taxes and debts and even the government traded commodities for its purchases. At various times between 1683 and 1700, the Pennsylvania Assembly conferred the status of money on hemp, flax, wheat, rye, barley, Indian corn, tobacco, pork, and hides. The system obviously had some disadvantages. Many of these commodities were perishable. The quality of the goods might vary. Trade between colonies was hampered as each colony placed a different value on the same commodity.

Pennsylvania next resorted to paper money to satisfy its monetary needs. In 1723 Pennsylvania issued 15,000 pounds in paper money, with the stipulation that the paper would be guaranteed. This system worked well for many years, but as expenditures increased, such as during the crisis of the French and Indian Wars, inflation depreciated the value of Pennsylvania's paper currency. On the average in the late colonial era, a pound of Pennsylvania currency was worth only about 70 percent of a

Opposite page: *Philadelphia became the social and cultural center of the colonies and then the new nation. Fine homes on lower Chestnut Street bespoke new wealth and the gradual appearance of a middle class whose money and enterprise would fuel the industrial growth of the 1800s.*

Above: *Headhouse Square was originally a market, much like today's Lancaster farmer's market. Later, investors and planners envisioned a major terminus for every stage and canal route in the state. They never counted on railroads. Today it is a major tourist attraction on South Street.*

Above: *There were a number of private banks operating in Pennsylvania in the late eighteenth and early nineteenth centuries. Stephen Girard, who owned a successful mercantile business in Philadelphia, purchased the building of the Bank of the United States in 1812 and started his own bank. Girard's Bank is pictured here. From Scharf and Westcott,* History of Philadelphia, *vol. III, 1884*

Above, left: *A circa 1770 engraving depicts a colonial counting house—a pillar of early Pennsylvania commerce. Note the ships in harbor and cargo pictured— symbols of much ventured, much gained. Courtesy, The Library Company of Philadelphia*

Opposite page: *The Bank of North America was Pennsylvania's first true bank. Founded in 1781, the bank is America's oldest. This building stands on 3rd Street in Philadelphia. Courtesy, Pennsylvania State Archives*

pound sterling.

Though note issues, loans, and other banking functions were carried on by the provincial government, there were no banks in Pennsylvania before the American Revolution. Finally, to help meet the financial needs of the war, the first bank was organized on July 17, 1780. This institution was, strictly speaking, not a bank but a group of private subscribers organized to aid the federal government in an emergency. Out of this organization developed the first true bank in 1782, known as the Bank of North America. It has continued under a state charter and is now the oldest bank in America.

Once the precedent had been established, the banking system developed rapidly. In 1791 the federally chartered First Bank of the United States opened its main office in Philadelphia. In 1813 the Pennsylvania legislature authorized the chartering of forty-one new banks, of which thirty-five were in operation within two years. Besides the chartered banks there were an unknown number of uncharted private banks. The chartered banks enjoyed greater public confidence because of the controls designed to guarantee the safety of their financial operations.

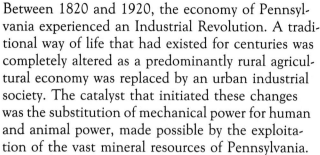

PART II
Evolution of an Industrial Titan:
1820 to 1920

Between 1820 and 1920, the economy of Pennsylvania experienced an Industrial Revolution. A traditional way of life that had existed for centuries was completely altered as a predominantly rural agricultural economy was replaced by an urban industrial society. The catalyst that initiated these changes was the substitution of mechanical power for human and animal power, made possible by the exploitation of the vast mineral resources of Pennsylvania.

A complex industrial society evolved in which the component elements—mining, manufacturing, transportation, agriculture, business—reinforced each other. When one component changed, there was a change in each of the others. The nineteenth and early twentieth centuries were a dynamic period that permanently altered the character of life in Pennsylvania.

Few areas of the world possess greater natural resources than Pennsylvania. Beginning in the early 1800s, these vast resources began to be exploited at a rate beyond the imagination of earlier times. Annual production of bituminous and anthracite coal was measured not in thousands of tons but in millions of tons. Petroleum, unknown in commercial quantities before 1859, was produced in millions of barrels. Forest resources were exploited not to clear new land for farms but to produce lumber products for an industrial society.

The development of manufacturing was the most important change in the way people earned their living. With the creation of the factory system, hundreds of workers were employed in a single plant. As a result, new patterns of settlement evolved. In the eighteenth-century rural economy, the population was widely and fairly evenly dispersed, with small commercial centers serving the needs of the farming community. In the new industrial society, large numbers of people were concentrated in manufacturing centers. Urban population grew rapidly, and by 1900 Pennsylvania had fifty-four cities with a population of more than 8,000.

A prerequisite for the growth of an industrial society is the development of a transportation network. A manufacturing system requires the assembly of vast quantities of fuel and raw materials and efficient distribution of the finished product. During the nineteenth century the network of turnpikes gave way to canals, and these, in turn, were replaced by the railroads. The development of Pennsylvania's railroad network between 1850 and 1900 was fundamental to the industrial evolution of the state. Few places in the world possessed a more diverse network of rail lines.

Throughout most of history, the average family possessed only the most rudimentary material necessities. During the nineteenth and early twentieth centuries, two major forces complemented each other in encouraging the expanded production of factory goods. First, the population of Pennsylvania increased from 1,049,000 in 1820 to 8,720,000 in 1920, providing an expanding potential market. Second, coupled with the population increase was a general rise in purchasing power. In 1860 the average worker earned $1.00 to $1.50 a day; by 1920 the $5.00-a-day wage was widely accepted. The increase in total wages paid in manufacturing—from $37,163,000 in 1850 to $263,375,000 in 1890 and $1,406,066,000 in 1920—indicates the growth in the purchasing power of factory workers. The standard of living of Pennsylvanians, despite temporary setbacks during times of economic depression, rose dramatically with the development of an industrial economy.

The changing industrial environment demanded new business practices. To serve the growing economy, the organizational scale of business was greatly enlarged. Capital requirements became so great that they could only be met through corporate financial institutions. Bank capital became the leading source of financing for new industrial enterprises, and the corporation became the basic structure for the development of any sizable business venture.

While mining and manufacturing were experiencing revolutionary changes, agriculture was also dramatically altered by the evolving industrial society. The pioneer Pennsylvania farmer produced grain, livestock, and other products that were needed to make his family self-sufficient. Only a small portion of the farm produce was marketed. Traditional agriculture was not so much an industry as a way of life. With the growth of a large urban population, the farmer had, for the first time, an economic incentive to produce much more than could be consumed by the family. To accomplish this, a new system of agriculture evolved. The new era began with the development of machinery, operated first by horse power and later by mechanical power. Not only could more land be cultivated, but the emphasis shifted to commodities that could be sold in the urban industrial markets.

The nineteenth and early twentieth centuries were Pennsylvania's greatest period of rapid economic growth. Exploitation of the state's vast natural resources provided the foundation for the expand-

The Bessemer converter, seen here in an 1880s Pittsburgh steel mill, removed carbon and other impurities from molten pig iron cheaply and efficiently. Drawing by Charles Graham. From Harper's Weekly, *April 19, 1886*

ing industrial economy. Great industrial empires were created by such dynamic leaders as Andrew Carnegie and John D. Rockefeller. The economic opportunities in the new manufacturing centers were considered superior to those in the country and acted as a magnet drawing people to urban life. Although economic progress was intertwined with horrible working conditions in the mines and factories and such urban problems as inadequate housing, sewage disposal, and impure water, it was nonetheless a time of advancing expectations. The vast majority of the people improved their standard of living, and hope for the future was high.

Chapter Four
Exploitation of a Rich Natural Heritage

The greatest single factor favoring Pennsylvania's development of an industrial economy between 1820 and 1920 was its vast storehouse of natural resources. Of these resources, the mineral fuels—bituminous coal, anthracite, petroleum, and natural gas—provided the power base for a manufacturing economy. Pennsylvania led all other states in value of minerals produced between 1820 and 1920. Besides minerals, the timber resources of the state provided the basis for major lumber and leather-tanning industries, and agriculture provided the raw materials for a major food-processing industry.

Besides providing the power base for manufacturing, exploitation of the state's resources provided the basis for general economic development. Entire regions were dominated by a mineral economy, and in many areas settlement patterns reflected the presence of mineral resources. Where the resources were greatest, as in the anthracite region, large cities developed. In the bituminous fields, scores of mining towns developed to exploit the coal reserves. In areas where the resources were depleted quickly, as in the oil and lumbering areas, population grew rapidly and declined rapidly. As a result Pennsylvania possesses many ghost towns, but the strategically located towns have persisted, serving permanent local and regional economies. In many of the larger towns and cities, manufacturing has replaced mining as the major source of employment.

Because the natural resources were primarily consumed outside the mining and lumbering regions, the development of a transportation network was essential. The development of the railroads in nineteenth-century Pennsylvania reflects the localization of the state's natural resources. In the anthracite region, for example, railroads were built for the single purpose of transporting coal to distant markets. In the bituminous region, the great trunk lines of the Pennsylvania, the New York Central, and the Baltimore and Ohio were served by a vast net-

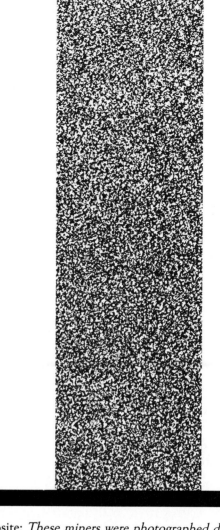

Opposite: *These miners were photographed drilling at the Cornwall iron mine. Iron was initially an important ore for Pennsylvania, but the exploitation of the Mesabi Range in Minnesota crippled iron mines in the East. Courtesy, Pennsylvania State Archives*

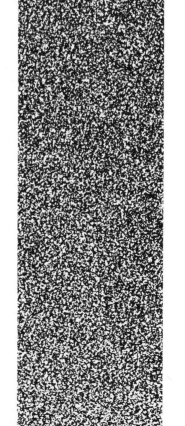

work of independent feeder lines extending into every nook and cranny of the coal region.

BITUMINOUS-COAL INDUSTRY

Bituminous coal is Pennsylvania's most important mineral resource. The availability of this major fuel has been a principal factor in the industrial prominence of the state. During the nineteenth century and well into the twentieth, Pennsylvania was the nation's leading coal-producing state.

The bituminous coalfields of Pennsylvania lie at the northernmost extension of the great Appalachian Coalfield. Coal is found in portions of thirty-three of the state's sixty-seven counties, and the total area underlain exceeds 13,000 square miles. The bituminous-coal beds, deposited during the late Paleozoic Era, are contained in strata that range in age between Pennsylvanian and early Permian. Thus, the coal-bearing measures are approximately 260 to 310 million years old. The geologic structure of the coalfields is characterized by nearly horizontal to gently undulating broad northeast-southwest trending folds. Structure axes are separated by two to four miles, with the flanks dipping on the order of one to fifteen degrees.

The coal-bearing Pennsylvanian and early Permian stratigraphic sections range in thickness from 1,200 to 3,000 feet. Major rock types within these sections are shale, sandstone, limestone, claystone, and, of course, coal. Approximately fifty named coal beds are recognizable in the coalfield, but only eight of these maintain sufficient continuity and quality to be of economic importance throughout the entire coalfield. These, in order of economic importance, are: Pittsburgh, Upper Freeport, Lower Kittanning, Lower Freeport, Upper Kittanning, Waynesburg, Sewickley, and Middle Kittanning. Most of the coal beds average less than five feet in thickness, although some attain a local thickness of seven to eleven feet. The majority of the coal beds have been mined locally where seam thickness and quality have enabled profitable operations.

Coal quality varies both locally and regionally throughout the bituminous coalfields of Pennsylvania. Regional metamorphism was greatest on the eastern edge of the field. Consequently the coal beds exhibit a general progression from east to west, from low-volatile bituminous (fixed carbon between 78 and 86 percent) to medium-volatile bituminous (fixed carbon between 68 and 78 percent) to high-volatile bituminous (fixed-carbon content less than 69 percent). That is, the fixed-carbon content decreases, and volatile matter increases, from east to west. The majority of reserves in Pennsylvania are moderate to high in sulfur, from one percent to more than 3 percent, and have a moderate to high ash content of from 8 to 15 percent. The heat value of the coal normally ranges between 10,000 Btu/lb to 14,000 Btu/lb on an as-received basis. Most of the coal beds in Pennsylvania can be used to produce coke in the by-product ovens.

Estimates of the original in-place reserves of bituminous coal in Pennsylvania, prior to mining, range between seventy-five and ninety billion tons. It has been estimated that since mining commenced in the eighteenth century, between ten and twenty billion tons of coal have been mined in Pennsylvania, accounting for about 20 percent of the total amount of bituminous coal mined in the United States. Estimates of total recoverable reserves of bituminous coal in Pennsylvania (underground and strip mineable reserves) range between twenty and thirty billion tons. If coal is mined at the rate of 100 million tons per year, some 250 to 350 years of bituminous-coal production may still be realized from Pennsylvania's coalfields. The recoverable reserves of bituminous coal in Pennsylvania account for about 6 percent of the potentially economically mineable coal in the United States, which is estimated to be about 438 billion tons.

HISTORY OF COAL PRODUCTION

Production of bituminous coal began with the first settlement in western Pennsylvania. The first known mention of coal was made in 1751 of an outcrop in the valley of the Kiskiminetas River, and the first definite mention of the

Pittsburgh seam was made by Captain Adam Stephen in 1754. The early coal mines supplied fuel for domestic heating and cooking and for such pioneer activities as the blacksmith shops. The first recorded export of coal from the region was in 1803, when 350 tons of coal were shipped from Pittsburgh as ballast in the ship *Louisiana* to New Orleans and then on to Philadelphia, where it sold for 37.5 cents a bushel.

Production grew steadily but slowly until the western Pennsylvania iron and steel industry began requiring great supplies of coke. Total production was only 1,305,000 tons in 1877, but in 1878 it rose to 12,500,000 tons. From then on tonnage mined increased rapidly, to an all-time peak production in 1918 of 177,217,000 tons. Employment in the bituminous fields reached its peak in 1914, when 196,038 miners produced coal. Employment declined slightly during World War I, but production increased because of longer workdays. During these four decades of growth, Pennsylvania dominated the U.S. bituminous-coal industry, and as late as 1915 the state was supplying one-third of the nation's coal needs.

Until the 1870s coal mining in western Pennsylvania was widely dispersed. The near-surface coal seams were readily accessible, and the cost of transporting a bulky, relatively low-cost fuel favored local development to satisfy local demands. With the growth of iron and steel and allied industries in southwestern Pennsylvania, however, the industry concentrated there, and Fayette, Westmoreland, and Allegheny counties assumed leadership positions. Between 1881 and 1917 Pennsylvania mines produced 3,111,245,000 tons of bituminous coal. Of this total, Fayette County produced 18.6 percent, Westmoreland 18.5 percent, and Allegheny 12.8 percent. Thus, during this thirty-six-year period, these three counties produced 49.9 percent of the state's coal.

The rapid growth of the coal industry and allied coke industry in Fayette and Westmoreland counties was determined by the position of the Pittsburgh coal bed. Coal from this seam was recognized at an early date as being physically and chemically nearly perfect for producing

beehive coke. With a carbon content of 57 to 60 percent, volatile matter 30 to 35 percent, moisture content under 2 percent, ash content less than 8 percent, and most important, a sulfur content under one percent, it was an ideal coking coal. No other coal bed in the United States had comparable coking qualities.

Besides the excellent quality, accessibility and a large reserve were important factors localizing the beehive-coke industry. The Pittsburgh coal bed underlies all of southwestern Pennsylvania. In Fayette County it was eight to eleven feet thick, and the original reserve of 1.9 billion tons was considered virtually inexhaustible.

Coke was produced right at the mine. In the beehive coking process, the gaseous and liquid hydrocarbons were burned off and destroyed so that only the carbon material remained as coke. In this way a ton of coal was reduced to 1,200 to 1,300 pounds of coke. The reduced weight and bulk of coke as opposed to coal greatly lowered the cost of transporting the fuel to the blast furnaces. From the late 1870s until World War I, the coke region of Fayette and Westmoreland counties, known as the Connellsville Beehive Coke Region, supplied essentially all of the coke consumed in western Pennsylvania, northern West Virginia, and eastern Ohio, and more than 85 percent of the coke for other iron and steel districts of the United States. The peak output of the region was reached in 1916, when more than 40,000 coke ovens were in operation, converting 33,792,000 tons of coal into 22,486,000 tons of coke.

As coal mining and beehive coke making developed, all other economic activities in the region were relegated to a place of minor importance. After 1880 about 75 to 80 percent of the wage earners in the region were employed in the coal-mining and coke industries. In the decade from 1900 to 1910, it is estimated that more than 80 percent of all capital investments in the region were in the coal and coke industries. The railroad pattern of the area was developed essentially to serve the coke industry, for the location of the ovens was largely determined by the availability of rail transportation.

At the peak of operation, about 25,000 car-loads of coke were hauled from this area daily. From 1880 to after 1910, because of the immense coal and coke freight, the southwestern division of the Pennsylvania Railroad was more profitable in proportion to its length than any other part of the company's lines. No other area of the state was more completely dominated by a single economic endeavor.

Although the Connellsville Region produced the fuel for blast furnaces, an important primary iron and steel industry did not develop. That industry centered in the valleys of western Pennsylvania, at the point of greatest advantage in transportation for the assemblage of iron ore and coke and the marketing of the finished products. The expanding coal and coke industry, nevertheless, created an economic boom in the area that lasted for about half a century. As a result the population of the region expanded remarkably. In Fayette County the population rose from 58,000 in 1880 to 188,104 in 1920, and in Westmoreland County during the same period population increased from 78,036 to 273,568. This was an increase of approximately 35 percent for each ten-year period, or about twice the rate of increase for the state as a whole.

The distribution of population was largely determined by the location of the coal and coke industries. The increased population did not concentrate in the larger towns and cities, but in the small mining settlements known locally as "patches." These settlements were normally company towns with poorly constructed houses and minimal amenities. A company store supplied the necessities for the mining population. The towns were bathed in smoke from the belching beehive ovens, and the polluted air created one of the dirtiest industrial environments in the nation.

If the growth of the beehive industry was spectacular, its decline was even more striking. After 1916 beehive coke production decreased rapidly, until by the early 1930s the industry had essentially disappeared from the region. The decline of the coking industry in the Connellsville Region is attributable to a number of

factors, the most important of which was the change from the beehive to the by-product method of coke production. This new process eliminated the tremendous waste of liquid and gaseous hydrocarbons inherent in the beehive oven. During the period from 1907 to 1916, it is estimated that beehive ovens wasted $50-million worth of hydrocarbon products annually.

The growth of the by-product coke process was modest in the United States until World War I, but after that it reached a position of dominance in less than five years. By 1923 by-product ovens were supplying more than 80 percent of the nation's coke requirements. This rapid growth was due to the demand for such valuable hydrocarbon products as explosives, coal-tar dyes, and medicines. The change from the beehive to the by-product process of coke production ranks high among revolutionary changes in modern industry.

The change in coking processes resulted in a complete change in the location of the industry. With using the by-product method, the coal must be processed at the place where the coal gases and liquids can be utilized. Since coal gases are used for heating blast furnaces, open hearths, power stations, and other plants, by-product ovens are nearly always built near the site of the primary iron and steel industry.

Opposite page *In burning coal in coke ovens, only soft coal was used, which irreparably hurt the anthracite (hard coal) industry. Coke was and is an important component of modern steel making. This photo, taken near Connellsville, dates from about 1885. Courtesy, Pennsylvania State Archives*

Above: *When coal seams were depleted, operations moved on and abandoned their rail lines. Courtesy, Pennsylvania State Archives*

Thus there has never been a by-product coke industry in the Connellsville Region.

The Connellsville Region also declined as a source of coal. After fifty years of increasing coal production, it was becoming evident that the most accessible areas had been mined. Many of the older mines were exhausted, and new mines were needed to maintain production. A survey of the Pittsburgh coal bed in Fayette County showed that about 78 percent of the original deposit, or about 1.5 billion tons, had been mined or lost to production.

With the decline of the mining and coke industries, the Connellsville Region began a period of economic difficulty. The small coal-mining and coke towns did not present a physical or cultural environment that attracted new enterprises. Because of lack of economic opportunity, the region gradually lost population. The mining economy did not provide a sound base for other economic development.

TECHNOLOGY AND LABOR

Mechanization of the coal-mining industry proceeded slowly, lagging far behind the great technological advances of many other nineteenth-century industries. The early mining techniques were crude and simple, characteristically labeled "pick-and-shovel labor." Because many coal seams outcropped on the hillsides, early miners using picks and shovels dug directly into the seam. If the coal was beneath the surface, they dug a shaft to the seam and hoisted the coal with crank and windlass. Before the use of pumps, when a shaft accumulated too much water, another shaft was sunk to the coal seam.

Very early in the mining operation, a systematic method known as the "room-and-pillar method" was devised to extract the coal from the nearly flat-lying seams. In this procedure, patterned after the "board-and-pillar" system of Europe, a main entry was driven to the coal seam. From the main entry, headings were driven at right angles. From these headings, again at right angles, the coal was removed, creating open rooms. Blocks of coal called pillars were left standing between rooms to prevent the mine roof from caving in on the working areas.

As the main entry became longer, the mining of coal became more difficult. The miner could no longer carry the coal from the mine, and a system of animal-drawn coal cars evolved. For many years labor was the most important factor in coal mining. Using his pick, the miner would break the coal from the seam. The broken lumps of coal were then shoveled into a small cart to be hauled from the mine by a donkey.

One of the first major inventions to aid in the mining process was the "miner's squib," an explosive charge of black powder that loosened the coal from the seam. Unfortunately this simple process of blasting coal off the solid seam was not only dangerous but produced too many small-size lumps of coal. In 1877 the air cutting machine was developed to undercut the face of the coal, providing a sufficient expansion area to control the effect of the blast. The air drill was introduced in 1889. The work pattern now consisted of undercutting, drilling the blast hole, blasting, and loading. Electricity was introduced into the mine operation in 1887, with the electric locomotive replacing the donkey to haul coal from the mine. The electric cutting machine was invented in 1890, but the electric drill did not become available until 1914. All coal was hand loaded in the mine until after 1920.

Because of a lack of mechanization, the miners' productivity, expressed in tons per man per day, remained low, and by 1918 had reached only four tons. A number of factors contributed to keeping productivity low. Labor was cheap and plentiful, so there was little incentive to increase productivity. Most of the mines were small, employing from one to no more than a few hundred miners, so there was little investment in research and development.

The coal mines were extremely dangerous places to work. There were thousands of accidents every year and a total of 9,449 fatalities between 1902 and 1920. The worst year for mine fatalities was 1907, when 806 miners were killed. Mine safety was given little consideration. Many of the miners who escaped accidents contracted black lung, a disease caused by coal dust accumulating in the lungs. Be-

A mechanical lever at the top of the mine shaft gave each carload of coal a shove that sent it rolling down into the breaker. If gravity proved inadequate, the miners had to take matters into their own hands. Courtesy, Bookmakers, Inc.

At the turn of the century electricity greatly changed the work of miners. It became possible to haul more coal with fewer men, run more powerful elevators, and improve lighting. Still, early wiring sparked often and caused explosions. This Keystone View Company shot was taken in a mine near Scranton. Courtesy, Pennsylvania State Archives

Opposite page: Matthew Hale Carpenter (1824-1881) was one of the defense attorneys in the trial of John Siney and Xingo Parks. Carpenter later went on to become a United States senator. From Cirker, Dictionary of American Portraits, Dover, 1967

Below: Despite new machinery, manual labor in the nineteenth century remained a big part of mining coal. Courtesy, Pennsylvania State Archives

cause the mines were damp and wet, rheumatic problems were commonplace among miners.

Although working conditions were at times intolerable, unionization of the miners was slow to develop. The mine owners engaged in a ceaseless war against the unions. One of the earliest attempts at organizing a miners' union in Pennsylvania came in 1873, when John Siney called a convention in Youngstown, Ohio, to form a national union. Siney created the organization known as the Miners National Association of the United States. To combat the new organization, mine owners compelled workers to sign "yellow-dog contracts" if they wanted to keep working. Siney's response was: "Sign them on the same grounds Galileo took before the Inquisition, exclaiming, 'But it does move after all!'"

As Siney struggled to preserve the union, the operators turned to the law to destroy it. Siney and Xingo Parks, one of his organizers, were indicted by a western Pennsylvania grand jury for violation of the state's criminal conspiracy law. The case was based on ancient legalism from English common law stating that the joining of men in a union to raise wages was unlawful. Two renowned lawyers, Matthew Carpenter of Wisconsin and Benjamin Butler of Massachusetts, came to the Clearfield County, Pennsylvania, courtroom to defend Siney and Parks. The only evidence at the trial consisted of speeches, printed documents, and the union constitution. Newspapers from across the country reported the proceedings to a national audience.

The defense attacked the conspiracy law that had long since been repealed in England. The argument closed with these words:

If you convict John Siney and Xingo Parks under this law, will it be, in the minds of a reading and intelligent public, John Siney or Xingo Parks, or the county of Clearfield and the State of Pennsylvania that is disgraced? This I leave to you, gentlemen of the jury, by your verdict to decide.

The prosecution's viewpoint was summed up by

the statement of Pennsylvania state senator William A. Wallace:

Shall this court and this jury fear to punish these men for a criminal violation of our law because the counsel for the defense says our law is old? . . . By the testimony of those men, John Siney and Xingo Parks, did assist, in this combination of miners, for the purpose of raising wages, and it is your bounden duty under the provision of the law to bring in a verdict of guilty.

The jury found Siney not guilty, but ruled against Parks on one count of inciting a riot. Cheering crowds carried Siney on their shoulders through the streets of Clearfield. Nevertheless, the mine operators continued to harass and control the miners, and the union's attempts at organizing were terminated in 1876.

Although there were a few local unions, the next national union did not evolve until 1890, when the United Mine Workers of America was organized. While many of the early attempts at unionization of the coal miners were based on the brotherhood of man, the United

Mine Workers' constitution stressed practicality. The first objective of the new organization was to secure proper wages for the miners. A second goal was safety, to "reduce to the lowest possible minimum the awful catastrophes which have been sweeping our fellow craftsmen to untimely graves by the thousands." There were also demands for an eight-hour day and for laws to prevent the hiring of children under fourteen to work in the mines. The final goal was labor peace by arbitration and conciliation.

The United Mine Workers was fortunate in having a series of strong leaders who welded the miners into a unified body. The first organizers, such as John McBride and John B. Rae, were consummate politicians who were able to woo rival factions into agreement. While they were the chief draftsmen of the practical objectives of the union, they also possessed the ability to inspire men. In 1899 John Mitchell became president of the United Mine Workers. Although he was a practical leader, his idealism, combined with hard work, caught the imagination of the miners and the nation. He unified the miners by preaching the brotherhood of man, saying, "The coal you dig isn't

Slavic or Polish or Irish coal. It's just coal."

In response to this magnificent leadership, the major coal areas, especially within Pennsylvania, were unionized in a short time. By 1903 the union had attained a membership of 173,000 and a treasury of one million dollars. Mitchell was forced to resign in 1908 because of his moderate policies, but by that time the membership had reached 273,000. Within a few years, John L. Lewis, the greatest leader of the United Mine Workers of America, emerged, becoming president of the union in 1919.

The United Mine Workers—created out of the poetic aspirations of men like Daniel Weaver, John Siney, and John Mitchell and the political practicality of men like John McBride, John B. Rae, and John L. Lewis—became one of the most remarkable institutions in America. These men shared a dream of changing the unbearable working conditions of the miner by battling the established rules of the industry. The union established its own government, a kingdom within a kingdom. It exerted a compelling influence over the lives of the miners who joined it, and at the peak of its power it was able to force a confrontation with the nation. During World War I, despite the need for coal in the war effort, the coal miners followed the leadership of John L. Lewis to a man. The miners believed that they had to take drastic action in order to achieve their goals of better working conditions and higher wages and Lewis molded thousands of men into one.

The United Mine Workers of America, led by Lewis and wielding vast amounts of money, political power, and influence, remade the American labor movement. Its achievements in establishing a health and welfare fund marked the beginning of a restructuring of American social security, providing health care, hospitalization, medical benefits, and pensions to the working population. Men from the UMW went on to create the Congress of Industrial Organizations, the United Automobile Workers, and the United Steelworkers.

Why did the United Mine Workers of America become the premier union in the nation in the early twentieth century? Possibly it was be-

Opposite page: *John Mitchell (1870-1919) became the United Mine Workers' president in 1899. His statement, "The coal you dig isn't Slavish or Polish or Irish coal. It's just coal," helped unite the miners. When Mitchell resigned in 1908, union membership numbered 273,000. From Cirker,* Dictionary of American Portraits, *Dover, 1967*

A district meeting of mine workers brought John L. Lewis (center) to Shenandoah, Pennsylvania, in 1938. The meeting was held in the town's stadium. Photo by Sheldon Dick. Courtesy, U.S. Dept. of Agriculture FSA Collection, Library of Congress

cause the dangers faced by every miner moved him nearer to brotherhood. In the mines there was a sense that every man's life depended upon his neighbor. Possibly the drab and desolate life of the shabby mining towns, while it sometimes brought despair, also created the overwhelming desire for a better life. Perhaps it was because the dangerous work of the miner produced strong, vibrant leaders who were able to challenge antagonistic employers, too often concerned solely with profits at the expense of human suffering. Most likely it was a combination of all these powerful ingredients that unionized an overwhelming percentage of the mines of Pennsylvania.

ANTHRACITE MINING

Pennsylvania's anthracite fields occupy some 484 square miles of a ten-county region in northeastern Pennsylvania. Three of the fields occupy valleys or basins (Northern, Western Middle, and Southern fields), whereas the Eastern Middle Field occupies a plateau-like tableland. The Northern Field of 176 square miles extends through Luzerne, Lackawanna, and small portions of Susquehanna and Wayne counties. The largest cities in the Northern Field are Scranton and Wilkes-Barre. The Eastern Middle Field, centering on Luzerne County with extensions into Schuylkill, Carbon, and Columbia counties, has an area of only thirty-three square miles. Hazleton is the urban center of this field. The Western Middle Field occupies ninety-four square miles in Northumberland, Columbia, and Schuylkill counties. The largest urban center is Shamokin. The Southern Field is the largest in area, occupying 180 square miles. It extends northeast-southwest in Schuylkill, Carbon, Dauphin, and Lebanon counties. Pottsville is the largest settlement.

The Pennsylvania anthracite fields are geologically complex. The coalfields have been subjected to intense folding of the rocks into synclines and anticlines in which thrust faulting is common. The structural complexity increases from north to south. Thus in the north the folds are open and symmetrical, while in the

south they are tightly folded with associated high-angle faults.

More than 200 seams of coal have been mined in the anthracite fields. The original reserve of coal was 24.4 billion tons, of which 8 billion tons have been mined. Of the 16.4 billion tons that remain, about another 8 billion tons could be recovered by modern mining methods. However, the reserves are not evenly distributed. Reserves in the Northern Field have largely been depleted or have been flooded after mine abandonment, whereas the Eastern, Western Middle, and particularly the Southern Field have significant reserves that may be economically recoverable by modern mining technology.

DEVELOPMENT OF THE ANTHRACITE ECONOMY

The first recorded use of anthracite in Pennsylvania was in 1769, when Obadiah Gore used it in his blacksmith shop in Wilkes-Barre. In 1777 the first shipment of anthracite outside the coalfields was made from the Wyoming Valley down the Susquehanna River to Harrisburg. In 1782 the first coal-mining company, the Lehigh Coal Mining Company, was organized to surface-mine coal in Carbon County, where it had been found accidentally the year before. Anthracite was first used as a home-heating fuel in 1808, when Judge Jesse Fell of Wilkes-Barre designed a furnace grate that would withstand the intense heat produced by burning anthracite. However, the use of anthracite increased slowly because of the difficulty in igniting it, the relative abundance of firewood, and the many problems involved in transporting the fuel to market. Annual anthracite production did not exceed one million tons until 1837.

The first major market for anthracite was in the smelting of iron ore. The anthracite furnace was larger than the charcoal furnace, and in the late 1830s it assumed a major role in supplying the growing American iron market. By 1841 a dozen anthracite furnaces were in operation in eastern Pennsylvania, with four more in New Jersey. Because there was a limited

This Carbon County coal town view dates from around 1920. Courtesy, Pennsylvania State Archives

market for iron in the anthracite region, the coal moved southeastward toward the iron ore and the ultimate market. The Lehigh Valley was the center of the new industry. By 1860 half a million tons of anthracite iron were produced in the United States, more than half of it in Pennsylvania. Anthracite was beginning its twenty-year reign as the chief furnace fuel. After about 1880 coke produced from bituminous coal assumed the leading role, although as late as 1915 a score of American blast furnaces were still using anthracite mixed with coke.

Because the cost of anthracite was almost twice that of bituminous coal, it was eliminated from those market areas in which the cheaper fuel could be used. As the industrial iron market declined, however, the use of anthracite for home heating increased. Anthracite was considered a nearly perfect home-heating fuel. Once ignited, it provided an even, constant heat with minimum care. Because of the high carbon content, it produced a large amount of heat and very little smoke. With its low ash and sul-

phur content, anthracite was a particularly clean-burning fuel. As the forests were depleted in New England and the East Coast, a new domestic heating fuel was needed, and anthracite was the fuel nearest to these expanding markets.

Because the anthracite market was outside the coalfields, the first prerequisite for its use was the development of a transportation system. Early pioneers in anthracite production were hindered by prohibitive land-transportation costs to the eastern Pennsylvania markets. With the completion of the Schuylkill Navigation Canal and the Delaware and Hudson Canal in 1827, and the Lehigh Canal in 1829, anthracite became the most important commodity moving on the canals. By 1846 the canal system of the anthracite region consisted of 643 miles of waterways. Canals greatly reduced

Above: *Convinced that there was a great future in mining and transporting anthracite coal, Josiah White (pictured here) and his partner, Erskine Hazard, made possible the navigation of the Lehigh and the growth of the valley's anthracite coal industry. From M.S. Henry,* History of the Lehigh Valley, *1860*

Above right: *The Lehigh Coal and Navigation Company's chief engineer and superintendent, E.A. Douglass, oversaw the most specialized canal in the United States while responsible for the Lehigh's upper grand section. From M.S. Henry,* History of the Lehigh Valley, *1860*

Opposite page: *The Lehigh Valley's industrial development was spurred by the work of the Lehigh Coal and Navigation Company, which was incorporated in 1822. Seven years later the Lehigh Canal was completed. From the Pennsylvania Canal Society Collection, Canal Museum, Easton, PA*

shipping costs, giving anthracite a competitive advantage over other fuels in Eastern Seaboard cities.

The regional canals were in turn superceded by the railroads. The canal companies themselves were among the earliest investors in the anthracite railroads, which were built initially to carry coal from the mines to the rivers and canals. The Mauch Chunk Railroad, completed in 1827, was the first steam railroad in Pennsylvania and the second in the nation. By the Civil War period, railroads had largely replaced canals for transporting anthracite.

Because virtually all of the anthracite produced was transported out of the region, railroads developed rapidly. As early as 1846 there were 436 miles of track in the anthracite region. This figure increased to more than 1,000 miles in 1863 and by 1873 reached 2,290 miles, representing a capital investment of $128 million. In 1900 there were ten railroad companies operating in the coalfields, each of them controlling coal lands.

When anthracite production reached a magnitude that proved profitable to railroads, com-

petition among carriers arose. Because the mine capacity was always greater than the market demand, the railroads in order to reduce competition and increase profits gradually purchased the coal lands. By combining the mining and distribution of coal under a single company, the railroads were able to achieve a monopolistic control of the anthracite coal industry. The benefits to the companies of this control included a more efficient transportation system, the elimination of coal agents and thus cheaper marketing of coal, the working of the most profitable collieries and shutting down of the most expensive mines, lower management costs through centralization, greater control over coal prices for maximum profit, and finally, greater control over labor.

THE ANTHRACITE MINER
The words on one miner's tombstone reveal the intensity of feeling of many nineteenth-century anthracite miners:

Fourty years I worked with pick and drill

Down in the mines against my will
The Coal King's slave, but now its passed;
Thanks be to God I am free at last.

The hazards of anthracite mining were great. Deep in the bowels of the earth, sometimes knee-deep in water, tens of thousands of men mined seams of coal sometimes no more than a few inches thick, always fearful of cave-ins, rock falls, explosions, and fires, and terrible death by suffocation. When an accident occurred, death frequently came mercifully quick. In 1911, for example, when 175,098 miners were employed in the coalfields, there were 699 fatalities. At times when the mine was hopelessly entombed, there was the agony of burial alive. In most mining settlements there was not a single family that had not lost some member in the mines—father, son, or brother.

Life in the mines began at an early age. The Pennsylvania legislature in 1885 made it illegal to hire boys under fourteen years of age for underground work, or twelve years in surface jobs. In 1903 the ages were raised to sixteen and

Above: *Located on the Lehigh River, Mauch Chunk (renamed Jim Thorpe) prospered from the anthracite coal-mining operations in the surrounding mountains. The town manufactured the machinery needed for the mining, transporting, and shipping of coal. From M.S. Henry,* History of the Lehigh Valley, *1860*

Opposite, top: *When the colliery was operating, miners took an open-cage elevator into the mine. Each miner wore a kerosene-burning helmet torch and carried a lunch pail. The cold drink on the top of the pail helped keep the rest of the lunch cool. Courtesy, Book-makers, Inc.*

Opposite, bottom: *These miners and their boss were photographed at Hazleton about 1900. Their lamps burned oil, which could start underground fires. Courtesy, Pennsylvania State Archives*

fourteen, respectively. The law, however, was little enforced. Parents, eager for additional income, consistently filed false affidavits on their sons' ages with local magistrates, who received a 25-cent fee for each document. Many of the boys began working in the mines when they were only six or seven years old.

The young boy advanced through a type of apprentice system in learning the necessary skills to become a full-fledged miner. The first job was in the breaker, a towering wooden structure. The coal was carried to the top of the breaker and fed into tiers of chutes. The boys straddled the chutes on narrow planks and picked out the slate and other refuse as the coal swirled by. Sometimes older men who could no longer function as miners also worked as breaker boys. This gave rise to the regional refrain, "Twice a boy and once a man is the poor miner's life."

The workday in the breakers averaged ten hours, and a work week was six days. In the days before water was used in processing, the dust was so thick in the screening room that

the boys could barely see beyond their reach. They wore handkerchiefs over nose and mouth, and most chewed tobacco to keep from choking. When mechanical breakers were introduced, the noise was unbearable. Bleeding and mangled fingers were common, for the use of gloves was usually forbidden as it decreased the efficiency of the boys' work, and besides, they were too expensive. The sorry plight of the breaker boys is dramatically portrayed in the poem "Over the Coals" by James Sweeney Boyle:

Over the ice they pull the coals
Their fingers rent by a hundred holes;
You may trace the path torn digits shed.
Their heads are bowed and their bodies cramped.
A painful look on their features stamped;
Their knees are pressed against aching breasts

Above: *Lewis Hine photographed these breaker boys in 1911 in South Pittston. Though the Pennsylvania legislature passed a law in 1903 prohibiting boys under fourteen years old from working in the breakers or in other mining-related surface jobs, the law was not really enforced. These boys worked about ten hours a day, six days a week. Courtesy, National Archives*

Opposite page: *A young boy working in the mining industry in the nineteenth century would usually begin his "apprenticeship" in a coal breaker like this one. Here the coal was crushed, freed from culm (slag), sorted, and washed. Courtesy, Wyoming Historical and Geological Society*

Till bones are bent in the tender chests;
And lungs are crushed in their chambers tight . . .
In sorrow they slave where the massive screen
rolls,
So fearfully, tearfully over the coals.

From the breakers, boys went into the mines at the age of twelve to fourteen, to work for a few years as door boys. The heavy wooden doors, located in gangways and headings, controlled ventilation, but they had to be opened and closed to allow the passage of mule-drawn coal cars. The boys had to sit in the damp darkness for hours on end, and still stay alert and listen for the approaching cars. This lonely life frequently was the beginning of such health problems as rheumatism, arthritis, and lung disease, but it instilled a sense of responsibility and courage, traits necessary for survival in the mines.

The next step in becoming a miner was to advance to the position of driver boy, or mule driver. It was now the boy's responsibility to move the coal from deep in the mine to the breaker. This was a difficult task, for many of the mine tunnels were at steep angles to reach the steeply pitching coal lying in synclines and anticlines. The mule was an excellent animal for hauling the cars as it was small, surefooted, and could pull a heavy load. The driver boys had the responsibility of caring for the animals. In the mines there was the impression that the mules received better treatment than the miners.

If a boy survived these introductory years, he then became a miner. As one observer noted, "Young boys labored at tasks which stunted their bodies, ground their brains, and warped their souls." They entered adulthood as hardened and calloused men, quick to violence and brutality, seemingly stoic and even indifferent in the face of suffering and death.

Because working conditions were horrible and the monetary rewards slim, there were continuous disputes between labor and the mine owners. Under these conditions, the miners fought back as best they could, organizing mutual-assistance societies. The largest of these was the Ancient Order of Hibernians, formed to "promote friendship, unity, and true Christian charity" among its members, but also the spearhead of Irish-American labor and political action.

Early attempts at unionization in the coalfields were met with opposition—a combination of anti-Catholicism, ethnic hostility, class antagonism, and economic degradation of the miners. During the early 1860s there were more than forty killings, all of them unsolved, most of them related to labor strife.

Labor-related terrorism involving destruction of mine property, however, could not solve the fundamental problems. Most Irish workers

Fresh goat's milk supplemented these Pottsville miners' lunches about 1907.

turned to unionism to improve their economic situation. After many failures, a strong union organization began to evolve in the 1870s. At the same time Franklin Benjamin Gowen, president of the Philadelphia and Reading Railroad, moved to consolidate the railroad company's control of mining. In 1873 he met secretly with the heads of major anthracite railroads, and they drew up a trust agreement that included fixing the price of coal at five dollars a ton and dividing the market among themselves.

Control over the industry also required control over labor. The labor dispute came to a head with the Long Strike of 1875, which lasted more than five months and resembled a war more than a strike. Gowen's tactics were ruthless. Strikebreakers, protected by security forces, were brought into the region by the trainload. The union was infiltrated by spies and its every move anticipated. As violence intensified, the Molly Maguires, a secret society organized about 1857, were allegedly at the forefront of the miners' terrorism. The strike ended when the resources of the union were exhausted and the miners could no longer battle the overwhelming power of the mine owners, the railroads, and the state. At the end of the strike, those miners not blacklisted were allowed to return to work, at a 20-percent cut in pay, in the nonunion mines.

The aftermath of this strike was disastrous to the union movement and the Molly Maguires. The final demise of the Mollies began in the Schuylkill County courthouse in Pottsville on May 4, 1876, when five men went on trial for the murder of a policeman. All were found guilty in a sensational trial and hanged.

Although only a few of the Mollies escaped hanging or imprisonment, peace did not return to the fields. In 1877 a wave of railroad violence and riots swept the region. These acts of destruction and civil difficulties gradually ran their course, and the miners gained some rights. The United Mine Workers finally organized the coal anthracite workers in 1897, and while the mine operators continued to oppose unions, more than 85 percent of the miners had joined the union by 1900. Miners who knew little of the workers' trials in the 1870s and 1880s flocked into the organization. They heard their fathers speak of past failures but believed they could do better, and the United Mine Workers became a power in the settling of labor problems. Working conditions, though still harsh, gradually improved.

PETROLEUM INDUSTRY

The world's petroleum industry began along Oil Creek at Titusville, Pennsylvania, on August 27, 1859, when "Colonel" Edwin L. Drake drilled a well and discovered oil at a depth of sixty-nine feet. The discovery came at a time of growing world demand for a better illuminant than candles and a better lubricant than whale oil, and the early oil industry grew rapidly. Land bordering Oil Creek was soon leased, and latecomers were forced to secure holdings on the valley slopes. From 1859 to 1864 the oil region was confined to the valley of Oil Creek and an area extending forty miles up and down the Allegheny River. The wells of 1860 produced more oil than anyone had ever seen before, but they were small when compared to the flowing wells of 1861. The first of these wells, known as the "Fountain," had a flow of 300 barrels a day. With each new well the excitement increased. Where there was once a vast wilderness, there now appeared, as if by magic, the most intensive activity. Towns sprang up overnight in the vicinity of prolific producers.

In 1864 production in the lowland areas began to taper off, and new discoveries were sought. Because the individual oil pools were relatively small, the boundaries of the oil region were rapidly enlarged, until by the mid-1870s oil was being produced from the Bradford field on the New York boundary to the borders of West Virginia and Ohio in the southwest.

Production increased rapidly, from about 3,200 barrels of crude petroleum in 1859 to 3,056,606 barrels in 1862. With the expansion of the producing area, production rose to 10,910,000 barrels in 1874 and reached an all-time high in 1891 of 31,000,000 barrels, or about 83 percent of the nation's output. The development of the oil resources was nevertheless a precarious endeavor. Between 1859 and 1874 it is estimated that 10,500 wells were drilled, of which only 3,250 were productive. The oil-producing horizons were not continuous, so that many wildcat wells did not tap oil-bearing formations.

TECHNOLOGY AND TRANSPORTATION
With the discovery of oil, a totally new industry came into existence. Not only did drilling techniques have to be developed, but new transportation, refining, and marketing systems had to be created. The Drake well was drilled with a simple percussion bit. Soon, however, more efficient and powerful drilling methods were devised. The early derricks were only twenty to thirty feet high, but by the mid-1860s they reached a height of fifty-six feet to sustain the heavier drilling tools. In the early years the weight of drilling tools was about 600 pounds, but this rapidly increased to 1,600 to 1,800 pounds. These heavier tools were able to drill a hole to the oil sands at a much faster rate. Larger casings were also used to control drilling and water. Production was revolutionized with the introduction of the oil-well torpedo in January 1965 at a well near Titusville. When the torpedo was lowered into a well and exploded, a large pocket was created at the bottom of the well and the oil sands shattered so that oil could more easily flow into the well. This increased oil production enormously, and the torpedoing of wells became one of the established practices in oil production.

After the peak year of 1891, oil production began a gradual decline. It was apparent to the oil producers that most of the large pools had already been discovered. Oilmen who a few years before had produced oil with no regard for conservation practices now began to realize that the future looked bleak and to seek ways of increasing production.

As early as 1880, John F. Carll, geologist of the Second Geological Survey of Pennsylvania, had suggested that an oil field could be rejuvenated by flooding the oil sands. "The flooding

Above: *This early oil field near Lamertine, complete with derricks, sprouted up among well-kept lawns. By the mid-1860s, about the time this photo was taken, oil derricks stood close to sixty feet high. Courtesy, Pennsylvania State Archives*

Opposite page: *When the flow of oil in a petroleum well became sluggish, the well was "shot." To shoot a well, a blast of nitroglycerine was discharged in the bottom of the well, usually resulting in streams and sprays of oil shooting forth like a geyser. The Pennsylvania well pictured was shot with eighty quarts of nitroglycerine. If, after a blast, the oil did not spout forth, that would mean the well had become unprofitable.*

of an oil district is generally viewed as a great calamity," he wrote, "yet it may be questioned whether a larger amount of oil cannot be drawn from the rocks in that way than by any other, for it is certain that all the oil cannot be drawn from the reservoir without the admission of something to take its place." However, the introduction of water into one well, thereby increasing the production of others, was probably accidental. In some depleted wells the casing was removed without proper plugging, and in others the casing corroded, admitting fresh water from shallow horizons to the producing sand.

Because most of the oil fields were extremely small, they did not lend themselves to secondary recovery of oil by water flooding. Only the Bradford field, with its large area of uniform oil-producing sand, lent itself to this method. However, it was not until about 1905 that production began very slowly to increase. At that time the laws of Pennsylvania required that all abandoned wells be plugged to prevent fresh water from entering the oil sands; thus those producers who practiced flooding had to do so illegally. By 1921 flooding had become so prevalent, and so much political pressure had been exerted, that the Pennsylvania legislature passed a special act legalizing the practice when applied to the Bradford Third and certain other specified ranks. Production from the Bradford field then rose rapidly from about three million barrels to a second peak in 1937 of seventeen million barrels, representing more than 90 percent of the state's total production.

The Bradford oil field became the testing area for secondary-recovery methods. The earliest method is now known as the circle flood. A number of abandoned wells were selected. Water injected into these wells spread out more or less in a circle, pushing the oil outward into producing wells. The greatest disadvantage of this early method of flooding was the irregular spacing of the wells. Because there was no definite pattern of wells, pockets of oil were frequently bypassed so the oil could not migrate to the producing wells.

A more efficient method, the line flood, was

introduced in 1922. Under this method, two rows of oil wells were staggered on both sides with an equally spaced row of water-intake wells extending across a productive tract. This method demonstrated that the greater the pressure exerted on the oil sand, the larger the ultimate yield.

The line flood was used until 1928, when a still more intensive method of secondary recovery was introduced. This is known as the five-spot method because the arrangement of the wells is similar to the five spot on dice. The water-intake well is in the center, surrounded by four producing wells. Water injection under pressure began in 1930. The techniques for secondary recovery developed in the Bradford oil field are now employed throughout the world.

Because liquids had previously been transported only in small quantities, a new method of transportation had to be devised for petroleum. Initially the oil was put in barrels at the wells and hauled to shipping points by long processions of teams—a laborious and costly endeavor. The extension of the railroads into the region made possible the introduction of the tank car. In 1865 two wooden tanks, each holding forty to forty-five barrels of oil, were placed on an ordinary flatcar. The experiment proved successful, and by the spring of 1866 hundreds of tank cars were in use. This type prevailed until the iron boiler tank car appeared in February 1869.

The development of the pipeline to transport oil came with the prolific production of oil at Pithole in 1865. This experiment also proved successful, and within a short time many other pipelines were in operation within the oil region. It was not, however, until the large production from the Bradford oil field that pipelines were considered for long distance transportation of oil. In 1878 the largest pipeline in operation was three inches in diameter, and oil had not been pumped for a longer distance than thirty miles. The prevailing system was to transport the oil by pipeline from the dispersed oil fields to the railroads and then move it by tank car to the Atlantic coast and Midwest refineries.

To gain an economic advantage over the Standard Oil Company controlled by John D. Rockefeller, the independent producers and refiners decided to try replacing costly rail transportation with long-distance pipelines. In 1878 the Tidewater Pipe Company was formed to build a pipeline from the Bradford oil field to Williamsport, where the oil would then be transported by the Reading Railroad to the East Coast refineries. Construction of the pipeline was one of the greatest engineering endeavors of the time. Besides the problem of laying the pipeline, an entirely new set of specifications was necessary for such items as gate valves, flanges, unions, and ells that could withstand the high pressures necessary to move the oil. In addition, a new system of pumping engines had to be developed, capable of moving oil not only across great distances but also over the high ridges of the rugged Allegheny Plateau. Pumping stations were placed from twenty to thirty miles apart along the pipeline route. On May 29, 1879, oil was placed in the pipeline at Bradford, and seven days later it flowed into receiving tanks at Williamsport. The pipeline was a success, and a new era began in oil transportation.

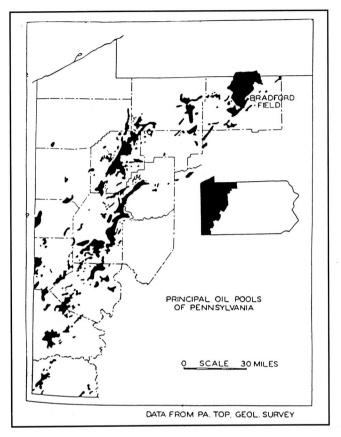

PRINCIPAL OIL POOLS
OF PENNSYLVANIA

0   SCALE   30 MILES

DATA FROM PA. TOP. GEOL. SURVEY

Oil fields are found in western Pennsylvania from the New York border to the southwestern portion of the state.

It became immediately evident that the old system of short pipeline haulage followed by long-distance rail haulage could not compete economically with the new, cheaper mode of transportation. John D. Rockefeller had been exceedingly skeptical concerning the success of so long a pipeline, but once he saw the results he promptly took action. He instituted a program for the construction of trunk pipelines that amazed the oil region.

By the end of June 1879 the Standard Oil Company had bought a right-of-way from the Bradford field to Bayonne, New Jersey, and was laying a pipeline directly to the East Coast. At the same time a pipeline was laid to Philadelphia to serve this area's refineries. These were six-inch lines with a daily capacity of 10,000 barrels each. Almost simultaneously new four-inch pipelines were laid from the Bradford field to Buffalo and Pittsburgh. The Pittsburgh line connected with the pipeline to Cleveland. By 1881 all parts of the oil region were connected by trunk lines to the Eastern Seaboard and Midwest refineries.

With the success of the Tidewater pipeline and the completion of the trunk system of the Standard Oil Company, Rockefeller recognized that if the Standard Oil Company was to maintain its position, no other independent outlet could be allowed to develop. Tidewater survived the competition of Standard Oil. However, to control the operations of the independent company Standard bought a minority interest in the company in 1883 to secure a voice in the operating policies of the company. This led to a compromise. It was agreed to divide the pipeline operations of the eastward moving oil. Standard received 88.5 percent and Tidewater 11.5 percent of the business. Tidewater regarded it as a final recognition of independence and Standard now knew that it controlled the vast amount of the oil movement. Tidewater thrived under the agreement, and by 1911 the company had paid more than 2,000 percent in dividends to its investors. The company expanded, becoming a combined producing, transporting, refining, and exporting corporation with oil leases and property throughout the United States and several foreign countries.

All attempts by independent companies to maintain other pipeline companies faced the powerful opposition of Standard Oil. For example, early in 1880 the Buffalo Pipe Line Company was organized by a group of independent oilmen, and on August 24, 1881, a pipeline was completed from Bradford to Buffalo. Immediately, Standard Oil started a price war with the independent refineries in Buffalo that was so devastating that the pipeline was sold to Standard Oil interests on January 23, 1882. These practices continued throughout the 1880s, and by 1890 Standard Oil had gained a monopolistic control of all transportation from the Pennsylvania oil fields.

With the control of transportation, Standard Oil developed a monopolistic system for controlling markets. From 1875 to 1910 more than 90 percent of the refined petroleum products sold in the United States were Standard Oil brands. The organization was so conceived as to refine all of the oil that could be produced to supply both domestic and foreign markets. There was no attempt to control the oil producers. Rather, the Standard Oil viewpoint was that oil production was too decentralized and the individual producer too small, and that oil would be pumped from the wells at the maximum rate if the producer had a market. Standard Oil's control thus came in the marketing process.

With the increasing supply of oil, an intensive program was developed to market the products throughout the United States. The country was divided into major regions, and these were further divided into divisions, sections, and subsections, thus extending marketing control to the local outlets. Because the American market was not large enough to absorb the domestic oil production, the world market was developed with the same systematic intensity as the domestic market. In the two decades prior to 1900, about 70 percent of American oil went abroad.

The solidification of Standard Oil's monopolistic position in the United States and its development of foreign markets came only after the elimination of domestic competition with independent companies, bitter contests with foreign competitors, and the resolution of difficult problems involving trade barriers, heavy taxes, antiquated methods of distribution, strange local regulations and customs, and national prejudices. Standard Oil's control of the Pennsylvania oil industry was complete until the company was dissolved by the Supreme Court's famous antitrust decision of 1911. By that time, however, vast new oil fields had been discovered not only in the United States but in foreign countries, and major new companies were being organized. Standard Oil never again achieved the monopolistic control over an oil region held by John D. Rockefeller in Pennsylvania in the late nineteenth and early twentieth centuries.

Above: *After the Civil War, oil boomtowns sprang up in western Pennsylvania. This is possibly Pithole, one of the most famous. Courtesy, Pennsylvania State Archives*

Opposite page: *Glade Run, pictured around 1870, was one of the ephemeral oil boomtowns. Structures went up almost overnight and vanished when the place was no longer profitable. Courtesy, Pennsylvania State Archives*

The Pennsylvania oil industry provided the technological and economic foundation upon which the modern oil industry rests. Pennsylvania's oil industry was supreme during the kerosene era that lasted from 1859 into the early twentieth century. The world has a great heritage from these early beginnings when oildom existed only in Pennsylvania.

PITHOLE: OILDOM'S FIRST GREAT BOOMTOWN

The discovery of petroleum has always held the potential of creating great wealth. As a result, each new field acted as a magnet drawing people to it. Hundreds of oil boomtowns sprang up in the oil region of western Pennsylvania. Of these ephemeral boomtowns, none was more spectacular than Pithole in the forests of Venango County.

When oil was discovered at Pithole on January 7, 1865, it was one of the wildest and most isolated regions in western Pennsylvania. The

few pioneers who lived on the scattered farms eked a bare existence from the land by raising buckwheat and hunting deer. Their homes were log cabins. Money existed largely in the imagination. The only stranger that passed from farm to farm was the itinerant peddler with a few outside necessities.

With the drilling of each new well in early 1865, it became evident that a major oil pool had been discovered. Many of the wells were free-flowing, producing 50 to 500 barrels of oil per day. News of the possibility of great wealth spread like wildfire throughout the eastern United States. By May hundreds of people were rushing to Pithole, which presented inducements to not only developers, but to oil field adventurers, keen shysters, unscrupulous stock jobbers, needy laborers, and dishonest tricksters.

During the summer of 1865, a number of mammoth wells were brought in. On August 2 the Grant well began to flow at 800 barrels per day. On August 28 the largest well of the pool began to flow at 1,300 barrels. For each new producing well, six dry holes were drilled, but these were disregarded. By September more than 100 wells had been drilled on the sixty-five-acre Holmden farm, the initial area of discovery. The production of the pool was more than 5,000 barrels a day—two-thirds of the entire production of the oil region.

With the possibility of "striking it rich," the first act of the stranger was to invest in some oil venture. Fabulous prices were paid for land that ordinarily would have been worthless. One farmer refused $800,000 for his farm, reportedly saying, "I don't keer to hev my buckwheat tramped over, but you kin hev it next winter fur a million." Many wells were sold on the spot without any investigation, for $100,000 and half the oil. A favorite scheme of promoters was to sell seventeen-sixteenths of each well. Speculators came from all parts of the mining world, and Pithole stock was found on many European exchanges.

The greatest speculative transaction occurred

in July 1865, when two speculators named Duncan and Prother obtained a thirty-day option at $1.3 million on the Holmden farm—a farm that would have sold for no more than $1,500 six months earlier. The buyers expected to turn around and sell the farm to New York speculators for $1.6 million. Difficulty was encountered in raising the initial purchase money, and when the money was finally obtained in Chicago, it had to be transported to Pithole. As a result the buyers reached the boomtown to make payment after the sun had set on the thirtieth day. The real estate agents refused the money, claiming that the contract had expired with the setting of the sun. A suit was immediately filed in the United States District Court in Pittsburgh, but differences were adjusted without the need for a trial. Duncan and Prother then sold the farm in the middle of September for two million dollars.

One of the greatest problems faced in the development of the Pithole pool was the transportation of the oil to market. Up until this time oil was loaded in barrels and hauled by horse teams to the streams of the region for transportation by water. As long as the pioneer petroleum territory was limited to Oil Creek, teamsters could handle the short haul to water transportation, but now that development was extending into the uplands, this means of transportation had many drawbacks. The poor condition of the roads, exorbitant charges (up to $3.15 per barrel for hauling oil that sold for less than $2 a barrel), and the production of oil at a greater rate than could be hauled from Pithole led to the attempt to develop a new means of transportation.

Although there had been previous attempts to carry oil through pipelines, they had all been unsuccessful because of poor pipe, leaky lead joints, and faulty pumping machinery. On September 5, 1865, an oil buyer named Van Sicle began laying a pipeline from Pithole to Oil Creek. It was completed on October 7, at a cost of $100,000 to lay the five miles of pipe and erect three pumping stations. In testing the line, eighty-one barrels of oil were forced through the pipe in one hour, doing the day's work of 300 teams working ten hours. The teamsters were infuriated, for they saw that they would soon be eliminated as an essential part of the oil industry. Within two weeks of the completion of the pipeline, 1,500 teamsters had left Pithole. The completion of this successful pipeline was one of the greatest technological advances of the early oil industry. Soon pipelines were being laid in every portion of the oil region.

Amidst the drilling, Pithole evolved as one of the most striking "mushroom cities" in the history of the American oil industry. On May 24 there was one building under construction. When Pithole was incorporated as a borough on September 30, 1865, the population was estimated from 12,000 to 15,000 and the land valued at fifty million dollars. Pithole had one of the most unusual land-tenure systems ever devised. Within the town limits lots could not be purchased. Instead, they were leased for three years, with the privilege of removing the buildings on the expiration of the lease or selling them to the owners of the land. If the lease extended for five years, all buildings and improvements went to the owners of the land without compensation. Despite this peculiar arrangement, the lots were immediately leased.

Pithole had the appearance of a gigantic city of shreds and patches, not a brick or stone house in it. The odor of new lumber, fresh paint, and pungent petroleum was everywhere. Hotels, saloons, drinking and gambling dens, brothels, and boardinghouses were built by the score. The plan of architecture was known as golgothic, in that all of the display was on the front. Each building had its own individual character—one had a splendid sign, another was papered, and another had neither sides nor floor.

At night Pithole gave the impression of a place gone mad. Light streamed from every crack of the poorly constructed buildings. The barrooms and inns were a mass of oil producers, workmen, speculators, teamsters, mechanics, farmers who had sold their farms for thousands, town dandies, swindlers, soldiers, prostitutes, and hotel keepers, all drinking, carrying on business, and carousing. Everything indicated disorder, disarray, and indifference to all except the one grand objective of making money. It was a place where man lived for the day, with no thought of conservation of resources.

With population increasing by the hundreds each week, food and water shortages developed. In June 1865 an enterprising individual hauled a wagon load of groceries to Pithole and from a day's transactions made $700. Tough beef, bread, and black coffee were the staple foods. The problem of drinking water was a serious one, for the local water was polluted. Enterprising individuals hauled water from distant springs and sold it for ten cents a drink, or a dollar a gallon. Hard liquor was much cheaper than water, and as one driller put it, "The whiskey is bad, but to drink the water is certain death."

As Pithole grew, it developed some of the conveniences and luxuries of an older community. A post office, established on July 27, 1865, was soon handling 10,000 pieces of mail a day and was exceeded in importance only by Philadelphia and Pittsburgh. The pioneer daily paper of Venango County, the *Pithole Record,* was first published on September 25, 1865. A water system was designed in September and constructed at a cost of $25,000. The first municipal elections were held on December 11.

The first religious services were conducted in July in an unfinished hotel by a Presbyterian and a Methodist minister. A campaign was started to raise money for a church, which was built in March 1866. For those who preferred the stage, a theater was constructed with a seating capacity of 1,100. The interior decorations were splendid, and the center chandeliers of glass crystals were bought from Tiffany's in New York. Many of the nation's leading stage companies played there, and world-famous speakers lectured from its platform. A number of social organizations were also founded. The Swordsman's Club, for example, gave many concerts and balls in 1866 and 1867. Invitations to these affairs were sought by all oildom. Many wanted better means of travel, and a railroad was completed from Oil City to Pithole on March 10, 1866.

Fires were always a major problem in Pithole.

The first major one occurred on October 8, 1865, when twelve buildings were destroyed. In the next year sixteen major fires destroyed more than $500,000 worth of property.

The rapid growth of Pithole had astounded the world, but its decline was even more fantastic. The first shock to the speculative bubble came late in August 1865, when the wells on the Holmden farm stopped flowing. In the early part of 1866, despite frenzied effort to keep production up, it decreased rapidly. By January 1866 the daily production at Pithole had fallen to 3,600 barrels, by December 1866 it was down to 1,800 barrels, and by early 1867 it was less than 1,000 barrels. After having produced about 3.5 million barrels from less than 100 acres, the pool was exhausted.

When oil production declined, the town was abandoned in a few months. The Danford House, built for $50,000 on a lot subleased for $14,000, was sold in 1868 for $16 and torn down for kindling wood. By 1876 only six voters remained. The derricks were gone, the buildings had been removed or burned, and the only evidence that a great city had once existed were the deep ruts cut by wagons on what was once Holmden Street. Although Pithole was the epitome of oildom's boomtowns, scores of other ghost towns marked the once reckless exploitation of a great resource in western Pennsylvania.

LIMESTONE AND THE PORTLAND-CEMENT INDUSTRY

The Lehigh Valley in eastern Pennsylvania was the birthplace of the American portland-cement industry in 1875. Although limestone deposits are found throughout the United States, the Lehigh Valley is one of the few areas that contain a natural "cement rock." This is an impure limestone that contains about 75 percent calcium carbonate and 20 percent silica alumina and iron oxide, the remaining 5 percent consisting of unimportant earth materials. Users of portland cement long believed that the limestone of the Lehigh Valley produced the highest-quality cement in the nation.

The cement industry was raw-material oriented, with the cement mills situated right on the impure limestone deposits. The fuel for heating the limestone in the process of turning it into cement came originally from the nearby anthracite region. This area was particularly well situated to serve the expanding industrial market of the eastern United States.

Initially, however, the Lehigh Valley portland-cement industry grew only slowly. Two factors appear particularly important in retarding its rapid development. First, the natural cements, such as pozzolana, had gained a national reputation as quality products, and many builders preferred to use them. Second, portland cement was imported from Europe, and until about 1890, could be brought to the United States and sold at a price below that of the American product. These foreign cements had gained a good reputation, which gave them a preferred market.

By the 1890s, however, Lehigh Valley cement was gaining wide acceptance. It was being sent to every section of the country and had even developed a small export market. As a result, production increased from 57,150 metric tons in 1890 to 1,447,000 in 1900. At this time Pennsylvania produced about 80 percent of the nation's total output. After 1900, as the national market expanded and technological progress made it possible to use a wider range of raw materials, many new plants were constructed in other states. Although the Lehigh Valley increased its output in absolute terms, its relative position declined. By 1920 the region produced only about 26 percent of the total U.S. output.

With the growth of the Lehigh Valley cement industry, a series of cement towns evolved. In Northampton County the towns of Northampton, Nazareth, Martins Creek, Bath, and Stockertown; and in Lehigh County, Coplay, Cementon, Egypt, Ormrod, and Fogelsville owed their existence to cement. These towns extend in a belt about thirty miles long but not more than a mile wide, outlining the extent of the outcrop of cement rock. They are one-industry towns, dedicated to production of a single product.

The cement industry is a heavy industry requiring much space. At all stages of cement production, mechanization rapidly replaced hard labor in the early twentieth century. Large quantities of cement rock are blasted down in a single charge from large, deep nearby quarries. The rock is conveyed to a crusher, where it is pulverized into small particles. These fragments are fed into rotary kilns, where they are converted into hard clinkers. Enormous amounts of heat are needed to attain the high temperatures required to convert the raw materials into cement. After the hard clinkers are removed from the kilns, they are repulverized in ball mills to form cement. The powdered cement is fed into special bags and loaded onto freight cars at the rate of 20,000 bags or more per day.

The cement operations, with the crushing of

The village of Portland, located one mile north of Coplay, was so named because its only industrial establishment was a Portland cement works. The kilns pictured at top converted pulverized rock into hard clinkers which were removed and recrushed to form powdered cement. From Frank H. Taylor, Autumn Leaves Upon the Lehigh

limestone and the cement clinkers, are extremely noisy. Dust rises from the quarries and mills, covering not only the plant but entire neighborhoods, giving them a white, powdery appearance. Thus the cement industry and assorted settlements in the Lehigh Valley constitute a unique industrial landscape.

SLATE INDUSTRY

Two slate deposits have been quarried in Pennsylvania—one in the Lehigh Valley of Northampton and Lehigh counties, and the other in the Peach Bottom area of southeastern York County. Of these, the Lehigh Valley is by far the more important. Along a narrow outcrop of slate, there developed a series of small towns—Bangor, Pen Argyl, Slatington, Windgap, Walnutport, and several smaller boroughs—whose

economy was dominated by slate quarrying. The first slate was quarried in the early nineteenth century, and the industry flourished well into the twentieth century.

Although some of the deposits are horizontal, most have deep dips and sharp folds so that the quarries often exceed 500 feet in

Limekilns like this one were common in eastern Pennsylvania, and their ruins are still visible, even in modern industrial parks. These furnaces were used to reduce naturally occurring calcium carbonate to lime. The kiln pictured was located near Newtown in Bucks County in the late nineteenth century. From the collection of the Spruance Library of the Bucks County Historical Society

Above: *At the old Grenoble Quarry of N.E. Arnold near Newtown, rock was hauled to waiting cars for transport to the crushing facilities. From the collection of the Spruance Library of the Bucks County Historical Society*

Opposite, top: *The mechanization of Pennsylvania industry in the latter half of the nineteenth century was a discontinuous process. While ships and factories used new steam power and electricity, many basic industries found it more economical to rely on manual and horse-drawn power, such as at N.E. Arnold's Grenoble Quarry in southeastern Pennsylvania. The quarry stands near what is now Interstate 95. From the collection of the Spruance Library of the Bucks County Historical Society*

Opposite, bottom: *This Lehigh Valley slate quarry excavation measured 240 feet deep, 300 feet wide, and 820 feet long. Smoke from the massive amount of coal used to process slate caused the sky above the excavation to darken. From Frank H. Taylor,* Autumn Leaves Upon the Lehigh

Massive hoisting equipment hauled slate from the pits as seen in this 1865 drawing. Slate quarried from excavations in the town of Slatington was shipped to destinations all over the United States and Europe. From Frank H. Taylor, Autumn Leaves Upon the Lehigh

depth. The slate was hauled from the pits in great blocks, requiring massive hoisting equipment. It was an impressive sight to see tons of rock dangling over the open pit as it was hoisted to the surface. In splitting the rock into sheets, cleavage was an all important property. The shaping, sizing, and finishing processes were carried on in inconspicuous sheds.

The quantity of waste in processing slate is enormous. From 60 to 80 percent of the slate quarried ends up in refuse piles. Consequently the great piles of waste are even more conspicuous in the landscape than the slate pits. Many of the refuse piles are 75 to 100 feet high and cover surprisingly large areas.

Aside from a small production of slate granules in the Peach Bottom area, all of the Pennsylvania slate products came from the Lehigh-Northampton district. By far the most important product was roofing slate, followed by structural and sanitary slate, slate for blackboards, electrical slate, slate granules, and several other items. The slate products were marketed largely in Pennsylvania and the northeastern states.

The slate industry reached its zenith early in the twentieth century. Since then the industry has been beset with many problems. Less expensive substitutes, particularly for roofing and blackboards, greatly reduced the demand for slate. Because slate is a heavy product, transportation costs were high, restricting the market potential to a smaller region. Finally, slate came only in a dark gray color and many home owners wanted colored roofs. This style preference could only be satisfied by man-made roof shingles. As a result, the slate industry has declined to a remnant of its past importance.

About 1910 the textile industry began moving into these slate towns, as it did in many eastern Pennsylvanian towns, seeking lower labor costs than could be found in the more highly organized industrial centers. The textile industry of the slate towns began as distinctly parasitic endeavors based on low-cost female labor. By the 1930s, however, textiles had grown in importance so that they employed twice as many workers as the slate industry.

The textile industry has declined to insignificance in recent times, and the towns are now residential communities.

IRON ORE

As early as 1683 William Penn mentioned that the colony possessed deposits of iron ore. The first iron ore was mined in Pennsylvania in 1716, when Thomas Ritter erected a bloomery forge, known as Pool Forge, on Manatowny Creek in Berks County. The iron industry of the entire pioneer era was based on local iron-ore deposits. The production of iron ore increased with the advancing westward settlement and the construction of forges and furnaces to satisfy the local needs of settlers.

The Cornwall ore hills in southeastern Pennsylvania were the most productive in the state. Located in Lebanon County, they comprised three deposits of nearly pure magnetic ore. Production was continuous from about 1740 until the mines were flooded during Hurricane Agnes in 1972. The area yielded more than a million tons of ore before 1848. Between 1853 and 1864 production totaled 1,351,717 tons, and from 1864 to 1907 output was more than 20,000,000 tons. Production peaked in 1889, when 769,200 tons of ore were mined in a single year.

In the late eighteenth century, iron production moved westward, becoming the principal industry in the Juniata Valley region. By 1850 the industry had developed to such an extent that Huntingdon, Centre, Blair, and Mifflin counties together had a total of forty-eight furnaces, forty-two forges, and eight rolling mills. For many years the Juniata Valley was one of the principal iron-mining regions of the nation. Iron manufacture and iron mining spread widely throughout western Pennsylvania, and the iron-ore production of the Allegheny Valley by the 1840s and 1850s rivaled that of the Juniata Valley.

In 1880 iron ore was being mined in thirty-four counties of Pennsylvania by 358 establishments, for a total output of 1,820,561 tons. The leading counties were Lehigh, Lebanon, Berks,

Blair, Northampton, Cumberland, Fayette, York, and Lancaster. Pennsylvania ranked first in the nation in the production of iron ore, and the output of Pennsylvania mines in 1880 was nearly half the national total. With the dynamic growth of the iron and steel industry in southwestern Pennsylvania, the local iron-ore deposits were too small to supply the industry's needs. Only the massive iron ore deposits of the upper Great Lakes in Michigan and Minnesota were sufficiently large to meet the growing demands. By 1900 Pennsylvania's mines had ceased to be of importance in supplying the raw material for the iron and steel industry of the state.

LUMBERING INDUSTRY

When the first settlers arrived in Pennsylvania, they found a forested land. Every pioneer Pennsylvanian was, in a sense, a lumberman. Before he could have a farm, he had to clear the land. Although most of the timber was burned in the clearing process, there was also a local demand for lumber. To build the early settlements, logs were sawed into timber by water-powered and family-operated sawmills. Because transportation was difficult, the mills were widely scattered, serving nearby markets only.

For decades local sawmilling served the needs of Pennsylvania, but about 1860 there arose a growing demand for lumber in distant markets. Forest areas began to be exploited by lumbermen rather than farmers. Because logs were massive and heavy, and land transporta-

Around the turn of the century steam power was utilized in logging. This 1890 photo was taken in Potter County. Courtesy, Pennsylvania State Archives

tion lacking, the streams became the highways for the movement of logs from the forest to the sawmills and even on to the market areas.

The first area to develop a lumbering economy was in the north-central portion of the state where the West Branch tributaries of the Susquehanna River drained thousands of square miles of virgin forests. This was an area of magnificent coniferous forests of which the white pine was supreme. Many of these superb trees stood 150 feet tall and yielded more than 5,000 board feet of lumber.

The development of vast white pine and hemlock forests on the deeply dissected plateau of north-central Pennsylvania was totally dependent on the use of water transportation, for land transportation was essentially nonexistent. Although the streams were sufficiently large to float the logs, a means had to be devised to secure the logs that came rushing down the northern tributaries of the Susquehanna. As John Franklin Meginness points out in his history of Lycoming County, men were initially stationed in boats to watch the Susquehanna day and night and catch the logs as they floated downstream. The captured logs were formed into a crude raft which was anchored to the shore. At night huge fires on the riverbank lighted the water to enable the log catchers to see the logs. At times flatboats were stationed in the middle of the streams to aid in the log catching. The work was not only extremely dangerous but ineffective, for a large percentage of the logs were lost as they were swept downstream during the high waters in spring.

More effective control over the movement of logs was achieved with the development of the lumber boom stretching across a stream or river. The boom was an arrangement of log cribs, built log-cabin fashion, resting on the river bottom and weighted down with tons of rocks. Between the cribs were strung chains or logs, each one fastened to its neighbor by sturdy iron couplings. When the boom was closed, all logs were caught until the boom was filled. To release the logs, one end of the boom was opened and the logs escaped through a sort of double gate, where "boom rats" armed with long pikepoles and wearing boots with sharp calks were stationed to keep the logs moving and identify the logs belonging to different owners. Identification was made possible by the owner's brand that was burned into both ends of each log. Some 700 different brands were registered in Williamsport during the heyday of the lumber era.

A number of booms were built on the Susquehanna and even its tributaries at such places as Lock Haven and Linden, but the greatest of them all was the Williamsport boom. This boom was more than six miles long, stretching diagonally from one shore to another, and was

Above: *One of the few up-down sawmills in Perry County at the turn of the century, this mill had a capacity of 300-700 board feet. Courtesy, Pennsylvania State Archives*

Right: *Sawed lumber could be seen piled high in Potter County in 1890. Courtesy, Pennsylvania State Archives*

Opposite page: *Logs are shown floating behind a boom in the Susquehanna River. When the boom is opened, the logs float down the river to the sawmills along the riverbank. Courtesy, Pennsylvania State Archives*

*Logs are being loaded on flatcars at this lumberyard.
Courtesy, Pennsylvania State Archives*

Opposite: *The Porter Locomotive Works of Pittsburgh
specialized in building light locomotives for logging
railroads. This 1883 engine is typical of the company's
logging locomotives. From Matthias N. Forney,* Recent
Locomotives, *1886*

Opposite, bottom: *The Lackawanna Lumber Company
operated a 4-4-0 logging train in the late nineteenth century. Courtesy, Pennsylvania State Archives*

Below: *Massive loads of heavy logs were pulled by specially constructed engines. These lumber cars were photographed in central Pennsylvania about 1910. Courtesy,
Pennsylvania State Archives*

the major collection point for the entire West Branch basin. When the flood of 1889 broke the boom, it is estimated that 300 million board feet of lumber went whirling down the river. Temporary sawmills were built along the river to turn the captured logs into boards.

The great lumbering era of northern Pennsylvania began about 1860 and ended shortly after 1900. The importance of lumbering in the region is most vividly shown by the activity generated at Williamsport by the Williamsport boom. In 1862 a total of 196,953 logs went through the boom, producing in the local sawmills 87,863,621 board feet of timber. The lumbering era reached a peak about 1885, when 1,850,951 logs produced 225,847,555 board feet of lumber. After that production steadily declined.

Williamsport was not only the supreme transit center, but a sawmill and wood-milling center. During the peak years there were twenty-five great sawmills operating day and night. Nowhere else in the world had so much lumber been seen. For miles along the riverbank, sawed lumber was piled mountain high. Lumber-planing mills turned out doors, sashes, shelving, and a multitude of other wood items. A vast complex of wood-working shops lined the river shore. Not all the lumber could be processed at Williamsport, and lesser centers de-

veloped at Lock Haven, Montoursville, Muncy, Montgomery, Watsonville, Lewisburg, and elsewhere.

LOGGING RAILROADS

The next stage in the Pennsylvania lumber industry came with the development of the lumber railroad. As the timber was cut away from the streams, the lumbermen could no longer depend on water routes and spring thaws for the movement of timber. Large forest tracts still remained in Pennsylvania after 1890, and the industrial logging railroads penetrated the most isolated areas. At the end of the nineteenth century, these railroads supplied the wood for more than 600 sawmills, tanneries, and wood chemical companies. The first known lumber railroad began operations in 1864 in Jefferson County, and the last one was abandoned in Elk County in 1948.

The logging railroad added a new dimension to the lumber industry. In contrast to the water transportation era, the logging railroad did not develop great centers of processing. The railroads were normally short spurs, from three to possibly thirty miles in length, built to exploit the timber of a small area. A discontinuous network of these lines developed throughout the state wherever forest stands were exploited.

The logging railroads were distinctly different from the regular railroads. They ran on a flimsy track of light steel or wood rails and were able to negotiate sharp curves and steep grades. Because their usefulness ceased, once a small tract of timber was extracted, the railroads were cheaply constructed. The engines were specially constructed, however, because they had to pull massive loads of heavy logs at low speeds for short distances. Many were made in local machine shops and were essentially one of a kind. Because the market for these locomotives was small, factory production was always limited.

Although any single lumber operation was quite small, the penetration of hundreds of tracts by the logging railroads produced a vast quantity of lumber. Besides the production of lumber, the hemlock forests of Pennsylvania provided the basis for a large leather-tanning industry. The processing of hides was one of the earliest major industries of Pennsylvania, and by the early 1870s there were more than 500 small tanneries in the state. But with the increased availability of tanning extract from hemlock bark, combined with the growing demand for leather caused by the rapidly expanding population and industrial needs, large tanneries began to be constructed. Ultimately 120 large tanneries were built, 65 of them combining to form the United States Leather Company. These tanneries were not limited to the

Left: *Roulette in Potter County was a company town of the Grey Chemical Company. The chemicals produced were consumed primarily by the local tanning industry. Courtesy, Pennsylvania State Archives*

Above: *On the steep ridges of central Pennsylvania righting an overturned locomotive meant building a timber pile, lifting with a crane, and building the pile higher. It was not an easy task. Courtesy, Pennsylvania State Archives*

Above: *Hauling logs in winter was not a welcome job for neither man nor beast in the 1890s. Courtesy, Pennsylvania State Archives*

Opposite, top: *Composed of a kitchen, bunkhouse, mess hall, store, office, barn, and blacksmith shop, this logging camp, like most, was a ramshackle wooden place. Courtesy, Pennsylvania State Archives*

Opposite: *These men stood ready to move huge logs circa 1899. Courtesy, Pennsylvania State Archives*

forest region, but were also located in major leather market areas such as Philadelphia and Pittsburgh.

LUMBER CAMPS

The timber resources were located in the most isolated areas of the state. These forested lands were sparsely populated, and huge tracts had no settlements. To exploit the forest, new settlements had to be created. In contrast to the petroleum boomtowns of the nineteenth century, where the prospect of immediate great wealth attracted thousands to a new town, the forest tracts held no such promise. To develop a forest tract only a small settlement was required. Because the practice of the day was to remove the trees as quickly as possible and move to a new tract, the settlements gave little appearance of being permanent. There was no consideration for the future because the common viewpoint was that the timber resources could never be exhausted in the vast forests of the nation. There would always be another tract of timber to exploit. The industry was continuously migratory.

The lumber camps were thus small, at most a few hundred people. The buildings were crude, originally built of logs, later of unseasoned boards and planks. Because the population was predominantly male, there was normally a bunkhouse and mess hall. Bunks were crude wooden shelves, and the loggers slept on straw ticks. The mess hall contained a long wooden table and plank seats. The cook prepared simple but nutritious food. In the bunkhouse there may have been a sitting room kept warm by a round-bellied stove kept piping hot during the long, frigid winters.

For the logger, it was a rough, rugged life. He worked from sunup to sunset for less than a dollar a day plus meals and lodging and continually faced the threat of accidents and loss of life or limb. In spite of the legend and lore of the mighty woodsman with his axe, life was cheap and expendable. Indeed, the only thing cheaper than human life was the forest land itself.

The logging operations were extremely dangerous. The trees were felled by "choppers," and the partially cut trees often "jumped" from their stumps, crushing the workers. When the trees crashed to the ground, many a lumberman was crushed to death by falling timber. Getting the logs out of the forest was a difficult job. The first step was for "swampers" to cut crude trails to the nearest stream. The logs were dragged by oxen or teams of horses. In moving the logs the heavy chains could break, or on steep slopes a log might suddenly shoot forward creating a disaster for man and animal.

By spring the logs stretched for miles along the stream waiting for the first thaw. As the thousands of logs rushed downstream in the swirling waters, logjams would occur. From the bottom of the stream, the logs were piled high above the surface. Soon a great dam of water and logs was created. When this happened, lumbermen walking on the logjam tried to find the key logs causing the jam. Freeing the logs was like playing a game of jackstraws with massive tree trunks. Working with cant hooks, the lumbermen pulled and pushed the key logs until the entire mass of logs was released. At times dynamite was required to move the logs. At the moment of release, the mountain of logs again rushed downstream. And if, in that instant of time, the lumbermen did not reach shore, it was the end of them.

Left: *As winter's snows melted into spring, logs to be floated downstream to sawmills could be found for miles along streams. Courtesy, Pennsylvania State Archives*

Above: *Charcoal production took days and was wasteful of timber, but produced a major fuel for smelting iron ores in small local furnaces. Courtesy, Pennsylvania State Archives*

The exploitation of Pennsylvania's forests was a dynamic period in the history of lumbering. Hundreds of small settlements were built. When the forests were gone, there was no other economic activity to sustain their existence. Many were destroyed by fire. Some were moved to new forest locations. But many simply disappeared over time. The roll call of ghost towns is almost endless, and many have passed into oblivion with no record that they ever existed. Only a few of the lumber camps and leather-tanning centers have survived to the present day as small commercial and recreational centers serving large sparsely populated second- and third-growth forest regions.

Above: *Austin, a logging settlement in Potter County, appeared to be a stable little town in this 1926 view. By 1927, however, it was gone. Courtesy, Pennsylvania State Archives*

Opposite: *Norwich in McKean County, an active lumber town in this photo, had disappeared completely a year later. Courtesy, Pennsylvania State Archives*

Chapter Five

Manufacturing: Core of the Industrial System

In the nineteenth century manufacturing underwent revolutionary changes, as mechanical power replaced human and animal power and the factory replaced the traditional handicraft system. The increased use of mechanical energy raised productivity while decreasing the cost of goods. For example, while it took hundreds of hours to produce a few yards of cloth using human energy, the same task could be accomplished in a few minutes on a power loom.

Because energy was the catalyst that altered traditional manufacturing methods, Pennsylvania, with its great reserves of bituminous and anthracite coal and petroleum, possessed a great natural advantage in the development of modern manufacturing. Once the exploitation of these resources began, human ingenuity played an even greater role. Hundreds of inventions for all types of manufacturing provided the foundation for the establishment of new technologies. Combined with these endeavors were new concepts in the structure and organization of the industrial system. Where once it required decades to change the industrial system, the pace of change accelerated almost beyond measure. The growth of manufacturing created a new era in the economic structure not only of Pennsylvania's but of the nation's economy.

In the change from a rural to an industrial society, manufacturing played a key role. In 1850 there were only 146,000 workers in manufacturing. This number increased to 387,000 in 1880, to 733,000 in 1900, and to 1,135,837 in 1919. The capital investment in manufacturing during the same period rose from $94,473,000 to $6,177,729,000, and the value of manufactured products rose from $155,044,000 to $7,315,702,000. Manufacturing employed only 6.3 percent of the state's wage earners in 1850 but about 25 percent by 1919. In 1919 Pennsylvania ranked as the second most important state in manufacturing, exceeded only by New York. Pennsylvania employed 12.4 percent of the nation's manufacturing workers while New

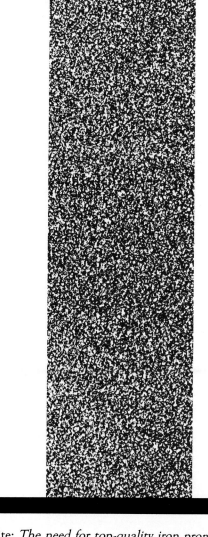

Opposite: *The need for top-quality iron prompted the building of the Chester Rolling Mill, shown here circa 1876. The mill was built for the sole purpose of supplying the Delaware River Iron Ship Building and Engine Works. From Asher and Adams,* Pictorial Album of American Industry, *1876*

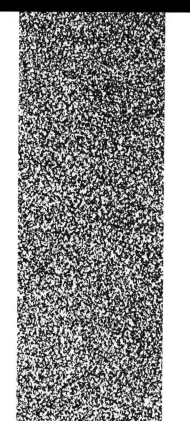

York had 14 percent.

Pennsylvania developed a highly diversified manufacturing economy in the nineteenth and early twentieth centuries. The production of iron and steel (blast furnaces, steelworks, and rolling mills), with 25 percent of all workers in manufacturing, occupied a premier position. The textile industry was second in importance, with 13.5 percent of the wage earners. No other single industry accounted for as much as 7 percent of the total employment in manufacturing. Other principal types of manufacturing were foundry products and machinery, railroad-car repair and manufacture, apparel, tobacco products, glass, bricks and tile, leather products, printing and publishing, and coke production.

Pennsylvania was a leader in many types of manufacturing. It stood first among the states in employment in blast furnaces, steelworks and rolling mills, iron and steel forging, structural-iron works, railroad-car repair and manufacture, cement, glass, coke, knit goods, silk manufacture, and tobacco products. It occupied second place in foundry and machine-shop manufac-

ture, petroleum refining, newspaper printing and publishing, leather products, liquors and malt brewing, women's apparel, and carpets and rugs, and third place in chemicals, men's clothing, book printing and publishing, and woolens and worsteds.

The leading manufacturing center of Pennsylvania was Philadelphia, which accounted for about 45 percent of the state's manufacturing workers in 1890. Although the number of workers in Philadelphia grew from 260,264 in 1890 to 281,105 in 1919, the city's percentage of the state total declined to 25 percent. This reflects the growing importance of manufacturing throughout the state and the relative decline of a single, dominant center.

Manufacturing in Philadelphia was very diversified. Textiles were a major industry in the city, but other important industries included foundries and machine shops, locomotives, chemicals, petroleum refining, shipbuilding, drugs, leather boots and shoes, apparel, and electrical machinery. It would be difficult to find a single category of manufacturing that was not represented in Philadelphia.

In southeastern Pennsylvania such counties as Bucks, Montgomery, Chester, Delaware, Berks, Lancaster, and York developed manufacturing to serve regional markets. They were diversified manufacturing centers, but on a lesser scale than Philadelphia. Of these new growth centers, Delaware County was most important, with employment in manufacturing increasing from 13,719 in 1890 to 67,396 in 1919. York, the westernmost of these counties, also grew rapidly, from 8,391 workers in 1890 to 25,127 in 1919.

Pittsburgh, in Allegheny County, was the second major manufacturing center in Pennsylvania. The growth of this center came with the expansion of the iron and steel industry late in the nineteenth century. In 1890 Allegheny County had 97,657 workers, or 17.1 percent of the state's total. By 1919 the total had risen to

Above: *In 1912 the Shrenhat Toy Company of Philadelphia employed these women to assemble dolls. At the time, Philadelphia was the leading manufacturing center of Pennsylvania with virtually every category of manufacturing represented. Courtesy, National Archives*

Opposite page: *Snellenberg's clothing cutting room is shown here circa 1910. Snellenberg's was a famous store on Market Street in Philadelphia until the 1950s. Courtesy, Pennsylvania State Archives*

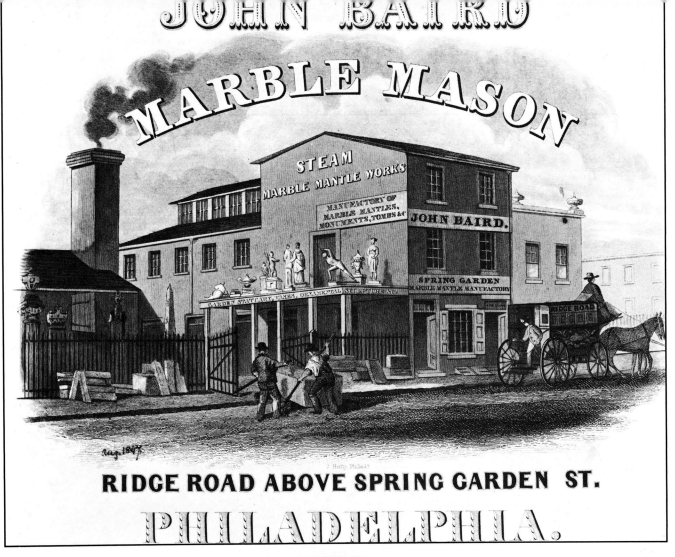

RIDGE ROAD ABOVE SPRING GARDEN ST.

Opposite: *In 1847 marble mason John Baird of Philadelphia advertised his Steam Marble Mantle Works. Pennsylvanians have always preferred to build with stone. Pollution, however, has eaten away many of the older stone Philadelphia buildings. Courtesy, The Library Company of Philadelphia*

Opposite, bottom: *Philadelphia woodworkers Hale, Kilburn and Company occupied 86,000 square feet and employed 250-300 workers in 1876. The firm, which produced photo and picture frames, walnut moldings, mantel and mirror frames, the "Champion" Folding Bedstead, and other pieces of wood furniture, prided itself on producing "the very highest class of work . . . rapidly and cheaply." From Asher and Adams,* Pictorial Album of American Industry, *1876*

Below: *Hale, Kilburn and Company's "Champion" Folding Bedstead is shown here partially unfolded. The company stated in an 1876 advertisement that "the changes from closet to bed or from bed to closet are readily made, requiring neither great strength nor special skill." From Asher and Adams,* Pictorial Album of American Industry, *1876*

173,561, but similar to Philadelphia, the area had experienced a relative decline to 15.2 percent of the state's total manufacturing workers. Besides iron and steel, Pittsburgh-area manufactures included foundry and machine-shop products, glass, fabricated metals, pipe, bridges, and processed foods. Manufacturing also grew rapidly in a number of nearby counties. Between 1890 and 1919, employment in manufacturing increased in Beaver County from 4,891 workers to 24,474, in Westmoreland County from 6,247 to 31,066, and in Lawrence County from 2,816 to 20,329.

In many of the smaller cities, iron and steel and associated industries dominated manufacturing. In western Pennsylvania these centers included Johnstown, New Castle, Duquesne, McKeesport, Sharon, Braddock, and DuBois. In eastern Pennsylvania, Reading, Steelton, Harrisburg, Bethlehem, Pottstown, Lebanon, and Phoenixville were major iron and steel centers.

Because of the widespread railroad network

The jewelry manufacturing firm of Hagstoz and Thorpe built the Keystone Watch-Case Manufactory on Nineteenth above Wylie Street in Philadelphia. Depicted here as it appeared in the early 1880s, the factory was composed of a five-story building and a six-story building connected by bridges. The watchcases manufactured by the firm were composed of a layer of composition metal sandwiched between two layers of gold. Thus, the cases were stronger, more durable, and less expensive than those made of all gold. From Scharf and Westcott, History of Philadelphia, *Vol. III, 1884*

Above: *Limousine bodies were built in this early twentieth-century Pittsburgh factory. Pittsburgh was Pennsylvania's second major manufacturing center when this 1912 photo was taken. Courtesy, National Archives*

Opposite page: *James Hall of Union County and his primitive tar pits were photographed about 1920. Each of the small pits yielded about two quarts of oil and two and one-half gallons of tar. Together the two pits yielded about seven dollars worth of products. Courtesy, Pennsylvania State Archives*

in the state, a number of cities developed rail-road-car repair shops, and in a number of places these shops provided the leading manufacturing industry. The most important of these centers was Altoona, with not only repairing but construction of locomotives and railroad cars. Other railroad-car repair centers included Meadville, Dunmore, and Chambersburg.

Petroleum refining was important in such places as Oil City, Titusville, Warren, Bradford, Freedom, and Franklin, reflecting the availability of oil from nearby fields. Major textile towns outside Philadelphia included Scranton, Wilkes-Barre, Allentown, Easton, Columbia, Sunbury, and Shamokin.

RISE OF THE CORPORATE ORGANIZATION

The change from handicraft industries to the factory system was accompanied by a shift toward large-scale corporate organizations, especially after 1870. The demands for capital investment and the growth of national and even international markets were primary factors in fostering these organizational changes.

The term "corporation" originated in England when partnership agreements were extended to include several owners. Corporate organization was first practiced in banking and transportation. These early corporate organizations were based on state-authorized charters, and on occasion there were state subscriptions to the stock providing a semi-partnership with government. Legislation enacted by the Pennsylvania Assembly with regard to corporations was usually dictated by special interests seeking to secure special advantages and promote their own growth. These practices were vigorously criticized, and the new state constitution of 1873 sought to curb them. Article III specified that the General Assembly "shall not pass" any local or special law "creating corporations or amending, renewing, or extending the charter thereof." The incorporation of business enterprises was then transferred to the jurisdiction of the courts.

The striking growth of manufacturing, mining, and transportation required such huge sums of capital that it could no longer be supplied by a few wealthy individuals, and it became necessary to secure the resources of large, established banking institutions to provide sufficient capital for the growing enterprises. By 1900 at least two-thirds of American business was organized on a corporate basis, and Pennsylvania was a leader in these endeavors.

The United States manufacturing census of 1900 provided the first report on "industrial combinations." It found a total of 185 corporations controlling more than a dozen major fields of industrial enterprise. Of these industrial combinations, forty were in iron and steel, indicating that Pennsylvania was a leader in the development of corporate structures. Pennsylvania had 358 iron and steel plants and mills involved in these combinations, compared to 227 in New York, the next largest state.

The classic example of industrial consolidation and economic integration was United States Steel (Big Steel). This corporation was formed by the merger of ten great steel companies with a capitalization of $1.4 billion, or nearly twice its actual worth. Corporate assets included 149 steel plants, 84 blast furnaces, 1,000 miles of railroads, 112 Great Lakes vessels, and vast resources of coal, iron ore, and limestone. The headquarters of United States Steel was in Pittsburgh, and most of its works were within 100 miles of this city.

LABOR AND LABOR ORGANIZATIONS

The expanding industrial economy was a magnet that attracted European laborers in vast numbers. The reformer Henry George stated of Pennsylvania in 1886, "It may be doubted if there is on the earth's surface another area of 43,000 square miles, which, considering all things, is better fitted by nature to yield large returns to labor." The state's labor-intensive industries drew huge numbers of immigrants from many countries, bringing with them a great diversity of ethnic, linguistic, social, and religious customs.

Of all the immigrants who came to the United States, more went to Pennsylvania than any other state except New York. In 1860 more than 430,000 Pennsylvania residents, about 15 percent of the state's population, were foreign-born. In 1920 the figure was 1.4 million, or about 16 percent of the total population. Although the immigrants came largely from rural areas, almost all sought jobs in mines or factories. Because the immigrants were frequently not welcomed by the earlier settlers, ethnic neighborhoods were a common feature of urban areas.

Many of the immigrants flocked to areas where their friends had settled. In 1920 Russians were the largest immigrant group in Philadelphia, followed by Irish and Italians. Poles concentrated in Allegheny, Luzerne, Lackawanna, and Schuylkill counties and the cities of Wilkes-Barre and Chester. Italians settled in Washington, Fayette, and Montgomery counties and the city of Scranton. Austrian immigrants were concentrated in Westmoreland and Cambria counties and in Johnstown. Hungarians were found largely in Northampton County and the cities of Bethlehem and McKeesport. The largest Irish settlement was in Delaware County. Yugoslavians were found in largest numbers in Beaver County, and the Germans concentrated in Erie County and in the cities of Pittsburgh and Erie.

The immigrants that arrived from Europe be-

Above: In this view of the banks of the Monongahela at Pittsburgh stand some of the city's blast furnaces, while in the background, across the river, are the rolling mills. In the blast furnaces iron ore, limestone, and coke were converted to pit iron and, later, steel. In the rolling mills the steel was rolled into rails, bridge beams, and hundreds of other things.

Above right: A steel ingot glows on the table of a blooming mill about 1890. By this time steel making was a complicated process. Large ladles or pails poured the molten steel into molds. It was then covered with sand and cooled. A large crane lifted ingots out of the molds and placed them on a blooming table (photo). The table would then drive the hot ingot through one of the template openings on the "blooming" machine behind it, where it would be pared down to several sizes of finished steel. Courtesy, Pennsylvania State Archives

with its mammoth industrial concentration in the river valleys, became, like Germany's Ruhr Valley, a citadel of heavy industry. Pittsburgh became so closely associated with the iron and steel industry that most people came to think of this city as the steel capital of the world.

Within this region the iron and steel industry was concentrated along the river valleys. Railways hugged the riverbanks, which provided the least grade for the movement of heavy raw materials and finished products. The river systems themselves provided the lowest-cost transportation routes, bringing coal, coke, and limestone from the mines and quarries to the iron and steel mills and transporting the finished steel by barge to New Orleans and the Gulf Coast. The movement of raw materials and iron and steel products made traffic on the Monongahela River the heaviest of all rivers in the United States.

The riverside location of the iron and steel mills was of considerable value, too, because of their tremendous consumption of water. It would have been nearly impossible to have satisfied the water requirements of the iron and steel industry in this region from underground wells.

Although the river valleys proved the most desirable location for the iron and steel indus-

Above: *Andrew Carnegie (1835-1919), who had emigrated to the United States from Scotland with his family in 1848, began his teen years in Allegheny (later Pittsburgh). After having worked in a cotton factory, a telegraph office, and for the Pennsylvania Railroad, Carnegie formed the Keystone Bridge Company in 1865. Within eight years, however, he decided to devote his energies to the steel industry. In 1889 he consolidated his steel holdings into the Carnegie Steel Company. By 1900 Carnegie Steel produced 25 percent of the nation's steel. Carnegie, however, believing that wealth should be used for the public good, sold his business to United States Steel in 1901 and devoted the rest of his life to philanthropy and the promotion of peace. Photo by Charles H. Davis and E. Starr Sanford. Courtesy, National Portrait Gallery, Smithsonian Institution, Washington, D.C.*

Opposite: *Construction on Carnegie's Edgar Thomson Works in Braddock began in 1873. This view of the works dates from about 1910. Courtesy, Pennsylvania State Archives*

try, there were a number of disadvantages to this location. The massive plants of the iron and steel industry required large amounts of space. The narrow ribbons of land along the rivers soon became congested, making expansion difficult, and a number of mills were forced to establish branches in various portions of the valleys. In many places, such as McKeesport, Carnegie, Etna, Monessen, and Aliquippa, the giant works were situated near the center of the city, creating problems of noise, dirt, grime, and congestion.

Although the initial dominance of this area was based on the availability of beehive-coking coal and accessibility to iron ore by lake freighter, other factors also fostered the growth of the iron and steel industry. The great market for iron and steel stretched from Boston to Chicago, and southwestern Pennsylvania, lying in the middle of this area, occupied a supreme market position. Railroad development, centering on this region, gave supreme accessibility. Thus new industries were attracted to the area not only to be near the basic raw materials but also to save on freight charges in the transportation of the crude steel.

In its heyday the near-monopolistic Pittsburgh iron and steel industry was able to discourage competition, by means of a controlled freight-rate system known as "Pittsburgh Plus." Its primary purpose was to localize the industry in the region by discouraging growth elsewhere. Under this system, if a Kansas City, Missouri, buyer purchased steel from a Gary, Indiana, plant, he paid the f.o.b. Gary price and also the freight rate (the "plus") that would have been assessed against shipment from a Pittsburgh mill. In 1900 the cost of producing iron and steel was lower in the Pittsburgh region than anywhere else in the country. Shortly after 1900, however, the cost of producing iron and steel in a number of places, notably the Chicago region, fell below that of Pittsburgh. As a result of this system of freight charges, however, Pittsburgh continued to possess a tremendous competitive advantage over all other regions. This advantage continued to exist until 1924, when the U.S. Supreme Court declared the discriminatory freight-rate system illegal, replacing it with a multiple-basing-point system. Under the new system, a single freight rate was charged for movement of iron and steel within a region, but if the iron and steel moved to another region the rate charged was for the two regions.

The iron and steel industry was organized by a number of industrial and financial giants. Of these Andrew Carnegie was the supreme leader. Carnegie was born in Scotland in 1835, the son of a poor cloth weaver. The father brought the family to Pittsburgh, where they lived for a time in a relative's home. As a youth Carnegie became a messenger boy in a telegraph office, where he learned to operate a telegraph. With this skill Carnegie attracted the attention of Thomas Scott, then superintendent of the Pittsburgh Division of the Pennsylvania Railroad, who hired him as a telegrapher for the railroad. He advanced rapidly and at the age of twenty-four was made superintendent of the Pittsburgh Division of the Pennsylvania Railroad. Carnegie remained with the railroad from 1853 to 1865, when he entered the iron and steel business by joining the Keystone Bridge Company. In the following years he made a small fortune in oil and in selling railroad securities in Europe, and he gained the reputation of a dashing young Pittsburgh entrepreneur.

Carnegie was one of the first to recognize the great advantage of steel over iron and to foresee that steel would replace iron products. In 1873 he began building a huge steelworks, the Edgar Thomson Works at Braddock, Pennsylvania, to manufacture Bessemer steel. Soon after, the open-hearth process of producing steel was introduced from Europe, and again Carnegie was in the forefront in developing this new technology in his mills. Open-hearth steel had greater strength and was of more uniform quality than Bessemer steel.

With his success, he merged a number of small companies into the Carnegie Steel Company, and for the next thirty years its growth epitomized the success of the American steel

Above: *Born in 1862, Charles M. Schwab was an inno-vative, ingenious steelworker who became president of the Carnegie Steel Company in 1897, the first president of the United States Steel Corporation in 1900, and chairman of the Bethlehem Steel Company in 1903. Though his fortune once neared $200 million, Schwab lost all of it in unwise investments and died insolvent in 1939. Oil painting by Joseph Cummings Chase. Cour-tesy, National Portrait Gallery, Smithsonian Institution, Washington, D.C.*

Opposite: *Many large companies took a paternalistic view of their employees. Here, a Bethlehem Steel domes-tic educator instructs a worker's family on the finer points of keeping house. Courtesy, Hagley Museum and Library, Wilmington, Delaware*

industry. Carnegie created a magnificent in-dustrial steel complex. By the 1890s he had purchased or leased the most valuable Lake Su-perior iron ores. The Connellsville coke region was initially developed by Henry Clay Frick, who joined Carnegie in 1882 and became his chief executive officer in 1889. Carnegie se-cured the services of some of the most notable industrial leaders of the day—among them, Charles M. Schwab, one of the nation's leading shipbuilders, and Captain William R. (Bill) Jones, an ingenious inventor and inspirational leader.

The Carnegie Steel Company was for most of its existence a limited partnership, not a cor-poration. Its stock was not publicly sold but was held by only a few individuals, who thus reaped all the profits. In 1900 these profits amounted to forty million dollars, of which Carnegie's personal share was twenty-five mil-lion dollars.

Carnegie not only possessed great organiza-tional ability but demonstrated considerable courage and daring in acquiring new properties and pioneering new methods. With his enor-mous resources, he could afford to experiment with new techniques and to expand during pe-riods of economic decline. With the return of prosperity, he could undersell his competitors and ultimately buy them out. By 1900 he had gained a near-monopolistic position in the in-dustry. At the turn of the century, it is estimat-ed that the Carnegie Steel Company produced between 25 and 30 percent of the nation's steel, including half of the structural steel, half the armor plate, and 30 percent of the rails.

In 1901 Carnegie sold his company for $250 million to J. Pierpont Morgan, who organized the United States Steel Corporation. Carnegie conceived of himself as a trustee of wealth that others had created. In the last two decades of his life, from 1900 to 1919, he gave $350 mil-lion to philanthropic projects in the United States and Britain, including the famous Car-negie public libraries.

Two other modern iron and steel centers emerged during the nineteenth century: Bethle-hem, in eastern Pennsylvania, and Steelton, a

suburb of Harrisburg. These centers trace their origins to the colonial period, when bog iron ore and charcoal were the basic raw materials. Of the two, Bethlehem emerged as a major industrial center, concentrating on the manufacture of steel. The Bethlehem Steel Corporation dominated the industrial structure of that city, employing more than half of all workers, and nearly three-fourths of the city's workers were in the metal and metal-product industries.

The iron and steel mills stretching along the Lehigh River presented a spectacular view of a heavy metallurgical complex. Blast furnaces belching smoke and flame and surrounded by huge piles of iron ore, coke, and limestone, batteries of coke ovens, vast rolling mills, and auxiliary buildings dominated the landscape. Because of the massive assemblage of raw materials and marketing of finished products, railroads were also a conspicuous part of the landscape.

The raw materials for Steelton and Bethlehem were assembled from diverse areas. The coking coal came primarily from western Pennsylvania by railroad, and the iron ore came from Cornwall, Pennsylvania, the Adirondacks, and the Lake Superior deposits. Limestone came from the massive deposits in the Great Valley physiographic region of central Pennsylvania and water was obtained from the Susquehanna and Lehigh rivers.

THE TEXTILE INDUSTRIES

Textiles as a group—silk, cotton goods, knit goods, and woolens and worsteds—comprised the second most important industry in Pennsylvania. Employment increased steadily from 79,500 in 1890 to 154,000 in 1919, when Pennsylvania produced about 15 percent of all the textiles manufactured in the United States. Although the textile industry as a whole continued to grow slowly after 1900, a number of branches such as woolens and worsteds began the long decline that textiles have experienced in Pennsylvania in the twentieth century. As wage rates increased in the older industrial regions, textiles were among the first industries to migrate to lower-cost producing areas.

Of the various branches of the textile industry, the manufacture of silk was preeminent. In 1880 Pennsylvania ranked fifth in the United States, accounting for 8.5 percent of the total value of silk produced. By 1900 it had risen to second place, with 29 percent of the total, and by 1919 Pennsylvania was the leader among the states, with 33 percent of total output by value. The industry was localized in Philadelphia, Scranton, Allentown, Easton, and a number of smaller centers.

The manufacture of silk has a long history in Pennsylvania. Silk culture started in 1750, when a filature for reeling silk from cocoons was established under the patronage of Benjamin Franklin and others. In 1793 the making of fringes, laces, and tassels began in Philadelphia, expanding by 1815 to include trimmings, naval sashes, and ribbons. Power looms were introduced in 1837 for weaving ribbons and narrow goods. About 1839 the culture of silk was abandoned, and output was confined to silk manufacture. By the twentieth century, broad silks were the principal products. The growth of the silk industry was particularly noteworthy between 1880 and 1900. During this period many towns offered financial inducements to attract the industry.

In the knit-goods branch of the industry, Pennsylvania specialized in the production of hosiery. The German Palatines who settled in Germantown, a suburb of Philadelphia, introduced the making of hosiery about 1698, and the industry developed in the Philadelphia area. By 1810, when the state's production totaled 107,508 pairs, Philadelphia accounted for about one-half of the total. Throughout the nineteenth and early twentieth centuries, Pennsylvania's hosiery output was first in the nation. In 1919 the state contributed 34.4 percent of the quantity and 40.5 percent of the value of all hosiery made in the United States. In the nineteenth century the industry concentrated on producing cotton hose, but early in the twentieth century the demand for silk and woolen hosiery grew. Between 1909 and 1919 the value of silk hosiery grew from 4 percent to

60 percent of the total. Although hosiery still constituted about 66 percent of the value of knit goods in 1919, underwear, fancy knit goods, and knitted cloth were growing in importance.

The woolen industry was one of the more traditional branches of the textile industry. During the pioneer period the women of the family produced woolen cloth for family consumption in most homes in the state. The manufacture of woolen goods was first established by English millers in the Schuylkill Valley, in small factories using hand looms, and by 1850 Pennsylvania produced more yarn than any other state. With the development of fac-

Though child labor was technically illegal, factories making textiles employed teenagers for long hours and low wages at the hardest work. This young woman was photographed at the Sauquoit Silk Manufacturing Company in Philadelphia in 1918. Courtesy, Pennsylvania State Archives

Above: *A lone young woman winds bobbins with woolen yarn in a Philadelphia factory as rows of bobbins seem to stretch forever. About 1909 the industry peaked and then declined due to competition from other areas brought on by the state's higher wages and declining sources of local wool.*

Left: *Caleb Cope and Company of Philadelphia was an importer and jobber of silk goods. This view of the firm's Market Street store is reproduced from an 1854 issue of Gleason's Pictorial Drawing-room Companion.*

tory production, the industry concentrated in Philadelphia. By 1870 the state ranked second in the manufacture of both woolen and worsted goods, with about 18 and 36 percent, respectively, of the nation's output by value. The woolen and worsted industry reached its peak about 1909 and then began to decline as competition from other areas increased. High-cost production in Pennsylvania, due primarily to higher wages and declining sources of local wool, placed the state at a cost disadvantage, and the industry began its migration to newer centers.

In the nineteenth century Pennsylvania became the carpet and rug center of the nation. In 1850 the state ranked third, with products valued at 21 percent of the national output. By 1870 the state ranked first, with 45 percent of the nation's total, and this share increased to 48 percent in 1900. After 1900, however, the industry began to decline, and by 1919 production, measured in square yards, was less than half the state's peak output. The decline of the woolen industry, which provided the basic raw material for carpet and rugs, affected the industry adversely. Also, Philadelphia had gained its reputation in the production of ingrain carpets. As demand for Brussels carpet grew, the Philadelphia manufacturers were slow to follow the fashion of the day, and the industry developed in new centers.

Of the various branches of the textile industry, cotton-goods production has been of relatively little importance in Pennsylvania. In 1900 the state ranked fifth in the nation, but produced only about 7 percent of the total output. The cotton-goods industry was concentrated in the New England states. Pennsylvania was noted for certain specialty items, however. The use of cotton for decorative fibers originated in Pennsylvania, and its cotton tapestries and chenille curtains gained national markets.

FOUNDRY PRODUCTS AND MACHINERY

Pennsylvania's third largest source of manufacturing employment was the foundry-products and machinery industry. These industries were

At the turn of the century the textile industry was still the leading industry in Pennsylvania. Advances in machinery meant less labor, but the factories still went South in the face of rising wage scales. The wool loom pictured was at Hardwicke and Magee Company in Philadelphia. Courtesy, Pennsylvania State Archives

Opposite, top: Pittsburgh's Atlas Iron Works produced the giant shears depicted in this 1875 drawing from Frank Leslie's Illustrated. By the 1880s the machine shops and foundries of Pittsburgh made over ten million dollars worth of products.

Opposite, bottom: Stationary engines like this one were produced at the Erie City Iron Works in fourteen different sizes, varying from 8 to 125 horsepower. The iron works also manufactured portable engines, boilers, and circular saws and could outfit an entire mill on short notice. From Asher and Adams, Pictorial Album of American Industry, 1876

reversing bloom mill, and the first continuous-hot-strip mill. Pittsburgh was also the headquarters of the United Engineering and Foundry Company, for decades the world's largest designer and maker of rolls and rolling-mill equipment for the steel industry. This was one of the earliest international firms, as it was affiliated with the Davy-United Engineering Company, Ltd., of Sheffield, England. The Rockwell Company was another of Pittsburgh's early leaders in the metal-products industry. Without these and other companies, the iron and steel industry could not have developed.

Pennsylvania was also a center of textile-machine production to serve the expanding textile industry of the state. The H.W. Butterworth and Sons Company of Philadelphia, established in 1820, pioneered in the development of complete textile mills. A major center of textile machinery was Reading. There two German immigrants, Henry Janssen and Ferdinand Thun, began building braiding machines in the 1890s. This venture became the basis for the Textile Machine Works, which developed the first practical machine in this country for making full-fashioned hosiery. Many other types of textile machinery were developed in Pennsylvania to meet the needs of the industry.

Many of the new industries of the nineteenth century developed plants in Pennsylvania. Of these none was of greater importance than the electrical-machinery industry. By 1900 the Census of Manufactures listed nearly 100 manufacturers of some type of electrical apparatus. The manufacture of electrical machinery and apparatus was one of the state's fastest-growing industries after 1900 and was a major factor in Pennsylvania's leadership in the machinery field.

Of Pennsylvania's many leaders in the development of the electrical-machinery industry, the most prominent was George Westinghouse of Pittsburgh. He was not only a major inventor of new electrical machinery but a corporate leader who founded one of the nation's largest electrical-machinery companies. The original Westinghouse Electric and Manufacturing Company was formed in 1886 in a small factory in

established early and expanded rapidly after 1880. By 1919 employment totaled more than 71,000 in foundry products and machinery, 24,200 in electrical machinery, and 3,670 in machine tools.

Because this was a period of great technological innovation, foundry products and machinery were in constant demand. The heavy castings and forgings produced by Pennsylvania's iron and steel industry provided the foundation for the machine age. The Mackintosh-Hemphill Company of Pittsburgh, founded in 1803, was a leader in producing machinery for the iron and steel industry. Noted for its ability to build complete rolling mills, it also designed the machinery for the first large tin-plate mill. The same company produced the machine equipment used in the first Garret rod mill, the first

Above: *In his Pennsylvania laboratory, with his more than 400 patents, George Westinghouse contributed more to the age of electricity than anyone, including Thomas Edison. From Cirker,* Dictionary of American Portraits, *Dover, 1967*

Opposite: *Standing beneath what appears to be a cloth-draped lightbulb, an American Sheet and Tin Plate Company worker trims tin plate. Courtesy, Pennsylvania State Archives*

Pittsburgh, with 200 employees producing thirteen products.

The first electric light bulb was invented by Thomas A. Edison in his New Jersey laboratory and test-proved on October 21, 1879. On July 4, 1883, in Sunbury, Pennsylvania, Edison conducted the first successful experiment in using a three-wire electrical circuit to light an entire building. The use of electricity was hampered, however, by its dependence on direct current transmission, which could not transport the electricity more than a few feet. The inventive genius of Westinghouse solved this problem by developing the alternating current. In the late 1880s he secured patent rights for the alternating-current electrical transformer just invented in Europe and then refined the transformer in his Pittsburgh laboratory. Using his alternating current, Westinghouse demonstrated how an entire town could be lighted in Great Barrington, Massachusetts. In 1893 he received the contract to provide the electric lights for the Chicago World's Fair. In the same year he installed three of his alternating-current generators at the Niagara Falls generating station. Within three years electricity generated at Niagara Falls was carried to Buffalo.

Westinghouse made many other contributions to furthering the use of electricity. In the 1890s he developed a steam turbine for producing electricity, and in 1898 he began using the turbines in his own factories. By 1905 Westinghouse had introduced the use of electricity in a steel mill, and in 1906 a railroad line was electrified. In 1920 the Westinghouse organization launched the world's first radio broadcasting station, KDKA in Pittsburgh. No single person, including Thomas Edison, contributed more to the development of the electrical age through inventions and technological innovations and the manufacture of electrical machinery and apparatus than George Westinghouse.

In addition to the Westinghouse company, Pennsylvania had a number of other leading electrical-equipment manufacturers. The General Electric Corporation built major plants in Philadelphia and Erie. This giant had its origin

The Disston saw works of Philadelphia employed about 2,000 workers when this photo was taken circa 1916. The men here are using hand files to finish saw blades. From the Philadelphia Commercial Museum Collection, Pennsylvania State Archives

in Philadelphia in the Thomson-Houston Electric Company organized to supply electricity to Philadelphia. Associated with this endeavor was Elihu Thomson, a Philadelphia high school teacher of chemistry and mechanics, who was a pioneer inventor of many electrical devices in the 1880s. A group of Philadelphians in 1892 established the Philadelphia Storage Battery Company, later to become the Philco Corporation, one of the world's largest producers of electrical equipment. Another large manufacturer of electrical equipment was the Sylvania Electric Products Company, with headquarters in Emporium.

With the modernization of the agricultural economy, there was a growing market for machinery and tools. Although Pennsylvania was not a leading manufacturer of agricultural machinery, many small companies produced farm implements. One of the largest of the companies was A.B. Farquhar, founded in 1856 in York, which produced much of the machinery for the farms of southeastern Pennsylvania. A well-known manufacturer of hardware and hand tools was Henry Disston and Sons of Philadelphia, founded in 1840.

With the development of machinery came a demand for precision instruments, and Pennsylvania was a leader in the manufacture of control instruments. The Brown Instrument Company of Philadelphia, later an affiliate of the Minneapolis-Honeywell Company, illustrates the development of the instrument industry. Its origin dates from 1859, when a young English engineer and draftsman, Edward Brown, came to the United States. The instruments used at that time to measure variation in pressure and temperature were extremely crude, and Brown recognized the need for greater precision. During his lifetime Brown developed many measuring devices, including the expansion pyrometer, thermometer, and pressure gauges. The Robertshaw Thermostat Company was founded in 1899 to manufacture thermostats for domestic and industrial use. The company soon became a maker of precision instruments and controls for a wide range of industries. These industries rely heavily on research and development to maintain a competitive position, and Pennsylvania has been a leader in these endeavors.

LOCOMOTIVES AND RAILROAD CARS

The fourth largest industry in the state during the period of great expansion of manufacturing was the production of locomotives and the repair and building of railroad cars. The tremendous growth of railroads in the nineteenth century provided the basis for the locomotive and car industry. Because the Pennsylvania Railroad, with its headquarters in the state, served a large region in the northeastern quadrant of the United States, the Pennsylvania industry had a large regional market, and the quality of Pennsylvania locomotives and equipment provided the basis for a national market.

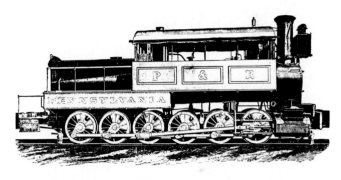

Top: *Henry R. Campbell of Philadelphia completed his first eight-wheel locomotive in 1837 for the Philadelphia, Germantown and Norristown Railroad. From James Dredge,* A Record of the Transportation Exhibits at the World's Columbian Exposition of 1893

Above: *Workers at the Philadelphia and Reading Railroad's repair shops built the* Pennsylvania *in 1863. This fifty-ton pusher engine, which was designed to help trains up steep grades, was the world's largest locomotive for a time. From Matthias N. Forney,* Recent Locomotives, *1886*

Above: *Matthias W. Baldwin, a former jeweler, established the Baldwin Locomotive Works in the 1830s. His first locomotive,* Old Ironsides, *was not a great success: the newspapers called it a "fair weather" locomotive, since its light weight did not give it the tractive power needed to draw a loaded train on wet, slippery rails. Other ventures, however, were more successful. During Baldwin's lifetime, his Philadelphia-based company built over 1,500 locomotives. From Scharf and Westcott,* History of Philadelphia, *Vol. III, 1884*

Above right: *The Baldwin Works built this anthracite-burning "camel back" freight locomotive in 1880 for the Philadelphia and Reading Railroad. It was called a "camel back" because the cab sat atop the central portion of the boiler. From Matthias N. Forney,* Recent Locomotives, *1886*

One of the first steam locomotives was built in Pennsylvania by Matthias Baldwin in Philadelphia in 1831 for the new railroad being constructed between Philadelphia and Germantown. The engine, built partly of iron and wood, became known as "Old Ironsides." Baldwin succeeded so well that by 1866 at the time of his death he had built 1,500 locomotives for the American railroads. The Baldwin Locomotive Works, later becoming the Baldwin-Lima-Hamilton Corporation, was a major builder of steam locomotives. Many other companies built locomotives in Pennsylvania including the Pennsylvania Railroad.

Besides locomotives a number of major companies built railroad equipment. The American Car and Foundry Company, with its main plant at Berwick, was an early builder of equipment for American railroads. Founded in 1840, it was the oldest company of its kind in the nation. The Edward G. Budd Company, incorporated in 1912 at Ardmore, near Philadelphia, was a pioneer in the building and design of streamlined cars, including the high speed cars used on the Pennsylvania Railroad between New York and Philadelphia. Budd built the pioneer Burlington Zephyrs running between Chicago and Denver.

OTHER MANUFACTURING

During the nineteenth century Pennsylvania developed one of the most diversified industrial bases of any state in the nation. It is difficult

Several locomotives under simultaneous construction were an everyday sight at the Baldwin Locomotive Works erecting shop about 1900. From the Philadelphia Commercial Museum Collection, Pennsylvania State Archives

Luxury items such as perfume have been popular in Pennsylvania since William Penn's time. R. and G.A. Wright, perfume manufacturers, druggists, and importers of "fancy articles," issued this elaborate advertisement in the mid-nineteenth century. Courtesy, Library Company of Philadelphia

to find a category of manufacturing that was not represented. Among the smaller but nonetheless important industries were food processing, papermaking, printing and publishing, glassmaking, aluminum, and shipbuilding.

As the industrial age advanced, an increasingly urban population could no longer depend on home-grown produce and home-processed meats, and demand grew for commercially prepared foodstuffs. Although certain types of food preparation, such as bakeries, were widely distributed and served local markets, Pennsylvania developed a number of companies that were nationally, and even internationally, known.

Of the processors of food products, Henry J. Heinz became the Pennsylvania leader. As a

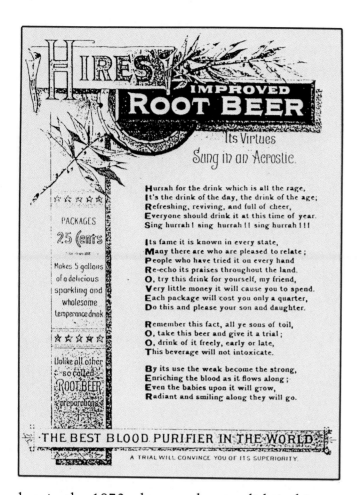

Above: *Henry John Heinz (1844-1919), a native of Pennsylvania, grew up in Pittsburgh and Sharpsburg. After working for his father in a brick-making business, he started a fresh produce business. Then, in 1876, he, a brother, and a cousin formed the F and J Heinz Company to make and sell prepared food products such as soups, pickles, and ketchup. The company was reorganized in 1888 as the H.J. Heinz Company, and in 1905 the firm was incorporated with Henry Heinz as its president. Heinz passed away in Pittsburgh fourteen years later. From Cirker,* Dictionary of American Portraits, *Dover, 1967*

Above left: *The Charles E. Hires Company, located at 48 North Delaware Avenue in Philadelphia when this advertisement appeared, referred to its Hires Improved Root Beer as "the best blood purifier in the world."*

boy in the 1870s, he grew horseradish in his mother's garden, grated it, and sold the prepared product in the neighborhood. By the time he was sixteen, he was growing and canning vegetables and selling them in the Pittsburgh market. His prepared horseradish was the first specialty product of the famous "57 Varieties" that became the slogan of the Heinz company. Freshly grated horseradish made dull food palatable and good food—such as beef and raw oysters—better. This was the beginning of a series of products that Heinz produced to enliven the food at the dinner table.

In 1888 the H.J. Heinz Company was formed to increase production and reach a wider market. By the early 1900s Heinz had built one of the country's biggest and most profitable businesses, manufacturing more than 200 products. It was the nation's largest producer of pickles, vinegar, and ketchup; the largest grower and processor of cabbage and sauerkraut, pickling onions, and horseradish; the second largest producer of mustard; and the fourth largest packer of olives. With headquarters in Pittsburgh, the company had nine branch factories in six states, thirty-eight salting houses in nine states, a branch company in London, and agencies around the world. It was the only company of its kind that manufactured its own bottles and had its own private railroad and tank cars. The company employed 2,800 full-time workers, plus some 20,000 others engaged in growing crops for processing. The Heinz Company was built without mergers and with the purchase of only two or three small companies.

Heinz assembled products from throughout the world, including raisins and green olives from Spain, figs and dates from the Middle East, currants from Greece, fresh fruits and sugar from the West Indies, whole spices from the East Indies, and mustard seed from England, France, and Italy. From American distilleries came scores of thousands of used oak kegs and barrels to be scraped clean of charcoal and reused for kraut and vinegar. (Federal law did not permit reuse of kegs by distilleries.)

The H.J. Heinz Company contributed greatly to the technology of producing pure foods in quantity. Advances in the canning process were noteworthy. Originally the food was inserted in a hole about the size of a silver dollar in the top of the can, which was then capped and soldered shut. In this process there were many possibilities for contamination and spoilage of the food. The Heinz laboratories devised a process in which a machine deftly fashioned a cylinder open at both ends, the sides being rotated together and crimped in a lapped double-lock seam. A bottom was then crimped and doubled-locked onto the can. After the can was filled, the top was put on in the same manner and the can placed in the pressure cooker. One machine could turn out 40,000 of these cans—airtight, with no "leakers"—in a ten-hour day. Heinz believed that for the food-processing industry to produce pure foods and earn the confidence of the public, there had to be a partnership with a federal regulatory agency. The company thus became a major force in the passage of the Pure Food and Drug Act of 1906 and other legislation that followed.

Another famous producer of specialized food products in Pennsylvania was Milton S. Hershey. Hershey was born on a farm in Dauphin County in 1857. He learned to make candy in small plants in Lancaster, but was unsuccessful for many years in establishing his own business. Finally, at the Chicago World's Fair in 1893, he was impressed by a German exhibit of chocolate-making machinery. He bought the machine and began making caramel candy in Lancaster. It was a most successful venture, and in 1898 Hershey sold the caramel business for one million dollars.

Hershey and his major partner, William F.R. Murrie, then decided to erect a new plant to produce chocolates. They situated the plant in Dauphin County, in the heart of a dairy region, so that milk, the most perishable of the raw materials, could be obtained locally. The first chocolate was produced in 1905, and the present Hershey Chocolate Company founded in 1910. By 1920 the Hershey Company was using about one-tenth of the world's crop of cocoa. No candy bar became better known than the Hershey chocolate bar.

Above: *These 1910 photos show Dauphin County residents enjoying the scenery at Hershey Park. The park, like the town of Hershey, is the property of the Hershey Chocolate Company.*

Right: *On the reverse side of this Wilson-Cass Company advertisement appear testimonials from medical doctors, the president of Philadelphia's Old Ladies' Home, and Mrs. Ann Jane Garrett of the Home for Destitute Children that extol the virtues of the company's Health Biscuit. All agreed that the biscuits were nutritious and easily digested.*

Opposite page: *Milton S. Hershey (1857-1945), a Dauphin County native, served an apprenticeship with a Lancaster confectioner before forming the Lancaster Caramel Company in 1888. At the turn of the century, Hershey sold his company for one million dollars, and three years later formed a company to manufacture chocolate bars. The town of Hershey grew up around the chocolate factory, and the Hershey Chocolate Company became the world's largest manufacturer of chocolate products. Hershey died in 1945 in the town that bears his name. From Cirker,* Dictionary of American Portraits, *Dover, 1967*

The town of Hershey is a model industrial settlement. Hershey controlled the building of the town by developing residential areas and providing the utilities and services until the Derry township government assumed responsibility. The homes were always privately owned. Present growth is still largely controlled because the Hershey Trust still owns the majority of undeveloped land. In 1907 Hershey Park was opened as an amusement center for the chocolate company employees. It has become a major amusement center in eastern Pennsylvania. The M.S. Hershey Foundation operates the Hershey Educational and Financial Center. Within the area the Milton Hershey school is a 10,000-acre institution that houses and educates 1,250 boys and girls from broken and needy families. The Hershey Medical Center of the Pennsylvania State University opened in 1970 with a $50-million contribution from the M.S. Hershey Foundation.

The growing dairy industry of Pennsylvania was the basis for the establishment of several large companies. The history of the Supplee-Wills-Jones Mill Company illustrates the importance of a growing urban market. In 1804 Joel Woolman started a one-man milk route in Philadelphia. He owned and milked his own cows. By 1843 Woolman's original market had grown so large that his successor, Joseph L. Jones, began purchasing milk from dairymen to supply the Philadelphia market. In the 1870s George Supplee enlarged the milk-collecting area and improved distribution in the city, thereby controlling a larger share of the market. At the same time the greater capital made possible the use of the newest technologies. For example, about 1895 the glass milk bottle replaced the milk pail in deliveries, and in 1898, with the development of pasteurization, many of the health problems associated with contaminated milk disappeared. In 1925 the Supplee-Wills-Jones Company became affiliated with the National Dairy Products Corporation, the largest producer of dairy products in the nation.

Pennsylvania was also the home of many early ice-cream companies. The Breyer Company, now one of the largest in the eastern United States, was begun by William Breyer of Philadelphia in the late 1860s. He produced ice cream in a home freezer and sold the product in the local neighborhood. To attract attention, his small wagon had a brass dinner bell that told his customers the ice-cream man was on their street. The enterprise proved a success, and the company now has a marketing organization that serves at least seven states.

The making of paper was one of the earliest industries developed in Pennsylvania. The first paper mill in the United States was built in Germantown in 1693. The industry flourished, and in 1880 Pennsylvania ranked third among the states. The leading counties were Philadelphia, York, Blair, Elk, and Erie.

As the market increased, there was a continued incentive to develop new technologies to utilize a greater variety of raw materials and improve the quality of the paper. In 1816 the first steam-powered paper mill in the United States began operation in Pittsburgh. In 1830 Wooster and Holmes, of Meadville, secured patents for making paper from whitewood and hemlock. The process for making white paper from straw was developed at Flat Rock Mills in 1854. J.A. Roth of Philadelphia patented in 1857 the process of treating wood fiber with a combination of sulfuric acid and chlorine bleaching agents. In 1863 M.L. Keen of Royersford patented a process for making pulp from wood, and in the following year Richard Magee of Philadelphia patented a method for making quality writing paper.

The type of paper produced in Pennsylvania changed in response to new technology, the availability of raw material, and market demands. In the early part of the nineteenth century, the mills of Pennsylvania produced all types of paper, including that required by the newspapers of the state. By 1900 there was essentially no newsprint made in the state. This change was due largely to the lack of spruce, the wood best suited for newsprint manufacture. There was also a growing concentration on quality papers, including book paper.

The printing and publishing industry is also

one of the oldest in the state. The first printing press was erected in 1686, about four years after the first English settlement. Publication of the first magazine was attempted by Benjamin Franklin as early as 1741. The first Bible printed in the United States, except those printed in the Indian language, was from the press of Christopher Sauer of Germantown in 1743. A daily paper was printed as early as 1784, and by 1810 seventy-three newspapers were published in Philadelphia. By the early nineteenth century, it is estimated that half a million volumes were printed annually in Philadelphia.

By 1900 Pennsylvania firms accounted for about 10 percent of the nation's printing and publishing output. Among the leading book publishers were the Winston and Lippincott publishers of Philadelphia. The L.B. Lippincott Company, founded in 1792, published a wide range of books including fiction, nonfiction, reference books, children's books, and books of religious interest. The Winston Company, founded by John Winston in 1884, developed an international reputation for its Bibles, children's books, dictionaries, and other reference books. The Curtis Publishing Company, organized by Cyrus H.K. Curtis of Philadelphia in 1891, ranked as one of the foremost publishers of magazines. In addition to the *Ladies' Home Journal* and the *Saturday Evening Post,* one of its early publications was *The Farm Journal,* the leading rural periodical in the nation.

Pennsylvania became noted for a wide variety of printing and publishing techniques. Bookbinding, engraving, stereotyping, electroengraving, and blank book printing were techniques developed early in Pennsylvania. The Gladfelder Company of York was an early leader in the production of fine papers, and Edward Stern & Company of Philadelphia was noted for fine book printing.

The glass industry was one of the earliest industries in western Pennsylvania, filling a fundamental need for containers not only for Pennsylvania but for the western migrating settlers. The industry centered in Allegheny, Westmoreland, Washington, and Armstrong counties. The first glass plant west of the Alle-

Founded by John W. Forney in 1857, The Press *of Philadelphia was at first issued as a four-page folio. By 1884, when this engraving appeared in Scharf and Westcott's* History of Philadelphia, *the paper's editorial and news staffs numbered almost 500.*

Left: *Cyrus H.K. Curtis is pictured here circa 1890, the year he formed the Curtis Publishing Company. Unlike most publishers of his time, Curtis relied on revenue from the sale of ad space and also paid popular authors top-scale fees for their contributions. From Cirker,* Dictionary of American Portraits, *Dover, 1967*

Below: *One of Philadelphia's major white-collar employers in the early part of this century was the Curtis Publishing Company. In 1916, with 3,000 employees and 1,800 office personnel, the company had the largest nongovernmental office force in the city at that time. Shown here is the composing room, where publications such as the* Saturday Evening Post *and* Ladies' Home Journal *were produced. From the Philadelphia Commercial Museum Collection, Pennsylvania State Archives*

Glass lamp shades were more popular at the turn of the century than today. Workers in this Pittsburgh factory are making shades for both gas and electric lights. Courtesy, Pennsylvania State Archives

Above: *Workers at a Pittsburgh plant blow and mold glass objects around 1899. The man seated in the foreground holds the mold shut while the blower fills the glass with air to shape the final product. Courtesy, Pennsylvania State Archives*

Opposite page: *In February 1886, when he was only twenty-three, Charles Martin Hall succeeded in separating a pure sample of aluminum from a batch of alumina— a process that could produce the metal inexpensively. Four years later, Hall became a vice president of the company that would become the Aluminum Company of America (ALCOA). Courtesy, Oberlin College. From Cirker,* Dictionary of American Portraits, *Dover, 1967*

ghenies was built by Albert Gallatin at New Geneva, on the Monongahela River, in 1797. By 1810 there were at least eight glass factories in western Pennsylvania. The industry was oriented to raw materials and fuel supplies. Bituminous coal was the first major source of energy to produce glass, but as natural gas became available, it became an important source of energy. The first successful use of natural gas to manufacture glass took place at a large glass factory at Creighton, near Pittsburgh, in 1883. High-quality glass sands were also available, particularly in Juniata and Fayette counties. Further, there was an abundance of fireclay suitable for making bricks to line furnaces in western Pennsylvania and eastern Ohio. By 1870 Pennsylvania was the leading glass-producing state, with about 52 percent of the nation's output, based on the value of the product. Although the total value of Pennsylvania's output continued to increase, its relative position declined as other states developed new glass industries.

The modern aluminum industry was born in Pittsburgh in 1886, when chemists Charles M. Hall and Arthur Vining Davis perfected the electrolytic process, the passing of a direct electric current through molten cryolite-alumina. Until then aluminum, first discovered in 1825, was a novelty—a rare metal more costly than silver. The new technique meant that aluminum could be produced cheaply.

The next problem was that of producing it in commercial quantities. Hall and Davis were able to secure initial financial backing from Captain Alfred Hunt of Pittsburgh to build a smelter in the city. On Thanksgiving Day, 1888, the first shiny new ingot of aluminum was made at the Smallman Street plant of the Pittsburgh Reduction Company. The output was about fifty to sixty pounds per day initially, and the market was limited entirely to the use of aluminum for household utensils.

By 1891 the demand had grown so large that a new factory was built at New Kensington, thirty miles north of Pittsburgh, on the Allegheny River. The high cost of electrical energy in the region, however, caused the reduction plant to be dismantled and moved to Niagara Falls in 1895. The fabrication plant remained at New Kensington.

Andrew W. Mellon, a Pittsburgh banker and financier, recognized the value of aluminum and invested in the small company. As the company grew, Mellon and his family became the principal stockholders. In 1907 the company became the Aluminum Company of America, Alcoa, the only producer of aluminum in the United States for decades.

Another traditional industry in Pennsylvania dating from the colonial era was shipbuilding. With its vast forests and tall trees for masts, the Delaware River offered a prime location for the wooden shipbuilding industry. The famous Cramp Shipbuilding Company, organized in

1830, became a leader in wooden ship construction. As the wooden ships were replaced by new iron and steel vessels, the Pennsylvania shipyards were in the forefront of technological innovation. In 1872 the Cramp Company changed its name to the William Cramp and Sons Ship and Engine Building Company, and the firm became noted for its steel ships equipped with powerful steam engines. Cramp, a leader in developing innovative new engines, built the first triple expansion engine and the first three-screw propeller vessel.

When the American navy was enlarged late in the nineteenth century, such Pennsylvania shipbuilders as William and Charles Cramp, John Roach, and Horace See became leading naval architects and builders. Many of the vessels that saw service in the Spanish-American War were built in Pennsylvania shipyards. As of 1900 Pennsylvania ranked first among the states in shipbuilding, with 28 percent of the nation's tonnage coming from its shipyards. The Delaware was the world's second largest shipbuilding center, next to the River Clyde in Scotland.

154

Above: *To speed warship construction, Pennsylvania shipyards practiced assembly line construction. There are enough parts laid out in this yard for ten ships.*

Opposite, top: *These workers at Charles Cramp and Sons were conscious of being the best shipfitters anywhere in 1918.*

Left: *World War I introduced American shipyards to antisubmarine warfare. The Philadelphia and Chester yards turned out dozens of the legendary "four stacker" destroyers. The vessel in the background is already wearing "warpaint" and has steam up. These sturdy ships could be found in various navies as late as 1950.*

At Hog Island workers built ships to the latest naval architecture specifications. In this case, a worker is caulking the seams of part of a ship's inner bottom. Courtesy, Pennsylvania State Archives

Opposite, top left: *In the mould loft of the Hog Island Shipyard during World War I, each piece of the proposed ship was laid out in full-scale mock-up. Courtesy, Pennsylvania State Archives*

Opposite, top right: *Philadelphia's shipbuilding industry received a great boost when, during World War I, the United States government awarded a contract to the American International Shipbuilding Corporation to construct a huge shipyard on Hog Island. Courtesy, Pennsylvania State Archives*

Above: *Under the War Emergency Act of 1917-1918, Pennsylvania's Hog Island Shipyard built merchant ships faster than any yard in the world at that time. Courtesy, Pennsylvania State Archives*

Opposite page, bottom: *Hog Island in the Delaware River was a test site for applying assembly line procedures to military construction in 1918. The hulls of merchant vessels, all in identical states, are visible among the derricks. Courtesy, Pennsylvania State Archives*

FINANCIAL AND COMMERCIAL INSTITUTIONS

Pennsylvania's transformation from a rural to an industrial economy required the development of new financial and commercial institutions. In order to build the new industrial complexes, vast amounts of capital were required, the accumulation of which was only possible through major financial institutions. By the end of the nineteenth century industrial management was no longer oriented to the factory site, but was concentrated in the central business districts of the industrial cities. The industrial corporations located their management offices near banks and other commercial facilities. In turn, banking facilities secured capital from a wide variety of sources in order to provide monies for the expanding economy.

The concentration of business activities in a central location changed the structure of Pennsylvania's cities. In Pittsburgh, for example, the concentration of business in the central business district changed the appearance and the functions of the "downtown." Space became increasingly scarce and buildings increased in height with the first true "skyscraper" being built in 1895. By 1912 twenty-seven such structures had been built. At the same time there was a dramatic decline in population in the central business district. The population of the four central wards declined from 21,439 in 1850 to 8,217 in 1900. In 1870 there were thirty-four churches in these wards, but by 1910 only eleven remained. In contrast, the tax assessment figures rose rapidly after 1880 when residential land was re-classified for business. Industry, finance, and commerce were the cornerstones of the growing metropolis, with finance and commerce concentrated in a

small urban core.

ESTABLISHMENT OF MODERN BANKING

The development of modern banking in Pennsylvania began with the Omnibus Act of 1814. Prior to this time banking offices in Pennsylvania were found only in Philadelphia, Lancaster, Easton, Columbia, Wilkes-Barre, Harrisburg, York, Chambersburg, Washington, and Pittsburgh. Banking was concentrated in the east and was very restricted west of the Susquehanna. The development of banks in the state had been limited by a number of governmental regulations. Banking companies incorporated under the laws of other states were forbidden to do business in Pennsylvania by an act of the legislature, enacted on March 28, 1808. Further, a supplemental Act of 1810 prohibited any unincorporated banking association from receiving deposits, discounting notes, or issuing notes of circulation.

Because of the expanding economy, however, there was a growing desire on the part of many businessmen to expand banking opportunities. There was also a growing need for banking to extend beyond the traditional urban financial centers. To accomplish this, the legislature in 1814 passed the act which became known as the "Omnibus" Banking Act. This act resulted in a virtual explosion of the number of banks in Pennsylvania. The act authorized the establishment of forty-one banks in twenty-seven different banking districts. (Formerly there had been only twelve banks operating in just ten communities in the state.) Of the forty-one new banks authorized, thirty-nine received charters, but only thirty-seven opened for business. By 1822 eleven of the banks had forfeited their charters because of their inability to redeem their notes on demand in specie so that only twenty-six remained active. The Omnibus Act also made special provisions for unchartered banks operating in Pennsylvania in order to expand their activities.

The Omnibus Act specified many provisions that later became standard in banking procedures. No bank was to owe more than double

Opposite page, top: William Cramp (left) built wooden ships and later his son, Charles Henry (right), produced iron and steel vessels. From Cirker, Dictionary of American Portraits, *Dover, 1967*

Left: Ike Gillete was a clerk for many years at the Cramp shipbuilding yard in Philadelphia during its heyday.

the amount of paid-in-capital, with the exception of money deposited for safekeeping. Other major provisions were: dividends not exceeding the net profits were to be declared at least twice a year, in May and November; the discount rate was limited to one half of one percent for thirty days; banks could hold only such real estate as was necessary for the convenient transaction of business; banks were not to purchase or hold any stock except their own and that of the stock of Pennsylvania corporations and stock of the federal government; banks were not to issue notes of a smaller denomination than five dollars; and banks were required, upon sixty days notice, to lend the state 10 percent of their capital at no more than 6 percent interest for a period of five years.

The Omnibus Act was modified by the Banking Act of 1824. While this act changed certain details, its main impact on banking was to end the mass chartering of banks in Pennsylvania. From this time on, the legislature authorized the incorporation of banks, one at a time, under special charters, and charters were extended or renewed on an individual basis. By 1836 there were seventeen chartered banks in Philadelphia and thirty-two in the rest of the state.

PENNSYLVANIA'S ROLE IN THE NATION'S BANKING

Pennsylvania played an active role in the development of the national banking systems from its origin late in the eighteenth century. The original Bank of the United States, chartered in 1791 in Philadelphia, was forced to close on March 3, 1811 due to relentless opposition by advocates of state banking. But it was soon evident that the country had destroyed the only viable national banking system that it possessed. The numerous small local banks were simply unable to handle the fiscal operations of the national government. Many prominent bankers who opposed renewing the charter of the first Bank of the United States later recognized the need for renewal, but it was a Pennsylvanian, Alexander J. Dallas of Philadelphia,

who spearheaded the efforts to establish the second Bank of the United States. By the Act of 1816 the bank was established and it opened on January 7, 1817 in Carpenters' Hall in Philadelphia, the same location the original bank had occupied. On April 5, 1819 the cornerstone for a new building was laid at a new state. It was then, and still is, one of the finest examples of Greek and Georgian architecture in the United States.

Philadelphia soon became the recognized core of the federal banking system. Branch offices were established, one of which was in Pittsburgh. The bank experienced many difficulties during its early years. In 1823, Nicholas Biddle, a member of an old and distinguished Philadelphia family, was appointed president of the bank, and he established policies that brought it solvency. This was accomplished primarily by an increased use of domestic bills of exchange and of branch drafts. Although Biddle had little practical experience in banking, his great intelligence and industrious nature made it possible for the bank to enjoy a long period of successful operation. The second Bank of the United States was the forerunner of the Federal Reserve System of today. Its notes gradually replaced those of the local banks, thus providing the country with a uniform currency. Because the revenue of the federal government at that time consisted mainly of taxes on imports, and these were deposited in the Bank of the United States, the bank was the sole depository of the federal government.

By the time the bank applied to be rechartered, in 1832, much opposition had developed. The popular mistrust of large-scale banking found an uncompromising champion in Andrew Jackson. He not only vetoed the renewal bill of 1832 but after his re-election he weakened the bank by having its funds transferred to various state banks. The Philadelphia banking community recognized that the removal of the bank would have a very adverse economic effect on the city, and sent a delegation to Washington to confront President Jackson. The President listened to the Philadelphia spokesmen briefly and then said, "Andrew

Jackson would never recharter that monster of corruption . . . sooner than live in a country where such a power prevailed, he would seek an asylum in the wilds of Arabia." The bank ceased business under its national charter on March 3, 1836.

The disappearance of the second Bank of the United States was not only important in national and Pennsylvania banking history, but it represented the great economic and social repercussions beginning to shape the economy of the nation. Andrew Jackson was a representative of the populist tradition. His administration was made up of officials who were opposed to wealthy urban businessmen. They represented an agrarian way of life that was being altered by the industrial revolution. In this evolution they became the spokesmen for laissez-faire economics. The demise of the second Bank of the United States was the first dramatic evidence of the triumph of this doctrine over economic conservatism and governmental controls. The establishment of free enterprise provided the dominant economic theme for Pennsylvania's and the nation's economy in the nineteenth century.

The activities of the second Bank of the United States did not end when the federal charter expired. Rather, it continued to operate under a state charter granted by the Pennsylvania legislature on February 18, 1836. This act was a strange piece of legislation entitled, "An Act to repeal the State tax on real and personal property, and to continue and extend the improvements of the State by railroads and canals, and to charter a State bank to be called the United States Bank." This bank charter, authorizing the United States Bank of Pennsylvania differed little from that of the federal charter, except that it was to run for thirty years and the bonus to be paid for the charter was exceptionally high. The bank was to pay the state an immediate bonus of $2,500,000 and $100,000 annually for twenty years for the support of schools. It was to loan the state up to $1,000,000 a year in temporary 4 percent loans and $6,000,000 on state bonds payable in 1868 at 4 percent; and it was to subscribe

$640,000 to railroads and other improvements. Personal taxes were repealed and $1,368,000 was to be appropriated out of the basic funds for various public works.

Most banking historians agree that the continuation of the second Bank of the United States under a Pennsylvania charter was the work of Nicholas Biddle. Biddle resented the discontinuance of the federal charter and wanted to prove, if not to Jackson, at least to the people, that he was capable of managing a large banking operation and that such an institution was needed for the economic welfare of the nation. In the political process to obtain a state charter there is evidence that the charter was secured by political manipulation and legislative bribery. This contrasts greatly from the manner that Biddle managed the Bank of the United States, for it was recognized that he would not tolerate corruption or bribery. Although Andrew Jackson had repeatedly charged Biddle with corruption, on all occasions the second Bank of the United States had successfully refuted the charges. In contrast, the United States Bank of Pennsylvania during its short life was noted for its political manipulation and unsound financial practices.

Although the United States Bank of Pennsylvania operated with Nicholas Biddle as president and under the same management, its functions were drastically changed. The Bank of the United States had a federal charter and operated as a national institution; the United States Bank of Pennsylvania was a state institution with no national prerogatives or responsibilities. This changed the manner in which Nicholas Biddle functioned as a chief executive. As president of the Bank of the United States he was a conservative administrator ever mindful of overseeing a national institution. In contrast, as president of the Pennsylvania bank he was seized with irrational, impetuous, and grandiose ideas that were manifested in erratic and imprudent policies. These policies evolved into a series of rash investments, apparently a desperate attempt at empire building. The bank began to promote enterprises everywhere and enter into unworkable financial contracts. In a

161

As a concluding anecdote, Nicholas B. Wainwright wrote in his book *The Philadelphia National Bank: A Century and a Half of Philadelphia Banking*:

In March 1842 . . . a distinguished English visitor arrived in the city and was driven to the United States Hotel on Chestnut Street. 'We reached the city late that night,' wrote Charles Dickens, 'when looking out of my chamber-window, before going to bed, I saw on the opposite side of the way a handsome building of white marble, which had a mournful ghost-like aspect, dreary to behold.' On rising in the morning the author expected to see throngs of people passing in and out of that monumental edifice. But the doors remained tight shut. Surprised, Dickens inquired the identity of the building, and learned that 'it was the Tomb of many fortunes, the Great Catacomb of investment, the memorable United States Bank.'

When the charter was not renewed on the second Bank of the United States in 1836 the United States was left without a national banking system. As a consequence there was little or no regulation of credit resulting in a wildly fluctuating currency. The economy was thus subject to economic depressions such as those of 1837 and 1857. It became evident that the financial system could not function effectively without some form of central control.

The National Banking Act of 1863 was passed by Congress to meet two urgent governmental needs. First, the government needed a safe and uniform system for circulating its currency. Second, the Civil War was in progress and the federal government required a market for its bonds in order to carry out its military objectives. The National Act authorized a system of banks to be chartered by the federal government with the stipulation that these banks purchase government bonds.

With the passage of the act, the first federal bank was established in Philadelphia on June 20, 1863. Initially the state banks of Pennsylvania were reluctant to relinquish their state charters. They feared that they would be breaking the

little more than a year, loans on stocks increased from $4,800,000 to over $20,000,000. As a consequence the bank had to secure loans from foreign countries. But instead of retrenching, the bank continued to borrow upon past notes and bonds to the extent of $23,000,000 more. It seemed impossible for the bank, and particularly Biddle, to refuse a loan to anyone. Bonds from Mississippi, Michigan, Florida, and even the Republic of Texas received approval.

When Nicholas Biddle retired as president of the bank in 1839 he declared the bank prosperous. In 1840, however, the lack of assets raised many questions as to the financial soundness of the bank. In 1841 the bank failed, largely due to Biddle's mismanagement. He defended his actions in a number of legal suits and was acquitted in every case. The stockholders, however, lost everything when the bank failed. Shares that stood at 126 when the charter was granted in 1836 were priced at 1 7/8 when the bank closed. Biddle died in 1844, some say of a "broken heart." It was a sad end to a man who had once guided the country in its establishment of a central banking system.

state banking laws unless the state legislature provided an enabling act, for the changeover meant a huge tax loss to the state for the federal banks could not be taxed by the state. In 1864 the Pennsylvania legislature passed the necessary enabling legislation. But Governor Andrew Curtin signed the act only when the banks making the conversion to federal charters surrendered the certificates that represented the premium on gold recently lent the state by the banks. The certificates were surrendered to help the Commonwealth pay interest in specie on its bonds. The good faith of the Commonwealth had been pledged for their redemption, but now the governor asked that they be cancelled. The state banks agreed and the enabling act became law on August 22, 1864.

The National Banking Act acted in a number of ways to bring stability to the nation's financial situation. The reserve requirements were strengthened; the issuance of circulating bank notes was regulated and systematized; and there was a more stringent examination of banks, which reduced the number of failures. As a result of the National Banking Act, the number of state banks decreased in Pennsylvania from ninety-four in 1863 to a low of six in 1867. In contrast the number of national banks rose from fifteen in 1863 to 198 in 1868 and to 426 in 1898. The number of state banks remained small for several years, but began to increase in the 1870s.

The National Banking Act created a dual banking system in the United States. A bank could choose to be a part of the state or federal system. The federal government, however, did attempt to provide an incentive for state banks to join the federal system when in 1865 an amendment to the National Banking Act was passed which levied a tax of 2-to-10 percent on state bank notes. Although the initial reaction of banks throughout the country was to abandon their state charter for a federal charter, the widespread demand for banking facilities created a need for state as well as federal banks. Nevertheless, in contrast to national trends in the 1860s where state banks were

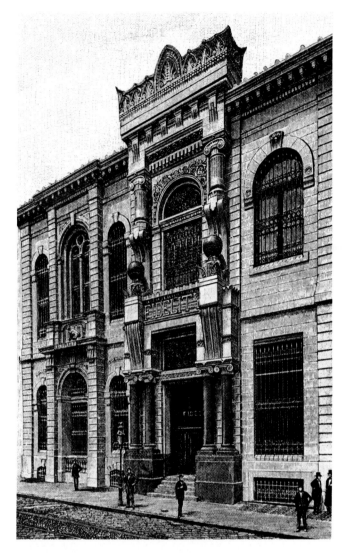

Above: *The Fidelity Insurance, Trust, and Safe Deposit Company was located at 329 Chestnut Street in Philadelphia. The company was incorporated in 1866, three years after the National Banking Act was passed to provide a safe, uniform system for circulating currency. From Scharf and Westcott,* History of Philadelphia, *Vol. III, 1884*

Opposite page: *A native Philadelphian, Nicholas Biddle (1786-1844) was elected to the Pennsylvania State Legislature in 1814, appointed a director of the Bank of the United States by President Monroe in 1819, and then served as president of the Bank of the United States for nearly two decades. Biddle, who was the editor of the first American literary journal,* Port Folio, *in 1812, was an extremely precocious child. He entered the University of Pennsylvania when he was only ten years old. From Cirker,* Dictionary of American Portraits, *Dover, 1967*

about twice as numerous as federal banks, Pennsylvania had nearly twice as many federal banks as state banks. This trend was changed in the 1870s when in 1871 twenty-eight state banks were chartered, thirty-four more in 1872, and again thirty-four in 1873.

By the early twentieth century it was becoming evident that the National Banking Act of 1863 was outmoded. The financial disturbances of 1893 and 1907 provided evidence that the continued financial stability of the nation was contingent upon the revitalization of the central banking system. In 1908 Congress appointed a National Monetary Commission to consider a new banking structure. After three years of study the Aldrich Plan, named after Senator Nelson W. Aldrich, chairman of the commission, recommended the creation of a National Reserve Association of fifteen banks. But many felt that this plan reflected the interests of business too strongly. After much discussion a compromise was finally reached that resulted in the Federal Reserve Act of 1913.

This act created a banking system that combined central and regional controls. Central authority was vested in the Board of Governors of the Federal Reserve System in Washington. Board members were appointed by the President with the consent of the Senate. Regional control was divided among Federal Reserve Banks, strategically located throughout the country in Federal Reserve Districts. These banks were owned by the banks in the district belonging to the federal reserve system. All national banks were required to be members, and state chartered and private banks could become members if they adhered to certain regulations. Each member bank was required to subscribe a certain percent of its capital and surplus with its regional Federal Reserve Bank.

In the establishment of the Federal Reserve Districts the act provided that there should not be fewer than eight or more than twelve districts, each to contain a Federal Reserve city with a Federal Reserve Bank. In 1914 the Organization Committee announced the creation of twelve districts. In general, state lines were followed in developing districts. Pennsylvania

was an exception. All of Pennsylvania east of the western boundary of McKean, Elk, Clearfield, Cambria, and Bedford counties, together with the states of New Jersey and Delaware, constituted District No. 3 with Philadelphia as the Federal Reserve city. The remainder of Pennsylvania was included with Ohio as well as certain counties in northwestern West Virginia and the eastern part of Kentucky to form District No. 4 with Cleveland as the Federal Reserve city. Pittsburgh had hoped to become the center, with a Federal Reserve Bank. Although it protested the ruling, it did not succeed in reversing the decision. In 1917 Pittsburgh did succeed in securing a branch bank and the disappointment was somewhat eased. The division of Pennsylvania into two districts reflected the difference in the economy between eastern and western Pennsylvania.

The Federal Reserve System has influenced the banking institutions in a number of ways. It provided for a safer and more elastic system of currency. It mobilized bank reserves more effectively; it created a discount system for commercial loans and established an open market for commercial paper; it provided a more satisfactory check clearance system; and it strengthened the examination and supervision structure for national banks.

BANKING FIRSTS IN PENNSYLVANIA

Pennsylvania was a leader in the establishment of a number of different types of banking institutions. The Commonwealth was the location of the first incorporated commercial bank in America, the first Bank of the United States, the first mint, the first life insurance company, the first mutual savings bank, and the first savings and loan association.

On February 2, 1816 the first mutual savings bank in the nation, the Philadelphia Saving Fund Society, began to receive deposits. Shortly after the Philadelphia savings bank was established two others were founded in New York and Boston. The leader in organizing the Philadelphia Saving Fund Society was Condy Roquet, who was also the president of the Pennsylvania Company for Insurances on Lives and Granting Annuities.

The mutual savings banks were organized to encourage saving among people of modest means. These banks provided a safe facility where comparatively small savings could be deposited and earn a small interest rate. At that time regular banks and other institutions frequently did not accept small amounts or at best were not enthusiastic about small individual accounts. The mutual savings banks were most popular in the growing manufacturing and commercial centers. In the agricultural, lumbering, and mining areas where comparatively small numbers of wage earners had limited needs for a savings bank the mutual savings banks did not flourish.

Pennsylvania was also the home of the first savings and loan association in the United States, located at Frankford, an industrial suburb of Philadelphia. The English settlers in this small town originally known as Oxford worked in the textile and tanning mills. As the town grew, the new residents needed housing. Records indicate that many of the inhabitants were familiar with the building societies that existed in Britain, and a building society was proposed for Frankford. To meet the need the Oxford-Provident Savings and Loan Association was established in 1831.

The original savings and loan associations differed from the mutual savings banks in that they were designed primarily to help solve home financing problems. The constitution of the Oxford-Provident stated its purpose was "to enable contributors thereof to build or purchase dwelling houses." There is also a difference between savings and loan associations and mutual savings banks in the manner in which they accept savings; a bank, whether it is a commercial or mutual savings bank, receives money for deposit. In contrast, savings and loan associations receive funds in savings accounts, which usually constitute shares in the association. In other words, savers who place money in a bank are depositors, but are shareholders in a savings and loan association. These savers in a mutual savings bank collect interest on a deposit while in a savings and

loan association the saver collects dividends as a shareholder. Savings and loan associations and mutual savings banks differ fundamentally from commercial banks in that neither of them by law can provide such services as checking accounts or installment lending.

The savings and loan associations of the state have made a major contribution to the home building industry. They have been a major factor in creating economic stability in many areas.

ANDREW W. MELLON, PREMIER FINANCIER

Pennsylvania's growing industrial sector spawned great industrial leaders, and the creation of numerous financial empires was a direct result of the genius of such men as Andrew W. Mellon. Mellon was born in Pittsburgh in 1855 and after attending the Western University of Pennsylvania (University of Pittsburgh) he began his career in 1872 as a manager of a lumber business near Mansfield, Pennsylvania. In 1874 he returned to Pittsburgh to enter his father's banking business. He was so successful that in 1882 his father transferred ownership of T. Mellon and Sons Bank to him. In the next twenty years he built a great banking empire. In 1899, Mellon, together with Henry Clay Frick, founded the Union Trust Company of Pittsburgh. In 1902 the T. Mellon and Sons Bank was incorporated as the Mellon National Bank with Andrew W. Mellon serving as president until 1921.

The Mellon bank provided the financial backing for the creation of some of the largest corporations in the nation. One of its earliest financial endeavors was the backing of the infant aluminum industry in Pittsburgh. In 1896 Mellon became a partner of Edward Goodrich Acheson to form the Carborundum Company. In 1901 when the prolific oil strike was made at Signal Hill in Texas, Andrew Mellon helped found the Gulf Oil Corporation. This was the first major oil company to provide competition to the oil empire of John D. Rockefeller. He also helped found the Union Steel Company, which later merged with United States Steel,

Financier Andrew W. Mellon backed the founding and growth of companies such as ALCOA and Gulf Oil. The head of Mellon National Bank is pictured here in 1923, when he served in President Harding's cabinet. Possibly the greatest Secretary of Treasury since Alexander Hamilton, Mellon strongly advocated the "trickle theory" and the belief that America's business is business. Oil painting by Sir Oswald Hornby Joseph Birley. Courtesy, the National Portrait Gallery, Smithsonian Institution, Washington, D.C.

the Standard Steel Car Company, and the New York Shipbuilding Company. With two young engineers, Mellon formed a construction company that built the Panama Canal locks, the Hell Gate and George Washington bridges, and the Waldorf-Astoria Hotel. He controlled the Pittsburgh Coal Company and when he saw the value of Heinrich Kopper's by-product coke ovens (the ovens recovered vast quantities of hydrocarbon materials that had previously been lost to produce a wide variety of chemical products) he, with three of his associates, purchased in 1918 the American assets of the German-controlled company at a very low price. In all, Mellon held directorships in more than sixty-two corporations.

Andrew W. Mellon exemplified the archtype of the modern financial capitalist. He was certainly among the most important financiers in the United States in the period from 1890 to 1930. His appearance and manner, however, belied his powerful position. Physically, Mellon was slight and frail. With his dark suits, of which the coat was always buttoned, and his black tie and socks he presented a somber appearance. He smoked small, black-paper cigarettes, gingerly puffing them down to the last one-eighth inch of tobacco. He was always serious and he smiled only on the rarest occasions. When shaking hands only the tips of his fingers touched the other person's hand. As one reporter derogatorily stated, Mellon looked like "a tired double-entry bookkeeper who is afraid of losing his job." Another said Mellon reminded him of "a dried up dollar bill that any wind might whisk away."

In 1921 Mellon left the presidency of the Mellon bank to become secretary of the treasury under Warren Harding, a position he held under the Coolidge and Hoover administrations until 1932. When Mellon went to Washington he left the world of commercial banking. Many of his friends could not understand how a man of Mellon's power and status in the world of financial and corporate affairs could relinquish this for a career in government service.

Andrew Mellon possessed a strong conviction that service to his country was an absolute obligation of every citizen. To enter government service he sacrificed much in the financial world. Forbidden by law to engage in any business or commerce while serving as secretary, Mellon resigned the directorships in the corporations he served as well as the presidency of Mellon National Bank. He sold his bank stock to Richard G. Mellon, his brother, who became the president of the bank. During his years at the treasury, he immersed himself totally in the financial problems of the country and of the world.

Although Mellon was not particularly well-liked by the general public, he was regarded with awe and fascination by friend and foe alike. Throughout the 1920s presidents and fellow cabinet members looked to Mellon for guidance in domestic and international financial policies. One of his contemporaries in the government remarked that Mellon was the only cabinet officer in American history to have three presidents serve under him.

Mellon established a firm financial policy for the nation during his term of office. When he took office, the national debt was at an extremely high level due to spending during the World War I period. Between 1921 and 1929 the debt was reduced from $24 billion to $16.2 billion. Andrew Mellon initiated many new policies at a time of great financial growth. He believed that taxes of individuals with high incomes should be reduced so that the wealthy could reinvest their money in productive enterprises. Consequently, he convinced Congress to lower the tax rates. He opposed the veteran's bonus and the McNary-Haugen farm relief bills, believing that they would be a drain on the treasury with little investment going into productive endeavors. In contrast, he approved the Agricultural Credit Acts of 1921 and 1923, for these bills encouraged increased agricultural production.

Mellon was the government spokesman for "big business" in the Republican administrations of the 1920s. His conservative policies were influential in setting the stage for the economic boom of the 1920s, but many later came to believe that these policies also set the stage

for the ensuing stock market crash in October 1929. Under the Hoover administration his financial policies were attacked and he lost much of his earlier prestige. Because of increasing pressure, he resigned as secretary of the treasury in 1932 and Hoover appointed him ambassador to Great Britain. He held this post only until 1933 when Franklin D. Roosevelt became president.

Andrew W. Mellon was a financier in the mold of the late nineteenth and early twentieth centuries. He exemplified the rugged individualist. One of his last major contributions to the nation came in 1937 when he gave his vast art collection to the government and provided the funds to build the museum which became the National Gallery of Art in Washington.

EVOLUTION OF MODERN MERCHANDISING

Pennsylvania's changing economic structure also changed its method of merchandising goods. The development of the industrial city created a mass market for the growing amount of manufactured goods being produced. In addition, the expanding economy provided the average citizen with an increased purchasing power. The size of the market for manufactured goods was further enlarged by the state's expanding railroad network.

It was during this period that the department store evolved. Of the innovators in retailing, John Wanamaker of Philadelphia was an outstanding leader. He became one of Pennsylvania's most successful nineteenth-century merchants. After only a grammer school education he began work in 1852 as a stock boy in a clothing store in Philadelphia. In 1854, because of a dispute over a window display, he became a stock boy at a rival clothing store, and in a few years became manager of the men's furnishings department.

With this experience, Wanamaker, with a partner, Nathan Brown, opened a men's clothing store in the Oak Hill district of Philadelphia. By 1868 the Oak Hill store was the largest men's clothing store in the nation, and the

167

following year Wanamaker established John Wanamaker and Company and located on fashionable Chestnut Street. In 1876 he moved his store to the abandoned Pennsylvania Railroad freight station, which had over two acres of floor space. To utilize some of the space he added women's clothing to his line.

Since 1876 was the year of the Philadelphia Centennial Exposition, thousands of visitors came to the "Grand Depot" to buy clothing, but possibly more important, they spread the word across the nation of the value of mass marketing clothing. After the fair, Wanamaker could not interest other merchants in renting space in the Grand Depot. Consequently he

Innovation and continual reorganization brought success to John Wanamaker, founder of one of the first department stores in the country. Besides introducing a "new kind of store," Wanamaker was also a pioneer in using business advertising and in implementing full-refund policies. He is shown here circa 1900. Engraving by E.G. Williams & Bro. From Cirker, Dictionary of American Portraits, *Dover, 1967*

developed what was no doubt the world's first department store by developing in a single unit a cluster of specialty shops with 129 counters and 1,400 stools where customers could sit while selecting their purchases. At the same time, Roland Hussey Macy and Samuel Lord and George Washington Taylor were developing department stores in New York. By 1888 Wanamaker's store was possibly the largest store in the nation, with more than 5,000 employees. In 1911 on Wanamaker's golden jubilee, stores were located not only in Philadelphia but New York, London, and Paris with more than 13,000 employees in the organization.

The department store revolutionized the marketing of goods in the late nineteenth century. In its evolution, the first step was the introduction of a large single-line establishment to replace the traditional general store. The concentration on a single line of goods provided economies of scale in financing, advertising, and management. The single-line store purchasing in quantity could bypass the wholesaler and then secure higher quality goods at a lower price. It was logical, once a management system was in operation, to add other lines of merchandise. In due time the store developed numerous divisions selling all types of goods.

As was typical of so many industrialists, financiers, and merchants in the nineteenth century, Wanamaker was active in politics. In the 1888 presidential campaign he was a major fundraiser, and for his efforts, President Harrison appointed him postmaster general in 1889. Wanamaker was a strong believer in the "spoils system" and distributed patronage to loyal party members. He sought political power by organizing an insurgent movement against Quay's political control of Pennsylvania politics in the early 1890s. He failed to destroy the power of Quay, which likely lost him the Republican nomination for senator in 1896 and governor in 1928. In building his merchandising empire he believed in the Horatio Alger rags-to-riches philosophy of his day that anyone could be economically successful through hard work and strong religious convictions.

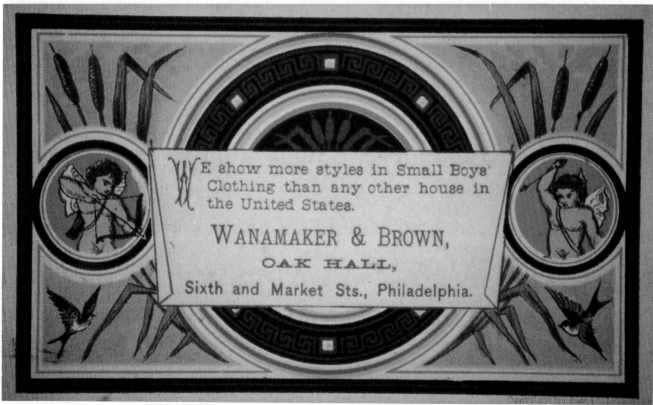

WE show more styles in Small Boys' Clothing than any other house in the United States.

WANAMAKER & BROWN,

OAK HALL,

Sixth and Market Sts., Philadelphia.

Top: *In 1876 Wanamaker developed the first department store in the abandoned Pennsylvania Railroad freight station. From James D. McCabe,* Illustrated History of the Centennial Exhibition, *1876*

Above: *While in partnership with Brown, Wanamaker distributed business cards such as this one.*

170

Left: *A bituminous coal mine and plant in Indiana, Pennsylvania, was depicted by painter Carrie Pattison. Courtesy, College of Earth and Mineral Sciences Museum and Art Gallery, The Pennsylvania State University*

Top: *Artist Lawrence Whitaker painted this view of an entrance to a small Pennsylvania coal mine. Courtesy, College of Earth and Mineral Sciences Museum and Art Gallery, The Pennsylvania State University*

Above: *The Ohio and Monongahela rivers have always been major outlets for the coal industry, despite the speed of trains. In this rare, hand-colored postcard, a fleet of stern wheelers are lining up to push coal barges. Courtesy, Pennsylvania State Archives*

172

Opposite, top: *The secondary recovery of petroleum in the Bradford oil field is depicted in this Christian J. Walter painting. Courtesy, College of Earth and Mineral Sciences Museum and Art Gallery, The Pennsylvania State University*

Left: *Oil wells dotted the western Pennsylvania landscape in the nineteenth century. Painting by Clarence McWilliams. Courtesy, College of Earth and Mineral Sciences Museum and Art Gallery, The Pennsylvania State University*

Above: *Quarriers are depicted hard at work in the Millard Quarry in Annville, Pennsylvania. Painting by Saverio DiMagno. Courtesy, College of Earth and Mineral Sciences Museum and Art Gallery, The Pennsylvania State University*

Below: *As steel became America's lifeblood, the machinery got bigger, the men fewer. Operations were perhaps less dramatic in 1900 than in 1840, when whole gangs worked the forges. Courtesy, Pennsylvania State Archives*

Bottom: *Heavy industry and economic expansion were the focal points of American cultural identity in the heady years of westward expansion after the Civil War. The steel mills and foundries of Pennsylvania symbolized that identity more than anything else.*

Below: *A somewhat romanticized painting shows a Pittsburgh steelworker pouring molten metal into a mold. Painting by Carl Walberg. Courtesy, College of Earth and Mineral Sciences Museum and Art Gallery, The Pennsylvania State University*

Left: *The Pittsburgh Steel Company boasted that its steel fence had "the weld that held" in this circa 1910 advertisement.*

Below: *Companies such as Stillman and Allen's Novelty Iron Works in Philadelphia grew rapidly in the 1820s and 1830s in response to the sudden and phenomenal demand for steam machinery of every sort. The steam technology developed by such Pennsylvania plants, for locomotives in particular, remained basically unchanged until the demise of steam power in the early twentieth century.*

Andrew Carnegie's Eliza Mill was a fiery apparition not only at night, but also in labor relations. Here, Frick and Carnegie made their stand against unions. Eliza, Homestead Steel, and other mills figured in the violent course of labor history. Courtesy, Pennsylvania State Archives

In response to heavy demand for fabric, Pennsylvania became one of the nation's leading textile centers by 1800. Mass production to meet that demand was only possible with the development of new machinery such as the loom pictured here. It swiftly replaced traditional cottage industry and attracted rural labor to the cities.

The Adelaide Silk Mills of Allentown are depicted on this postcard printed in Germany.

U. S. 466. Allentown, Pa. Adelaide Silk Mills.

Above: *In Pittsburgh during the first decade of the twentieth century, boys in their early teens could learn the craft of glass blowing in the city's glass factories. Courtesy, Pennsylvania State Archives*

Above: *While Edison turned out ideas, George Westinghouse turned out dynamos and other electrical equipment. Pictured here around 1905 is the Westinghouse turbine factory. Courtesy, Pennsylvania State Archives*

Top right: *Shipbuilding has been an important Pennsylvania industry since the eighteenth century. This colored etching depicting the building of the frigate* Philadelphia *dates from 1799. Etching by William Birch. Courtesy, The Historical Society of Pennsylvania*

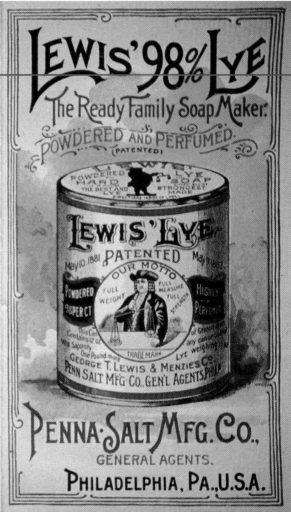

LEHR HIGH GRADE PIANOS

MRS. LESLIE CARTER

MISS HELLYET.

Manufactured by H. LEHR & CO., Easton, Pa. OVER

Above and right: *Easton's H. Lehr and Company produced pianos and organs. The company stressed on the reverse of these advertisements that its instruments contained "every perfection" and that "there is no necessity to buy a clearer instrument, while a cheaper one would be unsafe."*

Opposite page: *Philadelphia's Pennsylvania Salt Manufacturing Company produced Lewis' 98% Lye, while Pittsburgh's Fleming Brothers turned out Kidd's Cough Syrup and Mikado Cologne.*

TRY AND YOU WILL BUY
THE LEHR SEVEN OCTAVE ORGAN.
PIANO-STYLE

MANUFACTURED BY
H. LEHR & CO., EASTON, PA.

179

Main Plant and
General Offices: PITTSBURGH, U.S.A.

This page: *The famous H.J. Heinz Company has been in Pittsburgh for more than a century. Pictured here are the main plant and general offices (above) and Heinz employees packing pickles in the 1890s (right). Courtesy, Pennsylvania State Archives*

Opposite page: *Philadelphia has long been one of the nation's foremost producers of food products, and creative advertising has always played a large role in the marketing of both major and minor brands.*

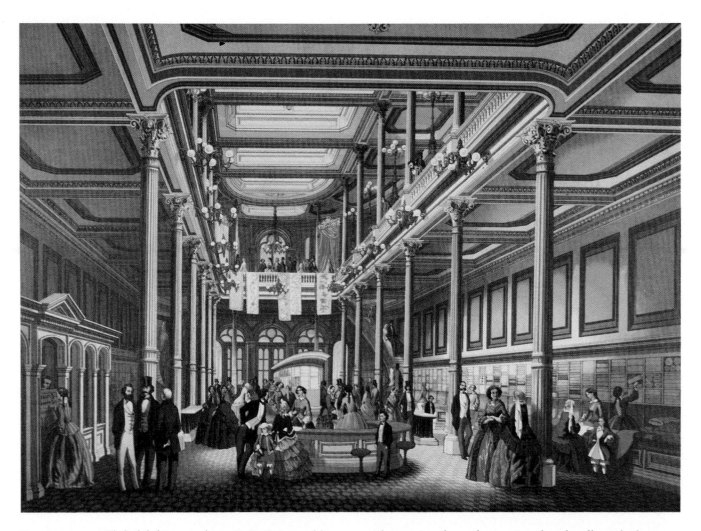

Opposite, top: *Philadelphia merchant D.S. Ewing sold the New Home Sewing Machine from his Chestnut Street store.*

Left: *William H. Weiss of Bethlehem sold dry goods, notions, and groceries. Why he chose this graphic of a one-handed sea captain, buxom woman, and brokenhearted cupid to advertise his business is a mystery.*

Above: *An elegantly appointed and well-stocked store greeted patrons of L.J. Levy and Company's Dry Goods establishment on Chestnut in Philadelphia. Lithograph by L.N. Rosenthal after Max Rosenthal, 1857. Courtesy, The Historical Society of Pennsylvania*

Chapter Six
Transportation for an Industrial Economy

The transformation of the economy of Pennsylvania from one dominated by agriculture to one in which industry was preeminent required a revolution in the means of transportation. Without the development of an efficient transportation system, the movement of fuels and raw materials to the factories and the distribution of the finished commodities would not have been possible. The building of canals and improvement of waterways was the initial step

in this transportation revolution. But the dominance of canals lasted barely twenty-five years before they were superseded by the railroads.

The early 1820s saw a wave of canal building in the United States. To the north of Pennsylvania, the famed Erie Canal was being built to give New York access to the agricultural Midwest. To the south, Baltimore merchants were making surveys for a ninety-four-mile canal from Baltimore to

York Haven to tap the resources of the Susquehanna Valley in Pennsylvania. It was recognized that if Philadelphia was to prosper, a direct canal route focusing on Philadelphia was needed to compete successfully for the western trade.

The first canal route in Pennsylvania, between Reading on the Schuylkill and Middletown on the Susquehanna River, was considered as early as 1762, but the Union Canal between these two points was not completed until 1827. This route, following a series of low-lying valleys, was planned to give Philadelphia a water route to the Susquehanna. Although the canal was used to transport wheat, rye, flour, whiskey, iron, coal, lumber, stone, salt, and manufactured goods, it proved only a modest success. With the completion of the Philadelphia and Columbia Railroad in 1834, as part of the Pennsylvania Canal, traffic on the Union Canal was greatly reduced.

A legislative commission appointed in 1824 reported that a lock system of canals was feasible from Philadelphia to Pittsburgh, except for thirty-six miles between Hollidaysburg and

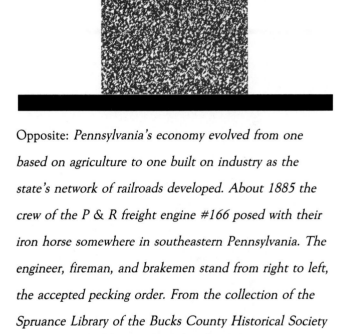

Opposite: *Pennsylvania's economy evolved from one based on agriculture to one built on industry as the state's network of railroads developed. About 1885 the crew of the P & R freight engine #166 posed with their iron horse somewhere in southeastern Pennsylvania. The engineer, fireman, and brakemen stand from right to left, the accepted pecking order. From the collection of the Spruance Library of the Bucks County Historical Society*

185

Barges carried coal throughout the Lehigh Valley's river and canal system and kept the iron mills' furnaces burning.

Johnstown—the section over the Allegheny Front and the eastern edge of the Allegheny Plateau. Although the United States had no railroads at this time, it was decided that the only possible solution was to construct a railroad over the mountainous area to haul the boats between the two canal points. Work was begun on the Pennsylvania Canal in 1826, one year after completion of the Erie Canal, and was finished in 1834.

This transportation route west from Philadelphia combined railroads and waterways. A railroad was built from Philadelphia to Columbia on the Susquehanna River. The central section, from Columbia to Hollidaysburg, consisted of 15.8 miles of slack-water navigation and 156 miles of canals, extending along the valleys of the Susquehanna and Juniata rivers. The third section was the Allegheny Portage Railroad between Hollidaysburg and Johnstown. To extend the canal over the Allegheny Front would have required 100 locks each with a fourteen-foot

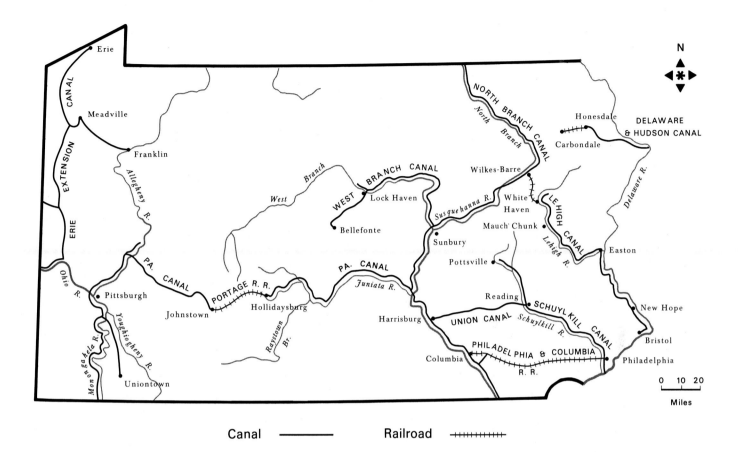

Canal ———— Railroad ++++++++++

lift. The traverse of the Allegheny Plateau would have been equally difficult. A water route was thus completely impractical. Instead, an incline railroad was built to raise boats 1,398 feet from Hollidaysburg to the top of the Allegheny Front. The railroad was then extended to Johnstown. Finally, the western portion of the canal extended 104 miles from Johnstown to Pittsburgh, following the deep, narrow, meandering valleys of the Conemaugh, Kiskiminetas, and Allegheny rivers. This section required the construction of ten dams and sixty-one locks.

With the completion of the Pennsylvania Canal, a network of connecting canals was built along rivers wherever feasible. One canal extended northward along the Susquehanna from the Juniata to Northumberland, connecting with a railroad to Elmira, New York. From Northumberland another canal was built along the West Branch of the Susquehanna to Lock Haven, with an extension to Bellefonte. These

The Pennsylvania Canal from Harrisburg to Pittsburgh, including the Portage Railroad, provided the water route linking eastern and western Pennsylvania. Other canals were developed to provide transportation routes within eastern and western Pennsylvania. Prepared by the Deasy Laboratory of Geographics, Dept. of Geography, The Pennsylvania State University

Above: *Easton, on the Delaware and Lehigh rivers, was a transportation crossroads where a double bridge connected the New Jersey Central and the Lehigh Valley railroads. From M.S. Henry,* History of the Lehigh Valley, *1860*

Opposite page: *The ferryboat* William E. Doron *plied the Delaware between Bristol, Pennsylvania, and Burlington, New Jersey, in the 1880s. Bridges in the wider parts of the river were a rarity until the 1920s. From the collection of the Spruance Library of the Bucks County Historical Society*

canals tapped regions producing anthracite and iron products and the white-pine forests of northern Pennsylvania. Along the Delaware River, a canal from Bristol to Easton and on to Mauch Chunk (Jim Thorpe) and Stoddartville served the southern anthracite fields. Many canals were projected in western Pennsylvania, but only a few of them were actually built. The most important of these was the canal from Beaver on the Ohio River northward along Beaver Creek to New Castle and on to Erie, ultimately connecting with the Mahoning Canal of Ohio.

Although major canal projects began later in Pennsylvania than in other states, Pennsylvania became a leader in canal building. By 1830 the United States had 1,343 miles of canals and other artificial water routes in operation and another 1,828 miles under construction. Of these totals, Pennsylvania had 480 miles completed, 250 miles in the process of construction, and another 368 miles projected. By 1838 Pennsylvania had a total of 788.5 miles of canals completed and another 133.75 miles under construction. At the peak of the canal era, about 1852, there were 1,024 miles of canals and 314 miles of unfinished improvements in the waterway system of Pennsylvania.

Above: *The Lehigh Coal and Navigation Company lasted longer than any other canal company in the state. Its principal canal still parallels the Delaware River, where rides on canal boats are still available. Courtesy, Pennsylvania State Archives*

Right: *Canal boats were pulled by a mule over viaducts and along railroad tracks. Canal life gave rise to a particular culture in northeastern Pennsylvania. Courtesy, Pennsylvania State Archives*

Above: *The popularity of canal boats and barges in Pennsylvania didn't wane until the 1900s. These boats were built near Pittsburgh around 1875. They carried coal and other "slow" freight more cheaply than did railroads. Courtesy, Pennsylvania State Archives*

Opposite page, top: *Sam Scheetz was a lock attendant on the Lehigh and Delaware Canal in 1889 when J.A. Johnson took this bucolic photo. From the collection of the Spruance Library of the Bucks County Historical Society*

Opposite: *Sturdy mules in special harnesses pulled canal boats and barges in Pennsylvania until 1937. Canals were never particularly profitable, yet remained popular for slow, bulky cargo. From the collection of the Spruance Library of the Bucks County Historical Society*

Although Pennsylvania built an extensive canal system, the waterways failed to achieve the movement of traffic expected. It became evident within a few years that the Pennsylvania Canal, the main link in the system, would never be the profitable route that had been anticipated. The weak link was the Portage Railroad. Because goods had to be transferred from boats to rail cars and back again, costs were high and the speed of movement greatly reduced. Local traffic was normally more important than through traffic, which was directed to the Erie Canal rather than the Pennsylvania Canal.

The canals of Pennsylvania encountered many problems. Many of them were poorly located to secure large volumes of traffic. Although the Pennsylvania Canal served economically developed areas at its eastern and western terminals, the central section passed through an area of limited development. Similarly, the canals of the north and west branches of the Susquehanna served thinly populated areas. The regions best served by canals were those that produced bulky, low-value commodities, such as the anthracite region, where canals carried great volumes of coal. Canals serving the agricultural regions of southeastern Pennsylvania, by contrast, had peak loads during harvest periods and long periods of little activity. Unlike railroads, canals could not adapt quickly to frequent improvements in technology. Finally, canals were closed by ice during a considerable period of the year, and at times lack of water made navigation difficult.

The chief competition to the canals came from the railroad. The Pennsylvania Railroad Company was incorporated in 1846. Between 1846 and 1854 the railroad built its major route between Philadelphia and Pittsburgh, essentially following the route of the Pennsylvania Canal. To avoid competition, the Pennsylvania Railroad purchased the Pennsylvania Canal and operated it for some time. By 1864, however, the western section from Pittsburgh to Johnstown had been abandoned. The central section in the Juniata Valley was abandoned in 1899, and the Susquehanna River section in 1900. By 1872 most of the canals in Pennsylvania had been purchased by railroads.

By 1906, of the 1,200 miles of improved rivers and canals that the state and private corporations had developed in Pennsylvania, 908

miles had been abandoned. In eastern and central Pennsylvania only two canals, the Schuylkill and Lehigh, and the improved portion of the Delaware River still provided water transportation. In western Pennsylvania all the canals had been abandoned, and only the improved natural waterways of the Ohio River system were still able to meet the competition of railroads.

THE RAILROAD ERA

Pennsylvania was the pioneer in railroad building in the United States. As early as 1809 a short line about a mile long was built in Delaware County to haul stone from a quarry, and in Armstrong County in western Pennsylvania a short line was built in 1819 to haul materials from blast furnaces. Short coal lines were also

Right: *Though the coming of the railroad meant progress to some, others viewed it as a road to ruination and destruction. This poster was circulated in Philadelphia in 1839 to "forbid this outrage!" Courtesy, National Archives*

Below: *Trains were not required to have safety equipment, such as brakes, until the end of the nineteenth century. As a consequence, the public was generally callous about the railroad's dismal safety record. Courtesy, Hagley Museum and Library, Wilmington, Delaware*

BALLOONS MAY BE MADE REALLY USEFUL.
BIG IDEA FOR WESTERN RAILROADS! HOW THEY MAY SAVE THEIR PASSENGERS FROM REAR-END COLLISIONS AND THEMSELVES FROM HEAVY SUITS FOR DAMAGES!

MOTHERS LOOK OUT FOR YOUR CHILDREN!
ARTISANS, MECHANICS, CITIZENS!

When you leave your family in health, must you be hurried home to mourn a

DREADFUL CASUALITY!

PHILADELPHIANS, your RIGHTS are being invaded! regardless of your interests, or the LIVES OF YOUR LITTLE ONES. THE CAMDEN AND AMBOY, with the assistance of other companies without a Charter, and in VIOLATION OF LAW, as decreed by your Courts, are laying a

LOCOMOTIVE RAIL ROAD!

Through your most Beautiful Streets, to the RUIN of your TRADE, annihilation of your RIGHTS, and regardless of your PROSPERITY and COMFORT. **Will you permit this!** or do you consent to be a

SUBURB OF NEW YORK!!

Rails are now being laid on BROAD STREET to CONNECT the TRENTON RAIL ROAD with the WILMINGTON and BALTIMORE ROAD, under the pretence of constructing a City Passenger Railway from the Navy Yard to Fairmount!!! This is done under the auspices of the CAMDEN AND AMBOY MONOPOLY!

RALLY PEOPLE in the Majesty of your Strength and forbid THIS

OUTRAGE!

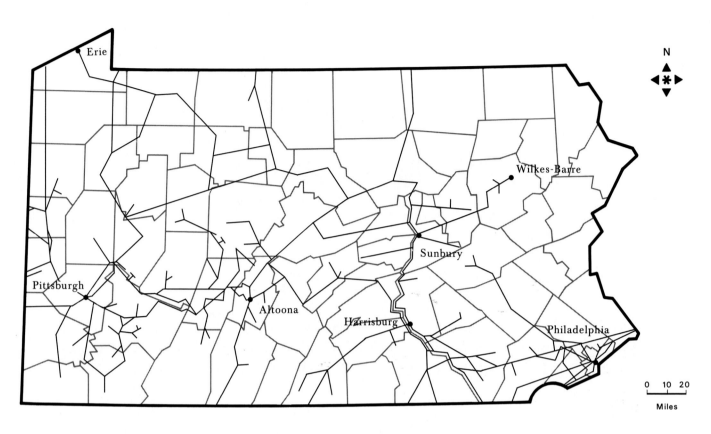

Pennsylvania Railroad ————

built to connect anthracite mines to canals. By 1840 there were more than thirty-six lines, varying from seven to fifty miles in length, mostly in the east.

THE PENNSYLVANIA RAILROAD

In the 1830s, in order to supplement the developing canal network, Baltimore, New York, and Boston secured railroad connections to the Midwest. It soon became evident that Philadelphia required access to the western markets not provided by the Pennsylvania Canal. When state aid was not forthcoming, a group of Philadelphia merchants formed a company and on April 13, 1846, secured a charter to build a railroad from Philadelphia to Pittsburgh, to be known as the Pennsylvania Railroad.

The Pennsylvania Railroad Company succeeded in establishing the cross-state system. The line was completed to Hollidaysburg by 1850 and reached Pittsburgh in 1854. In 1852 Israel Andrews, a businessman, wrote, "As a through route, both for trade and travel, there

Above: The main line of the Pennsylvania Railroad extended from Philadelphia to Pittsburgh. Other routes were developed to exploit the resources and provide services to the expanding economy. Prepared by the Deasy Laboratory of Geographics, Dept. of Geography, The Pennsylvania State University

Right: Before diesel engines, everything on the railroads worked by steam power. Special work tracks had to be laid to accommodate this old Bucyrus steam shovel on a Pennsylvania Railroad line around the turn of the century. Above it is a steam-powered drill for dynamiting. Courtesy, Pennsylvania State Archives

is hardly a work of the kind in the United States possessing greater advantages or a stronger position." With the Pennsylvania Railroad, Philadelphia now had a route that could compete successfully with those of other eastern cities.

The Pennsylvania Railroad continued to expand its system. In the 1860s a line was extended to Chicago, and another line to St. Louis connected these cities to the Atlantic seaboard. The Pennsylvania leased the Philadelphia and Lake Erie Railroad. Extending through the rich forests and oil fields of the state, this line opened an area in which economic development had long been retarded.

GROWTH OF THE RAILROAD NETWORK
Besides the Pennsylvania Railroad there were a number of other important railroads in the state. The expansion of anthracite production created a demand for railroads to serve that area. The Reading Railroad was established to market anthracite from the southern fields to southeastern Pennsylvania and the Delaware

River terminals. The Lehigh, the Lackawanna, and the Delaware and Hudson were the major routes to the northeastern states.

Pennsylvania's railroad network was completed between 1860 and 1900. It blanketed the state, so that by 1900 only a few areas were more than ten miles from a railroad. These areas included Fulton and Bedford counties in the south central, Pike County in the northeast, and small areas of Bradford and Susquehanna counties in the north-central portion of the state.

Track mileage increased dramatically each decade. In 1860 the state had 2,598 miles of railroads. In 1874-75 the Department of Internal Affairs reported a total trackage of 8,960 miles, of which 1,806 miles were double track. In 1901 the Annual Report of the Bureau of Railways listed 10,697 miles of main-line railroads. Including sidings, spurs, and other lines, the grand total would have been about 25,000 miles of track.

In 1900 Pennsylvania railroads carried 478,684,683 tons of freight. More than half of

this tonnage consisted of mineral products, primarily anthracite and bituminous coal. It is obvious that railroads were the key to the rapid expansion of mining in the state. The location of coal deposits, in turn, was a major factor in determining the basic rail network of the state.

The topography of Pennsylvania has played a major role in the pattern of transportation. In most of the state the rail lines have been forced to follow the natural drainage lines. Only in the southeastern plains country could routes ignore the lay of the land. In the Ridge and Valley province, the routes follow the valleys, crossing from one valley to the next through water gaps. In the Appalachian Plateau the railroads are largely confined to the river valleys. The meandering streams may lengthen the mileage of many railroads by as much as 50 percent. The topography is so rugged in many sections of the state that the number of potential routes is highly limited. The Pennsylvania Railroad achieved a dominant position in the state by obtaining rights-of-way along the most strategic valley routes. Once a right-of-way had been obtained, the possibility of competition was slight.

Expansion of the railroad system stopped abruptly in 1900. In that year only slightly more than 100 miles of new track were laid, and for several decades the track mileage remained virtually unchanged. In 1909 Pennsylvania had a total of 11,200 miles of main-line tracks, and in 1932 the mileage was slightly less than 11,100 miles. The great era of railroad building was at an end.

There were a number of reasons for the stoppage in expansion of the rail network. First, the fine network of trunk lines plus short spurs to isolated areas provided a complete network, with frequent passenger schedules and extensive local freight service. Second, the advent of motor vehicles focused attention on the improvement of the state's road network. As the road system expanded, the need for passenger service declined. Abandonment of the short lines began after World War I and continues to the present day.

Pennsylvanians made many contributions to railroad advancement in the nineteenth century. In the pioneer period of railroading, coal and wood competed in fueling the locomotives. General William Palmer, an employee of the Pennsylvania Railroad, was instrumental in developing a firebox system that could use bitu-

Opposite page: *Railroad lines multiplied in western Pennsylvania in proportion to the steel industry's growth. Where lines crossed, viaducts were built with new concrete techniques. An unusual aspect of this photo is the relaxed pose of the two men, which was highly unusual in early photography. Courtesy, Pennsylvania State Archives*

Above: *On the Pennsylvania Railroad lines in the western part of the state, tunnels and overpasses had to be built efficiently to meet the needs of the growing line. To build a tunnel, a wooden core was laid down first with the brickwork laid over it. A steam winch, guided by the crew, hauled it out when the mortar set. Courtesy, Pennsylvania State Archives*

Above: *Thomas Alexander Scott (1823-1881) was president of the Pennsylvania Railroad and Union transportation officer during the Civil War. From Cirker,* Dictionary of American Portraits, Dover, 1967

Above right: *During the Civil War, bridge and railroad engineer Herman Haupt (1817-1905) helped facilitate the movement of military supplies to critical war zones. Courtesy, Brady Collection, National Archives. From Cirker,* Dictionary of American Portraits, Dover, 1967

Left: *Using a steam-powered drill, a railroad crew prepares to blast for a new road in western Pennsylvania. Courtesy, Pennsylvania State Archives*

minous coal. This was a major advancement over the use of wood as a fuel. The inventions of George Westinghouse, including the air brake and uniform switch and signal systems, revolutionized railroading by solving the problems of controlling the speed of trains. During the Civil War such railroad men as Frank Thomas and Thomas Scott of the Pennsylvania Railroad and Herman Haupt of the Reading line developed transport systems that facilitated the movement of military supplies to critical war zones.

The railroads required a large number of supporting industries to function effectively, most notably the iron and steel industry. By the 1880s a significant percentage of the steel produced in Pennsylvania was used to make rails. Such companies as Baldwin (the builder of locomotives in Philadelphia), the Pressed Steel Car Company, the Pullman Standard Manufacturing Company, and the American Car and Foundry Works (builders of freight and passenger rail cars), made major contributions in improving the movement of goods and people by rail transportation.

Above: *Baldwin locomotives were the work horses of Pennsylvania's heavy industry for a century. Whether on big freight locomotives or small work engines, the crews were a race apart from other workers. Though poorly paid and working as long as forty-eight hours on one trick, they were a proud elite. Courtesy, Pennsylvania State Archives*

Opposite, top: *The Pennsylvania Railroad's Altoona shops (pictured in 1885) were the largest in the world. They serviced thousands of items of rolling stock a year. They remain one of Conrail's principal yards. Courtesy, Pennsylvania State Archives*

Opposite: *As chief engineer of the Pennsylvania Railroad, John Edgar Thompson was responsible for locating the line through Blair County. Later president of the PRR, Thompson believed the Juniata Valley was, without rival, the best throughway for his railroad. From the Pennsylvania Railroad collection. Courtesy, Pennsylvania Historical and Museum Commission, Dept. of Archives and Manuscripts*

ALTOONA: NINETEENTH-CENTURY RAILROAD CENTER

In the building of the Pennsylvania Railroad from Philadelphia to Pittsburgh, the Allegheny Front of the plateau country presented a great topographic barrier. Additional engine power was required to move up this steep grade, and a site was chosen at the foot of the grade to provide the necessary facilities. The first railroad shop was built on a nearby farm in 1850. This was the beginning of the city of Altoona and ultimately the site of the largest railroad shops in the world.

For the next seventy-five years, the railroad dominated the economy of Altoona. The railroad shops grew with the growth of the Pennsylvania system. By 1855 the shops extended for more than a 1,000 feet along the tracks. Until 1866 the shops were engaged in the repair and rebuilding of locomotives and the

Top: *During the 1880s the Class K locomotive was one of the fastest express locomotives operating in the United States. The 10, the Class K prototype, was built at the Altoona shops in 1881. From Matthias N. Forney,* Recent Locomotives, *1886*

Above: *The Pennsylvania Railroad's Altoona shops produced the 400 in 1885. It was the first Class R series locomotive. From Matthias N. Forney,* Recent Locomotives, *1886*

building of railroad cars and bridges, but in that year the building of new locomotives began. In 1869 the locomotive and car shops were separated. Although the original shops were constructed to overcome a topographic barrier, the locomotive and car shops soon expanded to become the major facilities serving the entire Pennsylvania Railroad network. Throughout the remainder of the nineteenth century and on into the early twentieth century, the facilities grew with the needs of the entire system. To maintain and improve the quality of railroading, the Pennsylvania Railroad established a test department and chemical laboratory to select the best materials and prepare standard specifications. Thus many of the major improvements in American railroading originated in the Altoona shops.

Dominated by the Pennsylvania Railroad, Altoona exemplified the one-industry town. As the railroad expanded, the population grew until it numbered some 80,000. The influence of the railroad extended into every phase of community life. The earliest volunteer fire department was organized to protect not only the town but also the railroad shops. In 1853 the Pennsylvania Railroad sponsored the Altoona City Band, the city's oldest musical organization. In 1855 the railroad built the Logan House to provide travelers with the best accommodations for a break in the journey from Philadelphia to the West. This "mansion in the wilderness" was pronounced by an English traveler of the day to be "better than any in Europe and equal to any in America." The Altoona Mechanics Library and Reading Room Association was formed in 1858 and for several years occupied a railroad building. Concerned with the health of the shopmen and their families, the railroad joined with the community in building a hospital in 1885. The railroad was also instrumental in developing the cricket field and clubhouse, at first for cricket only but later for all sports. Altoona was a company town, and the company was the Pennsylvania Railroad.

THE TROLLEY-CAR ERA

While long-distance transportation was provided by the railroads, urban and interurban transportation in the nineteenth and early twentieth centuries evolved from the horse-drawn to the electric-powered trolley car. This mode of transportation was well developed by the 1880s. In 1887 the state's trolley system carried a total of 184,000,000 passengers—nearly as many as the railroads. Street-railway trackage totaled 520 miles, and 10,900 horses were still used to move the trolleys. The system continued to expand, and in 1901 there were 2,168 miles of tracks on which 580,000,000 passengers moved—about twice the number of passengers carried by the Pennsylvania steam railroads. By this time the horse-drawn cars had essentially disappeared, and electric power moved the

In the Altoona shops in 1888 a locomotive could be assembled in sixteen hours and fifty minutes. From top to bottom, these engravings take us from the commencement of work on the locomotive to having the boiler in position to placing the wheels under and the cab in position to the point where the locomotive is ready for a trial run. From Railroad Gazette, *August 31, 1888*

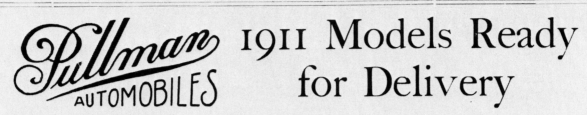

Pullman AUTOMOBILES

1911 Models Ready for Delivery

ADVANCE INFORMATION BULLETIN MAILED ON APPLICATION

From the commencement of the manufacture of the PULLMAN car, seven years ago, its makers have had in mind the single aim of producing an all-purpose machine, which will withstand the severest strains to which an automobile can be subjected.

This company early recognized the fact that the ultimate car which would please the American people, should be a machine which would show the finest performance in tests for durability and reliability. Such a machine is the type which best meets the requirements of the man of family in America, who wants to buy an automobile which will take him to a designated point without subjecting him to the annoyance and disgust of delays on the road for repairs and adjustments.

Pullman Performances Prove Its Perfection

In every endurance contest in which it participated in the 1910 season, the PULLMAN made a clean score. Not only has it demonstrated the maker's claims for it as an unexcelled reliability machine, but it has proven that in hill-climbing ability it is unbeatable at a similar horse-power rating and price.

DEALERS: Write for 1911 Proposition. Good territory in Penna still open.

PULLMAN MOTOR CAR COMPANY

Licensed under Selden Patents

YORK, PA.

Above: *In the 1910 York City Directory, the Pullman Motor Car Company announced that its 1911 models were available for purchase. The increasing use of private automobiles in the first two decades of the twentieth century led to the eventual demise of streetcars and trolleys.*

Left: *Horse-drawn wagons and carriages compete with an electric trolley car for space on a congested cobblestone street in Philadelphia in 1897. Courtesy, National Archives*

streetcars.

The rise of trolley transportation was due largely to the inventive genius of John G. Brill and later his son Martin. The J.G. Brill Company was one of the first companies to build a horse-drawn car for the embryonic Philadelphia street-railway system in 1869, and in 1886 the company built the first electric-powered trolley. The Brill trolleys became so famous that they commanded a world market.

The trolley car reached its zenith in the early twentieth century. Electric streetcars provided service not only within urban communities but between them, linking cities by means of a system of interurban lines. Trolleys provided frequent, rapid service at reasonable rates, and suburban life now became a possibility. The trolley system lasted until it was superseded by the private automobile. After 1920 the streetcar system gradually declined, and by the 1940s it had virtually disappeared, although remnants of the system persist to the present day.

Chapter Seven
Agriculture in the Industrial Age

The development of an industrial economy brought vast changes in the state's pioneer agricultural economy. In addition to forces for change within the state, Pennsylvania had to adapt to a changing national pattern of agriculture. Although the population of Pennsylvania grew rapidly after 1820, bringing increased demand for agricultural products, this demand was frequently met by products produced outside the state. The Pennsylvania farmer now had to compete on a national level.

Although agriculture remained an important endeavor, its relative importance in the state's economy declined sharply. Between 1820 and 1920 employment in agriculture declined from about 80 percent to less than 20 percent of the state's total work force. The number of farms and the total area under cultivation peaked in the 1880s and declined continuously thereafter. Pennsylvania was evolving in character from a rural-dominated society to one in which urban life was of growing importance. At the same time dynamic changes—technological, economic, and cultural—were taking place within the agricultural sector.

The nineteenth century witnessed the development of animal-powered machinery. As late as 1840 animal power was used only for plowing, harrowing, and hauling crops to the barn. The planting of grain and grass seeds was done by hand; grass was cut with a scythe; grain was reaped using a sickle or cradle and threshed with a flail. W.M. Jardine, secretary of the U.S. Department of Agriculture in the 1920s, observed, "Could the farmer of Pharoah's time be suddenly re-incarnated and sat down in grandfather's wheat field he could have gone to work with a familiar tool. Then, within a period of fifty years, we covered ground in methods of crop production where fifty centuries had left almost no progress."

The golden age in the development of farm machinery occurred between 1840 and 1860. By 1860 patents had been granted for the basic

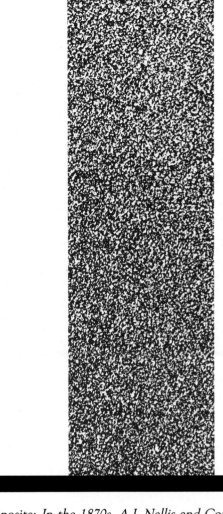

Opposite: *In the 1870s, A.J. Nellis and Company of Pittsburgh patented this method of conveying hay and straw, which required the use of Nellis' Original Harpoon Horse Hay Fork, believed by some to be the greatest labor-saving agricultural instrument developed at that time. With the fork, one man could do the work of three in a quarter of the time. From Asher and Adams,* Pictorial Album of American Industry, *1876*

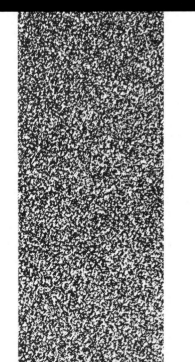

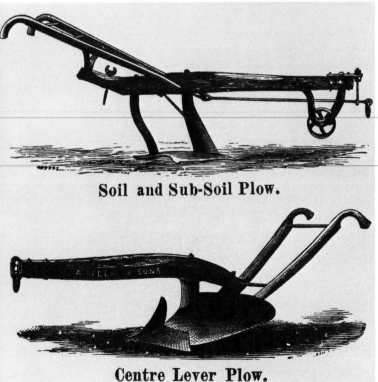

Soil and Sub-Soil Plow.

Centre Lever Plow.

This page: *In the mid-1800s, Pittsburgh was a farm-machinery manufacturing center. The Pittsburgh Globe Plow Works, established in 1828, became one of the largest plow manufacturers in the United States. Some of the company's plows are shown at left. The factory pictured above was built in the 1870s. From Asher and Adams,* Pictorial Album of American Industry, *1876*

Right: *Once sickles and scythes were all the Pennsylvania farmers had for reaping, then came the horse-drawn reaper, shown circa 1890. The efficient tractor and powered combine were still thirty years away. Many such machines are still in use in Amish country around Lancaster and other central counties, where farmers achieve yields comparable to fully mechanized farms! From the collection of the Spruance Library of the Bucks County Historical Society*

principles of most of the modern farm machinery of today. Developments since then have been mainly refinements to improve these basic designs. Among the many animal-powered machines developed during this period were the sulky plow, spring-tooth harrow, sulky cultivator, steel roller, hay mower, grain combine, corn husker, grain drill, dump hay rake, hay fork, and grain thresher. Major farm-machinery manufacturing centers developed in Pittsburgh, Philadelphia, the Schuylkill Valley, York, and Waynesboro.

Until about 1870 oxen predominated as the source of animal power. The ox was a more powerful animal than the horse and was favored in clearing new land. After the stumps and rocks had been cleared from the fields, and with the improvement of roads and transporting of more produce to market, the horse began to replace the ox. Most of the new farm machinery was designed for horsepower. Although the substitution of mechanical power for horsepower began with the introduction of the gasoline tractor about 1905, these early tractors were huge and cumbersome and little used until the small, light, general-purpose tractor appeared after 1925.

FARM LABOR

The changes in farm labor between 1820 and 1920 were fully as significant as changes in the techniques of production and methods of marketing farm produce. With the introduction of machinery, the requirements for human labor were greatly reduced. With the development of a highly commercialized agriculture and an evolving rural social structure, the work of the farmer's wife and family declined. At the same time there was a need for more skilled labor.

Looking like the roll of a player piano, this homemade machine shelled dried corn in the late 1800s. From the collection of the Spruance Library of the Bucks County Historical Society

occasionally a "hired girl," who lived on the farm and became practically a member of the family.

All farm children had responsibilities on the farm. The small boys kept the kitchen woodbox filled. The girls gathered the eggs, not only from the chicken coop but hunted for them in other places such as the haymow. From these simple tasks they graduated to more important farm work. By the age of ten or twelve, they were performing the work of adults. The milking and making of butter was always done by the women on the farm.

During harvest time additional labor was re-

quired. This labor was supplied by employing both men and women for a few weeks. Sometimes neighbors exchanged services. Expert harvest hands, particularly cradlers, commanded high wages. In 1850 a cradler was paid from seventy-five cents to a dollar a day for work from sunrise to sunset. During the harvest period the farmer's wife had the responsibility of preparing huge meals for the field hands.

Because farm wages were below those of many other jobs, shortages of farm labor developed from time to time. In the 1850s, when labor-saving machinery had not yet come into general use, Pennsylvania farm labor seeking higher wages migrated to the California Gold Rush, to railroad construction jobs, and to Midwestern farms. Thousands of farmers, especially from the rugged Appalachians, left the old homesteads to establish new homes in distant places. Although this was a period of great emigration from Europe, most of these new settlers found work in the expanding urban areas and the mines of the state.

During the Civil War period, the shortage of farm labor became acute. In 1862 the editor of *Farm and Gardener* warned,

The withdrawal of nearly a hundred and eighty thousand able-bodied men from our state is a subject for most serious thought . . . We see but a single remedy, labor-saving machinery . . . . Those who have used the flail must secure the thresher; the scythe must everywhere give way to the reaper. The horse-power must do the work of men.

The wages of farm labor rose dramatically to two dollars or more a day.

From 1870 to about 1900, with the introduction of machinery, farm labor once again became plentiful. Correspondingly, wages fell. In 1880 the State Board of Agriculture reported that the average wage was 71 cents a day plus board, the estimated value of which was 31 cents a day. The average wage by the year, with board, was $12 a month. Harvest hands averaged $1 a day with board. By 1900 farm wages had risen only slightly. The average wage

Above: *Using a portable wheel, a steady hand, and a sharp eye, an itinerant grinder sharpens a drawknife. With manual tools so common, everyone from railroad workers to small farmers needed the grinder's services. From the collection of the Spruance Library of the Bucks County Historical Society*

Opposite: *Captain John S. Bailey, maker of sundials, is pictured here in his shop in Buckingham in 1901. His dials have traditional slogans, such as "Tempus Fugit" (time flies) and "I Mark Time, Dost Thou?" From the collection of the Spruance Library of the Bucks County Historical Society*

was now 85 cents a day plus board, the estimated value of which was 35 cents. The average for yearly employees was $13.58 a month with board, and harvest hands averaged $1.35 a day with board.

After 1900 the farm-labor problem once again became acute. In 1902 the Pennsylvania State Secretary of Agriculture observed,

The wonderful development of the manufacturing, mining, commercial, and transportation industries has drained the country of help until, in some localities, it is impossible to hire labor at any price which the farmer can afford to pay. More women have been working in the fields this year than perhaps ever before in the history of the State.

As a result, wages rose rapidly. Between 1900 and 1910 the wages expended for labor by the Pennsylvania farmer increased by at least 50 percent.

During the World War I period, economic prosperity plus the Selective Service Act of 1917 again created great farm-labor shortages. Although the demand for food increased, many farms produced less rather than more food. Farmers did not ask to be deferred from military service, as many occupational groups had done. Fired by patriotism, many urban youths, both boys and girls, volunteered for farm work. Many rendered satisfactory service, but others did not. By 1918 the labor situation had reached so critical a stage that deferments from military service were being granted. The labor shortage on Pennsylvania's farms continued well into the 1920s.

WESTERN COMPETITION

As agricultural development moved westward in the nineteenth century, competition developed between the Pennsylvania farmer and those farther west. Soon after 1840 this competition from the Midwest grew rapidly, and the livestock industry of Pennsylvania had to adjust to changing economic conditions. In the early nineteenth century, the livestock industry was

widely distributed over the state. As competition increased, however, the least favored areas declined and regional patterns of concentration began to evolve.

Hogs were among the earliest animals produced on the farms of Pennsylvania. By 1840 it is estimated that 1,504,000 hogs were distributed throughout the state, with the greatest concentration in the southeast. After 1850 the number of swine declined sharply. It is estimated that it cost six cents to produce a pound of pork in Pennsylvania, compared with only two cents in the Midwest. The center of production shifted westward, with Cincinnati, known as Porkopolis, becoming a major processing center. Swine continued to be raised on Pennsylvania farms for home consumption and for the local market.

In the 1870s, with the rise of dairying in the southeastern counties, the number of swine grew rapidly. Butter was produced on the farms for the local market, and the skimmed milk and buttermilk were fed to the hogs. This increase was short-lived, however, for in the 1880s creameries developed and farm production of butter declined sharply. The supply of skimmed milk diminished, and it was difficult and expensive for farmers to haul the buttermilk back to the farm from the creameries. Pennsylvania soon became a net importer of pork. In 1923 the Pennsylvania Department of Agriculture reported, "The rural population alone consumes annually 224,000,000 pounds of pork which is approximately 64,000,000 pounds more than is produced in the state."

The beef-cattle industry also experienced problems associated with low-cost meat production in the Midwest. In the 1830s Chester County was named the fat-cattle capital of the nation. The area's rich bluegrass and clover were considered ideal pasture for fattening cattle. In 1846 the editor of *The Cultivator* magazine observed,

The Eastern part of Pennsylvania is becoming every year more and more engaged in the grazing business but little attention is paid to raising cattle, the graziers depending almost al-

together for a supply of beef cattle from Ohio, New York and other states . . . . The number fattened annually in this [Chester] county is believed to be between 40 and 50 thousand head.

After 1850, however, the industry in Chester County began a rapid decline. In the Midwest good pastureland could be bought for a dollar an acre, while in Chester County an acre cost from $30 to $100.

With the decline in grass fattening, the center of the beef industry in Pennsylvania shifted in the 1870s to Lancaster and adjoining counties where grain feeds were available. As Frederick Watts wrote in an 1879 report on Pennsylvania agriculture,

[Stock] is brought from the West, purchased in the fall, fed with hay, corn, and oats during the winter, and sold in the months of March, April, and May. The farmer finds that the increase of weight and price of cattle fed is the most profitable mode of disposing of his corn and oats and increasing the quality and quantity of his manure.

The industry reached its greatest importance about 1890, but output varied considerably after this date depending upon price and demand for beef.

In the early nineteenth century, small meat-packing establishments were widely distributed over the state. Without refrigeration, fresh meat could not be transported great distances. With the development of refrigeration, however, the small packing plant was doomed. The first shipment of meat in refrigerated cars from Chicago to the East occurred in 1869. By 1910 the meat-packing industry in the state was concentrated in Philadelphia, Pittsburgh, and Lancaster. These three centers processed more than 85 percent of the dressed livestock of the state. Practically all of the meat sold in the small cities came from the Midwest or from local farms. Most rural and small-town people still raised cattle and pigs for home consumption.

Sheep production thrived in Pennsylvania in

The beef-cattle industry concentrated in southeastern Pennsylvania with Lancaster County the center of production. The Alderney bull, one of which is pictured here, was among the type of cattle raised for its beef in the state. From Lewis F. Allen, American Cattle: Their History, Breeding and Management, *1868*

the early nineteenth century. In the 1830s a demand for fine Merino wool developed, and by 1840 nearly every farm in Pennsylvania had a flock of sheep. Wool production was concentrated in the southwestern counties, while in the southeast there was a thriving mutton industry. Sheep production reached its zenith about 1850, when 1,822,000 sheep were reported on Pennsylvania farms—about 8 percent of the national total.

After 1850 the sheep industry experienced a steady decline. Competition from western farmers was devastating. It was estimated that it cost one to two dollars a head to raise sheep in Pennsylvania, compared with twenty-five to fifty cents in the Midwest. The Tariff Acts of 1846 and 1857 reduced the duty on imported wool to about one-half that of the Act of 1842, and foreign wool was soon imported in greater quantities. As population grew, destruction of sheep by dogs became another limiting factor. Sheep production gradually declined in

Above: *A Wyoming Valley farmer loads grain on his wagon for transport to market. Courtesy, Pennsylvania State Archives*

Right: *On this gristmill in northwestern Pennsylvania, internal-combustion machinery was hooked up to the old waterwheel once the millrace was filled in. Courtesy, Pennsylvania State Archives*

the state, except in the rugged pasturelands of Greene and Washington counties.

Wheat was the major cash crop on Pennsylvania farms and was thus most affected by the growth of production in the Midwest. After 1850 Pennsylvania yielded the distinction of being the leading wheat-producing state in the nation. By 1860 western competition had grown to such an extent that many farmers questioned the continued production of wheat. The sharpest decline occurred in the Appalachian hill country. Wheat remained an important crop in the farm system of southeastern Pennsylvania, however, because it fit well into the prevailing rotation scheme, served as a nurse crop for grass, and provided straw for bedding.

CHANGING AGRICULTURAL PATTERNS

As the diet of Pennsylvanians improved in the nineteenth century, there was a growing demand for a greater variety of food products. Most significant was the rise of the potato from a feed for livestock to one of the principal human foods by 1900. From about 1830 to the end of the century, potatoes were grown in small acreage by general farmers. By the 1840s production totaled between nine and ten million bushels, with Washington County the leading producer. The potato-loving Irish immigrants who flocked from famine-stricken Ireland in the 1840s encouraged production. In spite of blight, disease, insect pests, and rot during many years, the potato industry thrived,

Above: *The Piedmont Dairy Farm of New Castle advertised the fact that it "sterilizes all cans and bottles." F.E. McConnell managed the farm when this postcard was made.*

Opposite: *The Alderney (top) and short-horn (bottom) both figured prominently in Pennsylvania's dairy industry in the late 1860s. By 1900 the state's dairy industry had become a highly organized commercial enterprise. From* Lewis F. Allen, American Cattle: Their History, Breeding and Management, *1868*

and in the twentieth century the potato became the leading cash crop in the state.

The dairy industry of Pennsylvania came into existence about 1830. Over the next seventy years it was transformed from a home farm industry to a highly organized commercial enterprise. The products were primarily butter and cheese until late in the nineteenth century. Fluid milk began to compete with butter about 1870, but did not become a major product until after 1900. The demand for milk increased with the urban population as city dwellers were no longer able to keep cows. In the early 1860s Louis Pasteur discovered that harmful bacteria could be destroyed by heating milk to a temperature of 140°F, but its application was long delayed as the general public little recognized the value of preventive disease controls. It was not until the eradication of bovine tuberculosis in 1895 and the introduction of pasteurization after 1900 that milk was recognized as a safe food for human consumption, and soon after that milk replaced butter as the leading dairy product. With education, the health value of milk was recognized, and it became accepted as a staple of the diet.

Until the 1850s vegetable gardens were al-

Above: *Surplus apples became apple butter in one of the popular cottage industries of 1885. Apple butter continues to be a popular commodity. From the collection of the Spruance Library of the Bucks County Historical Society*

Opposite page: *The seated man in this 1880 photo of a cider mill is making wooden barrel hoops with a drawknife. From the collection of the Spruance Library of the Bucks County Historical Society*

most wholly for home consumption. Only after 1850 did market gardens develop in the vicinity of the larger cities, such as Philadelphia and Pittsburgh. Fresh vegetables then became an increasingly important part of the average urban dweller's diet. The market grew so significantly that by the 1890s vegetables were being transported in refrigerated cars from distant agricultural centers. With the decline of wheat as a cash crop, a number of farmers near city markets began to develop commercial gardens and to produce a great variety of vegetables. Most notable after 1875 was the rise of the tomato, which had previously been considered poisonous.

Until the middle of the nineteenth century, fruit production was primarily for the making of drinks, such as cider, and the feeding of hogs. After 1850, however, most farms had an area devoted to orchards producing apples, cherries, pears, plums, and other fruits, mostly for home and local consumption. With the decline of grain crops as principal sources of cash income, farmers turned to fruit as well as vegetable production as a major source of income. Rapid transportation plus refrigeration expanded the market for Pennsylvania fruit growers. Another milestone was the introduction of spraying about 1890, at a time when growers were becoming disheartened by the rapidly increasing hordes of pests. At the same time the development of cold storage meant that fruit could be marketed over a period of many months. These factors, along with a growing urban population and a growing recognition of the health value of fruits, helped bring about the rise of commercial fruit farming.

Between 1840 and 1940 the acreage devoted to tobacco increased more, proportionally, than that of any other field crop. In 1840 a total of 2,740 acres yielded 385,000 pounds of tobacco;

Henry C. Mercer was fascinated with occupations, no matter how trivial, and he carefully recorded all he could find. In this case, it's making apple butter in a giant cauldron. From the collection of the Spruance Library of the Bucks County Historical Society

by 1940 these figures had increased to 33,700 acres and 50,586,000 pounds. In 1840 tobacco was raised for domestic consumption in nearly all parts of the state. After 1900 tobacco production was limited to a few commercial areas and had disappeared from most general farms. In 1840 York County was the leader, with three times the output of Lancaster County, but by 1860 Lancaster County had become the leader, and by 1920 it was producing about 90 percent of the state's total.

Tobacco became the main cash crop in Lancaster County, following corn in the rotation of about three-quarters of the county's farms. Tobacco requires soils of high fertility, preferably limestone, heavy manuring, and heavy application of commercial fertilizers rich in potash. It also requires much more manual labor than

Left: *In the nineteenth century apples were grown in Pennsylvania, first for local consumption and later for markets farther away. The 1857* Book of Commerce *stated that "the pippins of New York, New Jersey, and Pennsylvania are the richest in flavor of any apples known in the United States." From Uriah Hunt,* The Book of Commerce by Sea and Land, *1857*

Below: *Tobacco has long been a part of Pennsylvania's economy, and the word "stogie" comes from "Conestoga." In this Reading warehouse, pictured about 1895, cigar filler is being dried. Courtesy, Pennsylvania State Archives*

Above: *A turn-of-the-century cigar store was a colorful place where the storekeeper frequently made special orders. From the collection of the Spruance Library of the Bucks County Historical Society*

Opposite page: *In 1889 a schooner carrying hay on the Delaware River near Bristol must have been an odd sight, but hay was a cheap bulk cargo, unprofitable for rail shipment. From the collection of the Spruance Library of the Bucks County Historical Society*

any other staple crop in Pennsylvania, as well as highly specialized skills in production, curing, and marketing. This crop fits well into the hardworking cultural patterns of the Amish, Dunkards, and Mennonites of the Lancaster region. These ultra-conservative groups are forbidden by their churches to use tobacco and carry on a crusade against it as religious groups, but they produce the crop as it brings a better return to their high-priced land than any other. Because of the exacting labor requirements and the depletion of the soil, most farmers commonly produce only four to five acres of tobacco annually.

The type of tobacco produced in Lancaster County is known as broadleaf and is used almost exclusively as cigar filler. The industry began about 1828, when several farmers near Ephrata rolled the leaves into cigars or "stogies" (Conestogas), which they sold in country stores at the modest price of five for one cent. Until after 1890 the cigars were handmade, mostly on the farms or in small craft shops. Although the first machine to produce cigars was invented in 1860, factory manufacture did not begin to displace hand wrapping for many decades. The hand-wrapped cigar was considered far superior to those produced on a machine. The first automatic cigar-making machine that was really successful was put into operation in 1919.

TRANSPORTATION AND MARKETING

Advances in transportation and marketing between 1820 and 1920 greatly influenced the farming system of Pennsylvania. The period witnessed many transportation changes, including the end of droving, the rise and abandonment of canals, the rapid expansion of railroads, and the construction of improved highways with the coming of motor vehicles.

Improvements in transportation created not only opportunities but problems for the Pennsylvania farmer. Competition from Midwestern farmers began with the development of the railroads and the invention of the refrigerated car. Compounding the problem of competition

from the low-cost agricultural areas of the Midwest, the railroads gave preferential freight rates to competitors from the western states. In 1880 M.C. Beebe, a member of the Pennsylvania State Board of Agriculture, complained, "A carload of Texas steers . . . will be hauled from Kansas City to New York for a less sum, absolutely, than the same line of railroad will charge for hauling a carload of Pennsylvania cattle from Greenville to Altoona." Preferential freight rates did not change until after 1887, when the Interstate Commerce Commission was created.

The development of better transportation was a major factor in the change from self-sufficient to commercial agriculture. Farmers increasingly produced excess food that was sold to the growing urban population. Because of western competition, the Pennsylvania farmer began to specialize in the production of certain perishable commodities, such as milk, eggs, fruits, and vegetables. General farm crops—

with the exception of corn and wheat, which could be used to feed poultry and livestock—declined in importance.

As urbanization grew, farmers marketed a constantly increasing percentage of their produce directly to consumers. The simplest form was direct sale at the farm. With the development of roads and the automobile, farm roadside markets developed rapidly. With the development of commercial farming, a wholesale marketing system evolved. Philadelphia and Pittsburgh became major wholesale distributing centers, and produce was shipped to smaller cities from these centers. Warehouses were erected at the terminals, where sales and auctions were held.

AGRICULTURAL ORGANIZATIONS

During the pioneer era farmers were isolated, and exchange of information occurred largely within local communities. After 1840, with im-

Philadelphia's wholesale produce market was located on Dock Street, an area of crowded confusion as photographed in October 1920. From the Philadelphia Commercial Museum Collection, Pennsylvania State Archives

provements in transportation, meetings of farmers from different parts of the state, and even the nation, became more frequent. As farmers began to cooperate, agricultural societies developed and began to speak out on behalf of Pennsylvania agriculture. Only the Old Order Amish and Mennonite farmers remained independent, being ordered by their church to remain outside the growing organizational structure.

The Philadelphia Society for Promoting Agriculture was first organized by gentlemen farmers in 1785. Its meetings were sporadic until about 1840, when monthly meetings and annual exhibitions were organized. It was the principal education organization for Pennsylvania agriculture until 1851, when the State Agricultural Society was formed. This new organization sought to be a scientific body as well as an organization of working farmers. However, because of faulty organization and the selection of poorly qualified scientists, the society proved unable to achieve its high goals.

After 1870 the Order of Patrons of Husbandry, better known as the Grange, assumed the leadership among agricultural organizations, not only in Pennsylvania but in the nation. The original objective of the Grange was educational, but the organization soon embarked on a great variety of cooperative enterprises. These included purchasing and selling fire and life insurance, banking, and manufacturing farm and home equipment. The Grange was not only a major economic force in farm life but a potent social factor in rural communities. The monthly meetings not only discussed farm problems, but provided such social activities as dancing, picnics, suppers, athletic events, and local entertainment. Since its origin, the Grange has been a consistent voice for the betterment of economic, social, and educational conditions in rural Pennsylvania.

In addition to the general farm organizations, a number of specialized organizations developed, including the Pennsylvania Horticultural Society, the State Dairymen's Association, the Pennsylvania Fruit Growers Society, the Livestock Breeders Association, the State Potato Growers Association, and the State Nut Growers Association. Each of these organizations developed its own specific programs. The State Horticultural Association, organized in 1827, was responsible for bringing many ornamental plants, including the poinsettia, to the United States. The State Potato Growers Association stressed cooperative marketing as well as education.

County agricultural societies flourished after 1851, when the legislature provided that the state would contribute to each county organization a sum equal to the dues collected from its members, provided that the amount did not exceed $100. The importance of the county organizations varied greatly. Many were active for a short period and then disappeared, but they did serve a local need and advance the education of the agricultural community.

AGRICULTURAL FAIRS

The agricultural fair began in medieval Europe as a vehicle of commerce and trade. In contrast, the first agricultural fairs in Pennsylvania were primarily educational in nature, and they soon evolved into commercial endeavors. The "golden age" of Pennsylvania fairs was between 1850 and 1870, when they were the chief means of communicating new ideas on farming, including new types of crops and livestock and advancements in farm machinery.

The early fairs were local, but in 1851 the first state fair, organized by the State Agricultural Society, was held in Harrisburg. In its early years the state fair was held at many locations. Most of the exhibitions were provided by county agricultural societies. In the 1890s interest declined, and after forty-six consecutive fairs, it was discontinued in 1898. Although there were attempts to revive the fair, legislative action did not occur until 1923, when the present-day State Farm Products Show in Harrisburg came into existence. The fair, held early in January each year, was an early success and now draws hundreds of thousands of visitors yearly.

The county and community farm fair began to flourish after state support was provided under the charter of the State Agricultural Society. By 1857 there were seventy-one county and community organizations holding exhibitions, and by 1892 the number had grown to eighty-one. These fairs provided a wide variety of activities, including contests such as corn shucking, horse pulling, and plowing. Over time, the amusement side of the fair grew in importance. Side shows and livestock demonstrations and judging increased. There were demonstrations by boys and girls of farm handicrafts, and women entered their foods, decorative quilts, and household handiworks to be judged. Parades, athletic events, horse racing, and educational talks became part of the show activities. At some fairs tent cities arose where the local people gathered for the period of the fair. It was a time of fine community spirit, and for many it was the major event in rural life.

PART III
Evolution of the Post-Industrial Economy:
1920 to the Present

As an economy evolves, it advances from the primary stage, based on development of virgin resources, to the secondary stage, in which manufacturing is the major catalyst of growth, and finally to the tertiary stage, in which services become the dynamic force in the economy.

As Pennsylvania's economy has evolved, each of these sectors has undergone changes in order to remain economically viable. In the primary activities, agriculture has moved from subsistence farming during the pioneer era to a diversified agricultural system in the nineteenth century to more specialized activities, such as dairying, in the twentieth century. In the great era of manufacturing, fuel resources and other raw materials were major factors in determining the location of industry. Today skilled labor and transportation facilities, as well as the amenities provided by a particular region, are of overriding importance.

In the nineteenth and early twentieth centuries, the great growth industries were iron and steel, textiles, clay and glass products, and leather. Today these industries are in decline, and if the manufacturing economy of Pennsylvania is to prosper, they

The waterways of Pennsylvania have facilitated the transport of raw materials and manufactured products since the eighteenth century. Photo by Jack Wolf

must be replaced by the growth industries of the late twentieth century—high-tech industries such as electronics and instruments. The "smokestack" image is gradually being replaced by the well-landscaped plant in a modern industrial park. Regions that developed in the past must adjust to new and continually changing factors that determine the location of economic activities. Only those regions that have the ability and the will to adjust to modern economic conditions will survive and prosper. An economic environment must be created that reflects present-day trends and developments.

As the economy has matured, the tertiary industries have become the dynamic generators of employment. A prosperous population demands better services in wholesale and retail trade, banking and finance, transportation, and a wide variety of personal services including health, recreation, social and legal services, and education. Most of these service activities require specialized training. They must be nurtured if Pennsylvania is to provide the way of life desired by the modern American family.

The economy of Pennsylvania, with its labor force of five million, remains of major importance in the industrial system of the United States. Many factors provide the foundation for a prosperous future. The labor force is not only large but highly skilled, and a highly developed infrastructure is in place. The educational system of Pennsylvania provides well-trained individuals who understand the modern industrial system and how they can be a part of it. The state has long been known for its industrial and financial leaders, and this tradition continues to the present day. In the tertiary activities, the state has been a leader in providing medical and health services. Pennsylvania's economy has been built on challenge and change. Pennsylvanians have recognized this challenge in the past and look with confidence to the future.

Chapter Eight

Mineral Resources: Modern-Day Trends

The exploitation of Pennsylvania's mineral resources in the nineteenth and early twentieth centuries was a major force in the development of the state's economy. The importance of minerals was so great that large areas were known as anthracite, bituminous, and petroleum regions. Thousands of people were attracted to these areas for the single purpose of developing the natural resources, and from these economic activities a permanent economy evolved.

During the twentieth century the importance of minerals in the state's economy has declined significantly. The exploitation of petroleum and anthracite is no longer of any significance. Only the mining of bituminous coal remains important to the economy of western Pennsylvania. In the 1980s mineral exploitation employed about one percent of the state's total labor force.

Pennsylvania's position as a mineral producer has also changed significantly. As late as the 1920s, Pennsylvania produced about one-quarter of the value of minerals in the United States, remaining the leading state in value of production until the early 1930s. From the early 1930s until the early 1950s, Pennsylvania's mineral production was exceeded in value only by that of Texas, and Pennsylvania was still producing about 10 percent of the nation's mineral wealth. By 1960 Pennsylvania had fallen to fourth place, dropping to seventh place in 1970 with only 3.6 percent of the nation's total. By the 1980s Pennsylvania had fallen to tenth place. Of a national total of $179 billion in mineral production in 1982, Pennsylvania produced $3.7 billion, or about 2 percent. About 85 percent of the minerals produced in Pennsylvania are fuels, primarily bituminous coal, and the remainder are largely nonmetallic minerals such as sand, gravel, limestone, and slate.

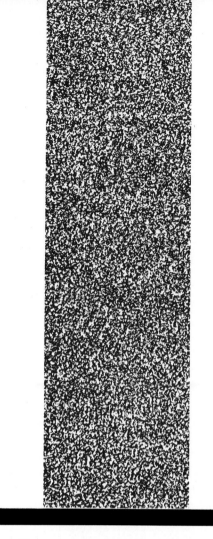

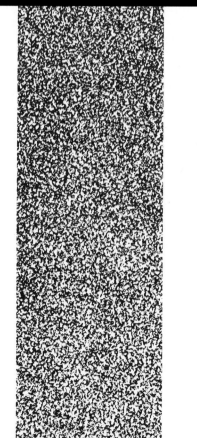

Opposite: *Electric coal cars in the anthracite regions made mining easier and safer when compared to mule-drawn, flame-lit equipment. Courtesy, Hagley Museum and Library, Wilmington, Delaware*

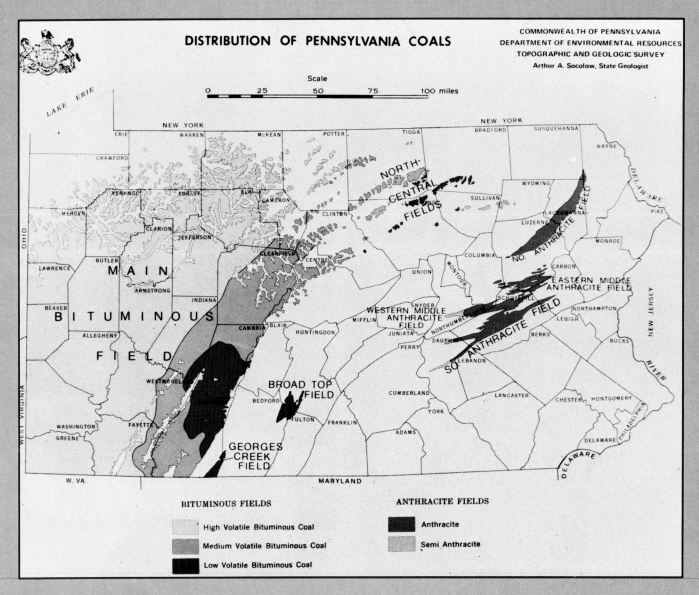

The bituminous coalfields of Pennsylvania cover all or
part of twenty-three counties in western Pennsylvania.
The anthracite fields are located in northeast Pennsylvania. Courtesy, Department of Environmental Resources,
Commonwealth of Pennsylvania

BITUMINOUS COAL: FOUNDATION OF THE MODERN MINERAL ECONOMY

Bituminous coal remains Pennsylvania's most important mineral resource. Its modern history has been characterized, however, by great fluctuations in production. As a result the industry has long exhibited economic instability. Company failures are common and unemployment an endemic problem. In the nation's search for a sound energy policy, the great coal deposits of Appalachia, including Pennsylvania, have been relegated to a minor position.

Bituminous-coal production in Pennsylvania reached its all-time peak in 1918, when 177,217,800 tons were produced. Since then distinct production trends can be recognized. The first was a long period of decline from 1918 to 1961, when production dropped to 63,171,000 tons. The second period, characterized by rising production, occurred from 1961 to 1979, when output reached 89,166,800 tons. The present trend is marked by a disastrous decline to 68,000,000 tons in 1983 and 60,000,000 tons in 1985. The lack of market for high sulfur coal plus the falling oil prices have drastically affected the Pennsylvania coal industry.

During the long period of decline, there was considerable fluctuation of output. In the 1920s the trend was steadily downward, to a low of 142,351,000 tons in 1929. With the onset of the Great Depression, production declined rapidly to a low of 74,162,000 tons in 1932 and, after a brief recovery, to a second low of 76,881,000 tons in 1938. During World War II, as petroleum and natural gas became scarce because of military demands, coal once again became important in supplying the nation's energy needs, and production rose rapidly to 144,408,000 tons in 1944. For a short time in the postwar period, coal production remained high to satisfy not only domestic needs but world energy demands. In the 1950s, however, production declined rapidly to its low output in 1961.

The basic reason for the decline of production in Pennsylvania was the growing competition from petroleum and natural gas. Many traditional markets for coal were greatly reduced or essentially disappeared. At the beginning of the twentieth century, when coal was the dominant fuel, domestic heating consumed from one-quarter to one-third of bituminous production. By the 1950s bituminous coal as a domestic heating fuel had declined to insignificance. Coal was the leading fuel for locomotives well into the twentieth century. With the development of the diesel engine, however, coal was completely replaced by diesel fuel in operating locomotives. The use of coal as an industrial fuel also declined, with petroleum and natural gas making great inroads in manufacturing. Metallurgical coke can only be made from bituminous coal, but this market also declined as blast furnaces became more efficient, requiring less fuel for each ton of ore smelted. In the 1980s the decrease in iron and steel production has greatly reduced demand. The major consumer of coal is the public utilities, but even here competitive fuels have become important.

Besides competition from petroleum and natural gas, a number of other factors have adversely affected the Pennsylvania coal industry. Pennsylvania was one of the first states in which the vast majority of coal miners were members of the United Mine Workers of America. There were frequent strikes, and ultimately the price of coal rose as union demands were met. To combat rising costs, coal companies began to exploit the coal resources of such nonunion areas as West Virginia and Kentucky. The southern Appalachian fields, although farther from the large markets, possessed high-quality coals and enjoyed a lower ton-mile freight rate. Most important, however, were the lower wage scales. By 1927 the expansion in the nonunion fields was so great that they could supply the entire country's needs without the output of the unionized areas. Although the southern fields were gradually unionized, excessive production capacity remained and excessive competition continued.

After 1961 production of coal began a modest recovery. In the 1960s the demands for electricity grew rapidly, and coal supplied a portion of the fuel for this growing market. By 1970 Pennsylvania's coal production stood at 80,091,000 tons. In 1972 the oil crisis of the 1970s began, and with a scarcity of petroleum the demand for coal increased. Although the Clean Air Act depressed the market for Pennsylvania coal, production rose modestly to a high of 89,166,000 tons in 1979.

By 1980, however, petroleum supplies had once again become available, the economy had adjusted to the sharp rise in prices, and the market for coal declined rapidly. In the 1980s, as the world glut in petroleum became more pronounced, the price of petroleum fell rapidly, from an average price per barrel of about thirty-five dollars in 1979 to under fifteen dollars in February 1986. By 1985 coal production in Pennsylvania had declined to a level of the 1880s output.

In addition to market factors, legislation at various levels of government has become increasingly important in determining both the overall demand for coal and regional patterns of production. Of greatest significance for Pennsylvania's bituminous-coal industry have been the Federal Clean Air Act of 1971 and Coal Mine Health and Safety Act of 1969.

THE FEDERAL CLEAN AIR ACT

One of the earliest attempts at controlling the burning of coal was made by the Pittsburgh City Council in 1955. Pittsburgh was long known as the "Smoky City." To eliminate air pollution, the city council passed legislation that prohibited the burning of coal within city limits unless smoke-control equipment was installed. Because costs were prohibitive, the burning of coal for domestic heating, in factories, and by the railroads essentially stopped.

In 1971 the federal government passed the Clean Air Act. Its central purpose is to control the pollution of the atmosphere. As the nation's population has grown and its consumption of fuels expanded, the quantities of solid and gaseous contaminants have increased at an alarming rate.

Implementation of the Clean Air Act was the job of the federal Environmental Protection Agency (EPA). On December 23, 1971, the EPA issued air-pollution control regulations for the emission of sulfur dioxide (SO_2), oxides of nitrogen (NO_x), and particulates (fly ash). Of greatest significance to the Pennsylvania coal industry were the standards for emission of sulfur dioxides from coalfield plants using high-sulfur coals. These standards varied according to the sulfur content and the thermal content of various coals, as well as the degree of urbanization of the surrounding area. However, the result was that most coals in Pennsylvania could only be burned if the sulfur content was reduced. Depending on the form in which the sulfur occurs, this requires a complex and costly precombustion cleaning process and/or removal by scrubbers during the burning process.

As national demand for coal increased in the early 1970s, the low-sulfur coals of the nation were sought to reduce costs. In essence the EPA regulations created two regional markets for coal: high-sulfur versus low-sulfur coals. Most western coals, such as those found in Wyoming, Montana, Colorado, North Dakota, South Dakota, Utah, New Mexico, and Arizona, and a few eastern coals, primarily in eastern Kentucky, are low-sulfur coals that can comply with the clean-air standards without costly cleaning and emission controls. Most coals in Appalachia, including Pennsylvania, and the Midwest can only be burned when the sulfur content is reduced.

In 1970 bituminous-coal production of the United States was 602,932,000 tons. Six states —West Virginia, Kentucky, Pennsylvania, Illinois, Ohio, and Virginia—accounted for 83.8 percent of the total. By 1982 coal production had increased to 793,474,000 tons, but the share of these six states had fallen to 61.2 percent. Clean-air standards and the cost of compliance were producing significant regional changes.

Between 1970 and 1982 total bituminous-coal production rose by 131.6 percent. Of the twenty-four coal-producing states, twelve experienced a growth rate higher than the national average—nine of them in the West. The twelve states that had a rate of growth below the national average were located entirely in Appalachia and the Midwest. Of the western states, Wyoming had the greatest increase, from 7,272,000 tons in 1970 to 108,360,000 in 1982, a rise of about 1,400 percent. Of the eastern states, West Virginia experienced the largest absolute and comparative decline, with a drop in production from 144,072,000 to 127,499,000 tons, or 11.5 percent. Pennsylvania's coal production declined from 80,491,000 tons to 74,066,000 tons, or about 8 percent.

Thus the western states with their low-sulfur coals have experienced remarkable growth, at the expense of the high-sulfur coal states of Appalachia and the Midwest. Despite the decline, however, the bituminous-coal industry has survived in Pennsylvania for three reasons: (1) the utilization of the coal in electric-power plants, usually in areas of low population where the high-sulfur coals can be burned after cleaning; (2) the production of coking coal; and (3) the expansion of the export market.

THE FEDERAL COAL MINE HEALTH AND SAFETY ACT

Since the beginning of the coal-mining industry, technological progress and union pressures have sought to make it a less hazardous occupation. National health and safety standards were not established, however, until the passage of the Federal Coal Mine Health and Safety Act of 1969.

The purpose of this act was "to provide more effective means and measures for improving the working conditions and practices in the nation's coal or other mines in order to prevent death and other serious physical harm, and in order to prevent occupational diseases originating in the mines." The act established mandatory health and safety standards and required each operator of a coal mine and every miner to comply with the established standards. These requirements cover such matters as inspection of roof supports, ventilation, combustible materials and rock dusting, electrical equipment, trailing cables, grounding, voltage distribution, trolley and trolley feeder wires, fire protection, blasting and explosives, hoisting,

emergency shelters, and mine communication. The act also contained provisions for expanding research and training programs aimed at preventing coal-mine accidents and occupationally caused diseases in the industry.

To enforce the regulations, inspection of underground and surface mines is required on a regular basis. The purposes of these inspections are: (1) to obtain and disseminate information relating to health and safety conditions; (2) to gather information on mandatory health and safety standards; (3) to determine whether a danger exists in a mine; and (4) to determine whether the mine operation is in compliance with the mandatory health and safety standards.

If after an inspection of a mine, it is found to be in violation of the Health and Safety Act, a citation is issued to the operator. Each citation describes the violation and specifies the length of time, usually ninety days, the operator has to rectify the violation. If the violation is not corrected, the mine inspector is required to issue an order to remove all persons in the area affected by the violation until it is corrected. In some instances this means closing the mine.

If a mine is found to be in violation of the Health and Safety Act, not only must the violation be corrected, but a penalty is also imposed. The basic penalty is not more than $10,000 for each violation. Any operator who fails to correct a violation may be assessed a civil penalty of not more than $1,000 for each day during which the violation continues. Any operator who willfully violates a provision of the act is liable to a fine of not more than $25,000 or imprisonment for not more than one year, or both. For a second conviction the fine is not more than $50,000 or imprisonment for not more than five years, or both. Other penalties can also be imposed for noncompliance with the act.

The Coal Mine Health and Safety Act has been a major factor in bringing about numerous structural changes in the industry. With the implementation of the act, a long-range trend of increasing productivity has been re-

Above: *Though these miners had the benefit of using pneumatic tools and other modern mechanical equipment,the work remained dangerous. Courtesy, Pennsylvania State Archives*

Right: *A coal miner is shown at work in a Latrobe, Pennsylvania, mine. Photo by Jack Wolf*

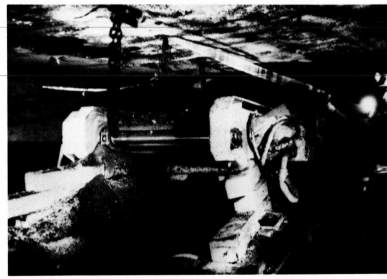

Right: *Coal is cleaned and processed from deep mines in modern colliers. Thus a portion of the sulfur is removed before the coal is burned, reducing the cost of removing sulfur in the burning process. Photo by E. Willard Miller*

versed. The principal reason seems to be the amount of labor needed to implement health and safety measures, as opposed to the actual mining of coal. This decline in productivity has had a differential impact on underground versus surface mining.

In underground mining, productivity—expressed as average tons produced per man per day—increased from 6.5 tons in 1955 to a high of 14.2 tons in 1969. Since then productivity has declined in underground mines to about 7.9 tons per man per day. In surface mining, productivity rose from 14.5 tons in 1955 to a high in the early 1970s of 24.9 tons per man per day. Since then productivity has declined to about 17 tons per man per day. The loss of productivity in surface mining has been less extreme because of the greater complexity of underground mining.

Between 1950 and 1960 employment in the bituminous coalfields declined from 94,514 to 33,396—as a result of increasing productivity

as well as a decline in coal production from 103,439,000 tons to 65,595,000 tons. In 1961 underground production in Pennsylvania was only 41,958,000 tons and employment had declined to 22,950 miners. Although underground production rose to its modern peak in 1969, when 56,055,000 tons were produced, employment continued to decline in the 1960s to a low of 17,710 in 1970. This continued decline reflects higher productivity because of greater mechanization.

The long downward trend in employment in underground mines was halted in 1970. Between 1970 and 1979 employment in underground mines rose to 23,535, an increase of nearly 33 percent. This reversal in the traditional employment trend occurred at the same time as coal production in underground mines declined from 55,930,000 tons in 1970 to 43,450,000 tons in 1979, a decrease of more than 22 percent.

Surface-mine employment experienced trends

Many coal mines are located close to waterways so that coal can be loaded directly into barges. Water transportation remains the lowest cost mode of transporting coal. This coal dock was located at Harmarville, Pennsylvania. Photo by E. Willard Miller

similar to those in underground employment, declining steadily from 10,810 in 1950 to a low of 4,130 in 1969. During the period from 1969 to 1979, however, employment rose to 10,190, an increase of 146.6 percent. During the same period, surface production rose from 21,652,000 to 45,116,000 tons, an increase of 108.4 percent. Though production was increasing, employment increased at a significantly higher rate.

These labor trends clearly reflect the trends in productivity. In underground mining, the increase in employment is directly related to the implementation of health and safety measures. In surface mining, the increase in employment is related both to that and to the greater demand for labor in implementing conservation programs such as land reclamation.

Trends in the number of underground and strip mines also reflect the changing economic conditions of the times. From 1955 to 1970 the total number of underground mines declined from about 1,350 to 245, reflecting decreasing production and increasing productivity. The number of mines continued to decline in the 1970s to a low of 144 in 1979. In the 1970s, with the implementation of high-cost safety standards, only the most modern and productive underground mines were able to survive economically. The average production of underground mines increased from 225,880 tons in 1970 to 301,040 tons in 1979. With the decline in coal production in the 1980s, the number of underground mines continued to decrease to 129 in 1983.

In contrast to the rapid decline in the number of underground mines, the number of surface mines remained nearly stable in the 1950s and 1960s, varying from year to year from about 550 to 700. During the 1970s the number increased from 780 in 1970 to a peak of 1,864 in 1978. Since then the number of surface mines has declined steadily to 1,062 in 1983.

The closing of many of the old underground mines reflects the economic problems of meeting federal health and safety standards. Further, with a depressed market for high-sulfur coals and the huge capital outlay required to develop a new mine, few new underground mines have been developed in recent years. The capital outlay for a small underground mine is now about $100 million. In contrast, a small surface mine can be put into operation for a few million dollars. An underground mine to be profitable must have an operating life of about twenty-five years or more. A surface mine may have an operating life of only a few months to a few years. Thus while the initial cost of new underground mines and the maintenance cost of old underground mines have caused their decline, the low initial cost and the lower cost of maintaining health and safety standards at surface mines have encouraged the development of the surface-mining industry. As a result, the relative importance of these types of mining has changed.

Strip mining began about 1915 but remained relatively unimportant until the 1940s. During World War II, strip-mine production in Pennsylvania rose from 2,808,000 tons in 1940 to 26,675,000 in 1945, representing an increase from 2.5 to 20.4 percent of total coal production in the state. From 1945 to 1970 production remained relatively stable at an annual output of twenty to twenty-five million tons, or about 25 to 30 percent of total coal production. In the 1970s, however, as the cost of underground production increased, strip-mine production rose to slightly more than 50 percent of all the bituminous coal mined in Pennsylvania.

These structural changes in the bituminous-coal industry have had a marked effect on the location within the state of both underground and surface mining. Between 1968 and 1979 underground coal production in Pennsylvania decreased from 54,645,000 to 43,350,000 tons, a decrease of 20.6 percent. Of the sixteen counties involved in underground production, thirteen experienced a decrease in production greater than the statewide average, and only three counties did better than average. Of these three, only Indiana County experienced a major absolute increase, from 5,724,000 to 10,112,000 tons. This was a direct result of the construction of a mine-mouth thermoelectric power plant that was able to use the high-sulfur coals of the area.

The thirteen counties whose production declined more than 20.6 percent were widely distributed. Most significant was the decline in importance of underground mining in the traditional counties of Cambria, Westmoreland, Allegheny, Washington, and Greene in southwestern Pennsylvania. The greatest decline occurred in Westmoreland County, where production fell from 2,709,000 to 539,000 tons, a decrease of about 80 percent. The underground mines of this area were old, and the cost of bringing them into compliance with federal health and safety standards was too high. As a result, many mines were abandoned. Underground mining persists, however, because of past capital investments, the availability of skilled miners, the remnants of a traditional market, a growing export market in the 1970s, and an established mining infrastructure.

During the same period, from 1968 to 1979,

surface-mine production in Pennsylvania rose from 20,512,000 to 45,116,000 tons, an increase of 120 percent. Of the twenty-five counties that had surface mines, however, thirteen experienced a growth of production greater than the statewide average, while twelve counties experienced below-average growth. Conflicting forces were thus shaping the regional pattern of production within Pennsylvania.

Surface mining was traditionally concentrated on the northern borders of the Pennsylvania coalfields, where the coal seams were near the surface and were easily mined by small draglines. In southwestern Pennsylvania, where the coal seams were deeper, underground mining dominated. Since 1968 this regional pattern has changed. The major growth in surface mining has occurred in counties that have experienced the greatest loss in underground mining. Surface-mine production in Westmoreland County, for example, increased from 242,000 tons in 1968 to 1,686,000 tons in 1979, an increase of nearly 600 percent. A number of factors have influenced this trend. The increased size of draglines has made it possible to mine the deeper coal seams from the surface. With the decline of the underground mines, an abundant supply of miners is available, and the infrastructure of the underground industry remains available to the surface operators. Even where the coal lies deeper, surface-mined coal is less costly today than coal from deep mines.

The counties in which production declined between 1968 and 1979 were largely concentrated on the northern margin of the coalfield. Many of the easily accessible shallow coal seams had been mined. Moreover, the coals in that area have a high sulfur and ash content. Most of the stripping operations were small and did not have coal-preparation facilities to reduce the sulfur content of the coals.

Counties with surface mines are widely distributed throughout the state, reflecting the ease with which strip mining is able to adjust to changing economic conditions. The regional pattern of strip mining over time is dynamic, reflecting the industry's attempt to produce coal where the profit margins are greatest. Thus

the coal industry has had to face not only the overall problem of declining production but also significant regional shifts within the state. This situation has exacerbated the economic hardships at particular locations where mining is declining. Further, the growing importance of strip mining has not only reduced the demand for labor but has changed its basic character. Finally, the industry has had to face a series of environmental problems, whose cumulative history has aroused state and national concern only in recent years.

STRIP-MINE LAND RECLAMATION

Strip mining—the process of removing an overburden of rock from an underlying mineral resource—is one of the oldest methods of mining. Open-pit mining for such minerals as iron ore, limestone, and slate has been practiced for hundreds of years, but the mining of coal by stripping is a relatively modern phenomenon. The development of this type of mining, which requires the movement of tremendous quantities of earth because of the relative thinness of coal seams, became important only after the development of the large power shovel in the 1930s.

Top: *The initial step in strip-mining is to remove the top-soil. This soil is then stored so that in the recovery operation it can be spread over the strip-mined area to facilitate the planting of trees or grass. Photo by E. Willard Miller*

Opposite page: *The huge draglines, with buckets of thirty to eighty-five cubic yards or more, remove the rock above the coal seams. Photo by E. Willard Miller*

Above: *The coal companies build roads to the strip mines that consist of broken stone and are extremely muddy after rain. Because the huge trucks carry from five to more than fifteen tons of coal, constant upkeep of the mine roads is required. Photo by E. Willard Miller*

In the mining process bulldozers first remove the weathered surface materials, and then large power shovels or draglines remove the bedrock. The largest of these draglines in Pennsylvania has a capacity of more than eighty-five cubic yards and can move overburden to a depth of several hundred feet. After the overburden is removed, the coal is mined by smaller shovels and loaded onto trucks.

The advantages of strip mining over underground operations are many. One acre of coal three feet thick will produce by stripping operations approximately 5,000 tons, whereas in deep mining the average recovery will be 3,300 tons or less. From 80 to nearly 100 percent of the coal can be recovered by surface mining, whereas underground mines recover only 40 to 60 percent of the seam being mined. Because of the efficiency of surface mining, the average surface mine produces two to three times the amount of coal of an underground mine per shift per day. Investment in strip-mining machinery is high—a modern dragline costs more than ten million dollars—but the salvage value is much greater than that of underground equipment. In strip mining the interval between initial investment and full production is comparatively short, whereas an underground mine may require two to four years of preparatory work before production begins. Finally, because danger is minimal in open-pit operations, insurance for the surface miner is significantly lower than for underground miners.

Although the ravages of strip mining have long been evident in Pennsylvania, a comprehensive survey of the amount of land disturbed by mining did not occur until the 1970s. Based upon high-altitude aerial photography, the U.S. Geological Survey's Geographic Information Retrieval and Analysis System (GIRAS) prepared land-use maps on which the strip-mined areas were plotted.

The amount of stripped land varies greatly from county to county. In the anthracite region, the largest amount of stripped land occurs in Schuylkill County, where 10.2 percent of the total land area has been stripped, followed by Lackawanna County with 5.4 percent. In the bituminous fields, Clearfield County leads with 9.8 percent of its area stripped, followed by Clarion with 6.8 percent, Armstrong 5.4 percent, Lawrence 3.5 percent, Cambria 3 percent, Somerset 2.7 percent, and Indiana 2.5 percent.

Although the percentage of land that is actually stripped in a county may be relatively small, large tracts of land in close proximity to the direct stripping operations are also affected. In the hill country of western Pennsylvania, the coal frequently outcrops on the side of a hill. Strip mining follows the contour of the hill and proceeds into the hillside until the overburden becomes too thick for economic operations. Vast areas may be scarred by these narrowly mined strips of land.

To the average citizen the most striking feature of strip mining is the destruction of scenic beauty by the presence of unsightly spoil banks. In the early days of strip mining, however, the prevailing attitude among landowners and strip miners was that the land in Appalachian Pennsylvania had little value and therefore did not justify the cost of reclamation. The abandonment of farmland began in western Pennsylvania about 1890, long before strip mining was practiced, and there was little public or private interest in reclaiming spoil banks on land that had little or no economic productivity. As land became unproductive, farmers sought to have their land strip mined to secure a windfall profit, often at retirement time. Although forests

Opposite page: *To get an idea of the size of a dragline, look at the workman at lower left. In strip-mining, new technology and the use of larger machinery makes possible the mining of coal.*

Above: *Many of Pennsylvania's coal regions have been scarred by strip-mining. While this form of mining is profitable, rigorous laws now require reforestation measures.*

Following page: *Strip-mining devastates the landscape by leaving behind piles of rock known as spoil banks. Then pools of water, which are normally acidic due to the reaction of sulfur minerals with them, create a weak sulfuric acid and dot the depressions. All vegetation is destroyed in the mining process. Photo by E. Willard Miller*

are the natural vegetation of western Pennsylvania, there was little interest in recovering the land by reforestation. The strip-mined areas were dispersed and relatively small, so that a solid forest stand was difficult to achieve, and interest by major lumber companies was minimal. Finally, the rugged coal-mining regions of western Pennsylvania were so isolated, and the tourist industry so little developed, that the esthetic value of the region was largely unappreciated.

The first legislation regarding strip-mine reclamation in Pennsylvania was enacted in 1945. The Pennsylvania Bituminous Coal Open Pit Mining Conservation Act, the most comprehensive of its day, required that each mining company deposit a filing fee of $100 for each stripping operation and post a bond of $300 per acre to be stripped, with a minimum of $3,000. Liability under the law was for the duration of open-pit mining at each operation and for a period of five years thereafter. This initial act required each strip-mine operator to

cover the exposed face of the unmined coal within one year after completion of mining and to level and round off the spoil banks sufficiently to permit the planting of trees, shrubs, or grasses. The slope of the leveled area was not to exceed forty-five degrees. After the leveling was completed, the miner was to plant the stripped area to the specifications of the commonwealth's Department of Forests and Waters. If the operator failed to comply with these regulations, he forfeited all or part of the posted bond.

Although this law appeared to provide the necessary regulations for the reclamation of strip-mined land, it was largely ineffective. First, forfeiture of the required bond was not a sufficient penalty to induce land reclamation. The cost of reclamation was estimated to be from two to six times the posted bond. As a result, at least 80 percent of the bonds were simply forfeited by the mining companies. Second, even when the bond was forfeited, there was no legal means of preventing the same mining

company from securing another concession to strip mine a new area. As a consequence, violators of the law continued to strip mine other areas. Third, reclamation of stripped land presented difficulties not previously encountered in the revegetation of an area. The average coal-mining company had no real interest in reclamation, and the methods used for revegetation were largely ineffective. On many strip-mined areas where the spoil banks were leveled and planted in trees, from 60 to 100 percent of the trees died within a year after planting. Finally, state inspection of strip-mined sites was nonexistent or at best superficial. As a consequence the state has a heritage of strip-mined areas from the past that have never been reclaimed.

To make these controls more effective, the Pennsylvania Surface Mining Conservation and Reclamation Act was passed in 1963 and revised in 1968, 1971, 1972, and 1974. The present act is recognized as a model law for the control of strip mining and was used to formulate the federal strip mining law of 1977. The present Pennsylvania law requires that the mining company secure an operator's license and a mining permit, post a bond, and provide a reclamation plan before strip mining can begin. The reclamation plan must include the following: (1) a statement of the best use to which the land was put prior to surface mining; (2) the use that is proposed for the land after reclamation; (3) where conditions permit, the manner in which topsoil and subsoil will be conserved and restored, or if these conditions cannot be met, what alternative procedures will be adopted; (4) where the proposed land use so requires, the manner in which compaction of the soil and fill will be accomplished; (5) a complete planting program, including trees, grasses, legumes, and shrubs, or a combination approved by the state Department of Environmental Resources; (6) a detailed timetable for the accomplishment of each step in the reclamation plan, and the operator's estimate of costs; (7) the written consent of the landowner, allowing access to the land for five years after mining ceases, in order to restore the land;

(8) a certificate of insurance certifying that the applicant has in force a liability-insurance policy of not less than $100,000; (9) the manner in which the operator plans to direct surface water to prevent it from draining into the pit; (10) a practical method of avoiding acid mine drainage and preventing avoidable siltation or other stream pollution; and (11) the application of health and safety rules necessary for the safety of the miners and the public.

The great problem in strip mining is the restoration of the land after power shovels have removed the coal. In the coal areas of western Pennsylvania, the greater portion of the overburden consists of shale, a compacted clayey rock. It is weak mechanically and slowly weathers into clay, thus gradually providing soil material. In many districts sandstone layers are also encountered. Sandstones are mechanically much stronger than shales and in spoil banks may form a jumble of boulders that resist weathering for very long periods. When limestone or liming shales occur in the overburden, they tend to neutralize the acidic waters and thus aid the growth of vegetation.

The spoil banks usually contain a number of minor materials that retard plant growth. Pyrite, an iron sulphide, is commonly found near the top of the coal seams. After the earth is overturned in the stripping operation, pyrite is frequently found near the surface of the spoil banks. When exposed to air and moisture, these particles decompose to iron sulphates and on further oxidation and hydration form rusty iron oxides and sulfuric acid. The acid, though hastening the weathering process, hinders plant growth. Soluble alumina formed by the reaction of acid on shales is likewise harmful to plants. Where pyrite is abundant, a much longer period of weathering is needed before planting can be successfully undertaken.

The quantity, quality, and distribution of the spoil-bank waters are also important factors in revegetation. The irregular surface of the leveled areas may have numerous clay depressions where water collects for long periods after rains. In these places trees may be completely covered for several weeks and are usually drowned. In

dry periods these clay tracts usually become hardpans. In other areas the material may be exceptionally porous, and the surface becomes desiccated quickly. The acidity of the water depends on the presence of pyrites and the rapidity of weathering, usually varying from pH 3.0 to 6.0.

Revegetation of the spoil banks in western Pennsylvania has traditionally been achieved by planting trees, which are better able than other plants to survive in an acid soil or where the topsoil is thin or nonexistent. The red, Banks, shortleaf, and pitch pine, Norway and white spruce, and hemlock are commonly used. The shortleaf and pitch pines are particularly suitable for sandstone and acid shales. If the soils are highly acidic, Japanese larch is one of the better trees to plant. In a number of places where the soil is moderately acid, red oak and black locust are particularly satisfactory if a quick cover of vegetation is desired. These trees develop a surface litter of two to three inches in six to nine years, stabilizing the spoil bank.

The black locust also has an abundance of nitrogen-fixing nodules on its network of fibrous roots, which stimulate plant growth in the soil. In both the anthracite and bituminous fields, most plantings have been of a single species. However, mixed plantings of several species are generally more desirable because of the greater protection from insect and disease attacks and the benefit of site improvement. Furthermore, if the season of planting is less favorable to one species than to another, mixed stands offer less likelihood of complete failure.

Although Pennsylvania has long had state-mandated recovery of strip-mined lands, there is still much controversy concerning the effectiveness of the reclamation procedures. In the early 1980s the state had only fifty-one inspectors to cover the entire coal region. Some mines had not been inspected for more than a year. The lack of proper inspection resulted in mining and reclamation violations, such as failure to replace the topsoil properly, silting from the mining operations, and lack of control of

Left: *The final process in restoring the strip-mined area is to provide a vegetation cover. In Pennsylvania pine trees are planted on many reclaimed areas. This area of pine trees is about ten years old, and the recovery is well underway. Photo by E. Willard Miller*

Opposite page: *The Pennsylvania strip mine law requires that the spoil banks be leveled to the original contour of the area. In this process bulldozers level the spoil banks, cut down any high walls created by the draglines, and in the final step, the topsoil, which was initially stored, is spread over the newly leveled area. Photo by E. Willard Miller*

acid mine drainage. By the late 1970s and early 1980s, mining had become so intensive in some areas that problems of pollution were virtually inevitable. State law forbids the Department of Environmental Resources to renew the annual mining license of a company with environmental violations, but this law was violated to some extent at the height of stripping operations in the 1970s. When strip-coal production declined in the late 1970s and early 1980s, many mining companies declared bankruptcy before reclamation of the land had occurred. Many of these areas have not been restored.

ACID MINE DRAINAGE

Acid mine drainage is one of the oldest problems in the coal region. The presence of acid water was recognized as early as 1803, when T.M. Morris, a pioneer farmer, noted that spring water issuing from hills with coal seams "is so impregnated with bituminous and sulfurous particles as to be frequently nauseous to the taste and prejudicial to health." Acid mine drainage began with the first mining operation, and it is estimated that 80 percent of the acid mine-drainage pollution today comes from abandoned mines. Within the bituminous region, acid mine drainage is coincident with the

mining of the Allegheny, Conemaugh, and Monongahela group coals.

Pennsylvania has the most widespread mine-drainage problem of the Appalachian coalfields. Of the estimated 6,000 tons of mineral acidity entering Appalachia's waters daily, it is estimated that 2,750 tons, or about 46 percent, enter the streams of Pennsylvania. This means that more than a million tons of acid water pour into Pennsylvania's streams every year. About 2,300 miles of the state's waterways are polluted by acid drainage, including the river systems of the Monongahela, Allegheny, Conemaugh, Kiskiminetas, Clarion, Loyalhanna, Susquehanna, and Schuylkill.

Acid mine drainage results in the deterioration of surface-water and groundwater systems by lowering the pH, reducing the natural alkalinity, and increasing the total hardness by the presence of iron, manganese, sulfates, aluminum, and other dissolved and suspended solid concentrations. The quantity and quality of mine-drainage pollutants produced from a mining operation depend upon such factors as whether the mine is active or inactive; the hydrologic, geologic, and topographic features of the surrounding terrain; the type of mining method employed; and the presence of air, water, and iron sulfides.

Acid water from underground mines is normally at a constant flow. In contrast, the discharge from surface mines is often intermittent, generally occurring during and after periods of precipitation. Runoff in stripped areas may find its way directly to surface streams, or it may be trapped in pools for a period and only reach a stream during high-water periods. These concentrated "slugs" of acid are particularly damaging to aquatic life in streams. Between flush-out periods, the pools in stripped areas often drain slowly into the backfill to emerge as mine-drainage seepages downslope from the mining operations. Another major source of acid drainage is from refuse materials from mines and coal-preparation plants. These refuse dumps are also sources of fine coal and silt pollution common to streams in the coal region.

Attempts to control acid mine drainage were limited until the passage of the Pennsylvania Clean Streams Act of 1967 and the federal Water Pollution Control Act of 1972. The federal law, amended in 1977, is now known as the Clean Water Act. Its basic objective "is to restore and maintain the chemical, physical and biological integrity of the nation's waters." The major goal is to eliminate the discharge of pollutants into navigable waters.

The Pennsylvania Clean Streams Act requires that discharged waters shall have a pH of not less than 6.0 nor greater than 9.0, and that such wastes shall not contain more than 7.0 mg/l of dissolved iron. The law also requires mine operators to submit to the Department of Environmental Resources (DER) an application for a drainage permit for their proposed operations indicating how they plan to control acid drainage during the active operations and how acid discharges will be prevented after completion of mining. All plans must be approved by the DER. Active coal operators must report monthly the quantity and quality of discharges from their operations. Penalties, such as forfeiture of posted bonds, can be applied if acid mine wastes are discharged. Nonetheless, drainage from many of the active, and particularly the abandoned, mines does not meet the water-quality standards required by law.

The technology is available to control acid mine drainage, either by the prevention of acid formation or by corrective measures after its formation, but these processes are costly. Modern estimates indicate that several billion dollars are required to clean up the streams of western Pennsylvania. The three basic methods of water-pollution control available to coal-mine operators are treatment, abatement, and prevention through selective mining.

Treatment methods include neutralization, reverse osmosis, ion exchange, renovation, and the mixing of acidic discharges with alkaline streams. Neutralization and precipitation mechanisms are fundamental to each of these methods.

Neutralization of acid water by using lime or limestone is the most common technique. The nation's first lime neutralization plant was built in 1966 on Little Scrubgrass Creek in western Pennsylvania. The disadvantages of this process include the problem of disposing of the sludge of iron hydroxides and calcium sulfate, the expense of purchasing and applying the reagents, the need to add these reagents for as long as the treatment is required (which may be decades), and the increase in hardness of the treated water.

By mixing the acidic fluids with non-acidic fluids (reverse osmosis) many of the dissolved particles can be removed from the acid water. However, the reagents must be continually added, the energy expense is high, and the resulting brine must be discarded. The first ion-exchange plant was built in 1968 at Burgettstown in southwestern Pennsylvania. Ion-exchange resins substitute bicarbonate ions for sulfate ions in the acid water, but this process also has the disadvantages of expensive reagents that must be continually added and solid residues that must be discarded. Soils have also been used as a medium for the renovation of acid mine waters. In tests, calcareous soils have proved most effective in order to neutralize the acidic conditions. Finally, the mixing of acidic discharges with alkaline streams works both to dilute and to neutralize acid waters.

Abatement techniques are designed to prevent or reduce the production of acid waters. Because acid formation depends upon the presence of oxygen, water, and pyrite, most abatement techniques attempt to remove one of the required reactants. This has proved to be a difficult task. Deep-mine sealing has proved unsuccessful in reducing the flow of water from the mine and in preventing oxygen from entering the mine. The burial of acid-producing material in surface mines is normally not practical because of the large quantities involved. Reclamation of the surface, however, has usually succeeded in reducing the acid discharge from the mine. Another technique involves reducing the rate of pyrite oxidation by inhibiting the catalyzing effect of the iron-oxidizing bacteria. Increasing the pH in the neighborhood of the bacteria by spreading limestone on top of the soil has been found to be an effective method of inhibiting acid reactions.

The final procedure involves development of mining at non-acid-producing sites. Current surface-mining laws require that overburden deposits be analyzed in an attempt to predict possible acid pollution. However, because the factors that control acid-water development are not well understood, the present procedures have met with variable and unpredictable results.

The problems caused by acid water in rivers and lakes have been widely studied. The flora and fauna are reduced and sometimes eliminated by acidic conditions. Each fish species is vulnerable to a different level of acidity. When the pH level falls below 6.5, brook and rainbow trout disappear. The females lay eggs, but the eggs do not hatch in acid water. When the acid level reaches pH 5.0, smallmouth bass, walleye, and lake trout have no future. Finally, at about pH 4.0—acidity 1,000 times stronger than neutral water—only chubbs, rock bass, and herring survive. Besides the impact on the fish community, acidity affects the total stream ecosystem. Algae and higher plants are reduced to a few tolerant forms. Sensitive macroinvertebrates, including the majority of mayflies, stone flies, and caddis flies, are unable to tolerate the al-

tered physical and chemical environment.

The quality of water is a major factor in its utilization. Acid water restricts recreational uses in many regions. A number of communities depend on streams for their water supply; acid drainage can destroy this source of water. Water quality is also a factor in industrial location. Acid conditions reduce the usability of water in many manufacturing processes. Acid pollution of streams may qualify as the most significant problem in terms of severity of damage for recreational and industrial use.

MINE SUBSIDENCE

In deep mining, the removal of substantial quantities of coal creates a void which, under certain conditions, may result in subsidence at the surface. As the roof of the mine falls into the void, cracking and caving of the overlying rock progresses upward. Earth movement at the surface can result in many different types of damage. Building foundations and walls may be cracked or displaced. Railroad tracks may be pushed out of alignment. Highways may crack or subside unevenly, creating a roller-coaster effect.

Subsidence damage is normally greater in urban than in rural areas. Forest lands are little affected by mine subsidence. Damage to croplands may be limited to local depressions and cracks, and the surface can be reclaimed with minimum cost. The most serious effect is the loss of groundwater sources—wells, springs, and ponds. The water table may be lowered, affecting the supply of water to crops and livestock. This may be a permanent change, and the farmer must adjust to a different water regime.

Because subsidence begins as soon as deep mining occurs, the subsidence problem in Pennsylvania is more than 150 years old. To provide some relief to individuals in old coal regions, the Anthracite and Bituminous Coal Mine Subsidence Fund was created by the Pennsylvania legislature in 1961. Any individual could purchase insurance giving protection against mine subsidence. In 1982, the fund wrote 1,650 new policies, bringing the total number of policyholders to 17,500 and total coverage to $645 million. In the same year the fund paid forty-eight claims totaling $281,707. The Mine Subsidence Division of the Department of Environmental Resources oversees the program.

To control subsidence, the Pennsylvania legislators in 1966 passed the Bituminous Mine Subsidence and Land Conservation Act. The act specifically provided protection for (1) public buildings, churches, hospitals, schools, and the like; (2) any dwelling used for human habitation; and (3) any cemetery or burial ground.

The Bureau of Surface Mine Reclamation established the guidelines to control subsidence. In all deep mines, 50 percent of the coal must be left in place in uniformly distributed pillars which cannot be smaller than 6.1 x 9.1 meters (20 x 30 feet). No mining can occur if the overburden is less than 30.5 meters, and pillars cannot be extracted between two support areas when the distance between them is less than the support cover.

This law has prevented subsidence in modern mining operations. However, billions of tons of coal were mined before the 1966 act was passed, and much of this mining, especially in the anthracite region, was in highly urbanized areas. To solve the traditional problem of subsidence, the void in the deep mine can be filled with mine wastes. Red ash, a nonflammable residue from culm banks, is commonly used, as is fly ash, the coal waste from electric-power generating stations. Sand is also utilized. These procedures can reduce surface subsidence up to 50 percent, but usually at a high cost. In the late 1960s eleven mine-filling projects in the anthracite fields cost more than seven million dollars. Because of these prohibitive costs, such projects have filled only a few of the abandoned mines in the coalfields of Pennsylvania. It is less costly to pay damages as subsidence occurs through the insurance fund established in 1961.

MINE FIRES

Coal-mine and culm-bank fires are a major problem in the coal regions. Presently there are more than 200 mine fires that have been burning for years, a few for decades, throughout the United States. In addition, there are some 500 culm-bank fires. These fires exist in both the bituminous and anthracite fields of Pennsylvania. A number of them were started by spontaneous combustion, but most have resulted from carelessness by burning of rubbish near the mines or culm banks. In some instances a mine fire has ignited culm banks and vice versa. Once a coal seam or culm bank has been ignited, it is extremely difficult to extinguish. Sufficient oxygen is normally available for smoldering and burning to continue until all of the fuel is exhausted. Underground mine fires sometimes smolder for years unnoticed, feeding on vestigial coal seams. Eventually these noxious and poisonous gases break through the surface.

Since 1965, when the program Operation Scarlift began in Pennsylvania, there have been serious attempts to extinguish the fires in culm banks. To put out a fire in a surface culm bank requires the removal of the burning hot spots. High-power water guns have become the principal equipment in extinguishing the blazes. To reach the burning materials, thousands of tons of material must be moved by draglines. The largest burning culm banks in the United States are in the anthracite region and the oldest mining areas of Appalachia. The Huber Bank at Ashley covers ninety-seven acres, and the Glen Burn Bank at Shamokin is hundreds of feet high and a mile long. In the Morvine Bank north of Scranton, nearly 2.5 million tons of smoldering, fiery culm were removed over four years of reclamation operations. In the past twenty years, at least thirty-three burning, abandoned refuse piles have been eliminated in Pennsylvania.

The control of underground fires is more difficult. The normal technique is to seal the mine, shutting off the supply of oxygen, then fill the mine with refuse materials. This process has proved successful in controlling a number of fires, including one of the largest underground fires, known as the Cedar Avenue project in Scranton. Operation Scarlift extinguished the fire, and Cedar Avenue has once again become

deeper surface mining. A number of the strip pits are now more than 400 feet deep. Mining with the larger equipment results in a far more complete removal of remaining coal reserves. In a number of places the coal being stripped is the pillar-and-barrier remnants of previous deep-mining operations. This residual of 35 to 50 percent of the bed had been left to support the deep mine.

The larger equipment is also more environmentally sound. The mining is done in a transverse fashion, across the coal basin. The dragline operates at the bottom of the pit. As it removes overburden lying above the coal seam, it rotates 180 degrees and drops the spoil material to its back, resulting in near-concurrent backfilling. As the cut is opened in the direction of stripping operations, a relatively flat terrain is left, posing less of an erosion problem. Bulldozers can more easily level the land, and revegetation can begin immediately when mining stops.

TRANSPORTATION EVOLUTION
Because 85 to 90 percent of the anthracite mined was marketed outside the coalfields, an extremely dense network of railroads developed as output increased. The Reading (originally the Philadelphia and Reading), the Erie, the Delaware and Hudson (D&H), the Delaware, Lackawanna, and Western, the Wilkes-Barre and Eastern (Erie), the Lehigh and Susquehanna (Central Railroad of New Jersey), the Lehigh Valley, the Lehigh and New England, and the Pennsylvania Railroad all served sections of the anthracite fields. With the exception of the D&H, all are now part of Conrail. From each of the major lines, spurs were built to the producing underground mines.

In 1917 a total of 88,147,050 tons of coal—100 percent of total marketed production—were transported by rail. The remainder was consumed in local trade or used at the colliery. Railroads remained the principal carrier of coal until the 1950s, when they carried about 85 percent of the traffic. Since then trucks have become increasingly important. By 1983 these proportions were nearly reversed, with trucks

hauling 79 percent and railroads 21 percent of the anthracite to market.

A number of factors account for this shift in the method of transporting coal. As deep-mine production declined, output was not sufficient to make up a full trainload of coal. The railroad network deteriorated, and a great many of the mine spurs were abandoned. As strip mining increased in importance, it was not worthwhile to build rail lines to these often short-lived mines. Thus the coal had to be hauled from the mine by trucks. Sometimes the trucks moved the coal only a short distance to railroad-loading platforms, but as road systems improved producers found it more cost-effective to move the coal all the way to its final market destination by truck.

EXPORT MARKETS
Eastern Canada was a traditional market for Pennsylvania anthracite. The cold winters and lack of domestic fuel sources provided the basis for Canadian imports of anthracite. In 1917 a total of 5,917,000 tons of anthracite, or 98 percent of all exports, were shipped to Canada. This was approximately 6 percent of the entire 1917 anthracite production.

As the domestic market declined, the export market became more significant, rising from about 10 percent of total production in 1960 to about 15 percent in 1980. Since 1980 exports have become the major factor in maintaining the small production that still exists. In recent years about 45 percent of Pennsylvania's anthracite has been exported. Canada remains the largest importer, but its relative importance has declined. It now takes about 70 to 75 percent of the exported coal, but a few thousand tons are also sent to Western European countries, Latin America, and Japan. Much of this coal is consumed on American overseas military bases. Regrettably, however, total exports are so small that they are unable to sustain any significant anthracite industry.

A UNIQUE ENVIRONMENTAL PROBLEM
In the anthracite fields are hundreds of abandoned mines. Since the mid-1970s these old

mines have been used as favored dumping grounds for extremely toxic chemical wastes. Because the mines are deep, the waste disappears immediately. This practice has been fostered by a lack of state legislation to control waste disposal. The wastes come not only from Pennsylvania but also from New Jersey, as the New Jersey legislature has enacted stiff penalties for illegal hazardous-waste disposal in that state. Chemical-disposal companies truck the toxic residues to the isolated, abandoned mine sites and dump the wastes into the mine shafts.

In most of the coalfields, tunnels were dug to great depths to lower the water table, thereby permitting deeper mining. In many of the abandoned mines, there are virtual underground streams. The chemical wastes move rapidly through the abandoned mine tunnels and quickly enter the streams and rivers that drain the region.

In the late 1970s toxic chemicals from an unknown location were released from mine-drainage tunnels into the Susquehanna River, forming an extremely toxic and potentially explosive slick thirty-five miles long. Workers cleaning up the hazard had to wear protective gear. Some of the chemicals, including dichlorobenzene, penetrated the water systems of some of the river towns. Although this spill was cleaned up before immediate damage was done to the environment or to humans, the danger of long-term toxic wastes seeping into river systems is yet largely unknown. The additive nature of the effects of chemical wastes may ultimately contribute to dramatic increases in human cancer, social problems, and ecosystem catastrophes.

ECONOMIC AND SOCIAL CONDITIONS

With the decline of the anthracite industry, the economic and social structure of the region is in a state of transition. These changes have occurred relatively gradually, for the decline in coal production did not occur precipitously. Miners and coal companies long shared the hope that the decline was only temporary and that the coming years would be better. Unfortunately, this has proved to be a false hope.

Above: *In the latter part of the nineteenth century many eastern European immigrants worked in the anthracite fields. This Orthodox church in Mt. Carmel reflects their heritage. Photo by E. Willard Miller*

Top: *This small Quaker State oil refinery at Emlenton, Pennsylvania, produces lubricating oils as well as other refined products. Photo by E. Willard Miller*

Opposite page: *Northumberland County's Glen Burn mine had a gravity-operated rail line. Courtesy, Pennsylvania Bureau of Travel Development*

The decline in population reflects the erosion of economic opportunities over an extended time period. The population of the four major anthracite counties—Lackawanna, Luzerne, Northumberland, and Schuylkill—reached a peak in 1930 with a total of 1,119,515. In each of the censuses since then, the population of the region has fallen, reaching a low of 831,998 in 1980. Many of the small mining settlements have virtually disappeared, but the decline in the major cities has also been significant. The population of Scranton, the largest city, has declined from 143,433 in 1930 to 88,117 in 1980, and that of Wilkes-Barre during the same period from 86,626 to 51,551.

Despite significant outmigration of the labor force, unemployment has plagued the region for decades. In the 1950s and 1960s, unemployment rarely fell below 10 percent. A state report in 1961 revealed that unemployment compensation was the major single source of income for the Scranton/Wilkes-Barre district, totaling twenty-eight million dollars. It is virtually impossible to estimate the social-service costs to the public due to the decline of the mining economy in this region. The decline has certainly affected the economic life of the local people, but it has also affected the rest of society, which pays for the economic problems through the tax system.

The lack of economic opportunity is reflected in many measures in the census reports. In 1979 the Census of Housing revealed that household income in the anthracite counties was among the lowest in the state. The average household income in 1979 for Schuylkill County was $13,334, Luzerne $13,977, Northumberland $12,788, and Lackawanna $14,239. By contrast, average household income in the noncoal counties of southeastern Pennsylvania were: Lancaster, $17,835; York, $18,347; Cumberland, $19,219; and Montgomery, the highest in the state, $22,387.

The houses of the anthracite region are considerably older, on the average, than those in the rest of southeastern Pennsylvania. In the four anthracite counties, 60 percent of the houses were built prior to 1939, compared to about 35 to 40 percent of the houses in other southeastern counties of Pennsylvania. The median value of the houses is also among the lowest in the state. In 1979 the median value of a house in Northumberland County was $31,000, Schuylkill $25,200, Luzerne $36,300, and Lackawanna $42,700; in nearby noncoal counties the median values were $50,200 in Lancaster County, $46,800 in Cumberland County, and $56,600 in Lehigh County. About 20 percent of the houses in the anthracite counties have one or more individual air coolers, compared to about one-third of the houses in nearby noncoal counties.

During the period of rising anthracite production, the economy was overwhelmingly dominated by coal. In 1924, for example, the total value of production from mining and manufacturing in Luzerne County was $277,058,000, of which anthracite accounted for $198,501,000; in Lackawanna County the figures were $173,348,000 and $109,780,000, respectively. Anthracite did not provide the basis for a manufacturing economy similar to that of the bituminous-coal industry. The male population worked in the mines. By tradition no woman could work in the mining industry. To utilize female labor, textiles became the first major industry in the region. It was a "parasitic" industry, taking advantage of the unused labor supply, and wages were low. Girls and women provided between 80 and 90 percent of the textile industry's labor force, which represented 50 to 60 percent of all employment in manufacturing. Tobacco and leather, also parasitic industries, were much less important, employing from 3 to 8 percent of the region's workers. A number of other industries existed mainly to serve the mines. Powder and explosives were the most important products of the chemical industry, and the metal and metal-products industries were primarily engaged in producing equipment for the mines.

With the decline of mining and the rise of unemployment, manufacturing was not attracted to the region. Despite unemployment, coal miners were reluctant to accept factory jobs. The miner was a highly skilled individual, and factory work did not provide equally skilled opportunities. The miners were unionized, and average wages were higher in mining than in manufacturing. Manufacturers were not attracted to a high-cost labor area. As the miners lost their jobs, the women of the region earned sufficient money to maintain the household, and large numbers of miners remained outside the labor force. Unfortunately, however, just as anthracite production began to decline, the textile industry began its migration to lower-cost production areas in the southeastern states. As a result the textile industry, which had provided 57 percent of all manufacturing employment in Luzerne County in 1924, declined to 40 percent in 1950 and only 5 percent in the 1980s. Similar declines occurred throughout the anthracite region.

With the decline in textile manufacturing, the employment of women shifted to the apparel industry. Because this industry required more labor and thus had a higher value added in the process of manufacturing, it could absorb slightly higher labor costs. The apparel industry provided increasing employment from the 1930s until the mid-1960s, when the peak was reached. During that period employment in the apparel industry in Luzerne County increased from 6 percent to about 40 percent of the total. The industry concentrated on such low-fashion items as overalls, shirts, and blouses.

Since the mid-1960s the apparel industry has declined in importance with the growing importation of clothing from Hong Kong, South Korea, and many other foreign sources. Between 1965 and 1982 employment in the apparel industries in the four leading anthracite counties—Lackawanna, Luzerne, Northumberland, and Schuylkill—fell from 45,490 to 27,645. The decline of the apparel industry, along with the continued decline of the textile industry, has been the major factor in the decrease in total manufacturing employment in these four counties from 113,347 in 1965 to 89,679 in 1982.

No significant new industries have entered the anthracite region in the past twenty years. The manufacture of fabricated metal products, machinery, and electrical machinery continues on a small scale, and the newer technological industries such as electronics and computers are insignificant. In spite of considerable regional efforts to attract industry through special inducements, the results are not encouraging.

While employment in mining has nearly disappeared and manufacturing has declined significantly the tertiary industries—transportation and other public utilities, wholesale and retail trade, finance and insurance, and the service industries—have exhibited a dynamic growth in employment. Between 1962 and 1982 employment in these industries in the four major anthracite counties rose from 88,599 to 140,595. The greatest increases occurred in the service industries, where employment rose from 26,619 in 1962 to 58,241 in 1982. The biggest increases of all were in health services.

The tertiary industries have brought a considerable degree of stability to employment in the anthracite counties. The population now appears to have stabilized, unemployment has declined, and job opportunities are expanding. A region normally progresses from a primary to a secondary and finally to a tertiary economy. It appears as if the secondary phase of manufacturing has been partially bypassed in the anthracite region, with the economy evolving from one dominated by primary activities to one in which tertiary activities provide the major growth potential for the future.

PETROLEUM AND NATURAL GAS: TWILIGHT OF AN INDUSTRY

The petroleum and natural-gas industries of Pennsylvania are important only to the local economy. In the modern period petroleum production reached its peak in 1937, then declined to a low of 2,564,000 barrels in 1978. As a response to the high price for Pennsylvania crude, production increased again to 3,950,000 barrels in 1983.

Although oil is produced in twenty-two counties of western Pennsylvania, three counties—Warren, McKean, and Venango—account for about three-fourths of the total. Pennsylvania is characterized as a "stripper well" producer, with an average output per well per day of about .5 barrels of oil. Production per well ranges from .1 barrel to rarely more than 3 barrels per day. The number of oil wells is still remarkably large, although the number has declined significantly from 28,806 in 1976 to 20,739 in 1983. Once a well has been drilled and placed in production, maintenance costs are minimal and production continues until a very small amount of oil is produced daily. The landowners also encourage continued production, for most receive royalties of one-eighth of the output. In a depressed economic region, the small oil income is welcome.

A number of local trends are evident within the oil region. Secondary oil recovery began in the Bradford field of McKean County, and this area long dominated production. As the Bradford oil sands near exhaustion, however, production in this area has declined from 1,302,034 barrels in 1976 to 827,935 in 1983. During the same period, the number of producing oil wells

has declined from 13,271 to 6,709. In contrast, production in nearby Warren County has risen from 465,154 barrels in 1976 to 1,207,129 barrels in 1983, and the number of wells has increased from 3,972 to 5,089.

Because several hundred wells are drilled each year, Pennsylvania will continue to produce a small quantity of oil for many more years. Proved reserves total more than fifty-five million barrels. Quality oil is sought by the local refineries to produce specialty products. Because of the small local production, however, the refineries must import oil from other oil regions.

Natural gas is more important than oil production to the local economy. Natural gas is found at much greater depths than petroleum. Some wells are more than 10,800 feet deep. Unfortunately the natural gas is found in "pockets." As a consequence one well may be a major producer, while another well drilled only a short distance away may produce nothing. Because of the depth of the wells, drilling costs are high, and exploration is essentially limited to large companies with major assets. As demand for natural gas has increased, production has risen from an average of 85 billion cubic feet output per year in the late 1960s to about 120 billion cubic feet per year in recent years.

A number of environmental problems have been created by the oil industry. To secure the oil from the producing horizon the oil is moved into the well by water flowing through the oil seam. In this process there may be from 10 to more than 100 times more water than oil that must be pumped from the well. After pumping the oil into a barrel it floats on the surface of the water, for oil is lighter than water. The water is then removed from the bottom of the barrel and must be disposed of. This water is normally contaminated with such impurities as salt, sulfur, and iron. In the past the contaminated water drained into the streams of the area causing ecological damage. The clean stream laws now require that the contaminants be removed before the water enters the streams of the region.

Chapter Nine

Agriculture: The Era of Specialization

Pennsylvania agriculture has experienced great changes since the colonial period. Economic forces not only within the state but in the nation as a whole have molded the present agricultural system. During the colonial period Pennsylvania farmers not only produced for a home market but, because of the bountiful harvests, soon made Pennsylvania the breadbasket of the nation. During the nineteenth century general farming dominated, with the typical

farm producing a great variety of crops and livestock. As other farming regions developed, however, competition increased, and each region began to produce agricultural products that brought the greatest economic returns. As a result, in the twentieth century general farming has declined in Pennsylvania, being replaced by a system of specialized agriculture in which the dairy and poultry industries dominate. Each sector of the agricultural economy has adjusted to this specialization.

Agricultural products, with an annual value of $2.675 billion, make an important contribution to the economy of the state. About 72 percent of this total comes from livestock products, of which dairy products and poultry are most important, and the other 28 percent from crops. Of the crops, feed crops such as corn and hay make up 30 percent of the total, fruits 15 percent, and vegetables about 8 percent. Mushrooms are the single most important crop, accounting for about 19 percent of total crop income.

Although Pennsylvania stands in twenty-third place among the states in total agricultural production, it places among the leaders in dairy and poultry production. In number of milk cows and volume of whole milk sold, Pennsylvania stands fifth, exceeded only by Wisconsin, California, New York, and Minnesota. In poultry products, the state is the fourth largest producer of eggs and the eleventh largest producer of broilers. Because corn provides a basic feed for cows and chickens, Pennsylvania is the twelfth largest producer in the nation.

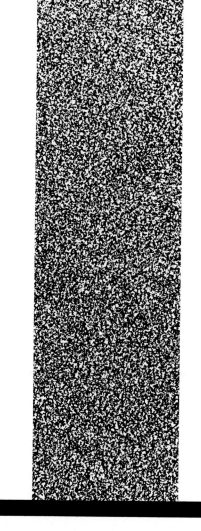

Opposite: *Dairy farms may be found in most of the counties of Pennsylvania, including Green County, where this photo was taken. Photo by Jack Wolf*

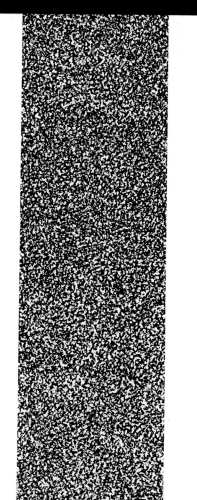

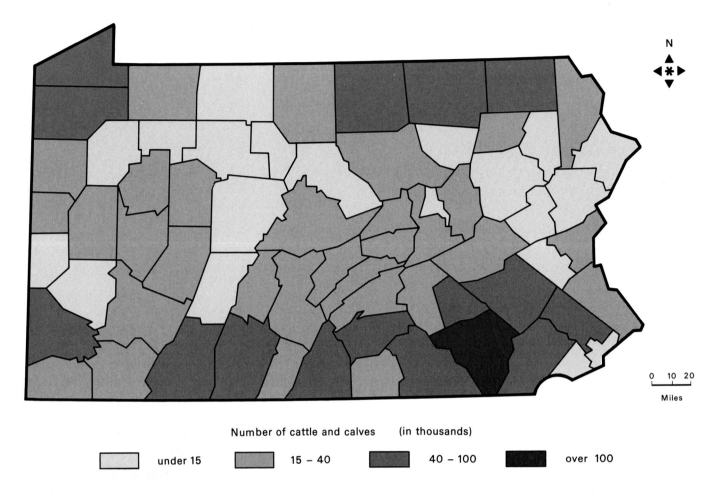

Number of cattle and calves   (in thousands)

under 15   15 – 40   40 – 100   over 100

Above: *Southeastern Pennsylvania has the major concentration of cattle and calves with Lancaster County accounting for about 14 percent of the state's total. Bradford County in northeastern Pennsylvania is the second largest county with about 4.5 percent of the state's total of 1,970,000 livestock. Prepared by the Deasy Laboratory of Geographics, Dept. of Geography, The Pennsylvania State University*

Opposite: *A dairy farm's large barn allows cattle to be kept on the bottom level during cold weather and hay to be stored in the upper part. The barnyard is used to exercise the cattle during the winter months. Photo by E. Willard Miller*

THE DAIRY INDUSTRY

The dairy industry dominates the agricultural activity of most Pennsylvania counties. Farm sales of milk products, dairy cows and calves, cull cows, and surplus grain and hay provide about 55 percent of all farm cash receipts. The state's 15,000 commercial dairy farms employ about 27,000 workers, and an additional 12,000 are employed in the 220 dairy plants processing milk and manufacturing milk products. This is about one percent of total employment in the state. Because Pennsylvania produces about 20 percent more milk than it consumes, it is an important supplier of milk to the northeastern milk market, particularly New Jersey and metropolitan New York.

Trends in the Pennsylvania dairy industry are closely related to changes on the national scene. Most significant has been the decrease in the number of dairy farms in Pennsylvania, from 32,500 in 1958 to about 11,000 in the

1980s—an average annual decrease of about 3 percent. The small dairy farms have become uneconomical and have been purchased by larger dairies or simply abandoned. The total number of milk cows has also declined, from 900,000 in 1958 to about 700,000 in the mid-1980s. The major decline occurred in the 1960s, and the number has remained nearly stable since 1970. The number of milk cows on commercial farms has increased to about 95 percent of the total, in contrast to the once large number of milk cows on farms producing fluid milk for home consumption.

Although the number of milk cows has decreased, milk production has risen, from 6.5 billion pounds in 1958 to about 8 billion pounds in the 1980s, for an average annual increase of about 3 percent. This increase in total production is due to the rise in milk production per cow. In 1958 the average annual milk production per cow was 7,240 pounds, but by the 1980s this figure had risen to more than 11,250 pounds. In 1958 no herd averaged more than 650 pounds of butterfat annually, but by 1984 a few herds were averaging more than 900 pounds of butterfat. The acreage per dairy farm has increased from an average of 175 in the mid-1950s to more than 245 today, while a more intense feeding program has raised the milk and butterfat production.

There has also been a decrease in the number of processing plants, from 511 in 1957 to fewer than 200 in the 1980s. As transportation of milk has improved, milk can be collected from more distant farms and a larger market area served. The larger plants have the advantages of economies of scale in processing larger quantities of milk. In marketing the milk, the quart glass bottle has nearly disappeared, being replaced by paper or plastic containers in quart, half-gallon, and gallon sizes. This innovation reduces the cost of cleaning the glass containers.

CHARACTERISTICS OF DAIRY FARMING

The Pennsylvania dairy farm is typically a family-operated business. The average dairy farm has

a labor force equivalent to about two persons and a herd averaging sixty cows. About 75 percent of the dairy labor force is provided by the farm family. Even on larger farms with ninety to a hundred cows, 50 percent or more of the labor is provided by the family. The farm operator manages the business as well as providing labor for crop production.

The modern dairy farm is highly mechanized. Specialized equipment includes pipeline milkers, milking parlors, bulk milk tanks, silo unloaders, and manure gutter cleaners. This mechanization makes possible an increase in the number of cows without increasing the labor force. To illustrate, traditionally manure was hauled daily from the barn to the fields. This resulted in loss of nutrients, damage to soil structure, and difficulties of hauling during winter months and rainy periods. Now an increasing number of dairy farmers are building storage facilities to hold manure for four to six months. The manure is then spread on the fields at the time of its maximum value.

Increased land values, more expensive machinery and equipment, improved barns and sheds, larger silos, larger herd size, and increased livestock values have all combined to

Above: *Harrisburg's Farm Show Complex provides the perfect setting for livestock shows. Photo by Allied Pix Service, Inc.*

Top: *Silos and barns such as these in Bucks County dot the rural Pennsylvania landscape. Photo by Jack Wolf*

greatly increase the capital investment of the modern commercial dairy farm. Since the late 1960s the average investment in land, livestock, machinery, feed inventories, and supplies has risen from $2,000 to about $75,000 per cow. This amounts to an investment of $375,000 for a typical fifty-cow dairy farm.

Capital to finance a dairy farm must be secured primarily by the owner-operator, and sources of loan money are very important. The average dairy farm has a debt of 25 to 35 percent of its total asset value. Total assets of the dairy farms have risen significantly in recent decades.

SOUTHEASTERN AND CENTRAL DAIRY REGION

The dairy industry has its greatest concentration in the region that extends westward from the Delaware River to Altoona, State College, and Williamsport. This region has the most productive farmland in the state, as well as the greatest population density providing the larg-

Pennsylvania farmers sometimes sell their fresh produce directly to the consumer from roadside stands such as these. Photos by Jack Wolf

est market potential. The dairy farms are family-sized, with dairying supplemented by the production of poultry, hogs, beef cattle, and fruit and vegetables.

Within this region Lancaster County is the outstanding farming county of the state. This single county produces about 46 percent of the eggs, 38 percent of the broilers, 35 percent of the hay, 34 percent of the milk, 21 percent of the field and forage crops, and 37 percent of the swine of the state. Today the value of livestock products totals nearly $400 million annually. The second most important county, Franklin, produces about $78 million annually.

Lancaster is endowed with a remarkably favorable physical environment for farming. Large areas are level to gently rolling, with the richest soil in Pennsylvania. These physical attributes combined with the fine market location create a most favorable agricultural environment. The dairy industry provides the core of the Lancaster farming economy. Chickens, as egg produc-

Above: *A decorated barn in the vicinity of Ephrata became the subject of this John Collier 1942 photo. From the U.S. Dept. of Agriculture FSA Collection, Library of Congress*

ers or broilers, are the second most common feature on Lancaster farms. More than 80 percent of the farms raise chickens. On some farms chickens are grown primarily to supply the family with eggs, meat, and a small cash income. At the other extreme are the poultry farms where chickens are raised by the thousands in multistory buildings. These large commercial enterprises are highly specialized, producing no other farm product. Feed is not raised on these farms but purchased from outside sources. The poultry industry is now highly mechanized, and broilers are fed a highly concentrated feed to produce meat in the shortest possible time.

Next to dairy cattle and poultry, swine and beef cattle play a lesser role on the farm. Swine are fed corn and skim milk, so that their distribution correlates well with corn and dairy cattle. Beef cattle are raised in greatest numbers in the tobacco areas. The labor goes to the production of tobacco, which is labor-intensive, rather than livestock which requires little attention. Lancaster County also has one of the largest population of horses and mules in the nation, as the Amish people use animal rather than motor power for plowing, harrowing, cultivating, and harvesting crops.

Although Lancaster County is not recognized as a truck-farming area, a great variety of vegetables is produced. Vegetable production is widely distributed, including a small area on the Susquehanna River where early vegetables dominate. On many farms vegetable growing is simply an extension of the farm garden plot. Tomatoes, which cover about 6,000 acres, make up about one-third of the country's vegetable acreage. Potatoes are produced on about 4,000 farms, mostly for family use.

Tobacco is the major specialty crop in Lancaster County. It is grown on many farms in plots of one to not more than five acres. The acreage is limited by the quantity of labor on the farm. Tobacco culture requires great amounts of labor not only during the growing season for planting, cultivation, control of tobacco worms and insects, and picking the individual leaves at harvest time, but also during the curing period in the barn, as the tobacco leaves must be

Opposite, top: The Sheely family of Arentsville, Adams County, owned this picturesque round barn, which was photographed by Sheldon Dick in 1938. From the U.S. Dept. of Agriculture FSA Collection, Library of Congress

Above: Jay Reich, Jr., whose father was a Farm Security Administration client, fills a milk can while working on his family's Lancaster County farm. This 1938 photo is by Sheldon Dick. From the U.S. Dept. of Agriculture FSA Collection, Library of Congress

Above: *Many Pennsylvanians still purchase produce and meats at large year-round farm markets like this one in Lancaster. Courtesy, Pennsylvania Commonwealth Media Services*

Left: *Because swine are fed corn and milk, they are well suited for the dairy farm. Photo © 1982 Tom Weigand, Inc.*

Below: *Tobacco farming is centered in Lancaster County. In early spring the tobacco plants are started in seedbeds to protect the fragile plants from frosts. Photo by E. Willard Miller*

Bottom: *Tobacco is planted in rows and cultivated to control weed growth. This Lancaster County tobacco field was photographed in early summer. Photo by E. Willard Miller*

Below: *In early fall the leaves are picked individually from the tobacco plant. In order to dry them initially, the leaves are placed in open racks in the field during the harvesting period. Photo by E. Willard Miller*

Above: *The process of drying tobacco leaves continues in the barn. To allow circulation of air through the barn, the structure's sides are opened. The drying process, which requires several weeks, must be done indoors to protect the tobacco leaves from fall rain showers. Photo by E. Willard Miller*

Opposite: *An Amish farmstead in Lancaster County houses three generations of a family in a single home. Photo by E. Willard Miller*

individually hung in drying barns for several weeks before they can be marketed. Because tobacco is a soil-depleting crop, and the cost of farm labor is rising, tobacco acreage has declined from about 40,000 in 1950 to 13,000 in recent years. Some Amish farmers will not grow tobacco as they do not want to associate themselves in any way with the evils of tobacco.

THE AMISH: TRADITIONAL FARMERS
Within the farming economy of southeastern Pennsylvania, centering on Lancaster County, are communities of Amish and Mennonite farmers who maintain farming traditions of the past. These groups have a heritage based on the practices begun in sixteenth-century Europe.

The Amish agricultural system began when the Anabaptists were disenfranchised politically in Europe and began to devise distinctly different methods of farming. They began the then revolutionary practices of crop rotation, stable

The Pennsylvania Dutch region encompasses some of the country's most colorfully named towns. Photo © 1982 Tom Weigand, Inc.

Opposite page: *Amish farms range in size from 30 to 120 acres. This farm is located in Intercourse. Photo by Arnold J. Kaplan/Berg & Associates*

Left: *Amish-owned Summerfield Farms is located near New Wilmington, Pennsylvania. Photo by Jack Wolf*

Below: *The Amish farmer utilizes the energy of draft horses or mules to work his farm. Photo by Arnold J. Kaplan/Berg & Associates*

Above: *Tobacco hanging in a Churchtown barn to dry became the subject of this 1930s photo by Sheldon Dick.*

Top: *Arthur Rothstein shot this Lancaster County barn which doubled as a billboard in 1941. Both photos from the U.S. Dept. of Agriculture FSA Collection, Library of Congress*

feeding of livestock, irrigation of pastures, the use of natural fertilizers, and the growing of clover and alfalfa as a means of restoring soil fertility. The Amish farmer transferred these practices to his new homeland in Pennsylvania.

The way land is used has a spiritual significance to the Amish and Mennonites, who see the land as providing not only sustenance but the pleasantness and orderliness of life. The soil must not be defiled but must receive proper cultivation and fertilization. The care of the soil is based on Biblical interpretation—that man is to till the soil not only for his fulfillment but also his pleasure (Genesis 2:15); that the earth belongs to the Lord and it is the responsibility of man to care for the earth on behalf of God (Psalms 24). Thus the Amish believe that they are the stewards of the land for an absentee landlord. This stewardship is continuous, ending only with the day of reckoning when man is required to provide an account to God.

To the Amish the most desirable occupation is farming. If this is not possible, a rural job is next to be preferred. The primary goal of the Amish farmer is not to make money, but to

PUBLIC SALE

Live Stock and Farm Implements

Saturday, March 14th, 1942

Will be sold on the premises, along the road leading from Lauber's School House to Witmer's Garage, formerly Zook's Woolen Mill, the following, to wit:

Two Horses

One thereof a single line leader;

ONE MULE

Single line leader;

Eight Short Horn Cows

All milking;

STOCK BULL   3 Yorkshire Sows

SEED HOG; 14 SHOATS;

100 Chickens, 6 Guineas
6 Muscovy Ducks

Allis-Chalmers W. C. TRACTOR, on rubber, with cultivator attachment; **2 Tractor Discs; Harrow; 18-in. Plow; 2 Bottom 14-in. Plow; 2 Manure Spreaders;**

Hay Loader; New Idea Wagon; 3 two-horse Wagons; Spring Wagon; John Deere Side Delivery Rake; 2 Mowers; 2 Cultivators; Potato Digger; Corn Planter; Tobacco Planter; Grain Drill; Cultipacker; Denlinger Hammer Mill; 3 Shovel Harrows; 2-hole Corn Sheller; 2 Hay Ladders, one with carriage; 2 (15-H. P.) Westinghouse Motors, with starter; Minnich Tobacco Press; Straw Cutter; 40-ft. Extension Ladder; 22-ft. Fruit Ladder; Platform Scales; Hog Self-Feeders; 2 Range Shelters; 2 Hog Range Houses; 2 Brooder Stoves; Water Tank; 1,000 bushels Corn; 100 bushels Kathadin Potatoes, certified last year; 7,000 Tobacco Lath; 2 Walking Plows; Lumber; Concrete Blocks; Fire-Wood; Galvanized Roofing; Hay Rope and Carriage; Slings; Hooks; Pulleys; Harness; Collars; Shovels; Crobars; Chicken Coops; Wire Fence; Barb Wire; 2 Tobacco Ladders and many other articles not mentioned.

Public Sale of a Complete Line of Household Goods will be held at the same on Monday, March 2nd.

Sale to be held on Saturday, March 14th, 1942, at 12 o'clock, when terms and conditions will be made known by

John L. Halligan, auct.
D. G. Ranck, clerk.

ELMER J. MARTIN

No Dinner Served.

Auctions offering livestock and farm implements were held regularly during World War II. From the U.S. Dept. of Agriculture FSA Collection, Library of Congress

Right: *For road transportation the Amish farmer drives a horse-powered buggy. Photo by Jack Wolf*

Opposite page: *A windmill and waterwheel are more than just picturesque on this Strasburg farm. They are also functional. Photo by Arnold J. Kaplan/Berg & Associates*

Below: *Some Amish farmers harness gasoline-powered motors to horse-drawn farm equipment. Photo by Jack Wolf*

support himself and his family on the land with a minimum of interference from the outside world. In the sixteenth century Menno Simons established the creed of the Amish family: "Rent a farm, milk cows, learn a trade if possible, do manual labor as did Paul, and all that which you then fall short of will doubtlessly be given and provided you by pious brethren."

Amish agricultural practices reflect these long-established traditions. In southeastern Pennsylvania the Amish originally settled on farms of from 100 to more than 400 acres, but gradually the size of their holdings was reduced so that they could be managed by family labor. At first they sought areas of limestone soil which they recognized as superior to other soils. Over time, however, the Amish found that high productivity did not depend on limestone soils but on the care with which the land was nurtured.

Traditionally the Amish farmer preferred general farming, producing a variety of crops and livestock. Crops included corn, wheat, oats, rye, a variety of hay crops for feeding, and a great variety of vegetables and fruits. The typical farm also has horses, mules, dairy cattle, beef cattle, hogs, poultry, and sheep. The products from such a farm provide the Amish with a high degree of self-sufficiency.

Amish farming is, however, not immune to general economic forces affecting agriculture. Population pressures have forced the Amish to

develop more specialized farm enterprises and to assess the influence of technology on Amish values. The average-size Amish farm today is about 84 acres, with a range from 30 to 120 acres. It is a common practice for the Amish to divide their farm to keep the younger generation on the land. They also buy farms from non-Amish farmers as they become available.

Diminishing farm size and the high price of land have forced the Amish into a more intensive use of the land. Cash crops have become increasingly important. A traditional cash crop of the Amish is tobacco, which they began cultivating about 1838. In 1930 possibly 85 percent of the Amish farms had a tobacco crop. Tobacco has decreased in importance, however, and today it is produced on no more than one-third of the Amish farms. Although tobacco yields about 2,000 pounds per acre and provides a high income, it is a soil-depleting crop. In recent years milk, poultry, and tomatoes have replaced tobacco as cash farm products.

A major characteristic of Amish farming is the low demand for energy. The Amish use less energy than any other group of farmers to achieve the same yields. Rejecting the use of tractors, they use mules and horses instead. The Amish farmer believes that tractors compact the soil so that drainage is poorer, crop roots will not penetrate as deeply, plowing must occur later in the spring, plant nutrients are more difficult to incorporate into the soil, and crop yields are reduced.

The Amish farmer normally has six draft horses or mules and one or two light horses for road transportation. Belgian and Percheron horses are most prized as draft animals. Each Amish area has a number of horse dealers who raise or deal in horses. Auction sales are major events where farmers not only buy and sell animals but keep abreast of trends, prices, and general farm news. These gatherings are also a time for storytelling, joking, and development of comradeships.

The Amish have made some adaptations to modern farming. In all changes, however, decisions are painstakingly made so that a balance is maintained between the traditional culture of

Above: *A cornucopia of produce fills this Amish-owned roadside wagon. Photo by Arnold J. Kaplan/Berg & Associates*

Opposite page: *Amish farmers gather at auctions not only to buy and sell, but also to talk and joke. The auction these farmers attended took place near New Wilmington, Pennsylvania. Photo by Jack Wolf*

the Amish community and modern farming methods. Amish farmers may have purebred dairy herds and use artificial insemination, but they are not permitted to have the livestock registered. Membership in dairy-herd associations is discouraged because it would draw "too much attention from the world" and, possibly more important, would entail too much record keeping and "paperwork."

Some types of machines are now permitted on the Amish farms. In the Lancaster area, where the presence of an industrial society is evident, some accommodations have been made to modernization. Milking machines and bulk milk tanks operated by diesel engines are utilized, but pipes connecting the milk machines to the bulk tanks are not permitted. Gasoline-driven motors may also be harnessed to traditional horse-drawn farm implements. Amish repair shops now buy old tractors and adapt them to horse-drawn equipment, mount-

Above: *The children of the Plain People are provided a fundamental education in reading, writing, and arithmetic in one-room schoolhouses. This rural school is located near Intercourse, Pennsylvania, in the heart of Lancaster County's farming lands. Photo by E. Willard Miller*

Opposite: *Quilting is a time for socializing for these Amish women. Photo © 1980 Tom Weigand, Inc.*

pairing harness, and maintaining the farmstead are most important. The midday meal is served about eleven o'clock. After a short rest the activities of the morning are continued. Supper is served between four and five o'clock. After supper the daily chores of feeding the animals and milking the cows must be done. In summer the men will work in the fields until dark. Bedtime is between nine and ten o'clock. Work takes place only on weekdays. Only the most essential work, such as milking the cows and feeding the livestock, is done on Sunday.

Because of a high birth rate and a limited supply of land in Lancaster County, the Amish have been forced to make difficult decisions in the past few decades. One alternative is to migrate to new areas and establish new communities. Since 1964 the dispersion of the Amish has been dramatic. The first group left Lancaster County for Adams County in 1964. In succeeding years they were followed by groups to Centre County (1967), Union (1970), Franklin (1971), Cumberland (1972), Clinton (1973), Montour (1974), York (1975), Lycoming (1976), and Dauphin (1978). Other groups have migrated to northwestern Pennsylvania and the Midwest, particularly Ohio, Indiana, and Iowa, and some have gone to Canada.

Another alternative is to pursue nonagricultural occupations while still remaining Amish. This is possibly the most difficult alternative. Until 1954 any farmer from Lancaster County who took a factory job was excommunicated. This meant being cut off from any contact or communication with any Amish person; his own wife and family were forbidden to speak to him. Population pressures have since altered this policy. However, when the Amish cannot farm, they make every attempt to enter closely allied trades within the community, becoming carpenters, cabinetmakers, blacksmiths, harness makers, and the like. Other traditional occupations include butcher, sheepshearer, shoemaker, beekeeper, plumber, horsetrainer, tool sharpener, carpet maker, and orchard grower.

The final alternative is to continue to divide the land so that each farm becomes smaller. This practice is occurring today, resulting in

ing the motors on the traditional chassis of the hay mower, rake, corn picker, and other implements. Self-propelled grain combines have not been adopted by the Pennsylvania Amish. Within the Amish community there is considerable variation from group to group as to what types of modern machinery can or cannot be used.

The Amish farming system is based on labor provided primarily by the family. Few Amish farmers hire farm laborers from the community. The prevailing feeling is that hired help does not know enough to perform farm tasks nor do they work hard enough. On an Amish farm the workday begins between four and five o'clock in the morning with milking and chores around the barn. Breakfast is served about five-thirty. In the summer the tasks of plowing, seeding, cultivating, and harvesting then begin. In winter feeding the livestock, hauling manure, re-

some fundamental agricultural changes because of the need to use the land more intensively. Dairying and poultry production can be expanded, but with less land to produce feed, most feeds have to be purchased. Some Amish have established mechanized poultry and hog barns on small plots of ground. After purchasing farms at high interest rates, with payments amounting to as much as $40,000 to $50,000 a year, they find that mechanized hog, poultry, and dairy barns are required to meet those payments. As these trends develop, some Amish farms are beginning to resemble agrifactories, and the traditional image of a peaceful, rural environment is threatened.

NORTHEASTERN DAIRY REGION

Northeastern Pennsylvania is a land of rolling, glaciated hills. The topsoil is thin and acidic in most areas. The topography becomes increasingly rugged toward the south and west, and agriculture is limited to a few level upland areas and narrow river floodplains. Large patches of woodlands exist throughout the entire region in the more rugged areas and areas of poorest soils.

This dairy region is characterized by large barns, silos, and a high percentage of pastureland. Alfalfa and hay occupy the largest percentage of cropland. Corn is produced on the better soils and in the less rugged areas. Because grain production is limited, feed concentrates must be purchased from outside the region. The northeastern farmer must also sell more heifers than the dairy farmers of southeastern and central Pennsylvania, since the land will not support as high a milk-cow density.

The population density of the area is low, and most of the milk is sent out of the region, transported by truck. New York, Philadelphia, and the anthracite cities are the main market areas. Some of the milk is processed into cheese and butter, and a small portion is used to produce condensed and evaporated milk.

Closely allied to the dairy industry is the production of broilers and eggs. Because chicken production requires little land, all of the land can be given over to the dairy industry,

and since the market for broilers and eggs is the same as for milk, the same marketing system is effective for both products. Poultry raising thus provides an important supplement to the dairy farmer's income.

NORTHWESTERN DAIRY REGION

The dairy industry of northwestern Pennsylvania resembles that of northeastern Pennsylvania. The glaciated country is well suited to alfalfa and grass production, and grains are limited to the better lands. Here the milk is marketed largely in the Pittsburgh area; little of it goes to Buffalo or Cleveland because of stiff competition from the dairy farmers of New York and Ohio. Excess milk is converted into butter, cheese, and condensed milk. Here, too, the poultry industry has developed in conjunction with the dairy industry. The land is not used intensively, and large tracts remain as woodlands.

SOUTHWESTERN DAIRY REGION

The dairy industry in the rugged area of southwestern Pennsylvania provides milk for Pittsburgh and the heavily populated industrial valleys of western Pennsylvania. Farms are situated on the plateau uplands and in the valley floodplains. This is one of the least intensively farmed regions in the state, and large tracts of woodlands remain. As in other dairy regions, poultry production is found on many farms. A large percentage of the land is devoted to alfalfa and hay crops, while production of corn is limited to the better lands. The area does not produce sufficient feed for its poultry and livestock industries and buys feed from outside the region. In many places farmland is being abandoned as production costs rise and profits diminish.

Within the southwestern dairy region are the remnants of the Pennsylvania sheep industry, in Greene and Washington counties, which together have about 25 percent of the state's sheep. The remainder are widely scattered throughout the state. Merino sheep were imported into the region in the early 1800s. Because general farming could not compete with other areas in the state and with the Midwest, sheep provided the hill farmers with a source of income. Sheep thrived on the grass-covered hills, and the value of the wool made it possible to absorb the high cost of transportation from the isolated farms. Sheep raising required little labor, and the sparsely populated area could support the industry. The wool of the area commanded a high price as the flocks were maintained with high-grade breeding stock.

In spite of many favorable factors, however, the sheep industry has long been in decline in the region. The growth of the mining industry, with its higher-paying jobs, has attracted many farmers away from sheep raising. In recent years the number of sheep-killing dogs have increased, cutting into the farmer's profits. The demand for wool has also decreased as synthetic fibers have grown in importance. Finally, the availability of lower-priced wool from other areas of the world makes wool production in

Dairy cows graze on an Oakdale, Pennsylvania, farm. Photo by Jack Wolf

southwestern Pennsylvania less and less competitive. The specialized sheep farms may soon disappear from Pennsylvania.

Above: *This dairy farm with cornfield is located in Greene County. Photo by Jack Wolf*

Opposite: *Pennsylvania's milk processing plants provide the consumer with milk in plastic bottles or paper cartons. Photos © 1982 Tom Weigand, Inc.*

MARKET STRUCTURE

The milk produced on Pennsylvania dairy farms is transported from farms to processing plants by bulk tank trucks. Ninety-eight percent of the milk meets the sanitary requirements for fluid consumption. Most of the fluid milk that does not meet these standards comes from farmers such as the Amish whose religious doctrines prohibit the use of modern technology on the farms. These farmers sell their milk at a reduced price to cheese factories. Besides the sanitation problem, Amish farmers have consistently refused to allow milk to be picked up by trucks on Sunday. Many firms agree to pick up the Sunday milk on Monday morning if proper cooling and storage are assured. Larger firms, however, do not want this type of uneven delivery and refuse to buy milk produced by the

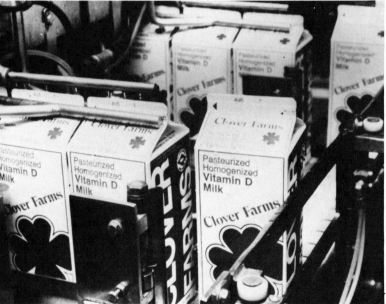

Amish.

Most of the milk produced in Pennsylvania comes from family-operated farms, and at least twenty-four dairy cooperatives operate in the state. Most of the milk that is marketed moves through the major regional cooperatives, which assemble milk from large areas.

Home delivery of milk has virtually disappeared in the past thirty years. Supermarket chains and convenience stores are playing a more significant role in marketing milk. The large chains use centralized plants to supply their stores. Because shopping is not uniformly distributed throughout the week and dairy cows produce a daily uniform supply, there are some distribution problems. Some milk is stored in tanks, but at times milk must be sold to manufacturing plants. Cooperatives attempt to coordinate the supply.

In the 1950s a new marketing strategy developed as dairy farmers began selling milk directly to customers from their own farm stores. These operations became known as "juggers." Relatively wide margins existed between the price paid to farmers for milk and the price of milk in the retail market. Although the price of milk is controlled by the Pennsylvania Milk Marketing Board, an exception to the milk-marketing law allows a dairy farmer to sell milk directly to the consumer and escape price regulations as long as the milk comes exclusively from the farmer's own dairy herd. By the late 1970s it was estimated that about 280 dairy farmers had established farm stores.

In the 1980s there has been a decrease in jug sales. A number of factors seem to have played a role in this decline. First, the margin between the price paid producers for milk and the retail price has declined, reducing the profit margin of the juggers. Second, many juggers purchased dairy-plant equipment from small milk plants that were closing down. Many of these plants are old and outdated, and farmers have decided it is not worth replacing the equipment to continue jugging operations. Finally, the high cost of gasoline makes it unattractive for city dwellers to drive long distances to farm stores to purchase a single low-cost item. Although juggers are only a small part of the total milk market, they sometimes play an important role in local markets.

MILK PRICING

The price of milk is strongly influenced by the federal price-support program, by federal milk-marketing orders, and within the state by the Pennsylvania Milk Marketing Board.

Under the federal price-support program, the U.S. Secretary of Agriculture is required to set a support price for commercial-grade milk. Since 1973 the law requires that the minimum price be set at 80 percent of parity. To implement this law, the Commodity Credit Corporation purchases certain dairy products at prices calculated to generate the desired price for milk on the farm. The products purchased include cheese, butter, and nonfat dry milk powder. These products are sold back into commercial channels or given to people on welfare programs.

The dairy price-control program has a number of unique features. First, there have never been any direct production controls similar to those for wheat, cotton, and other crops. Second, the government does not buy milk but rather the products of milk. Although these products can be stored for short periods, they differ greatly from grains and cotton in their long-term storage and transportation requirements. When dairy products are purchased, the government depends on market competition to benefit the dairy farmer.

The federal government also controls milk prices through the federal milk-marketing order program. Under this program the price of milk is determined according to the way it will be used. The market revenues are then "pooled," and payments are made to farmers at the blend prices. The price of Pennsylvania milk is determined by three federal orders: 36 (Eastern Ohio/Western Pennsylvania), 4 (Middle Atlantic), and 2 (New York/New Jersey). Of these regional divisions, the Middle Atlantic area takes about 40 percent of Pennsylvania's milk, New York/New Jersey about 33 percent, and Eastern Ohio/Western Pennsylvania only 18 percent. The remainder is regulated exclusively by the Pennsylvania Milk Marketing Board.

The Pennsylvania Milk Marketing Board consists of three members appointed by the governor and approved by the senate. The board regulates prices at wholesale and retail levels for all fluid milk marketed within the state. The state is divided into several marketing regions, each with its own price structure.

PROBLEMS OF THE DAIRY FARMER

A number of problems and issues face the modern dairy farmer. One major issue is the high investment needed to acquire a dairy farm sufficiently large to achieve efficiencies of scale. A farm of seventy-five to a hundred cows now requires an investment of more than $500,000. Investment costs are particularly critical to the new dairy farmer.

Other problems are involved in transferring a viable dairy operation to the next generation. This demands adequate estate planning, which usually requires professional assistance. Partnership agreements between father and son are commonly used in Pennsylvania to transfer dairy operations.

As dairy farms increase in size, there is a growing concern about the availability and skill of hired labor. At the same time operational procedures have become more complex and difficult. Dairy farmers need to develop better personnel-management skills for handling and training hired labor.

The system of records and accounts, an important part of any business, is frequently weak on dairy farms. In the past records were kept in account books, but these traditional methods are giving way to the computer. Today's commercial dairy farms are big business, in amount of investment and financial transactions, demanding higher levels of business-management skills.

In a time of rising prices, keeping costs under control remains a constant problem. The U.S. index of prices paid by farmers for production items, interest, taxes, and wages in 1979 was 2.6 times that of 1967. In recent years the escalating costs of energy have presented serious financial problems.

The continually changing market situation is a constant concern. Within the market structure, cooperatives play a significant role. Increased transportation costs present both advantages and problems, as milk located near a market becomes more valuable than milk from a more distant source. The distance between farm and processing plant may be critical to the ultimate profit of the dairy farm.

A long-discussed issue is whether milk prices should be maintained by parity measures or other means. Critics of parity pricing argue that there is no logic for maintaining the relationship of prices received and prices paid over a period that began in 1910. This system may inhibit change necessary for a modern industry. One group of farmers would prefer the use of "target prices" based on the current cost of producing milk. Another alternative would be a direct-payment system under which dairy farmers would receive an income supplement if the market price of milk fell below a predetermined target level. A third option is to impose controls on supply through production and marketing quotas. Another possibility is a "hybrid" program that combines direct payment and supply control. Finally, some farmers would like to see the entire federal and state price-support system dismantled and let prices be determined in the marketplace.

THE POULTRY INDUSTRY

Pennsylvania is one of the leading poultry-producing states in the nation. With 18 million chickens producing 4.7 billion eggs annually, the state ranks fourth in the United States, exceeded only by Georgia, California, and Arkansas. Annual commercial broiler production is between 100 and 115 million, placing the state eleventh in the nation. The total live weight of chickens sold from the commercial farms each year varies from 450 to 470 million pounds. The gross income from broilers is about $120 million. Another 80 million laying chickens are sold annually, for a value of $13 million. Pennsylvania commercial hatcheries produce more than 150 million chicks annually. The gross annual sale of poultry from Pennsylvania farms

The poultry industry is concentrated in southeastern Pennsylvania. Lancaster County is the center of the industry with about 45 percent of the state's 23,800,000 chickens. Prepared by the Deasy Laboratory of Geographics, Dept. of Geography, The Pennsylvania State University

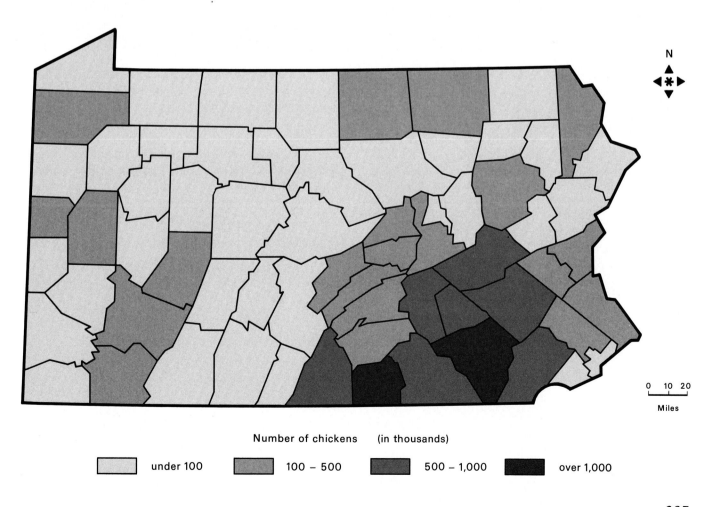

N

Number of chickens   (in thousands)

under 100   100 – 500   500 – 1,000   over 1,000

Above: *Specialized turkey farms have been developed in Pennsylvania to satisfy the large urban market of the East. Photo by E. Willard Miller*

Opposite: *A young girl washes eggs to be sold at the Tri-county Farmers' Cooperative Market at DuBois. This Jack Delano photo was shot in Falls Creek, Pennsylvania, in 1940. From the U.S. Dept. of Agriculture FSA Collection, Library of Congress*

Chickens, which occupy little space on a farm, provide the dairy farmer with a major supplemental income. Photo © 1982 Tom Weigand, Inc.

is about $450 million.

Although every county in the state produces chickens, the major producers are also the leading dairy-farming counties. Of a total of 23,800,000 chickens in the state, Lancaster County has 10,555,000, or about 45 percent. Other major poultry counties are Bradford, Wayne, Dauphin, Perry, Schuylkill, Adams, Cumberland, Franklin, York, Berks, Chester, Lebanon, and Montgomery, each of which has a chicken population of more than 300,000. Together these fourteen counties have about 83 percent of the chickens in the state.

Chickens are produced in two types of farming systems. One is as an adjunct to dairy farming. Chickens provide a major supplementary income on dairy farms. They fit into the farming system in that corn is a major feed for both dairy cattle and chickens. Chickens occupy little space, leaving the land for the cattle.

Further, the market for milk is the same as the one for eggs.

The second type of poultry farming, which is becoming increasingly important, is the specialized commercial chicken farm producing thousands of broilers and/or eggs. These highly mechanized operations, in many ways resembling factory production, are best developed near the great urban markets of eastern Pennsylvania and adjacent states. They occupy little space. The chicken feeds are not produced on the farm but are purchased from the lowest-cost sources. Large trucks deliver the eggs and broilers each day to the nearby markets.

The poultry industry of Pennsylvania and adjacent states experienced a major problem late in 1983 when avian influenza was confirmed in forty-six hen (layer) and broiler flocks in Lancaster County. The disease is characterized by high mortality in broilers and great reduction in egg production in layers. The cause of the disease is a virus that originates from respiratory exudates and feces. The disease is spread when equipment, coops, vehicles, and people are contaminated with exudates and feces. Medication and vaccination of flocks were found to be of no value. Quarantining the areas of the disease was the only means found to prevent its spread. Within the areas of the disease, extreme precautions were instituted to prevent its spread. Clean-out crews had to remove their clothing before leaving poultry farms, and trucks could not visit poultry farms if they had recently been in an avian-flu area. The only means of controlling the avian virus once it had infected a flock was to kill the chickens. In spite of all precautions, in the eleven months the disease existed about nine million chickens were destroyed in Pennsylvania alone, and more than seventeen million in 452 flocks all together in Pennsylvania, Virginia, and adjacent states. Federal indemnities totaled $41.9 million, plus an additional $22.6 million in federal support costs, for a total cost of $64.5 million. On May 29, 1985, avian influenza was officially declared eradicated from the United States by U.S. Department of Agriculture animal-health officials. However, in

Above: *This picture of shocked corn in Centre County was taken in the 1940s before the use of modern corn pickers. Corn is now harvested mechanically in the late fall after the ears are dried in the field. Prior to this, each individual stock of corn was cut by hand, shocked in the field for the corn to dry, and each ear was shucked individually. Mechanization has shortened a very laborious process of harvesting corn. Photo by E. Willard Miller*

Opposite page, top: *Getting ready for winter in Cumberland County still means storing corn in wire silos for cattle. Courtesy, Pennsylvania Bureau of Travel Development*

Bottom: *This Lancaster County cornfield was photographed in 1938 by Sheldon Dick. From the U.S. Dept. of Agriculture FSA Collection, Library of Congress*

January 1986 avion influenza once again was reported in eastern Pennsylvania, and in this single month 250,000 chickens were destroyed. Strict measures are being applied to control the spread of the disease and lessen the damage to the poultry industry. The trends in field crops in Pennsylvania reflect the evolution from general farming to concentration in the dairy and poultry industries. Patterns of production have changed, with animal-feed crops dominating and cash-crop production experiencing a notable decline. Although field-crop production in Pennsylvania ranks low among the states, most Pennsylvania farms produce some field crops. On most farms from 60 to 80 percent of the feed grains, 85 percent of the hay and alfalfa,

and more than 90 percent of the corn silage are consumed by animals on the farm where they are produced. Wheat, rye, and soybeans are grown mainly as cash crops.

CORN

Of the grains grown on Pennsylvania farms, corn occupies a premier position. Although the acreage devoted to corn has decreased from about 1.5 million acres in 1920 to about 1.2 million acres today, the average yield per acre has increased from forty-five to ninety-five bushels. As a result annual production has increased from about 65 million to more than 110 million bushels. Corn now occupies between 35 and 40 percent of the cropland devoted to field crops.

With the development of the dairy industry and the need for livestock feed, corn consumption has grown rapidly. In addition to the acreage of corn grown for grain, more than 400,000 acres produce silage. While grain-corn yield may vary considerably due to such factors as

drought or frosts, silage production remains relatively stable.

The stability of corn-silage production reflects the importance of silage in the dairy farmer's feeding program. Farmers will normally produce the maximum corn silage their silos will hold; when the silos are filled, the remaining corn is harvested as grain. Because corn si-

lage is bulky, relatively low-cost, and expensive to transport, it must be grown locally and stored close to the feeding stalls. If the corn yield varies, the farmer can sell the excess grain, as there is a national market for corn.

HAY CROPS
Hay crops occupy the largest crop acreage in Pennsylvania—about 45 percent of the total farmland. There crops consist of alfalfa, alfalfa-grass mixtures, and other legume-grass mixtures.

In the twentieth century there has been a very significant shift to alfalfa and a decline in grass acreage. Alfalfa did not become an important hay crop until about 1930, when 99,000 acres were produced in the state. Production increased rapidly to about 850,000 acres by 1970 and has remained nearly stable since then. In contrast, grasses reached their peak importance about 1890, when 3,250,000 acres were in production, but have gradually declined to about 1,130,000 acres in 1985.

The increase in acreage of alfalfa is due to its higher yield. Between 1948 and 1978 alfalfa yields averaged 42 percent higher than other hay yields. In addition, alfalfa normally has a higher protein content and sometimes a higher energy content than other hay. Acreage and

yield changes have increased alfalfa production between 1948 and 1978 two and a half times while other hay production has decreased almost one-third.

Because of the yield and quality advantages of alfalfa over other hay crops, it may seem surprising that its acreage has remained stable. A number of factors have prevented further expansion. First, alfalfa has much higher costs of production than other legume-grass mixtures. It requires more machinery use, expert management, and labor because of the large number of cuttings. Second, and also a crucial factor, alfalfa production generally requires more fertile and better drained land than other legumes. In Pennsylvania the amount of land on which alfalfa can grow effectively is limited, and alfalfa must compete with grains, particularly corn, for these good lands.

WHEAT
During the nineteenth century Pennsylvania was one of the major wheat-producing states. Since then there has been a steady decrease in acreage, from a peak of 1,475,000 acres in 1900 to less than 250,000 acres in recent years. Annual output is now about 8 million bushels. Several factors are responsible for the decline in wheat production. Competition from producers in the Midwest and Great Plains placed Pennsylvania at a cost disadvantage. Possibly more important was the need to produce crops, such as corn, for the dairy industry. Corn is a superior feed for livestock and chickens compared to wheat, and it has a higher yield per acre than wheat. Wheat is essentially a cash crop.

In the nineteenth-century diversified cropping system, wheat played an important role in crop rotation. Since crop rotation has declined, there is a reduced need for small-grain nurse crops. Most farmers now seed alfalfa and other hays directly on prepared fields. Use of no-till methods to plant hay crops is also increasing.

As the production of wheat has declined, the availability of straw has also declined. As a result straw prices have increased relative to corn and hay, and the comparative position of wheat

Above: A migratory thresher moved from farm to farm to thresh wheat and other grains until the World War II period. Photo by E. Willard Miller

Opposite page: *A stockpile of corn stands ready to be consumed by the livestock living on this Strasburg, Pennsylvania, farm. Photo by Arnold J. Kaplan/Berg & Associates*

has improved slightly. This factor is relatively insignificant, however, as straw has been replaced for bedding on many farms by chopped cornstalks or rubber mats.

OATS

Although oats are a feed crop similar to corn, its acreage has declined consistently over the past century, from 1,310,000 acres in 1890 to about 300,000 acres in recent years. Yield per acre has increased from about 25 to nearly 60 bushels, so that total production has experienced a much less drastic decline. Annual production varies from 16 to 20 million bushels.

As a livestock and poultry feed crop, oats has to compete for land with corn. The average yield per acre of oats, by weight, is about one-third less than for corn. Oats has its best chance of competing with corn on the poorer, more acidic upland soils where corn yields are the lowest. Because oats has a higher protein value than corn, many horse owners prefer to feed oats. Some farmers will continue to produce some oats because they need straw, and some farmers use oats as a nurse crop in establishing a field of alfalfa and hay.

BARLEY AND RYE

Barley is a minor grain crop in Pennsylvania because the cold winters in northern and western Pennsylvania destroy the crop for many years. Even in southern Pennsylvania winterkill can occur. In recent years about 125,000 acres have been planted, producing about 6 million bushels of grain. When winterkill does not occur, barley provides an excellent livestock feed crop, and the straw is an additional bonus. Barley also thrives on poorer soils than corn. With a slowly declining acreage, however, barley is of little importance to the farm economy of the state.

In the 1800s rye was an important farm crop in Pennsylvania, with acreage sometimes exceeding that of oats. Total acreage is now less than 20,000, and production is 650,000 bushels. Because rye is neither a competitive feed crop nor a profitable cash crop, it has essentially disappeared from Pennsylvania farms.

Right: Feed corn is a leading Pennsylvania agricultural product. Photo © 1982 Tom Weigand, Inc.

Far right: Pennsylvania's annual wheat output numbers about 8 million bushels. Photo © 1982 Tom Weigand, Inc.

Below, right: A view of the beautiful and wealthy rural community of Ligonier, home to Arnold Palmer, appears here. Photo by Jack Wolf

SOYBEANS

Soybeans are a relatively new crop in Pennsylvania. The first soybeans were grown in the early 1930s, but the crop was not widely accepted for many years. Gradually the acreage increased, from about 16,000 in 1965 to 175,000 in 1984, while the yield per acre has increased from about 20 bushels to more than 30. There is little indication that soybeans will become a major crop in Pennsylvania. The proportion of livestock to cropland in Pennsylvania is large, and farmers usually find it more profitable to use cropland for feed production than for cash crops such as soybeans. Another limiting factor is that soybeans must compete with both corn and alfalfa for the more valuable agriculture lands.

SPECIALIZED AGRICULTURAL REGIONS

A number of small areas have developed specialty agricultural products within the dairy regions of Pennsylvania. These regions exist because of a unique physical environment combined with excellent market conditions. In these areas specialty crops provide from one-third to one-half of the total farm income.

MUSHROOM CULTURE

The mushroom industry of Pennsylvania is concentrated in Chester County in the vicinity of Kennett Square and West Chester. In this

small area 70 to 80 percent of the mushroom crop of the nation is produced. Mushroom culture was introduced from France in the early 1900s. It was a gourmet food that was first accepted by the wealthy who lived in the suburban "Mainline" of Philadelphia. A few farmers developed mushroom culture as an income supplement to the dairy industry.

As a taste for mushrooms developed, the Chester County area was well suited to serve the expanding market. There is no climatic or soil requirement for growing mushrooms. Originally the season was from October to May. During the summer the growing sheds become too warm. With air conditioning the temperature is controlled in the sheds, and the growing season now extends throughout the year. Horse manure from the Philadelphia area provided the original soil base for mushrooms. This material has now been replaced by cooked grains. Because mushrooms are highly perishable, the nearby Eastern Seaboard provided the major market area. With the development of refrigeration and fast express trucks, however, the mushrooms are now marketed nationwide. The industry has developed so significantly that it is now a specialty farming endeavor not associated with other farming activities.

Mushroom culture occupies little space. In southern Chester County clusters of long windowless mushroom sheds extend side by side under a continuous roof. Each of the sheds has its own gable, along which runs a ventilator. These sheds provide a distinct appearance in the region. Mushroom production is a labor-intensive industry, as the crop must be harvested daily. The mushrooms are graded by size, and the fresh mushrooms are marketed within a few hours. Once the mushrooms were only marketed fresh, but in recent years a significant percentage of the crop is canned.

As the mushroom market has grown, the structure of the industry has changed. Originally the mushrooms were marketed by the mushroom farmers themselves. Next came the small companies with regional markets. In recent years large companies have developed a national market for both fresh and canned mushrooms, and these giants now dominate the industry. For decades, when only the fresh product was sold, the region had no competition from foreign sources. Since the late 1970s foreign competition, particularly from China, has developed for canned mushrooms. As a consequence the Pennsylvania industry has been depressed, with output declining from an

Above: *Mushrooms, which are harvested daily, are then graded and marketed within a few hours. Photo © 1982 Tom Weigand, Inc.*

Opposite page: *Sulky driver Del Miller owns this horse farm in western Pennsylvania. Photo by Jack Wolf*

all-time high of $158,138,000 in 1980 to less than $140,000,000 in the mid-1980s.

Mushrooms are produced in a few other places in the state. The caves near West Winfield, Butler County, and in a few abandoned coal mines in western Pennsylvania are small centers of production serving a regional market in the western portion of the state.

SOUTH MOUNTAIN FRUIT REGION

In the foothills of South Mountain in Adams, Cumberland, and Franklin counties lies the most important apple-producing district of the state. It is an extension of the Great Valley apple-growing belt of Maryland, Virginia, and West Virginia.

Fruit orchards began as a supplement to general farming after 1870, supplying the farmers with fruit and also serving a small local market. As late as 1900 Franklin County ranked as only the nineteenth most important county in the state in apple production, and Adams County was not even among the top twenty-five. Commercial orchards were virtually non-existent in the South Mountain area. Early in the twentieth century, however, rapid changes occurred in fruit production because of the growing demand for fruits in the eastern cities and the development of rapid railroad transportation.

The development of the fruit industry is thus a response to a desirable physical environment and a nearby major market. The commercial orchards are planted in the foothills of South Mountain on sites with sufficient slope for good air drainage, to protect against late spring frosts. This same type of site provides excellent water-drainage conditions, a prerequisite for fruit growing. Most fruit orchards are planted at elevations of 600 to 800 feet, but a few are found as high as 1,000 feet. The soils of the foothills are also favorable to fruit production, with gravelly loams that are deep and well drained. A limiting factor is the steepness of the slopes, making plowing to control weed growth difficult and causing problems of slope wash.

Originally many orchards were planted near

railroads, since carload shipments were the rule and railroads were the only means of transportation. The eastern slopes of South Mountain possessed a transportation advantage in reaching the eastern markets, so that the industry had its greatest concentration in Adams County. This concentration continues, although trucks have replaced railroads in transporting the fruit to market. The change in transportation, which occurred in the 1930s, greatly affected the type of apple grown, as the apples were no longer packed in barrels but in basket containers. This permitted a diversification in apple varieties. Varieties produced today include Delicious, Mackintosh, Rome, York Imperial, and Galia. Besides apples, other fruits have grown in importance, including pears, plums, cherries, and especially peaches. Within the area it is said, "From Jacks Mountain to York Springs the apple is king and the peach is queen."

Because of the growing market, the orchards have increased greatly in size, and many today are more than 100 acres in size. As a result general farming and dairying have declined in importance. A number of towns have developed as marketing centers, including Biglerville, Bendersville, Gardners, Guernsey, and Orrtanna in Adams County; Longsdorf, Boiling Springs, and Bowmansdale in Cumberland County; and Quincy, Fayetteville, Scotland, and Mont Alto in Franklin County.

With the rapid growth of the apple industry, production exceeded the fresh-market demands. In the 1930s about one-half of the apple crop was canned or made into cider, vinegar, and other apple products. As the fresh-fruit market has expanded and quality control has reduced the culls and low-grade apples, the processing industry has declined. In Adams County the number of workers in processing plants has declined from 1,446 in 1970 to 997 in 1983.

This district is one of the major tourist areas of the state during the apple-blossoming time, when the hills are covered with a canopy of pink. Apple-blossom festivals have become a major attraction for the East Coast traveler. Because the orchards are planted at varying

Above and opposite, top: *The varieties of apples grown in the state include Delicious, Mackintosh, Rome, York Imperial, and Galia. Photos © 1980, 1981 Tom Weigand, Inc.*

Right: *Many fruit farms on the Erie Lake plain sell their produce from markets along the highways. The high quality of the fruit fresh off the farms provides the incentive for urban dwellers to seek these roadside stands. Photo by E. Willard Miller*

elevations, the blossoming is extended over several weeks. In late summer and early fall, fruit stands attract the visitor who wants to purchase fresh fruit directly from the orchards.

LAKE ERIE FRUIT AND TRUCK-FARM REGION

The Lake Erie fruit and truck-farm region is part of a larger area that extends from Buffalo to Toledo along the shores of Lake Erie. The Pennsylvania portion is particularly noted for its grape vineyards, concentrated in the two distinct areas of Girard and North East. These two areas produce about 85 percent of the state's grape output. Besides grapes, the Lake Plain has orchards of apples, cherries, peaches, plums, and other fruits. A wide variety of vegetables are grown, including tomatoes, cabbage, sweet corn, and potatoes.

The physical environment is most favorable for the production of fruits and vegetables. Lake Erie has a notable influence on the climatic regime of the shore. In spring the cool water retards the blossoming of fruit trees and vineyards until danger of frost is past. In autumn, the warm lake waters delay the first frost until about October 31. The long growing season is especially favorable to grape production, for it ensures the development of a high sugar content making the grapes particularly desirable for juice.

Grape production is a year-round industry. In the autumn after the first hard frost, the bare vines are pruned. In early spring, when the freezing and thawing of winter have passed, the stakes supporting the trellises are driven firmly into the ground, and the wires supporting the new growth are stretched anew. As the vine grows, it is tied to the wire by twine. The vineyards are fertilized several times during the growing season, and the ground between the rows of grapes is shallow-plowed to control weed growth. During the summer the grape vines must be sprayed to control insects and blight. Grapes are harvested by machine if they are to be used for juice and jellies. If the grapes are to be sold fresh, a special grape shears is used to cut each cluster from the vine. Government inspectors examine and grade all grapes.

More than 95 percent of the grapes grown are of the Concord variety; Niagara, Worden,

Below: *Pumpkins, among the state's varied field crops, are harvested in the fall. Photo © 1982 Tom Weigand, Inc.*

Bottom: *The Erie Lake plain is the leading grape-producing region in Pennsylvania. The cool lake water in spring retards budding of the vines, and the warm lake water in fall provides nearly a 200-day frost-free growing season. Photo by E. Willard Miller*

Right: *The farmer working his fields may become a rare sight as residential, commercial, and industrial activities encroach on the country's farmland. Photo by Allied Pix Service, Inc.*

Below: *The contour plowing of fields in Pennsylvania transforms the agricultural landscape into a verdant mosaic when viewed from the air. Photo © 1982 Tom Weigand, Inc.*

Golden fields provide the foreground for this central Pennsylvania farm scene. Photo by Allied Pix Service, Inc.

and other types are of very limited importance, chiefly for local use. Though some of the grapes are marketed as table grapes, most of the crop is used for juice. The Welsh Company purchases most of the grapes produced. The emphasis on juice production has greatly retarded the development of a local wine industry.

Next to grapes, cherries and apples are the most important fruits. The region has long been noted for producing several tons of Maraschino cherries from its red sour cherry crop. This specialized industry has long experienced competition from foreign imports, but superior quality has maintained the industry. The most important vegetable crop is cabbage, and Erie outranks all other counties in the state in this crop. Tomatoes are grown chiefly for juice. Besides fruits and vegetables for processing, there is a considerable local and regional market for fresh produce. The region is also noted for its dairy and poultry products.

The fruit and vegetable industries of the Lake Plain are labor-intensive, and migrant workers—mainly Puerto Ricans and Mexicans—are a fundamental part of the labor supply during the intense harvesting period. Many of the farms have buildings to house the migrant workers during their several weeks' stay each year.

DECLINING AGRICULTURAL LAND USE

Agricultural land use in Pennsylvania has changed over the years, principally because of declining productivity and competing land uses.

In the nineteenth century large areas of rugged, low-productivity land were cleared. These rugged areas with their thin acidic soils were not only environmentally poor, but also lacked economic advantages to compete in a commercial system. In the dairy and poultry industries, the products are sold off the farm, often to

markets hundreds of miles away. As population was sparse in the rugged regions, local markets were meager. Transportation facilities in these areas were poorly developed, so that wider markets remained inaccessible. Further, as the fertility of these areas diminished, crop yields were lowered and income declined. Land abandonment in some of these areas began in the 1880s and 1890s. The rugged lands of the Appalachian Plateau, especially the Allegheny Mountain section of central Pennsylvania and the dissected High Plateaus of northern Pennsylvania, have large tracts of abandoned farmland. Much of the land has reverted to brush, and in places a second or even third growth forest has evolved.

Large tracts of farmland in the state are being lost to agriculture as residential, commercial, and industrial activities seek rural sites. In the past fifty years, suburbanization has been one of the great cultural forces in America. A countrified city environment has developed, particularly in southeastern Pennsylvania. As suburbanization occurs, land values increase, and agriculture can no longer compete. Farmland is sold for other purposes, and agriculture disappears. The process of land conversion has become so rapid that there is grave concern that the farm economy will be irreparably damaged. Legislative action is now being considered to protect the best farmland in the state.

The mining industry has also affected agricultural land in specific areas of the state. Although underground mining may produce great piles of debris, the area covered is small. Surface strip-mining covers broad areas and also affects adjacent land. There was little reclamation of stripped areas until recent years, and large tracts of unproductive land remain as an unwanted heritage from the past.

As a result of these physical and economic forces, the acreage of farmland in Pennsylvania has declined from a maximum of 19,791,000 acres in 1880 to a present-day low of about 8,000,000. Croplands have experienced corresponding declines, from 13,423,000 acres to about 4,300,000. Each year more agricultural land goes out of production.

Chapter Ten

Manufacturing in a Mature Economy

In the nineteenth and early twentieth centuries, the growth of manufacturing played a dominant role in the expanding economy of Pennsylvania. Between 1900 and 1919 manufacturing employment grew from about 660,000 to an initial peak of 1,135,000, then remained essentially stable throughout the 1920s. In the economic depression of the 1930s employment in manufacturing declined to about 850,000, but during World War II it increased sharply to

more than 1.4 million. Manufacturing employment in Pennsylvania peaked in the mid- to late 1960s at more than 1.5 million, a level it maintained throughout most of the 1970s. In the late 1970s employment began to decline, and by 1985 more than 500,000 manufacturing jobs had been lost in the state.

Although employment is declining, Pennsylvania remains a major manufacturing state. Pennsylvania ranks sixth in the nation in output of manufactured goods, exceeded only by California, Texas, Illinois, Ohio, and New York. In 1982 the state produced manufactured goods valued at $103 billion, consuming $56.5 billion worth of raw materials and generating a total payroll of $23.3 billion.

The factors that attracted industry to a region in the nineteenth century, such as local fuels and markets, have been dramatically altered in the twentieth century.

A major factor in the development of industry in Pennsylvania was the availability of low-cost energy from bituminous coal. Nineteenth-century industry was characterized by high energy consumption. The smoky environment was a sign of prosperity, and many of the industries with their extravagant consumption of energy were known as "smokestack" industries. As fuel costs have risen in the twentieth century, plants have become more energy-efficient, and total consumption of energy has declined. For example, the consumption of coal in the processing of a ton of iron ore has declined from about two tons to one ton. Fuels can be imported from distant sources, and the local availabili-

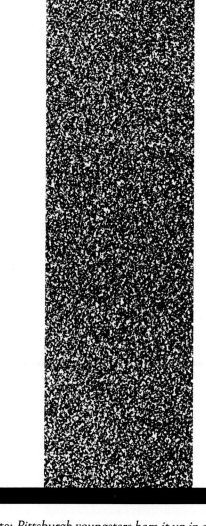

Opposite: *Pittsburgh youngsters ham it up in a homemade swimming pool in 1938, while a billboard advertising Iron City Beer looms in the background. Photo by Arthur Rothstein. From* The Depression Years, *Dover, 1978*

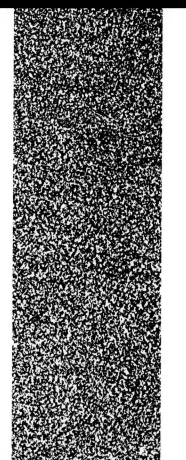

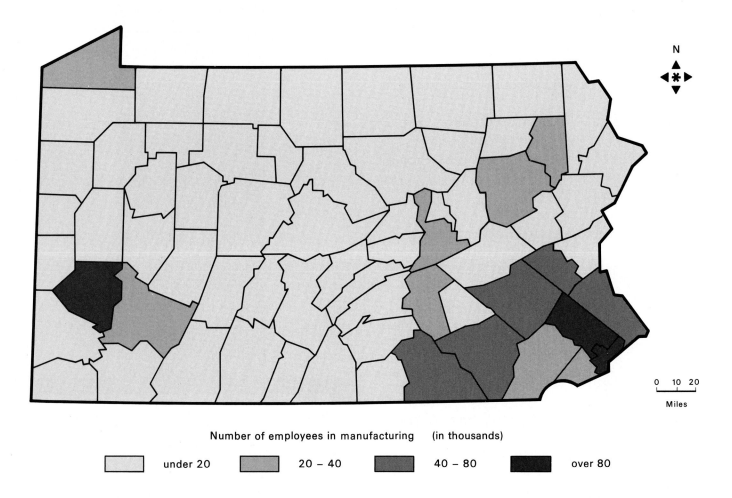

Number of employees in manufacturing   (in thousands)

under 20   20 – 40   40 – 80   over 80

Employment in manufacturing is concentrated in south-eastern and southwestern Pennsylvania with Philadelphia and Allegheny counties as the dominant centers. Prepared by the Deasy Laboratory of Geographics, Dept. of Geography, The Pennsylvania State University

ty of fuel is no longer important in the choice of a manufacturing site. It would be difficult to find a single manufacturing company that has developed in Pennsylvania in the past quarter-century specifically because of local power sources.

Nineteenth-century industry was labor-intensive. Industry was at a much lower techno-logical level, and unskilled and semiskilled work-ers performed numerous industrial tasks. The growing population of Pennsylvania, supple-mented by vast numbers of immigrants, pro-vided a pool of low-cost labor. In the twentieth

century there is a growing efficiency in the use of human labor, and humans have been re-placed by machines in many plant operations. It is now recognized that a robot can produce a better product in many plants than human la-bor. Wages have risen over the decades in the mature industrial regions, and many plants have migrated to the newer industrial areas of the na-tion and the world seeking low-cost labor. A critical factor for the continuance of manufac-turing in Pennsylvania is the growing importa-tion of industrial goods from low-cost labor areas.

A hundred years ago it took only a relatively small amount of capital to start an industry. A limited amount of low-cost equipment was needed, and an industry could thrive with a small output of goods. As industry became in-creasingly complex, more capital was needed, and today high capitalization characterizes most modern industrial plants. Because advances in modern industry are extremely rapid, a large

316

capital investment must be made in research and development to remain competitive. Small firms rarely have these resources and either disappear or are purchased by larger companies if they have a unique product with market potential.

Originally industry was limited to satisfying local and possibly regional markets, and these were important factors in plant location. Cost of transportation was only a minor factor. Because many industries now seek world markets, low-cost transportation is often an important consideration. However, in the nineteenth century much of the industrial output was heavy and bulky, whereas many twentieth-century growth industries, such as electronic equipment and instruments, produce items that are small and extremely costly. These products can withstand the costs of distant transportation.

REGIONAL PATTERNS OF MANUFACTURING

In 1983 about 85 percent of the manufacturing in Pennsylvania was concentrated in twenty-six counties, each of them with 10,000 or more workers employed in manufacturing. Seventeen of these counties—those that developed major industries in the nineteenth century—are now experiencing a decline in manufacturing. The other nine counties have developed industry only in the last half-century, and these are the state's growth regions today.

GROWTH REGIONS
In southeastern Pennsylvania nine counties—Bucks, Chester, Lehigh, Lancaster, Cumberland, Dauphin, Franklin, Montgomery, and York—form the largest region in the state where manufacturing employment has grown. Between 1965 and 1983 total manufacturing employment in these six counties increased from 331,400 to 371,200. Montgomery County—adjacent to Philadelphia, where the largest decrease in manufacturing employment occurred—experienced the greatest growth, with employment rising from 80,200 to 90,700 between 1965 and 1983. In the past quarter-

century this growth belt has gradually moved westward.

The industrial structure of the southeastern Pennsylvania growth region consists of industries that have experienced their greatest growth in the last half-century. The machinery industry has increased its work force in the nine counties from 31,600 in 1965 to 44,400 in 1983. During the same period employment in instruments has grown from 6,700 to 18,800, in electric and electronic equipment from 27,700 to 35,500, and in printing and publishing from 9,700 to 25,900. The industries that experienced great growth in the nineteenth and early twentieth centuries, such as textiles, apparel, paper, chemicals, leather, primary metals (particularly iron and steel), and glass products are of little or no importance in the industrial structure of this region.

A series of factors have encouraged growth in this region. Of the utmost importance has been the migration of skilled labor, including engineers and scientists, to the suburban areas. The availability of relatively low-cost land for industrial plants, including large parking areas for employees, has also been important. The emphasis on high-value-added industries ensures that the final products are competitive in national and world markets. The development of a modern transportation network has been crucial for rapid assembly of raw materials and distribution of finished products. Finally, the development of amenities such as parks, golf courses, riding academies, and recreational centers has provided a gracious living environment.

DECLINING REGIONS
The greatest decline in manufacturing employment in Pennsylvania between 1965 and 1983 was in Philadelphia and Delaware counties, where employment dropped from 316,600 to about 150,000. During the same period employment in manufacturing in Philadelphia and Delaware counties dropped from 40 percent of the state's total employment to about 22 percent. The first industries to decline in Philadelphia and Delaware counties were those that had dominated in the nineteenth century, most

notably the textile and apparel industries. In the past twenty-five years, textile-mill employment has dropped from 19,000 to about 5,700, and the apparel industry has experienced an employment decrease from 45,000 to 17,700. Other older declining industries include paper and printing, tobacco, leather products, fabricated metals, and lumber products. These declining older industries have not yet been replaced by new, twentieth-century industries. In fact every major category of industry (the twenty two-digit Standard Industrial Classifications) has declined in Philadelphia in the past twenty-five years. For example, employment in machinery declined from 29,300 workers in 1960 to 9,600 in the early 1980s; in electrical machinery, from 25,500 to 8,500; and in instruments, from 7,400 to 3,400.

The decline in manufacturing in Philadelphia and Delaware counties is due to a wide range of factors. The nineteenth-century industries such as textiles, apparel, leather, tobacco, paper, and printing have not been able to compete economically with other regions, and plants have either gone out of business or migrated to other regions. The twentieth-century industries such as machinery, electronic and electrical equipment, transportation equipment, and instruments grew until the 1950s but have experienced a decline in the past thirty years. The general economic environment of decline has been caused by many factors including old and antiquated plants for which renovation is too costly, lack of space for new plants, migration of high-quality labor to the suburbs, high wage rates, high cost of land and taxes within the urbanized areas, a high crime rate in the industrial districts, transportation congestion because of an antiquated road system, and a lack of modern amenities such as parks, recreational facilities, and cultural events.

A second major region of declining employment is in southwestern Pennsylvania, centering on Allegheny County (Pittsburgh) and including the surrounding counties of Beaver, Mercer, Washington, and Westmoreland. Employment in manufacturing in these five counties declined from 316,000 in 1965 to 172,100 by 1983. Allegheny County experienced the greatest decline, from 190,000 to 103,000 manufacturing employees. These southwestern counties have long been dominated by the primary metals (iron and steel) and allied industries. Employment in the primary metals declined from 127,800 in 1965 to 42,500 in 1983, and in such allied industries as fabricated metals from 23,100 to 13,600. Other industries with declining employment include food processing, electrical machinery, and stone, clay, and glass products.

A third major area of decline comprises the four counties—Lackawanna, Luzerne, Northumberland, and Schuylkill—that are the heart of the anthracite region. Manufacturing employment in this region declined from 113,247 in 1965 to 83,668 in 1983. The apparel industry, which dominated manufacturing in the region, experienced the greatest decline in employment, from 45,490 to 25,289. Textile-mill products, which experienced their greatest decline before 1960, showed a further drop in employment from 9,343 to 5,521.

A number of isolated counties that had 10,000 or more manufacturing employees in 1983 experienced major declines after 1965. Northampton and Lebanon counties each experienced significant decreases in the iron and steel and apparel industries, with the total number of employees declining from 62,750 to 40,200. In Berks County employment declined from 53,950 in 1965 to 48,100 in 1983 due primarily to a decline in employment in the textile and apparel industries from 13,850 to 8,000. In Lycoming County significant declines in employment occurred in the textile, apparel, furniture, and leather industries, reducing the manufacturing employment total from 18,670 to 14,330. Blair County experienced a modest decline in employment, from 12,460 to 10,525, resulting primarily from decreased employment in food, paper, leather, and fabricated metals. A decrease in manufacturing employment in Erie County, from 38,800 to 34,000, reflected a decline from 15,060 to 9,800 workers in primary metals, fabricated metals, and electric and electronic equipment.

MANUFACTURING IN RURAL PENNSYLVANIA

Of the forty-one counties that had fewer than 10,000 manufacturing employees in 1983, twenty-seven experienced a decline and thirteen an increase in manufacturing employment between 1965 and 1983. Employment changes, whether growth or decline, entailed fewer than 1,000 employees in twenty-three of the counties. In 1965 employment varied from 157 in Pike County to a maximum of 21,448 in Cambria County. By 1983 the range had narrowed, from 242 employees in Forest County to 9,750 in Butler County.

Of the forty-one rural counties, Cambria County experienced the greatest decrease in manufacturing employment, from 21,448 in 1965 to 7,558 in 1983. The greatest gain was in Wyoming County, from 1,060 to 3,700. There was thus a considerable geographical shift in manufacturing employment. In most counties the growth or decline was largely attributable to changes in employment in one or two industries.

Of the thirteen counties that lost more than 1,000 manufacturing jobs, the greatest declines occurred in Cambria, Lawrence, and Butler, where the primary-metal industries decreased in importance. In Armstrong and Fayette counties, the decline in the clay and glass industries was most significant. In Venango, McKean, and Warren counties, the decline of the petroleum industry led to a decline in the machinery industries. The migration of an aircraft company to Florida was a major factor in the loss of employment in Clinton County. In Columbia County employment declined in the textiles industries, and in Cameron County in electric and electronic equipment.

Of the thirteen growth counties, only four gained more than 1,000 manufacturing jobs, and only one, Wyoming, gained more than 2,000. The growth in Wyoming County was due to the establishment of a single paper company. In Centre County the presence of the Pennsylvania State University has provided a scientific and technological environment to attract such high-value-added industries as

instruments, electronics, and glass products. Similarly, in Bradford County the major employment growth occurred in instruments, and in Jefferson County in electric and electronic equipment.

No one type of industry dominates manufacturing in these forty-one primarily rural counties. In some cases the factors that have attracted industry to adjacent urban areas have had "spillover" effects in nearby rural counties, as in the location of primary metals in western Pennsylvania and textile mills in eastern Pennsylvania. In other industries—such as lumber and wood products, pulp, paper, and allied products, and petroleum refining—the impetus for development has been the local availability of resources.

In most counties a given industry is dominated by a single plant. For example, in 1979 one plant employed 3,144 out of a total of 3,772 primary-metal workers in Butler County; one plant employed 1,922 out of 2,348 fabricated-metal workers in Mifflin County; and one paper mill employed 2,556 out of 2,559 workers in that industry in Wyoming County. If employment declines in the major plant, the economic consequences are severe. Although the company town as such has disappeared, the economy of many towns remains tied to a single industry.

Because most rural Pennsylvania counties have only one or two manufacturing centers, a single industry frequently dominates manufacturing in a county. For example, in 1983 the machinery industry accounted for 39 percent of all manufacturing employment in Venango County; electric and electronic equipment for 44 percent of employment in Elk County; and stone, clay, and glass for 44 percent of the employment in Armstrong County. The dominance of a single industry has discouraged the diversification of manufacturing in a number of counties.

Of the factors discouraging industrial growth in rural Pennsylvania, the lack of a labor supply is paramount. The rural Pennsylvania population is small, and scientifically and technically trained workers are in particularly short supply.

In rural Pennsylvania many workers travel fifty miles or more to their place of employment. Many sections of the region are poorly served by transportation facilities. The sparse rural population provides only a limited market, and when products are marketed outside the region, the lack of adequate transportation facilities—both roads and railroads—presents a severe problem. Capital is also limited in rural Pennsylvania, so that outside resources are required to establish a large plant.

The future of manufacturing in rural Pennsylvania is a major issue in the total economy of the state. The economic degeneration of some urban areas has created a need to re-appraise how economic activities might be better distributed. The fundamental importance of manufacturing to the economic stability of a large portion of rural Pennsylvania makes these areas a key element in the total industrial structure. Manufacturing employment has been more stable in rural Pennsylvania than in the urban counties. Nevertheless present-day trends give little indication that major new manufacturing centers will evolve in rural Pennsylvania. Future growth in manufacturing is most likely to occur in those industries that require a limited supply of semiskilled to skilled labor producing products of low bulk and relatively high value that can be marketed nationally.

INDUSTRIAL STRUCTURE

The basic industrial structure of Pennsylvania manufacturing was established in the nineteenth and early twentieth centuries. The major industry in 1920 was primary metals, dominated by iron and steel, with about 20 percent of total employment. Other major industries included textile-mill products, apparel, fabricated metals, and food and kindred products.

The great growth industries of the nineteenth and early twentieth centuries are the ones that have experienced the greatest decline in employment. Primary metals have declined from about 20 percent of total employment to less than 10 percent. In 1983 apparel and kindred products had more employees than any

Farm Security Administration photographer Jack Delano photographed this Croatian steelworker in the hall of the Steel Workers Organizing Committee in Midland, Pennsylvania, not quite a year before the United States entered World War II. From the U.S. Dept. of Agriculture FSA Collection, Library of Congress

other industry in Pennsylvania, with about 11 percent of the total, but were declining rapidly. Other major industries, in order of importance in 1983, were machinery (10 percent), electric and electronic equipment (9 percent), fabricated metals (8.5 percent), food and kindred products (8.4 percent), and printing and publishing (7 percent). These seven industries employed nearly two-thirds of all manufacturing workers in Pennsylvania.

Of the twenty two-digit Standard Industrial Classification industries, thirteen experienced declines in employment greater than 15 percent between 1965 and 1983. Tobacco products showed the greatest decline (85 percent), followed by primary metals (59 percent), leather products (also 59 percent), textile-mill products (45 percent), apparel and related products (40 percent), petroleum and coal products (38 percent), furniture and fixtures (28 percent), stone, clay and glass (26 percent), transportation equipment (25 percent), miscellaneous industries (25 percent), electronic and electrical equipment (21 percent), food and kindred products (19 percent), and fabricated metals (19 percent).

Arthur Rothstein, another FSA photographer who travelled the country documenting the Depression era with his camera, photographed some out-of-work Midland steelworkers playing cards at the Congress of Industrial Organization headquarters in July 1938. From the U.S. Dept. of Agriculture FSA Collection, Library of Congress

TOBACCO PRODUCTS

The tobacco industry today is a mere remnant of its previous importance. Employment has declined from 11,100 in 1965 to about 1,700 in 1983. Two factors are important in the near disappearance of this industry, which was dominated by the production of cigars. First, the production of tobacco in Lancaster County has declined greatly in recent years, thus greatly diminishing the raw-material base. Second, and possibly more important, the traditional cigar-making industry of southeastern Pennsylvania was labor-intensive. The cigars were largely handmade in small factories. As machine production of cigars developed in other states, Pennsylvania's high-cost handmade cigars could not compete. Because the factories were small, there was not sufficient capital to purchase the high-cost cigar-making machinery. Soon cigar making will be an historical industry of Pennsylvania's past.

PRIMARY-METAL INDUSTRIES

The iron and steel industry constitutes about 90 percent of the primary-metal industries of the state. The basic regional centers of this industry were established in the nineteenth century. The greatest of these centers was southwestern Pennsylvania, with the adjacent steel centers of Youngstown and Wheeling. This area produced about 70 percent of the nation's iron and steel early in the twentieth century. Isolated centers of primary iron and steel production also developed at Bethlehem, Steelton, and Morrisville in eastern Pennsylvania.

Since early in the twentieth century, the relative importance in the nation of southwestern Pennsylvania's iron and steel industry has declined. Several factors have favored the decentralization of the U.S. iron and steel industry. Possibly the most important of these was the country's mammoth economic growth. The market increased so greatly that it was no longer feasible to supply the demand for iron and steel from a single region. Major new industrial centers required nearby sources of iron and steel.

As the nationwide market developed, an important technological advance aided the decentralization of the steel industry. Until about 1920 coke for the steel industry was made mostly in beehive ovens, which were localized in the Connellsville region of southwestern Pennsylvania. Between 1910 and 1925, however, the wasteful beehive process was largely replaced by the by-product coke oven. In the beehive oven the only product was about 1,000 pounds of coke per ton of coal. In the by-product oven the yield was about 1,200 pounds of coke, plus 10,000 cubic feet of gas, 7.1 gallons of tar, 2.4 gallons of oil, 20 to 25 pounds of ammonium sulfate, 5 to 6 pounds of liquid ammonia, and a little toluol. Since 1930 beehive ovens have been important producers of coke only during periods of national emergency when by-product ovens could not meet the demand.

The by-product ovens had a number of advantages over the older beehive process. They not only saved the valuable coal tars and gases but made possible a wider distribution of the coke industry. A much greater range of coals could be used, and the coal supply became geographically decentralized. Because the gases from by-product ovens were used to preheat the blast furnaces as well as the plant, these ovens were developed at iron and steel plant sites instead of mine sites, where the beehive ovens were located. It thus became advantageous to transport coal to the market-oriented iron and steel plants.

The market-orientation advantage was enhanced as blast furnaces became more efficient. In the nineteenth century it normally required two tons of coal to smelt one ton of iron ore. Today only about one ton of coal is required to smelt one ton of iron ore. Fuel orientation is thus basically eliminated.

Another factor in decentralization was the alteration of the preferential "Pittsburgh Plus" freight-rate structure. With the rapid growth of the industry, particularly during World War I, it was no longer possible to maintain this artificial rate structure, which was finally declared illegal by the U.S. Supreme Court in 1924. Under the multiple basing-point system that

Right: *In January 1941 this union member distributed copies of* Steel Labor *near the James and Laughlin Steel Company entrance in Aliquippa. Photo by Jack Delano. From the U.S. Dept. of Agriculture FSA Collection, Library of Congress*

Below: *Aliquippa steelworkers leave the plant at the end of an eight-hour day shift in 1938. Photo by Arthur Rothstein. From* The Depression Years, *Dover, 1978*

Left: *The Pittsburgh Mercantile Co., the company store of Jones and Laughlin Steel in Aliquippa, was photographed by John Vachon in January 1941. From the U.S. Dept. of Agriculture FSA Collection, Library of Congress*

Right: *The iron and steel industry, represented by the pouring of molten metal, constitutes about 90 percent of Pennsylvania's primary-metal industries. Photo © 1981 Tom Weigand, Inc.*

Below: *Cornwall, Pennsylvania, is a town built in the nineteenth century at the height of the mining of the Cornwall iron ores. Because the iron ore deposit was large, substantial stone houses were built for the miners. Mining operations were abandoned in 1972 due to flooding of the mines from Hurricane Agnes. The town now exists as a small residential community. Photo by E. Willard Miller*

took its place, a number of centers were established (including Chicago and Birmingham) to serve as regional basing points for freight rates. Prices for iron and steel were quoted in terms of the nearest "government basing point," plus the appropriate charges for transportation and extras. This system in effect established a number of regions within which a plant or group of plants enjoyed a competitive freight advantage. Only when an iron and steel shipment crossed a regional boundary did freight rates increase.

Both the single and multiple basing-point systems were sources of considerable controversy. The major criticism was that the basing-point system provided the basis for geographic price discrimination because it eliminated interregional price competition. After twenty-four years of operation, the multiple basing-point system was also outlawed by the U.S. Supreme Court, and the system was abandoned in 1948.

Since 1948 the price of steel at any destination has been determined by the f.o.b.-mill pricing policy. This system is based on the price of steel plus freight charges from the point of origin to the point of destination. As a result a number of companies in the 1950s built plants in new areas to compete in the steel market. A notable example in Pennsylvania was the new U.S. Steel plant at Morrisville, north of Philadelphia—the first primary iron and steel plant built by this firm on the Atlantic coast. With the abandonment of the regional basing-point system in 1948, the U.S. Steel Corporation found itself at a cost disadvantage in marketing steel in the Atlantic coast region.

Changing sources of raw materials have also had an adverse effect on the Pennsylvania iron and steel industry. Although the original reserve of high-grade iron ore in the Lake Superior ore ranges was enormous, huge demands for more than a century have reduced the supply of high-grade ore, so much so that the industry is facing a depletion problem. Low-grade taconite ores are being mined in the Lake Superior area and enriched before being shipped to the iron and steel plants. As a consequence new

Opposite page: *In the nineteenth and early twentieth centuries beehive ovens produced the coke to fuel the nation's iron and steel industry. The coal was placed in the upper portion of the oven. A fire was then lit beneath the coal. As the coal heated, the hydrocarbon gases escaped from the top of the oven. At the moment the gases were removed from the coal, the process was stopped by pouring water on the hot coals. The nearly pure carbon that remained was the resistant coke used in the blast furnaces to melt iron ore. The beehive ovens near Connellsville operated for a short time during the World War II period of high coke demand. Photo by E. Willard Miller*

Above: *A huge vat of molten steel is poured into a mold at the Jones and Laughlin plant in Pittsburgh in 1942. Courtesy, National Archives*

sources of ore have been developed in Canada, Venezuela, and Brazil. Because these ores enter the United States through port cities, there has been a growing tendency to build new iron and steel plants at such port cities as Baltimore and Houston.

Government policies have also encouraged the decentralization of the American iron and steel industry. Iron and steel plants have been constructed in strategic locations under government subsidies during national emergencies. For example, the Fontana plant east of Los Angeles was built by the U.S. government during World War II to supply steel to West Coast shipyards and other war plants. Pennsylvania secured no government aid during World War II to expand its iron and steel industry.

With the decentralization of the iron and steel industry, the relative position of the Pittsburgh-Youngstown region declined. In 1947 this region produced 39.5 percent of the nation's steel, but by 1969 it was producing only 27.5 percent of the total steel output. The Pittsburgh district had declined from 26.3 to 19.1 percent of the total, and the Youngstown district from 13.2 to 8.4 percent. During the period from 1947 to 1969, the Chicago district maintained a nearly constant relative position, producing about 20 percent of the nation's total. With the decline in importance of the Pittsburgh district, Chicago became the nation's leading steel-producing district in 1960 and has maintained its lead ever since.

The absolute production of steel in the Pittsburgh district actually increased with the major rise in national output from 84.78 million tons in 1947 to 141.24 million tons in 1969. Output of the Pittsburgh district grew from 33.48 million tons to 39.54 million tons, and that of the Youngstown district 11.19 million tons to 11.86 million tons. During the same period, however, steel output in the Chicago district rose from 16.95 million tons to 28.24 million tons.

Beginning in the early 1970s, the challenge to the Pennsylvania iron and steel industry has come not from further decentralization but from increases in foreign imports. The world

iron and steel industry has grown enormously. New overseas plants are more modern than those in Pennsylvania, and indeed most other parts of the United States. Not only can they produce steel at a lower cost, but lower wages add to their vast advantage. Further, in many countries, including Belgium, the United Kingdom, Italy, France, South Africa, Brazil, and many Third World countries, the national government heavily subsidized state-owned mills.

Initially the American steel industry did not consider imports a serious threat to the future of the industry, and little consideration was given to producing cheaper or better steel. Each year thousands of tons of steel sheet were rejected by U.S. automakers. There was no price bargaining between the buyers of steel and the steel companies. Banking on the consumer's willingness to absorb price increases, the companies chose to pass costs on rather than disrupt the pattern of business as usual.

American steel makers generally have not developed new technology, devoting only minimal expenditures to research and development. Meanwhile automakers, the largest consumers of steel, have been seeking to make weight reductions in their automobiles. Having achieved most of the cost-effective weight reductions that are possible through design changes, the auto companies are particularly interested in using thinner, high-strength steel treated for corrosion resistance. Since 1975 General Motors has increased its consumption of galvanized steel by 250 percent, while its use of zincrometal (steel coated with a zinc-rich paint) has increased by 500 percent. These new steels are largely foreign imports.

The high cost of American steel can be attributed largely to the high cost of labor. During the 1970s the steel companies bought labor peace with overgenerous settlements that widened the cost differential with foreign steels. In 1984 steelworkers in the United States earned $22 an hour, including fringe benefits. In contrast, a Japanese steelworker received $12 an hour, a British steelworker $8, and a Korean steelworker $2 an hour. The American steelworker makes considerably more than the average American manufacturing worker—35 percent more in 1970, and a great deal more than that today. If the 1970 differential was restored, the steelworker's wage would be reduced to $16 an hour, still much higher than in foreign countries.

The billions of dollars that went for higher wages were not used to modernize U.S. steel mills. The greatest cost benefits could have been realized by installing more continuous casters, which eliminate two steps in making semifinished slabs ready for the rolling mill and reduce the cost by as much as $80 a ton. In addition continuous-cast steel has a smoother finished surface desired by automobile companies. The United States casts about 25 percent of the steel it produces, while Japan casts about 80 percent of its production. As a result the automobile companies reject a higher proportion of American steel for use in cars. In recent years the Ford Motor Company has rejected 4.5 percent of its American purchases, compared with only 3.5 percent of the sheet steel produced in Europe and only one percent of Japanese steel.

As a response to steel imports, two types of steel industries have developed in the United States. The older integrated mills producing nonspecialty steels have taken the brunt of the import problem. In contrast, smaller plants, known as mini-mills, have flourished and are producing a greater share of the nation's steel. Two decades ago the integrated steel companies, such as U.S. Steel and Bethlehem Steel, had 95 percent of the market for nonspecialty steels. Because of the growth of imports and mini-mill production, they now supply only 22 percent. Most integrated mills are operating at about 60-percent capacity, and most are losing money.

The mini-mills are expanding for a number of reasons. Technologically they are at the forefront of the world's steel industry. The plants are modern, and the nonunion work force earns up to $9 an hour less than members of the United Steelworkers Union. Foreign steel producers cannot compete with steel produced by the mini-mills because mini-mills use scrap

as their sole raw material, and scrap is cheaper in the United States than elsewhere. Combining this advantage with modern plants and simplified work practices that reduce the amount of labor, the mini steel industry is world competitive. The mini-mills, now with about 20 percent of the steel market, have made inroads into the light structural and wire business as well as rods, bars, and even some types of pipe. However, the mini-mills are too small to compete with the high-volume flat rolled products used to produce such products as automobile fenders and tin cans.

In Pennsylvania the Allegheny Ludlum Corporation in Brackenridge is a magnificent example of a company producing specialty steels. Since 1980 it has been the largest specialty-steel producing company in the United States. In its completely modern plant, it has achieved a 35-percent increase in productivity—tons produced per person per hour—within the past five years. Quality control is a top priority of this company, which produces 126 standard grades of stainless steel and 400 variations. When alloys are added to the stainless steels, the number of different steels can total in the thousands. The products of Allegheny Ludlum are marketed throughout the world.

Although there are a number of mini steel companies in Pennsylvania, the industry is still dominated by the traditional integrated companies. As a result the iron and steel industry in Pennsylvania has experienced a significant decline in recent years. Employment in the primary-metals industry, which is about 90 percent iron and steel, has fallen from 241,189 in 1965 to 99,278 in 1983. The future of the industry in Pennsylvania will rest on the integrated companies' closing old plants and abandoning antiquated practices. A recent study by Merrill Lynch notes that high-priced labor inefficiently used accounts for a $150-a-ton difference between the cost of producing steel in a U.S. plant compared to a Japanese integrated mill. The Pennsylvania iron and steel industry is undergoing a period of transition. These changes are part of a global division of labor increasingly taking place in many industries, as product lines are parceled out across international borders.

The decline of the iron and steel industry has had serious repercussions on the economy of cities dominated by this industry. In September 1985 Clairton, a city fifteen miles south of Pittsburgh on the Monongahela River, laid off its entire fourteen-member police force, ten-member fire department, and five members of its clerical staff in the municipal office. Many of the streetlights of the city have been turned off. Since 1980 Clairton's total revenue has dropped from $3.1 million to $2.4 million, even though the city has revised taxes to the legal limit and imposed new or higher service fees. The single reason for this decline is the loss of revenue from the United States Steel Corporation. Between 1983 and 1985 the company's total payments to the city have dropped by 50 percent. In an attempt to balance the books and persuade the banks to renew its line of credit, Clairton has, in the words of one official, "closed the city."

The financial problems of Clairton are common to many towns in an area that has come to be known as the Rust Belt. McKeesport, which has a projected $700,000 operating deficit in 1985, has laid off five police officers and two clerical workers. West Homestead has laid off nine of fourteen employees in its public-works department. With jobs scarce, many residents have moved out of the region, and some cities have become virtual ghost towns. Property values have plummeted. In Clairton homes that sold for $50,000 ten years ago are now on the market for $25,000—and not selling. With the decline in home values, revenue from property taxes also decreases. In Clairton, for example, each tenth of a cent of the real-estate tax raised $28,200 in 1985, compared with $48,000 five years earlier.

The residents of the area have a sense of futility. As one retired steelworker in Clairton put it, "There's no future. It's a dirty, rotten shame. It's been just a wonderful city, just a wonderful city." Barbara Hafer, an Allegheny County commissioner, stated after a tour of the steel towns, "The crunch is on. The police have

always been sacrosanct. If you lose your police, its a bellwether of death." Raymond C. Siniawski, president of the Steel Valley Council of Governments, observes, "Everybody is trying to do more with less. But it's getting more difficult. After you patch potholes for so long, you have to pave the streets. But we can't afford that." Charles W. Bartach, a policy analyst with the Northeast-Northwest Institute, a Washington-based center for economic and environmental research, concludes, "It's a bleak picture. Many of these towns aren't going to make it. They're going to have to go through bankruptcy and let the chips fall where they may."

LEATHER AND LEATHER PRODUCTS

In the eighteenth and nineteenth centuries, the tanning of leather was a major industry in Pennsylvania. During the pioneer period the hides were soaked in a solution of water and bark obtained from oak or chestnut trees. The skins were preserved by the tannic acid contained in the bark. The leather was then finished by making it either dense and firm or soft and pliable, according to the needs of the customers. During the nineteenth century there was little change in the process, except for the substitution of coniferous bark in northern Pennsylvania. The operation, although a simple one, was extremely slow, taking from nine months to a year to complete. The labor was unskilled, except for the boss tanner, who by sight, touch, and smell determined when the skins had turned to leather. The tanneries were small and widely scattered in the forest regions.

The tanning industry has declined greatly in Pennsylvania, and in 1982 only 1,100 employees remained. A number of factors have been responsible. First, the development of tanning concentrates meant that tanneries could be located at the source of the hides rather than near the trees needed for bark. Tanning concentrates are distillates of tannic acid made by cooking the bark at its point of origin. The extract is then shipped in concentrated form to the tanneries, where it is diluted to about 10 percent of its original strength. Second, and more important, was the invention in the 1880s of a tanning material derived from the mineral chrome. This new tanning material replaced the tannic acid from bark in most tanneries. A third factor was the development, at the end of the nineteenth century, of large meat-packing establishments with centralized slaughtering and packing plants. Large-scale tanneries developed at these centers in the Midwest to utilize these centralized sources of hides.

The final factor in the decline of Pennsylvania's tanneries was the formation of large leather companies. The United States Leather Company, organized in 1893, comprised of six companies controlling about 150 establishments. It was the first corporation in the United States with a capitalization in excess of $100 million, and it controlled at the outset about 60 percent of the sole-leather production of the country. In 1899 the American Hide and Leather Company was formed by combining twenty-three companies, and in the early 1900s it controlled about 75 percent of the United States upper-leather output. Both companies consolidated operations by dismantling inefficient plants and transferring production to better-located and better-equipped sites. In the process most of Pennsylvania's tanneries disappeared.

In the twentieth century the making of footwear employs between 75 and 80 percent of the workers in the leather industries. Employment in footwear manufacture in Pennsylvania reached a peak about 1965, when 31,500 workers were employed, declining sharply thereafter to only 11,200 in 1982. Imported shoes have devastated the American industry. Today there is no major region of shoe production in Pennsylvania. In 1982 small shoe factories were found in twenty-nine counties, with Luzerne, Lancaster, York, and Berks the leaders. Pennsylvania produces about $434 million worth of footwear, generating $90 million in annual wages for its production workers.

TEXTILE-MILL PRODUCTS
The textile industry of Pennsylvania was well developed in the nineteenth century, but has experienced a long decline in the twentieth century, along with other states of the Northeast. The decrease in employment has been particularly sharp in recent years, declining from 67,500 workers in 1965 to 37,200 by 1983, while the number of establishments has declined from about 740 to 450. Of these 450 establishments, about 180 have fewer than twenty employees. Nonetheless the industry provided $353 million in wages in 1982, with a total output valued at more than $2.2 million. Knit goods accounted for 55 percent of the total value, synthetic fibers and silk 10 percent, and carpet and rugs 9 percent.

The industry is concentrated in a few counties. In 1965 the six leading counties—Philadelphia, Berks, Montgomery, Luzerne, Lackawanna, and Schuylkill—had 57 percent of the state's textile-mill employment. In 1983 these six counties remained the leaders but had only 43 percent of total textile-mill employment. Philadelphia, the leading county, has experienced the greatest decline in employment, from 17,700 in 1965 to 5,700 in 1983. Employment in the six counties declined from 38,900 to 16,200 between 1965 and 1983.

The textile industry is traditionally migratory, always seeking areas of lower-cost production. The first textile industry in the United States was localized in the Northeast. In the late nineteenth century, however, the industry began to develop in the Piedmont region of North and South Carolina and Georgia. One commonly cited reason for the migration southward is that the industry was seeking the source of its raw material. In the early twentieth century the access to cotton, lowering transportation costs of raw materials, did give an advantage to the Piedmont mills. As the industry grew, however, local cotton sources were no longer adequate. A large percentage of the cotton is now imported into the Piedmont from the Mississippi lowlands and as far away as western Texas. The transportation-cost advantage has disappeared.

In the past few decades, natural raw materials have declined greatly in importance in favor

The textile industry, one of the first industries to develop during the colonial period, was widely distributed throughout eastern Pennsylvania by the nineteenth century. In the anthracite region the wives and daughters of the coal miners provided the dominant supply of labor for the textile industry. This knitting mill in the southern anthracite field in Pottsville was typical of textile plants built in the nineteenth century. The plants were located in urban residential areas to be near their source of labor. Most of the many-storied and inefficient plants have disappeared. Photo by E. Willard Miller

of synthetic fibers. In the 1980s synthetic fibers make up about 76 percent of the total textile output in the Piedmont, cotton 23 percent, and wool only one percent. Thus the textile industry is less and less raw-material oriented.

Initially the southern railroads offered special low shipping rates on finished cotton products to offset their competitive disadvantage in terms of distance to the northern market. Early in the twentieth century, however, the railroads reverted to their normally higher rates for finished goods, so that southern plants actually operated at a cost disadvantage in shipping to northern markets. Thus transportation-cost differentials, on either raw materials or finished goods, cannot adequately account for the growth of textiles in the Piedmont.

The South probably had little advantage over

the Northeast in the cost of constructing and equipping factories. Although materials and labor are somewhat less expensive in the South, thus reducing construction costs, the cost of equipping factories is greater because textile machinery must be secured from Pennsylvania and New England.

A more significant factor in explaining the growth of the southern textile industry and the inability of the Northeast, including Pennsylvania, to compete is the sizable differential in labor costs between northern and southern mills. In the textile industry wages and salaries represent the largest share of mill costs, averaging about 25 percent of the value of the product. Lesser costs include raw materials, depreciation, fuel and power, taxes, marketing, and management.

Because of the high proportion of labor costs to the value of the products and, even more significantly, because these costs constitute the major share of the mill margin, textiles are labor-cost oriented. The favorable differential in labor costs for the South was and is the result of both lower wages and higher productivity of textile workers. In the 1920s it was estimated that the wages of textile workers in the Carolinas were 20 to 30 percent lower than in Pennsylvania. The differential in wages has declined, but it still exists. In 1972 the average hourly earnings for cotton-textile workers were $2.62 in North Carolina, as compared with about $3.10 in Pennsylvania. The differentials have narrowed because of the influence of unions, government regulations pertaining to minimum wages, and the general increase in the level of the southern economy.

Just as the labor-cost gap was narrowing between Pennsylvania and the South, competition began with foreign producers such as Korea, Hong Kong, Singapore, and many other developing nations. Labor costs in these areas are as little as $1.00 per hour for textile workers. In the past few years, an increasing flow of foreign textiles into the United States has been devastating to the nation, including Pennsylvania.

The U.S. government has long recognized the adverse effect of textile imports on the American industry and has gradually moved from supporting the concept of free trade to promoting controls. Until the 1950s foreign competition was small. A few tariffs were in effect, but most textiles were free to enter the United States. As foreign competition developed, the U.S. textile industry, later joined by the apparel industry, began to pressure the federal government for protection from imports. In 1961 the first bilateral trade agreement was negotiated with Japan to control imports of textiles and apparel. Since then many bilateral and multifiber arrangements have been negotiated. These controls, however, have not limited the flow of textiles into the United States.

Even if wages were comparable in the South and in foreign countries, the Pennsylvania textile industry would still be at a disadvantage because of its lower productivity. The work assignments are larger for southern and foreign workers. This is due partly to less union control, and in some instances, particularly in foreign countries, to more modern plants and machinery. Foreign workers are less conscious of delegated work loads and have been more amenable to scientifically designed job assignments. In addition, the tempo of technological change has been rapid, and management in the South and in foreign countries has been more willing to experiment with new technologies.

The textile industry in Pennsylvania is at a critical stage of its existence. In 1982 capital expenditures in the Pennsylvania textile industry totaled only $41 million. Plants are old and are not being modernized. There are essentially no funds for research and development. The Pennsylvania textile industry must adjust to both domestic and foreign competition if it is to survive.

APPAREL AND OTHER TEXTILE PRODUCTS

Apparel and other textile products are among the oldest and most important industries in Pennsylvania. In the 1970s this industry became the largest employer in the state, surpassing primary metals. Employment in the apparel industry increased steadily until the mid-1960s,

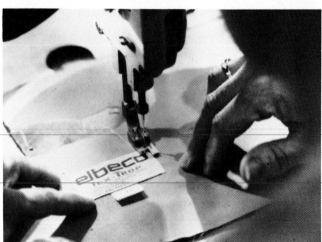

when 178,000 workers were engaged in producing clothing and other textile products.

The first center of production in the state was Philadelphia. The apparel industry has traditionally been an urban industry. It was a labor-intensive business, and manufacturers sought areas where huge numbers of immigrant women were willing to work for low wages. New York was the principal garment center on the East Coast, but other large cities also developed apparel industries. Besides the availability of labor, Philadelphia was well situated in relation to the East Coast market. A general rise in standards of living beginning in the nineteenth century provided further impetus for the expansion of the needle trades.

A second center of the apparel industry developed in the twentieth century in the anthracite region. As the textile industry began to decline in this region, the apparel industry developed and grew. Textile establishments were readily converted to the production of clothing, and textile workers were easily trained to manufacture low-style garments. The anthracite region was also well situated to serve the massive

Above: *The state's apparel industry ranks as one of Pennsylvania's oldest and most important industries. Photo © Tom Weigand, Inc.*

Top: *Handmade quilts are sold each year at the Kutztown Folk Festival in July. The quilts range in price from $100-$400. Courtesy, Pennsylvania Commonwealth Media Services*

East Coast market.

After World War II there began a migration of the apparel industry away from the major urban centers, where the industry had become highly unionized, in search of lower-cost labor and lower taxes. This movement favored not only the anthracite counties, but also other areas of southeastern Pennsylvania. By 1965 a total of fifty-nine counties in Pennsylvania produced apparel and other textile products. About two-thirds of the state's garment workers were concentrated in the eight counties of Philadelphia, Northampton, Luzerne, Lackawanna, Schuylkill, Lehigh, Lancaster, and Berks, with employment in most other counties varying from fewer than 50 to little more than 1,000.

Since the mid-1960s employment in this industry has decreased from 178,000 in 1965 to 107,300 in 1983. Employment in Philadelphia County alone fell from 44,600 in 1965 to 17,200 in 1983. This decline in employment can be largely attributed to the growing importation of foreign clothing. The cost of materials and labor, which make up about 75 percent of the cost of a garment, are much lower in Hong Kong, South Korea, Taiwan, Singapore, and many other Third World countries than in the United States. As Pennsylvania apparel becomes noncompetitive with foreign imports, the plants are abandoned.

The present-day apparel industry of Pennsylvania generates a payroll of about $1.1 billion annually and ships products worth $3.55 billion. The industry is characterized by the small size of its plants. In 1982, of the 1,725 establishments in the state, 1,179 had fewer than twenty employees. Because of the smallness of the plants, capital reserves are highly limited. If a company cannot sell its products quickly, it has few reserves to continue in the future.

The production of women's and misses' outerwear, including dresses, blouses, suits, and coats, employs about 45 percent of the state's apparel-industry workers. Men's and boys' furnishings, including suits, shirts, underwear, ties, trousers, and work clothing, contribute an additional 30 percent of employment. A wide variety of other textile products, including children's wear, hats and caps, gloves, curtains and drapes, textile bags, and robes and dressing gowns, make up the remaining 25 percent.

PETROLEUM AND COAL PRODUCTS

Within the category of petroleum and coal products, petroleum refining accounts for 95 percent of total employment and value of production. The remainder consists of paving and roofing materials and miscellaneous products.

The petroleum-refining industry of the world began in 1859 with the discovery of oil at Titusville, Pennsylvania. Within a few years the petroleum-refining industry was localized on the oil fields of western Pennsylvania, as well as in eastern Pennsylvania on the Delaware River estuary. Within the state, this regional pattern persists to the present day.

Because the petroleum fields of Pennsylvania produce little oil, the refineries in western Pennsylvania are small, producing specialty products of which lubricating oils are most important. The major refining center of Pennsylvania is on the shore of the Delaware River in Philadelphia and Delaware counties, where foreign oils are processed for the Eastern Seaboard market. Petroleum refining is now one of the most highly automated industries in the world. With increasing automation, employment in petroleum refining has decreased from 9,900 in 1967 to only 6,600 in 1982. During the same period the value of the petroleum products refined has risen from $1.2 billion in 1967 to $9.8 billion in 1982. Only primary metals and food and kindred products contribute a greater value of output to the state's economy.

Petroleum refining will continue to be a major industry in Pennsylvania thanks to the huge market for petroleum products. Because foreign crude oils are processed at the break in transportation, the industry will remain highly localized in the port area of southeastern Pennsylvania.

FURNITURE AND FIXTURES

The furniture and fixtures industry has traditionally been small in Pennsylvania, accounting for about 1.8 percent of manufacturing employment in the state. Between 1965 and 1983 em-

Above: *The Anchor Hocking glass factory is located near Pittsburgh. Photo by Jack Wolf*

Right, top: *The eerie beauty of a Pennsylvania refinery at night creates a spectacular sight when viewed from the air.*

Right: *A Venango County oil refinery stands silhouetted against a twilight sky. Courtesy, Pennsylvania Bureau of Travel Development*

ployment declined from 25,547 to 18,314, a loss of 7,233 jobs, or 28 percent. In 1982 the industry bought $526 million of raw materials, and the value added in the manufacturing process was $638 million. The total value of output for this industry was thus $1.16 billion.

About 55 percent of the state's furniture and fixture industry has long been concentrated in the six counties of Philadelphia, Montgomery, York, Erie, Luzerne, and Lycoming. Philadelphia County, which has the largest employment, has also experienced the greatest decline—from 4,984 employees in 1965 to 2,784 in 1983, a loss of 2,200 jobs, or 44 percent. As a result Philadelphia County's share of the industry, in terms of employment, has declined from about 20 percent to 15 percent. The location of this industry in Philadelphia, Montgomery, York, and Luzerne counties reflects a market orientation to major population centers. The industry in Lycoming and Erie counties was originally oriented to raw materials, and these centers remain producers mainly of wood furniture.

The industry is characterized by small plants. In 1982, of the 410 establishments, 238 had fewer than twenty employees. Household furniture, with 202 establishments, produces about one-third of the total value of output. The furniture is utilitarian and consists of wood, metal, and upholstered items, mattresses, and bedsprings. In contrast to the large number of household-furniture establishments, only 36 establishments produce office furniture, but their output is valued at 25 percent of the total. About 90 percent of the office furniture is metal. Partitions and fixtures, about half metal and half wood, make up another 30 percent of the state's total output.

Although the industry provides a relatively small number of jobs, it generates a total payroll of $300 million, produces products valued at more than $600 million, and is important in the local economy of a number of counties.

STONE, CLAY, AND GLASS PRODUCTS
Stone, clay, and glass products are traditional industries of Pennsylvania. A wide variety of

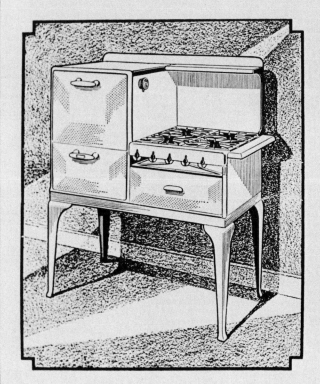

Above: Erie's Odin Stove Manufacturing Company ran this advertisement in 1930 listing the reasons to buy its Odin Gas Ranges: "for faultless cooking and baking . . . economy and quality . . . beauty and style." Soon the Depression would make the purchase of items such as this gas range a luxury.

Opposite page: Among its numerous products offered in 1930, the Pittston Stove Company presented the Pittston Duplex stove (top left), with its six cooking holes—two for coal and four for gas ($281); the Pittston Hotel Steel Range (bottom left), with its two ovens, which burned hard or soft coal or coke ($340); the Happy Thought Range (bottom right), which burned coal or wood ($240); and the Pittston Pipeless Furnace (top right), with galvanized casings, duplex register, water pan, wall regulator, check damper, poker, and radiation shield. The furnace ranged in price from $202 to $308, depending on the size of its fire pot.

items are produced, including flat glass, glassware, cement, pottery, plates, stone, a variety of abrasives, mineral wool, and nonclay refractories. Each of these products has a different geographical concentration. The cement industry has its greatest concentration in eastern Pennsylvania, in the traditional centers of production of the Lehigh Valley, whereas glass production is concentrated in the southwestern part of the state.

Employment in these industries has declined from about 56,000 in 1965 to 41,000 in 1983. One reason is that these industries, particularly cement and glass, have become highly mechanized, evolving from small-scale to large-scale production. As the plants become larger, their efficiency increases and the labor force decreases. Because the products are heavy and bulky, a market orientation is important to reduce transportation costs. As the economy of the United States has grown, these industries have become increasingly decentralized, and

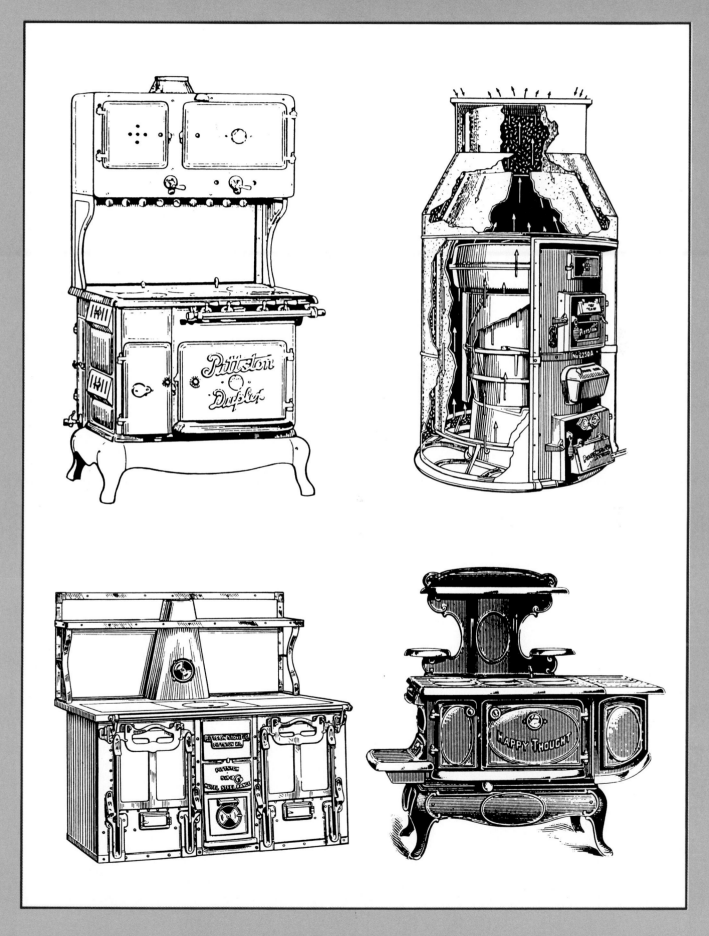

Above: *The cement industry has its greatest concentration in the eastern part of the state. Pictured here is a concrete mixing facility. Courtesy, Pennsylvania Commonwealth Media Services*

Left: *Pennsylvania is richly endowed with raw material and fuel providing the basis for its large cement industry. Courtesy, Pennsylvania Commonwealth Media Services*

Opposite page, top: *The American Portland cement industry began in the Lehigh Valley of western Pennsylvania late in the nineteenth century. The natural cement rock of the region was the major factor in its localization. This cement plant at Northampton shows the large amount of space required for the quarrying, crushing operations, kilns, and storage silos needed to produce cement. Photo by E. Willard Miller*

Bottom: *The clay deposits of Pennsylvania provide the raw materials for a clay products industry. These clay pipes, produced in kilns at a plant in Clearfield, are marketed throughout the eastern United States. Photo by E. Willard Miller*

the market for products produced in Pennsylvania has declined.

Within Pennsylvania, employment in these industries is widely dispersed in forty-seven counties. As in many other industries, the traditional centers of production have experienced the greatest drop in employment. Between 1965 and 1983 employment in Allegheny County declined from 6,300 to 2,700, in Lehigh County from 1,100 to 490, and in Armstrong County from 3,550 to 1,500. In many other counties, however, employment has remained steady or has risen slightly. The stone, clay, and glass industries together have an annual value of output in excess of $3.45 billion and provide $650 million in wages.

TRANSPORTATION EQUIPMENT

In the nineteenth century, during the expansion of the railroads, Pennsylvania was a major producer of steam engines, coaches, and rolling stock. In the twentieth century, when the coal-fired engine gave way to the diesel and then

the electric engine, Pennsylvania lost its advantage in engine production. Pennsylvania was also a major producer of Pullman cars, but as the railroads of the nation curtailed this type of service, the demand for Pullman cars disappeared. Finally, with the decline in freight service, the demand for rolling stock has been greatly reduced.

In 1982 the transportation-equipment industry paid wages to production workers of $813 million and produced output valued at nearly $5.8 billion. Of the different branches of the industry, motor vehicles and equipment are most important, with about 36 percent of the output, followed by railroad equipment with 22 percent, aircraft and parts with 17 percent, and ship and boat building and repair with about 10 percent. The industry employed about 56,000 workers in 1983 down from 74,700 in 1965.

The transportation industry has traditionally been highly concentrated. Today the seven leading counties account for about 70 percent of the state's total output. Within each of these counties, one or two companies dominate production, controlling from one-half to more than 90 percent of total output. In Delaware County the Sun Shipbuilding and Dry Dock Company and the Boeing Vestal Company together employ about 97 percent of the county's transportation-equipment workers. In Lehigh County the industry is dominated by Mack Trucks. However, in January 1986 Mack Trucks

These interior and exterior scenes were shot at the Altoona shops during various eras of the twentieth century. The World War II era is represented by the photos on this page—workers in front of a T-1 locomotive (top) and men assembling trucks for gondola cars (bottom). On the opposite page we see a post-World War II view of the plant closing for the day (top) and a Depression-era shot of a man painting a passenger car (bottom). All photos courtesy, Pennsylvania Historical and Museum Commission

closed operations at one of its Allentown plants and plans to build a new plant outside the state. Friction between the company and the automotive union was primarily responsible for closure of the Pennsylvania plant. The General Electric Company has a major railroad-equipment plant in Erie County and two plants producing guided missiles and space vehicles in Philadelphia and Montgomery counties. In York County AMF Incorporated produces motorcycles. In Philadelphia County the Budd Company produces motor-vehicle parts and railroad equipment. The only automobile company in Pennsylvania is Volkswagen of America in Westmoreland County. In contrast to most Pennsylvania industries, in which many plants have fewer than twenty employees, the typical transportation-equipment plant has hundreds or even thousands of employees.

Pennsylvania has not developed major centers of manufacturing for twentieth-century transportation equipment. The automobile industry is centered in Michigan, and later assembly plants have been built in other states. The aircraft industry has been concentrated in other states such as California, Kansas, and Washington. Most of the small companies have left Pennsylvania, including the Piper Aircraft Company, which discontinued operations at Lock Haven in Clinton County in 1983 to consolidate its operations in Florida. Nor has Pennsylvania been a major producer of parts for either the automobile or aircraft industries. The dominance of nineteenth-century industries, such as iron and steel, textiles, glass, and leather, was so great in the state that the new industries that evolved in the twentieth century sought new centers of development.

ELECTRIC AND ELECTRONIC EQUIPMENT

In the nineteenth century Pennsylvania was a leader in the invention and production of electrical machinery. The Westinghouse Electric Corporation in Pittsburgh was one of the first major electrical-machinery companies. With its more than 3,000 employees, it continues to play a major role in this industry today.

Above: *Electronics manufacturing is Pennsylvania's primary high-tech industry. Courtesy, Pennsylvania Commonwealth Media Services*

Left, top: *In the invention and production of electrical equipment, Pennsylvania continues its nineteenth-century tradition in modern-day production of electronic equipment. Photo © Tom Weigand, Inc.*

Left: *The electric and electronic equipment manufacturers of Pennsylvania produce a great variety of products. Photo © 1984 Tom Weigand, Inc.*

Right: *As the Northeast recoups its losses to the Sunbelt, Pennsylvania seeks to attract new high-tech companies to the state. Courtesy, Pennsylvania Commonwealth Media Services*

Above: *Dr. Hetenyi, a research engineer at the Westinghouse Electric and Manufacturing Company in Pittsburgh, was photographed by Marjory Collins in June 1943 as part of an assignment for the U.S. Office of War Information. Courtesy, Library of Congress*

Above right: *Computer tapes, once widely used, have been replaced in most office environments with disks. Printouts, however, remain in use. Photo © Tom Weigand, Inc.*

Electric and electronic equipment is one of the major industries in the state, with annual production in excess of $7 billion. The industry annually consumes $2.9 billion worth of raw materials and pays wages totalling more than $1 billion. A wide variety of electric and electronic products are produced in Pennsylvania. Electronic components and accessories make up about one-third of the state's total output, electric distributing equipment about 16 percent, electrical industrial apparatus about 14 percent, electric lighting and wiring equipment another 14 percent, and communication equipment 10 percent.

Employment in the electric- and electronic-equipment industries has declined from 114,000 in 1965 to 90,300 in 1983. The greatest declines have occurred in the two major producing counties, with employment dropping from 23,800 to 7,400 in Philadelphia County and from 12,600 to 7,100 in Allegheny County. Other counties with significant declines in employment include Elk (from 4,200 to 3,100), Lehigh (from 7,300 to 5,600), and Westmoreland (from 4,300 to 1,400).

While the traditional centers of these industries are experiencing a decline in employment, a number of small new centers are developing in the state. In the industrial-growth counties of southeastern Pennsylvania, employment in the electric and electronic industries grew between 1965 and 1983 from 2,200 to 5,100 in Bucks County, from 2,000 to 2,800 in Cumberland County, from 6,100 to 8,800 in Montgomery County, and from 1,400 to 4,300 in York County. The typical plant in these growth counties has fewer than 100 workers, and most of the plants produce a single product.

The electronics industry is among the most complex and rapidly changing of all industries of modern times. Research and development are fundamental to continued existence. Pennsylvania's electronics industry has not been in the forefront of modern development as have the major centers in Massachusetts and California. The electric and electronic industries of Pennsylvania will continue to produce basic products but need a revitalization to compete successfully with other states.

FOOD AND KINDRED PRODUCTS
Food and kindred products are a basic industry in Pennsylvania. In 1982 the industry processed raw materials worth $8.3 billion. The value added in the manufacturing process exceeded $4.9 billion, and the total value of output was more than $13.2 billion.

A wide variety of food items are produced in the state, with no single branch dominating the industry. Bakery products account for the largest share of employment, with about 19 percent of the total, followed by meat (16 percent), sugar and confectionary products (also 16 percent), preserved fruits and vegetables (13 percent), beverages (10 percent), dairy products (9 percent), grain-mill products (6 percent), and miscellaneous foods (10 percent). The largest single food processor in the state is the Heinz Company, located in Pittsburgh. About one-third of statewide employment in canned fruits and vegetables is concentrated in Adams County.

In the period from 1965 to 1983, employment in the food industry declined from 103,300 to 83,700. The area of greatest decline was in Philadelphia, where employment decreased from 26,600 to 13,600—a loss of 13,000 jobs, or two-thirds of the entire statewide decrease. The small food-processing operation, such as the neighborhood bakery, was unable to survive in Philadelphia, as name-brand products forced the high-cost specialty shops out of business. The large food processors could achieve economics of scale, producing products of high quality at a lower cost with far fewer employees. Future employment in the food industry will depend on the degree of mechanization that the industry achieves.

Although Philadelphia remains the largest single center of food processing, with about 18 percent of the state's employment, the industry is highly decentralized. In the 1980s fifty-one of the state's sixty-seven counties possess some type of food-processing industry. Because many products, such as baking and confectionary products, are highly perishable, the industry is market oriented. Producers of perishable goods serving regional markets have developed fleets of fast delivery trucks.

As employment has declined, the number of food-processing establishments has decreased even more. In 1947 there were 2,789 establishments, with an average of thirty-seven workers. By 1982 the number of businesses had decreased to 1,225, but the average number of employees was sixty-nine. Although total employment has declined, the industry has become more highly mechanized, with the result that production has been maintained and even increased in certain types of food processing.

FABRICATED-METAL PRODUCTS
The fabricated-metal industry produces an annual output valued at about $7.6 billion, using $3.8 billion worth of raw materials and paying wages of more than $1.2 billion. The industry developed along with the iron and steel industry in the nineteenth century, and Pennsylvania today produces a wide variety of fabricated-metal products. Fabricated structural metal

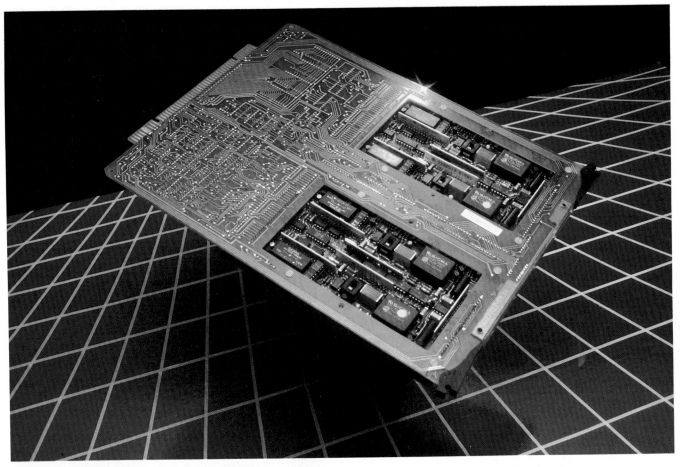

Above and left: *About one-third of Pennsylvania's total output of electric and electronic products is made up of electronic components and accessories. Components are used on printed circuit boards such as those pictured. Photos © Tom Weigand, Inc.*

Opposite, top: *The state's food industry produces a wide variety of products, including snack foods such as pretzels and chips. Photo © 1982 Tom Weigand, Inc.*

Bottom left: *Sugar and confectionary products account for 16 percent of the food items produced in Pennsylvania. Pictured here are Luden's Peppermint Patties. Photo © 1980 Tom Weigand Inc.*

Right: *Lab testing is a necessary part of candy production. Photo © 1980 Tom Weigand, Inc.*

products account for about 35 percent of the total; metal forgings and stampings, 16 percent; screw machine products, 6 percent; metal cans and shipping containers, also 6 percent; cutlery, hand tools, and hardware, 4 percent; ordnance and accessories, 3 percent; and miscellaneous items, about 30 percent.

Employment in the fabricated-metal industry declined from 106,000 in 1965 to 83,800 in 1983. Major declines occurred in those counties where the industry had initially been concentrated. Employment dropped from 23,200 to 10,400 in Philadelphia County and from 15,600 to 8,700 in Allegheny County. Other counties with significant decreases in employment were Montgomery, Erie, Westmoreland, and Delaware.

A number of other counties—including Lancaster, York, Luzerne, Lackawanna, and Lebanon—experienced a modest growth in employment. The industry is widely distributed in fifty-two of the state's sixty-seven counties. Al-

Opposite, top: *Reese's Pieces, those delicious candy-coated chocolate morsels, are among the confectionary products of the state. Photo © Tom Weigand, Inc.*

Opposite, bottom: *The Hershey Kiss is one of the most well-known and well-loved food products made in Pennsylvania. Photo © 1982 Tom Weigand, Inc.*

Above: *The refining of maple sugar takes place at Keim's Kamp in Somerset County. Courtesy, Pennsylvania Bureau of Travel Development*

Above: *Wineries are becoming increasingly popular throughout the state. Courtesy, Pennsylvania Bureau of Travel Development*

Left: *Pennsylvania's fabricated metal industry produces $7.6 billion of products annually. Pictured is a Beryllium copper strip. Photo © 1981 Tom Weigand, Inc.*

though the basic pattern of production has not changed greatly in recent years, most of the new plants are being built outside the old industrial areas.

STABLE INDUSTRIES

Three industries—paper and allied products, machinery other than electrical, and chemicals and allied products—experienced employment declines of less than 15 percent between 1965 and 1983. These industries are considered stable, for while some areas have experienced sharp declines in employment, new areas of production have given them economic vitality. These industries are also experiencing increased productivity in a number of their branches.

PAPER AND ALLIED PRODUCTS

The manufacture of paper and allied products is another traditional industry in Pennsylvania. The early industry was noted for its production of quality paper. In the twentieth century, however, the production of paper in paper mills has declined greatly, and by 1982 only 20 percent of employment was in this branch of the industry. The largest center of paper production is in Wyoming County, where a single plant employs about 50 percent of the state's total of 7,600 paper-mill workers. Other plants are located in such counties as Clinton and Erie. These plants are raw-material oriented.

Plants producing converted paper products, such as envelopes, bags, stationery, sanitary paper, and paperboard containers and boxes, are widely distributed in thirty-eight counties. Of a total of 346 plants, 224 have fewer than twenty employees. These products are bulky and have a low value, so that the market for most of these items is local and regional. Philadelphia has the largest number of employees in paper products, but employment there declined from 9,100 in 1965 to about 4,700 in 1983. A major factor in the decline of the industry is the high cost of operating a plant that produces a low-cost product in an expensive urbanized area. The industry is seeking lower-cost producing centers. Although employment throughout the state has declined from 40,000 in 1965 to 36,500 in 1983, a number of counties, including Luzerne, Berks, Huntington, Lackawanna, and Westmoreland, have seen an increase in employment. In 1982 employees in the paper-products industry earned wages of $375 million and produced products valued at more than $2 billion.

MACHINERY OTHER THAN ELECTRICAL

Pennsylvania was an early producer of machinery for use in such industries as primary metals, glass, cement, textiles, transportation, and petroleum refining. With an annual output valued at $9 billion, machinery is exceeded only by primary metals and petroleum refining in overall value of production. The industry consumes $3.7 billion worth of raw materials and pays wages totaling more than $1.4 billion. Employment grew steadily in the twentieth century to a peak of about 135,000 in 1975. Since then, however, employment has dropped sharply to about 100,000.

Employment trends have varied throughout the state, with some areas experiencing major declines and other areas modest increases. The counties experiencing the greatest declines have been Philadelphia County, where employment dropped from 20,200 in 1965 to 5,900 in 1983; Delaware County, from 9,100 to 3,700; and Allegheny County, from 11,500 to 9,100. During the same period significant increases in employment occurred in Bucks County (from 2,050 to 6,023), Chester County (from 2,300 to 4,300), Lancaster County (from 4,100 to 5,600), Westmoreland County (from 3,800 to 4,200), and York County (from 6,800 to 10,300).

A wide variety of machinery is produced in Pennsylvania. General industrial machinery is most important, with 22 percent of the output, followed by construction of related machinery (19 percent), metalworking machinery (12 percent), refrigeration and service machinery (9 percent), special-industry machinery (also 9 percent), and office and computing machinery (6 percent). The machinery establishments vary greatly in size. Of the 2,540 plants in Pennsyl-

The SKF roller bearing factory in Philadelphia employed many Swedish-American workers, including this man. Marjory Collins photographed SKF employees in the spring of 1942 for the U.S. Office of War Information. Courtesy, Library of Congress

Right: Of all the chemicals produced in the state, pharmaceuticals account for the largest percentage. Here we see a production line in a pharmaceutical company. Courtesy, Pennsylvania Commonwealth Media Services

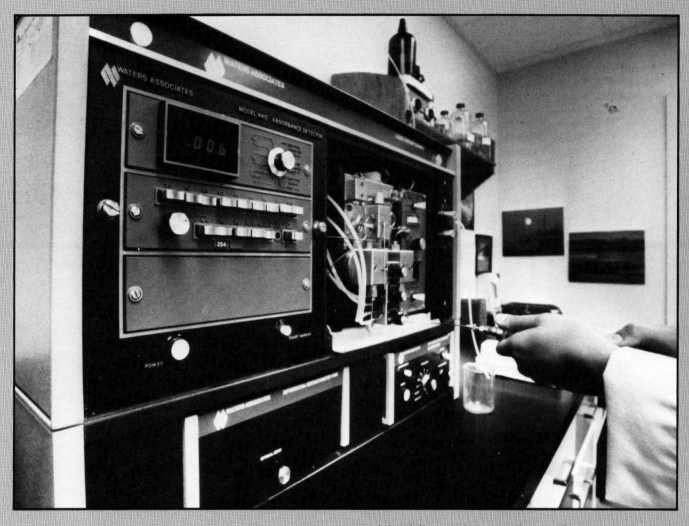

*Of the different segments of Pennsylvania's instruments
and related products industry, measuring and controlling
devices constitute about 45 percent of total output.
Photo © 1982 Tom Weigand, Inc.*

In Blair County's Veeder Root plant an employee assembles meters for gasoline pumps. Courtesy, Altoona Chamber of Commerce

employees.

Instruments and related products are high-value-added items. In 1982 the cost of materials was $871 million, while the value added was nearly $1.8 billion. This industry is not oriented to fuel sources or raw materials. With its high-value small-bulk products, the industry serves national and worldwide markets with relatively little concern for transportation costs. Above all the industry is oriented to highly skilled labor, including scientists and engineers. Pennsylvania is ideally suited to experience continued growth in the development and manufacture of instruments and related products.

RUBBER AND MISCELLANEOUS PLASTIC PRODUCTS

Pennsylvania's rubber and plastics industries employ about 30,000 workers—80 percent of them in plastics, and the rest in the production of rubber footwear, fabricated rubber products, and a small output of tires and inner tubes.

The plastics industry has developed since World War II and in recent years has become increasingly dispersed. In 1965 sixteen counties had plastic factories; by 1983 this number had grown to forty-one. Employment in individual counties remains relatively small, with no county having more than 3,300 workers. Of the 645 plants in 1982, 309 had fewer than twenty employees. In 1982 the plastic-products industry produced an output valued at more than $2.1 billion and provided more than $300 million in wages.

The plastics industry is best developed in the less industrialized areas of the state and has had its greatest economic impact in rural areas. Raw materials and energy are of little importance as location factors. Plants and equipment needs are modest, so that capital investments are low. A labor force can be rapidly trained to operate the simple machines. The product is light, so that it can be transported to distant markets. Thus the industry seeks sites where production costs are minimal. The demand for plastic products is increasing, and the growth pattern of the immediate past suggests that

Pennsylvania will continue to be a major producer of these products.

LUMBER AND WOOD PRODUCTS

There are no great lumbering centers in Pennsylvania today similar to those at the end of the nineteenth century. Employment in the industry has grown, however, from 13,500 in 1965 to 17,600 in 1983. Annual wages total $170 million, and output is valued at $1.13 billion annually.

The industry is highly decentralized, distributed among fifty-eight counties. Thus the average employment per county is only 303, with actual totals ranging from 50 to 1,500. The industry is based on the raw material of local forests. Timberlands in Pennsylvania were extensively lumbered in the late nineteenth century, and by the turn of the century the state's forests had been reduced in area from 28.5 million acres to about 11.5 million acres, or about 40 percent of their original area. As the loggers moved to other states and farmland was abandoned, the regeneration of the forests began. Forests now cover about 18 million acres, or 58 percent of the state.

The present forests of Pennsylvania are not the same as the virgin forests. Most of the conifers are gone, and the predominance of hardwoods, especially maples and oaks, gives the modern forest a character and appearance entirely different from that of the past. Although many trees are of timber age, most of the trees are still ten to twenty years away from full maturity. In 1982 the U.S. Census of Manufactures reported 194 logging camps and contractors in Pennsylvania, of which only 5 had twenty or more employees. There were also 431 sawmills and planing mills, of which only 64 had twenty or more employees. These operations are migratory. The timber developer moves into an area, cuts the mature trees, and then moves to another tract. Because of the high cost of transporting logs, it is more economical to move operations to the raw-material source. Because the timber is hardwood, major products include cabinets, hardwood veneers, containers, mobile homes, and prefabricated

Left: *An employee at a Grantville sawmill gets ready to add another board to the stack. Photo by Allied Pix Service, Inc.*

Below: *Small migratory sawmills secure logs from a local region and move to a new logging area when the timber is depleted. This sawmill and associated lumberyard were located near Milroy, Pennsylvania. Photo by E. Willard Miller*

wood buildings.

As the hardwood forests mature in the near future, employment in lumbering and the wood-products industry will increase modestly. The wood-products industry is likely to remain oriented to its raw-material base, thus tying it to rural areas where other employment opportunities are limited.

PRINTING AND PUBLISHING
The printing and publishing industries have experienced significant growth in the past few decades, with employment growing from 54,600 in 1947 to 65,400 in 1965 to 71,600 in 1983. About 30 percent of the employment is in newspapers, about one-third in commercial printing, and about 10 percent in book publishing.

The industry is highly decentralized. A total of 302 newspapers are scattered around the state, ranging from the large metropolitan dailies to the weekly county papers in rural areas. Of the 2,186 printing and publishing establishments throughout the state, 1,624 have fewer than twenty employees. Most of the commercial printing establishments serve a local or regional market.

Trends in printing and publishing are geographically diverse. In Philadelphia County employment has declined from 27,250 in 1965 to 15,740 in 1983. As the local economy of Philadelphia has declined, the demand for printing and publishing has also declined. In contrast Montgomery County, adjacent to Philadelphia, has experienced an increase in employment from 1,940 to 5,260 during the same period. Most of the economically growing counties of southeastern Pennsylvania have increased their employment in printing and publishing. This industry closely reflects the economy of an area. When business is prospering, demand for the products of printing and publishing is high. Conversely, during economic recessions the demand declines.

GOVERNMENT INDUSTRIAL ACTIVITIES

In order to encourage the development of industry in Pennsylvania, the state and federal governments have passed a number of laws and established a number of agencies over the years. Among these government programs are a wide range of incentives including loans, establishment of scientific and technological programs and industrial training programs, and the development of the infrastructure of a region in order to attract new industry.

The Commerce Act passed by the Pennsylvania General Assembly in 1939 was one of the earliest laws in the state specifically designed to promote business, industry, and commerce. Thousands of Pennsylvanians were unemployed, and state lawmakers believed that an administrative program was needed to aid the depressed economy. Under this act the Department of Commerce became the first state government agency designated to seek solutions to the ailing economy. The powers granted under the act were broad-based, including the location and development of new industries, the development of technical and scientific studies useful to the growth of industry, the development of natural resources, the encouragement of commerce with foreign countries, and the conducting of a program of information, advertising, and publicity relating to economic development. The Commerce Act actually had little influence on the economy of Pennsylvania because with the advent of World War II the state's economy flourished.

The Pennsylvania Industrial Development Authority was created in 1956 with the power to allocate funds for and make secured loans to industrial-development agencies. The authority grants loans to develop projects in critical economic areas of high unemployment, with the goal of improving economic conditions and fostering the health, morals, and general welfare of the people. Pennsylvania lawmakers recognized that when economic opportunity declined, people migrated out of the depressed region, thereby reducing the tax base and impairing support for education and other government services.

The Pennsylvania Industrial Development Authority consists of ten members, including

ERIE LITHOGRAPHING & PRINTING COMPANY

ERIE, PENNA.

THE FACTORY SERVICE BUILT

COLOR LITHOGRAPHY BY EVERY KNOWN PROCESS

The Great Depression had already begun when this Erie Lithographing and Printing Company advertisement appeared in 1930. The company prided itself on its service and by its ability to produce color lithography "by every known process."

the secretaries of the pertinent Pennsylvania government departments. The authority is responsible for determining critical economic areas from applications submitted by local and regional development agencies. When a development plan is approved, loans are made to the appropriate development agencies from the state's Industrial Development Fund, initially funded at $5 million and increased over the years.

The Pennsylvania Industrial Development Authority has been active in developing cooperative programs between state government and local communities since its origin in 1956. In its first six years of existence from May 1956 to July 1962, 238 projects were financed in areas of chronic unemployment with the help of loans provided to local non-profit community development organizations. The 238 projects were located in 80 communities spread across the state. It was estimated that new job oppor-

Left: *More than 300 newspapers are printed throughout the state. The press of* The Morning Call *of Allentown is pictured here. Photo © 1984 Tom Weigand, Inc.*

Right: *A graphic artist attempts to match inks. The number of Pennsylvania's printing and publishing businesses exceeds the 2,000 mark. Photo © Tom Weigand, Inc.*

tunities in plants built or expanded with the help of the PIDA totaled 39,517. Additional jobs in services and sales made possible by the new factory jobs totaled an estimated 29,242.

From 1956 to 1962 there were 130 new plants built in 61 depressed areas. These endeavors represented teamwork between communities, financial institutions, utilities, the Bureau of Industrial Development of the Department of Commerce, and the Pennsylvania Industrial Development Authority. Besides new plants there was also the expansion of 108 existing plants. Emphasis was placed on aiding growth industries in order to assure future stability of industry in the state. It was estimated in 1961 that the annual payroll created in industrial expansion by the six-year efforts of PIDA was $145,611,043. The loans granted by PIDA between 1956 and 1961 totaled $30,782,297. During the same period, local communities, banks, and other financial institutions provided $58,600,626. The total cost of the new and expanded plants financed by the Authority's help totaled $89,382,923. This amount of construction in itself acted as an economic stimulant to areas of chronic unemployment.

The Pennsylvania Industrial Development Authority has continued to expand its efforts. During the fiscal year July 1970 through June 1971, the PIDA approved 81 projects in 31 counties with loans totaling $24,326,676 in projects costing a total of $78,141,352. These projects had a planned increase in employment of 6,905 and an annual payroll of $52,373,257. In the 1984 calendar year there were 182 projects approved in 42 counties. During 1984 PIDA loans and commitments totaled $69,427,495 for plants costing a total of $151,342,936. The estimated increase in employment was 7,690 with an increase in the payroll of $126,355,080. It has been a policy of the Authority to have a wide geographical distribution of the projects. In 1984 Allegheny County had a total of fourteen projects while Bucks, Lackawanna, and York each had eleven. In the other thirty-eight counties the number of projects varied from one to eight. Within individual counties the loans varied in 1984 from $149,913 in Centre County to $6,062,538 in

363

Allegheny County. The total project costs also varied greatly from $408,035 in Centre County to a high of $23,428,810 in Luzerne County. The increase in the estimated payroll varied from $144,000 in Snyder County to $8,589,586 in Luzerne County. The figures vary greatly from county to county over the years depending on the industrial activity in a particular year.

The Appalachian Regional Development Act was passed by the federal government in 1965 in an effort to improve the economy of Appalachia. In the implementation of the act, Pennsylvania became a member of the Appalachian Regional Commission, whose functions include conducting investigations, research, and studies on the resources of the region; forming local development districts; providing a forum for considering the problems of the region; sponsoring demonstration projects designed to foster regional productivity and growth; and encouraging private investment in industrial, commercial, and recreational projects.

The programs of the Appalachian Regional Commission are directed toward the development of the infrastructure of the region in order to create a favorable industrial environment. Of these programs, the creation of the Appalachian Development Highway System has been paramount. Other programs have included demonstration health facilities, land stabilization, conservation and erosion control, mining-area restoration, water-resource surveys, sewage-treatment works, and vocational-education facilities.

To implement the Appalachian programs more effectively within the state, the Pennsylvania General Assembly in 1984 passed the Capital Loan Fund Act. Using funds made available under the Appalachian Regional Development Act of 1965 and the Public Works and Economic Development Act of 1965, this act provides for loans, loan guarantees, and other programs for capital development projects undertaken by small businesses and industries.

Pennsylvania's Site Development Act was passed in 1968 to provide state grants for the construction, rehabilitation, alteration, expansion, or improvement of site-development projects. Assistance is directed primarily to the acquisition of land located in designated impoverished urban areas. Applications for aid may come from any eligible municipality, municipal authority, industrial-development agency, or state agency. The site-development plan must be approved by the Secretary of Public Welfare, and the loan may not exceed 50 percent of the cost of the project.

In the mid-1960s Pennsylvania began to explore ways in which existing information could be used to solve scientific and technical problems throughout the Commonwealth. Out of these meetings the Pennsylvania Technical Assistance Program (PENNTAP) was established to assist in the transfer of known scientific and technical information to solve existing industrial problems. PENNTAP is approved by the Pennsylvania Department of Commerce and the Continuing Education Division of the Commonwealth Educational System of the Pennsylvania State University. As an aid to business and industry in Pennsylvania, PENNTAP receives requests from local governments, agencies, and municipalities.

When PENNTAP began as an active organization, the prevailing theory was that simply pointing out the existence of new or improved technologies would be sufficient—that their adoption would follow automatically. Experience has proved this theory to be erroneous. A system has evolved that provides not only information but technological development through personal, cooperative interaction. An advisory council from a diversity of backgrounds guides the operations of PENNTAP, pinpointing problems that lead to new efforts. Besides a full-time director, there are eleven full-time technical specialists on the staff: a chemical engineer, a geologist, a metallurgist, an ecologist, five technologists, an electrical engineer, and a technical research librarian. Each of these technical specialists is a faculty member of the Pennsylvania State University. Each specialist's college is responsible for the academic and technical content of the information that is disseminated. PENNTAP also utilizes the Pennsylvania State University Commonwealth Campus system and the forty-six members of the Continuing Education field staff in twenty-four locations throughout the state.

The mode of operations of PENNTAP can be divided into two basic types: problem solving and problem prevention. In problem solving, a typical problem goes through six steps. The potential user begins with a question or problem, which is then analyzed by technical specialists. Once the parameters of the problem have been determined, the technical specialist searches all available resources. The data are then compiled for the user, and the technical specialist remains ready to answer questions. Finally, after the relevant technology has been applied, the program is evaluated.

A second major contribution of PENNTAP is the application of new technology to prevent problems from occurring. The first step is the recognition that a problem could develop. After observation of the existing system, pilot programs are devised incorporating new technology in cooperation with the user. Once the relevant technology has been applied, the program is evaluated to assess its potential. In essence PENNTAP serves as a link between industries that need assistance on technical problems and the technological resources that can provide answers and solutions.

In 1982 the Pennsylvania General Assembly created the Ben Franklin Partnership Fund under the Pennsylvania Science and Engineering Foundation. This new legislation amended previous acts of 1929 and 1970. The duties of the Pennsylvania Science and Engineering Foundation (the Ben Franklin Partnership Fund) are to stimulate basic and applied scientific research and development and to foster scientific and technological education in Pennsylvania in order to promote the state's economic growth and welfare. To implement the program, technological centers have been established at a number of universities, including Lehigh University, the Pennsylvania State University, the University of Pittsburgh, and Carnegie Mellon University, in order to provide advanced research and development technology, training, education, and related activities. A basic goal is

to provide facilities that will lead to the development of new technologies that will, in turn, create new jobs. Efforts are also made to link labor, business, university, and government in order to promote industrial diversification. Programs include the establishment of technology parks devoted to research and development.

In addition to state agencies that have encouraged industrial growth in Pennsylvania there are over 125 community development organizations. The basic purpose of these groups is to inform companies about the industrial advantages of their community. In order to attract industry many types of subsidization schemes have been implemented. The traditional inducements include direct loan programs, free industrial sites, municipal plant financing, and tax abatements and concessions. More recent subsidies include local revenue bond issues to support industry, direct financial assistance using public funds to finance industry, low interest mortgages, and the development of chartered development credit corporations. The basic types of subsidies vary little from place to place.

The operation of a local industrial promotion program has a number of aspects. One of the first steps is the preparation of a data book listing information pertinent to the localization of manufacturing. Making initial contacts with industrial prospects and arranging visits to the community are also necessary considerations. The efforts of the promotional groups in Pennsylvania now usually extend to other endeavors. For example, the evaluation of the physical appearance of the community may be critical in attracting new industry. Good hotel facilities, well-paved and well-lighted streets, good schools and hospitals are now recognized by Pennsylvania communities as necessary inducements for industrial growth. This is particularly true when a firm plans to move its executive staff to a new location. The local industrial development agencies now recognize that many aspects of the cultural and economic environment of the community not directly associated with manufacturing are important in attracting new industries.

Chapter Eleven

Rise of the Tertiary Economy

In 1790, when the first U.S. Census was taken, about 90 percent of the population of Pennsylvania was engaged in primary activities, mostly in agriculture. By 1920, following a century of rapid industrialization, primary activities (including agriculture, mining, and lumbering) employed only 18 percent of the state's workers; secondary activities (including manufacturing and construction) had grown to 41.6 percent; and tertiary activities (including commerce and services) employed 40.4 percent of the state's workers. In 1985 Pennsylvania had a total work force of about five million, of which only about 2.7 percent were engaged in primary activities and 24.8 percent in secondary activities (20 percent in manufacturing and 4.8 percent in construction). Tertiary activities now provide about 72.5 percent of the state's total employment, or more than 3.6 million jobs. Clearly, the economic future of

Pennsylvania rests on developing these tertiary activities.

Tertiary activities today dominate the economic structure of Pennsylvania. They not only have the largest employment, but are the growth sectors of the economy. As primary and secondary activities decline in employment potential, the tertiary activities provide job opportunities for the unemployed. The five major categories of tertiary activities, with their respective shares of total employment, are: services (56 percent); retail trade (21 percent); transportation and public utilities (10 percent); finance, insurance, and real estate (7 percent); and wholesale trade (6 percent).

The service functions are the most rapidly growing sector of the tertiary activities and now employ more than 2 million workers in the state. Within this category, growth has been most dynamic in the areas of health and government services. Other major service functions include education, business and repair services, recreation and entertainment, personal, social, and legal services.

Health services have experienced dynamic

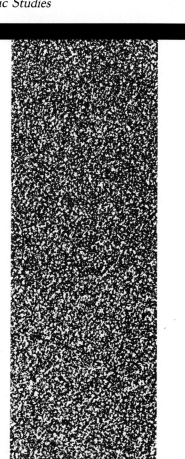

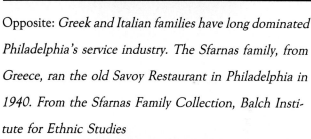

Opposite: *Greek and Italian families have long dominated Philadelphia's service industry. The Sfarnas family, from Greece, ran the old Savoy Restaurant in Philadelphia in 1940. From the Sfarnas Family Collection, Balch Institute for Ethnic Studies*

growth in the past two decades, with employment increasing from about 120,000 in 1965 to 370,000 in 1983. Every county in the state has experienced growth in this field. In contrast to the general trend of employment in Philadelphia County, employment in health services grew from 23,850 to 73,125 between 1965 and 1983. In Allegheny County, the second largest in the state in terms of health services, employment grew from 21,500 to 58,000. In many counties the percentage growth was even more spectacular. For example, during the same period health-services employment grew in Montgomery County from 7,300 to 28,500, or 290 percent, and in Bucks County from 2,100 to 11,500, or 447 percent. Particularly important was the expansion of health services in the smaller counties. For example, employment in health services increased from 160 to 800 in Wayne County and from 40 to 220 in Pike County. Health services are now being provided in the most sparsely populated sections of the state.

About 216,000 health-service workers, or 58 percent of the total, are employed in hospitals.

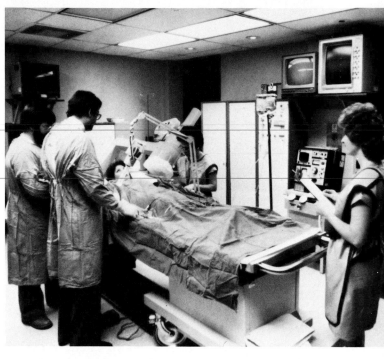

Another 39,000 are physicians, 19,000 are dentists, 3,200 are osteopaths, 58,000 are nurses, 12,100 provide outpatient care, and the remainder perform a variety of health-related services. In 1982 there were 297 hospitals in the state—226 general hospitals and 71 specialized

Left: *The Harrisburg Polyclinic Medical Center is one of three teaching hospitals in the Harrisburg area.*

Opposite, top: *Complete health and research services are available at Allegheny General Hospital.*

Opposite, bottom: *The cardiac-catherization laboratory at Lee Hospital in Johnstown is a great asset to the community.*

institutions. These specialized institutions are increasingly important in treating health problems such as rehabilitation after strokes and heart attacks, psychiatric disorders, and special diseases. In 1982 the general hospitals had 54,616 beds, and the specialty hospitals 20,751. A total of 1,835,994 patients were admitted to general hospitals, representing 154 admissions per 1,000 population in the state.

Pennsylvania has developed a number of distinctive health programs. Foremost of them is the program to provide compensation for the occupational diseases—black lung and other respiratory ailments—of coal miners. In 1978-79 there were 14,559 cases, with payments totaling $16,510,000. With the decline of the coal-mining industry, these figures have decreased significantly. In 1982-83 there were 9,119 cases (2,952 of them in the anthracite region), and payments totaled $9,885,000 (including $3,177,000 in the anthracite region).

The state of Pennsylvania has eleven centers to house and treat the mentally retarded. In 1983 there were 6,073 residents in these centers. In addition there are seven smaller units for the severely mentally retarded, housing 537 residents. The largest centers are at Polk (1,185 residents) and at Selinsgrove (1,038). These centers and units are widely dispersed throughout the state to serve various regions.

In the coming years the greatest demands for health services will be in the care of the elderly, the application of sophisticated technology in medical procedures, the prevention of disease, and the containment of costs without jeopardizing the quality of care. A major change affecting future health services was introduced by Medicare in 1983, when payments to hospitals became based on a fixed amount for a particular diagnosis. Since the hospital must bear the loss if the cost of treatment exceeds the fixed Medicare payment, hospitals are now taking greater care in the patients they admit and the length of hospital stays. The pressure on hospitals to economize is creating a need for discharge planners, outpatient services, home health workers, and financial managers. New jobs are developing for social workers with public-health training who can evaluate the capital requirements of hospitals to meet changing health-services needs. The need to operate in a more businesslike way is forcing Pennsylvania hospitals to adopt sophisticated information systems, creating new opportunities for data processors, health-care consultants, and software vendors.

It is still too soon to predict the impact these developments will have on the health-care field, but it is clear that employment prospects remain dynamic and job opportunities will become increasingly diversified. While there will continue to be a great demand for specialists, there will also be a demand for generalists in providing patient-oriented health-care services.

GOVERNMENT SERVICES

As the citizens of the Commonwealth have demanded more government services, employment in this area has grown steadily. In 1950 there were 338,000 workers in government offices. By 1964 this figure was 487,000, and in 1980 it was 729,000.

Of these 729,000 government workers, 170,000 were employed by the federal government, another 170,000 by the state, and 389,000 by local governments. These employees provided services in a wide range of areas, including agriculture, natural resources, manufacturing, and social activities. There is every indication that additional government services in the future will require continued growth of employment.

Opposite, top: *A modernistic fountain highlights Johnstown's Main Street East Municipal Complex. Photo by Robert B. Milnes*

Left: *The courtyard at Pittsburgh's City Hall provides a pleasant atmosphere for a break from the office. Photo by Robert B. Milnes*

Above: *The Pennsylvania State Capitol in Harrisburg, completed in 1906, overlooks the Susquehanna. As of 1980, about 170,000 people were employed by the state. Photo by Allied Pix Service, Inc.*

Most teachers in the state's schools are responsive to the needs of each student.

EDUCATIONAL SERVICES

In the 1980s more than 400,000 persons are employed in meeting the educational needs of Pennsylvania's citizens. This level of employment has remained nearly stable for the past decade.

In 1983-84 enrollment in elementary and secondary public and non-public schools totaled 2,134,185, of which 1,131,517 were in elementary schools and 1,002,668 were in secondary schools. In addition in 1982-83 there were 395,190 students enrolled in vocational education, of whom 233,242 were at the secondary level, 80,130 were post-secondary students, and 81,818 were adults. These vocational-education programs include agriculture, business, health occupations, marketing, occupational home economics, technical, and industrial. The combined expenditure of general funds (excluding non-public schools) for 1982-83 by all school districts, area vocational/technical schools, and special schools in Pennsylvania was $4.64 billion, up from $2.51 billion in 1973-74. The current expenditure per pupil for all public

Left: *Benjamin Franklin Elementary in Harrisburg, housed in this modern school building, is appropriately named after one of the state's most historical figures. Photo by Robert B. Milnes*

Right: *The majestic "Cathedral of Learning" exemplifies the intellectual endeavors of the University of Pittsburgh. This is an institution respected worldwide for the excellence of its programs.*

Below: *Internationally renowned Duquesne provides quality liberal arts and professional educations.*

schools was $2,628.52 in 1982-83.

Pennsylvania has an exceptionally well developed system of higher education. Enrollment in 1983 in institutions of higher education totaled 550,639, or about 4.5 percent of the state's total population. The land grant institution of the state is the Pennsylvania State University. This university plus the University of Pittsburgh and Temple University make up the state-related Commonwealth Universities, with a combined budget of $1.15 billion. In addition there are fourteen publicly supported state universities serving regional areas, plus about fifty-five private colleges and universities in the state. Total expenditures of these institutions in 1983 was more than $3.9 billion.

RECREATIONAL SERVICES
Recreation is no longer limited to the leisured wealthy but has become a fundamental part of most people's lifestyles. Recreation takes many forms, varying from a leisurely drive in the

Robert Morris College offers students undergraduate and advanced degrees in business administration.

country on Sunday afternoon to a bowling league on Friday nights to a two-week vacation sometime during the year. It has been estimated that one of every eight dollars spent in Pennsylvania is for recreational pursuits.

Pennsylvania possesses a wide variety of recreational attractions in its natural environment, historical past, and cultural diversity. Its varied topography, from the lowlands in the east to the ridge and alley country in the center to the rugged dissected mountains of the north and west, provide a wide variety of scenery. In the mountains are superb trout streams and some of the country's most varied hunting. There are many isolated regions providing solitude to the camper and nature lover.

As one of the original thirteen states, Pennsylvania has experienced a long and vital historical development. It was in Philadelphia that the American nation was born. Pennsylvania's pioneer forts protected the westward movement of population. In the Civil War the key battle

Above: *The Altoona campus of The Pennsylvania State University is situated in a lovely area of the state.*

Opposite, top: *Hunters in northeast Pennsylvania take time out to warm up with a hot drink. Photo by Bill Croul*

Bottom: *Fallsington Day in Bucks County is an annual event that harkens back to colonial times. Photos by Bill Croul*

of Gettysburg occurred on Pennsylvania soil. The state also played a fundamental part in establishing the Industrial Revolution in America. The best of the past is preserved in re-created villages, outdoor and indoor museums, and buildings maintained in their original state.

The state also boasts a wide range of cultural attractions, including summer theaters, folk festivals, and county fairs. The state's cultural diversity ranges from the Pennsylvania German farms to the sleek new skylines of renaissance cities. The federal government has played an important role in the development of the state's recreational areas. Six federal agencies are involved in the management of outstanding natural and historic recreational resources throughout the Commonwealth.

The National Park Service administers eight national historical parks and sites and one national recreation area in Pennsylvania. The Delaware Water Gap National Recreation Area, encompassing 20,277 acres, was authorized by Congress in 1962. This area preserves relatively unspoiled land on either side of the Delaware River. Valley Forge National Park was transferred from the Commonwealth to the National Park Service in 1976. This park commemorates the site where George Washington's Continental Army encamped in the bitter winter of 1777-78. Other national parks are the Johnstown Flood Memorial, Allegheny Portage Railroad, Hopewell Village, Gettysburg Battlefield, Eisenhower Farm, Fort Necessity Battlefield, and Independence National Historical Park, which includes structures and properties in Philadelphia associated with the American Revolution.

The U.S. Fish and Wildlife Service administers the Lamar and Allegheny national fish hatcheries, which together produce about 460,000 stream and lake trout annually, thus providing Pennsylvania anglers with superb recreational fishing. The Erie National Wildlife Refuge was established in 1959 as a resting and breeding place for migrating fowl. The Tinicum National Environmental Center was established in 1972 to protect the last remaining fresh-water tidal marsh in the state.

The U.S. Army Corps of Engineers is responsible for the construction and operation of navigation, beach-erosion control, and major drainage and flood-control projects. However, because so many recreational activities involve water, there is increasing emphasis on the recreational possibilities of these projects. A total of 65,000 acres of lake area behind dams built by the corps now provide additional recreational opportunities for Pennsylvanians.

The U.S. Forest Service manages the Allegheny National Forest, an area of 508,593 acres providing water, timber, wildlife habitat, and recreational opportunities. Within the area are 165 miles of trails, 762 camping sites, 561 miles of streams, and 7,752 acres of lakes for fishing, boating, and swimming.

The U.S. Soil Conservation Service administers programs of soil and water conservation, many of which affect recreational facilities directly or indirectly. State fishing, wildlife, and park agencies are eligible for assistance.

The Federal Energy Regulatory Commission has licensed a total of eleven hydroelectric-

Above: *A number of historic villages have been reconstructed in Pennsylvania to preserve the state's cultural heritage. The houses, stores, barns, shops, and other structures in Bedford Village have been reassembled from existing buildings in south central Pennsylvania. Photo by E. Willard Miller*

Left: *An early nineteenth century farmhouse kitchen was reconstructed in Bedford Village. Photo by E. Willard Miller*

Opposite page: *A fisherman wading in a central Pennsylvania stream takes advantage of the state's superb recreational fishing. Photo by Bill Croul*

Left: *Suits of armor are among the many exhibits at the Mercer Museum in Doylestown. Photo by Bill Croul*

Opposite, top: *Valley Forge, one of the nation's major military parks, was the site of the encampment of the Continental Army during the winter of 1777-1778. George Washington, the commanding general, had his headquarters in a stone farmhouse. Photo by E. Willard Miller*

Bottom: *The Gettysburg National Military Park has been established to commemorate the battle that occurred in early July 1863. Along the twenty-five miles of highways within the park are reminders of the battle. Photos by E. Willard Miller and Bill Croul*

Below: *Among the holdings of the Philadelphia Museum of Art are the John G. Johnson Collection of Western European Masters, modern art, works from Persia and China, and a group of paintings by Eakins. Photo by Bill Croul*

Top: *To commemorate the soldiers who fought in the Battle of Gettysburg, over 2,000 monuments and markers have been erected throughout the battlefield. Photo by E. Willard Miller*

Above: *As a pioneer outpost, Fort Necessity played a role in determining whether the British or the French would ultimately control the interior of America. Photo by E. Willard Miller*

Left: *Children play on a cannon on the Gettysburg battlefield. Photo by Bill Croul*

Top: *The Museum of Art, Carnegie Institute, founded in 1896, houses exhibition galleries, ancient and decorative arts collections, and the Carnegie Museum of Natural History. Photo by Jack Wolf*

Above: *Bucks County's Mercer Museum is built around Henry Mercer's collection of nineteenth-century crafts. Photo by Jack Wolf*

power projects in Pennsylvania. These power plants not only produce electricity but provide opportunities for swimming, boating, hiking, and many other outdoor activities. A number have educational centers to provide information to the public.

The state government has a number of agencies involved in the development of natural, historical, and cultural sites. These agencies acquire, develop, and manage lands for recreational use.

The Bureau of State Parks manages the state park system, which offers a wide variety of land- and water-based recreational activities. Evolution of the system began in 1893 with the creation of Valley Forge State Park. Over the years additional parklands have been acquired through a combination of legislature appropriations and private funding. In 1955 Pennsylvania had 45 state parks; by 1985 the system had grown to a total of 110 parks encompassing more than 272,840 acres. The modern park system was developed by Maurice Goddard, Secretary of the Department of Environmental Resources, in the 1960s. His goal of having a state park within twenty-five miles of every

Pennsylvanian has been nearly accomplished, and today the Bureau of State Parks has 1,200 permanent employees. Millions of people visit these parks annually. The most frequented state park is Presque Isle on Lake Erie, with an attendance of 4,438,000 in 1983, followed by Pymatuming in Crawford County with 4,422,000.

The Bureau of Forestry, through its twenty state forest district offices, manages 2,040,798 acres of state forest land. In addition to providing a large quantity of timber, these lands provide low-density recreation such as hiking, backpacking, camping, skiing, hunting, fishing, picnicking, and horseback riding.

The Pennsylvania Game Commission was created by an act of the legislature in 1895. Today the commission owns and manages more than 1.2 million acres of state game lands, which are used for public hunting and other compatible forms of recreation. The first state game land of 6,000 acres was purchased in Elk

Above: *Pennsylvania's state park system encompasses more than 270,000 acres. Point State Park, located in Pittsburgh, is pictured here. Photo by Robert B. Milnes*

Opposite, top: *Boating on the state's rivers and lakes is a pleasurable pastime enjoyed by many Pennsylvanians. Photo © 1982 Tom Weigand, Inc.*

Bottom: *Pinchot Park in York County provides the perfect setting for sailing. Photo by Allied Pix Service, Inc.*

Above: *Summer concerts at Point State Park entertain Pittsburgh residents and visitors. Photo by Jack Wolf*

Right: *Boyce Park in Monroeville offers downhill ski facilities.*

Opposite page, top: *Visitors to Washington Crossing State Park take in a spectacular panoramic view of the park and the Delaware River. Photo by Bill Croul*

Bottom: *Skiers ride the lifts on Doe Mountain in Macungie, Lehigh County, Pennsylvania. Photo © 1983 Tom Weigand, Inc.*

County in 1920. Prior to that all game refuge and public hunting grounds were in state forests. The commission sets policies for hunting, such as the length of the season and maximum kill. The commission also maintains six state game farms for the breeding of birds, such as pheasants, turkeys, and mallard ducks, to supplement natural production.

The Pennsylvania Fish Commission dates from 1866 and is responsible for rules and regulations governing fishing. The first fish hatchery was established in 1873, and the state now operates twelve hatcheries. Each year the commission stocks more than 5 million trout in nearly 100 lakes and more than 900 streams totaling 5,200 miles in length. A total of 70 waterways patrolmen and more than 600 deputy patrolmen enforce the state's fishing regulations.

The Pennsylvania Historical and Museum Commission is responsible for the care, preservation, and maintenance of fifty-five historic properties, including museums such as the William Penn, Fort Pitt, Lumber, and Drake Oil Well; industrial sites such as the iron-producing Curtin Village and Cornwall iron furnace; historical buildings such as the Daniel Boone

homestead, Daniel Bradford house, Pennsbury Manor, and Joseph Priestley house; military memorials such as Bushy Run battlefield, Flagship Niagara, Fort Loudon, and Pennsylvania Military Museum; and such special historical places as Old Economy Village, Ephrata Cloisters, and Old Mill Village.

Pennsylvania municipal governments have the prime responsibility for providing daily recreation programs and facilities for local residents. A total of 175 municipalities have park and recreational agencies with full-time directors. There are 850 recreation boards whose members assist 937 municipalities in administering recreation and park services. School authorities and specially designated township supervisors or borough councils carry the responsibility for numerous smaller communities.

Although long-distance recreational travel is increasing, Pennsylvania citizens continue to seek and find the majority of their leisure activities close to home. Since 1964 more than half of the state's municipalities have received one or more federal or state grants for acquiring land, developing new facilities, or making renovations or additions to existing neighborhood recreational sites.

Private capital has also played a major role in the development of recreational facilities in the state, including bowling alleys, health spas, skating rinks, and virtually all other indoor facilities. Private capital is also responsible for the construction of hotels and motels for tourists throughout the state.

The Pocono Mountains have long been recognized as a major recreational area. This region, lying in east central Pennsylvania on the New Jersey border, possesses a combination of natural features that has encouraged resort development. The Poconos are a dissected, glaciated upland averaging 1,500 to 2,000 feet above sea level, ensuring a cooler climate than in the East Coast lowland areas. The summers are pleasantly cool, and the cold winters with heavy snowfall and persistent snow cover are favorable for winter sports. Because the area is not suitable for agriculture, a forest covering prevails. The heritage of the glacial epoch is a land of many lakes and waterfalls.

The resort industry is central to the economy and the cultural environment of the area, which features large resort hotels and many small motels and inns. Much of the land is held in large hunting and fishing preserves that are "posted," forbidding public hunting and fishing. The streams of these private preserves are stocked with trout and the lakes with bass, and users pay a fee for the privilege of hunting or fishing on the land.

The major centers of the resort industry are the resort hotels. Some are located on the beaches of the lakes, some on famous trout streams, others at picturesque waterfalls such as the famous Buck Hill Falls, while others are isolated in the high plateau country. They are centers of intense utilization in the midst of isolated forest. These resorts have tennis courts, golf courses, indoor and outdoor swimming pools, hiking trails, riding stables, and several restaurants with evening entertainment. Many

Above left: *An outdoor restaurant in the Poconos offers a relaxed atmosphere in which to enjoy a meal. Courtesy, Pennsylvania Commonwealth Media Services*

Above: *The Pocono mountain region abounds with lakes such as Lake Wallenpaupack, pictured here as it looked in late winter. Photo © Tom Weigand, Inc.*

Left: *Golfers have their pick of courses throughout the state. Courtesy, Pennsylvania Commonwealth Media Services*

Opposite page: *A wild turkey stands his ground in north-eastern Pennsylvania. Photo by Bill Croul*

Above: *Two joggers run along a path lined with brilliantly colored fall foliage. Photo © Tom Weigand, Inc.*

Above left: *A replica of the Drake oil well is located at Titusville at the Drake Museum. The discovery of large quantities of oil at a depth of fifty-nine feet was the catalyst that sparked an energy revolution that has changed the economy and culture of the world. Photo by E. Willard Miller*

Left: *Pittsburgh residents experience the thrill of riding the roller coaster at Kennywood Park. Photo by Robert B. Milnes*

Left: *A young boy fishes in mirror-like Tulpehocken Creek at Grings Mill in Reading. Photo © Tom Weigand, Inc.*

of the hotels and motels cater to the honeymoon trade.

The Poconos are situated in the middle of the metropolitan East Coast and are served by three interstate highways. Interstates 80 and 84 cross east-west through the southern and northern borders of the region, respectively, and Interstate 380, know as the Pocono Extension, cuts diagonally across the area connecting 80 and 84. The Poconos are thus accessible by superhighways to millions of East Coast urban dwellers.

The Poconos are a year-round resort region. The height of the season is summer, when visitors stay from a single day to more than a month. Because of the vast numbers returning to the cities on Sunday evenings, traffic jams are common on the highways. In the fall visitors come to view the spectacular color of the leaves of the hardwood trees, and hunting draws thousands to the region. From December to April winter sports include skiing, tobogganing, sledding, skating, and dogsled riding. In recent years more visitors are coming to the Poconos in winter simply to enjoy an indoor vacation in the luxury hotels. After April 15 fishermen flock to the area to fish in the well-stocked streams.

Besides the commercial hotels and inns, thousands of vacation homes have been built in the area. Despite the great tracts of isolated forests, the large crowds have encouraged the growth of small curio shops and restaurants that tend to destroy the beauty of the natural environment, and development controls are necessary if the area is to be preserved as a natural recreational region.

Other recreational regions are found in the South Mountains and the Laurel Highlands of the Appalachian Mountains. These and other recreational areas provide an increasingly urban population the opportunity to spend some time in a natural environment.

WHOLESALE TRADE

Wholesale trade was one of the major industries of the pioneer era, and it continues to

Above: *Once a railway station, the Grand Concourse in Pittsburgh is now a popular dining spot. Photo by Robert B. Milnes*

Opposite page: *Station Square's Freight House Shops in Pittsburgh offer consumers a number of specialty items. Photo by Robert B. Milnes*

play an important role in the modern-day economy. Between 1965 and 1983 employment rose from 194,500 to 235,500, an increase of about 21 percent. Durable goods account for about 57 percent of this employment and nondurable goods 35 percent, with administrative personnel making up the remaining 8 percent. The annual payroll increased from less than $1.2 billion in 1965 to more than $4.8 billion in 1983.

The total number of wholesale trade establishments increased from 62,890 to 67,350, an increase of only 7 percent from 1965 to 1983, with little change in the distribution or size of establishments. Establishments with one to three employees represented 40 percent of the total in 1965 and 44 percent in 1983. An additional 23 percent had four to seven employees, both in 1965 and in 1983. In 1965 there were only seven establishments with more than 500 employees; by 1983 the number had risen to sixteen.

Wholesale trade is represented in every county of the state. However, the number of employees per county in 1983 varied from 14 to 37,983. Between 1965 and 1983 fifty-eight of the state's sixty-seven counties experienced some growth, and in eight other counties the employment losses were small. Only Philadelphia County experienced a major decline in wholesale-trade employment from 62,794 to 37,299, for a drop of 25,495 or about 40 percent. The loss of employment in wholesale trade in Philadelphia reflects the declining importance of manufacturing in the local economy. The decline of employment was particularly large in wholesale trade of such durable goods as machinery, electrical goods, metals, and lumber. In wholesale trading of nondurable goods, employment declines were concentrated in groceries, drugs, paper products, and apparel and notions, reflecting the general decline in the economy of Philadelphia.

Wholesale-trade employment increased most in those counties that experienced the greatest growth in manufacturing. Chester County has become a major wholesale-trade center, with employment increasing from 1,750 in 1965 to 13,960 in 1983. Major employment growth also

occurred in Montgomery (12,400 to 25,750), Bucks (2,000 to 11,300), Lancaster (4,400 to 8,500) and Berks (3,740 to 7,930). The growth of employment in wholesale trade was small in Allegheny County, from about 35,700 in 1965 to 37,983 in 1983, but with the great decline in Philadelphia, Allegheny County became the largest wholesale-trade center in the state.

RETAIL TRADE

The distribution of retail sales is closely related to the distribution of population in the state. Only the smallest hamlets and townships lack some type of retail establishment. Between 1965 and 1983 total employment in retail trade grew from 520,700 to 731,850, and the annual payroll increased from about $1.7 billion to $6.7 billion.

The growth of employment however, was not evenly distributed among the different sectors of retail trade. Employment in eating and drinking establishments rose from 108,000 to 210,000, accounting for nearly one-half of the total increase. With the rise of fast-food, low-cost restaurants, many more people were eating out in 1983 than in 1965.

The second largest area of growth was in food-store employment, which rose from 80,400 in 1965 to 126,000 in 1983. This period has seen the growth of mini-marts, serving local neighborhoods in towns and cities with basic necessities. These small mini-marts are modern versions of the street-corner stores found in most neighborhoods prior to World War II. Areas of more modest growth in retail-sales employment were building materials and garden supplies (from 18,800 to 21,120), automobiles (from 72,260 to 77,760), apparel and accessories shops (from 39,300 to 44,800), and furniture and home furnishings (from 21,200 to 23,680). Employment in miscellaneous retailing increased from 54,000 to 92,000.

The only decline in retail-trade employment between 1965 and 1983 occurred in general-merchandising stores, where employment decreased from 109,000 to 101,000. The general-merchandising store selling a wide variety of products is being replaced by video, computer, card, and other specialty stores. The large department stores in city centers also experienced a decline.

Between 1965 and 1983 the number of retail establishments in Pennsylvania increased from 62,870 to 67,350. There was a modest trend toward larger retail establishments, in terms of number of employees. Establishments with one to three employees represented 58 percent of the total in 1965, but only 51 percent in 1983. About 21 percent of all establishments had four to seven employees, and another 14 percent had eight to nineteen employees; both of these percentages were unchanged between 1965 and 1983. Establishments with twenty to forty-nine employees rose from 4.5 percent to 7.9 percent of the total, and those with 50 to 99 employees increased from 1.0 percent to 2.7 percent. However, the number of retail establishments with 500 or more employees declined from 61 to 28 percent.

Every county in the state experienced some growth in retail-trade employment except Philadelphia County, where employment declined from 109,600 in 1965 to 88,600 in 1983. The greatest portion of this loss was in general merchandising, where employment fell from 28,500 to 10,200, especially in department stores. Another major area of decline was in eating and drinking establishments, where employment fell from 27,000 to 21,600. As the economy of Philadelphia County declines, the luxury of

eating in a restaurant is no longer possible financially for many people. Other retail sectors that lost employment included food stores, automobile dealers, furniture and home furnishings, and fuel and ice dealers. Only in apparel and accessory stores and in miscellaneous retailing was there a slight increase in employment.

The major growth counties in the area of retail trade were those that were experiencing the greatest economic growth. Employment in retail trade increased in Montgomery County from 31,150 to 57,850 (an increase of 86 percent), in Lancaster County from 13,642 to 26,334 (93 percent), in Cumberland County from 6,460 to 15,900 (146 percent), and in Bucks County from 13,270 to 35,000 (164 percent). These counties of rapid overall growth experience the greatest increases in eating and drinking establishments and in the modern mini-mart food stores.

In most of the rural counties, retail trade is not well developed. The small market potential discourages the growth of retail establishments, and in many of these areas the practice of "eating out" has not become a part of the social customs. Employment in restaurants is very modest, and modern marketing establishments such as shopping centers have not been developed in rural counties.

Future employment in retail trade will be determined largely by the general economic prosperity of the state. In times of economic depression, retail sales contract; in times of prosperity, retail sales expand.

FINANCE, INSURANCE, AND REAL ESTATE

Pennsylvania has long been one of the major financial centers of the nation. Finance, insurance, and real estate remain dynamic sectors, with an overall growth in employment from 160,600 in 1965 to 253,712 in 1983, and an increase in annual payroll from $790 million to $4.625 billion. The 1983 employment total was approximately 47 percent in financial institutions, 37 percent in insurance, and 15 percent in real estate, with financial institutions growing more rapidly than the other two sectors.

In 1982 there were 3,146 banking institutions in Pennsylvania, with assets totaling

Opposite page: *The almost 200-year-old Philadelphia Stock Exchange, the nation's oldest, is the fastest-growing exchange in the country. The PHLX building is located at 1900 Market Street. Courtesy, Philadelphia Stock Exchange, Inc.*

Below: *Philadelphia, the fourth-largest U.S. city, is a commercial, banking, insurance, and transportation center. Photo by Jack Wolf*

$144.5 billion. These institutions vary greatly in size, from those with assets of a few million dollars to those whose assets are in the billions. Pennsylvania is a major banking center, having 21 of the 300 largest banks in the nation. The largest in the state is the Mellon Bank of Pittsburgh, with deposits alone totaling over $15 billion. Of the twenty-one largest banks, six are in Philadelphia, four in Pittsburgh, two each in Wilkes-Barre and Harrisburg, and one each in Reading, Norristown, Lancaster, Allentown, Butler, Malvern, and Warren.

State banks have assets totaling more than $59 billion, national banks $54 billion, and other financial institutions $30 billion. A total of 155 state banking institutions in 1982 included 91 bank and trust companies, 46 banks, 8 saving banks, 5 trust companies, and 5 private banks.

Savings and loan associations are well represented in the state. A total of 205 institutions under state regulation in 1982 had a combined membership of 2,468,732 and assets of nearly $10.7 billion. In 1977 there were 304 associations, of which only 152 were insured; by 1982, of the 205 associations, 203 were insured. This trend has guaranteed the soundness of the savings and loan associations and made them much more attractive to depositors. In 1982 there were also 79 federal saving and loan associations with 3,369,851 members and assets of nearly $15.7 billion.

Credit unions have also thrived in Pennsylvania. In 1982 there were 1,355 federal credit unions with 1,546,143 members and assets of nearly $2.7 billion, plus another 192 state credit unions with 320,556 members and assets of $446 million. In contrast to other banking establishments, the state consumer discount companies have experienced a modest decline in recent years, from 1,268 institutions with assets of $1.8 billion in 1978 to 929 institutions with assets of $1.6 billion in 1982. As of 1982 there were twenty-eight pawnbrokers in the state of which sixteen were in Philadelphia, with total assets of only $8 million.

Banking institutions are widely distributed throughout the state. The only county without a single institution in 1982 was Sullivan County. The great centers of banking are Allegheny County, with 439 financial institutions, followed by Philadelphia (377), Montgomery (173), Luzerne (130), Erie (122), and Westmoreland (120).

The banks and financial institutions of Pennsylvania operate under the legislative act, the Banking Code of 1965, and the later amendments. The purpose of the code is to provide for the safe and sound conduct of banking institutions and to assure public confidence in these organizations. The banking powers of the financial institutions are specifically stated.

The most important change in the 1965 code was enacted by the legislature in 1982. The code was modified permitting banks to operate statewide. Banks were permitted to widen their operations by the merger of banks throughout the state. Between 1982 and 1985 sixty-one mergers were completed and at least thirty-six new holding companies were formed. The change in the code occurred because the need for new bank capital was growing faster than the ability of an individual bank to raise new capital. Banks did not want to dilute shareholder equity by selling additional stock. The only means of acquiring new capital was by merging a number of banks. Mellon Bank of Pittsburgh with total assets in 1983 of $26,400 million has been active in merging with banks throughout the state. It has acquired CCB Bancorp of State College ($565 million), Girard Bank of Philadelphia ($4,800 million), and Northwest Pennsylvania Corporation of Oil City ($718 million). PNC was formed by the merger of Pittsburgh National Corporation of Pittsburgh and the Provident National Corporation of Philadelphia (combined assets of $12,200 million). It has since acquired Marine Bancorp of Erie ($888 million) and Northeastern Bancorp of Scranton ($1,400 million).

The mergers have financially benefited both the larger and smaller institutions. The larger bank acquires a local market base while the smaller partner acquires the capital and services needed to compete with other financial institutions in its region. In an era when electronic banking at the commercial and consumer level has made independently operated systems redundant, such mergers can also result in significant economies of scale. For example, following the merger of PNC and Marine Bancorp, the smaller bank abandoned its automated teller machine system and became a part of the PNC's automated network.

The code change has strengthened the soundness of the Pennsylvania commercial banking system by reducing the threat of banks to attempt to obtain additional resources through volatile purchased funds. By permitting banks to secure funds through mergers, Pennsylvania banks can seek additional funding from depositors as opposed to purchased funds. The 1982 Act has allowed banks to provide a quality service by drawing on each merger partner's expertise, in offering competitive interest rates, and sophisticated financial advice.

TRANSPORTATION: HIGHWAYS

Pennsylvania has had a long history of develop-

ing new and better transportation systems. In the pioneer era, the improved turnpikes were the ultimate means for transporting passengers and freight. In the first half of the nineteenth century, a network of canals was developed to facilitate the movement of people and freight. The canals disappeared with the coming of the railroads, and by the end of the century railroads blanketed the state.

In the twentieth century, motor vehicles have largely replaced the train as the mover of people and the carrier of freight, and a dense highway network now extends throughout the state. The development of Pennsylvania's highway system can be divided into three stages: first, the establishment of the state's road system;

All roads and main streets of the state highway system are shown on this map, and there is no indication of road importance. Note that there are wide differences in the density of roads in Pennsylvania. The rugged highland areas have a sparse pattern while the lowlands and resource areas have a well developed road network. Courtesy, Pennsylvania Dept. of Transportation

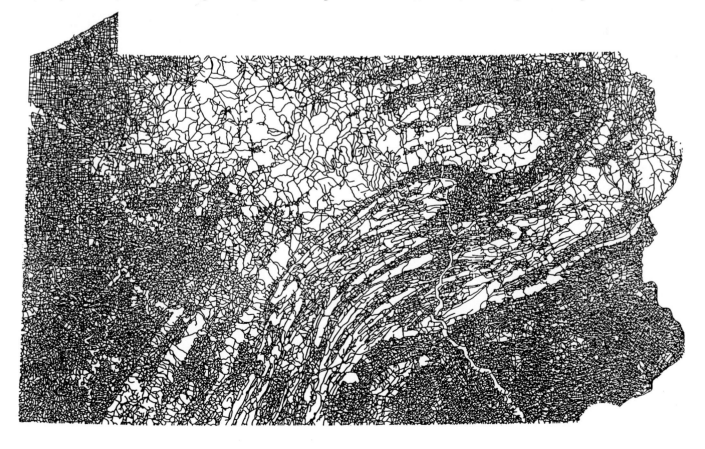

Above: *Pennsylvania's steel industry continues to supply the framework for road improvements. Courtesy, Pennsylvania Commonwealth Media Services*

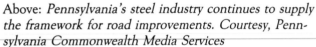

Above right: *Parkway East in Pittsburgh leads in and out of the city. Photo by Jack Wolf*

Opposite page: *U.S. 219 enters Pennsylvania from New York at Bradford, goes southward through Du Bois and Johnstown (where it is shown here), and runs into Maryland south of Meyersdale.*

second, the creation of a network of United States highways extending across the state and connecting with adjacent states; and third, the development of the interstate highway system. Pennsylvania today has about 106,000 miles of highways, of which the state has primary responsibility for 44,800 miles. The remainder are roads controlled by townships, counties, boroughs, and cities.

THE STATE HIGHWAY SYSTEM

With the development of the railroad network in the nineteenth century, roads were neglected. Prior to 1900 less than 5 percent of the state's 80,000 miles of roads could be classified as even fair, and there were no improved roads in rural districts. Under the road law of 1836, which was still in effect in the 1890s, county courts were empowered to appoint township su-

pervisors, usually farmers with no training for the job. The supervisors could levy and collect taxes, but a citizen could work out his road taxes at the rate of $1.50 a day. Work was done at the convenience of the individuals, and the roads remained nearly impassable.

In the 1890s many citizens began to press for better roads. The Hamilton Road Bill of 1897, providing an appropriation of $1 million to repair the state's roads, and the report of the Road Commission to the General Assembly in 1899 led at last to the passage of the Sproul-Roberts Act of 1903. This legislation created a Department of Public Highways and was the first important step toward a state highway system. To demonstrate the value of paved roads, sixty-four short, object-lesson macadam roads were built throughout the state. When requested by local road commissioners, the Department of Public Highways was required to prepare plans for construction of all main highways in the district. Two-thirds of the cost was paid by

the state, and one-third by the local government. After 1910 farmers began to use automobiles and thus added their voice to the swelling chorus demanding better roads.

The next forward step was the Sproul Road Act of 1911. Senator William C. Sproul, who later became governor, is known as the "father of good roads" in Pennsylvania. The 1911 Act reorganized the State Highway Department and greatly extended state aid. The state took over 8,855 miles of main highways connecting the principal cities and towns and assumed responsibility for their reconstruction with "durable material" and their maintenance. The state also purchased all toll roads that were a part of the state highway system. The Sproul Act initiated a complete survey of all roads of the state, which became the basis for the present state highway system. To secure funds for highways, a legislative act of 1913 stipulated that all money obtained from the licensing of motor vehicles was to be used exclusively by the State

Top: *In 1900 a state road crew used horse power to help get the job done.*

Above: *This state road in eastern Pennsylvania was merely dirt with a few rocks thrown in by accident. Both photos from the collection of the Spruance Library of the Bucks County Historical Society*

Opposite page: *The United States routes and interstate highways provide the basic east-west, north-south routes across the state. Prepared by the Deasy Laboratory of Geographics, Dept. of Geography, The Pennsylvania State University*

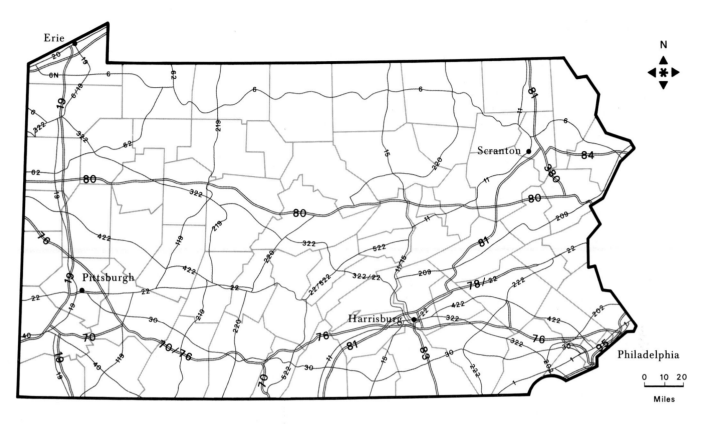

Interstate highway ══════ U.S. highway ─────

Highway Department. During this early period most of the funds were expended for urban highways, but gradually the rural areas gained improved roads.

Federal aid to improve Pennsylvania's roads was initiated by an Act of Congress in 1916. In 1917 Pennsylvania received $230,644 from federal sources, to be matched by state appropriations. In the 1920s funds for road improvements grew rapidly. During the administration of Governor Sproul (1919-1923) more than $120 million was expended, and in the administration of John D. Fisher (1927-1931) the amount exceeded $235 million. By 1929 the state had assumed responsibility for all borough streets that were part of state highway routes, and for county bridges on such routes. By 1930 the state was responsible for the maintenance of 13,500 miles of highway.

Most of Pennsylvania's main routes had been improved by 1930, but most of the rural roads remained gravel or dirt. In 1931 Gifford Pinchot campaigned for governor on the issue "Take the farmers out of the mud." During the first

year of his administration, more than 1,500 miles of township dirt roads were lightly surfaced with bituminous material, at a cost of $5,000 a mile compared to $40,000 a mile on primary roads. In the 1930s the state assumed responsibility for about 20,000 miles of township roads, providing much-needed tax relief to the townships. By 1940 there were 18,314 miles of "Pinchot roads," and the state's modern highway network had been established.

UNITED STATES HIGHWAYS

Federal legislation in 1916 provided that a state could designate not more than 7 percent of its total highway mileage as part of a federal highway system, thereby creating a federal-state highway partnership. Under this system the states had the primary responsibility for choosing the routes for development, planning individual projects, and establishing priorities. As a project developed, the Federal Highway Administration's Bureau of Public Roads guided, reviewed, and approved each step. Federal funds, which had to be matched by state funds, were

The Pennsylvania Turnpike bridge over the Delaware links the New Jersey and Pennsylvania turnpikes. Photo by Bill Croul

apportioned to each state by legislated formulas. The funds were made available six months before the fiscal year for which they were authorized, enabling states to plan their highway projects and ensuring continuity of development. Between 1917 and 1971 more than $3 billion in federal highway funds were apportioned to Pennsylvania.

Several major east-west and north-south routes were selected as federal highways in Pennsylvania. On the northern border of the state is U.S. Route 6. This route begins at Milford on the New Jersey border and winds westward north of Scranton to Warren. A north branch enters Ohio from Erie County, and a south branch enters Ohio through Meadville and Crawford County. This road traverses some of the least developed regions of the state.

In central Pennsylvania three federal highways cut diagonally across the state. U.S. Route 22 extends from Allentown-Bethlehem to Harrisburg and on to Pittsburgh, leaving the state at Steubenville, Ohio. U.S. 322 enters Pennsylvania at Chester, extends northwest through Harrisburg, and leaves the state in Crawford County. U.S. 422 begins at Philadelphia and winds its way through Reading to Harrisburg. From Harrisburg to Ebensburg it follows U.S. 22, then stretches westward through Butler and enters Ohio west of New Castle. In southern Pennsylvania U.S. 30 starts in Philadelphia and passes through Lancaster, York, Gettysburg, Chambersburg, Bedford, and Greensburg to Pittsburgh, meeting U.S. 22 westward to Steubenville, Ohio. In southeastern Pennsylvania U.S. 202 begins at Lambertville on the Delaware River, extends through Norristown and West Chester, and leaves Pennsylvania north of Wilmington, Delaware.

Six routes extending north-south across the state, as well as a few shorter routes, were also designated as federal highways. In the east U.S. 11 extends across the state from Binghamton, New York, to Hagerstown, Maryland. U.S. 15 enters Pennsylvania from Emmitsburg, Maryland, and extends to Harrisburg, up the Susquehanna River to Williamsport, and on north to the border at Corning, New York. In central Pennsylvania U.S. 522 extends through the valleys of the Ridge and Valley Province from Hancock, Maryland, to Sunbury, and U.S. 220 extends from Cumberland, Maryland, through Altoona and Williamsport to meet the New York border just east of Elmira.

In western Pennsylvania U.S. 219 enters Pennsylvania from New York at Bradford, goes southward through Du Bois and Johnstown, and enters Maryland south of Meyersdale. U.S. 119 branches off from U.S. 219 at Du Bois and extends southward through Greensburg and Connellsville to Morgantown, West Virginia. On the western border of the state, U.S. 19 extends from Erie to Pittsburgh and then southward to Morgantown, West Virginia. In northwestern Pennsylvania U.S. 62 extends from Sharon to Franklin, Oil City, and Warren and leaves Pennsylvania south of Jamestown, New York.

The federal routes were established prior to 1940, and except for small sections, they are two-lane highways that wind over the hills and valleys of the state. Many of the interstate highways, such as routes 70, 76, 78, 79, and 81, parallel the U.S. routes, and in a few places the U.S. routes have been rebuilt to interstate standards. To recognize the importance of the U.S. routes, many of them were given specific names. U.S. 6 was named the Grand Army of the Republic Highway; U.S. 322, the Lakes to Sea Highway; U.S. 30, the Lincoln Highway; U.S. 422, the Benjamin Franklin Highway; U.S. 219, the Buffalo-Pittsburgh Highway; U.S. 22, the William Penn Highway; and in recent years U.S. 220 has come to be known as the Appalachian Thruway.

THE PENNSYLVANIA TURNPIKE

The problem of crossing Pennsylvania from east to west has persisted since the pioneer era. The Pennsylvania Canal attempted to solve the problem by hauling boats over the highest ridges by means of an incline railroad. During the railroad era of the nineteenth century, the railroads followed the stream valleys wherever possible, but at times tunneled through the ridges. The Pennsylvania Turnpike was not only the first four-lane long-distance highway in the nation, but it provided a low-grade route through the mountains of central Pennsylvania. The turnpike extends for 327 miles, from Philadelphia on the east through Pittsburgh to a point on the Ohio line a few miles south of Youngstown.

The origins of the Pennsylvania Turnpike date to the late 1830s, when surveyors began seeking an easier grade and a shorter route across the mountain barriers. During the great railroad-building era of the 1880s, the South Pennsylvania Railroad Company was formed to build a railroad across the state. Some of the greatest railroad-empire builders of the day were interested in the project, including Cornelius Vanderbilt and his son William H. Vanderbilt, J. Pierpont Morgan, Jay Gould, George M. Pullman, and John Jacob Astor. Construction of the railroad began in 1883, and contracts were awarded for nine tunnels and piers for the bridge across the Susquehanna River at Harrisburg. For almost two years construction work on the tunnels and right-of-way were pursued energetically, but in 1885 the Pennsylvania Railroad bought the South Pennsylvania Railroad and work on the new railroad was abandoned.

In the 1930s survey-crew reports indicated that the abandoned South Pennsylvania Railroad route was "the best ever devised between the Ocean and Ohio." In order to stimulate the economy and provide jobs for the unemployed during the Great Depression, plans were set in motion to develop the highway. Harry Hopkins, federal Works Progress Administration head, became interested in the project and initiated surveys to determine the cost of building the central mountainous section. The Pennsylvania Turnpike Commission was created by the state legislature in May 1937, with the simple instruction to build a turnpike from Middlesex in Cumberland County, about eighteen miles west of Harrisburg, to Irwin, about twenty-four miles east of Pittsburgh, a total distance of 160 miles.

The commission first sought to have a New York investment company purchase the $60 million in bonds required for construction. However, there was no market for the securities. To salvage the project President Franklin D. Roosevelt, who saw the value of a high-speed route for military purposes if war developed in Europe, ordered two federal agencies to provide the funds. The Reconstruction Finance Corporation, headed by Jesse Jones, underwrote a $35-million issue of turnpike bonds, and the Public Works Administration, under Harold Ickes, provided an outright grant of $29.1 million to the commission.

In September 1937 the commission secured title to the nine tunnels of the abandoned South Penn Railroad, and on October 27, 1938, construction of the first section began in Cumberland County. Twenty-three months and five days later, on October 1, 1940, the 160-mile-long "Across the Barrier" section of the Pennsylvania Turnpike was opened to traffic. The job involved some 155 primary and subcontractors from eighteen different states. Six of the nine original railroad tunnels were completed, and one new one was built.

To complete the turnpike, the 100-mile Philadelphia Extension to the east was begun in October 1948, and the 67-mile Western Extension to the Ohio line in October 1949. The eastern section was completed in 1950, and the western section in 1951. The Northeast Extension, from Philadelphia to Scranton with a tunnel at Allentown, was opened in 1957.

The original turnpike was built as a four-lane highway with no divider between the eastbound and westbound lanes. The seven tunnels were to carry one lane of traffic each way, a reasonable plan at the time in light of the projected traffic of 1.3 million vehicles a year. But the public response was far more favorable to this pay-as-you-go road than state officials had predicted. In the first year of the completed 160-mile Allegheny Mountain stretch, 2.4 million vehicles used the new highway, providing an income of nearly $3.5 billion.

The highway was a marvel of construction. Most of the route was free of sharp curves, and the maximum grade of 3 percent meant that truckers could keep their rigs in high gear the entire way. To achieve this low-grade route, 53.3 million cubic yards of earth and rock were moved, cutting off ridges and filling in valleys. With increasing traffic the turnpike has been continually improved. In the 1960s three tunnels were eliminated, and the remaining four on the original route were given an additional tunnel to provide a complete four-lane route. Because the original turnpike did not have a divider strip, a median guard rail was installed along the entire length of the toll road to provide additional safety.

Traffic on the turnpike has grown steadily. In 1983 a total of 62,908,000 passenger vehicles and 9,088,000 commercial vehicles entered the thirty interchanges from Philadelphia to the Ohio border. An additional 6,246,000 passenger cars and 771,000 commercial vehicles used the Northeast Extension from Philadelphia to Scranton. The forerunner of all superhighways continues to be a major traffic route in Pennsylvania.

THE INTERSTATE HIGHWAY SYSTEM

The nation's interstate highway system came into being in the mid-1950s, when the Eisenhower administration recognized the need for a national network of superhighways. The plan this time was not to improve existing roads, but to build a completely new system of highways, with federal funds providing 90 percent of actual construction and right-of-way costs and states providing the remaining 10 percent. The federal funds came from the Highway Trust Fund, created by the Highway Revenue Act of 1956 as a depository for taxes on motor fuels and other highway-related levies, which were to be used solely to finance the federal share of the interstate system. No funds were provided directly from the general budget of the U.S. Treasury.

The Pennsylvania Turnpike was designated as Interstate 76, one of the few highways in the United States not specifically built for the system. It remains the only interstate toll highway in Pennsylvania. A second east-west highway was built in central Pennsylvania as Interstate 80, better known as the Keystone Shortway. In addition a number of north-south interstate highways have been constructed in the state.

In eastern Pennsylvania Interstate 81 extends from the Maryland border at Hagerstown through Harrisburg, Hazleton, Wilkes-Barre, and Scranton and leaves Pennsylvania at the New York border south of Binghamton. This new highway parallels U.S. Route 11. Branching off from Interstate 81 at Harrisburg are interstates 78 and 83. Interstate 78 extends to Allentown-Bethlehem and the New Jersey border, and 83 extends southward to York and on to Baltimore, Maryland. At Scranton two routes branch to the east. Interstate 380, known as the Pocono Extension, extends through the Poconos and connects with Interstate 80. The other route is Interstate 84, extending to Port Jervis on the New York border and providing access to New England. East Coast Interstate 95 follows the Delaware River from Trenton through Philadelphia and on to Wilmington, Delaware.

In the central and western part of the state, Interstate 70 enters Pennsylvania north of Hancock, Maryland, and connects with Interstate 76 at Breezewood. It follows Interstate 76 west to New Stanton, then branches off and leaves the state at the West Virginia border east of Wheeling. Interstate 79 provides the major north-south route from Erie through Pittsburgh, leaving the state at the West Virginia border north of Morgantown. Interstate 90 borders Lake Erie on the northwest.

In the construction of the interstate system, every effort was made to see that the roads did not go through urban areas, in order to reduce the cost of securing rights-of-way. The interstate system as originally visualized is now com-

plete. There are, however, vast areas in central, western, and northern Pennsylvania that are not served by a modern highway network.

INTERSTATE 80: THE KEYSTONE SHORTWAY

Linking the cities of Pennsylvania was a major factor in the establishment of the interstate routes, with the notable exception of Interstate 80. This route does not provide a connection between Pennsylvania cities. Rather it is a major link between New York and Chicago, and in Pennsylvania it extends through an area of limited economic development.

A direct route across central Pennsylvania was first considered in 1938 by a group of Williamsport community leaders who wanted tourists from the Midwest to go through their community on the way to the New York World's Fair in 1939. By placing a ruler on a map, they discovered that a short route from Cleveland to New York via Williamsport would cut seventy-five miles from any other combination of highway routes across Pennsylvania. The route linking a number of highways was advertised in more than 145,000 Short Route folders distributed to all parts of the nation through automobile clubs. The increased traffic brought a substantial amount of new business to Williamsport and convinced the city leaders that a new highway should be developed.

World War II delayed matters, and it was not until 1952 that, again in Williamsport, a committee was formed titled the North Pennsylvania Turnpike Committee. The objective of the committee was the construction of a self-sustaining toll road through central Pennsylvania with Chicago and New York as the terminals. In the next few years the committee obtained the support of automobile clubs, chambers of commerce, and other community groups. Although local interest was high, the proposed highway generated only limited interest in official quarters.

In 1954 a new organization was formed with a broader geographical representation, ultimately becoming known as the Keystone Shortway Association. The first act of the new organization was to seek the assistance of the Bureau of Business Research of the Pennsylvania State University in order to document the critical need for a cross-state highway. This survey revealed that the depressed economy of the region lacked an adequate transportation system to assemble raw materials and ship out manufactured products.

The Williamsport organization served as a model for other groups that developed across the state. In 1954, an election year, both parties adopted campaign planks supporting the Keystone Shortway, and in 1955 the legislature overwhelmingly authorized construction of a cross-state toll road with terminals at Stroudsburg on the east and Sharon on the west.

With the signing of this act, Governor George Leader authorized the Michael Baker engineering firm to prepare a report comparing the economic advantages of the more northerly U.S. Route 6, which had already been designated as a link in the newly authorized federal interstate highway system, with those of the proposed Shortway. Baker's study suggested that the Shortway would serve the state better than Route 6 because it had twice the population and number of industries, producing twice the value of manufactured goods, as did the communities along the more northerly route.

As a result the governor recommended that, rather than proceeding with the Shortway as a toll road to be constructed unilaterally by the state of Pennsylvania, the proposed route be included instead in the new interstate system. This recommendation was presented at two public hearings before the U.S. Bureau of Public Roads in Washington, and on May 22, 1957, the Shortway was approved for inclusion in the interstate network.

Public hearings for the construction of segments began, and in 1958 ground was broken in East Stroudsburg for the first section. The second segment began in 1959 near Corsica in Clarion County. It was soon realized that state funds were insufficient, and in 1961 the state legislature passed a two-cent gasoline-tax increase to provide needed monies. With this additional support construction proceeded, and

the 313-mile route across the central part of the state was completed by 1970.

The physical obstacles to construction of I-80 made it one of the most difficult highway-building projects in the eastern United States. Particularly spectacular was the "Big Rock Cut" in Centre and Clinton counties. In a stretch of 4.9 miles, rock excavation totaled almost 7 million cubic yards. Presplit blasting, in which the sides of the cuts are nearly vertical, was successfully used. Nearly 1.4 million square feet of presplit blasting was necessary, with the nearly vertical face standing 240 feet high. In order to bring the roadway grade from the adjacent valley to the proper elevation to insert the rock cuts, a 200-foot-high embankment was built using 6 million cubic yards of blasted rock. Another massive construction project was in the vicinity of Snow Shoe, Centre County. At the time, the contract of $9.3 million for the 3.5-mile link was the largest single road contract ever let in Pennsylvania. The 10-million-cubic-yard excavation was the largest earth-moving job in Pennsylvania history. An entire mountain was cut away to provide fill for a gorge so that the expressway could be kept to low-grade standards. Another section in the mountains of Centre County used 8 million pounds of explosives for blasting.

In Monroe County an unusual drainage problem along Pocono Creek was solved by a unique design. A system of double culverts had

Left: *The Harrisburg interchange of Interstate 81 is pictured here. I-81 extends from the Maryland border at Hagerstown and runs through Pennsylvania until exiting at the New York border south of Binghamton. Photo by Allied Pix Service, Inc.*

Right: *Keystone Shortway Association officers Confair, Heim, Ward, and Noyes met in April 1958, shortly before ground was broken for the Shortway. Courtesy, Grit Publishing Company*

Below: *The Keystone Shortway (I-80) appears here as it heads east toward New York City. The lower cloverleaf is the I-80 and Route 147 intersection, which links with the Susquehanna Beltway through Williamsport. Courtesy, Marlin D. Fausey and Michael G. Roskin*

to be constructed, connected by an open concrete flume, to drain water from the wide median strip. It has come to be known as the "Devil's Bathtub" and is a prime eye-catcher for those traveling I-80 in the Pocono resort area. In Luzerne County the relocation of Nescopeck Creek entailed moving more than a million cubic yards of earth, 80 percent of which required drilling and blasting before excavation.

One of the annoyances throughout most of the route was the presence of rattlesnakes and copperheads. Many chilling stories were related by survey parties as the route was determined, and when construction workers moved in for the clearing and grubbing operations, a sharp lookout was necessary to spot the snakes as they were dislodged from their dens. During the summer of 1966, when construction was advancing in Centre County, barely a day passed without reports of reptiles along the

Container cargo is unloaded at the Port of Philadelphia. Courtesy, Pennsylvania Commonwealth Media Services

right-of-way. In the Montoursville district emergency snakebite measures were established. Excellent cooperation was given by the Lewisburg Hospital, and luckless workers who were bitten rushed to the hospital for emergency treatment.

Interstate 80 has provided a direct corridor from New York City to the Midwest. Pennsylvania is fundamentally a transit area. At many of the interchanges services such as motel lodgings, restaurants, and gas stations have been developed, and these services have poured millions of dollars into the local economy. The Keystone Shortway has provided the incentive for new industrial projects in many adjacent small cities, as in the industrial expansion of Hazleton.

AIR TRANSPORTATION

Air transportation, of course, is strictly a twentieth-century phenomenon, and Pennsylvania was an early leader in this new mode of transportation. As early as 1908 aircraft were being designed and constructed by private individuals in the state, and by 1909 air shows were being held throughout the state. These pilots gained the attention of the public with breathtaking performances in frail wood and cloth machines. The Aero Club of Pennsylvania was organized in 1909 with ten charter members, and by 1910 it had grown so rapidly that it was incorporated. Today it is the oldest active incorporated organization of its kind in the United States.

To prove the durability of the airplane, races were organized, and interest was shown in aviation's possible commercial potential. A high point in aviation came in 1911 with a flight from New York to Philadelphia, covering the ninety miles in two hours and twenty-two minutes and demonstrating the airplane's ability to travel long distances.

THE ESTABLISHMENT OF AIRMAIL SERVICE

Commercial aviation had its formal beginning in 1918, when the U.S. government began airmail service from New York to Washington by way of Philadelphia. At that time none of the three cities had an airfield. In Washington the base of operations was the polo field in Potomac Park, about where the Jefferson Memorial is today. The Philadelphia junction was a farm field in Bustleton, next to the Lincoln Highway in northeast Philadelphia, and in New York the airfield was the infield at Belmont Park racetrack on Long Island.

The route was an immediate success, and the Post Office Department added another link from New York to Chicago via Cleveland. The route crossed Pennsylvania with stops about twenty to fifty miles apart. One stop for refueling in central Pennsylvania was Bellefonte, in the center of some of the most inhospitable terrain for fliers. The twenty-mile stretch across the Bald Eagle Ridge was known as the "Hell Stretch." There were no radio aids, and pilots complained that the rotating beacons were not much help because "on a clear night you didn't need them, and on a bad night you couldn't see them." Thirty-one of the first forty airmail pilots died in crashes. Although this air service crossed the state, it did not serve Pennsylvania, for the airmail route from New York to Chicago made no mail pickups or drops in the state. In 1920 Philadelphia was eliminated as a stop on the New York-Washington run, leaving Pennsylvania with no airmail service. In this early airmail era, Pennsylvania was essentially a transit area, but crossing the state involved tremendous flying handicaps, and overcoming them helped the industry advance through technical improvements.

THE AGE OF BARNSTORMING
By 1920 Pennsylvania was one of the leaders in "permanent" flying fields, with ground facilities at Altoona, Bellefonte, Bustleton (Philadelphia), Chester, Clarion, Clearfield, Du Bois, Essington, Everett, Gettysburg, Huntington Mills, Johnstown, Lebanon, Lehighton, Lewistown, Ligonier, Mt. Union, Philadelphia (Island Road), Pittsburgh, Stroudsburg, and Wilkes-Barre, plus the Essington seaplane base. The modern aviator can scarcely conceive of operating in the absence of regulations, or flying cross-country with neither navigation instruments nor ground support facilities at the end of the flight. For most flights there were no air charts except those published by local aero clubs or by Rand McNally. These contained many place names, but showed no terrain features essential for safe navigation.

Aeronautical aids developed rapidly in the 1920s. By 1922 there were excellent charts for a few areas. These experimental strip charts, drawn by the Airways Section Office of the U.S. Geological Survey, were nearly as accurate as modern aeronautical charts. They were not available to the public, however, but only to military aviators. The federal government also published an Aeronautical Bulletin containing a diagram of airports and existing facilities. Nevertheless, flying was hazardous. Alfred L. Wolf, a prominent aviator of the 1920s, describes a typical flight:

In flying from place to place, we had no airfields most of the time. Our technique was to swing low over a field at slow speed and look it over for ditches, hidden rivulets, and tree stumps, and to chase livestock off the landing area, then come back and make a low pass the other way, to double-check. We called it "dragging the field." We had no wind socks and no repair facilities if we stubbed a toe in a landing. Once off the ground from our home base, we were entirely on our own. For long trips we followed roads and railroads. Whenever we got lost, we would pick the largest field around, land, and ask where we were.

These were the pilots who proved that aviation had a future. They developed an enthusiasm for flying, and new records were set each year. Between 1921 and 1923, for example, an airplane altitude record of 34,509 feet was set, and a sustained flight of nearly thirty-eight hours was achieved.

In the 1920s there were many pilots who sought the thrill of flying, appearing at county fairs and other local gatherings to perform "stunts." These air shows were spectacular events, including parachute jumps and walking on the wings of the plane. To many, barn-storming across the state was the only means of earning a living, for there were few commercial opportunities in aviation, and the practice continued through the 1930s. The barnstormer played a major role in testing and improving planes and in the development of ground facilities.

THE DEVELOPMENT OF COMMERCIAL AVIATION

By the mid-1920s the airplane had advanced to the point where it was possible to develop a network of commercial routes. Prior to this time businessmen were reluctant to invest in aviation ventures, which were unregulated and frequently chaotic. The image of the barnstormer was one of instability and recklessness.

The transition of aviation from chaos to a disciplined profession required innovative legislation at the national level. In 1924 Representative Clyde Kelly of Pennsylvania introduced a bill in Congress, known as the Air Mail Act, authorizing the Postmaster General to designate airmail routes and to contract with private firms for their operation. This bill, which became law on February 2, 1925, authorized the federal government to create, define, and economically regulate the business of transporting persons or cargo on common air carriers. With the establishment of the commercial airmail routes began the vast system of scheduled air-lines, not only in Pennsylvania but throughout the nation.

A second piece of federal legislation, known as the Air Commerce Act of 1926, created a new agency, the Bureau of Air Commerce, in the Department of Commerce, to regulate the safe and efficient use of airspace. The new law provided for the licensing of pilots, aircraft, and aircraft components and established rules of the air, including enforcement provisions. These two acts brought discipline and responsibility to aviation.

Although a Pennsylvania congressman had sponsored the Air Mail Act, development of airmail routes in Pennsylvania was gradual. Only one of the initial routes was in Pennsylva-

nia, between Pittsburgh and Cleveland. By the early 1930s, however, the major cities and many smaller cities in the state were served by a growing network of routes.

Airports and other facilities in the state were gradually enlarged and developed. In 1928 the Avery Air Corps listed 183 "landing fields" in Pennsylvania, including 148 intermediate fields with improved landing strips, 5 federal, 15 municipal, and 15 commercial fields. In 1927 Governor Gifford Pinchot created a Pennsylvania State Bureau of Aeronautics and an advisory State Aeronautics Commission under the Department of Internal Affairs. In 1929 these two agencies were combined to form the State Aeronautics Commission.

By the late 1930s there were still many Pennsylvania communities without airmail service, for small airfields had not been developed. A solution to this problem came from Dr. Lytle S. Adams, a dentist in Irwin, a suburb of Pittsburgh, who invented a device that permitted an airplane to pick up a sack of mail without landing. Although Postmaster Farley was not greatly interested in experimentation, he agreed to have two routes in the "graveyard of aviation," where ground transportation was inadequate. All American Aviation (AAA) received the contract and began operations in 1939, linking fifty-four cities and towns in Pennsylvania, West Virginia, Ohio, and Delaware with the national airmail system. In the first year AAA flew 438,115 miles, made more than 23,000 pickups, and carried almost 75,000 pounds of mail over a 1,540-mile-long system. The system was successful and by 1941 had ninety-two pickup and delivery points in Pennsylvania alone, with major terminals at Pittsburgh and Philadelphia. The pickup points ranged from five to twenty miles apart, with the plane flying at heights that scattered pigeons from barns along the route. Although flying under instrument conditions was impossible, the pilots completed 94 percent of their scheduled flights, a remarkable performance considering the terrain and climatic conditions of the area.

The exploits of the pickup pilots have become legendary. Because stations were only five

to ten minutes apart, normal flights were at al-
titudes of less than 500 feet. One pilot enjoyed
flying under bridges, habitually zooming beneath the Westinghouse Bridge on the east side
of Pittsburgh. Another flier skimmed rivers,
touching the surface just enough to spin the
wheels of the plane, and still another who flew
low over railroad tracks had dozens of holes
put in the fabric of his airplane one morning as
track workers set off a blast at his approach.
The airmail pickup and delivery system was terminated in 1949, by which time it had become
outmoded.

THE DEVELOPMENT OF AIR-PASSENGER SERVICE

The first scheduled commercial passenger service in the United States began in 1926 in conjunction with the SesquiCentennial Exposition
in Philadelphia. Thomas E. Mitter, president of
the Philadelphia Rapid Transit Company, established a scheduled passenger service between
Philadelphia and Washington, and later on to
Norfolk. Although this service lasted only from
July to November 1926, the airline carried
3,695 passengers and flew 93,770 miles with no
mechanical delays. Of 688 scheduled trips, only
75 were canceled because of weather conditions.

During the 1930s the airmail carriers supple-
mented their income by carrying passengers.
Functioning without a mail subsidy was risky,
however, and few airline companies succeeded
as passenger carriers only. In 1930 C. Townsend
Ludington organized a passenger-carrying airline
that operated from New York through Philadelphia to Washington. The airline incorporated
as the New York-Philadelphia-Washington
Airline, but was simply known as the Ludington
Line. Its slogan was "Every Hour on the Hour."
During 1931 Ludington had 6,300 miles of
flying scheduled each day, out of a nationwide
total of 152,000. Ludington hoped that with
evidence of a profitable airline he would receive
an airmail contract on the New York-Atlanta-
Miami route in 1931, but the contract was
awarded instead to Eastern Air Transport. The
Ludington Line then floundered in the clutches

of the Depression and was sold to Eastern Air
Transport.

During the Depression of the 1930s and the
World War II period, development of passenger
carriers was of little importance. After World
War II, however, airplanes became larger and
safer, and the potential for a network of passenger routes became evident. The transition
from airmail airlines to the passenger airlines
required vast changes in personnel and operating techniques, as well as new types of planes,
and the Civil Aeronautics Board was charged
with regulating the air-passenger business. A
major economic change was the development
of independent airline companies.

In the post-World War II period, the Pennsylvania network consisted of three types of
carriers. The first were the national carriers
such as United, American, Eastern, and TWA;
a second group consisted of regional carriers
such as Pennsylvania Central (PCA) and Colonial; and third, there were a number of local
service or feeder lines. Philadelphia and Pittsburgh were the major modes of air service. A
number of smaller cities were served initially in
the 1950s by one or two airlines: Erie (American and PCA), Williamsport (TWA and PCA),
Scranton-Wilkes-Barre (Colonial), Allentown
(United, TWA, Colonial), Reading (Colonial),
Harrisburg (TWA and PCA), and Lancaster
(PCA and Colonial).

Many smaller communities wanted passenger
service, and in 1947 All American Aviation
(AAA) applied to the Civil Aeronautics Board
to provide passenger service to Bradford, Warren, Oil City-Franklin, Butler, Johnstown, Altoona, Lancaster, Connellsville-Uniontown,
and Harrisburg-York, in addition to Philadelphia and Pittsburgh. The application also re-
quested extensions to points in Ohio, West
Virginia, Maryland, Delaware, New Jersey, and
the District of Columbia. This was an ambitious request, as All American Aviation had
never carried passengers on its airmail pickup
routes. The CAB granted the request in part,
but with the stipulation that AAA terminate
mail-pickup services to all communities on
its passenger routes. This was a serious eco-

nomic penalty, and AAA countered with a proposal requesting passenger service to additional cities in Pennsylvania: Indiana, Du Bois, State College-Bellefonte, Lock Haven, Williamsport, Scranton-Wilkes-Barre, and Stroudsburg. The request was granted, and AAA became Allegheny Airlines in 1952. This airline gradually developed a national network of routes and in the late 1970s became US Air.

As air traffic increased at the major airports of Philadelphia and Pittsburgh, improvements occurred each year. The advent of the jet age required a major enlargement of the airports. Philadelphia and New York were selected to demonstrate the new Boeing 707 because these cities had the only runways on the East Coast capable of having the 80-ton, 140-passenger airplane land at a speed of nearly 130 miles per hour. To accommodate the larger planes, Philadelphia's main instrument-landing runway was extended from 5,000 feet to 7,500 feet in the late 1950s, and in the 1970s acres of unimproved riverfront were acquired to extend the runway to a total length of 10,000 feet. The terminal was also expanded. Philadelphia now has direct service to more than 100 cities and nonstop service to more than 50 cities. The airport handles more than 14 million passengers annually, and plans are underway to double this number by 1990. With five carriers operating out of the overseas terminals and domestic flights carrying millions of domestic passengers annually, Philadelphia is a major air-travel hub.

Pittsburgh's first major airport was completed in 1931. After a bond issue was approved, hills were leveled and 50,000 square yards of macadam paving were used to develop the Allegheny County Airport, which served as Pittsburgh's major air terminal for more than twenty years. After World War II, however, it became evident that a larger airport was needed. In 1946 the county commissioners secured a military-stopover airstrip in Moon Township, twelve miles west of downtown Pittsburgh, for a new airport. The Greater Pittsburgh Airport opened in 1951 and served more than a million passengers in its first year of operation. Both American and United airlines immediately rec-

ognized Pittsburgh as a prime new service point. The airport was renamed Greater Pittsburgh International Airport in 1977, when its international terminal was opened. The facility today handles more than 10 million passengers annually and is served by seven major U.S. air carriers, one Canadian airline, and eight regional or commuter air carriers. The Allegheny County Airport continues to serve nonairline aviation, handling more than 200,000 aircraft movements a year, averaging forty-five an hour between 7:00 A.M. and 11:00 P.M. each day.

MODERN TRENDS
The energy crisis of the 1970s altered the network of air travel in Pennsylvania, with Allegheny Airlines discontinuing service to a number of low-volume service points. In its place commuter services, provided by a number of airline companies using small planes of six- to thirty-passenger capacity, now connect these smaller centers to larger airports. In 1980 Pennsylvania's commuter airlines were first in the nation

USAir uses the Allegheny Commuter Terminal at the Greater Pittsburgh airport. Photo by Jack Wolf

in number of passengers carried, flying more than 16 percent of the national total in passenger miles. Four of these lines—Ransome, Pennsylvania Airlines, Altair, and Suburban—have been classified by the Federal Aviation Administration among the nation's top "large regional airlines." The others are classified as "small regional/commuter airlines."

In the 1980s personal travel in light planes for business and pleasure is economically feasible to and from locations in Pennsylvania that are more than fifty miles from a hub airport. The multimillion-dollar intercontinental jets and the smaller four- to ten-passenger business jet airplanes have proved a flexible and convenient combination in the conduct of corporate activities. The small, light plane has proven most efficient and practical for small businesses.

The future of aviation in Pennsylvania depends on the ability to adapt to high-cost energy. Technology is advancing, and powerful engines are being developed for smaller aircraft. These improvements should result in expanding the routes of regional and commuter lines, but few if any cities of the state will be added to the routes of national airlines.

RAILROADS

The railroad network of Pennsylvania was completed by 1900. By that time Pennsylvania had developed an integral network of lines and had become a central part of the seventeen-state system of the northeast quadrant of the United States. In the twentieth century the evolution of railroad corporate policy has been dominated by two crucial themes. First is the persistent problem of excess capacity, stemming first from extensive overbuilding in the nineteenth-century railroad era and then from the rise of competition from motor vehicles and air carriers. Second, in attempting to solve this problem, the railroads have moved steadily toward ever-greater reliance upon government action to deal with growing economic problems. These two themes are, of course, tightly interwoven and completely inseparable.

THE PENNSYLVANIA AND PENN CENTRAL RAILROADS

In the early twentieth century the Pennsylvania Railroad remained the dominant railroad in the state, not only serving a greater area but also carrying more passengers and freight than any other railroad. Its main line linked the two great urban areas, Philadelphia and Pittsburgh. By the 1920s it was becoming evident, however, that the Pennsylvania Railroad was in economic difficulty. Competition from the highways was challenging the near-monopoly of land transportation that the railroads had enjoyed since the Civil War.

As automobiles became common, travelers deserted the rails and did their traveling by car. While overall business declined, however, a strong demand continued for rush-hour service into and out of the central cities, such as Philadelphia and Pittsburgh. This produced the worst possible situation because it forced the railroad to maintain a large pool of equipment and a substantial labor force to operate a service that handled passengers only in the morning and late afternoon. For the rest of the time, the equipment and labor sat idle. The result was increasing passenger deficits that the railroad could not afford.

Competition was also developing with trucks for hauling freight. Unlike trucks, railroads have high terminal costs, as they are forced to maintain large marshalling and freight yards in many locations. Terminal costs remain the same no matter how far a commodity is shipped, a factor that works against short-distance rail shipments. Truck transportation is much more flexible. Trucks can pick up freight at its origin, reaching every part of a city or town, and they can move small shipments easily.

With the loss of passenger and freight service, the economic problems of the Pennsylvania Railroad became serious in the late 1920s. During this period of decline, the railroad management did not recognize the need for modernization in order to be competitive, and the railroad system deteriorated badly.

In the early 1950s the eastern railroads launched a campaign hoping to win public support for their struggle against the trucks. They hired a high-pressure public-relations firm, Carl Byoir and Associates of New York, to launch an attack on the trucking industry. At first the campaign appeared to be successful. When the Pennsylvania state legislature passed a Big Trucks Bill, raising from 50,000 to 60,000 pounds the maximum gross weight of truck and load, Governor John S. Fine vetoed the measure. Fine's veto meant that a reported $5 million worth of freight traffic in the state would be retained by the Pennsylvania Railroad.

In 1953 lawsuits were filed by both the truckers and the railroads, claiming that each side was vilifying and slandering the other. After a long series of court battles, in 1957 the courts declared for the truckers. The decision stated that the railroads had made "a deliberate attempt to injure a competitor for an illegal purpose by destroying public confidence in it." The Pennsylvania Motor Truck Association was awarded $852,000 in damages. Byoir was ordered to pay 20 percent and the twenty-four eastern railroads the other 80 percent.

By 1957 the Pennsylvania Railroad and the New York Central, whose major network was in New York but extended into northern Pennsylvania, had both suffered major losses, and the railroads began to recognize that if they were to survive, mergers would be a necessity. Initially it was envisioned that the Pennsylvania Railroad would serve as the core of one group, and the New York Central the core of another. Thus the historic competition would be preserved, while their chances of survival would be strengthened.

This type of organization did not materialize. Instead, on November 1, 1957, a joint committee of the two railroads was appointed to study a possible merger. More than a year later agreement had not been reached, and on January 12, 1959, the New York Central broke off negotiations. As the economic situation of the two railroads became increasingly desperate, however, the committee was reconvened on October 25, 1961, and agreement was quickly reached on key issues. The New York Central would sell its 20-percent interest in the Baltimore and Ohio,

and the Pennsylvania Railroad would divest itself of its one-third interest in the Norfolk and Western. The New York Central would be merged into the Pennsylvania Railroad, and the system would be called the Penn Central.

On January 12, 1962, the boards of both railroads unanimously approved the merger plan, and in May the stockholders overwhelmingly endorsed it. In August 1962 the Interstate Commerce Commission began hearings that would continue for fourteen months, with 461 witnesses producing 40,000 pages of testimony. A major concern of the ICC was that the Penn Central's size would be unmanageable. The railroad executives pointed out that because of the long period of decline the merged railroads would have fewer employees, freight cars, and locomotives than the Pennsylvania alone had had in past years. By merging it was hoped that the railroads could modernize and become profitable. On April 27, 1966, the Interstate Commerce Commission finally authorized the merger, providing that the new Penn Central organization would also take in the New York, New Haven, and Hartford Railroad. However, the U.S. Justice Department continued to oppose the merger until November 1967. Finally, on February 1, 1968, the merger was concluded.

Problems immediately became evident with the merger of the two railroads. The computer systems of the railroads had not been made compatible in advance, and data from the old New York Central could not be transmitted directly to Philadelphia, headquarters of the old

Pennsylvania Railroad and now of the Penn Central. The merged railroads were soon confronted with lost waybills, missing freight cars, clogged yards, and dissatisfied shippers, resulting in a serious decline in business. The equipment on both lines had deteriorated badly, but with continued losses there were no funds available to develop the hoped-for modernized, electronically operated system.

The Penn Central Railroad continued to lose money. Its operating losses for the first quarter of 1970 were probably the most disastrous in American railroad history. Receipts from rail operations totaled about $5 million a day, but operating costs were more than $6 million a day. In June 1970 the railroad had liabilities of

Left: *The Pennsylvania Railroad's Broadway Limited runs from New York through Philadelphia and Pittsburgh to Chicago daily.*

Below: *A lone car sits in a Pittsburgh railway yard. Photo by Jack Wolf*

$748,974,320 and assets of $462,472,382, for a capital deficit of $286,501,938. The balance sheet showed cash on hand of only $7,308,130. Although desperate efforts were made to secure additional funds, the Penn Central was forced to declare bankruptcy on June 21, 1970.

The Penn Central was the biggest business failure in the history of the United States. If service had been discontinued, large areas not only of Pennsylvania but of the entire northeastern United States would have suffered. The Penn Central system thus continued to operate under the bankruptcy laws of the United States.

GOVERNMENT INTERVENTION

Because of the economic distress of the private railroad companies and their inability to provide necessary service, the federal government has increasingly been called upon to salvage the depressed railroads.

The first major federal act was the Rail Passenger Service Act of 1970, requiring that a "national integrated" system of passenger service be established, thus creating Amtrak. For decades the private railroads had neglected passenger service, which had become increasingly unprofitable. In 1970 the private railroads lost $400 million operating what was left on their passenger fleet. The rail system had deteriorated to such an extent that on one stretch of the Penn Central system in Pennsylvania unwary passengers were sometimes thrown out of their dining chairs.

The Amtrak passenger system serves eastern Pennsylvania with a major route that extends from Boston to New York, Philadelphia, and Washington. A second route extends across the state from New York through Philadelphia and Pittsburgh to Chicago, stopping at Lancaster, Harrisburg, Lewistown, Huntingdon, Altoona, and Johnstown. A third route, originating in Washington, enters Pennsylvania in the southwest, stops at Connellsville and McKeesport, and connects at Pittsburgh to the New York-Chicago route. A fourth route crosses northwestern Pennsylvania on the Buffalo-Chicago route, stopping at Erie.

The East Coast corridor route through Philadelphia is the major passenger route in the nation. Nineteen trains in both directions operate weekdays between New York and Philadelphia. Pennsylvania's east-west route has two trains daily: the *Pennsylvanian* from New York to Pittsburgh, and the *Broadway Limited* from New York through Philadelphia and Pittsburgh to Chicago. Two trains run from Washington to Chicago daily.

Because the track and other facilities had long been neglected on the Boston-to-Washington route, Amtrak has sought to make this route a showplace of modern American railroading. Between 1977 and 1985 more than $2 billion has been spent on reconstruction of Amtrak's main line in the Northeast Corridor. The *Metroliner,* the deluxe train of the route, has finally achieved speeds for short distances of 120 to 125 miles per hour, speeds approaching those of the Japanese and French "bullet trains." Since 1977 Amtrak has replaced the old joined rails with quiet seamless ones and has installed concrete ties for greater stability. Every grade crossing between Washington and New Haven, Connecticut, has been eliminated, and selected stretches of the right-of-way have been fenced off. The signaling system has been modernized. Immovable curves, bridges, and tunnels, plus the need to run freight and commuter trains on the lines, keep the trains from achieving even higher speeds. Except for the Japanese and French bullet trains, however, "this is the state of the art railroad in the world," states Dennis F. Sullivan, Amtrak's vice president of operations and management.

The Amtrak system was conceived to provide passenger service between the largest American cities. As a consequence vast areas of the state do not have passenger-train service. In the late twentieth century, only the highway and the automobile serve the many local communities that had railroad passenger service in the nineteenth century.

In the 1970s not only the Penn Central but four other railroads with lines in Pennsylvania—the Reading, Erie Lackawanna, Lehigh Valley, and Central Railroad of New Jersey—

The GG-1 electric locomotive, designed by Raymond Loewry and engineered by John V.B. Duer, was introduced by the Pennsylvania Railroad in 1934. This photo was taken in Harrisburg during World War II, where the GG-1 was the principal means of intercity travel at the time. Reliable and durable, some of these locomotives are still in service. Courtesy, Historical Society of Dauphin County

declared bankruptcy, as did the Boston and Maine and the tiny Ann Arbor Railroad. Despite strong opposition to nationalization of these six lines, no other solution could be found, and in January 1974 Congress passed the Regional Rail Reorganization Act. This new law established the United States Railway Association, out of which the Consolidated Rail Corporation (Conrail) was formed.

Since 1974 Conrail has provided service on more than 80 percent of the rail lines in Pennsylvania. Private railroads no longer provide a statewide system but serve regional areas. The Baltimore and Ohio has the most extensive network in western Pennsylvania, with tracks from Pittsburgh to Wheeling in the south and Buffalo in the north. The Pittsburgh and Lake Erie and the Bessemer and Lake Erie are specialized freight lines in western Pennsylvania. Short routes entering Pennsylvania but originating outside the state are the Norfolk and Western, the Western Maryland, and the Delaware and Hudson.

Recognizing that the rail system had seriously deteriorated, the new law provided an initial outlay of $2.2 billion to renovate the system. Between 1976 and 1981 the government spent $3.3 billion in federal grants for modernization.

Besides the effort to improve the lines, there was also a major effort to reduce the mileage. Between 1974 and 1982 the entire mileage of

Conrail was reduced from about 30,000 to 15,000 miles. In Pennsylvania railroad mileage was reduced from 8,064 to 6,961, and employment from 44,000 to 33,000. The lines that have been abandoned were branch lines with low traffic density, many of them in the anthracite and bituminous regions where truck traffic has replaced the railroad. In the anthracite area the abandonment of lines is due to the near-disappearance of anthracite production. In other places the number of tracks has been reduced, as on the famous Horseshoe Curve west of Altoona, where a reduction from four tracks to three is adequate for today's reduced volume of traffic.

Conrail was originally responsible for numerous commuter trains, and it was required to serve Amtrak under the same general terms as other railroads. Amtrak is much less dependent on Conrail than it was on the Penn Central, however, because under the law that created Conrail, Amtrak had to buy or lease all passen-

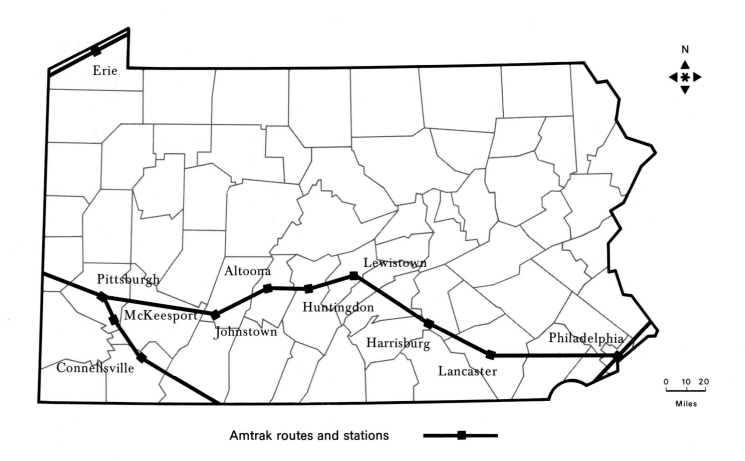

Amtrak routes and stations ━━━■━━━

ger equipment. Over the years Conrail has reduced its commuter service and is now a freight-
service organization.

The Conrail system lost money until 1981.
In the last six months of 1981, however, Conrail reported a profit of $830.6 million on rev-
enues of $1.9 billion. The streamlined Conrail
has received no government funds since 1980.
In 1983 the railroad had a profit of $250 mil-
lion. As soon as Conrail became profitable, the
federal government wanted to return the railroad to private ownership, and in 1982 the
U.S. Department of Transportation began seeking a buyer. According to federal stipulations
Conrail could be sold to a corporation, to the
public in a stock offering, or to railroad employees.

In June 1983 the railroad employees—members of seventeen unions plus nonunion workers—made an offer to purchase Conrail for $2
billion, including $500 million in bank loans.
The employee group planned to sell 20 to 30
percent of the railroad stock to the public. The
U.S. Department of Transportation, concerned
that the employees did not have sufficient
funds to maintain the railroad and that it
would once again need government aid, rejected
the offer. The Norfolk and Southern Railroad
has prepared offers for Conrail, but as of 1986
only the U.S. Senate had opposed the sale.

THE FUTURE OF PENNSYLVANIA'S RAILROADS

The railroads of Pennsylvania have experienced
a long period of adjustment, and a major re-
trenchment from their dominant position in
the nineteenth century has become a necessity.
Railroad service has been greatly reduced or
eliminated in areas that were uneconomical,
and equipment and facilities have been greatly
improved. Because of these changes the railroads are more economically solid in the 1980s
than they have been in the previous sixty-five
years. The railroads have become an integral
part of the total transportation system of the
state.

Above: *Pittsburgh's 16th Street Bridge crosses the Allegheny River to the H.J. Heinz Company. Photo by Jack Wolf*

Opposite page: *The major Amtrak route crosses Pennsylvania from Philadelphia to Pittsburgh as part of the network from New York and Washington on the east coast to Chicago and St. Louis in the Midwest. Prepared by the Deasy Laboratory of Geographics, Dept. of Geography, The Pennsylvania State University*

PERSPECTIVE

The economy of Pennsylvania has been built on change. In the process of change, some industries have declined while other industries have grown. If the economy is to remain dynamic it must be recognized that redundant industries will decline and in certain instances even disappear. These industries must be replaced by industries that serve the needs of the population today. The patterns of growth established in the nineteenth and early twentieth centuries will not provide the key to the future. The late twentieth century is one based on an advanced technology. The past industrial economy of Pennsylvania must thus be based on the modern factors of growth. We now exist in a world economy and Pennsylvanians must recognize both the perils and advantages of such a society.

417

PART IV
Keystone Enterprises

The "Keystone State," Pennsylvania was the center of the Atlantic coastal arch of American colonies and the focus of its strength. From the Friends' meetinghouses and countinghouses of Philadelphia, to the deep mines of the coal region, to the iron forges and steel furnaces of Pittsburgh, Pennsylvania has been the business and industrial keystone of the nation for more than 250 years.

Pennsylvania is a miniature United States, with an economic self-sufficiency enjoyed by few countries of the world. It is a microcosm of the United Nations, enjoying an ethnic diversity that is uniquely American.

Here are lush farms and orchards, great universities, innovative medical centers, battered but still proud smokestacks, and exuberant high-technology industries. Here are apple packers, airlines, automotive manufacturers, banks, and bologna makers. Pennsylvania firms lead the nation in such fields as cabinetry, chocolates, communications, computers, cranes, engineering, glass, paints, industrial ceramics, petrochemicals, pharmaceuticals, potato chips, pretzels, textiles, and tool and die manufacturing— among others. In commercial activities from agriculture to Zippo lighters, you have a friend in Pennsylvania.

Since the seventeenth century, people have come to Pennsylvania from everywhere. Quaker and Amish, Catholic and Protestant and Jew. They came for religious freedom, political freedom, and economic freedom. They knew that the streets of America were not paved with gold. They hoped only for a chance to plow the fields and pave the streets and build the factories.

While British, Dutch, and Swedish politicians disputed early rights to the region, French Huguenots and German Lutherans fled religious persecution and came to Pennsylvania. Indentured servants and ambitious young journeymen came too.

They came to Pennsylvania to become citizens of the New World. With them they brought knowledge, skills, discipline, and the willingness to work hard. Commonwealth craftsmen produced the finest furniture and fabrics in the colonies. Pennsylvania's artists painted the portraits of the nation's founding fathers.

Her architects created unique American adaptations of traditional forms. Her doctors established America's first medical school.

From the beginning, the business of Pennsylvania was business. Benjamin Franklin wrote the rules, and Pennsylvania lived by them. "A penny saved is a penny earned." "Waste not, want not." "Remember that time is money." "Keep thy shop, and thy shop will keep thee."

Pennsylvania bankers like Haym Solomon, Robert Morris, and Albert Gallatin financed the revolution and set fiscal policy for the new nation. Not that everyone was happy with it. Out on the Western Pennsylvania frontier, Scotch-Irish farmers grew dissatisfied with their new "national" government's taxation and took arms against it in the Whiskey Rebellion. The farmers lost.

Later, Philadelphia banker Nicholas Biddle struggled with President Andrew Jackson for control of American economic affairs. (The President won.) America was a nation on the move, and Pennsylvania artisans and businessmen blazed the trail. To cross the Columbia River, Pennsylvania engineers built the longest covered bridge in the world. In Conestoga Township, wagon builders fashioned a vehicle that could carry freight throughout the East, and that in modified form would cross the mountains and the prairies. Those who rode the Conestoga wagons carried the wonderful long, extraordinarily accurate rifles made by inventive Pennsylvania gunsmiths.

The railroads would follow along paths worn deep by the wooden wheels of the Conestogas. Matthias Baldwin built the engines in Philadelphia, and the Erie Railroad became America's first long-haul line. The first sleeping cars appeared on the Philadelphia to Harrisburg line. Throughout the nation, trains ran on rails and bridges built with Pennsylvania steel. A new era of railroad safety was introduced when George Westinghouse of Pittsburgh invented the airbrake.

In 1848 another immigrant family arrived from Scotland. The Carnegies settled near Pittsburgh, and their young son, Andrew, went to work for the Pennsylvania Railroad. With the help of Henry Frick and financing from the Mellon family bank, Carnegie Steel eventually controlled more than 25 percent of national production.

In the foundries of Reading, the textile mills of York, the coal mines of Wilkes-Barre, the glass factories of Manheim, and processing plants across the state worked immigrant Americans: Germans, Italians, Greeks and Turks, Hungarians and Poles, Czechs, Slavs, and Russians; refugees from famine, from poverty, from despotism, from frustrated hopes, from Communism, from war. Throughout American history they have come to Pennsylvania.

Oil poured out of the ground in a gusher that changed the history of the world. Pennsylvania's wealth of coal and natural gas had already made her America's dominant industrial state, but it was oil pouring from Edwin Drake's Titusville well in 1859 that smoothed the way to the twentieth century. The Pennsylvania oil fields became an industrial battleground as John D. Rockefeller's Standard Oil fought to consolidate thousands of independent drillers and refiners into a single giant organization—and subdued all but a courageous handful of them.

Confrontation is part of Pennsylvania's business history. In the face of increasingly concentrated industrial power, labor unions struggled to achieve safer working conditions, higher wages, and shorter hours. The campaigns brought bloodshed during the fight between coal mine owners and the radical (some still say criminal) Molly Maguires. The violence peaked at one of the most bitter strikes in American labor history, the Homestead Steel strike of 1892.

While less violent, the confrontation continued to be bitter. During the Great Depression, widespread unemployment and economic unrest threatened the state. As industrial distress deepened, labor leaders fought as much with each other as with management. The diversity of backgrounds and interests that had been the source of Pennsylvania's strength became the focus of its greatest problems. Only with the advent of post-World War II prosperity did tensions really relax.

Things are changing in Pennsylvania. The oil and gas fields are largely depleted now; there is less demand for coal and most of the great steel furnaces are cold. In their places are giant office buildings, industrial parks, communications centers, and warehouses. The stilled smokestacks stand in mute remembrance of once-upon-a-time while flickering video display tubes, glass and stainless steel laboratories, "clean room" assembly lines, and earth station antenna complexes point the way toward the future.

The organizations whose stories are detailed on the following pages have chosen to support this important literary and civic project. They illustrate the variety of ways in which individuals and their businesses have contributed to the state's growth and development. The civic involvement of Pennsylvania's businesses, institutions of learning, and local government, in cooperation with its citizens, has made the state an excellent place in which to live and work.

PENNSYLVANIA CHAMBER OF COMMERCE

Pennsylvania is proud that leading corporations in heavy industry, food and agriculture, fuels and chemicals, high-tech, transportation, communications, finance, medicine and pharmaceuticals, defense, automotives, and uncounted other sectors of the economy have made the Commonwealth their home.

Many giant corporations have grown in her great cities and thrived in her fertile valleys.

For much of the twentieth century, the Pennsylvania Chamber of Commerce has worked to maintain a healthy business climate in the state, supporting the free enterprise system and promoting activities and legislation to enhance the quality of life for Pennsylvania's people.

It all started on December 6, 1916, when 100 men from 35 cities representing 50 chambers of commerce met to form an organization "free from alliance with any political party" through which "men actively engaged in civic, industrial, and agricultural pursuits" could influence the legislature to "build up the interests of the state as a whole." Alba B. Johnson, president, Baldwin Locomotive Works, was elected the first chairman, an office he held until 1935.

The task proved more challenging than the chamber's leaders anticipated. One of the first issues to confront the infant organization was Prohibition. After extended research and debate, the chamber issued a detailed, 96-page report to guide the congressional delegation. It squarely straddled the issue. The chamber's guidance was accepted by the legislators—who split their vote evenly.

From its beginnings the chamber worked to ease friction between rural and urban factions, made itself a potent advocate of Pennsylvania's tourist attractions, and has helped to expan business and job opportunities in the private sector for the people of Pennsylvania.

In the 1920s the chamber was active in state and federal fiscal affairs, advocating restraint on appropriations and sound budgetary proce-

dures. The chamber also worked for adoption of the Administrative Code, which set the foundation for much of Pennsylvania's governmental affairs. Under chamber guidance, the Commonwealth adopted the Municipal Home Rule Amendment to the state constitution, a new Fiscal Code, and a Blue Sky Act regulating the sale of securities.

Since the mid-1930s the Pennsylvania Chamber of Commerce has concerned itself with state taxation and other legislation affecting the cost of doing business in the Commonwealth. It has focused attention on workers' compensation, unemployment compensation, industrial

Founded on December 6, 1916, the Pennsylvania Chamber of Commerce has provided seventy years of service "building the interests of the state as a whole."

relations, and all other business regulatory legislation.

The chamber's work continues today. Presently it supports tax revision and is working toward the adoption of health care cost containment, workers' compensation reform, product liability reform, truth and fairness in litigation, and extension of the Pennsylvania Turnpike. Current president of the Pennsylvania Chamber of Commerce is Clifford L. Jones.

SI HANDLING SYSTEMS, INC.

The old adage, "You can't get there from here," is never even whispered along the corridors of SI Handling Systems, Inc., a modern, state-of-the-art company settled in the pastoral countryside near Easton. Since it was founded in 1958, SI has been a leader in improving productivity in manufacturing plants and warehouses worldwide. SI supplies computer-integrated materials-handling systems to automate manufacturing and distribution operations worldwide.

SI's sophisticated handling and transport systems have been incorporated into the manufacturing process of such industry giants as General Motors, General Electric, IBM, Eastman Kodak Company, and Walgreens. The SI Cartrac®—a flexible, automated materials-handling and transport system—is an integral part of a totally automated assembly line.

A leading film manufacturer has installed the SI ITEMatic®, a revolutionary automated order selection system; the SI ITEMatic® distribution system has greatly reduced the distribution costs for a major retail

This Cartrac® automated handling system is being utilized by a manufacturer of photocopiers.

The SI ITEMatic® has proved a more efficient way to handle orders in this film manufacturer's warehouse.

drugstore chain with more than 1,000 drugstores and 80 independent restaurants in 30 states and Puerto Rico.

And many more SI systems—including the SIdewinder ™, an automated guided vehicle, and the SI Ordermatic, an exclusive system for the automated selection of full case items at temperatures of -10 degrees Fahrenheit—are being incorporated into in-

dustries as diverse as frozen foods, newspapers, and agricultural equipment manufacturing.

SI began in September 1958 with the concept of designing and selling automated systems to improve productivity. The original product, the Switch-Cart system, has been installed in over 1,000 facilities worldwide.

Starting in rented offices, SI began manufacturing in a cow barn and after several moves entered its present facilities in late 1963. Several expansions later, these facilities serve as headquarters for worldwide operations.

In addition to its Easton base, SI has offices in London, Bremen, and Tokyo, and affiliates in Australia, Canada, and throughout Europe. Jack Bradt, founder of SI Handling Systems, Inc., continues as chairman and chief executive officer.

The SIdewinder ™, a microprocessor-equipped unit load carrier for today's automated warehouses or factories.

SORDONI CONSTRUCTION CO.

In the winter of 1910 Andrew J. Sordoni borrowed a team of horses, purchased second-hand harnesses, and put down thirty-five dollars to buy a wagon. Then Sordoni, the youngest of twelve children of immigrant parents, worked twelve to sixteen hours a day hauling coal, digging cellars, and laying sidewalks before he returned home to do his own bookkeeping.

By this man and from these tasks Sordoni Construction Co. was formed.

Today, as the business celebrates its seventy-fifth anniversary, SORDONI is recognized as one of the nation's largest construction management and general contracting firms. It has grown from its base in Forty Fort to include offices in New York, New Jersey, and Massachusetts. The history of this company is rich with success stories that prove that opportunities are available through the free enterprise system.

By 1924 Sordoni Construction Co. was firmly established, and the firm hired a registered architect and several engineers to further strengthen its building team. This was a key move for the young enterprise because these professionals gave it the credentials to participate in the design-build type of construction, which remains a part of the company's business mix to this day.

While enjoying spectacular growth during those formative years, Sordoni launched his own political career, serving in numerous civic and public service positions. By 1926 he had been elected to the Pennsylvania State Senate, where he served three successive terms—two without opposition. As a result of his public service, the company's founder became known as "The Senator," a reference that lasted throughout his lifetime.

During the Great Depression Senator Sordoni proved that he was an innovative manager who could adapt to even the worst of times. While other businesses failed, he kept his business together by relying on earlier markets, such as sidewalk construction and other labor-intensive proj-

By 1912 SORDONI's reputation for quality and integrity had produced work for this crew of eight and for the teamsters, team, and wagon. Giving personal supervision is the company's founder, Andrew J. Sordoni, pictured in business suit.

ects. The firm also retrofitted its construction trucks to resume coal-hauling operations throughout Eastern Pennsylvania—this was a decision that allowed SORDONI to retain most of its employees during the Depression.

Like the two preceding decades, the 1940s were shaped by major national events. Once again, SORDONI adapted. During the early 1940s, when America's involvement in World War II was escalating, the company was busy with major construction projects for the war effort.

But the most significant turning point for the firm came after the war in 1946, when the senator's son, Andrew J. "Jack" Sordoni, Jr., returned home from serving his country as a fighter pilot to collaborate with his father. Jack Sordoni's skillful executive manner became the trademark of the business in the postwar era.

These years brought hundreds of construction projects to SORDONI, including a series of radio towers for the Western Union Telegraph Company built along the Eastern Seaboard. Other clients in the 1940s included Bethlehem Steel, Du Pont, B.F. Goodrich, IBM, Bell Telephone,

George F. Geisinger Memorial Hospital, F.W. Woolworth Company, and Pittsburgh-Corning Corporation.

During this period of rapid growth, the Sordoni family never failed to reach out to the community they served. In 1946 the Sordoni Foundation was formed. This charitable organization was originally conceived to assist with the education of children of working people—particularly coal miners. It soon broadened its scope to include support for social services, health care, arts, sciences, and numerous other community activities. An important mission of the Sordoni Foundation is economic education with public awareness of business, capitalism, and the free enterprise system.

The 1950s saw the heyday of large industrial construction projects and SORDONI earned an impressive segment of this market, including seven IBM projects, corporate headquarters for Metropolitan Edison Company in Reading, and two steel plants for Vanadium Corporation at Steubenville, Ohio.

In 1960 SORDONI celebrated its fiftieth anniversary, but soon suffered two tremendous losses. The founder, Senator Sordoni, died in 1963 and his son, Jack, died in 1967. Despite these losses the company's operations remained soundly structured, largely because Jack Sordoni had insisted on the development of a modern management organization designed to meet the needs of a rapidly changing

During the construction firm's fiftieth anniversary in 1960, three generations of the Sordoni family gather around the company's first truck. They are (left to right) William B., Andrew J. III, Andrew J. Jr., and Andrew J. Sordoni, Sr.

marketplace.

During this decade SORDONI reached beyond its established ways of operation to reflect a more economy-conscious industry. Management switched from its former "cost-plus" method of conducting business to competitive bidding and guaranteed-maximum-price contracts. SORDONI also formed several joint ventures, including a Caribbean operation to enhance its position to acquire new business.

In 1972 Andrew J. Sordoni III, Jack's oldest son and an officer of the firm since his father's death, became chairman of Sordoni Construction Co. He quickly organized a new team of professional managers who faced their first critical test later that year when floods caused by Hurricane Agnes virtually buried Wilkes-Barre. SORDONI's flood restoration work, largely funded by the federal government, reached into every cor-

ner of the community. The company hired more than 1,000 additional employees and managed a fleet of 165 pieces of heavy equipment to complete the flood clean-up. Some 400 men were involved solely with the intensive effort to construct temporary housing throughout the Wyoming Valley, and specially skilled crews worked on the renovation of flooded buildings.

One of Sordoni Construction Co.'s many prestigious projects in the 1980s is a multimillion-dollar expansion of the Owens-Illinois plant in Pittston.

The Agnes disaster created a need for new buildings as well, and SORDONI met the challenge by using techniques that produced efficient buildings at the lowest possible costs. These same management techniques were called upon when the company moved into hospital construction projects throughout the area, securing contracts valued at over $100 million.

As a result of its successful track record in health care and other construction, SORDONI emerged in the 1980s as a performance-proven organization offering an impressive array of services.

The firm's directors decided to increase its rate of growth by "exporting" its services into new markets. SORDONI opened full-service offices in the New York-New Jersey area in 1981 and in Boston in 1984. These facilities gave the company three full-service offices.

So, in its seventy-sixth year in operation, Sordoni Construction Co. has grown from a venture that started on a shoestring in 1910 with a borrowed team of horses and a $35 truck into a business of national proportions.

THE WHITEHALL CEMENT MANUFACTURING COMPANY

The Lehigh Valley is a veritable gold mine of minerals—its hillsides etched with veins of limestone, the earth below its surfaces crisscrossed with black rivers of anthracite coal. It was there that the American cement-manufacturing industry was born. At one time more cement industries were thriving in the Lehigh Valley than were grouped together anywhere else in the country. It is no wonder then that the Lehigh Valley is known as the cradle of the cement industry.

In 1911 a firm called The Whitehall Cement Manufacturing Company acquired what was originally Whitehall Portland Cement Company, which had discontinued operations in 1907. And since then, during a time when changes in the economy, technology, and competi-tion forced many cement factories to close, Whitehall has survived.

Today Whitehall Cement is one of six cement companies that continue to operate in the Lehigh Valley. The beginning of those businesses, and, indeed, the start of the cement industry in the valley, can be traced to David Oliver Saylor.

Saylor was born on October 20, 1827, in Hanover Township in Lehigh County. In 1866 he organized the Coplay Cement Company to manufacture natural cement. Soon he began to experiment with ways to produce portland cement, so named because its color closely resembles

---

The Whitehall Cement Manufacturing Company, at 5160 Main Street, Whitehall, in 1957.

the color of the cliffs found on the Isle of Portland, England.

In 1871 Saylor was granted a patent on his process, and five years later he received an award for his work at the Centennial Exhibition. Saylor died on July 21, 1884, but is still considered the moving spirit in the founding of the American portland cement industry. From Saylor's entrepreneurial spirit and own industry standards, cement companies tapping into the rich supply of limestone set up shop in the Lehigh Valley.

Just before the turn of the century Whitehall Portland Cement Company entered the portland cement industry with a plant at Cementon. After eight years of operation the firm shut down. A new business called Whitehall Cement Manufac-

turing Company took over in 1911.

Under Whitehall, a new quarry to provide additional raw limestone was opened, and extensive improvements and additions were made. When the company began operations the cement was shipped in wooden barrels and cloth sacks. The sacks were packed by hand, then sewn shut. Many times the deposits on the bags exceeded the cost of the cement. At that time the firm marketed its product through a limited number of distributors who in turn were responsible for its sale and distribution.

Over thirteen million tons of Whitehall cement were packaged and shipped by rail and by truck throughout the Northeast during the firm's first fifty years of business. Instead of one cement, Whitehall manufactured and stocked seven types. And by 1960 the company was no longer using cloth sacks to transport its product; over 80 percent of the cement was being shipped in bulk, with the remainder in paper sacks. In addition, Whitehall had established a complete sales force, with over 500

Today, still at the same location, with the most notable differences being the lack of stack emissions (as noted in the early photo), the advanced development of the quarry, and the absence of railroad facilities.

customers in all segments of the construction field.

During the next twenty years the product remained the same but the production process changed drastically. Whitehall converted its "dry" process kiln with waste heat boilers to preheater kilns. The first of three preheaters (the second one in the United States) was commissioned in 1956. The conversion to the preheater technology was necessary to make the process more fuel efficient as a means of offsetting the dramatic increases in energy costs in the 1960s and 1970s. As the years passed, Whitehall gained a reputation as a leader among cement companies willing to implement new manufacturing technologies.

As Whitehall approached its seventy-fifth anniversary, several concerns were paramount. High labor

costs were a factor as mechanization became necessary to keep production and product costs competitive as foreign markets began to export their cement products to the United States. In 1985 the firm employed ninety-seven hourly and sixty salaried workers. The company has kept pace with the changing environmental laws by installing and continually upgrading dust-emissions equipment to its plant, ensuring that the Lehigh Valley remains a clean and safe environment.

In 1981 General Portland Inc. purchased The Whitehall Cement Manufacturing Company. Whitehall became a wholly owned subsidiary of General Portland, and its stock was no longer publicly traded. The firm purchased a nearby quarry to ensure the supply of limestone in the production process and also expanded its storage capacity by about 80,000 tons. By 1985 The Whitehall Cement Manufacturing Company was producing 800,000 tons or 4.2 million barrels of portland cement annually.

425

POWER PIPING COMPANY

The corporate name is hardly a household word, but many households would have a hard time operating without the work of Power Piping Company of Pittsburgh and Donora. Power Piping, a wholly owned subsidiary of Harlan Electric Company (Southfield, Michigan), manufactures the heavy industrial piping systems needed by electrical power generators and similar industrial installations. From design to final approval, the firm furnishes, fabricates, and erects the heavy systems that run the companies that power America. Currently working in Georgia, Alabama, and Tampa, Florida, Power Piping has worked throughout the United States—and occasionally abroad—during its illustrious corporate history.

Power Piping Company's 829 Beaver Avenue corporate headquarters in Pittsburgh.

The business was founded in 1911 and acquired in 1936 by the Blaw-Knox Company, a highly diversified manufacturer of heavy industrial equipment. In 1963 Blaw-Knox was ready to terminate its power piping division and close the north side Pittsburgh plant. The 200 people working there would have become unemployed. Instead, Edward G. Prebor and Robert A. Patterson, both executives with Blaw-Knox, arranged for the plant, its inventory, and its order book to be purchased by C. Allen Harlan and Harlan Electric Company.

The new enterprise took the name Power Piping Company and became a totally autonomous subsidiary of Harlan Electric. Prebor, the former manager of sales for the Blaw-Knox division, became president of Power Piping and R.A. Patterson, the manager of construction under Blaw-Knox, became executive vice-presi-

dent of Power Piping. Prebor and Patterson brought in Bruce Hargett as chief accountant and assistant secretary of the corporation. "There are always fluctuations in the construction field," Prebor told the press, "but we have a good young team here and we intend to keep it together." As a result, 200 jobs were saved and Power Piping was launched.

C. Allen Harlan died in 1972 and was succeeded as president of Harlan Electric Company by his son, John M. Harlan of Bloomfield Hills, Michigan. John Harlan is also a vice-president of Power Piping along with two other Harlan Electric subsidiaries.

Power Piping has thrived since it became part of the Harlan corporate family. When it was purchased in 1963, its revenues were $1.5 million annually. In 1976, at the height of nuclear power plant construction,

the firm had gross revenues of $74 million. William J. Hoegel, vice-president since 1973 and formerly a manager and engineer with his service spanning from 1963, is directing Power Piping's sales and marketing program. Even under the depressed industrial conditions of 1984, Power Piping generated more than $40 million in annual revenues. And that labor force of 200 employees whose jobs were saved in 1963 now numbers almost 500.

Despite the fluctuations that are such an inherent part of heavy industry, Power Piping has experienced growth and expansion for much of its history. When first acquired from Blaw-Knox, mill work for U.S. Steel, Jones & Laughlin, and other Pittsburgh-based giants constituted more than 75 percent of its work load. R.A. Patterson led the firm's expansion into the electrical power generating field, and helped it move into the comprehensive systems approach that brought it the outstanding successes of the 1970s.

Power Piping is one of few companies in its field that is capable of providing a complete piping system, from concept to delivery. The firm's 120,000-square-foot pipe hanger fabrication plant provides supports to meet the diverse specifications required by both fossil fuel and nuclear power plants, as well as marine, chemical, processing, refinery, steel, and paper mill installations.

The pipe fabrication facilities are now also at the Donora location, where the latest welding techniques supplement the various cutting, bending, cleaning, and heat-treatment operations needed in fabrication of both stainless and high-carbon steels.

Most recently, Power Piping has become a leading fabricator of urethane cryogenic pipe supports made from POWERFOAM, a high-density molded rigid urethane foam specifically formulated and molded to meet exacting and precise specifications. These molded and insulated pipe supports are assuming an increasing role in the energy-conscious, high-

technology environment of contemporary industry.

The eighteen-acre Donora location was an abandoned U.S. Steel plant, originally leased in 1968 and later purchased with the assistance of the Washington County Industrial Development Authority and Middle Monongahela Industrial Development Association (MIDA). The Donora plant was expanded and modernized in 1972, and expanded again when a second building was acquired from Celco Industries. The third major modification to the Donora site was a new section joining the two existing buildings. It was completed in 1977. In 1984 Power Piping moved its hanger manufacturing operations from the Pittsburgh location to Donora. A 1985 expansion of the Pittsburgh facility will provide additional space for engineering, design, and executive offices.

William R. Patterson, an employee

The Donora plant is the site of Power Piping's pipe fabrication shop and pipe hanger shop operations.

with Power Piping since 1964 and executive vice-president since 1974, became president of the firm in 1981, taking over as chairman of the board and chief executive officer of Power Piping when his father died in 1982. Like his father, William Patterson is an active supporter of the Boy Scouts and of numerous Pittsburgh-area civic projects. He has led the firm to its consolidation and is now taking it down some new paths. In 1985 Power Piping acquired American Health & Diet, Inc., from American Diet Counselors of Salt Lake City. Currently under reorganization, the firm will become a wholly owned subsidiary of Power Piping.

The heart of Power Piping remains with the energy generation business. "The 1980s slowdown in power plant construction means that America will soon need to expand its generating capacity," says Patterson. "When that happens, Power Piping will be ready with skilled craftsmen, experienced engineers, and modern technology—ready once again to meet the needs of American industry."

GREENE, TWEED & CO.

The date was May 8, 1863, and there, tucked away on the inside pages of the *New York Tribune* and the *New York Sun,* was a small notice announcing the start of a new business that would merchandise wholesale hardware and mill supplies. The venture was founded along Murray Street by two brothers, J. Aston and John W. Greene, and their partner, Henry A. Tweed. Coming up with a name for their new enterprise was really quite simple: Greene, Tweed & Co.

Today Greene, Tweed is one of the nation's most sophisticated hydraulic seal manufacturers, employing over 300 people in four manufacturing facilities in the United States and three subsidiary companies in Great Britain, West Germany, and France. From its corporate headquarters in Kulpsville, Pennsylvania, the 123-year-old business offers a full range of fluid power and fluid-handling sealing elements. For instance, there could be just a handful of Greene, Tweed seals in a gun mount recoil mechanism. However, there were 4,000 of the firm's seals in the United States Space Shuttle *Columbia* when it blasted into space.

The company that now supplies parts for space missions once had to contend with the vagaries of the Civil War just to survive. In 1863 the Civil War was draining the North's economy, and the new business had a difficult time getting established. But the Union victory at Gettysburg gave both the North and Greene, Tweed the economic boost that it needed. By 1863 the firm was trading throughout the industrial Northeast, purchasing goods and then selling them to mills and hardware stores.

Greene, Tweed began its own manufacturing in 1872 with the acquisition of the Manhattan Packing Company. The firm then introduced internally lubricated packing, the first of many innovations, needed to contain the fluids being created by machines operating under greater temperatures, pressures, and speeds. The cotton-and-flax-braided packing

The founders (left to right): J. Aston Greene, Henry A. Tweed, and John W. Greene.

was known widely as Palmetto Packing. And the product, which was soundly endorsed when Rear Admiral Richard E. Byrd used it on his first Antarctic expedition in 1928, is still manufactured and in demand today.

With the onset of World War II Greene, Tweed joined the war effort, producing packings for military use and manufacturing gaskets for use in ship boilers. The company also developed a fluid power seal called the

The Greene, Tweed & Co. headquarters in North Wales in the early 1900s.

G-T Ring to be used in tanks and other military vehicles. The G-T Ring proved to be the forerunner of an entire line of Greene, Tweed seals that are known for their resistance to high temperatures, intense pressure, and reactive fluids.

A walk through Greene, Tweed's headquarters offers a quick glance at a business that combines engineering, research and development, product testing, and in-house tooling to form the multimillion-dollar corporation that it is today. From its tractor wheel-size, asymmetrical seals of superior urethane polymer to its double-acting, high-pressure piston seals tiny enough to fit around a finger, Greene, Tweed & Co. is a leading hydraulic seal manufacturer.

DUQUESNE LIGHT COMPANY

No one was quite sure what it would be good for, but in 1880, generating and distributing electricity seemed to be a promising commercial activity. Thomas Edison had just demonstrated that, at the very least, it provided a convenient, safe, and efficient form of light—a great advance over the gaslights then in widespread use. The idea was so promising that a group of Pittsburgh businessmen joined forces to capitalize the Allegheny County Light Company with $90,000.

The firm's first customers were the Pennsylvania Railroad and Westinghouse. Soon electric lights were chasing the darkness all over Pittsburgh. By the turn of the century 150 different local companies were offering electrical lighting to Allegheny County customers.

Duquesne Light Company was incorporated on August 5, 1903, by a group of businessmen intent on consolidating the industry. Under the leadership of Robert C. Hall, Howard McSweeny, R.H. Binns, and Shirley P. Austin, Duquesne Light expanded its territory and eliminated the competition through mergers and acquisitions.

The business grew rapidly, as did the technology drawing on the new source of power. The electrification of transportation (trolley lines) and industry was well under way by the second decade of the twentieth century. Duquesne Light became an industry leader in the technology of power transmission, distribution, and marketing.

Throughout the 1930s Duquesne Light continued its tradition of technological innovation. The great flood

A symbol of service in the 1920s was this Duquesne Light Company truck and the uniformed service employee. Duquesne Light traces its history back to the Allegheny County Light Company, which was chartered on March 6, 1880.

of 1936 forced the Reed, Brunot Island, and Colfax generating stations out of service, but within hours Duquesne Light had restored sufficient power to meet emergency needs—primarily through the interconnected grid system developed by Duquesne Light's own engineers and pioneered

The nuclear-fueled Beaver Valley Power Station, located along the Ohio River in Shippington, consists of two 833,000-kilowatt units operated by Duquesne Light Company. Unit No. 1 has been in operation since 1976. Unit No. 2 is under construction. Duquesne Light owns 47.5 percent of Unit No. 1 and 13.74 percent of Unit No. 2.

by the Pittsburgh utility in cooperation with neighboring systems.

Electrical appliances, radio, night baseball, television—all impossible before the era of electricity—became common through the 1930s, 1940s, and 1950s. Electricity had brought a new way of life, and Duquesne Light remained among the industry's most innovative leaders.

In 1954 Duquesne Light was selected to participate with the Atomic Energy Commission in the design and construction of Shippingport Atomic Power Station, the nation's first full-scale atomic power plant to be devoted exclusively to civilian needs.

The Shippingport Atomic Power Station has been generating electricity from nuclear fuel from 1957 to 1982. It also has proven to be an important source of research and development information. In many ways, Duquesne Light and Shippingport have provided the data and basic foundation of the entire commercial nuclear power industry. The plant currently is being decommissioned, a process that will be completed by 1988, closing this latest—but far from last—chapter in an outstanding story of innovation and dedication to the people and industries of Western Pennsylvania.

PENNSYLVANIA POWER & LIGHT COMPANY

February 12, 1985, marked the completion of an era for Pennsylvania Power & Light Company. On that date the Allentown-based utility placed in service Unit 2 of the Susquehanna Steam Electric Station, a nuclear power plant located near Berwick, and completed an era of power plant construction begun shortly after World War II.

With the 1.05-million-kilowatt generating unit and its twin Unit 1 in service, PP&L has met its construction needs for major generating capacity for at least the balance of this century. This exceptionally strong capacity position, based on an efficient mix of coal, nuclear, oil, and hydroelectric generation, opens up important opportunities for the firm to broaden the scope of energy services offered to its customers.

The strength of the company's generating capacity sets PP&L apart from most of the nation's electric utilities. In the years ahead the firm will emphasize the importance of this strong competitive position as a supplier of electric power to attract and hold job-producing businesses in the 10,000-square-mile area of Central-eastern Pennsylvania that the utility serves.

Reliable and competitively priced electric power is a vital economic development resource. As national trends clearly show, energy efficiency and improved productivity are increasingly being achieved in homes, businesses, and industries through the use of electricity because of its versatility and high end-use efficiency.

At the heart of PP&L's marketing and economic development effort is customer service. The overall effect of PP&L's programs in these areas is to provide opportunities to serve customers at a lower cost than otherwise would be possible. The objective of these programs is to facilitate the most effective operation of the PP&L

Pennsylvania Power & Light Company is headquartered in downtown Allentown.

system by achieving optimal levels of kilowatt-hour sales growth while managing relatively lower growth in future peak loads—the maximum demand for electricity at a particular point in time.

Over the long term, limiting growth in peak loads benefits customers by minimizing future requirements for new generating capacity. Also, the utility is actively studying additional methods of postponing the need for new central station generating capacity. Together with achieving added revenues through increased

With the operation of units 1 and 2 of the Susquehanna Steam Electric Station, PP&L has met its construction needs for major new generating capacity for at least the balance of this century.

sales, this will reduce future needs for higher rates, permitting PP&L to meet its long-term objective of holding increases in the price of electric service at or below the general rate of inflation.

Since its establishment in 1920, PP&L has been committed to meeting customers' needs for economical

and reliable electric service. Looking ahead to the remainder of the century, the firm fully recognizes that its more than one million customers make an economic choice each time they flip a switch to operate a work-saving appliance, enjoy entertainment, or improve productivity. Pennsylvania Power & Light Company intends to ensure that this essential resource, electricity, is available and economically priced for industrial growth, jobs, economic progress, health care, education, and personal comfort.

FADDIS BROTHERS, INC.

One day in 1947, newlyweds Leon and Virginia Faddis packed their belongings on the back of a 1946 Harley-Davidson motorcycle and drove thirteen miles to live in a house with a backyard barn that they had just purchased for $6,500.

On this six-acre tract of land just outside Downingtown, Pennsylvania, they would raise their family and start their own business. Today the family includes four children and eight grandchildren, the 1850 farmhouse has been expanded many times over, and there is an indoor swimming pool in the backyard. The business, Faddis Brothers, Inc., is one of the largest manufacturers of concrete lintels in the Northeast.

Leon and Virginia Faddis pose on the seat of their 1946 Harley-Davidson motorcycle.

A view of Faddis Brothers, Inc., includes the Faddis' first home (the brick house, center top), the steam-cure manufacturing facilities with solar-heated panels, and stacks of lintels on the grounds.

Seated in the upstairs office of the house where he and his wife first moved some forty years ago, Leon Faddis can look out his window and see the concrete lintels he produces—stacked in rows that look like so many popsicle sticks boxed together.

Nearly 2,000 truckloads of concrete lintels—the rectangular, concrete logs that span and usually carry the load above a doorway, window, or other opening—are produced here each year. But when Leon Faddis first settled in this house, he worked eight hours a day at the Downingtown Paper Company, and at night he would moonlight, hauling concrete blocks for employees at the paper company.

Before long he started buying loads of blocks and selling them for a profit. At night, he and Virginia would work on the 1939 Chevrolet truck they used for hauling. Leon still refers to Virginia as his first mechanic, his first partner.

In 1950 Faddis bought several trucks and hired his brother, Jim, to help him haul not only concrete blocks but concrete lintels, as well. In 1953, in the barn and sheds behind his house, Faddis started to manufacture the firm's own concrete lintels. By 1955 Leon had stopped working at the paper company to devote all of his efforts to the lintel business.

By this time James Faddis had joined his brother in the new venture and two corporations were established. Faddis Brothers, Inc., with James as president, manufactured the lintels. Leon Faddis was head of a retail building supply yard. One day, James approached a local block company, Fizzano Brothers, to see if it needed lintels. Fizzano Brothers challenged Faddis Brothers to make a lintel that was very strong, saying it would do business with the fledgling enterprise if the product was of high quality. So, in 1957, Faddis became the first lintel company in the area to begin to steam-cure lintels—a process that makes Faddis' lintels stronger than practically any lintel around.

And just how strong are these Faddis lintels? According to Leon Faddis, the average lintel being produced withstands 2,000 to 2,500 pounds per square inch. The lintels produced by Faddis Brothers have been tested to exceed 4,000 PSI.

Needless to say, Fizzano Brothers is still one of Faddis' largest customers. And to this day, Leon Faddis acknowledges that that challenge

Faddis Brothers, Inc., widely known for the manufacturing of concrete lintels, recently introduced Fence-Crete, a concrete wall concept that can be used for commercial or residential needs.

from Fizzano was the catalyst to create a strong, steam-cured lintel.

By the late 1950s there were nearly thirty people working for Faddis Brothers, Inc. In the early 1960s the manufacturing, storage, and living facilities were expanded to include some 100 acres, and Faddis lintels

The new line of Fence-Crete by Faddis Brothers, Inc., includes a concrete version of the split-rail fence.

were being sold in six states along the northeastern coast.

The operation has continued to expand. Today a walk through the manufacturing plant shows a modern facility where 8,000 to 10,000 feet of concrete lintels are dry-cast and steam-cured each day. The lintels are steam-cured in vast cooking ovens that reach 130 to 150 degrees Fahrenheit. The curing process takes anywhere from thirty minutes in the summer to three hours in the winter. Once they are cooked, the lintels are stacked and allowed to cure outdoors for twenty-eight days before they are shipped.

After James Faddis left Faddis Brothers in 1976, the retail business was renamed the Bee Supply Company; Leon's daughter, Leona, and her husband, Bob Mendenhall, now run the operation.

And in the 1980s Faddis expanded his venture to include a new line of concrete fencing called Fence-Crete. The product, which can be used for commercial or residential fencing needs, provides privacy and security and acts as a sound barrier. The fence requires no trenching, wall footings, mortar, or grout. With a variety of styles, Faddis plans to expand the Fence-Crete business in the future.

PENTAMATION ENTERPRISES, INC.

Pentamation Enterprises, Inc., marked its fifteenth anniversary in 1985, having already established an impressive set of credentials that belies its short history.

First, Pentamation is one of the five largest firms in Pennsylvania dedicated exclusively to computer software and services. And second, Pentamation is among the top 2 percent of all computer software firms in sales in the United States—a recognized leader in supplying computer systems, software, and services for the education community; the health care industry; local, state, and federal governments; the *Fortune* 1,300 companies; and major commercial and industrial firms. In fiscal year 1986 revenues reached forty million dollars.

Pentamation was incorporated in late 1969, and its name comes from the word "penta," which refers to the five people who started the company. In January 1970 the firm began operations with a staff of fifteen people. Today there are more than 600 employees.

During 1971 the company introduced "Pentamed," a terminal-based, hospital-processing service that provides reports for everything from census and inpatient and outpatient

billing to accounts receivable and inventory.

In 1972 the firm began providing information services not only to hospitals but also to the educational community when it assumed responsibility for the Middle Atlantic Educational and Research Center in Lancaster.

That same year the company organized its Facilities Management Ser-

More than 1,100 Pentamation systems are installed in health care institutions nationwide, including The Reading Hospital, one of the clients of Pentamation's Healthcare Systems Group.

Nazareth Area School District uses financial and student record-keeping systems from Pentamation's SYSTEM ELEVEN Division, the leading independent supplier of administrative software for school districts throughout North America.

vices group, the most comprehensive Pentamation service. In return for a fixed monthly fee, Pentamation assumes total responsibility for its clients' electronic data-processing functions. With the entire Pentamation organization as a resource, management is freed from concerns about data-processing operations, and has the additional confidence that changing information-processing needs can and will be met as they arise.

Other acquisitions during the next decade of the corporation's existence helped it build on its strengths and establish itself as a leader in providing computer systems, software, and services. And Pentamation's continuing growth in the competitive information software/services industry reflects a commitment to quality that has been a hallmark of the company's efforts since its founding fifteen years ago.

Pentamation Enterprises, Inc., is headquartered at One Bethlehem Plaza in Bethlehem, with offices of its operating divisions centered in Pennsylvania, as well as in Connecticut, Maryland, and Virginia. Sales and support offices are located nationwide.

T.W. PHILLIPS GAS AND OIL CO.

Thomas W. Phillips, a descendant of the Reverend George Phillips, a sixteenth-century founder of the Congregational Church in America, hoped to be a preacher. Frustrated in this desire by an injury to his lungs that weakened his speaking voice, Phillips turned his attention to the gushing Pennsylvania oil industry. One biographer suggests that he was led to his commercial destiny by a passage in the Book of Job: "And the rock poured me out rivers of oil."

In 1861, two years after Colonel Drake drilled the first oil well at Titusville, T.W. Phillips and his brothers went to Oil Creek to try their luck. At first it was excellent. Within a few years their holdings were among the largest in the oil country, but during the Panic of 1873 they discovered that oil is a slippery business. Mounting debts and the death of Isaac Phillips eventually forced the dissolution of the Phillips Brothers firm. Eventually, T.W. Phillips succeeded in paying the old debts. In 1896 he started a new firm, The Phillips Gas Company, later to become T.W. Phillips Gas and Oil Co.

Fiercely independent, Phillips refused to surrender to the pressures of John D. Rockefeller and the Standard Oil Trust. As with the other independent Pennsylvania oil producers, such resistance was emotionally and economically expensive, yet he persevered and thrived. From 1892 to 1896, Phillips served as a "trust-busting" progressive Republican U.S. congressman, and at the time of his death in 1912 his firm owned 850 oil and gas wells, 900 miles of gas pipelines, and held massive areas of Pennsylvania oil and gas lands under lease.

Today's T.W. Phillips Gas and Oil Co. is a vertically integrated natural gas public utility involved in the production, purchase, transmission, and distribution of natural gas. Serving Western Pennsylvania from its stately headquarters in Butler, T.W. Phillips has 50,000 customers in Allegheny, Armstrong, Butler, Clarion, Indiana,

T.W. Phillips, founder.

Jefferson, and Westmoreland counties. The closely held corporation is largely owned by descendants of T.W. Phillips. The current president is Phillips Wiegand, a great-grandson of the founder.

Almost 80 percent of the gas provided to T.W. Phillips' customers comes from Pennsylvania sources, one-fourth of that from T.W. Phillips' own wells, approximately 2,300 in number, located primarily in

Indiana, Clearfield, Jefferson, and Westmoreland counties. Because such a high proportion of the gas it sells is locally produced, the firm is able to charge lower rates than any major gas utility in Pennsylvania, and less than all but a few gas utilities in the entire nation.

The company still bears the imprint of T.W. Phillips' foresight and idealism. Parts of the original high-capacity pipeline network are still in use, still the basis of today's system. T.W. Phillips was also devoted to his community. He was a lifelong benefactor and trustee of Bethany College and other religious educational institutions. His family, and the company he founded, continue that tradition through active involvement in such organizations as the Butler YMCA, the North Street Christian Church, the Butler Area Chamber of Commerce, and the United Way.

The home office of T.W. Phillips Gas and Oil Co. has become an important landmark in downtown Butler.

SUN COMPANY, INC.

The year was 1886. Oil was booming, and Pennsylvania was still the nation's major oil region. That year the United States produced twenty-eight million barrels of crude, nearly 60 percent of the world's total output. For most oil men, kerosene was the principal product and the primary source of revenue.

There were two businessmen, however, who concentrated their efforts in the development of natural gas for use as a heating fuel. Joseph Newton Pew and Edward O. Emerson founded the Penn Fuel Company to provide natural gas service to the City of Pittsburgh in 1882. Two years later they sold their interest in Penn Fuel and incorporated a business to compete with it called The Peoples Natural Gas Company.

In 1886 Emerson and Pew sent Pew's nephew, Robert, to investigate the possibility of securing oil and gas leases near Lima, Ohio, the site of the first substantial oil discoveries outside the Western Pennsylvania oil regions. The leases were acquired, and in 1889 the partners used the name "Sun" for the first time when Sun Oil Line Company was incorporated in Ohio to deliver crude from that state's oil fields to the refineries springing up around Lima and Toledo.

It is from Robert C. Pew's 1886 investigation in Ohio that a leading energy firm called Sun Company, Inc., got its start. For it was that venture that moved the Pew-Emerson enterprise from a small, natural gas concern to a fully integrated oil com-

Sun Company opened its first service station in Ardmore in 1920. Today the firm has more than 500 service stations statewide and supplies nearly 10 percent of all gasoline sold in Pennsylvania.

pany and, ultimately, to what is today's Sun Company, Inc.

The new venture lost little time in expanding. A refinery was acquired in Toledo in 1894. In Texas, oil production followed closely on the heels of the 1901 discovery of the Spindletop oil field near Beaumont. The following year a refinery for processing Texas crude oil went into operation in Marcus Hook, Pennsylvania.

Sun Company's Marcus Hook refinery was built in 1901 to process into kerosene the oil that gushed from the Spindletop oil field in Texas.

Pew died in 1912, and for most of the next six decades his sons, J. Howard and Joseph N. Jr., directed the company through a period of steady growth.

Recognizing the pressing need for shipping during World War I, the firm established Sun Shipbuilding and Dry Dock Company in 1916, and launched the yard's first tanker the following year. Shortly thereafter world distribution of lubricants, which began in Great Britain in 1909, was further expanded with the formation of Netherlands Sun Oil Company in 1919. The firm began Canadian operations through a subsidiary, Sun Oil Company Limited, the same year.

Already established as a producer of quality lubricants, Sun moved into the retailing of motor products in 1919, steadily expanding this effort and its refining capabilities throughout the 1920s. Sun opened its first service station in Ardmore, Pennsylvania, in 1920.

In 1931 Sun pioneered long-distance pipeline transportation of products from the East Coast to inland markets, and in the mid-1930s provided leadership in developing the catalytic cracking process for producing high-quality fuels. The world's first commercial catalytic unit went into operation at Marcus Hook in

1937, setting the stage for Sun to play a major role in the production of high-octane aviation fuels during World War II.

Robert G. Dunlop replaced J. Howard Pew as president in 1947. During the postwar years the company embarked on a course that included the steady expansion of its marketing operations and a major move into foreign exploration and production. Key developments included the discovery of a major oil field in Venezuela's Lake Maracaibo in 1957. The following year Sun introduced the custom blending system for dispensing several grades of gasoline from a single pump.

In 1968 a new corporate entity was created when Sun merged with the Sunray DX Oil Company of Tulsa, Oklahoma. The move doubled the corporation's assets and for the first time extended Sun's refining and marketing operations beyond the Mississippi River. A major reorganization and redirection of the company followed. Dunlop advanced to chairman of the board in 1970, and H. Robert Sharbaugh was named president.

In 1971 a further reorganization saw the shareholders of Sun Oil Company, a New Jersey corporation, become shareholders of Sun Oil Company, a Pennsylvania corporation and non-operating parent. Two key operating subsidiaries were formed, with Sun Oil Company (Delaware) assuming responsibility for North American exploration and production and Sun Oil Company of Pennsylvania taking over domestic refining, transportation, and marketing.

When Dunlop retired as chief executive officer and chairman in 1974, Sharbaugh assumed the role of chief executive officer and the following year also became board chairman. During Sharbaugh's eight years as president, the company was reorganized into fourteen operating units and diversified into such fields as trucking, real estate, and high-technology information systems.

In 1976 Theodore A. Burtis was

Usually hidden beneath the ground, a Sun Company pipeline for moving petroleum products emerges at the Twin Oaks, Pennsylvania, pumping station to connect with pumps and storage tanks.

elected president and chief operating officer, with Sharbaugh continuing as chairman and chief executive officer. Early that year the word "oil" was dropped from the corporate name to reflect a growing involvement in non-petroleum energy resources. The name then became Sun Company, Inc.

The firm's purchase in 1979 of Elk River Resources, Inc., an eastern coal company with some 200 million tons of coal reserves, put Sun in the east-

Sun Company's 2,000-acre refinery in Marcus Hook is the third largest in the state, processing up to 155,000 barrels of crude oil each day.

ern coal business and positioned the company to be a major competitor in the national coal market. In 1980 Sun acquired the U.S. oil and gas properties of Texas Pacific Oil Company, Inc., for $2.3 billion. It was one of the largest transactions in the history of American business at that time. The move reflected Sun's back-to-basics corporate energy strategy and announced the firm's determination to place renewed emphasis on developing domestic oil and gas reserves. In 1981 Robert McClements, Jr., was appointed president and chief operating officer, with Burtis continuing as chairman and chief executive officer. In 1985 McClements assumed the chief executive officer's responsibilities. Burtis remained chairman.

During the early 1980s the company sold many non-energy assets and also divested those energy-related activities that did not fit into its long-range strategy. Sun also sold 25 percent of the outstanding common stock of its Canadian subsidiary, Suncor Inc.

Ranked in the top 5 percent of the *Fortune* 500 companies, Sun celebrated its centennial anniversary in 1986. For 100 years the firm, headquartered in Radnor, Pennsylvania, has been a major presence in the American business community. Sun approaches its second century committed to continuing its role as a major, broad-based energy producer and supplier.

DAY-TIMERS, INC.

Entertainer Bob Hope, scheduled to leave for a Christmas tour in Vietnam, refused to get on the plane until he could replace the Day-Timer he had lost. President Dwight Eisenhower used a Day-Timer, and actor Lorne Greene once wrote a seven-page letter extolling the virtues of his Day-Timer. A murder was solved in a mystery novel called *The Salamander Glass* after someone located the dead man's Day-Timer. And a lawyer once claimed that he won his case because he had dutifully filled out his Day-Timer.

As time-conscious people everywhere already know, the Day-Timer is a system that literally keeps track of time for those too busy to do it themselves. In its most basic form, the pocket Day-Timer takes a day and divides it into three parts:

appointments and scheduled events, to be done today, and a time record/services performed diary. There is room to record expenses, mileage, and important notes. At the top of every page, there is a perforated line, and when the day is over, Day-Timer lets you tear off the corner and turn the page into another organized day.

Over 3.1 million customers pledge allegiance each morning to the Day-Timer, and 92 percent of the people who buy one each year buy one every year. All of this delights the 600 employees at Day-Timers, Inc., a strictly mail-order business located near Allentown.

The origins of Day-Timers, Inc.,

The Day-Timers complex at One Willow Lane, East Texas, Pennsylvania.

can be traced back to 1939, when Warren Dorney started the Dorney Printing Company near Allentown as a hobby for his family. He set up his first printing press and equipment in a garage located behind the family's house. In 1949 Dorney built a two-story structure adjacent to his home to make room for the expanding printing business. When he died suddenly that same year, his wife and children formed a partnership and continued the business.

Meanwhile, an Allentown attorney named Morris Perkin had devised a time diary for lawyers. On a piece of paper Perkin would map out a daily time sheet, make duplicates, and distribute them to his lawyer friends. Before long, the lawyers couldn't live without them, and Perkin approached the Dorney Printing Company about

printing the diary. In 1952 Dorney began printing Lawyer's Day, the time record designed by Perkin. Several years later the Dorneys and Perkin merged.

Day-Timers soon published an entire family of diaries used by lawyers, accountants, business executives, and professionals in all fields. New products were added to the Day-Timers line each year, including time-saving business forms, personalized stationery and memos, as well as other business and executive needs.

Business grew at an annual rate of 15 to 20 percent as word of this unique time management concept spread through the testimony of satisfied customers. It wasn't until 1970 that Day-Timers published the first edition of a general catalog, printed in full color and encompassing its entire line.

In 1972 Day-Timers, Inc., became a wholly-owned subsidiary of Beatrice Companies, Inc., one of the fifty largest corporations in the United States. Two years later a series of expansions to the Day-Timers headquarters began, which brought the operating plant and corporate office space to its current size of 325,000 square feet. The installation of sophisticated data-processing equipment has helped to streamline Day-

Some of Day-Timers' current product line. Over 3.1 million people organize their time daily with a Day-Timer system.

Timers' ordering, production, shipping, and inventory operations.

And make no mistake. A Day-Timer will not be found on the shelves of even the most popular business or stationery supply shop. The classic Day-Timer and all accessory products are promoted and sold exclusively by direct mail.

The popularity of the Day-Timer

A variety of Day-Timer catalogs.

has made its name synonymous with time management organizers worldwide. More than 1,500 time management consultants now order Day-Timer kits and products to teach effective time management.

The firm currently manufactures more than twenty different formats of pocket and desk diaries. It also produces a complete line of time-saving forms, reply letters, business and personal stationery, and expense forms. In addition, the Day-Timer line includes printed certificates, bronze presentation plaques, customized binders and report covers, and a selection of executive accessories and gift items.

The bulk of the business, however, continues to be the sale of the popular desk and pocket Day-Timer. And stories of devotion to the product are often heard wafting through the corridors of corporate headquarters. Legend has it that once a devoted customer actually confessed to Day-Timers, Inc., that he could live without his wife—but not without his Day-Timer.

MOYER PACKING COMPANY (MOPAC®)

In the early 1900s a horse-drawn wagon with "A.F. Moyer—Butcher" painted on the side was a familiar sight in Franconia Township, a rural community in Eastern Pennsylvania. And in a collection of diaries and essays by Henry D. Hagey, one finds this description of Abram F. Moyer, Sr., the butcher who sold bacon, scrapple, lard, and beef:

"He would drive about the community ringing the bell on the wagon when he stopped. Recognizing his call, the neighborhood women would walk out to the road to inspect his meats. At the back of his wagon where the scale hung, he would cut the meat to the housewife's specifications. More than once his team ran off while he stood back there cutting meat, until he finally had longer reins attached so that they reached to the back of the wagon."

Moyer Packing Company's corporate headquarters in Souderton.

When Abram Jr. and Curtis joined their father's business, A.F. Moyer—Butcher became A.F. Moyer and Sons. Moyer's other two sons, Nelson and Jacob, eventually operated an animal by-products rendering business called North Penn Hide Company. In 1972 A.F. Moyer and Sons merged with North Penn Hide to become Moyer Packing Company, or MOPAC. And what had its origins in the back of a horse-drawn wagon has turned into the largest beef slaughterer and fabricator east of the Mississippi.

Based in Souderton, the largest facility of the present-day Beef Division of MOPAC is located on the original Moyer family homestead. A picture of the founder and his wagon still hangs on the office wall, a rare glimpse at the past in the modern facility where slaughtering and fabrication of meat is completed.

There, nearly 6,000 boxes of meat

Pineville is the site of one of MOPAC's three feed ingredient blending facilities.

MOPAC looks back fondly to the days of the horse-drawn wagon, although today's operation requires a fleet of tractor-trailers.

are prepared each day. And while A.F. Moyer slaughtered several animals a week to accommodate his door-to-door customers, approximately 1,500 cattle per day are slaughtered at MOPAC to meet today's marketing demands.

In less than thirty minutes after they are stunned and slaughtered, the cattle have been eviscerated, split into sides, weighed, and placed in coolers to chill overnight. After chilling they are presented to the U.S.D.A. for grading. The sides of cattle are then quartered before entering the fabrication plant for further processing.

Inside the fabrication unit, one box of beef is produced every four seconds. From catwalks overhead, visitors can watch as hundreds of highly trained employees bone and trim the meat, preparing traditional cuts of beef including those from the chuck, rib, loin, and round. Others package the product, and most cuts of beef are vacuum packed. A device called an Anyl-Ray Unit accurately measures the lean content of boneless beef and ground beef raw materials by analyzing a beef sample.

Inedible product is sent to MOPAC's Rendering Division for processing. The rendering business—acquired by Nelson Moyer in 1932 from his uncle, Irwin Kulp—started out as a small operation with just three employees and one cooker. Today MOPAC operates two rendering plants and three feed ingredient blending facilities. Rendering experts collect and process raw materials, producing high-quality finished products that are marketed worldwide. These include protein meals, tallows, greases, and cured hides and skins.

Together the Rendering and Beef divisions of MOPAC employ a total of 1,200 people, with sales of nearly $351 million in 1985. The privately held company buys 50 percent of its cattle in Pennsylvania during the summer, and a smaller percentage in Pennsylvania during the rest of the year. The remainder of MOPAC's cattle are purchased from approximately fourteen states and Canada. The beef and rendering products are shipped worldwide, with all domestic

The firm purchases a large number of its cattle in Pennsylvania.

shipping handled by MOPAC's own transportation department.

MOPAC has invested more than two million dollars over the past two years to develop modern wastewater-treatment facilities; all water and air released into the atmosphere from the MOPAC plants satisfy standards set by the Environmental Protection Agency.

Corporate headquarters remains in Souderton on the original 42-acre farm that Josiah Clemmer conveyed to Jacob Freed on March 28, 1885. It was there that Freed started his butchering and rendering business. On October 18, 1921, Freed conveyed his farm and butchering business to his son-in-law, Abram F. Moyer, who was married to his daughter Lydia. When Freed died in 1929, he left his rendering business to another son-in-law, Irwin Kulp, who was married to Susan, his youngest daughter. The four sons born to Abram and Lydia Moyer—Nelson, Jacob, Abram Jr., and Curtis—eventually controlled both businesses, which merged and became known as Moyer Packing Company on October 1, 1972.

A family business for over 100 years, MOPAC is currently represented by fourth-generation family members. The original homestead, with its white stucco walls and green shutters, has been maintained as a visitors' center, where each year thousands of people hear again the story of A.F. Moyer—Butcher.

DU-CO CERAMICS COMPANY

These products are everywhere—part of the industrial underpinning that we all take for granted, and trust for total reliability. Du-Co Ceramics Company of Saxonburg, Pennsylvania, is America's largest manufacturer of ceramic insulators, critical components of countless heating and electrical applications. Ceramic insulators hold the heating coils on a toaster, are part of every light bulb, of electrical switches in every house, every automobile, every telephone, every computer. Virtually everyone in the United States uses some product with Du-Co components every day.

Du-Co Ceramics was started by John J. Duke and Reldon W. Cooper in February 1949. A firm belief in the future of ceramics in industry, plus confidence in their engineering and technical knowledge, led the two men to their decision to go into business for themselves. Both were employees of another manufacturer of ceramic insulators, and thought that they could do better on their own. In pursuit of their American dream, they leased an abandoned slaughterhouse where Saxonburg bologna had once been made. Since that time the company has shown consistent growth, has diversified its product lines, and has maintained a research and development program for both quality control and the creation of new products.

Starting out was not easy. The two partners handled every part of the process, from soliciting orders, to manufacturing, through delivery. They did their own clerical work, purchased their own raw materials, mixed the clays, and watched over the furnace. "We out-hustled the competition," recalls Cooper. "We were small, and able to provide totally customized service. We had an outstanding delivery record, even though we had to work through the night sometimes to meet a commitment. We'd work twelve hours, then sleep for four, then go to work again."

Today Du-Co Ceramics has a full-time staff of 225 employees. The

Reldon W. Cooper, president and chief executive officer.

plant has 125,000 square feet of manufacturing space under roof, including the latest addition, completed in 1978. Computer-aided design and manufacturing speed the production process while guaranteeing the extraordinary precision required by modern high-tech applications. Since the death of John Duke the firm has been wholly owned by Reldon Cooper.

There are few standard parts in the ceramic insulator business. Virtually every order requires custom design and custom manufacturing. While many orders come in the form of comprehensive specifications, Du-Co is prepared to offer whatever assis-

tance a customer might require. The company designs and fabricates its own dies for all products. Insulators are a critical component that must be designed to cope with specific requirements involving both heat and electrical shock. They must also meet requirements specified by Underwriters Laboratory.

More than 200 tons of talc, clays, and such other raw materials as feldspar, magnesium oxide, silica, and zircon arrive at the Saxonburg plant every month. They come from Montana, Kentucky, and Tennessee; none are available locally. But as Cooper is quick to point out, almost all of the major end users of Du-Co products are located within 500 miles of his Saxonburg location. Du-Co customers include General Electric, Sylvania,

Westinghouse, Ford, General Motors, and countless other manufacturers of sophisticated appliances and components.

"The early years were difficult," recalls Cooper. "It took us eight to ten years to build up a reliable customer base. Expenses were higher than we expected; we had heavy debts; we had to learn to bid jobs properly as well as to deliver the product."

The modern ceramic insulator business is capital-intensive, requiring elaborate manufacturing machinery as well as skilled labor including ceramic engineers, tool and die makers, shipping and transportation experts, and research scientists. Materials must be precisely blended and pressed or extruded into precisely

specified shapes with narrow tolerances. Most are fired at temperatures around 2,400 degrees Fahrenheit. It all requires close supervision. "Even today," says Cooper, "if we lay back, things can go the wrong way real easily."

Du-Co has never "laid back." The firm started with a single tunnel kiln, a clay preparation area, and a few presses. When it added an extruder and additional cutting and machining equipment, it filled the available space. The next expansion required presses to be set up outside of the

Du-Co Ceramics Company, located in Saxon-burg, is America's largest manufacturer of ceramic insulators, critical components of countless heating and electrical applications.

old bologna factory, and construction of a new building began in 1950. Since that time Du-Co has experienced steady expansion and growth.

Cooper is an active worker on behalf of the American Cancer Association, a director of Allegheny Hospital, a dedicated Mason, Boy Scout leader, and supporter of the Butler Area Chamber of Commerce. His life is dedicated to "hard work and a deep commitment to whatever you are trying to achieve." He attributes his success to loyalty and support, the support that he and Duke gave to each other at the beginning, the loyalty of their employees and sales representatives, and the loyalty with which Du-Co Ceramics Company in turn supports its employees.

SOLID STATE EQUIPMENT CORPORATION

Over twenty years ago, in 1965, Solid State Equipment Corporation was founded in the living room of the home of Bob and Lynn Richardson. The founders believed (and still do) that the young and growing integrated circuit industry would require suppliers of fabrication equipment and supplies.

Integrated circuits, first invented and developed in the late 1950s, now include thousands of types of electronic devices that are used by the billions in computers, televisions, radios, watches, space vehicles, automobiles, airplanes—in every field utilizing electronics. The manufacture of integrated circuits involves complex processes utilizing the latest and highest technologies available to industry. Integrated circuits are manufactured all over the world.

Solid State Equipment Corporation was chosen as a name because its customers, integrated circuit manufacturers, produced devices designed on the principles of solid state physics. The combination of the words "solid state" with "equipment" seemed to state the purpose of the new firm. The company was therefore incorporated on October 28, 1965, as a Pennsylvania corporation.

The coffee table in the Richardsons' living room was moved aside and the space used to assemble the first machine. It was exhibited at an electronics industry trade show a few weeks later. Subsequently, the firm moved into its first office, comprising one room. The machine was in one corner, a desk in another.

Acceptance of Solid State Equipment's original product took years— not the few months anticipated. Competition from other techniques and firms proved difficult to overcome. Fortunately, the company prevailed.

Over the years, Solid State Equipment has grown to be a multi million-dollar international corporation with machine showrooms and inventories in Konstanz, West Germany, and Sunnyvale, California. The firm's main office and manufacturing facil-

Robert D. Richardson, president and chairman, and Lynn B. Richardson, secretary and treasurer, at the company's manufacturing facility in Fort Washington, Pennsylvania.

ity is located in Fort Washington, Pennsylvania.

Solid State Equipment now manufactures equipment and supplies for integrated circuit manufacturers, which include an advanced computer-controlled version of its initial product, an integrated circuit packaging machine. Also manufactured are integrated circuit processing machines, integrated circuit inspection machines, and components and chemicals for integrated circuit manufacturers.

The company's customers have grown from a very few to include hundreds such as IBM, Hewlett-Packard, Intel, AT&T, General Electric, Texas Instruments, and Philips. A point of special pride is Solid State

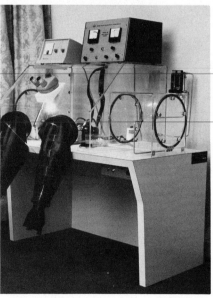

The first machine, an integrated circuit packaging machine, was assembled in the Richardsons' living room in early 1966.

Equipment's contribution to aerospace programs including everything

The 1986 version of the integrated circuit packaging machine incorporates many advancements, including software intensive computer control.

from Gemini, Apollo, the Space Shuttle, and the B1-B bomber. All have integrated circuits manufactured by the firm's equipment. High-reliability medical implants such as heart pacers also rely on equipment manufactured by Solid State Equipment.

The technology involved in the equipment manufactured by Solid State Equipment has dramatically evolved over the past twenty years. Early machines included air cylinders, electric solenoids, cams, and other electromechanical devices. Today computer software has replaced most of these components, resulting in equipment of superior reliability and capability. Machine controlled computer software development now dominates the company's product development programs.

A key factor contributing to the successful growth of Solid State Equipment has been its location in the Delaware Valley. The local availability of high-quality, long term personnel and suppliers of materials and services has been invaluable. The firm's auditor is Touche Ross & Co., its counsel is Dilworth, Paxson, Kalish & Kauffman, and its bank is The Fidelity Bank.

In the 1970s the company began an international worldwide marketing effort to generate export sales. In Europe, this proved successful to the point that Solid State Equipment was able to establish its own machine showrooms and spare parts center in Konstanz, West Germany, in 1981. The export effort continues to the present. For example, the firm received its first significant machine order from the People's Republic of China in early 1986.

Solid State Equipment Corporation remains dedicated to its customers and markets. It believes that its accomplishments in the past will lead to greater accomplishments in the future.

A modern, state-of-the-art, computer-controlled, integrated circuit processing machine manufactured by Solid State Equipment Corporation.

M&C SPECIALTIES COMPANY

Chances are, tucked away in the dash of your car, your office copier, your home tape deck, or some other piece of technical equipment, there's an unseen piece of tape that makes certain the machine works. And, chances are, that tape was converted, die cut, processed, printed, or packaged by a family-owned business just outside Philadelphia—a business that has in the past forty years sold adhesive products to everyone from Olympic athletes to orbiting astronauts to 80 percent of the *Fortune* 500 companies. Indeed, the top name in the specialty tape market is M&C Specialties Company of Southampton.

In 1944 Mary and Clyde Rauch took their $400 in savings and started a business. At first Clyde Rauch sold U.S. government surplus tape "to anyone who would buy it," says F. Clyde Rauch, one of six Rauch chil-

dren. Several years later M&C developed a working relationship with The 3M Company, acting as a distributor of its tape products. In 1950 M&C began to cut the tape, slitting the three-inch-wide tape into half-inch rolls. Mary Rauch was the official telephone operator, often holding a baby in her lap and taking orders from businesses within a fifty-mile radius of the first M&C headquarters on Cottman Avenue.

The company had soon earned the reputation as a business that could slit and cut tape to order. For M&C it was "the perfect niche. And the market expanded by itself," says

---

Clyde Jr. and Mary A. Rauch (center) gather here with (left to right) Donald M. Rauch, James J. Rauch, Jane Held, Kathleen Taylor, and Anne Mazzola.

James Rauch, the president of M&C from 1969 through 1979 and now director of western operations.

The M&C market, with literally thousands of tape products in its inventory, concentrates on six areas of products and services: die cutting, slitting and rewinding, laminating, printing, pressure-sensitive tapes, and safety-related products.

In the area of die cutting, M&C can custom design die cuts to exact configurations—any shape, any size, any pressure-sensitive or nonpressure-sensitive material. The die can hold exact tolerances for the most demanding standards of the electronics, automotive, and medical industries. An M&C die cut—supplied in rolls, individual pieces, multisheet pads, or to the customer's specifications—can be used as a sealant, cushion, insulator, conductor, or simply help elimi-

nate excess fastening hardware.

From its initial days of slitting 3M tape into narrow-width rolls, M&C is now equipped to slit all types of pressure-sensitive and nonpressure-sensitive materials. From thin films, paper, and cloth, to electrical, industrial, and medical tapes, the firm can slit any material ranging in size from five feet to 1/32 of an inch. In addition, the company can rewind the product to any length roll on the size or type core that the customer requires.

M&C provides web lamination on a myriad of materials, such as high- or low-density foams, cork and felt, thin film plastics, and coated cloths, as well as thin metals such as stainless steel, copper, and aluminum. In conjunction, the company offers a variety of printing options and maintains an extensive inventory of all major brands of industrial, electrical, and medical tapes. Its line of safety-related products includes a full line of discs and arrows, hazard stripes, safety signs, and nonskid material. And M&C, which currently employs 135 people, has expectations for continued growth.

Such diversification shows in the marketplace. M&C provided an adhesive pad for Olympic athletes who needed to monitor injuries; the pads, which conduct electricity through a stress-testing device, work when placed on the bottom of the athletes' feet. And when astronauts reported problems with static electricity in

The original location, from 1945 to 1955, of M&C Specialties Company at 4919 Cottman Avenue.

their spacecraft, NASA engineers called upon M&C to fabricate an adhesive pad that, when attached to the bottom of an astronaut's boot, reduced the static problem.

The tale of athletics to astronauts is one of the favorites swapped back and forth around the firm's conference table when the Rauch siblings and their mother, Mary, get together at their corporate headquarters for a review of the company's history. There's Don, the chief executive officer who joined the business in 1969; F. Clyde, also chief executive officer with a Ph.D. in chemistry who responded favorably in 1972 when his family asked him to leave his job as a chemist in Connecticut and join the business; and their sister Kathleen A. Taylor, production manager since 1977 and now vice-president in charge of manufacturing. James J. Rauch is director of M&C's western operations which are based in Phoenix, Arizona. Two sisters, Anne Rauch Mazzola and Jane Rauch Held, are not active in the business, although both worked summers at M&C; and Jane's husband, John, currently works for the firm. In addition, eleven of the fourteen third-generation Rauch family members have worked at M&C.

The company's founder, Clyde Rauch, died in 1971 at the age of

sixty-five. Even at that age he had plans to expand the business, and his family has moved forward with his dreams. In 1973 the new 35,000-square-foot headquarters in Southampton was built; in 1984 M&C doubled in size when a new 35,000-square-foot addition was completed. With products being shipped both nationwide and overseas, M&C sales figures totaled nearly thirteen million dollars in 1985.

The Rauch family remains close, and its members love telling business stories. One details the time in 1961 when Clyde and Mary Rauch made their first business trip to Milan, Italy, and a cabdriver was needed to help break the language barrier and negotiate a business deal. Another relates how Fred C. Cipriano came to work at M&C in the early 1950s and became Clyde Rauch's right-hand man and the company's general manager before retiring in 1972. Another tells how Matthew "Buddy" Horne, who is now the top foreman, once walked seven miles in the snow to start work at M&C.

And, of course, there is much in-house joking when the Rauch family is asked to explain what "M&C" represents. After suggestions of many outrageous interpretations of the initials, Don Rauch allows that his father often told people that M&C stood for manufacturers and consumers. But, truth to tell, M&C honors the company's founders: Mary and Clyde.

447

TELEFLEX INCORPORATED

In 1943 a company was founded with one product for one market: the helical cable, designed for the Spitfire, the legendary World War II fighter plane. This relatively simple, push-pull cable, in combination with a geared wheel, spawned a patented and highly successful family of mechanical control systems. This single product also formed the cornerstone for a new company called Teleflex Incorporated.

Teleflex Incorporated is an applications engineering firm dedicated to solving problems through the design, development, and marketing of specialized technologies. This has resulted in a profitable flow of proprietary products and services into economically and demographically diverse markets.

With corporate headquarters in Limerick, Pennsylvania, Teleflex employs over 2,000 people in thirty-two manufacturing and service facilities worldwide. Its business is divided into two segments: Technical Products and Services and Commercial Products.

The Technical segment serves the aerospace, defense, medical, and transportation industries. These products and services require a high de-

An employee checks a Pratt and Whitney JT8D Stator coated with SermeTel's process 5380.

gree of sophisticated engineering and are generally produced in limited quantities. The Commercial segment serves the automotive, pleasure marine, outdoor power equipment, and general industrial markets. These products tend to be less complex and are produced in much higher volume. Combined, the Technical and Commercial segments realized $155 million in sales in 1984, with $175 million in sales in 1985.

Teleflex Incorporated was founded in 1943 by M.C.C. Chisholm, who once said a mechanical control could

be as simple as a piece of string. Chisholm incorporated the business in Delaware as a subsidiary of Teleflex Limited, a Canadian corporation located in Toronto. Chisholm founded the company to pursue business opportunities under license rights to a British patent for a mechanical cable control device used principally in military aircraft at that time. He established his first Pennsylvania-based operation in 1958.

Though not as simple as a piece of string, some of the early aircraft-control products were relatively unsophisticated push-pull controls. Those early actuator controls, used in the legendary Spitfire and other World War II aircraft, were based on a patented system of a helix cable operating in a conduit that converted rotary to linear motion, or the reverse. The Teleflex system was unique in its simplicity, reliability, and maintainability; could operate in extreme temperatures under heavy vibration; and was lighter than alternate methods.

For fifteen years Teleflex focused on the development of mechanical control devices for military and commercial airframes and engines. As aerospace "vehicles" became more sophisticated, progressing first to jet aircraft and then to manned rockets for space travel, lubrication requirements for aircraft controls changed radically. Teleflex met the challenge with the identification and acquisition of a surface-coating process known as SermeTel. Through evolution of this technology, SermeTel emerged with coatings found to have important applications in the turbine engine aircraft market where fuel consumption was measurably reduced.

Today the Teleflex Defense/Aerospace Group consists of five basic segments offering a wide variety of technologies aimed at solving technical engineering problems associated with mechanisms, controls, materials, electrical interconnects, and coatings.

The Teleflex Sermatech International subsidiary offers a diverse

The STS Southeast/Gator-Gard Incorporated facility in Lantana, Florida.

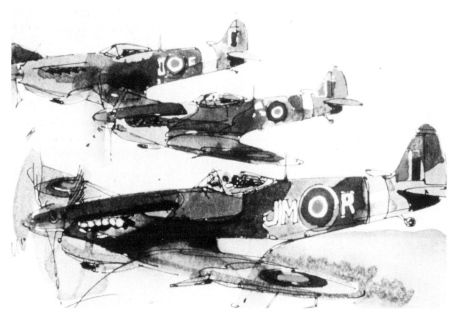

Teleflex's first contracts were during World War II for actuator controls used in the legendary Spitfire (shown here) and other World War II aircraft.

range of technical services and materials technology worldwide through a network that now claims eleven facilities in five countries. Sermatech provides clients with SermeTel®, Gator-Gard® high-energy plasma coatings, electron beam welding, computerized airfoil recontouring, and other technical services.

In 1958 Teleflex embarked on a course of diversification into the automotive, marine, and general industrial equipment markets—a course that would result in the acquisition of numerous companies and product applications. Today the firm is the leading worldwide supplier of mechanical and hydraulic steering systems for leisure powerboats and sailboats, as well as a significant factor in throttle and transmission control systems and instrumentation for pleasure boating. The new Teleflex SeaStar™ hydraulic steering system was introduced in 1984. In the American-built automobile market, Teleflex has developed, manufactured, and marketed a wide range of proprietary control products, ranging from controls for accelerator and transmission to park-lock devices.

In 1967 Teleflex acquired Trimflex, Inc., of Dover, New Jersey, the producer of Teflon® extrusions and other products for aerospace, industrial, and medical applications. This laid the groundwork for the day, nearly twenty years later, in 1984 when Teleflex reorganized several groups under the name Teleflex Medical Group, poised to expand its

Teleflex's Hoover Electric Division, in California, furnishes actuation systems for the Space Shuttle. Shown here is the Centaur.

development in medical disposable devices and specialized coated materials.

As a result of this reorganization, the Jaffrey, New Hampshire, facility has been equipped to manufacture sophisticated devices for the anesthesia and critical care market. Aries Medical Inc. in Woburn, Massachusetts, continues its development of highly sophisticated products that will be marketed to the cardiovascular and cardiac-assist markets. During 1984 the FDA approved the first product, the Teleflex Intra-Aortic Balloon Pump; this represents the most sophisticated product yet developed by the firm. And Teleflex plans to increase capacity at its Limerick, Ireland, operation in order to broaden current technology in tubing and components for the European market.

Looking to the future, Teleflex Incorporated has set its course to achieve these goals: to pursue international business expansion where proprietary technical advantages exist, to expand internal product development efforts, to carefully investigate acquisition opportunities, and to achieve $500 million in revenues by the end of the decade.

Teflon® DuPont Registered Trademark

GARLAND COMMERCIAL INDUSTRIES, INC.

Garland is a Pennsylvania company that is cooking on every burner—literally. Throughout the United States, the Caribbean basin, and South America, commercial cooking means Garland Commercial Industries, Inc., of Freeland, Pennsylvania. Garland is part of Welbilt Corporation, an international organization serving the food-service industry. Other Welbilt companies include Frymaster, Ice-O-Matic (ice-making equipment), Belshaw (doughnut makers), and Welbilt Commercial Industries (refrigeration and mixing equipment).

First manufactured in 1864, "Garland" was the trade name of a line of wood-burning stoves designed especially for the growing market of small roadside inns. The stove was produced by the Michigan Stove Company. Original nineteenth-century "Art Garland" stoves are now valued antiques, but visitors to the LBJ Ranch, birthplace of President Lyndon B. Johnson, will find an early twentieth-century model Garland stove still in use.

In the 1920s the Michigan Stove Company merged with Detroit Stove Works to become Detroit-Michigan Stove Company, the largest stove manufacturer in the world. The firm also built the largest stove in the world, a fifteen-ton wooden replica of its ever-popular "Garland" model built for the 1893 Columbian Exposition in Chicago. The size of a two-story house, the giant stove is now a historical landmark at The Henry Ford Museum, Greenfield Village, Dearborn, Michigan.

Welbilt acquired the Detroit-Michigan Stove Company in 1955, reorganizing it as Welbilt's American Garland Division and shifting its base of operations from Detroit to Maspeth, New York.

Reorganized as Garland Commercial Industries, Inc., the firm was brought to Pennsylvania in 1974, largely through the efforts of the Freeland Industrial Development Corporation and the Pennsylvania Industrial Development Authority. The move proved to be farsighted and imaginative, giving the company

A typical Garland installation for restaurants, institutions such as hospitals, and schools.

access to a rich labor market and outstanding shipping facilities. From its Freeland base, Garland has become one of the national leaders in the manufacture of commercial cooking equipment.

Garland engineering has been the keystone and focus of its growth. The company has become widely known and respected as an innovative leader in the design of gas and electric convection ovens, steam cooking equipment, broilers, fryers, counter equipment, and griddles. Garland customers include restaurants, hospitals, schools, and other institutions.

The president of Garland Commercial Industries, Inc., is Frank A. Radice, who has been with Welbilt since 1965 and with Garland since 1975. Garland operates a 161,000-square-foot plant in Freeland, and has acquired an additional 65,000 square feet of manufacturing and storage space in the spring of 1986. With a tradition that goes back 122 years, and a twelve-year history in Pennsylvania, Garland remains deeply committed to growth and to the future and to its Northeastern Pennsylvania community.

TRANSICOIL INC.

Imagine, for a moment, hundreds of magnetic coils wound together so tightly that when put together end to end they form a magnetic component no larger than a penny. Yet this coil has the ability to help fly an F-14 military aircraft.

In 1943 such a coil-wound component formed the cornerstone of a new venture called Transicoil Inc., a precision, custom hardware manufacturer that today designs, develops, and produces two broad-based product lines: servo components and controls, and panels and displays.

When it started in New York, Transicoil was primarily known as a supplier of servo systems and components to the military. But since World War II the firm's expertise and experience in servo technology has grown continuously. In fact, Transicoil now counts among its achievements the development and implementation of the torquer-pot concept (an integral assembly combining torquer and potentiometer) and the first size five (small enough to fit in the palm of your hand) rotating servo component.

During the firm's early years the demand for precision high-performance components influenced the development of a full line of rotating servo components—including servo motors, gear heads, generators and tachometers, synchros, resolvers, and servo amplifiers. In addition, Transicoil developed engineering and manufacturing technology to better package these components into precision assemblies and instruments.

To the layman, naturally, these precision components sound like words of a foreign language. But in very basic terms, Transicoil components look like shiny cylinders, filled with coils, microscopic components, and mechanisms so tiny they would fit on the tip of your finger. When combined, these units tell parts of very large machines how to interact.

For instance, Transicoil components are found in a full spectrum of markets: aerospace, military, marine, and industrial. So one might find a

Transicoil component in a 737's fuel management system, on the F-18's horizontal situation display, inside the zoom drive of a television camera, in the elbow of an industrial robot, or deep within a sophisticated medical scanner.

In 1980 Transicoil stepped into a new era when it acquired a U.S. avionics company that specialized in markets related to those already serviced by Transicoil, but through a very different technology: control/display panel manufacture for panel and instrumentation displays like those found in the cockpits of airplanes. From design to fabrication to assembly to production, Transicoil now incorporates state-of-the-art techniques to manufacture panels and displays for aerospace, military, and industrial applications.

By 1982 Transicoil was consolidated at one location in Worcester,

The Transicoil management team. Seated, from left: James R. Kennard, Charles G. Vinson, and Steven G. Pifer. Standing, from left: Mark M. Johnson, William J. Matthews, John D. DiCaprio, and Robert M. Hyatt.

Pennsylvania. Today it is the site of both corporate headquarters and manufacturing facilities. There experts use the latest in Computer Aided Design/Computer Aided Manufacturing (CAD/CAM), numerically controlled equipment, and certified photometric, magnetic, and electromechanical laboratory facilities to custom produce parts that might number from only five to 5,000 duplicates.

In June 1984 Transicoil was acquired from its Swiss parent corporation by seven people who now form the nucleus of the company's management team: James R. Kennard, president; John D. DiCaprio, vice-president/quality assurance; Robert M. Hyatt, vice-president/engineering; Mark M. Johnson, human resources director; William J. Matthews, vice-president/marketing; Steven G. Pifer, vice-president/finance; and Charles G. Vinson, vice-president/operations.

Current sales now exceed fifteen million dollars annually. More than 200 people work at Transicoil's Worcester headquarters, and over eighty are employed at the firm's wholly owned subsidiary in Malaysia.

FISCHER & PORTER

In March 1937 a freshly painted sign went up over the wooden double doors of a small brick garage in Philadelphia's old Germantown section. It read "Fischer & Porter Company," named for its founder, Kermit Fischer, and his only employee, George K. Porter. Inside this 4,000-square-foot building, the two men labored to develop a process for forming glass tubing that would be the cornerstone of their new venture.

Indeed, the production of these interchangeable glass tubes—long considered impossible—was the key to making a successful variable area flowmeter. Three months of persistent effort paid off when the first precision-tapered tubes were made by a reproducible process. The instrument, called a "rotameter," was no longer a handmade experimental device but rather a useful commercial product with tolerances reduced to a few ten-thousandths of an inch. It was the cornerstone Fischer was looking for on which to build his business.

Fischer & Porter is today a broadbased, sophisticated, worldwide corporation supplying automatic process-control instrumentation and systems to industries on every continent. The company designs, engineers, manufactures, and sells process-control instruments, equipment, and systems for the measurement, recording, and control of the flow of liquids and gases for industrial process control. Fischer & Porter supplies systems to

In 1937 Kermit Fischer began what would one day become a multimillion-dollar business in this Germantown garage.

the petrochemical, pulp and paper, food, metal mining, electrical power generation, marine, and pharmaceutical industries, and for use in municipal and industrial water, wastewater, and sewage treatment and distribution.

Fischer & Porter's line of products includes flow measurement instruments and instruments for mechanical and electronic use; analytical instruments; chlorinators; and analog, digital, and microprocessor based distributed control systems. Its newest distributed process-control system, the DCI-5000™, caps nearly five decades of continuous progress in flow and process-control expertise. In addition, the firm manufactures and sells laboratory and industrial glass products. Its clients range from paper companies that must control the pulp-bleaching process to city managers who must control the treatment of a metropolitan water supply.

Fischer & Porter employs over 2,900 people worldwide, from its

main plant in Warminster, Pennsylvania, to plants in many countries around the world. First listed on the American Stock Exchange in 1961, the firm now records yearly sales in excess of $160 million.

When Kermit Fischer died in Antwerp, Belgium, in 1971 the company's 65-year-old founder and driving force was the holder of eleven U.S. patents, the author of innumerable technical articles, and an active industrial and civic leader. The memory of Kermit Fischer, touring the plant with his faithful Labrador companion, Frosty, at his side, lingers as a reminder of how a multimillion-dollar worldwide corporation started with the dream of one man working in a Germantown garage.

Today Fischer & Porter is located in Warminster with headquarters in Horsham, Pennsylvania.

The Copa-X™ magnetic flowmeter installed in a pipeline.

SPIRAX SARCO, INC.

The dateline was Allentown, Pennsylvania, and the press release minced no words announcing what had happened on September 30, 1983: "The world's largest single resource for steam-related technology and equipment was introduced here today as officials of Sarco Company of Allentown and Spirax Sarco Engineering, plc, of the United Kingdom announced formation of the new organization to be known as Spirax Sarco, Inc., in the United States."

Before the press conference and dinner celebrations were over, A.C. Brown, chairman and managing director of Spirax Sarco Engineering, plc, and chairman of Spirax Sarco, Inc., reminded guests and dignitaries of one important fact. And that was that the formation of the new company actually marked the reunion of two businesses that had started out together in 1910. And those two firms began through the vision of one man, Clement H. Wells.

In 1910 Wells left his native England for America, settling in New York City and starting his career as a sales representative for Sanders Rehder & Co. It wasn't long before Wells established his own business called Sarco and began selling liquid expansion steam traps and temperature- and tank-control regulators.

Shortly after World War I Wells subcontracted with the Roller-Smith Company of Bethlehem to manufacture the regulators and traps. This

In December 1934 employees of the original Sarco Company posed for this group picture.

proved to be the beginning of the manufacturing program for Sarco products in the United States; until then most of these items had been imported from Germany.

Subcontracting continued at the Roller-Smith plant from 1920 to 1935, with steam-heating items such as boiler return traps, steam and water mixers, and float traps added to the inventory. In September 1935 forty-seven employees reported to work when Sarco opened its own manufacturing plant near Bethlehem.

Spirax Sarco's United States headquarters is at 1951 Twenty-sixth Street Southwest, Allentown.

In 1932 Wells reestablished his ties with England by forming Spirax Manufacturing. The name "Spirax" was chosen because it symbolized the spiral brass bellows inside the original Number 9 steam trap. The two companies that would eventually become one were now officially established by Wells on both sides of the Atlantic.

From the mid-1930s to today the separate histories of the two businesses reveal an array of expansions. In 1937 Wells founded Sarco Thermostats in England as a sales company. Eight years later he organized Sarcotherm Controls, Inc., in the United States to market a complete line of control systems for both steam and water heating. In 1952 Wells sold his interest in the companies he had founded to the employees. In 1962 Sarco Company, Inc., later acquired by White Consolidated Industries of Cleveland, Ohio, merged its operations in a new facility in Allentown.

In 1983 Spirax Sarco Engineering, plc, a publicly owned company in the United Kingdom since 1959, acquired Sarco Company from White.

And as Spirax Sarco, Inc., approached the seventy-fifth anniversary of the founding of Wells' first company, the union of the two organizations is still touted as the "perfect connection worldwide—reunited and continuing to be the world's largest resource for increasing the productivity of steam."

GALLATIN NATIONAL BANK

Gallatin National Bank was chartered on March 5, 1896, as the Second National Bank of Uniontown. The bank thrived as economic prosperity came to its Western Pennsylvania region, acquiring the Uniontown National Bank & Trust Company and the Third National Bank in 1930, and the First National Bank of New Salem in 1936.

Second National Bank continued its prudent policy of carefully controlled expansion over the next twenty years. In January 1953 the bank acquired the First National Bank of Perryopolis; in October it added a new office in Republic; by the end of the year it had 105 employees and assets of over thirty-five million dollars.

As the bank grew beyond Uniontown, it sought a new and more appropriate name, one that reflected its philosophy and its dedication to its expanding community of service. The Second National Bank of Uniontown officially became Gallatin National Bank on January 21, 1955.

Albert Gallatin of Fayette County, Pennsylvania, was an outstanding early American financier, diplomat, patriot, U.S. senator, member of Congress, and Secretary of the Treasury under President Thomas Jefferson. His policies included reduction of the national debt and support of the national bank of the United States. Gallatin is widely regarded as one of the most brilliant and successful statesmen of the Jeffersonian era.

Within the first year of its new identity, Gallatin National Bank acquired the National Bank & Trust Company of Connellsville, the First National Bank of Point Marion, the First National Bank of Dawson, and the First National Bank of Jefferson (taking the bank into Greene County). In April 1956 Gallatin added the National Deposit Bank of Brownsville. For a while it seemed that Gallatin Bank, which grew to assets of sixty million dollars, might lose its identity with Uniontown entirely, but other forces were at work, forces that would strengthen the ties binding Gallatin to its region.

A group of directors headed by Orville Eberly purchased a controlling interest in the bank on May 15, 1956. At the time, control of the bank was held by the Mellon family trust. When it became apparent that Pennsylvania law would not allow the merger of Gallatin Bank with Pittsburgh's Mellon Bank, the family trust offered the Gallatin directors an opportunity to purchase the bank's stock. Eberly was elected chairman of the board of Gallatin National Bank in 1957.

Eberly was the son of a coal mine superintendent, and he quickly demonstrated his own abilities under the earth. From a start as a coal mine electrician, he moved to mine fire boss, assistant mine foreman, and mine foreman. From there he became superintendent of the W.J. Rainey Company Old Home Mine and in 1929 general superintendent of the Kingston-Pocahontas Coal Company. During the Great Depression he demonstrated his talents as a businessman and investor, purchasing the Old Home Mine at McClellandtown in 1933 and establishing the Eberly Coal and Coke Company of Uniontown in 1936. With William E. Snee, he developed gas and oil resources while expanding his coal holdings.

Under Orville Eberly, new Gallatin offices opened in Fayette City and at the Connellsville Shopping Center. In 1958 the bank opened an office in Mount Pleasant, taking it into West-

Orville Eberly served as chairman of the board of Gallatin National Bank for twenty-one years, from 1957 to 1978.

Robert E. Eberly, Sr., chairman of the board.

G.R. Rendle, president.

The bank's New Salem office as it appeared in 1912.

moreland County. In 1962 Gallatin Bank entered the Somerset County communities of Meyersdale and Salisbury by acquiring the Second National Bank of Meyersdale. A branch in Richeyville, Washington County, was added in 1968. Orville Eberly retired in January 1978. By then the bank had twenty-five offices in five counties, almost 400 employees, and assets of $363,510,399.

Today Gallatin Bank has become one of the leading community banks in Southwestern Pennsylvania under its current board chairman Robert E. Eberly and president G.R. Rendle. The bank has forty-four offices in

Fayette, Greene, Somerset, Washington, and Westmoreland counties, and has more than doubled its assets in the past seven years. Much of the bank's growth can be attributed to Eberly's and Rendle's lending philosophy, which concentrates heavily on

This "Gallatin Country" billboard is from an award-winning advertising campaign. Pictured is Nemacolin Castle, located in Brownsville in Fayette County.

residential and commercial mortgages as well as installment credit to consumers and small businesses in its five-county area, a region that has become popularly known as "Gallatin Country."

Rendle has served as president of Gallatin Bank since June 1, 1975. He came to Gallatin after serving as vice-chairman of the board of the American Bank and Trust Company of Reading, Pennsylvania. His banking career spans more than four decades of service, and his expertise is currently being used by the Federal Reserve Board of Cleveland, of which he is a member of the Pittsburgh branch. Like the Eberlys, Rendle has played an active role in the Uniontown community, sharing his knowledge with numerous boards and civic organizations. Eberly and Rendle have seen total assets of Gallatin Bank climb to over $1.018 billion, but chairman Robert Eberly says, "The real assets of Gallatin National Bank are the people of this region."

People have found that Gallatin National and the Eberly family are also outstanding regional assets. Robert and Orville Eberly played a central role in the creation of Penn State University's Fayette Campus, and the Eberly Foundation continues to provide substantial scholarship aid for students at the Fayette Campus. In 1977 Penn State named the Eberly Classroom Building in honor of Orville Eberly.

Under Robert Eberly's stewardship, the bank and family have continued many of their philanthropic pursuits, but with a recognition of the new technological era. Gallatin Bank's network of automatic teller machines includes thirty-one outlets with more than 89,000 transactions each month. "We have to take advantage of the latest technology," says Eberly, "while maintaining an essentially conservative orientation." That philosophical commitment has created a long tradition of growth and community service, a source of great pride for Gallatin Country and for Gallatin National Bank.

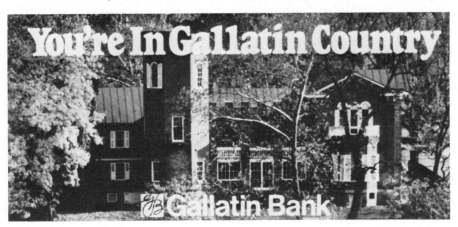

H.J. HEINZ COMPANY

Horseradish! Easily grown, difficult to process, and in widespread use, horseradish was Henry J. Heinz's first product. Instead of the green and brown glass then in common use, Heinz bottled his horseradish in clear glass so customers could see its purity and high quality for themselves. First he sold it door to door; then he wholesaled it to groceries, proving conclusively that superior quality will find a ready market—if it is properly packaged and promoted.

"The Little House Where We Began" is now in Michigan's Greenfield Village as a monument to American business acumen and the American Dream. It all began in 1869 in partnership with L.C. Noble. They planted three-quarters of an acre in Sharpsburg, six miles up the Allegheny River from Pittsburgh, took over the basement of the home from which the Heinz family had just moved, and hired three people to help process the horseradish. Harry Heinz was twenty-five years old.

Success came rapidly—too rapidly. Overexpansion, under financing, and the tempestuous national economy in those chaotic years following the end of the Civil War took their toll. Throughout 1875 Heinz worked desperately to save his business, which had operations throughout the eastern United States. By Christmas the firm was in bankruptcy. To start again, Heinz became a salaried employee of the new venture, a partnership formed by his brothers, his mother, and his wife. F.&J. Heinz Company was launched on St. Valentine's Day, 1876. Eventually, H.J. Heinz, who was responsible for about 80 percent of the debts, repaid every penny in full.

Over the next several years Heinz was able to repurchase much of the equipment and real estate that had been owned by the bankrupt Heinz & Noble. The new firm's pickles, horseradish, preserves, jellies, and canned fruits and vegetables quickly became popular with American housewives. So too did its chili sauce, vinegars, mustard, ketchup, fruit butters, mincemeat, and piccalilli. By the end of 1879 F.&J. Heinz had achieved financial stability and an enviable commercial reputation. There would be no looking backward.

Heinz remained devoted to his home state and region. The keystone symbol of Pennsylvania became an integral part of the Heinz product labeling—a tradition that is still continued. So too was the pickle symbol, proudly emblazoned with the name "Heinz."

In 1888 the organization changed its name to H.J. Heinz Company and began a series of expansions. Its salesmen continued to cover their territories in brightly painted wagons but started taking orders for future deliveries rather than actually selling goods directly. The firm began construction of its Allegheny City complex, just north of Pittsburgh. In 1892, at Muscatine, Iowa, the H.J. Heinz Company created the first of its network of branch factories located in prime agricultural areas.

His brilliant, nationally recognized success must have tasted very sweet indeed. H.J. Heinz moved himself and his family from Sharpsburg to the opulent Point Breeze section shared by such other successful residents as George Westinghouse, Henry Clay Frick, Thomas M. Armstrong, and Richard Beatty Mellon. H.J.

The H.J. Heinz Company's Pittsburgh facility. Heinz today has thirty-seven companies around the world, operating sixty plants in twenty nations and territories.

H.J. Heinz, founder.

In the early days employees wrapped Heinz products by hand.

Heinz and his firm had arrived.

The central concept of the H.J. Heinz Company, a commitment to use only the finest ingredients and methods, had taken the business to the top of its field. In an industry tainted by use and abuse of chemical additives and adulterants, Heinz remained dedicated to the purest and highest-quality ingredients and methods. He was one of the leading advocates of the Pure Food and Drug Act of 1906, and kept his factory open for tours of inspection by the public. Visitors were even given samples of Heinz products and a small lapel pin in the shape of a pickle.

Heinz understood that every housewife with a Mason jar and a home canner was potential competition. In response, he not only guarded his firm's reputation for quality but skillfully and imaginatively used advertising and promotion to make its

In 1888 the firm became known as the H.J. Heinz Company. Here barrels are delivered to be used in the firm's pickling process.

name a familiar part of the American scene.

Heinz personally created the "57 Varieties" concept in the early 1890s. The H.J. Heinz Company manufactured more than sixty products at the time, but Heinz liked the sound and sight of the numerals "57." In 1900 he provided New York City with its first large-scale electric sign, a forty-foot pickle. The numerals "57," cast in concrete ten feet high, decorated prominent hillsides across the country. The Heinz Pier became one of the great attractions of Atlantic City. An electric sign seventy feet tall spelled out "Heinz 57 Varieties."

Heinz took his business, its products, and its merchandising to Great Britain, opening the first of his foreign factories in London in 1905. His recipes proved as pleasing to foreign palates as to the American taste; Heinz today is made up of thirty-seven companies around the world, operating some sixty factories in twenty nations and territories.

The "57 Varieties" now covers

An array of old Heinz containers.

thousands of items that are marketed worldwide. Heinz is the leading producer of ketchup and the second-largest producer of canned soups and baby foods. Its Ore-Ida, Weight Watchers, and Star-Kist subsidiaries lead their own product lines and services. Heinz companies in Great Britain, Canada, Australia, the Netherlands, Portugal, Zimbabwe, China, France, West Germany, Venezuela, Japan, Italy, and Mexico help feed the world.

FERAG, INC.

The newspaper, stacked on a vendor's stand or tossed against the doorstep, is as much a part of everyday life as the morning cup of coffee. But few people, even those who devour every morsel of information a newspaper holds, ever stop to think about how the newspaper is put together. Between the time it rolls off the presses and the time its contents are read, the newspaper has been sorted, transported, collated with other printed material, and assembled into one neat package. And though newspaper readers rarely think about this process, a company named Ferag, Inc., was founded because Walter Reist could think of little else.

Reist founded Ferag AG in Zurich, Switzerland, in 1957. Today the Ferag name is synonymous worldwide with the state of the art in automated conveying, processing, and inserting systems. Every day millions of newspapers printed by hundreds of the world's leading publishing and printing firms rely on Ferag systems as important links in their total production chain.

Ferage, Inc. was established in 1969 as the American subsidiary of Ferag A.G. Starting with offices in Philadelphia, the company moved, in 1974, to the Keystone Industrial Park

Walter Reist, founder and owner of Ferag Group.

in Bristol to establish Ferag's own sales and administration office, plus a systems production facility. A 50-percent expansion of the facility will be completed in 1986. Today over 100 of the total 900 employees in the Ferag Group work at its American headquarters in Bristol, where publishers throughout the United

Ferag servicemen inspect a Rotadisc II Palletizing Station. Newspaper inserts can be stored on the discs and returned to palletizing and depalletizing stations as needed.

States and Canada can turn for their production needs.

The major components of the Ferag production system are best applied to very large commercial printers and newspapers with a circulation of more than 50,000. Several key innovations make up the firm's production system, including the single-copy conveying system, the Rotosert automatic inserting system, and the palletizing/depalletizing Rotadisc system.

The heart of Ferag flexibility is the single-copy conveyor, which grips each individual product from the press folder—at full press speed—and carries it without marking, pinching, or tearing. Each yellow gripper carries the product to any destination in the processing systems: direct to the stackers, to the inserters, to the palletizer, to checking stations, or to waste disposal. Microprocessor controls direct the flow and provide accurate product count.

Supplements, preprints, advertising brochures, and products such as stitched catalogs can be inserted into main jackets at press speeds with Rotosert inserting systems. Material to be handled is fed to a Rotosert drum from high-speed hoppers or from Ferag's own depalletizers. The insert system also efficiently handles off-line, preassembly of insert material (advertising supplements inserted into preprints, for example) to effectively increase the total number of inserts that can be accommodated during the on-line run.

The Rotadisc system is an entirely new product-handling technique for materials that have already been printed. The round, cylinder-like Rotadiscs roll materials onto cassettes that can then be handled and stored without any intermediate operations and at full production speed. Moreover, the copy can then be conveyed back to the processing units, unrolled, and fed back into the palletizing system when needed. Each Rotadisc holds up to 160,000 pages of copy. Such systems provide remarkable storage capacity for print-

ers; each cassette, even when completely rolled, is only slightly wider than the material it holds.

Philadelphia Newspapers, Inc., which publishes *The Philadelphia Inquirer* and the *Daily News,* is one of many newspaper industries around the world to incorporate the Ferag system into its printing and mailroom operation. And development of the Ferag system that those newspapers use actually began four years before the company was founded.

From his earliest years as an engineer, Walter Reist has been closely involved in the conveying and material-handling problem. Early on, he realized that the newspaper conveyor systems then available were inadequate to meet the demands of the increasing speed and quality of rotary presses.

By October 1953 Reist had invented the first nonsmudging gripper conveyor. The "gripper"—actually a double-gripper system that picked up materials as they came off the press and transported them smudge-free to the processing areas—started Ferag on the road to its present worldwide success.

By 1962 Ferag offered not only the gripper but also a counting system, stackers, stacker turners, belt conveyors, and diverters. This gave the company the ability to put the equipment together as an entire production system and was the first time copies from the press were handled automatically until they reached the inside of the truck. From that time on Ferag was planning complete mailroom systems.

The early 1970s brought several changes to Ferag. In addition to establishing its Pennsylvania base, the company established Ferag UK in England. At that same time Reist started to develop what is today called the "New System," the high-technology system that includes the single-copy conveying system, the inserting system, and the Rotadisc.

Throughout the Ferag system, it is widely held that the success of the corporation is made possible through Walter Reist's concentration on a single field, his constant attention to market demands, and his flair for providing precisely what his customers need. It is no surprise, then, to discover that Reist's approach to Ferag is reflected in one of his favorite phrases: "Nothing is a problem, only a challenge."

Ferag, Inc., an international company, has established its base in the United States at Bristol, Pennsylvania.

GOULD, INC.

Time was in Philadelphia when the use of electricity, indeed the very flip of a wall switch to turn on the kitchen lights, was synonymous with a firm called I-T-E Circuit Breaker Company. By the mid-1950s this corporation was one of the largest manufacturing firms in the city, and one of the top 500 corporations in the country.

Today what was once I-T-E is now part of the tapestry of Gould, Inc., a company that develops and manufactures information systems, computer-integrated industrial automation systems, instruments systems, defense systems, semiconductors, and other electronic components for worldwide markets. From its base in Philadelphia, Gould established a stand-alone division called the Systems Protection Division. And to understand how a division known as SPD evolved from the fabric of a company called I-T-E, one must start from the beginning, from the year 1888.

That was the year an electrical contractor and small manufacturer named Henry B. Cutter informally organized the Cutter Electrical and Manufacturing Company. Incorporated three years later, Cutter Electrical operated from a private residence at 27 South Eleventh Street and created the "double-push" wall switch

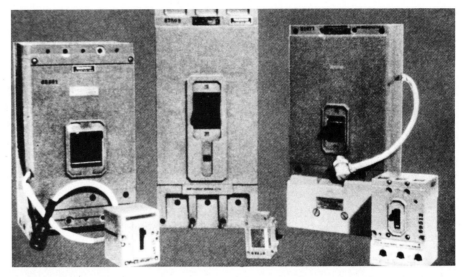

Present product line versions built for U.S. Navy vessels which most nearly resemble some of the early products built by SPD for general use.

for household use.

Working part time with Cutter was Walter E. Harrington, an inventor and chief engineer for the Camden Horse Railway, which was at the time in the throes of changing its company to electricity. Harrington became

SPD's current line of power circuit breakers, which provide much higher capacity ratings than former models. Power circuit breakers usually protect generators and important large loads on the ship's electrical distribution system.

interested in Cutter's circuit breaker, which was first introduced in 1890.

The first Cutter circuit breaker had a shunt fuse for interruption and resembled a black box of iron bars when attached to a wall. It worked on a principle called Inverse Time Element. Simply stated, the greater the overload or short-circuit current, the greater the necessity for opening the circuit. The greater the necessity for opening the circuit, the quicker it is accomplished. The inverse time element principle was the basis for almost all air circuit breaker development after 1890.

It wasn't long before Harrington convinced Cutter to start manufacturing his circuit breaker in a small factory at 1112 Samson Street. Soon the pair was joined by William M. Scott and A. Edward "Ned" Newton. Together the four men were the driving force behind the company's early growth.

During that time the inverse time element circuit breaker was continually refined. By 1905 the I-T-E principle was extended to the "Dalite" or direct acting limit inverse time element, which was particularly designed for low-voltage air circuit breakers. Each succeeding model expanded and improved the application of the product and allowed the company to grow. In 1908 the firm acquired the local switchboard builder, the Walker Electric Company, and added switchboards to its product line.

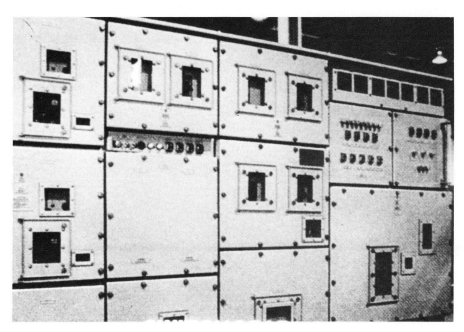

The switch gear, shown here, provides the housing for the circuit breakers and the site where cables are interconnected and control functions and decision making are automatically controlled.

In 1928 the business incorporated the concept of its original technology into a new name—the I-T-E Circuit Breaker Company. The original New Jersey corporation became a Pennsylvania enterprise in 1939. During the next thirty years many businesses were acquired, and product lines were added to and developed at I-T-E. Soon the company was a full-line supplier of electrical power distribution equipment, ranging from 120 volts to 600,000 volts. I-T-E had operations across the United States and in Canada, and by the mid-1950s was one of the largest manufacturing firms in Philadelphia.

The company merged with Imperial Eastman in 1967, and the resulting I-T-E Imperial Corporation added fluid power control to its product line. In 1976 I-T-E Imperial merged with Gould, Inc., which is based in Chicago.

From 1979 to 1982 the firm's Navy product lines were handled by various divisions within the company. In February 1983 Gould took several steps to consolidate its Navy products under one roof. First the firm

divested itself of several divisions that were originally part of I-T-E Imperial—the Distribution and Controls, and Switchgear divisions. With assets remaining from the divestiture, Gould formed the Systems Protection Division in Philadelphia. For the first

Gould, Inc., Systems Protection Division's new 165,000-square-foot facility in Philadelphia.

time in the company's history, one complete and separate business entity was responsible for its Navy product line: Gould SPD.

Since World War I—from the days of the battleship *Michigan* to today's Trident submarine *Michigan*—Gould SPD has given the Navy the edge it needs in systems protection technology. For both nuclear and conventional naval vessels, Gould SPD designs and manufactures the most environmentally suited complete line of circuit breakers, switchgear assemblies, and components. Gould SPD safeguards electrical distribution systems operating under real or simulated battle conditions, high shock impact, constant vibration, and high ambient temperature.

Today Gould SPD employs nearly 650 people and devotes 100 percent of its business to government contracts. From its headquarters in a modern, 165,000-square-foot facility located on twenty acres within the city, Gould, Inc., has continued the business that was first established here in 1888 by a man named Cutter.

MODERN GROUP LTD.

It might seem a bit unusual to walk into the lobby of a modern company and find—sitting there along with the ficus trees and chic couches—a bright, canary-yellow forklift truck.

But not so if the name of the business is Modern Group Ltd., a firm headquartered in Bristol that specializes in the sale and rental of industrial equipment.

Not only is Modern one of the largest distributors of a wide variety of Hyster Company forklifts, it also distributes an array of industrial warehousing and material-handling equipment. Modern's handling equipment is so diverse that company chairman Joseph McEwen likes to say that Modern services industries ranging from beer distributors to steel mills.

Modern is the privately owned holding company for six separate operations that comprise the Modern Group: Modern Handling Equipment Company of Pennsylvania, Modern Handling Equipment Company of New Jersey, Material Handling Equipment Company, Master Equipment Rentals, Modern HiLift Equipment, and Engines International.

Modern operates through twenty service and distribution centers throughout Eastern Pennsylvania, Delaware, New Jersey, and Maryland. In 1985 the firm reported sales and rentals in excess of fifty million dollars.

The company, which employs some 400 people in sales, service, and management, can trace its start to 1946, when another firm, called Rapistan of Pennsylvania, was formed to sell material-handling equipment—equipment ranging from conveyor belts to dollies. One year later Hyster Company, one of the largest forklift manufacturers in the nation, tapped Rapistan to be its distributor in Eastern Pennsylvania and New Jersey. In 1955 Modern Handling Equipment Company was formed to operate the Hyster distributorship, providing both sales and service of the Hyster products.

By 1963 Modern Handling operated out of four service branches in

Joseph McEwen, chief executive officer of Modern Handling Equipment Company since 1957 and chairman of the board of Modern Group Ltd. since 1979.

Pennsylvania and New Jersey. That same year Modern Rentals Inc., the forerunner of the current Master Equipment Rentals, was formed to rent the Hyster trucks. In 1966 Modern Handling Equipment of New Jersey was formed to operate the distributorships out of New Jersey,

with its headquarters in Hasbrouck Heights, New Jersey. Along the way Modern continued to open and expand service branches throughout the two states.

The mid-1970s brought several key changes for the company. In 1974 Master Equipment Rentals was formed in Wilmington, Delaware, to rent industrial equipment. Two years later Modern Equipment Handling Company of Pennsylvania moved its headquarters from Philadelphia to Bristol. In 1977 Material Handling Equipment was formed to sell allied material handling equipment. Three years later Modern Rentals was dissolved, and the remaining Modern companies were placed under the umbrella called Modern Group Ltd.

Modern expanded its umbrella a bit more in 1981 when it formed Engines International, and again in 1984 when it formed Modern HiLift Equipment to sell and rent aerial platform equipment. Along the way Modern Group Ltd. acquired four additional companies and merged them into its own corporate structure.

Modern Group Ltd.'s first branch operation was located in York, Pennsylvania, and dates back to the mid-1950s.

The glass-enclosed lobby of Modern's headquarters, dotted with various samples of industrial and material-handling equipment, offers a unique capsule of the firm's mission in the business world.

As a distributor of Hyster Company products for nearly forty years, Modern sells and rents hundreds of forklifts and industrial trucks and is one of the largest distributors of such products in the United States. Businesses that rent from Modern can expect a full service and maintenance agreement with the company, with servicemen stopping in regularly to inspect the equipment. Of course, not all of the company's forklift fleet could fit into its lobby. One of the largest forklift trucks distributed by Modern has a lifting capacity of 90,000 pounds.

The carts, dollies, ladders, aluminum conveyor belts, forklifts, and dock boards situated in the lobby represent only a small fraction of the firm's material-handling equipment supplies. From material handling in tiny corridors deep in warehouses to transporting bulky shipments from van to loading dock, Modern has top equipment to do the job.

Modern Group Ltd. is placing a growing emphasis on such high-technology avenues as automatic storage and retrieval systems and automatic guided vehicle systems. The firm has a staff of specialists who dedicate their full time and efforts to studying the latest developments in this fast-changing field. This expertise is then applied to the problems encountered by firms who are experiencing the need, through high-density storage and automated handling, to expand and streamline their storage of materials without resorting to the erection of additional buildings.

In 1985 Engines International was appointed the Northeast Regional Distributor for Perkins Diesel. Trading under the name of Perkins Engines Northeast, the company handles responsibilities for the distribution of Perkins industrial and mari-

This building, located at Broad and Champlost streets in Philadelphia, served as the company's headquarters from 1964 to 1976.

time diesel engines from Maine to Washington, D.C., in addition to representing other well-known engine manufacturers such as Continental and Briggs & Stratton.

One of the group's newest ventures is Modern HiLift, a firm engaged primarily in the rental of aerial work

Modern Group Ltd. has occupied its present headquarters, at the intersection of Route I-95 and the Pennsylvania Turnpike in Bristol, since 1976.

platform trucks. Outside the Bristol office a Condor 60N towers an impressive ninety feet in the air.

Modern Group sells and rents to a wide range of clientele—from the home owner who needs a cart or dolly to maneuver a bag of fertilizer around the backyard, to several firms that ordered their first Hyster forklift truck over twenty-five years ago and that now operate fleets of more than 100 trucks.

Joseph McEwen, who started with the company as a salesman in 1946, and who has been chief executive officer since 1957, smiles at the play on words as he repeats the company's motto, "Equip the *Modern* Way."

CHRISTMAN AIR SYSTEM

Take a free-wheeling entrepreneurial spirit and run it through the changing regulatory winds that have buffeted the American transportation industry in recent years. Toss in an old-fashioned survival instinct, a ton of hard work, and a stubborn refusal to quit when the road gets rough. That was Walter Christman's recipe for success at Christman Air System of Washington, Pennsylvania.

Christman was twenty-three years old and impatient when he started his own business on January 2, 1961. "I vowed that I would never treat my employees the way I had been treated," he recalls. He had a part-time assistant, a Chevy station wagon, and state certification to deliver packages, parcels, and messages in an area limited to seven miles around Canonsburg. He worked for hardware and grocery stores, charging thirty-five cents per delivery.

By 1962 Christman Trucking had become a contract freight carrier for Emery Air Freight—serving Allegheny County. In 1964 a second company, Christman Corporation, was formed as a real estate and stock holding company. In 1967 Emery cancelled its contract with Christman Trucking. To survive, Christman Corporation became Christman Air Freight, operating under regulation of the Civil Aeronautics Board. Christman Trucking continued operations under the authority of the Interstate Commerce Commission.

Then came deregulation and a series of massive changes in the transportation industry. This small firm was no longer able to compete in air freight services profitably, so, in order to survive, Christman took his business in a new direction—straight up. Christman Trucking became Christman Air System in 1978. The firm's white commuter aircraft with red and blue insignia began carrying both passengers and freight.

Today Christman Air System successfully competes with giant national transportation companies. "We're small at everything we do, but we do a lot of different things,"

Christman Air System's commuter airline is based in Washington, Pennsylvania, and serves five states and Washington, D.C., with seven aircraft including five turbo-prop commuter airliners carrying both passengers and freight.

says Walter Christman. The operation consists of an air freight carrier, a trucking line, and a commuter airline based in Washington, Pennsylvania, and serving five states and Washington, D.C.

"We've stayed in business by doing what other people wouldn't do," explains Christman. "We're small, specialized, and versatile. My son calls us 'a company in search of a business.' We've done whatever we've had to do in order to survive."

Christman Air System has not only survived—it has thrived. The firm now has seventy-five loyal employees, a fleet of trucks and tractor-trailers, seven aircraft (including five turbo-prop commuter airliners), and a seven-door terminal and operations center, plus a 12,000-square-foot hangar at Washington County Airport. "We're in business to make a living for ourselves and our employees," says Christman, "but we do it our way."

Christman Air System successfully competes with giant national transportation companies as an air freight carrier, a trucking line, and a commuter airline.

GILBRETH INTERNATIONAL CORPORATION

Although Gilbreth International Corporation's name is hardly a household word, its shrink bands have positioned it as the leader in heat-shrinkable packaging. Gilbreth's products and seals can be found on counters or inside the cabinets of nearly every home—wrapped around pharmaceuticals, cosmetics, food containers, and their caps. Printed by Gilbreth in many colors, these bands are used on bottles to label, decorate, and add tamper-evident protection. They are also used to decorate Christmas ornaments, label consumer batteries, seal lip balms, and for other diverse applications.

Founded in 1961 by two brothers, William J. and Jack Spiegel, Gilbreth was initially an import business. In 1965 Gilbreth became the first company to import the heat-shrinkable PVC.

Today over 300 employees work in two Gilbreth plants in Bucks County, Pennsylvania, with a combined square footage of 160,000 feet, producing heat-shrinkable film and con-

verting it into labels and seals.

Gilbreth has its own art department that creates the graphic designs for its customers. Its printing department has five rotogravure presses that print film in up to eight colors at speeds of 700 feet per minute.

The shrink bands are made by using either heat-shrinkable film or extruded seamless tubing, both made at the Gilbreth factory. The band shrink "memory" is produced by a Gilbreth process that expands the plastic film by 60 percent.

Shrink bands are sized just large enough to allow them to be placed over the length of the container as labels or over the cap and neck as tamper-evident seals. Applied by high-speed machinery, or manually, the band is exposed to a heat source that activates the band's "memory" and causes it to shrink and conform

Gilbreth International's headquarters is located on State Road in Bensalem.

tightly and smoothly around the container or cap.

Gilbreth's customers include leading pharmaceutical, cosmetic, food, and electronic manufacturers. Company sales exceed twenty million dollars per year.

"We consider ourselves big enough to do the job right, but small enough to care about every customer," says Edith M. Lichstein, who became Gilbreth's first employee in 1962. Today vice-president in charge of administration, she points out that Gilbreth was making tamper-evident seals some twenty years before the public demand for such seals. Gilbreth responded promptly when the Tylenol incident required tamper-evident protection for pharmaceutical products.

The firm, which started by importing, is now a fully integrated manufacturer selling through seven sales offices nationwide. The Skin-Tight Label, made by Gilbreth International Corporation, is found everywhere.

NEW HOLLAND SUPPLY COMPANY, INC.

Amish horse-drawn buggies run routinely along state Highway 23, the New Holland Pike. Alongside them run the brightly painted tractor-trailers of the New Holland Supply Company. But while the Amish farm folk are visiting local friends or business establishments, the New Holland trucks can be headed almost anywhere in the fifteen-state area served by this giant distributor of agricultural, pet, and rural-related supplies.

From the rocky fields of New England to the rolling prairies of Indiana, from the Canadian border to the gracious old plantation country of southern Virginia, New Holland Supply distributes products to dealers serving local farmers and rural home owners.

New Holland Supply offers the most complete product line of any rural supply distributor in the eastern United States. Its products run from Absorbine Hooflex (a horse care product) to Zodiak five-month flea collars for dogs; the firm's expanded line covers horse, pet, animal, lawn, garden, and hardware supplies as well as rural household goods, footwear, and clothing.

New Holland Supply was founded in September 1962 by George Weaver, A. Clarence Plank, Robert Schroll,

James D. Bradley and James L. Bradley in the office of New Holland Supply Company.

and John H. Hess. Hess was the manager responsible for the development of New Holland Supply from its creation until 1979, when it was purchased by James D. Bradley and his son, James L. Bradley. Hess still serves on the board of directors.

James D. Bradley is a Missouri na-

John Hess, one of the founders of the firm.

tive who has been active in the agricultural supply business since 1952. "I've spent my entire life on the farm and in agricultural distribution and manufacturing," he recalls proudly. His career included executive positions with Anchor Serum Company and DURVET, Inc., before he joined New Holland Supply in 1975 as executive vice-president.

The original business was located at the corner of Diller and Hoover avenues in New Holland, but that 2,000-square-foot building has since been removed. There were eight employees and a total annual payroll of $80,000.

The firm moved to its present location one-quarter mile west of New Holland on Highway 23 in 1964. A series of expansions have brought its current size to 116,000 square feet, but the warehouse's western wall is specially built to allow simple and efficient expansion.

The Bradley family purchased New Holland Supply in 1979. James D. Bradley is president and chief executive officer. James L. Bradley is executive vice-president and chief operating officer. Douglas Vertigan serves as corporate secretary and treasurer.

From the outside New Holland Supply looks like many other farm

supply stores (if you ignore the warehouses extending behind the low brick building in front). Park along the driveway, step through the inviting entry, and your first impression is confirmed. There are even a few customers browsing the spacious aisles, examining the orderly displays.

While it serves a few retail customers, primarily local Amish residents, this store is not intended to serve the public. It's there as a service to the firm's real customers, rural supply dealers from throughout New Holland's marketing area who arrive daily to learn display and sales techniques and to examine new products. The real action here is not in front of the counter, but through the "Staff Only" doors that separate the model sales room from the computer complex and warehouses that are the real New Holland Supply Company.

Behind those doors lie the warehouses, catalog production facilities, reference library, thirteen-bay transportation complex, and computers that allow New Holland Supply to ship orders within twenty-four hours of receipt. With the order goes a fully itemized invoice. "Our efficiency has allowed many of our dealers to shift their inventory burden to us. That's fine," says Bradley. "It means that

New Holland Supply offers one of the most complete inventories of agricultural, pet, and rural-related supplies in the eastern United States.

we're providing our dealers with good service. We like knowing that we provide them with the best service available."

Another unique service of New Holland Supply, what Bradley calls "the highlight of our year," is the firm's annual dealer showcase and

two-day buying show. Held each September at the Lancaster Host Farm Resort, it attracts dealers from throughout New Holland's fifteen-state region. It brings them together with 140 manufacturers for sales seminars and demonstrations.

New Holland Supply buys from 340 different manufacturers and delivers on a regular basis to 4,800 dealers. The latest product line expansion brought the company to 9,500 line items representing 2,500 different products. It's all managed with the aid of a sophisticated, state-of-the-art computer system that just went through its fourth major upgrade.

New Holland currently employs 24 full-time salespeople and a total of more than 100 employees. The Bradley family members are proud of their people. Prominently located plaques honor those with five, ten, fifteen, and twenty years of service. "Our dealers are our customers," says James D. Bradley, "and our employees are our best product."

The brightly colored tractor-trailers of the New Holland Supply Company are a familiar sight on the highways of a surrounding fifteen-state area.

REA AND DERICK, INC.

Follow the river valleys of Central Pennsylvania—the Susquehanna, Wyoming, and Lehigh. For more than a half-century, the people of that region have depended on Rea and Derick drugstores to provide them with prescription service, health and beauty aids, and first-quality merchandise. Starting from a single store in Sunbury, Rea and Derick spread throughout the Commonwealth, stretching into southern New York and northern Maryland.

Two partners, Scott C. Rea and George C. Derick, started that Sunbury store in 1920. The two young pharmacists were recent graduates from the Philadelphia School of Pharmacy and Science. They decided to combine their talents and training, opening a pharmacy that would be dedicated to community service and would give close attention to the "professional compounding of prescriptions." Their own business prescription succeeded, and before long Rea and Derick "Stores of Service" were seen throughout the Susquehanna Valley.

Rea and Derick built their chain by hiring top-quality pharmacists, managers, and employees, and allowing them to run individual stores. The owners' reputation for professional integrity and merchandising know-how helped to attract talented and devoted staff members as well as an extraordinary customer base.

The same river valleys that had nourished the growth of Rea and Derick almost devastated the chain in 1936. Floodwaters inundated Central and Western Pennsylvania, destroyed Rea and Derick's executive offices in Sunbury, and ruined drug stocks and other merchandise at more than twenty Rea and Derick stores. The partners dried their files, moved their headquarters across the river to Northumberland, and went back to work.

Northumberland is the site of the American home of Joseph Priestly, the British chemist who discovered oxygen. In 1874 the Priestly house became the birthplace of the Ameri-

Scott C. Rea

can Chemical Society. Northumberland is a scenic Central Pennsylvania town that looks like a Norman Rockwell painting come to life. Until the visitor actually arrives at the firm's block-long complex, only the appearance of a giant tractor-trailer moving through its quiet streets reveals the presence of Rea and Derick's offices and distribution center.

In 1964 the company experienced a series of major changes. First, the drugstore chain was acquired by the Acme Markets division of American Stores Company. Then the founders both retired from active leadership, and turned over the Rea and Derick presidency to a longtime Rea and Derick pharmacist, store manager, and district supervisor, Gorden H. Griffith. Griffith remained as president until his own retirement in 1975. During his ten years at the helm, Rea and Derick became one of the leading drugstore chains in the Commonwealth, with more than 100 stores.

American Stores Company was reorganized under the Skaggs Corporation of Salt Lake City, Utah, in 1974. It continued to prosper under

the new corporate umbrella; Paul A. Morelock took over as president in 1975. Val D. Buckmiller, a Skaggs executive, became president and chief executive officer in 1981.

The Skaggs Corporation maintained both the autonomy of the Rea and Derick operations, and its reliance on the basic concepts of the chain's founders. The chain continued to emphasize its pharmaceutical products and prescription service. "We've always been drugstores," says Rea and Derick executive Gib Loyn. "That's what we do best. We run drugstores, and we do it well." In 1982 Larry La Rock, another Skaggs executive, became president of the drugstore chain.

Skaggs sold the Rea and Derick chain to Peoples Drug of Alexandria, Virginia, in 1984. Peoples Drug is a wholly owned subsidiary of Imasco Corporation, a Canadian consumer products and services conglomerate. (Imasco also owns the Hardee's fast-food chain.)

There were 134 stores with a sales volume in excess of $200 million in the Rea and Derick chain when Peoples Drug assumed control. Peoples is

George C. Derick

reorganizing the chain, absorbing the stores in South-central Pennsylvania and Maryland into its own network, and changing them to the Peoples name.

The remaining eighty-five stores of the Rea and Derick chain will remain an autonomous division of Peoples, still headquartered and supplied from the Northumberland office and distribution center. Those stores are concentrated in the central Susquehanna Valley, the Pocono Mountain region, the Lehigh Valley, Wilkes-Barre, Scranton, Williamsport, and Sunbury.

With the Peoples acquisition, James L. Johnston became vice-president and chief operations officer of Rea and Derick. Johnston, a pharmacist, is a native Pennsylvanian from Blairsville. He has been with Peoples since 1965, most recently as a regional vice-president for the mid-Atlantic

In contrast to the 1930s store is this contemporary Rea and Derick drugstore located in a shopping mall.

region. He is expected to continue other Rea and Derick traditions as well, including the firm's tradition of controlled growth, careful selection of new locations, and an emphasis on outstanding prescription service.

As befits the contemporary international business environment, the corporate structure of Rea and Derick, Inc., is complex and involved.

Typical of the Rea and Derick stores of the day is Store No. 10 in Berwick. Photo circa 1930

But as befits the needs of its customers, Rea and Derick still thinks of its stores as neighborhood institutions. "Just as we were sixty-five years ago," says Loyn, "we're still family pharmacies."

LOCKHART IRON AND STEEL COMPANY

Charles Lockhart purchased the Long and Company steel plant at a sheriff's sale in 1890, and hired Thomas J. Gillespie as his general manager. The firm was one of the oldest in the McKees Rocks area, having been built in 1878 to make iron by the ancient process of "puddling." The small plant was enlarged by the addition of another finishing mill. Later the company purchased the adjacent property of the Russell Kress Box Factory. Under Gillespie's leadership, the Lockhart plant became the last great American mill to use the hand-puddling process to make wrought iron.

Puddling involved lining a small furnace with a paste made of iron ore and water. The furnace was heated to 2,700 degrees Fahrenheit, melting and refining the iron and forming a spongy ball that became the basis for later processing. During the World War I era the plant's products were in great demand, and Lockhart was staffed by more than 1,000 employees. But changing tastes and construction requirements eliminated

the need for this highly crafted product, and Lockhart closed its puddling furnaces, the last in the United States, in 1956. The plant ceased rolling wrought-iron products in June 1968.

Lockhart Iron and Steel was always quick to recognize industry trends and to position itself to meet new de-

Three generations, all named T.J. Gillespie, have served as presidents of Lockhart Iron and Steel Company.

mands. The company branched into steel warehousing in 1913. By the 1960s Lockhart had essentially become a metal-service center, providing a distribution system for the largest stock of hot- and cold-rolled carbon steel bars in the region. Lockhart also made itself a leading source of steel plates, sheets, reinforcing bars, structural shapes, and cold finished steel bars.

In August 1966 Lockhart purchased the Boiler Tube Company of America, and acquired the Fort Duquesne Steel Company in February 1969. As market requirements changed, so did Lockhart. It started distributing aluminum in 1959, sold the boiler tube subsidiary in 1979, and divested itself of the steel service center sector of its business in February 1985. In the meantime the firm had acquired N.L. Kimes Associates, a chemicals plant in 1982, purchased Watson Wood Products in 1983, and reaffirmed its commitment to aluminum by incorporating Lockhart Aluminum Inc. in December 1984.

Three generations of T.J. Gillespies have served as presidents of Lockhart Iron and Steel Company, a proud family and industrial tradition. Lockhart products have included the iron used in steam locomotives, the anchors and chains on countless ships, and the decorative wrought-iron fencing that surrounds the United Nations Building in New York City.

Lockhart Iron and Steel today is a modern diversified holding company with corporate interests throughout the East in real estate, equipment, chemicals, wood products, aluminum, and other sectors of business. Its roots run deep in the Three Rivers region, anchored in the oldest and finest crafts and traditions of the Pittsburgh iron industry.

The Lockhart Iron and Steel industrial complex is located in McKees Rocks.

FIRST EASTERN CORP.

On June 1, 1863, just four months after President Abraham Lincoln signed the National Banking Act, the First National Bank of Wilkes-Barre received Charter No. 30. Founded by James McLean, the institution began business with $51,000 of invested capital and a leased office in Wilkes-Barre's Chahoon Building.

Second National Bank of Wilkes-Barre received Charter No. 104 on September 19, 1863. The new institution was led by president Thomas F. Atherton. Second National Bank grew rapidly, acquiring the assets of Susquehanna Bank in October 1864, and reaching two million dollars in deposits by the end of 1889. Both national banks developed into strong institutions as the Wyoming Valley helped fuel the industrialization of Pennsylvania and the nation.

The Great Depression brought widespread unemployment and a virtual paralysis of the banking industry, but both institutions emerged on sound financial footing. As industrial production soared to meet the demands of World War II, they were prepared to meet the financial requirements of the Wyoming Valley and the seemingly insatiable needs of the war effort.

The postwar era was marked by acquisitions and mergers. Second National Bank of Wilkes-Barre purchased the First National Bank of Kingston in March 1951. On September 12, 1957, the First and Second National Banks of Wilkes-Barre consolidated to become the First-Second National Bank and Trust Company of Wilkes-Barre. Assets of the new institution surpassed fifty-seven million dollars.

First-Second acquired White Haven Savings Bank in 1964, Conyngham National in 1966, First National

The First National Bank Building, on the east side of Public Square, was occupied by the bank from 1876 to 1908.

of Bloomsburg in 1967, and First-Stroudsburgh National in 1971. On April 1, 1971, the directors changed the name of the institution to The First National Bank of Eastern Pennsylvania. Thomas Kiley became chairman of the board and chief executive officer, and Horace E. Kramer became president.

In July 1974 the institution merged with Berwick National Bank, taking the name First Eastern Bank, N.A.

In 1980 it acquired Southside National Bank in Catawissa and North Scranton Bank and Trust Company. In August 1982 the institution again reorganized with the creation of a one-bank holding company, First Eastern Corp. Scranton National Bank was acquired two years later.

The corporation now serves an area of almost 2,500 square miles with a population of more than 700,000. Under chairman, president, and chief executive officer Richard M. Ross, Jr., growth continues at a record-setting pace. Wholly owned subsidiaries include First Eastern Bank, First Eastern Life Insurance Company, First Eastern Realty, and Ideal Consumer Discount Co. Keystone Equipment Leasing (acquired in 1981) is a subsidiary of First Eastern Bank. By the end of 1985 assets exceeded $1.3 billion. The headquarters of First Eastern Corp. is at 11 West Market Street in Wilkes-Barre, next door to the site of the Chahoon Building where First National leased an office in 1863.

The four buildings that housed the Second National Bank of Wilkes-Barre before its merger with First National Bank of Wilkes-Barre to become First Eastern Bank, N.A. The building at upper left was constructed in 1908 and is the main office of the bank today. It is located at 11 West Market Street, Wilkes-Barre.

THE PEOPLES NATURAL GAS COMPANY

The great Haymaker well of Murrysville blew in on November 3, 1878, and with it came a new age, the gas age, for Pittsburgh and Western Pennsylvania. The roar of the well could be heard for miles, and when a lantern-carrying tourist moved a bit too close, the resulting flame turned night into day.

June 26, 1985, was Peoples Natural Gas Day in Pittsburgh. The governor of Pennsylvania, the mayor, state officials, and employees of Peoples Gas joined to commemorate the centennial of Peoples, the first company chartered by the Commonwealth of Pennsylvania to distribute natural gas. The firm was established by Joseph Newton Pew and Edward O. Emerson. The Pittsburgh entrepreneurs first became active in the gas business in 1882 and bought the pioneer Haymaker well in 1883. When Pennsylvania passed its Natural Gas Act in 1885, Pew and Emerson were first in line.

Pew, a one-time teacher and real estate speculator from Eastern Pennsylvania, was a gas pioneer not only in Pittsburgh, but also for the industry as a whole. His creation of the apparatus by which low-pressure gas could be compressed and pumped through pipelines freed the distribution network from reliance on wellhead pressure and made long-distance distribution possible. Pew's early policy decisions paved the way for making Peoples an outstanding, successful company.

Pew's partner, Edward O. Emerson, was also an accomplished businessman. His father, Charles O. Emerson, was a distinguished New York lawyer; his cousin, Ralph Waldo Emerson, was America's premier philosopher and essayist.

The early days in the gas fields were turbulent and sometimes violent. Pew and Emerson's rights to the Haymaker well were won over armed opposition. Private property owners fought to prevent Peoples from laying pipelines on their land; the City of Pittsburgh sued to stop what it claimed were unsafe practices. Competition

also came from other gas companies, including those owned by such other Pittsburgh power brokers as inventor/businessman George Westinghouse and financier Andrew W. Mellon.

John D. Rockefeller brought order to the Pennsylvania oil and gas fields in the form of his Standard Oil Company. One of Standard's companies, National Transit Company, purchased Peoples Natural Gas in 1903. The National Transit president, Calvin N. Payne, became president of Peoples.

It was the conservation-minded Payne who introduced the concept of having users pay for gas actually consumed. Before his adoption of metering, customers paid a flat rate for service and were free to use (and waste) as much gas as they chose.

To the public, the history of Peoples is a history of uninterrupted service, but to the company, it is a story of technological innovation and skillful management facing constantly changing legislative and regulatory environments. Court and commission rulings, the Pennsylvania Public Ser-

Many of The Peoples Natural Gas Company's fleet vehicles run on natural gas. More than 30,000 natural gas-powered vehicles operate in the United States, with a half-million such vehicles worldwide. Methane for the Western Pennsylvania transportation market is one of Peoples' new business targets.

vice Company Law (1913), the federal Public Utility Holding Company Act (1935), the Pennsylvania Public Utility Law, and other state and federal laws all helped change the shape of Peoples.

The aftermath of World War II ushered in Peoples' greatest era of expansion. Concern with the Pittsburgh environment brought demands for smoke-free air. Gas for heating, cooking, and industry use replaced dirtier fuels. The new Greater Pittsburgh Airport selected natural gas for its fuel needs—and Peoples to supply it. Returning veterans all wanted their own homes, and gas was their most popular fuel of choice. It was the company's golden age. Riding the crest of its postwar expansion program, Peoples moved its headquarters to the Gateway Center, the gleaming

downtown symbol of Pittsburgh's renaissance.

Since 1943 The Peoples Natural Gas Company has been a wholly owned subsidiary of Consolidated Natural Gas Company, but Peoples has preserved its own identity. The firm has traditionally cherished its public-service orientation and its dedication to education and civic service. Peoples' executives are also proud of the firm's long-standing reputation for compassionate and concerned treatment both of its employees and its customers.

Jack B. Hoey has been president of Peoples Gas since 1977. A native of Murrysville, where Peoples Gas was born, Hoey is aware of the organization's history and traditions, yet equally concerned with new challenges and demands. Among his first innovations was the introduction of the Facilities Information Management System, a computerized map-

FIMS—the Facilities Information Management System—has changed the way maps are drawn and transmitted. The Peoples Natural Gas Company is among the first utility companies in the United States to automate its method for recording pipeline and facilities information. On-line record keeping and retrieval helps the Pittsburgh-based firm maintain a safe and reliable gas distribution system.

ping and data-processing system that places Peoples on the technological frontier.

"Joseph Newton Pew and Edward O. Emerson would gaze with proud amazement at what they started 100 years ago. Their risk-filled investment has turned into a $300-million system," says Hoey. Yet with the decline of Pittsburgh's smokestack industries and America's new emphasis on energy conservation, the nature of the natural gas business has changed dramatically.

Hoey's emphasis is on promoting

the concept of natural gas as a viable solution to the energy problems of the future. Many of Peoples' vehicles run on natural gas, part of the fleet of more than 30,000 natural gas-powered vehicles operating in the United States, and the half-million such vehicles around the world. Says Hoey, "Our opportunities for growth and improved efficiency lie in developing nontraditional markets such as transportation, co-firing, and cogeneration."

"We always try to remember—as we develop new markets and confront greater competition—the importance of staying in touch with our traditional customers," says Hoey. "You can call yourself forward-thinking, and make all the right moves, but you'll never succeed in the long run if you don't keep customers satisfied. They've carried us through our first 100 years, and they'll keep us healthy in the future."

GEISINGER

The Geisinger health care system had its beginnings in the Pennsylvania community of Danville, a town of 5,500 located on a gentle turn of the Susquehanna River. Today it offers its services not only to that area but far beyond—to a 25,000-square-mile region with 2.3 million residents.

The Geisinger system's flagship is the Geisinger Medical Center, one of the nation's leading rural hospitals and clinics. Sixty-five miles north of the state capital at Harrisburg, Geisinger Medical Center is proud of its tradition of outstanding service. The facility remains dedicated to fulfilling the mission set for it when it was created in 1915 by Mrs. Abigail A. Geisinger, the wealthy heiress of a Pennsylvania coal-mining fortune.

Almost three-quarters of a century has passed since Mrs. Geisinger met with three of her fellow townspeople in the parlor of her Danville home and revealed her dream of building a modern general hospital as a tribute to the memory of her husband. Mrs. Geisinger, then eighty-five years old, gave the three men a broad, general

Ground-breaking ceremonies for the George F. Geisinger Memorial Hospital. Abigail A. Cornelison Geisinger is flanked by the original hospital board.

charge: "Make my hospital right; make it the best."

Geisinger's share of the rural health care market has evolved from its seventy years' experience in Central and Northeastern Pennsylvania. The Geisinger system reflects a hard-earned reputation for quality and the efficient and successful management

of diverse physician groups.

To meet the challenge of Central Pennsylvania's varied and wide-ranging geography, Geisinger has created a mixture of affiliated hospitals, medical group practices, managed hospitals, outreach clinics, and alcohol detoxification/rehabilitation ser-

At the age of eighty-eight, Abigail A. Cornelison Geisinger (1827-1921) completed her dream of building a modern general hospital as a tribute to the memory of her husband.

George F. Geisinger Memorial Hospital, 1915. The facility opened two weeks before the scheduled dedication to care for victims of a typhoid epidemic.

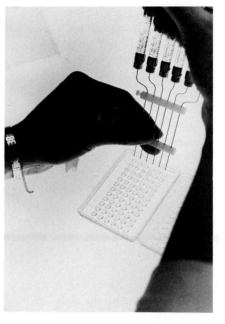

Geisinger Medical Center, 1986—a tertiary care referral center.

More than 240 active research projects are under way, and Geisinger broke ground in September 1985 for a new research building, part of a $57.5-million, ten-year investment in a program of basic research.

vices that are ideally suited to serve the health care needs of the Commonwealth's widely dispersed rural population. "If someone said to me, 'I want you to go to California and exactly replicate Geisinger,'" observes Henry Hood, M.D., the neurosurgeon who has been Geisinger's chief executive since 1974, "it just couldn't be done."

Geisinger reorganized itself in 1981, forming a system composed of the Geisinger Foundation and six corporate affiliates; since then, it has added three more.

The nine affiliates are:

Geisinger Clinic, a not-for-profit unit that employs the Geisinger medical staff, conducts medical education programs, and engages in biomedical research.

Geisinger Medical Center, one of only four rural hospitals in the United States that have more than 500 beds.

Geisinger Wyoming Valley Medical Center, a not-for-profit, open-staff, 230-bed community hospital that replaced two older facilities, sixty miles northeast of Danville, near Wilkes-Barre.

Marworth, a 72-bed alcohol treatment and rehabilitation center near Scranton, with a 56-bed adolescent treatment center under construction near Shawnee-on-Delaware.

Geisinger Health Plan, a health maintenance organization founded in 1972 and expanded in 1985.

Geisinger Medical Management Corporation, a for-profit subsidiary that provides management and health care consulting services.

Geisinger System Services, a not-for-profit corporation that provides management and consultative skills to support the other Geisinger affiliates. Among its services are financial and facilities management, legal

The lobby at the Geisinger Wyoming Valley Medical Center.

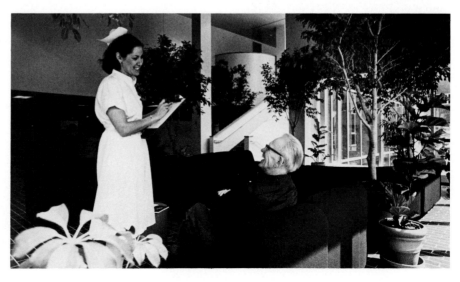

and computer services, management engineering, public relations, human resources, and development.

ISS, a major biomedical technology engineering company that operates throughout the mid-Atlantic states.

DePuy-Lenape, operator of joint-venture arrangements with Shawnee Development Corporation, Inc., to provide a facility for a primary care center.

In the work of the Geisinger Foundation and in the activities of its nine affiliates, the Geisinger style is apparent in day-to-day practice, attention to detail, and commitment to patient care. "We expect to be judged by how well we meet the comprehensive needs of the people in the region we serve," says Dr. Hood.

In founding her hospital, Mrs. Geisinger carefully selected the man she would make responsible for its administration. She retained Dr. Harold Foss, an able young surgeon who, at the time, was first assistant to Dr. William J. Mayo of the Mayo Clinic.

Dr. Foss had spent two years at the famed Rochester, Minnesota, clinic. The experience had strongly influenced his thinking about appropriate methods for delivering health care. In an early meeting with Mrs. Geisinger they concluded that "a project so splendidly conceived should be established, not solely as a community hospital, but as a medical center, fully equipped with the necessary apparatus required in modern diagnosis and treatment and staffed with specialists on full-time tenure who would serve a wide area."

Dr. Foss began immediately to hire salaried, specialty-trained physicians who would not engage in private practice. So, from its beginning, Geisinger was designed to be a center for outstanding health care serving a wide area.

Throughout its history the primary purpose of Mrs. Geisinger's medical center, and now the Geisinger health care system, has remained unchanged. That purpose is to provide clinical care to make sick people well again. Geisinger's growth and the demographic characteristics of its Central Pennsylvania community have led Pennsylvanians to depend on it as a regional tertiary care referral center.

The Geisinger health care system also has an abiding interest in preventive medicine, education, and ambulatory care. It operates primary care clinics at several sites in Central and Northeastern Pennsylvania. It was among the first to operate a rural health maintenance organization, and

Marworth is a 72-bed alcohol and chemical dependency treatment center located in Waverly.

it has recently expanded that HMO to serve even more residents of the Commonwealth.

Because of Geisinger, Danville—a nineteenth-century mill town of tree-lined curbs and square-roofed houses—has the highest per capita concentration of physicians in the United States. And, from the medical center, Geisinger's Life Flight helicopter airlifts emergency medicine teams to critically ill and injured patients throughout the region.

The Geisinger medical staff of more than 330 salaried physicians and surgeons represents fifty-seven clinical specialties. In addition, at

Geisinger's residency programs have attracted more than 2,000 young physicians.

Geisinger Medical Center in Danville, an average of more than 190 young physicians are always in training.

Since 1915 Geisinger has graduated more than 2,000 physicians and nearly 2,500 nurses. In 1973 it became a major teaching affiliate of the Pennsylvania State University College of Medicine. The eleven Geisinger schools, including medical technology, radiologic technology, nursing, and nurse anesthesiology, have graduated hundreds of students.

Geisinger employs 4,600 people, about 3,000 of them in Danville. Through those employees, the Geisinger health care system is involved in community activities, government, service clubs, and a variety of social agencies and civic programs.

Geisinger is, and always has been, a constructive participant in efforts to reduce health care costs. Its physicians treat the sickest of the sick; yet even as they work with cancer, perform kidney transplants, and do open-heart surgery, they strive to make sure that the care and treatment they provide are reasonably priced.

The organization is changing and expanding and is poised for more dramatic involvement in clinical and management opportunities. The Geisinger health care system is proud of its heritage and the progress it has made toward Mrs. Abigail Geisinger's original goal: "Make my hospital right; make it the best."

CONAIR, INC.

John C. Reib, a Venango County resident, was the head of a sales representative company serving the plastics manufacturing and processing industry. Reib had extensive experience building and selling molds for plastics processing before starting the sales company, and, when one of his principals discontinued manufacture of a piece of equipment, Reib saw his opportunity.

Using space borrowed from a previous employer and the help of three part-time employees, Reib chartered the Rainco Manufacturing Company on May 21, 1956, and began to assemble the units himself. His coura-

geous gamble paid off. In 1962 he leased an old dairy building in Franklin, Pennsylvania, and expanded his payroll to seven people. A year later he bought out his other investors and named the reorganized company Conair.

Conair is now recognized worldwide as a leader in the plastics industry. Its auxiliary equipment lines are marketed throughout the world and

---

The changing face of Conair is evident in these photographs of the corporate plant in Franklin, Pennsylvania, in 1965 (below) and 1984 (bottom).

the firm owns more than forty foreign and domestic patents on the equipment.

The corporate name, Conair, is widely believed to stand for "conveying plastics by air," but company insiders know better. At the time of its reorganization, Rainco had just purchased a new set of wooden letters for a sign. They cost sixty dollars and Reib had no intention of wasting them. He and his wife, Lille, scrambled the letters in search of a new company name—and found it. "Rainco" became "Conair."

Today Conair's Franklin plant employs 250 people. The corporation's other plants are located in Bay City, Michigan, and Uxbridge, Middlesex, England. Subsidiary and licensee operations are located in Mexico, Brazil, Canada, Australia, New Zealand, and Japan. Worldwide more than 450 people work directly for Conair, and over 150 independent sales representatives market the equipment lines.

Conair's future appears to be as brilliant as its past. In July 1984 the firm dedicated a 48,000-square-foot expansion to the Franklin plant, providing a modern showcase for the company and confirming its leadership both in the plastics industry and in the community.

The new plant and offices include computer-aided design equipment, computer-controlled machine tools and forming equipment, and word-processing networks. Also included are a demonstration room, featuring operating equipment displays, and a training and video studio section that the firm uses for its extensive educational activities.

John Reib and his employees remain active in local civic affairs. Reib has been an adviser on the board of the Venango County Area Vocational Technical School and was instrumental in establishing a local airport for Franklin. The company and its employees have also invested both time and money in such projects as establishing a tourist railroad and an industrial incubator to help stimulate the local economy.

MACK TRUCKS, INC.

It isn't often that a corporate name, a corporate symbol, and a corporate slogan become well known outside the corporate structure. But that is exactly what has happened with a company that has its world headquarters in Allentown. Its name? Mack Trucks, Inc. The corporate symbol? A burly, about-face, no-nonsense bulldog, the registered Mack Bulldog symbol. The corporate slogan, called to mind when describing strength and toughness? "Built like a Mack truck.®"

Mack Trucks, Inc., is one of America's largest producers of heavy-duty diesel trucks, as well as major product components. Over the years Mack has introduced innovations that have become industry standards—power steering, power brakes, rubber mounts for engine and transmission, air cleaners, oil filters, offset cabs for highway vehicles, and more. In 1985 the firm celebrated its eighty-fifth anniversary, capping a year when net income totaled seventy-five million dollars.

It all started in 1900, when the five Mack brothers, experienced wag-

Mack Trucks' world headquarters is at 2100 Mack Boulevard, Allentown.

on makers who experimented in self-propelled units, built and sold their first commercial motor vehicle. This twenty-passenger sight-seeing bus, powered by a Mack-built, forty-horse-power gasoline engine with chain drive, operated continuously for seventeen years in and around the New York City area. This Mack bus is considered the first bus in America, complete with a fringe on top. Mack produced approximately 150 similar vehicles from 1900 to 1914.

Before long Mack lay claim to a string of successful innovations. In 1910 the first motorized hook-and-

ladder fire truck was produced and delivered to Morristown, New Jersey. The Mack AB was the company's first standardized, high-volume model series, introduced in 1914. The AB filled the medium-duty role and incorporated many innovations particularly adapted to the times, including a choice of either chain or dual-reduction drive.

In 1915 the firm introduced the heavy-duty companion model to the Mack AB, called the AC Bulldog Mack. This hard-tire, chain-driven brute became a legend in its own time, produced through 1939 and serving 5,000 strong with the British and American troops in Europe during World War I. The AC, replete with a snub-nose hood that clearly resembled the snout of a bulldog, was distinguished by its incredible bulldog-like toughness and dependability. This characterization grew to encompass all Mack products, and, in 1922, the company adopted a specific form of the bulldog as its corporate symbol.

The Mack B Series, introduced in 1927, represented the first trucks developed by the company in response to the demand for larger-capacity, higher-speed hauling capabilities—a particular concern as trucks became

The AC "Bulldog" Mack, introduced in 1915, inspired the company to adopt the Bulldog® as its registered corporate symbol.

The Mack Ultra-Liner® model gives a whole new dimension to the familiar old expression "Built like a Mack truck."

more accepted as a mode of transportation. More than 15,000 Mack B Series trucks comprised the model run through 1941, representing one of the firm's most popular products.

Throughout the years there have been key innovations introduced in the Mack lineup to set it apart from its competitors. In 1938 the company was the first independent truck manufacturer to produce its own diesel engine, incorporating a number of patented features. The open-chamber, direct-injection Thermodyne® engine was introduced in the 1950s. The high-torque rise, con-

stant horsepower Maxidyne® engine revolutionized the industry in the 1960s and 1970s. And, in the 1980s, the Econodyne® six-cylinder and V-8 engines have raised Mack's commitment to efficiency and durability—and its concept of balanced design—to new heights.

In 1985 Mack introduced a new

Mack's Super-Liner® II, Magnum series.

Super-Liner® II premium conventional cab vehicle designed to appeal to the independent operator and small-fleet market segments. And its new Ultra-Liner® series is considered Mack's ultimate product achievement to date, a sleek blend of sophisticated technology with proven durability.

Mack trucks were once largely handmade. Today the units are built via assembly line, but most Mack trucks produced are equipped with major components designed and built by Mack. In fact, the company is the only heavy-duty truck manufacturer in North America engaged in the design, engineering, production, and assembly of its own major power train components: diesel engines, transmissions, and rear-axle carriers. The power train operation is located in Hagerstown, Maryland.

Product improvements and new designs are conceived and tested at the Engineering Development and Test Center (EDTC), located near Mack's world headquarters in Allentown. The EDTC sits inside a three-quarter-mile banked oval test track on sixty-two acres. Mack's truck assembly facilities are located in Allentown and Macungie, Pennsylvania, as well as Oakville, Ontario, Canada, and Brisbane, Queensland, Australia. A new assembly plant is scheduled for completion in Winnsboro, North Carolina, in 1987.

There are more than 800 Mack sales, parts, and service outlets nationwide, as well as similar outlets across Canada and around the world. The firm's association with Renault of France, one of the world's largest automotive and commercial vehicle manufacturers, has opened many new opportunities for both organizations as they share complementary resources in engineering and marketing.

Nearly 13,000 employees worldwide work at the company founded by the five Mack brothers. And, with a vital presence in more than eighty countries representing over 100 overseas outlets, it's a safe bet that the saying, "Built like a Mack truck," is heard around the globe.

THRIFT DRUG COMPANY

In the middle of the Great Depression, two Pennsylvania pharmacists, Reuben Helfant and Philip Hoffman, had faith in their idea. Both were University of Pittsburgh graduates, both owned drugstores, and they shared a vision. They invested almost $10,000 into their new joint venture, a chain of stores they called Thrift Drug.

Helfant and Hoffman opened their first store in Sewickley in May 1935 and a second in Bellevue two weeks later. "My husband was a dreamer," says Mrs. Hoffman. "He had faith that Thrift would prosper." Helfant and Hoffman both died in 1968, but their chain of drugstores has continued to grow. Today Thrift Drug has over 370 stores in 20 states, with some 200 outlets in Pennsylvania alone. Its operating performance has consistently made it a leader in the national chain drug industry.

The firm has grown both by opening new Thrift Drug stores and by acquisitions. In 1946 the eight-store Miller Drug chain of Ohio became part of Thrift, and West Virginia became the third Thrift Drug state. Expansion continued through the 1950s. The first store in Eastern Pennsylvania opened in West Chester in 1959. That same year witnessed Thrift's transformation to a

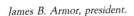

James B. Armor, president.

The soda fountains of a bygone era have been replaced by Thrift-Care displays, catalog desks, and pharmacy computers.

public corporation with its issuance of 75,000 shares of common stock.

Originally the only warehouse space required by Thrift Drug was the basement of the Bellevue store. As the chain expanded that space proved inadequate. The warehouse was moved to Pittsburgh's north side, and then to Sharpsburg. In 1968 newly appointed president Louis Avner moved it to the site of the current distribution center and executive office complex in Blawnox. The original 175,000-square-foot facility is now 285,000 square feet.

Thrift Drug became a division of JCPenney in 1969. Under JCPenney, Thrift Drug pursued a policy of aggressive growth, starting with its Treasury chain, first in Tennessee, then throughout the South. To complement the Pittsburgh distribution center, a 60,000-square-foot facility was built in Langhorne, Pennsylvania, in 1973. Two years later the Atlanta distribution center was built to help handle the accelerating volume of goods needed by the expanding chain. Along with the increasingly

complex distribution network came an electronic ordering system, bringing new efficiency to the entire system.

In 1980 J.B. Armor succeeded Avner as president. Armor began his career with JCPenney in 1948. Following a two-year stint in the U.S. Navy and studies at Duke University and the University of Oklahoma, Armor went to work in the Oklahoma City JCPenney store. He moved to San Diego in 1953 and was promoted to store manager in Alameda in 1960. Subsequent promotions took him to JCPenney's New York headquarters as a merchandise coordinator and merchandising department head for women's accessories, smallwares, and cosmetics in 1964.

Armor came to Thrift Drug in 1971, just two years after the chain had been acquired by JCPenney. His first assignment was as director of store operations, coordinating the installation of catalog order desks in Thrift Drug stores and increasing the authority and responsibilities of individual store managers. He was promoted to executive vice-president in 1976.

Under Armor's leadership Thrift Drug has achieved peak growth and

A Thrift Drug store in the 1940s.

operational efficiency. In an early reorganization, he developed a three-region structure with bases in Pittsburgh, Philadelphia, and Atlanta. He also consolidated the chain by acquiring new stores in Pennsylvania, Maryland, New Jersey, and Delaware, while divesting twenty stores in the Carolinas, Tennessee, and Alabama. His policy of aggressive, steady growth has resulted in continual expansion.

The Thrift Drug stores have also evolved over their half-century. During the early years stores were built at downtown locations. Later they opened mainly at suburban shopping malls. The smaller stores of the early days gave way to large, general merchandise centers in the 1970s. More recently Thrift has returned to a smaller facility, concentrating on more traditional drugstore merchandise.

Throughout its history the firm has continuously emphasized its prescription business—which still accounts for 36 percent of Thrift Drug's total sales. Most Thrift store managers are pharmacists, guaranteeing that the emphasis on prescriptions will continue.

A nostalgic look at Thrift Drug stores of the past would include elaborately trimmed windows and soda fountains, but those are gone now. In their place are Thrift-Care displays, catalog desks, and pharmacy computers. Thrift-Care, which began in June 1982, is a new concept, a home medical equipment program that rents or sells such products as wheelchairs and hospital beds. Customers receive free home delivery, assistance from trained technicians, and a 24-hour emergency service.

Another innovative program is Express Pharmacy Services, Thrift's new mail-order pharmacy that provides low-cost and efficient service to group plans such as Pennsylvania state employees, U.S. Steel, and Bethlehem Steel. Thrift is also moving to become a major contractor with nursing homes, currently providing prescription services to approximately fifty nursing homes in nine states.

Thrift Drug demonstrates both a continued awareness of the traditional services and products required of the community pharmacy, and a willingness to accept innovation and technology to meet new demands. The firm remains aware of its rich heritage, proud of its current growth, and excited by the promise of its future.

Over the past half-century Thrift Drug stores have evolved with the times but still concentrate on traditional merchandise and policies.

COLONIAL PENN GROUP, INC.

For more than two decades a company in Philadelphia has been a recognized leader in providing insurance needs for people who are fifty years of age and older. In fact, Colonial Penn Group, Inc., marked its twenty-first anniversary in 1984 with an impressive list of "firsts" that clearly illustrates its unique niche in the marketplace: the first company to offer non-underwritten health and life insurance to the fifty-plus market; the first to offer a guaranteed renewable auto policy to the fifty-plus market; and the first to develop travel services specializing in older travelers.

And though it is not based on statistical data, Colonial Penn could surely take credit for being "first" in the confidence of approximately 1.5 million policyholders over the age of fifty.

In the mid-1950s Leonard Davis, founder of Colonial Penn, and Dr. Ethel Percy Andrus, a retired high school principal who was concerned about the rights of the elderly, together made possible the first nationwide group health insurance program for the National Retired Teachers Association (NRTA). Subsequently, group health insurance was made available by Colonial Penn to the members of the American Association of Retired Persons.

On April 25, 1963, Davis founded Colonial Penn and that year the firm commenced its life insurance operations by acquiring all of the outstanding stock of Colonial Penn Life Insurance Company, formerly the William Penn Life Insurance Company.

Colonial Penn Life was a pioneer in offering, on a broad basis, modest amounts of guaranteed-issue individual life insurance to people age fifty and over. Moreover, the company helped pioneer the direct-market insurance field, with retirees and the elderly as its principal market. By 1984 more than fifty million insurance solicitations were being mailed out each year.

Colonial Penn's property/liability insurance operations began in 1966 when it acquired the American Maturity Insurance Company, a South Carolina concern, and later the Boston Indemnity Insurance Company. Colonial Penn Insurance Company, which resulted from the merger of those two businesses, provided the first automobile insurance program specially designed for qualified drivers age fifty and over. In 1971 the firm acquired Colonial Penn Franklin Insurance Company (then named National-Ben Franklin Insurance Company of Pittsburgh).

Colonial Penn's primary business is the development and marketing of personal lines insurance—property and liability, life and health—sold on a group or individual basis. The firm operates various other subsidiaries, including advertising, data processing, financial services, and real estate information services.

On December 31, 1985, Colonial Penn was acquired by FPL Group, Inc., of Miami, the parent of Florida Power and Light Company, the nation's fifth-largest electric utility. In March 1986 Colonial Penn moved into its new headquarters, Colonial Penn Plaza, located at Nineteenth and Market streets.

Colonial Penn Insurance Companies' headquarters is in Philadelphia's prestige location, Eleven Penn Center.

GRAPHIC ARTS, INC.

The Indian Chief is immediately distinctive, his head held high in profile to reveal a headdress made of white feathers with tips so rich and brown they look as though they have been dipped in chocolate. There is a crescent of fluffy down around his face, a beaded headband snug against his forehead. And at the very end of each feather, there is a burst of red, a fistful of firecracker-red plumage that tapers off into red streamers, dangling ever so gently away from the headdress and down the Indian's back.

The picture of this Indian represents a turning point in the history of Graphic Arts, Inc., a commercial printing company located in Philadelphia that was incorporated as a photoengraving plant on March 22, 1928. Ten years after it was incorporated, Graphic Arts printed the Indian head from original progressive proofs, making it the company's first four-color process effort produced through the offset process.

Throughout the years Graphic Arts has remained a specialist in four-

The Indian Chief—the first four-color process print produced through the offset process at Graphic Arts, Inc.

color process printing, with complete color departments and multicolor presses. And it has also remained a family business, with three generations of the same family directing the firm since its inception.

The business was actually started in 1922 by Raymond Neill, an artist with a local advertising agency, and four other men at a location along Twenty-second and Market streets. Incorporated in 1928 as Graphic Arts Engraving Company, the firm changed its name to Graphic Arts, Inc., in 1944. Two years later it chose Labor Day weekend to move to its present location at 4100 Chestnut Street, where today nearly seventy-five employees work in a facility with over 35,000 square feet of floor space.

In 1963 Neill's son-in-law, Fred W. Binder, joined the business, as did Binder's brother-in-law, Robert Koontz, Jr. Following Neill's death in

50 Years · Graphic Arts, Inc.

1928 1978

1967, Binder took over as president and treasurer of the company, and Koontz was named executive vice-president and secretary. Today both men have sons who work in the business.

Graphic Arts grew from what was primarily a photoengraving and letterpress printer to a commercial printing operation with the capacity for offset printing with up to five-color press runs. Commercial work ranges from brochures and magazine advertising inserts to greeting cards and display work for large corporations throughout the Delaware Valley. With seven highly sophisticated presses now in use, sales have grown from $800,000 in 1963 to over $8.5 million in 1985.

As a leader in Philadelphia's printing industry for more than a half-century, Graphic Arts, Inc., chose to honor its past when it celebrated its fiftieth anniversary in 1978. There, on the cover of the commemorative brochure, was a brilliant reproduction of the Indian Chief.

A single-color Harris press, one of the original offset presses purchased by Graphic Arts.

BRADFORD-WHITE CORPORATION

In the beginning there was the kettle. Put water in the kettle, put the kettle over a fire, and, before you know it, you have hot water.

For over 100 years a Philadelphia-based firm called Bradford-White Corporation has been striving to perfect the work of that fire-torched kettle by developing a full line of durable, energy-efficient water heaters.

Bradford-White manufactures water heaters, and only water heaters. Dating back over 100 years, Bradford-White is believed to be the oldest major water heater manufacturer in the United States, with annual international sales in excess of $100 million.

The firm traces its roots to 1881, when The Pennsylvania Range Boiler Company began manufacturing water-storage tanks in Philadelphia. Over the years The Pennsylvania Range Boiler Company has produced all kinds of tanks, including machine gun cooling tanks during World War II. When the war was over the firm produced its first gas water heater, with production commencing in a corner of the building at Twenty-fourth and Ellsworth streets.

A formal engineering department and sales force were added to The Pennsylvania Range Boiler Company, and nearly 140 people were employed by the late 1940s. In the early 1950s the business took a serious look at a

The officers of Bradford-White Corporation are (seated) Michael R. DeLuca, president; (standing, left to right) John T. Borzoni, vice-president/marketing; William A. Smith, vice-president/sales; and A. Robert Carnevale, senior vice-president.

problem that was having a detrimental effect on water storage tanks: corrosion. The answer to the problem was a glass lining that protected the metal interior of the tanks. It was developed by The Pennsylvania Range Boiler Company in 1951 and named Vitraglas. Vitraglas dramatically reduced the damage caused by corrosion, thereby substantially increasing the life of a water heater.

In 1959 The Pennsylvania Range Boiler Company was acquired by International Utilities (IU) General Waterworks, a Philadelphia-based corporation concerned primarily with utilities. IU began a million-dollar modernization and reorganization of the company and changed its name to Pennsylvania-Bradford Appliance Corporation.

While owned by IU, the new firm

set out to expand its water heater line by acquiring other companies, including the Pittsburgh-based Lawson Manufacturing Company, Hoffman, Fowler, Ever-Hot, Lovekin, and Waldorf. Later Pennsylvania-Bradford also acquired Jetglas and Republic. The corporation began selling nationally, and expanded its water heater line to include not only residential units but also commercial water heaters.

In the early 1960s Pennsylvania-Bradford was turning out 125,000 residential water heaters per year. The series of water heater manufacturing companies acquired along the way helped reinforce Pennsylvania-Bradford's marketing position, but they also taxed its already cramped production facilities. The answer was found in White Products of Middleville, Michigan, which had plenty of production capacity but limited distribution—the very opposite of Pennsylvania-Bradford's problem. In 1968 the two companies merged into Bradford-White Corporation. By the mid-1970s Bradford-White was producing 800,000 water heaters per year, with over 600 employees coast to coast.

In 1971 IU decided to sell Bradford-White. Michael R. DeLuca, then executive vice-president; Fred Pellegrini, then president; and a third-party in-

The forerunner of Bradford-White Corporation, The Pennsylvania Range Boiler Company, was located at Twenty-fourth and Ellsworth streets in Philadelphia. Photo circa 1945

vestor put together a leverage buy-out program and purchased the firm on January 28, 1972. When Pellegrini retired in 1982, DeLuca was named president of the now privately held company.

The firm maintains corporate headquarters, warehouses, and a small parts manufacturing operation in Philadelphia, with a large manufacturing facility in Middleville, about fifteen miles south of Grand Rapids. Factory service centers are located throughout the United States, including facilities in Atlanta, Boston, Dallas, Philadelphia, and Portland.

Today Bradford-White manufactures a complete line of residential gas, electric, oil-fired, and solar water heaters, as well as gas and electric commercial water heaters. The firm's deluxe residential energy-saving electric water heater—one of the more popular models—contains elements made of the finest magnesium oxide, incoloy sheath material, and nickel chromium wire to withstand operating temperatures up to 1,500 degrees Fahrenheit in air without damage. The heavy-gauge steel tank features

the exclusive Vitraglas lining, which is still considered an industry standard over thirty years after it was first introduced by Bradford-White. And now it is insulated with the company's Foamlock foam insulation, which has 175 percent more insulation effectiveness than fiberglass. Bradford-White water heaters are sold worldwide through its distribution network.

US Water Heater Company, a division of Bradford-White, offers nearly 100 different residential gas and electric models to the retail market.

In 1983 Bradford-White began a five-year program of modifications to its manufacturing operations that will both increase production capacity and further improve the quality of its products. President DeLuca, vowing to make the firm more visible in the marketplace, has outlined specific goals in distribution and delivery, competitive pricing, marketing, and product research and development. National advertising has been increased, and Bradford-White has a national spokesperson named Rocky Bleier, a former football star with the Pittsburgh Steelers.

For over 100 years Bradford-White Corporation has been an innovative and leading force in the water heating industry—and the firm is working hard to continue that tradition.

THE BELL TELEPHONE COMPANY OF PENNSYLVANIA

One day in 1877 a Philadelphia electrician named Thomas E. Cornish returned from a business trip to Boston with a new invention in his valise: Alexander Graham Bell's telephone. Before the summer had ended Cornish had obtained rights to promote the telephone in Philadelphia and had formed a business that he called The Telephone Company of Philadelphia.

The first two telephones in the state were installed in his home and Chestnut Street appliance shop. Cornish then hired two former telegraph company employees to install the first Philadelphia switchboard, and proceeded to run the first iron wire telephone lines to customers whose financial backing was critical to the success of his infant enterprise: E.T. Stotesbury, an important financier; Colonel Thomas A. Scott, president of Pennsylvania Railroad; and James E. Kingsley, proprietor of the city's leading hotel.

These five telephones were the crudely wrought forebears of the millions of sophisticated data and voice instruments that today use the local networks of The Bell Telephone Company of Pennsylvania. And while the telephone company has a history that can be traced back more than 100 years, Bell of Pennsylvania is actually a brand-new enterprise.

On January 1, 1984, pursuant to a court-ordered reorganization, Bell of

Short-distance toll calling is a major source of the company's revenue. This No. 4 ESS machine switches two and one-half million calls within the Philadelphia LATA daily.

Pennsylvania was divested from American Telephone & Telegraph Company (AT&T) and became a wholly owned subsidiary of the Bell Atlantic Corporation. The mission of the new entity was clear: to be the preferred source of low-cost, quality telecommunications services for the citizens of Pennsylvania. To understand this new chapter in Bell of Pennsylvania's history, one must look again to the beginning, back to entrepreneurial Cornish and his quest for telephone service, a quest that wasn't always easy.

Initial efforts to expand the infant telephone business in 1877 drew the ire of the wealthy and powerful telegraph company, which considered the building of telephone plants an infringement of its operations. In efforts to stop Cornish, his adversaries persuaded city officials to refuse Cornish permission to string his wires. His workmen were arrested, and he was warned to either quit or be driven out. Capitalists refused him money.

But Cornish persisted. In 1878 Philadelphia's first telephone exchange began with eight customers. That same year Cornish published the first telephone directory on four index-size cards, listing twenty-six subscribers. On September 18, 1879, Cornish and his backers were in-

corporated as The Bell Telephone Company of Philadelphia, and the telephone directory had swelled to 420 subscribers.

Meanwhile, telephone service was fast becoming a reality in Harrisburg, Pittsburgh, and other Pennsylvania cities. The first nine lines in Harrisburg were the work of Horace Clute, who founded the Pennsylvania Telephone Company. And in 1907 Cornish merged with Clute and several other utilities to become The Bell Telephone Company of Pennsylvania. When Thomas Cornish died in 1924, the business he started with five telephones counted 650,000 instruments.

History sparkles with tidbits of

Today's craftsmen splice optical fiber—the transmission medium that will bring Pennsylvanians information-age services.

Customized Bell service includes on-the-spot response to Centrex service customers' needs. Here a craftsman troubleshoots at Philadelphia's City Hall.

telephone lore. Alexander Graham Bell first unveiled his invention in 1876 at Philadelphia's Fairmount Park, where he won a Centennial Exhibition Award medal. One of the first transcontinental telephone lines was established between Philadelphia and San Francisco when, on February 11, 1915, the sound of three taps on

In the early days of Bell of Pennsylvania, it took a great deal of manpower to set poles.

the Liberty Bell was transmitted to San Francisco, where, in turn, a military bugler responded with the "Star Spangled Banner."

Today Bell of Pennsylvania—a Bell Atlantic Company that traces its history back to Cornish—provides 4.6 million Network access lines for homes and businesses. Led by Gilbert A.

The "Voice With a Smile" over the years has been the personality of Bell of Pennsylvania.

The Bell craftsman of yesteryear was equipped for any eventuality.

Wetzel, president and chief executive officer, the firm makes multimillion-dollar capital investments each year to provide advanced voice and data services to its customers.

Bell's flagship network, offering Centrex service, provides telecommunications for business customers both big and small. In fact, during Bell of Pennsylvania's first two years as a divested company, Centrex service was a solid revenue producer. More than 1,650 Centrex systems were sold in Pennsylvania's highly competitive telecommunications marketplace.

Looking to the future, Bell of Pennsylvania's mission continues to be to provide state-of-the-art telecommunications services to its customers. It is a mission not unlike the one held by Cornish, when he tucked a new invention, the telephone, into his valise and brought it to Philadelphia nearly 120 years ago.

487

PENNWALT CORPORATION

When it was founded by five Philadelphia Quakers in 1850, the Pennsylvania Salt Manufacturing Company
produced only one product—lye.

Today the Pennwalt Corporation is
a worldwide manufacturer of chemicals, health products, and specialized
equipment. And though chemicals
continue to be the core of its business, today a diversified Pennwalt
manufactures a myriad of products,
from a highly specialized piezo film to
twelve-hour controlled-release medicines and a revolutionary piece of
electronic equipment that is now being used to sort and grade more than
half of all the lemons grown in the
United States.

The story of this corporation's evolution begins in Natrona, where the
five determined Quakers founded the
Pennsylvania Salt Manufacturing
Company. The firm was able to declare its first dividend in 1863, and it
has not missed one since—the second-
longest dividend record of any industrial company listed on the New

York Stock Exchange.

By the beginning of the twentieth
century Pennsylvania Salt sold more
than twenty-five industrial chemicals
manufactured at three separate
plants. For the next sixty years the
company focused almost entirely on
chemicals and chemical specialty
products. In the first two decades of
the 1900s chlorine and caustic soda
became increasingly important to the
business. Indeed, Pennsalt, as the
company became generally known,
capitalized on the famous Gibbs Cell,
a process developed in 1904 by the
firm's technical director, Arthur E.
Gibbs. Through the Gibbs Cell,
chlorine and caustic soda were made
from brine.

By the mid-1930s Pennsalt was
selling chemical specialties, many of
which were derivatives of the industrial chemicals the company manufactured. Pennsalt was now selling its
products nationwide.

The expansion into precision capital
equipment became a reality in 1962

*Pennwalt's King of Prussia, Pennsylvania,
facility.*

when Pennsalt acquired Sharples
Corporation and in 1963 when it acquired the Stokes Corporation. The
firm expanded into the growing
health care field in 1966 by acquiring
S.S. White Company, a manufacturer
of dental supplies and equipment.
The 1969 merger with Wallace &
Tiernan expanded Pennsalt's health
business into pharmaceuticals. In addition, that merger also increased
Pennsalt's strength in both the chemicals and equipment businesses.

In 1969 the name Pennsalt Chemicals Corporation was changed to the
Pennwalt Corporation. A breakdown
of Pennwalt's current business activities clearly shows how much the once
exclusively chemical corporation has
expanded. In 1984 sales of over one
billion dollars came from these diverse
markets: health care (20 percent),
chemical process industry (26 per-

At the King of Prussia laboratories insects are raised in a controlled environment for the company's research into new and improved insecticides.

film. This unique film is being tested in a variety of electronic and tele-communications products where it converts electrical energy into vibrational energy and vice versa. It also converts thermal energy into electricity.

With headquarters in Philadelphia, Pennwalt Corporation employs more than 10,000 people worldwide, with sales offices and manufacturing facilities in twenty countries. The firm's annual meeting is frequently held in the auditorium of the Quaker-founded Friends Select School, adjacent to the Pennwalt Building at Three Parkway—an appropriate reminder of how the company first got its start.

cent), agriculture and food processing (18 percent), plastics (14 percent), environmental cleanup (9 percent), and other markets (13 percent). Put another way, more than 50 percent of Pennwalt's current business comes from products that have been added to the company's product line since the early 1960s.

One of the significant products is Kynar® polyvinylidene fluoride. Developed in Pennwalt's laboratories during the late 1950s, Kynar is an especially tough, versatile plastic that is resistant to chemicals and weathering. Its application focuses on three industries: architectural and construction; electrical and electronics; and chemical processing, where more than forty grades of Kynar are used. The construction of a $60-million plant in Thorofare, New Jersey, completed in 1985, has doubled Pennwalt's capacity to produce Kynar.

Pennwalt believes that the future prospects for Kynar are excellent. Kynar has achieved a compounded

growth rate of approximately 15 percent per year over the past fifteen years. This growth has been achieved by aggressively and continually developing new markets and applications. Currently one of the most sophisticated applications is Kynar® piezo

Kynar® piezoelectronic film, here being tested at the King of Prussia pilot plant, is lightweight, sensitive, durable, and easily fabricated into complex shapes. Its capacity to transform mechanical energy into an electrical signal and vice versa makes it an ideal transducer. Among the new products employing this unusual material is a muscle movement sensor that enables handicapped people to perform routine tasks more easily.

BOEING VERTOL COMPANY

In 1940 Frank Piasecki and some aviation associates gathered in Piasecki's garage in Sharon Hill, Pennsylvania, and organized a company called P-V Engineering Forum to study the design of a helicopter. And from this initial group of imaginative designers and enthusiasts evolved a business called the Boeing Vertol Company, now a division of the famed Seattle, Washington-based commercial jetliner manufacturer, The Boeing Company. Boeing Vertol is a leading manufacturer of military and commercial helicopters for domestic and international customers.

In fact, since 1943, the year Piasecki successfully flew his first helicopter, more than 2,500 helicopters, most of them tandem-rotor in design, have been produced by Boeing Vertol and its predecessor companies. That number includes thirty different models, the likes of which few early P-V Engineering pioneers could have imagined. After all, the first PV-2 was basically made of scrap materials and had one seat, one rotor, and one ninety-horsepower engine with a used Chevrolet transmission.

On April 11, 1943, Piasecki, holder of the first helicopter pilot's license issued in the United States, flew the PV-2, and the U.S. Navy awarded P-V Engineering Forum a contract to develop a helicopter. Thirteen months later the ten-passenger tandem-rotor XHRP-1 was a reality—the Navy's first large transport helicopter and the world's first tandem-rotor helicopter.

Two years later P-V Engineering won a U.S. Navy contract to develop a prototype utility rescue helicopter that became known as the HUP. Other military contracts followed and the company flourished. By 1946 the firm had built hundreds of piston-powered, tandem-rotor helicopters for both U.S. and foreign military forces.

In 1946 P-V Engineering Forum changed its name to Piasecki Helicopter Corporation and then, in 1956, to Vertol Aircraft Corporation. Four years later Vertol Aircraft was acquired by The Boeing Company,

The CH-46 Sea Knight is used by the U.S. Marine Corps for transport and combat assault duties. U.S. Navy (UH-46) missions include vertical replenishment—the transferring of cargo and personnel to combat ships at sea.

and became the Boeing Vertol Company.

The introduction of jet engines in the late 1950s led to designs for a new generation of helicopters. In 1962 Boeing Vertol launched its jet-age fleet of turbine-powered helicopters. The CH-46 Sea Knight, a military version of the commercial Model 107, was selected by the U.S. Marine

Corps for assault and transport missions. The U.S. Navy uses it for vital vertical-replenishment missions at sea. The CH-47 Chinook, a large tandem-rotor helicopter capable of carrying forty-four combat-equipped troops, was ordered by the U.S. Army; a total of 732 Chinooks were built for the Army during the 1960s and 1970s. Boeing Vertol is now

Offshore oil workers are preparing to board a Boeing 234. This aircraft is used in offshore-oil support in the North Sea and in the Navarin Basin off the Alaskan coast.

The V-22 Osprey, shown here in U.S. Marine Corps markings, has the unique capability to hover like a helicopter and then convert to the fast-forward flight (300 knots) of a turbo-prop airplane.

modernizing the Army's earlier-model Chinooks to the advanced CH-47D standard. A total of 436 CH-47Ds will be produced by Boeing Vertol through the early 1990s.

Boeing Vertol's International Military Chinook is an export version of the CH-47. Nearly 250 Chinooks are operated by fourteen foreign nations. Current customers include the Spanish Army and the United Kingdom's Royal Air Force. The Japanese Army and Air Force are receiving Chinooks co-produced by Boeing Vertol and Japan's Kawasaki Heavy Industries Ltd.

In addition, a version of the Chinook has now gone commercial, making it the largest passenger helicopter in the Free World. In November 1978 Boeing Vertol launched the Model 234 program in conjunction with British Airways Helicopters. The aircraft, which carries forty-four passengers, has been used to support distant offshore operations in Alaska and the North Sea oil fields.

The future of rotary-wing flight may well be shaped by a major new project jointly undertaken in 1982 by Bell Helicopter Textron and Boeing Vertol. The Bell-Boeing Team was awarded a contract for the preliminary design of a revolutionary tilt-rotor

aircraft for the U.S. Armed Forces. In January 1985 this aircraft was designated the V-22 Osprey. This unique aircraft will replace many existing helicopters and airplanes. Its wing-tip-mounted gas-turbine engines together with their prop-rotors rotate through ninety degrees to give the aircraft the flight characteristics of both a helicopter and a fast, fixed-wing turboprop airplane. The first flight of the V-22 is expected in June 1988, with initial deliveries to the U.S. Marine Corps scheduled for February 1992. All four U.S. military services are scheduled to receive Ospreys.

In June 1985 Boeing Vertol teamed with Sikorsky Aircraft of Stratford, Connecticut, to jointly bid to develop the U.S. Army's new light helicopter, called LHX. Current Army plans call for at least 4,500 LHX aircraft to replace its existing fleet of 7,000 light helicopters. The LHX will be produced in two versions, scout/attack and utility, and will feature automated advanced-technology systems permitting pilots to complete low-altitude missions day or night and in adverse weather. Associated with LHX are two important technology programs—electronics integration and composite materials manufacturing. One example from the research going on at Boeing Vertol is ADOCS—Advanced Digital Optical Control Systems. Eventually ADOCS may provide fiber-optics technology to allow pilots to fly by light.

An important, new high-speed tandem-rotor helicopter is undergoing testing at Boeing Vertol. The Boeing 360 is an all-composite aircraft about the size of the H-46 Sea Knight. The extensive use of composite materials in its airframe and rotor system, combined with the incorporation of the latest technological advances, prom-

ise higher payloads, productivity, and profitability for future Boeing 360 operators. The first flight of the 360 is planned for late 1986.

To keep pace with demand, Boeing Vertol has continuously expanded and improved its facilities, building a reputation for having one of the most advanced engineering and dynamics centers in the world. The main plant and office facilities are located on a 300-acre site just south of the Philadelphia International Airport in the suburb of Ridley Township. Boeing Vertol's campus-like complex has more than 2.6 million square feet of covered area devoted to the manufacturing of helicopters and aircraft subassemblies. Nearly 6,200 people work at the site.

Recent additions include a 350,000-square-foot integrated logistical support facility, which was completed in 1981. During 1985 the company added more than 250,000 square feet to office space and manufacturing and testing facilities. Construction activities during 1986 will add approximately 250,000 square feet of space, consolidating computer operations and expanding engineering laboratories, in order to keep pace with the increasing tempo of the V-22 Osprey tilt-rotor aircraft and LHX helicopter programs. Boeing Vertol's Flight Test Center is located in Wilmington, Delaware.

All of this adds up to an enormous helicopter manufacturing and testing facility, giving Boeing Vertol the physical resources it needs to continue its heritage of leadership in the design, engineering, production, and manufacture of rotary-wing aircraft.

The XHRP-X "Dogship," designed and built for the U.S. Navy in 1945, was the first helicopter produced under military contract.

PHILADELPHIA PHILLIES

Providence Wins.

That was the very small newspaper headline when the Philadelphia Phillies played their first game, a 4-3 loss to the Providence Grays. The date was May 1, 1883. The place was Recreation Park.

Today the "Phillies" is the oldest team name in the league, but it wasn't the first National League team to play in Philadelphia. That historical footnote belongs to a team called the Athletics that played the first league game in Philadelphia in 1876. However, due to financial troubles, the Athletics couldn't finish the season.

There was no National League team in Philadelphia until six years later, when Alfred J. Reach purchased the Brown Stockings from Worcester, Massachusetts, after the 1882 season. As president, Reach moved the team to Philadelphia and renamed it the Philadelphia Phillies. Four years after their first game the Phillies moved into a new park at Broad and Huntingdon streets, the Baker Bowl.

In 1911 a pitcher named Grover Cleveland Alexander was drafted from Syracuse and turned out to be the Phillies' first superstar. Led by Alexander's thirty-one wins in 1915, the Phillies captured their first National League pennant. Though Alexander won the first World Series game over the Boston Red Sox by a score of 3-1, the Phillies suffered four straight one-run defeats to lose the World Championship.

Fearing the loss of Alexander to the military service, the Phillies traded him after the 1917 season, a move that left the team without a formidable pitcher. Statistics tell the story. Between the trade and 1931 the Phillies finished as high as fifth place only once, despite a wealth of good hitters. There were Gavvy Cravath and Cy Williams, who won six and three home run titles, respectively. And in 1928 a slugger from Indianapolis named Chuck Klein came upon the scene.

A left-handed hitter, Klein became

Manager Harry Wright (black coat, top hat) and his 1887 Phillies. Wright, who managed the team from 1884 to 1893, won more games (678) than any other manager in team history.

the league's most dangerous hitter, especially in Baker Bowl. The right-field fence was just 280 feet from home plate, and Klein blasted 186 homers in his first five years. In 1930 the Phillies led the league with a team average of .315, yet lost 102

Dick Sisler (8) is mobbed by teammates after hitting a three-run homer in the tenth inning of the final game of the 1950 season to give the "whiz kids" their first pennant in thirty-five years.

games because of bad pitching.

Faced with money problems, good players like Klein, Lefty O'Doul, Pinky Whitney, Don Hurst, and others were eventually traded for cash and lesser players. Financial problems continued. Fire struck Baker Bowl in 1938, and the Phillies were forced to move to Shibe Park (later known as Connie Mack Stadium). Gerry Nugent was the owner then but he ran into financial problems and sold to William Cox in 1942. Cox didn't exactly bring the Phillies good luck. The owner was banned from the game after just one season for gambling.

In November 1943 Robert R.M. Carpenter bought the Phillies for $400,000 for his son, Robert Jr., who hired Herb Pennock as general manager. Pennock began building a farm system, and when he died in 1948, the Phillies were beginning to show promise. Young players such as Del Ennis, Richie Ashburn, Andy Seminick, Robin Roberts, Curt Simmons, and Granny Hamner started to develop, and in 1950 the Phillies rose to become National League champions for the second time. But the "whiz kids" were no match for the New York Yankees, who won the World Series in four straight games.

The baseball dynasty initially expected from these young players didn't develop, and in 1959 Carpenter brought in John Quinn as the new general manager. Quinn immediately hired a young manager out of the minor leagues, Gene Mauch. Mauch's 1964 Phillies—with Jim Bunning, Chris Short, Dick Allen, and Johnny Callison—led the league by six and one-half games with only twelve to go. The Phillies then lost ten straight games, and the longed-for pennant flag flew in St. Louis, not Philadelphia.

After more than thirty-two seasons at Connie Mack Stadium, the Phillies left the old park for the $50-million Veterans Stadium in 1971. Following that season Quinn made his final—and what many consider to be his greatest—trade, sending Rick Wise to St. Louis for left-handed pitcher Steve Carlton.

Carlton became the backbone of the franchise, winning twenty-eight games for a team that placed last in 1972. Paul Owens, the general manager, was team manager as well for the second half of the season, and a new team of "whiz kids" developed: Greg Luzinski, Larry Bowa, Bob Boone, and Mike Schmidt. Through a productive farm system and Owens' trades, the team climbed out of the cellar and won three consecutive division titles, beginning in 1976.

The World Series, however, continued to elude the Phillies. Pete Rose, a free agent, was signed with the hopes that he could help the club get over the hump. In 1980 manager Dallas Green, a former pitcher and farm director, was in the dugout as manager, and in August the team caught fire. On the strength of Schmidt's bat and reliever Tug McGraw's arm, the team won another title.

The play-off with the Houston Astros turned out to be one of the most gut-wrenching play-offs ever, as the Phillies—now dubbed the "comeback kids"—rallied after falling behind to win the play-offs, three games to two. The victory gave the team its third World Series appearance in the club's ninety-eight years. And on Tuesday,

Mike Schmidt (leaping) and teammates celebrate the Phillies' first World Series Championship in 1980.

October 21, 1980, the greatest moment in the history of the franchise occurred at precisely 11:29 p.m., when McGraw struck out Willie Wilson of the Kansas City Royals to give the Phillies their first World Championship.

In 1983, with veterans such as Rose, Carlton, Joe Morgan, and Tony Perez, the team repeated as league champions but lost to the Baltimore Orioles in the World Series.

Prior to the 1982 season the club, run by R.R.M. "Ruly" Carpenter III, was sold to a group headed by William Y. "Bill" Giles for over thirty million dollars. Giles became the Phillies' fourteenth president and brought in some young players who will play important roles in the future of the team.

Three Phillies—Alexander, Klein, and Roberts—have been enshrined in the Baseball Hall of Fame. And two more will be there once they take off the red pin-striped uniforms: Carlton,

the first left-hander to strike out 3,000 batters in the history of baseball; and Schmidt, the league's premier home-run leader, who was voted the greatest Phillies player by the fans in a 1983 poll.

The day that pair enters the Hall of Fame, the headlines will be much bigger than those after that very first game over 100 years ago.

Steve Carlton, acquired in a fortuitous trade, is the club's premier pitcher.

ANZON, INC.

"While still the brilliant British red-coats swaggered thru the streets of Colonial Philadelphia and shortly before the first Continental Congress met in Carpenter's Hall, a certain young gentleman, one Mordecai Lewis, was duly taken into the firm of Neave and Harman, and the firm became known as Neave, Harman and Lewis. This occured in 1772."

It is fitting, somehow, that the company where "one Mordecai Lewis" first worked would one day be steeped in history as rich as the words used to describe him in a magazine article in 1922. That company, in fact, is the oldest continuous manufacturing firm in the history of the United States. What's more, it is recognized as having the oldest continuous bank account on the North American continent, opened on January 16, 1782, just nine days after the Bank of North America opened its doors for business. The name of the company, which traces its origin back to the day Mordecai Lewis stepped into the Neave and Harman plant, is Anzon, Inc., located in Philadelphia.

Established in 1756, the firm of Neave and Harman was first involved in general merchandising, importing, and the sale of white lead and red lead for making paint. And, according to an advertisement in the *Pennsylvania Packet,* the business also sold "Gin in Casks and Choice Bordeau Claret in Cases of 50 Bottles Each, and Fine London Bottled Porter in Hampers."

In 1781 Mordecai Lewis assumed sole control of the business and changed its name to Mordecai Lewis & Company. Lewis is credited with opening the account at the Bank of North America in 1782.

Lewis had two sons, Mordecai and Samuel Neave Lewis. In 1806 the two brothers formed a partnership under the name M.C. & S.N. Lewis. The firm acted as an independent sales agent for the original Mordecai Lewis & Company and was located at 135 South Front Street in Philadelphia.

The firm entered the lead business

in 1829 when it acquired the lead works of Joseph and John Richards. Soon the company was manufacturing white lead and lead oxides, and producing linseed oil and colors.

In 1849 the factory's base of operation was moved to Thompson and Huntington streets. At that time Aramingo Creek bordered the property on the west side. Until 1900 canal barges made their way up the creek and unloaded at the plant. Eventually, however, the creek was converted into a sewer, and Aramingo Avenue was built over it.

In 1856 John T. Lewis, Mordecai's grandson, consolidated Mordecai Lewis & Company and M.C. & S.N.

Poster for advertisement dating back to the 1700s.

Lewis under the name John T. Lewis and Brothers. Some thirty years later, in 1888, the business was incorporated under the title of John T. Lewis & Bros. Company.

In 1889 National Lead Company acquired a controlling interest in the corporation. Two years later John T. Lewis & Bros. Company entered the metals field, acquiring a factory in Baltimore, Maryland, where Babbitt metals, solders, and similar metals were produced. During the two world wars the firm provided carloads of

John T. Lewis' original building dates back to the 1700s.

and red lead, from which the Dutch Boy line of paint materials were produced.

Through the years techniques and machinery were continuously refined; grinding machinery once produced white lead so fine that 100 grains were required to cover the head of a pin.

In 1972 the name National Lead Company was changed to N.L. Industries, Inc., and on October 16, 1979, the firm became known as Associated Lead, Inc., when it was bought from N.L. Industries, Inc., by L.I.G. (Lead Industries Group) of London, England. Eventually, L.I.G. changed its name to Cookson Group PLC.

Though the production of Dutch Boy paint was discontinued at the plant in 1978, Anzon, Inc., is now one of the nation's largest manufacturers of specialty products for the plastics industry, representing 65 percent of the U.S. market in plastic additives. This position was strengthened in 1984 when Anzon, Inc., purchased Envirostrande, Inc., a Massachusetts-based manufacturer of plastic additives.

Over the years numerous expansions and safety renovations have been made to the original 1860 building on Aramingo Avenue, where Anzon, Inc., is still based. In October 1985 Cookson combined Associated Lead with Anzon, a chemical company based in Freehold, New Jersey. The new corporation will be based in Philadelphia and has adopted a new name: Anzon Inc.

The last Lewis family members retired from the business in the 1940s, and there are no descendants of Mordecai Lewis working among the 100 employees at Anzon, Inc., today. But occasionally, when a historic event merits it, a company representative will don a wig, knee britches, and white silk stockings to play the role of Mordecai Lewis.

solder and Babbitt metal to the government, as well as batteries made with Lewis lead oxides.

The demand for lead oxides did not end with the war. Car batteries, plumbing, bathtub enamel, and even tubing for player pianos are just a few examples of the uses of Lewis products in everyday life. Throughout the early part of the twentieth century the company was one of the nation's major suppliers of lead and linseed oil products. Among its major products were lead oxides for automobile batteries and engine bearings, white enamel for plumbing fixtures, lead-type metals used in the printing trades, and Dutch Boy white lead

UNITED ENGINEERS & CONSTRUCTORS INC.

"The largest engineering and construction company in this country has been organized in Philadelphia." So began the press release issued on January 17, 1928, announcing the merger of four internationally known firms to form a new company called United Engineers & Constructors Inc.

The new venture was off to an auspicious start, with over $100 million in contracts. In addition to its headquarters in Philadelphia, United had offices in New York, Newark, Chicago, Los Angeles, Atlanta, Houston, Pittsburgh, Montreal, Buenos Aires, and Rio de Janeiro.

The four founding enterprises that combined to form United Engineers & Constructors dated from the 1880s: United Gas Improvement Company, Public Service Production Company of New Jersey, Dwight P.

Dwight P. Robinson, first president, from March 1928 through October 1931.

Edwin M. Chance, president from October 1931 until his death on November 26, 1954.

Robinson & Company, and Day & Zimmerman Engineering & Construction Company. Together they provided engineering and construction experience in industrial and commercial facilities, electric power production and transmission, manufactured gas facilities, highways and

railroads, irrigation projects, and water and wastewater treatment projects.

Dwight P. Robinson was United's first president. An electrical engineer with degrees from Harvard and MIT, he was a dynamic businessman who had started his own engineering and

During the 1930s United Engineers & Constructors had so many projects under way that it could have formed a city by itself. This artist's conception includes the Thirtieth Street Railroad Station, the Girard Trust Building, and Graterford Prison (in Philadelphia), plus projects in New York and other major cities.

construction firm in 1918. The chairman of the board of directors was Arthur W. Thompson, formerly president of the United Gas Improvement Company. That firm provided office space for the new company in its building at Broad and Arch streets, where United resided until its six-block move to South Seventeenth Street in 1975.

United expanded further in 1964, when Jackson & Moreland—the Boston-based engineering and construction firm founded in 1897—merged with the company. And, in 1969, United became a subsidiary of Raytheon Company, a diversified science and technology-based organization with annual sales in excess of $6 billion.

Today United Engineers & Constructors has about 3,000 employees with an additional 2,500 craft and contractor personnel located at construction sites. In addition to its Philadelphia home office, the firm maintains offices in Boston, Denver, and locally in Valley Forge, Pennsylvania.

The mainstay of the company continues to be the engineering and construction of utility and industrial power plants. The firm has designed and built numerous coal, lignite, gas, oil, and wood-fueled facilities, along with substations and transmission facilities. An early example is the $6.8-million Richmond Generating Station, built for Philadelphia Electric in 1931. Recent examples are the design and construction management of a 280-megawatt, coal-fired station for the Sunflower Electric Cooperative in Kansas, and a major oil-to-coal conversion project at Delmarva Power and Light's Edge Moor Station in Delaware, plus engineering and design of a large-scale electricity and steam cogeneration plant at a Union Camp paperboard mill.

The company also has widely recognized expertise in the design and construction of nuclear power plants. In the steel industry, United has also been recognized for its expertise in the engineering and construction of

iron ore beneficiation, steelmaking, and other metals facilities. Just two of the significant projects completed over the years are the 1948 design and construction of a $7.2-million, thirty-foot hot strip mill for Alan Wood Steel of Conshohocken, and the 1985 engineering for the $500-million installation of continuous steel casters at Bethlehem Steel plants in Baltimore, Maryland, and Burns Harbor, Indiana.

Moreover, the firm serves clients in the chemical, transportation, and manufacturing/research industries. The first subway system in Buenos Aires, Argentina, was built in 1930 by United Engineers & Constructors. More recently, United designed the traction-power system for the Metro system in Washington, D.C. Chemical projects range from the 1969 engineering and construction of a $20-million resin plant expansion for General Electric to the recent process design, engineering, and construction of flue gas desulfurization systems for Philadelphia Electric.

Over the years United has become known for the design and construc-

---

In a typical recent project, United provided engineering and construction management to Arizona Public Service Company for the $440-million installation of emission controls at the Four Corners power station.

tion of sophisticated research facilities. One of the major highlights was the design of NASA's Lunar Landing Research facility and the associated research vehicle to simulate the first moon landing.

At any one time United has approximately 250 projects at varying stages. Since the 1930s the company has no longer handled civil projects such as the construction of large office buildings. But from its early days United can take credit for the design and construction of some of Philadelphia's finest landmarks: the Barclay Hotel, the Thirtieth Street Railroad Station, and the Franklin Institute, to name a few.

United Engineers & Constructors has had an illustrious history since its founding in 1928. Today the company is involved in major power projects in Italy and India as well as in the United States. It is extending its skills into developing technologies through contributions to projects such as the Department of Energy's National Waste Terminal Storage Program and a new 1,000-ton-per-day waste-to-energy plant to be built in York County, Pennsylvania. In 1984 United Engineers & Constructors Inc. ranked twenty-eighth on *Engineering News-Record*'s list of the top fifty design-construction firms in the United States.

DANA CORPORATION

Pennsylvania's "Keystone State" nickname comes from the stone that holds an arch together and gives it strength. Dana Corporation is an industrial symbol of that heritage, producing frames, axles, springs, universal joints, and other parts for over-the-road tractors, trailers, dump trucks, farm machinery, and heavy construction equipment—critical components and services that keep vehicles—and industry—on the road throughout the world.

In 1982 the authors of *In Search of Excellence* identified Dana Corporation as one of their key group of America's best-run companies. They turned to Dana for lessons on decentralization, experimentation, personnel management, information management, and especially on productivity. Such recognition was not surprising to the Dana people. They have been demonstrating industrial excellence for a long time.

In the early 1900s Clarence W. Spicer, a young man from Illinois and an engineering student at Cornell University, developed a more effective method of transmitting power from an automobile engine to the wheels. The device was destined to revolutionize power transmission in automotive and other energy transmission-related industries. Spicer began manufacturing his patented Universal Joint with five people in a rented corner of a building in South Plainfield, New Jersey, in 1904.

Several years later Charles A. Dana, a lawyer and financier, became interested in the Spicer Company. Applying his organizational ability and business acumen, he began to build a larger corporation. His search to expand Universal Joint manufacturing led him to the Chadwick Engineering Works in Pottstown, which he purchased in 1919. Production of the Universal Joint began at this facility early the next year.

Eyeing continuing growth and progress, Dana turned his attention toward Berks County and the Parish Pressed Steel Company in Reading. This business, founded by Neff Parish in 1905, was producing heat-treated frames and component parts for vehicles to safeguard against assembly misalignment and breakage.

Reading was the hub of America's embryonic motor vehicle industry, and from its austere beginning in 1905 with three presses, the Parish Pressed Steel Company had become an important factor in the industry's progress. Parish frames formed the foundation for many famous vehicles: Pierce Arrow, Daniels, Mercer, Kaiser, and Frazer. The company's innovative approaches to building vehicular frames led Dana to purchase Parish Pressed Steel and make it part of the Dana Corporation in 1919.

Growth and progress have been synonymous with Dana since its birth early in the twentieth century. Through eight decades Dana Corporation has developed into a multiplant, multiproduct corporation, a worldwide leader in the manufacture and marketing of components and services for the vehicular and industrial markets, with a growing presence in financial services.

The Northeastern Parts Depot in Fogelsville was established in 1980 to service Dana customers in the NAPA distribution system and other independent warehouse distributors throughout the Northeast.

The newest Dana plant, completed in 1985, is the Spicer Heavy Axle assembly center in Lancaster. Like other Dana regional assembly centers, it is located close to the customer, permitting rapid and efficient shipment of assembled units. The Lancaster center serves Mack Trucks Inc. of Allentown.

The Northeastern Parts Depot, located in Fogelsville, supplies replacement parts to the automotive and truck markets. Established in September 1980, the facility employs thirty-two people.

Recognizing the quality of the work life and the work ethic of its people, Dana constructed its newest regional assembly center in Lancaster in 1985. This Spicer Heavy Axle assembly location employs eighty people and is one of the most technologically advanced facilities anywhere.

The Parish Division facility moved to its present location in Reading in 1925. It is situated on 110 acres with over 1.26 million square feet of floor space, and employs 2,400 people who are involved in the metal stamping and fabrication of chassis frames and components.

Dana's Trailer Products Division has a facility in Berwick where it produces leaf springs used on heavy-duty motor vehicles, farm machinery, and construction equipment.

Spicer Universal Joint Division's Pottstown plant employs 650 people. The plant manufactures Universal Joints and kits for both original-equipment markets and after-market sales.

Metal stamping and fabrication of chassis frames and other vehicular components are the responsibility of Dana's Parish Division, based in Reading. Situated on 110 acres with over 1.26 million square feet of floor space, the plant employs 2,400 people.

Today, with five facilities in Pennsylvania and more than 36,000 employees in 22 countries around the world, Dana Corporation competes as a top-quality manufacturer and marketer of products and product systems in these target markets: highway vehicles, automotive distribution, truck parts distribution, mobile off-highway, industrial equipment, and shelter and security.

Dana's market diversification means financial strength. The firm is a $3.5-billion corporation—and growing. Dana people are productive and committed to quality, and 70 percent of them are Dana Corporation shareholders. For eighty years Dana people have been committed to success in market growth, product development, and financial strength.

The Dana Style, which encourages the involvement and productivity of all Dana people, is the way the firm implements its commitment to leadership, technology, people, total quality, innovation, and global competition. That is the Dana Corporation tradition of excellence.

Dana's Trailer Products Division includes the facility in Berwick. C & M operations moved to Berwick from New York City in 1963. Acquired by Dana Corporation in 1970, the facility employs 100 people who produce leaf springs which are used on over-the-road tractors, trailers, dump trucks, farm machinery, and heavy construction equipment.

Spicer Universal Joint Division's Pottstown Plant employs 650 people engaged in manufacturing Universal Joints and kits for original-equipment-market and after-market sales. The plant dates back to 1919.

SEIZ CORPORATION

In a peaceful Pennsylvania borough called Perkasie, there stands a family-owned business that can design and engineer a steel storage rack system for warehouses. Known as Warehouse Storage Systems, the company also has two other wholly owned subsidiaries: Hi-Line Unit Handling Systems Company, engaged in engineering and design of conveyorized systems, and Steel Processing, Inc., which processes, pickles, and slits steel.

Seiz Corporation was founded in 1946 by Edward A. Seiz, a professional engineer who started the business along Pennsylvania Avenue in Hatfield. The firm, which Seiz originally called Hatfield Industries, initially concentrated on structural steel fabrication. As time passed, its direction changed to meet the needs of the material-handling industry and, ultimately, to the manufacturing of steel racks and related components. By 1966 the company had dropped the name "Hatfield" and was incorporated as the Seiz Corporation.

Indeed, Seiz ranks in the top five for sales among industrial rack manufacturers nationwide. The firm holds over 100 patents for storage devices, and its Hi-Line storage systems—a Gold Shield damage-resistant line of steel racks—is considered the Cadillac of industrial storage racking. These racks are uniquely resistant to the tremendous damage caused by forklifts.

Seiz did all of the engineering,

Seiz Corporation's current facility is located at the intersection of Hi-Line Drive and Ridge Road in Perkasie.

field training, and sales assistance himself. He concentrated on selling to the grocery industry which, with its high product turnover, seemed to have the most rack damage. Seiz did extensive testing and field surveying to develop the Gold Shield line of power-lock racks known by the trade name of Hi-Line. These products were marketed through a distributor network, rather than direct sales.

On June 15, 1974, Seiz, an original member of the Rack Manufacturers Institute and also one of its first presidents, was killed in a private plane crash near the company's manufacturing facility. The firm quickly

reorganized and continued the old philosophy of marketing through a distributor network—a network that today numbers more than 120 agents. Frederick G. Seiz, son of the founder, was named president, and his nephew, C. Gary Seiz, was named vice-president. Under its new president, Seiz expanded its manufacturing capabilities by more than ten times its original function, buying more machinery and updating existing equipment.

Seiz then began marketing its Hi-Line products nationally. With the support of the research and development departments, Seiz expanded its product line. Though the firm once marketed its products almost exclusively to grocery stores, its customers now include major distribution centers for clothing, pharmaceutical, and computer companies. Seiz' major division, Warehouse Storage Systems, accounts for approximately 75 percent of the business.

In 1946 Edward A. Seiz (left) founded the forerunner of Seiz Corporation.

VICTOR F. WEAVER, INC.

Victor F. Weaver, Inc., processes over forty million chickens each year.

New Holland, Pennsylvania, is in the heart of Pennsylvania Dutch country. Amish wagons drive along the highways, and quaint, small businesses dot the agricultural countryside. It may come as something of a surprise, then, when a visitor turns down South Custer Avenue and discovers the sprawling, modern corporate offices and industrial complex of Victor F. Weaver, Inc.

The company was born in 1937 at a small stand in the Sharon Hill Farmer's Market where Victor F. Weaver, with the help of his wife, Edith, dressed and sold seventeen whole chickens. Today the firm processes over forty million chickens each year. Victor F. Weaver is now chairman of the board, and his son, Dale M., is president and chief executive officer.

Through the 1940s the company remained a poultry retailer with stands at markets throughout Philadelphia. The 1950s brought supermarkets and Weaver's shift to the wholesale business. In 1956 the company began selling precut parts and frozen as well as ice-packed birds. Following the success of Weaver white meat chicken roll, the firm turned increasingly toward fully processed poultry.

In the mid-1960s Weaver introduced the first frozen fried chicken in the retail marketplace. In the early 1970s several expansions were made in the Weaver deli line. Later that same decade Weaver Dutch Entrées were added to the product line. The revolution in chicken took place in the 1980s, when boneless chicken products were introduced—first the Rondelet, and then Mini Drums, Chicken Nuggets, and Chicken Fillets.

Today Victor F. Weaver, Inc., is a prepared foods company specializing in poultry entrées. Weaver's frozen chicken products have become familiar to American cooks—and a staple part of our nation's new convenience-food-oriented way of life.

Weaver's food service products are also part of our highly mobile lifestyle, for Weaver provides processed frozen chicken to such familiar fast-food franchises as Kentucky Fried Chicken and Wendy's. The company also supplies processed frozen chicken to the kitchens of major universities, as well as hospitals and senior citizen residential communities nationwide.

Farmers throughout Lancaster and Lebanon counties grow the chickens to Weaver's high standards and rigid specifications. These arrive daily at the New Holland plant ready for processing; freshly processed and frozen products are also shipped daily.

The New Holland complex with its 1,600 employees is but one part of the Weaver Corporation. The company also has processing plants in Gainesville, Georgia, and Boaz, Alabama. The Central Farms Division is located in Fayetteville, North Carolina.

Until 1983 Weaver's distribution was primarily east of the Mississippi. Now its products are sold throughout most of the nation. Chicken Sticks, Chicken Rondelets, Mini Drums, Chicken Nuggets, Breast Fillets, and Thigh and Breast Fillet Strips have joined the line. For fifty years, "Nobody has known chicken like the folks at Weaver!"

Weaver's frozen chicken products have become familiar to American cooks and a staple part of the new convenience-food-oriented way of life.

THE PENNFIELD GROUP

They said it was the perfect marriage—the business partnership between two young tool and die makers named John and Carl who started a precision machining business in 1965. Today John F. Matczak and Carl F. Tate run a multimillion-dollar operation known as The Pennfield Group, with headquarters in the rural setting of Sellersville. From concept and design through casting and machining to final assembly and system engineering, The Pennfield Group offers a unique one-stop solution to customers from nearly every segment of industry and government.

The Pennfield Group is actually three companies, operating in three modern facilities with more than 200,000 square feet of manufacturing space and over 400 employees.

Pennfield Precision, Inc., the company that started in a garage, is the

group's leader. During the first several years of operation, Matczak and Tate relied on conventional turning and milling equipment to produce machined components. In 1968 the first piece of numerically controlled equipment was acquired. The following year the entire operation was moved to its present location in nearby Sellersville where, after major expansions in 1973 and 1979, it employs 175 people and services customers that include many of the major *Fortune* 500 companies.

In 1974 Pennfield Industries was formed to provide fabricating and assembly capability for the already rapidly growing precision machining operation. The company, located in Quakertown, designs, builds, installs, and services advanced automated production systems for defense and private industry. Here the latest

From left to right: Henry S. Zawila, president of Pennfield Industries; John F. Matczak, chairman of the board; Carl F. Tate, executive vice-president; Wolfgang Schmidt, president of Alcast Metals; Chester Orzechowski, vice-president/finance; and Jack Dibee, executive vice-president of marketing and sales.

state-of-the-art robotic technology and advanced integrated mechanical assembly techniques are applied to specific production requirements. The facility also has complete plating, painting, and finishing operations.

In 1975 Alcast Metals was acquired to supplement the aluminum sand-casting requirements for both Pennfield Precision and Pennfield Industries. Company officials like to say that at Alcast, "sand casting is practiced as an art." Indeed, from portable truck scales to nuclear sub-

The diversified world of The Pennfield Group—(clockwise) robotic welding (Pennfield Industries), addition of catalyst to bonding agent and control panel of computerized numerical control (CNC) machine (Pennfield Precision), and aluminum melt furnaces (Alcast Metals).

marine components, each Alcast job is completed to the highest standards of precision, economy, and quality control. In 1979 the operation was expanded to keep up with the increased demand from both outside customers and the two Pennfield enterprises that rely on the third component of their group for high-quality castings.

The Pennfield Group's three companies operate under the management team of Matczak, chairman of the board; Tate, executive vice-president; Jack Dibee, executive vice-president of marketing and sales; Chester Orzechowski, vice-president/finance; Henry S. Zawila, president of Pennfield Industries; and Wolfgang Schmidt, president of Alcast Metals. Celebrating its twentieth anniversary in 1985, The Pennfield Group reported sales of twenty-five million dollars—quite a jump from the $120,000 sales mark that Matczak and Tate celebrated during their first year of business.

John F. Matczak, the gregarious founder of Pennfield, says that the firm is always looking to expand—not only its actual operating facilities but its customer and business base as well. In fact, one diverse avenue that Matczak has taken over the past several years is thoroughbred horse breeding, through a fourth member of the Pennfield family called Pennfield Farms, Inc. Over the past three years Matczak says he has invested more than three million dollars in the farm, and expects to turn a profit within three to five years. One only has to listen to Matczak discuss his latest venture to realize that he relishes the horse-breeding business—particularly the pure sport and financial rewards it brings.

He and others on the Pennfield management team stress that they credit their success over the past two decades to a constant commitment to the customers' needs. As Matczak once said: "Our growth has come about over the past two decades because of our commitment to our customers in providing them with superior product and on-time delivery. We have never lost sight of the fact that our growth came about because of customer loyalty and our inherent sense of providing them with the best possible service. We intend to continue this tradition into the future."

PENNFIELD FARMS, INC.

In the rolling hills of Erwinna, a short distance from the banks of the Delaware River, there are barns paved with patterned red bricks, stalls made of walnut-stained planks, automatic watering devices, closed-circuit television cameras, pastures properly tested for mineral content, and shining, gold-like name plates for the prized stallions that live and breed there. Welcome to Pennfield Farms, Inc., almost heaven to some seventy-five horses that are part of a commercial breeding operation owned and managed by The Pennfield Group.

Founded by John F. Matczak in 1984, Pennfield Farms exists solely to breed and raise thoroughbreds that can compete successfully at the racetrack. On a farm that includes two facilities spread out over several hundred acres in rural Bucks County, Pennfield Farms stands stallions, boards and foals brood mares, raises weanlings and yearlings, prepares and consigns horses to sales, and breaks yearlings. The 24-hour staff of trainers, groomsmen, and stall hands also provide early training to young racehorses, while an affiliate, Pennfield Stables Ltd., handles racing syndication.

Pennfield Farms is home to some seventy-five horses that are part of a commercial breeding operation owned and managed by John Matczak.

The modern facilities, manicured pastures, and stunning thoroughbreds grazing in the distance are easily seen when visitors arrive at this pastoral setting, but another key element in Pennfield Farms is not so visible. And that is Pennfield Biomechanics (PBC).

Pennfield officials like to say that biomechanics advances the "breeder's art to state of the art" by adding a new dimension to breeding predictions and probabilities. Through a series of thirty-five different physical measurements fed through a computer, PBC's biomechanical analysis evaluates a horse's conformation and mechanics of motion. The results of these tests are used to determine the breeding and racing potential of the

thoroughbred.

Pennfield Biomechanics offers a variety of services: OPTIMATCH, a breeding service; a racing syndication consultation service that recommends purchases of racing stock that are structurally capable of becoming stakes performers; and a thoroughbred consultant contract that is designed to increase the probability of breeding and/or racing stake performers.

Pennfield Farms operates its facilities for horses that are privately owned as well as those owned by the farm. And, through a combination of highly trained personnel, modern facilities, and new technology, Pennfield Farms, Inc., plans to become the first name in commercial thoroughbred breeding.

Deanna Matczak, business manager of Pennfield Farms, Inc.

WEILER BRUSH COMPANY

The Weiler Brush Company is one of the leaders in the brush industry. With an active product list of 4,000 items, the firm designs and sells brushes to a wide range of industries that include oil exploration, construction, shipbuilding, automobile, rubber, metalworking, jewelry, and mold and die making. With the acquisition of the Joseph O. Flatt Company of Reading, Pennsylvania, Weiler has broadened its product line tremendously and will add the janitorial field to its list of markets. Econoline, the latest addition, is aimed at the home owner, and future markets include the electronics field.

The Weiler story demonstrates the promise of America. Raised in Pforzheim, Germany, Karl E. Weiler followed the tradition set by his father and was apprenticed in the art of brush making. He went on to receive his master's diploma, which authorized him to teach other apprentices. Weiler then came to the United States and worked for several years for leading manufacturers in the industry.

In 1944, with a capital of forty dollars, Weiler and his wife, Helmi, purchased a used foot press. In the basement of their home in Franklin Square, Long Island, Weiler designed a small brush for use in the jewelry industry. From that beginning the business grew and expanded. When a fire in 1952 nearly destroyed the plant, the Weilers built a new facility, and within one year the firm was again soaring ahead in the field of industrial brushes.

In 1957 the Weiler Brush Company moved to its new plant in Cresco, Pennsylvania. Room was needed to expand the business, and the Weilers chose the Pocono Mountains as the site because it reminded them of the Black Forest area of Germany. In addition to its beauty, the area offered room for future development and a good location in terms of freight and shipping.

The new plant grew quickly. Between 1957 and the present, five additions have brought the plant size to

During the past three decades Weiler Brush Company has grown from a one-man business to a leader in the industry.

60,000 square feet. Currently, another 10,000-square-foot addition is being planned.

In 1961 Karl M. Weiler joined his father's company, and in 1971 he assumed the presidency. His father retired in 1967, but Weiler has continued the family tradition, and the business remains a family concern. Elli Caracio, Weiler's sister, is the human resources director, and Ann Weiler, Weiler's wife, is the advertising manager. At the age of seventy-seven, Helmi Weiler is still active in the firm.

At Weiler Brush Company, everyone is considered part of the team that makes the business a success. Karl Weiler believes that the employees are the firm's most important asset.

Some of the innovations created by the Weiler team include the tooling process for heavy-duty industrial

brushes. The Weiler team has also designed and built the equipment used in manufacturing power brushes.

Recent additions at the plant include "E.T.," a robot added to the production line as a material handler and aid to the human worker. Recent product innovations include the Roughneck, a knot-type wheel brush used by the oil industry. Introduced in 1982, it soon became a top seller. In 1985 the Roughneck B.G., an encapsulated stringer bead brush, was introduced.

Community and civic involvement is part of the Weiler philosophy. The development of a unique education program is a recent achievement. In sponsoring Youth Day, Weiler Brush Company conducts a program for local high school students and teachers. The purpose of the program is to show students the skills needed in the working world and to demonstrate that what they are learning in school will be needed on the job. Youth Day has been successful, and there are plans to develop it further.

QUAKER STATE OIL REFINING CORPORATION

Oil City, the first capital of the petroleum world, is headquarters for Quaker State Oil Refining Corporation.

For Pennsylvania, the home state of the oil industry, there is nothing more natural than that one of its corporations adopt the state's nickname, Quaker State. For Quaker State Oil Refining Corporation, the name also signifies the unique type of crude oil originally produced from the world's first oil well in 1859.

Today Quaker State is the most recognized brand name in the American automotive products market, the motor oil preferred by nearly one out of four American motorists.

Now nearing the billion-dollar milestone of corporate development, and servicing virtually every community in the United States, Quaker State still makes its home in the small community of Oil City, close to its roots and its first wells. Oil City was the first capital of the petroleum world. At one time over 90 percent of the world's oil production flowed through it, and men such as John D. Rockefeller and Andrew Carnegie made their fortunes there.

Oil City and its surrounding communities became boom towns immediately after the discovery of oil there in 1859. Local wealth, growth, and violence exceeded that of the com-

bined gold rushes of the West. That period spawned many small companies, nineteen of which merged in 1931 to form the modern Quaker State Oil Refining Corporation.

The "Quaker State" trade name was first used in national advertising in 1914 to signify the highly stable and pure lubricants found in Pennsylvania crude oil. The Franklin Automobile Company would permit no other oil in its high-speed, air-cooled engines. It even included a two-gallon container of Quaker State oil under

the front seat of every new car—as a standard feature.

Geologists now realize that this unique crude oil is not limited to Western Pennsylvania, but includes adjoining portions of West Virginia, Ohio, and New York. It differs from other U.S. crude oils in three important ways: It yields more lubricant (over 30 percent compared to under 3 percent average for other U.S. crude oils) in the refining process; it contains virtually no impurities (such as the sulfur and asphalt commonly found in other crudes); and its molecular structure is naturally paraffinic (the best and most stable form), allowing it to better withstand heat and gases from internal-combustion engines.

Quaker State still makes most of its automotive motor oils from 100-percent Pennsylvania Grade crude oil. It is the only company that still labels Penn Grade motor oils.

While other oil companies moved from Oil City to new fields in Texas, Oklahoma, and elsewhere, Quaker State has preferred Pennsylvania as home for its corporate headquarters. Other corporate facilities, however, including mines, plants, warehouses, and other offices, are widely scattered throughout the United States and Canada. Quaker State is also active in twenty-six foreign countries.

In Pennsylvania, Quaker State maintains a research center in Seneca, a refinery in Farmers Valley, a wax refinery in Emlenton, a coal mine in

Quaker State's Congo, West Virginia, refinery.

Homer City, a crude oil production plant near Titusville, as well as distribution facilities in several other cities.

Major Quaker State facilities located outside Pennsylvania include two refineries in West Virginia; motor oil manufacturing plants in West Virginia, Mississippi, California, and in Ontario, Canada; coal mines in West Virginia and Utah; vehicular lighting equipment plants in New York; and docks in Minnesota and Ontario.

Quaker State's automotive products are distributed through approximately 1,500 warehouses. Besides lubricants, these include filters, undercoatings, car paint, interior sealants, car care chemicals, freon, antifreeze, and batteries.

Through Quaker State Minit-Lube, the company also owns or franchises over 100 fast-lube centers and over 100 fast-food restaurants, mostly in the western United States. Quaker State Minit-Lube was born in 1985 with the acquisition of Arctic Circle. Quaker State expects this sector of its operations to expand rapidly in the next few years.

Through its Heritage Insurance Group, headquartered near Los Angeles, the firm sells credit/life and credit/accident insurance, both marketed by automobile dealers throughout the nation.

Although Quaker State began as an oil refiner, it has evolved into a company primarily marketing consumer automotive after-market products. It considers the fuels produced by its drilling and refining operations as by-products of the production of motor oil.

Today's Quaker State has more in common with marketers of food and personal products than it does with fuel refiners. It relies heavily on advertising and promotional activities to expand its market. Some of the best Madison Avenue techniques were born in Oil City.

One of the production lines at the Congo, West Virginia, refinery.

Quaker State also pioneers innovations designed to improve product quality and consumer convenience, including the use of plastic bottles for motor oil, replacing the messy composite cans. Quaker State also developed the high-mounted stoplights now used in most models of Ford and Chrysler automobiles.

Quaker State's Pennsylvania employees enjoy unequaled outdoor recreational opportunities. Every form of summer and winter sports is available on a daily basis—not just at vacation time. Excellent housing is inexpensive and traffic jams are unknown. Nearby Pittsburgh and Erie provide a full range of cultural activities.

The Quaker State of Pennsylvania has provided Quaker State Oil Refining Corporation with an abundance of resources, excellent transportation, and creative and industrious people. The company has grown and prospered. The continued resources of state and company promise a future as productive as the past.

A Quaker State pumping jack near Bradford, Pennsylvania, the "high-grade oil metropolis of the world."

THE PRUDENTIAL INSURANCE COMPANY OF AMERICA

More than a century ago life insurance protection was far beyond the reach of most working people. Because of its high cost, few could afford this protection for themselves and their families, and many received a pauper's burial.

John F. Dryden, a young insurance salesman from Newark, New Jersey, saw a way to remedy this situation by making low-cost life insurance protection available to low-income families. Based on a system that had been successful in England, his idea was to sell life insurance policies that cost no more than a few cents a week. Known as industrial insurance, these policies would provide a decent burial and help families overcome the financial hardships that often followed the death of a breadwinner.

On October 13, 1875, Dryden, with the backing of some Newark businessmen, founded the Prudential Friendly Society—the first company in America to successfully sell weekly premium insurance designed for the workingman. Soon thereafter the name of the firm was changed to The Prudential Insurance Company of America.

In 1879, only four years after the corporation was formed, Prudential opened its first sales office in Pennsylvania on Walnut Street in Philadelphia. It was the firm's first venture outside New Jersey and was only the beginning for what was to become

John F. Dryden, Prudential's founder, served as its third president from 1881 until his death in 1911.

the world's largest insurance company.

As Prudential grew and prospered, it became apparent that the company needed a symbol, a symbol that would not only illustrate its financial strength and security but also depict the sense of stability and comfort it gave its policyholders. Many ideas

The company's Eastern Home Office, located in suburban Philadelphia, serves individual policyholders in eleven northeastern states and the District of Columbia.

were considered, and in 1896 the famous Rock of Gibraltar was chosen to represent Prudential. Since then the rock and its prominence in media and trade publications has made it one of the world's best-known trademarks.

By 1925 Prudential was poised to celebrate its fiftieth anniversary with more than eight billion dollars in life insurance policies in force and with operations in every state in the union as well as Canada. Pennsylvania continued to play a prominent role in the firm's continued growth through the Depression years and World War II. In fact, Prudential's first million-dollar policy was written for a prominent Philadelphia family. By 1948 there were fourteen sales offices in the Commonwealth, providing widespread insurance coverage.

Increasing demands on the Prudential headquarters in Newark and the need to serve policyholders on a more regional basis resulted in a decision to decentralize the company's operations. To that end, Prudential opened its first regional home office in Los Angeles, California, in 1948, and during the next twenty years set up similar regional operations in six U.S. cities and Canada.

The Central Atlantic Home Office, serving policyholders in Pennsylvania, Maryland, Delaware, and the District of Columbia, was the final step in the decentralization process.

Prudential's corporate headquarters in Newark, New Jersey, is located just a short distance from where the company was founded more than 110 years ago.

Established twenty miles outside of Philadelphia in 1969, the home office in Fort Washington was renamed the Eastern Home Office in 1984 and its operations were expanded to cover eleven states in the northeastern United States.

Today, after more than 110 years, The Prudential Insurance Company of America is the world's largest insurance company. With over 76,000 employees and assets of more than $100 billion, Prudential and its subsidiaries provide a wide range of financial products and services to millions of people throughout the United States, Canada, Europe, and the Far East.

Pennsylvania continues to play a pivotal role in Prudential's present and future growth. The company employs more than 11,000 people throughout the Commonwealth and its Eastern Home Office, the Central Atlantic Group Office, and a network of sixty-one local sales offices. In addition, it administers the American Association of Retired Persons Account, the largest group health insurance program in the nation insuring older Americans. With more than $2.5 billion invested in the Commonwealth, the company continues a strong commitment to Pennsylvanians.

The Prudential Insurance Company of America and its subsidiaries have changed markedly since John Dryden laid the cornerstone of the firm, founded on his goal of providing inexpensive life insurance protection for the workingman and his family. Yet one thing hasn't changed in 110 years. Prudential has remained dedicated to serving all its policyholders and "The strength of Gibraltar" prevails.

THE PRUDENTIAL HAS THE STRENGTH OF GIBRALTAR

The FLEET PROTECTS the NATION — PRUDENTIAL LIFE INSURANCE PROTECTS the HOME

This 1910 advertisement depicts Prudential's famous symbol, the Rock of Gibraltar, and the U.S. fleet.

BROCKWAY, INC.

There are few things in this modern world of ours that we take more for granted than packaging—plastic, metal, and glass—bottles, cans, and jars. They're all around us yet we rarely see them.

Hardly a day goes by when we don't reach for Brockway products. Budweiser beer and Dannon yogurt come in Brockway containers. So, too, do Coke and Pepsi and Wesson, Crisco, and Mazola corn oil. Gerber, Heinz, Welch's, P&G, Avon, Jergens, PPG and Olympic paints—all are Brockway customers, along with 1,000 other familiar producers of packaged goods.

And the Brockway name is reaching new fields, as well. Brockway Airlines operates a growing fleet of passenger aircraft to serve regional airports throughout the Northeast. The company also owns Crown Airways, which serves the Pittsburgh area as a franchised operator of Allegheny Commuter service in association with USAir.

Internationally, Brockway markets container technology and technologi-

cal services (including Brockway-designed production equipment) to container-manufacturing clients worldwide—from Canada and Mexico to South America, Europe, Australia, and the Far East.

Now a billion-dollar corporation, Brockway dates its origins to 1907, when the entrepreneurial spirit and technical expertise of a dozen glass-workers from New York combined with economic incentives offered by residents of Brockwayville, a small Northwestern Pennsylvania town. The glassmakers had helped to develop a semiautomatic bottle-forming machine. They pooled their resources for a total investment of $35,000 and purchased a financially troubled glass plant. The town later simplified its name and the company adopted it. The result: Brockway Machine Bottle Company, now known as Brockway, Inc.

The founding craftsmen proved

themselves as inventive as they were enterprising. They invented a feeder mechanism that made their bottle machines fully automatic, then consolidated their creations into a new machine that greatly increased production and virtually revolutionized glass container manufacturing.

Throughout the nation housewives were adopting processed foods provided by companies such as Pittsburgh's H.J. Heinz. Brockway's wide-mouthed containers met the need; they were also popular packaging for ink, salves, and other products. In the 1920s Brockway Sales Company was formed as the exclusive marketing agent for new narrow-neck containers that were becoming increasingly popular with food processors and pharmaceutical manufacturers.

In 1933 Prohibition was repealed. America again wanted bottled beer, wine, and liquor. Brockway stood ready to help meet the demand. Spirited sales stimulated the company to record growth and sales of $1.5 million—even when other industries

This is the earliest known photo (1907) of the original plant site in Brockwayville.

remained crippled by the Great Depression.

In 1941 Brockway expanded to nearby Crenshaw, building a brilliantly engineered plant designed to provide an uninterrupted production flow from batch house to packing line. The new plant became a model for the industry. Demand continued to grow during World War II as steel became too precious for packaging, and glass containers assumed new functions.

Brockway's growth has continued to be both dramatic and dynamic. Expansion took the firm to Muskogee, Oklahoma, for its third plant and to Lapel, Indiana, where it purchased Sterling Glass. Subsequent acquisitions included Demuth Glass in West Virginia and Tygert Valley Glass in Washington, Pennsylvania. During the 1950s Brockway also built plants in New Jersey and Minnesota.

The 1960s witnessed even more rapid growth. Brockway made its entry into plastic containers in 1960 with the purchase of Celluplastics, Inc., in Massachusetts. In 1964, with the purchase of six glass container plants from Continental Can Company, Brockway doubled its size and expanded its manufacturing network coast to coast.

And each year since, the company has reinvested tens of millions of dollars to maintain those plants in state-of-the-art condition.

Brockway executives believe that their key to success lies with the company's reputation for product quality and uniformity. Throughout the firm's expansion, it has maintained rigid operating standards and controls. That philosophy continues to guide the company's operations.

The firm's first plant manager alongside one of the original glass-forming machines installed at the Brockway plant. This was one of the first semiautomatic bottle-making machines in the industry.

The plastics division developed gradually through the 1960s and 1970s, and then in 1984 took a giant stride into the future when it tripled in size with the purchase of the eleven-plant IMCO Container Division of the Ethyl Corporation. Brockway's plastics division is headquartered in Richmond, Virginia.

Acquisition of Standard Container Company in 1979 brought Brockway into metal containers ranging from half-pint cans to 55-gallon drums. Atlanta-based Standard's plastic and metal containers are widely used for paints, joint cement, industrial mastics and other construction materials, agricultural chemicals, as well as some food and other consumer products.

The airline division, created in 1969, has experienced rapid growth in the 1980s in the turbulent wake of deregulation. Crown Airways links a half-dozen Pennsylvania, Ohio, and West Virginia communities with Pittsburgh. In 1983 Brockway acquired Clinton Aero of Plattsburgh, New York, and Air North of Burlington, Vermont. It consolidated the two into Brockway Air, which now operates as a Piedmont commuter, linking a number of key regional airports in New York State and New England with Boston, New York, Newark, Philadelphia, and Washington, D.C.

Under chairman and chief executive officer John A. Winfield and president and chief operating officer John J. McMackin, Brockway looks forward to an exciting future. Late in 1985 the corporate headquarters was moved to Jacksonville, Florida, as a further step in decentralizing the company's management operations and increasing the autonomy of the individual operating units. Brockway, Pennsylvania, however, will remain a keystone of the company's packaging operations. The firm's birthplace, it continues as the headquarters of its largest operating unit—Glass Containers—as well as the globe-circling International Division, and as the base for company-wide basic research and engineering activities.

WILKES-BARRE GENERAL HOSPITAL

Wilkes-Barre General Hospital, Northeast Pennsylvania's largest community general hospital, is committed to meeting the health care needs of the greater Wilkes-Barre community. That commitment, reflected in the institution's history, likewise represents its future.

Throughout its long and successful existence, Wilkes-Barre General Hospital has experienced and adapted to the many changes that have occurred both in the medical world and in the community it serves. But despite its years of continued progress and achievement, it has not grown away from its original mission: to be a general hospital for the community.

That mission has its origins in an appeal put forth in 1870 "on behalf of a hospital" by nine concerned area physicians who claimed that the Wilkes-Barre area (then a major regional mining center) required the "superior surgical and medical appliances as could be provided by a hospital." It was not until 1872, however, when a number of accidents needlessly claimed the lives of miners, that action was taken.

An organizing group first met in September of that year in the office of ex-Governor Henry M. Hoyt to plan the area's first hospital. On October 10, 1872, the twenty-bed Wilkes-Barre City Hospital (as it was originally named) opened in a rented factory building once used to manufacture weigh scales. It was conveniently located across from the Hazard Rope Works and near various industrial and mining communities. During its first three months of operation, a medical staff comprising two consulting physicians and two attending physicians, together with two matrons, admitted and treated a total of twenty-five patients, the majority for mining-related incidents.

For two years, until it began to receive state funding, the hospital was supported entirely by voluntary contributions from the families and industries of Wilkes-Barre. Examples of the community's support were duly noted each year by the following recorded donations: "Three geese, Mr. Burgunder. Six sheets, made and donated by St. Stephens Industrial School. One hundred glasses of jelly, Mr. E.P. Darling. One Turkey, H. Tuck and Co. . . ."

By late 1874 demands on the twenty-bed facility became so great that a larger building was needed. Two lots were offered to the board of directors in 1875, and a four-acre plot of land, donated by John Welles Hollenback, was chosen as the new site for Wilkes-Barre City Hospital. The land, located on River Street in the city's north end, remains the site of the hospital today.

The first institution built at that location was occupied on April 1, 1876, and was a quadrangle, two stories high with a large veranda at its front and an open court in the center. It contained sixty beds in its four female and five male wards, one operating room, a pharmacy, and separate dining rooms for male and female patients. The cost per patient, per day, was less than one dollar.

In 1887 skilled nursing had taken its place among the "gainful callings of life," and the Wilkes-Barre City Hospital's Nurses Training School opened. The school offered a three-year course of study in caring for the sick, and it graduated its first two nurses in the summer of 1890.

Wilkes-Barre City Hospital in 1876.

Ancillary growth began in 1902 with the opening of the X-ray department, which first introduced X-rays to Wilkes-Barre. Within one year the department admitted seventy-two patients to undergo "radiographs."

In 1925 the growing medical facility boasted a prominent nursing school, several new buildings that housed patient wards and services, and an active group of volunteers who devoted a great amount of time to helping with the hospital's day-to-day operations. Indeed, the institution's success in its early years was due largely to the Ladies' Auxiliary, known until 1908 as the Board of Lady Managers. In 1925 the hospital also assumed a new identity. A name change from Wilkes-Barre City Hospital to Wilkes-Barre General Hospital was made to emphasize its independence from local government.

It can be said that Wilkes-Barre General Hospital is synonymous with the word "growth." The period 1930 to the present has been a continuous cycle of renovation and addition.

The most dramatic changes began in 1959, when obsolete buildings were razed to make way for an emerging "new" hospital. Slowly Wilkes-Barre General was transformed from a cluster of individual settings to a single structure that would be continuously renovated and reconstructed. Growth was explosive during this period as new units and departments were born.

With the long period of renovation and expansion came the area's first Poison Control Center in 1959, nuclear medicine department in 1963, intensive care unit and electroencephalogram department in 1964, chest clinic and coronary care unit in 1966, and a 24-hour, seven-day-a-week emergency department in 1968. New administrative departments were created as well, and existing patient care departments were expanded and modernized. By 1970 the institution was ready for another major building phase.

Wilkes-Barre General celebrated 100 years of service to the community by once again responding to the community's needs. On June 23, 1972, Hurricane Agnes, the most devastating flood in the history of the Wilkes-Barre area, rendered over 80,000 persons homeless. With virtually the entire Wilkes-Barre region at a standstill, Wilkes-Barre General became a major emergency flood disaster hospital, admitting scores of patients from inundated hospitals in the flood-ravaged community. The emergency department's case load increased by 100 percent as people of all ages poured in for typhoid and tetanus shots as well as emergency

treatment. General's calm efficiency was praised by hospital president Thomas P. Saxton: "Everyone functioned normally, except at an accelerated pace—which is the highest praise of all."

New construction was again a major facet of hospital life in the 1970s and into the 1980s. As the result of a generous bequest to the hospital, the county's first radiation oncology center was created in 1974. Patient floors were added, departments were expanded, and the new East Tower opened in 1981. The $15-million Center for Intensive Care and Surgery, a three-floor, 45,000-square-foot addition to the hospital's north side, was completed in 1984 and combines modern facilities with sophisticated equipment to create a unique setting for surgery and specialized patient care.

As the institution's physical plant continued to grow to keep pace with the many technological advances in health care, its staff also experienced similar growth. The original handful of physicians who composed the

---

Today Wilkes-Barre General Hospital is Northeast Pennsylvania's largest community general hospital.

medical staff in 1872 has surged to almost 250 and encompasses more than thirty medical specialties and subspecialties. The employee population has grown to over 1,500, making General the county's largest employer. And the Auxiliary has continued its remarkable tradition of service to the hospital through volunteer programs and financial support.

The facility's corporate structure has also changed with the times. A 1982 reorganization established the Wilkes-Barre General Health Corporation with subsidiary organizations including the hospital, Heritage House, and Diversified Medical Systems. The new structure will ensure that the hospital and its related corporations can continue to effectively meet the health care needs of Northeast Pennsylvanians.

Wilkes-Barre General Hospital admits over 16,000 patients each year to its 444 beds, while also providing care for over 200,000 outpatients. This, of course, would not be possible if not for its unwavering philosophy emphasizing modern equipment and technology, expansion and modernization of the building, and a valued staff of highly skilled and caring health care professionals.

FORBES HEALTH SYSTEM

guests. To ensure the realization of this philosophy, Forbes developed the G.R.E.A.T. program: Guest Relations, Education, Awareness, and Teamwork. Forbes' employees provide a careful blending of medical expertise and modern technology with personal service and hospitality.

The facilities of the Forbes Health System include Forbes Regional Health Center in Monroeville; Forbes Metropolitan Health Center, Forbes Center for Gerontology, and Forbes Hospice in Pittsburgh; and Highlands Hospital and Health Center in Connellsville. The system is also affiliated with two Urgi-Care® centers and the innovative Forbes Life Style Center.

Forbes Regional Health Center provides care for more than twenty-

The Forbes Health System has a heritage rich in pioneering tradition.

In 1972 two well-established Pittsburgh hospitals with histories dating from the mid-1800s joined forces to enhance health care for area residents. This merger created the Forbes Health System, initiating a new era in health care for Western Pennsylvania.

The spirit of the Forbes Health System carries the determination of its namesake, General John Forbes, who carved the original Forbes Trail en route to Fort Duquesne during the French and Indian War. The founding hospitals were both located at key points along the trail.

Today the Forbes Health System is a 748-bed multi-institutional system spread throughout Western Pennsylvania, providing health care to more than fifty communities in Allegheny, Westmoreland, and Fayette counties.

Like a trail, the new system links different kinds of health facilities,

providing a continuum of care. This pioneering health care concept unites hospitals, skilled nursing facilities, home care services, urgent care centers, hospices, and other facilities in a single integrated system. By minimizing duplication and providing care in the most appropriate setting, patient needs can be met effectively, and at the lowest possible cost.

The key emphasis throughout the development and growth of the Forbes Health System has been meeting community needs for high-quality, affordable, personalized health care services. Forbes' health care centers provide preventive and ambulatory care, patient and consumer health education, and community outreach programs, in addition to traditional hospital services.

At Forbes, it is of primary importance that patients receive care with dignity and respect. Employees treat patients and visitors as personal

five communities in Allegheny and Westmoreland counties. The center offers regional services that include state-of-the-art diagnostic imagery, clinical laboratories, family practice, obstetrics, pediatrics, psychiatry, extensive outpatient care, emergency care, and graduate medical education.

Forbes Metropolitan Health Center, opened in 1984, provides medical services and health education programs to more than thirty communities in Allegheny County. Its programs emphasize cardiopulmonary medicine, rehabilitation, gastroenterology, orthopedics, general surgery, vascular surgery, internal medicine, emergency care, physical medicine, and family practice.

The Forbes Center for Gerontology addresses the special needs of the aging population through skilled nursing care for the individual who is discharged from a hospital but still requires professional health care services; intermediate care for individuals who are unable to function independently but do not require professional health care services; and residential living for individuals who are self-sufficient but prefer a structured living environment. To complete the trail, Forbes' hospice program cares for terminally ill patients and their families. Hospice care is provided by an interdisciplinary team dedicated to improving the quality of life for patients, through inpatient care, home care, and bereavement counseling.

Highlands Hospital and Health Center is the newest addition to the Forbes Health System's network of services. Formerly Connellsville State General Hospital, it was acquired by Forbes from the Commonwealth of Pennsylvania in September 1985. A wholly owned subsidiary of Forbes, it

Forbes Metropolitan Health Center in Pittsburgh emphasizes cardiopulmonary medicine, rehabilitation, gastroenterology, orthopedics, and general surgery, among other medical specialties.

provides care to more than twenty communities in Fayette County.

Two Urgi-Care centers extend the trail of Forbes' health services further into the communities served by the system. Urgi-Care was developed by the Forbes Health System and Western Pennsylvania Emergency Physicians, Inc., in 1982 to provide care for medical problems that require the attention of a physician, but do not require the extensive services of a hospital emergency department or the primary care provided by a personal physician.

As a multi-institutional system, Forbes has provided its operating units with centralized management expertise and shared services, including guest relations, finance, management engineering, human resources, marketing, public affairs, materiel management, patient accounting, risk management, planning, legal counsel, and data processing.

Centralized management is not only efficient, but also allows the

Forbes Health System to share its expertise in multi-hospital system development and its services with other health care providers. Through its parent company, Healthmark Corporation, Forbes can provide access to a wide spectrum of health care services with many advantages of regional and national linkages.

As its latest development (begun in June 1985), the Forbes Health System joined with The Racquet Club of Pittsburgh to open the Forbes Life Style Center, a health and fitness facility blending sports medicine, physical therapy, physical testing and evaluation, general fitness, and health education. While these programs are offered in The Racquet Club of Pittsburgh, they are applied with hospital technology, by a medically trained staff.

The Forbes Health System's pioneering tradition and commitment to quality, compassionate health care will guide it through the rapidly changing future of the health care industry. Visionary leadership, dedicated employees, and a solid guest relations philosophy will enable the Forbes Health System to continue to blaze new trails for health care delivery in Pennsylvania.

Forbes Center for Gerontology focuses on the needs of the aging population by providing skilled nursing, intermediate and residential care, and conducting research in gerontology. Forbes' hospice program was one of the first initiated in Pennsylvania and provides inpatient care, home care, and bereavement counseling to improve the quality of life for terminally ill patients and their families.

KENNAMETAL INC.

Making the materials that make the machines—that's the business of Kennametal Inc. of Latrobe—the largest American producer of hard carbide alloys. Applied research in chemical, metallurgical, and production techniques has made Kennametal tools and components the most durable in the world—capable of surviving against the most extreme of adverse industrial conditions including abrasion, corrosion-wear, and temperature.

The McKenna family involvement with the American metal industry stretches back to Robert McKenna, a coppersmith who came from Ireland to Pittsburgh in 1832. His sons reorganized his firm into A&J McKenna and then into Pittsburgh's A and T McKenna Brass & Copper Works in 1835. By 1899 the venture had evolved into the McKenna Brothers Brass Co.

In 1910 the McKenna family started the Vanadium Alloys Steel Company in Latrobe. It grew rapidly during World War I, producing tool steel and ferro-tungsten for the war effort. The ferro-tungsten was made under a new process covered by a patent granted to young Philip M. McKenna, who was then just starting his career.

Philip would prove to be an inventive and creative scientist, engineer, and businessman, but his ideas and ambitions were not fulfilled in the family firm.

Philip left Vanadium and started his own enterprise in 1938. Litigation over Philip's patent for a unique tungsten-titanium carbide composition, the material that would become

The corporate headquarters of Kennametal Inc. is located in Latrobe, where the company was founded in 1938. Kennametal has manufacturing facilities in Latrobe and at thirteen other U.S. locations. Subsidiaries or affiliates are located in Canada, England, Australia, Belgium, France, the Netherlands, West Germany, Italy, and Mexico.

known as Kennametal carbide, lasted until 1940 when it was settled by an amicable compromise favorable to young Philip. Philip's brother, Donald, and his cousin, Alex G. McKenna, became partners in the new firm which was named Kennametal after its chief product. Alex became the chief operating officer at Kennametal; he is currently chairman of the board.

Kennametal's twelve employees began operations within the Vanadium plant, and the young company moved to its present location in 1939. Its first building was a renovated garage. Today Kennametal has manufacturing facilities at Latrobe and twelve other domestic plants in six states as well as subsidiaries or affiliates in eleven foreign countries. President and chief executive officer of Kennametal is Quentin C. McKenna.

Kennametal products are critical to the international mining, metalworking, construction, and metallurgical industries. Manufacturers of en-

gines and turbines, farm machinery, oil field products, mining equipment, and countless other items from aluminum cans to aerospace products all rely on Kennametal components.

In the early years the future did not seem so bright. The metal industry was closely linked with German technology and tools; World War II forced Kennametal to premature self-reliance. Tax problems forced the business to incorporate (a break with the family's partnership tradition) in 1943. And the depressed postwar industrial economy of the late 1940s seriously threatened the young company. But new applications for Kennametal materials and the national economic expansion of the 1950s launched Kennametal into a period of rapid growth.

New coal-mining tools were developed using Kennametal carbide tips at the cutting points, and new, longer-lasting Kennametal-carbide-tipped percussion bits were made for faster drilling of hard rock. Kennametal carbide knives for the woodworking industry proved that they would outwear steel knives and won widespread adoption, while the line of Kennametal tools for the metalworking industry was expanded and improved.

Expansion continued through the 1960s. New applications were developed for Kennametal's hard carbide alloys, and several new compositions or "grades" of Kennametal carbide were introduced. The 1960s also witnessed the commercial introduction of Kennertium heavy tungsten alloys, Kengrip tire studs, DeVibrator vibration-damping units for boring bars, Kennametal carbide-edged snowplow and grader blades, new designs of Kenroc rock bits, and high-purity tantalum powders for electronic applications. As a climax to this decade of development, Kennametal brought an important new titanium-carbide-coated tungsten carbide to market.

Kennametal's Keziz process for the production of exceptionally high-quality carbide was publicly introduced in 1972, following six years of

secret development. Other significant new product introductions of the 1970s included the Kentrol line of inserts for metal-cutting tools, a mini-series of Kendex toolholders, and the company's first ceramic inserts for metal-cutting tools. The decade also witnessed Kennametal's accelerated growth in the international market.

The growth of Kennametal sales has paralleled the expansion of the company's innovative product lines. In 1974 sales topped $100 million for the first time. Only four years later sales passed the $200-million milestone. In 1980 they passed the $300-million mark, and the firm's growth continues.

Recent years have witnessed intensified overseas activities and research and development. In 1980 Kennametal acquired Erickson Tool Company of Solon, Ohio, and its subsidiary, Bristol Erickson Limited of Bristol, England; in 1981 the company entered the Asian market and strengthened holdings in Canada, England, and France. In 1985 Kennametal established new operating headquarters for Kennametal-Europe in Zurich, and for Kennametal Asia Pacific in Tokyo.

New products brought to market in the 1980s include Kyon 2000, a revo-

lutionary metal-cutting material combining high-speed cutting capability and impact resistance; KC950, a multi-layered ceramic-coated grade of tungsten carbide; and KT150, an ideal material for cutting steel under moderately light conditions at fairly high speeds. The introduction of Kyon 3000, a silicon-nitride (sialon) metal-cutting material, completed a major effort involving not only applied materials research but also manufacturing process technology.

Research and development of advanced cutting tool grades, comprehensive tooling systems, and wear-resistant materials continue to receive priority attention at Kennametal. The corporate objective is to remain at the forefront of this technology. It's a good bet that the company will continue to meet that goal; Kennametal Inc. is as hard and durable as the products it manufactures.

Kyon® 3000, new from Kennametal Inc., is a silicon nitride (sialon) material for metal-cutting inserts. The new material has been specifically engineered for high-productivity machining of cast iron, which is widely used in the automotive and heavy equipment industries for brake parts, engine blocks, and other components. A Kyon® 3000 insert, in a Kenloc® toolholder from Kennametal, is pictured here cutting cast iron at high speed on a metal-cutting lathe.

NATIONWIDE INDUSTRIES

Nationwide Industries, a company established twenty-two years ago in Bensalem, is perhaps best known as the manufacturer of Fix A Flat, a product sold in a can that does exactly what its name says: Through its air pressure and latex-base sealer combination, it helps fix a flat tire.

But the highly successful Fix A Flat, the number one seller among tire-inflation products, is just one of sixty products sold by Nationwide under the brand name SNAP, a line of liquid and aerosol chemical products that can be used to maintain every mechanical function that takes place under the hood of a car. And as Nationwide heads into its third decade of operation, some very important changes are taking place in the corporation—a business that in 1979 was sold by the three original founding partners to The Thompson Company, a diversified investment firm based in Dallas, Texas.

Nationwide is looking to expand its own product line through innovative new-product introductions and acquiring other branded consumer package goods products that will compliment its consumer-oriented business. Already, Nationwide is building a multiproduct line around two of its newest ventures: Outlaw, a horsepower booster, and Outlaw Oil Powerizer, two products that improve engine performance.

Through a complete redesign of packaging graphics, promotional material, and advertising campaigns, Nationwide plans to make its SNAP line of products even more prominent in the marketplace. The firm now manufactures and sells over fifty

The firm's management team consists of (left to right) Mark E. Simon, vice-president/finance; Wesley M. Buckner, president; Jerry Schlesinger, vice-president/sales; and Frank A. Masie, vice-president/operations.

million consumer packages of automotive chemicals each year. And, with a new management team positioned at Nationwide, the firm's 250 employees are hearing a new message. That message makes it clear that it is a new and improved Nationwide, one that is consumer conscious, and concerned with professional, action-oriented management, marketing and operation strategy, and the responsible and skillful development of staff members.

By the end of 1987 Nationwide will have completed a two-part, $7-million capital expansion program. This includes a million-dollar corporate headquarters in a new location in Bucks County where the firm will coordinate all management, sales,

marketing, financial, and customer services. The new, $6-million production facility in Ohio will combine two of Nationwide's plants previously operated in Columbus Grove and Pandora, Ohio. The new facility means that Nationwide will advance from twenty production lines producing fifty units a minute to four production lines with the capacity to produce 200 or more units per minute. This will provide better productivity, more capacity, and room for further expansion in the future.

The new Nationwide corporate headquarters in Bucks County.

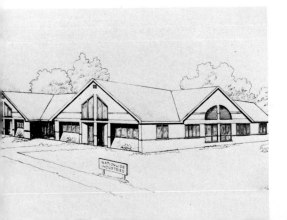

Nationwide's new $6-million manufacturing facility in Pandora, Ohio.

CIGNA CORPORATION

"Much like a prism . . . the focal point from which a broad spectrum of capabilities fans out to clients who are located in every corner of the globe."

It isn't every day that a company draws an analogy between the services it provides and the spectrum of colors created when light passes through a prism. But then again, the business that successfully does so is not just any business; it is CIGNA Corporation and its subsidiaries.

CIGNA is a major enterprise whose operating subsidiaries employ more than 47,000 people on five continents and provide a diverse range of insurance, health care, employee benefits, and financial services to businesses and individuals both in the United States and abroad.

CIGNA was formed in March 1982 from two giants in the industry: INA Corporation and Connecticut General Corporation. With over 300 years of experience between them, both companies brought to the union a history of leadership and innovation. INA was a world leader in the domestic and international property casualty industry; Connecticut General had its strength in the group life, health, and employee benefits industry.

The merger produced the largest investor-owned insurance organization in the country in terms of stockholders' equity and one of the largest financial services companies in the world. CIGNA subsidiaries include one of the largest writers of commercial insurance in the world, the second-leading carrier for group dental and long-term disability insurance, and the sixth-largest provider of group insurance in the nation. In addition, CIGNA's health care subsidiary is the largest investor-owned operator of prepaid health plans in the United States. CIGNA's presence in the international market is equally impressive—with professionals in all 50 states doing business in over 160 countries.

CIGNA has consistently enjoyed one of the highest client-retention rates in the industry—a reflection of its excellent service and its continued emphasis on maintaining solid, long-term relationships with its customers.

As of March 31, 1985, CIGNA Corporation assets exceeded forty billion dollars. Clearly, CIGNA is one of the premier diversified financial services organizations in the world.

CIGNA Corporation, whose operating subsidiaries employ more than 47,000 people on five continents, is headquartered at One Logan Square in downtown Philadelphia.

THE PENN MUTUAL LIFE INSURANCE COMPANY

John W. Hornor, founder.

For John Hornor, it was like a dream come true. The hardware merchant had been studying the concept of life insurance for over two years, expounding its theories and virtues whenever and wherever he could. So, on March 1, 1847, when eighteen people accepted Hornor's invitation to attend a meeting at the Merchant's Exchange in Philadelphia, the history of The Penn Mutual Life Insurance Company began.

It was a humble beginning, and the account of what happened was almost lost in the news of the day, as headlines related the more pressing accounts of Pennsylvanians fighting in Mexico alongside troops from the other twenty-nine states of the Union, and of the continuing debate on the issue of slavery.

But Hornor's presentation on life insurance, a relatively new concept in the United States in the 1800s, was so successful that he was elected secretary of a group that later became

The Penn Mutual Life Insurance Company, the first mutual life insurance company south of New York City and only the seventh in the United States.

The idea of a mutual company, without shareholders and with the benefits of favorable mortality, investment, and expense experience accruing directly to policyowners, appealed strongly to Hornor, and he became one of its foremost champions. The organization's founders, all Quakers, also viewed the concept of mutuality as an expression of the friendliness and justice that embodied the spirit of William Penn, and so they adopted his name for their new venture.

The twenty-seven men who applied for the Penn Mutual charter were named as trustees and took responsi-bility for overseeing the management of the company. Hornor assumed the responsibility of the day-in, day-out work because the trustees respected his mathematical skills and his ability to grasp complicated life insurance statistics. The trustees also agreed that if Hornor was successful, arrangements would be made for his compensation; the trustees themselves would serve without pay.

They also permitted Hornor to rent an office that measured fifteen square feet, with a small cellar below. A local tea merchant agreed to sweep

John E. Tait (left), president and chief operating officer, and Frank K. Tarbox, chairman of the board and chief executive officer, head The Penn Mutual Life Insurance Company.

and dust the office, wash the windows, and keep firewood nearby. In exchange, Hornor allowed the merchant to store tea in the cellar.

It was in that office that Hornor issued the first Penn Mutual policy—on his own life. It was a $5,000 policy, with an annual premium of $152.50, naming his wife as the beneficiary. Hornor's signature appeared twice on the page: on top as the applicant and on the bottom as the attesting official.

The twenty-seven founding members and original trustees were also the first policyholders. They insured their own lives and the lives of their relatives and friends. They agreed that all policyholders would share, on an equitable basis, the risks, expenses, and savings of the business. Each would pay an annual, semiannual, or quarterly premium. And at the end of the year, after obligations were met, each would have the benefit of any excess premium in the form of a dividend.

At the end of the first year, the number of policyholders had grown to 192. The following year the first dividend was declared. It consisted of 80 percent on the cash premium of the preceding nineteen months and in 1849 Penn Mutual issued its first mortgage and began its investment activities.

Although the company's roots were deeply tied to Philadelphia, Penn Mutual began expanding rapidly into surrounding Pennsylvania counties and even outside the state. In 1850 the firm contracted with its first agent outside of Pennsylvania, thus expanding its business into Indiana on March 12. Seven years later Penn Mutual again broadened its business to include New York.

The Penn Mutual of the 1980s is a diversified financial services institution, providing insurance and related financial services to policyowners nationwide through a variety of product distribution channels. Penn Mutual backs its commitment to its clients with a broad range of competitive products and services.

Throughout its history, Penn Mutual has always been an innovator. A recent example of this was the 1982 introduction of a Universal Life product. Universal Life provides competitive insurance protection combined with flexible premium payments and adjusted coverage during the life of the policy. Penn Mutual clearly established itself as a leader in the industry by becoming the first major mutual life insurance company to market this product.

In 1982 Penn Mutual also acquired Janney Montgomery Scott, a securities and investment firm that provides investment services to clients. Other companies in the Penn Mutual family invest in commercial and residential real estate, market fi-

The Penn Mutual Tower, home of The Penn Mutual Life Insurance Company, overlooks Independence Square.

nancial services to upscale professionals, and offer insurance products for the pension market.

Today The Penn Mutual Life Insurance Company ranks among the top twenty of all life insurance firms in the United States, and is the largest such firm chartered in Pennsylvania. With over four billion dollars in assets, insurance in force now exceeds $25 billion. Penn Mutual employs approximately 1,500 people at its 21-story home office complex in Philadelphia, and has 1,600 agents under contract throughout the United States.

PSFS

PSFS, the foundation of the Meritor Financial Group, is the largest bank headquartered in Philadelphia, the second largest in Pennsylvania, and among the top twenty-five banks in the nation based on asset size. Meritor, its parent, operates one of the largest mortgage banking networks in the United States and offers consumer credit services across the nation. More than one million customers in fifty states rely on Meritor for their financial services.

At the dawn of a new nation, however, PSFS began as an idea shared by twelve Philadelphia businessmen in the autumn of 1816. At that time banks would not accept the small deposits of the working people of the city, which had just begun to spread away from its founding site by the Delaware River.

These men drafted a plan for a new type of financial institution— one that would provide savings, security, and prosperity for the tradesmen and laborers who were building a new nation. On December 2, 1816, an entry of twenty-five dollars, the amount of the opening day's deposits, was made with quill pen in the first ledger book of the Philadelphia Saving Fund Society.

Through the years, as the port city of Philadelphia prospered, PSFS grew. It became the rock upon which individuals built their financial security. It became the first word in home mortgage financing for a growing population of immigrants.

Today 20 percent of all Philadelphia-area residents entrust their earnings to PSFS through its nearly 100 branch offices. And while consumer confidence has placed PSFS first among the city's home mortgage lenders, its reputation continues to grow as a competitive source of auto, personal, and student loans.

Businesses in Pennsylvania, New Jersey, and Delaware look to PSFS as a steady source of credit for expansion and other short- or long-term financing. And nearly 10,000 commercial customers rely on PSFS' quick and convenient cash manage-

The PSFS Building in Philadelphia—a National Historic Landmark. Photo by Lawrence S. Williams, Inc.

ment, checking, and investment services.

To meet better the challenges of a changing financial services industry, PSFS became a publicly held corporation in 1983 in the largest primary initial offering in Wall Street history. Today Meritor stock is held by more than 35,000 shareholders.

From the beginning PSFS has been intertwined with the growth of the Philadelphia area. Now Meritor builds on that foundation and its

Philadelphia heritage. But today it provides a growing array of convenient financial services nationwide. So PSFS is still growing, the way it has always grown: through sound, responsible management committed to excellence in providing financial services.

FIRST PENNSYLVANIA BANK N.A.

First Pennsylvania Bank N.A. has the distinction of being the oldest commercial bank in the nation. Its origins can be traced to the Bank of North America, whose charter was approved by the United States Congress on December 31, 1781.

The idea to establish the bank was born when Robert Morris, who only months before had been named superintendent of finance by the Continental Congress, agreed to oversee the formation and capitalization of a financial institution to provide a stable financing source for the fledgling colonial government. A board of twelve directors was subsequently named to help manage the affairs of the new bank, and they tapped Thomas Willing, a successful merchant, fellow board director, and a partner of Morris, as president of the institution. On January 7, 1782, the Bank of North America opened for business in a modest three-story building on the north side of Chestnut Street, a little west of Third.

Morris' plan for capitalization of the bank was simple. The sum of $400,000 was to be raised in shares of $400 each, payable in gold or silver. Wealthy colonists were invited to become subscribers, and they did, to the sum of $70,000. The list of original subscribers was impressive, and included such prominent American patriots as Benjamin Franklin, Thomas Jefferson, and John Paul Jones.

But $70,000 was a long way from $400,000, the bank's intended capitalization. Then, in a stroke of good luck, John Laurens, a special minister to the French Court, persuaded the King of France to personally guarantee a Dutch loan to America. Before long, the new financial institution was well on its way.

The Bank of North America's turbulent early years were dominated by financial tasks ranging from financing the Revolutionary War to making loans to the City of Philadelphia. However, under the leadership of Morris, the institution began to prove its worth in serving individuals as

Robert Morris, financier, Revolutionary War hero, and founder of the Bank of North America.

well as governments.

Several prominent Philadelphia financial organizations figured in the formation of the First Pennsylvania Bank as it is known today. One, the Pennsylvania Company for Insurance on Lives and Granting Annuities, was chartered by the state in 1812, principally as an insurance company to compete with British insurers who then dominated the American mar-

This building housed the original business office of the Bank of North America, the cornerstone of what would become First Pennsylvania Bank N.A.

ket. Its charter also empowered the firm to engage in banking activities, and by 1872 the directors of the company discontinued the insurance business and turned entirely to banking.

That decision proved to be a wise one. Benefiting handsomely from the synergism between trust activities and the more traditional forms of banking, the Pennsylvania Company expanded at a rapid rate. In 1929 it joined forces with the Bank of North America to form the base from which First Pennsylvania Bank N.A. has since evolved.

Three smaller mergers were effected during the 1930s. Immediately after World War II three more institutions were absorbed, and the name of the parent bank was changed to the Pennsylvania Company for Banking and Trust. The final link in the succession of major mergers was forged in 1955 with the acquisition of the highly respected First National Bank of Philadelphia.

First National had been founded in 1863 under the leadership of Jay Cooke, the legendary Philadelphia financier. First National Bank of Philadelphia was granted the first charter under federal legislation authorizing the creation of a new federally supervised banking system to operate side by side with state-chartered banks.

The institution was redesignated The First Pennsylvania Bank and Trust Company under its existing state charter. In 1969 First Pennsylvania Corporation, a one-bank holding company, was formed to broaden the scope of the firm's overall operation with the bank as its principal operating subsidiary. Finally, in 1974 the bank was converted from a state to a nationally chartered institution.

Today, with $5.5 billion in deposits, First Pennsylvania Bank N.A. continues to work to provide financial services through seventy branches in Southeast Pennsylvania and a regional market that extends from the New England states south to Virginia and westward inclusive of Ohio.

THE STROH BREWERY COMPANY

The Stroh Brewery Company is America's largest family-owned and -operated brewer. Founded in 1850 in Detroit, the firm has grown to include six breweries located throughout the United States. Following the tradition of eighteenth-century German brewers, the Stroh family has gained a reputation for excellence. German brewing techniques were the basis for the beer produced by The F.&M. Schaefer Brewing Co. and that foundation of quality brewing made Schaefer a natural choice to join the Stroh family.

In the spring of 1972 Schaefer's Lehigh Valley brewery began operations at its new facility. At the time the operation was called "the world's most modern brewery," a description earned by its prototype equipment that set the standard for the industry.

The distinctive building, with its glass front showcasing two enormous stainless steel kettles, has become a local landmark. Located at the intersection of routes 22 and 100, the 160-acre property had been farmed for generations by the Adams family. The brewery's hospitality room is decorated in Early American and Pennsylvania Dutch motifs, utilizing beams from the original house and barn.

When the brewery was owned by Schaefer, the hospitality room was known as the "Stein Room." It housed the Schaefer family's priceless stein collection, which has since been relocated and has become part of the Stroh stein collection at its corporate headquarters in Detroit, Michigan. Renamed Strohhaus, the hospitality room offers guests the opportunity to sample the various beers brewed at the facility.

In 1981 The F.&M. Schaefer Brewing Co. was acquired by The Stroh Brewery Company. Stroh has since expanded and improved the facility, investing thirty million dollars in additions such as the new brew house. The renovations enable the facility to produce Stroh's fire-brewed beer, using an Old World method that requires an open flame under a copper kettle.

At the Lehigh Valley facility, the firm produces several brands of beer, including Stroh's, Schaefer, Piels, and Schlitz. The acquisition of the Jos. Schlitz Company in 1982 made Stroh the third-largest brewer in the nation. Each Stroh brand has its own distinctive taste and individual brewing method. The Schaefer brand has the distinction of being America's oldest lager beer. Stroh brands are distributed in all fifty states and worldwide to Sweden, England, Korea, Puerto Rico, Guam, and other Caribbean islands.

The Lehigh Valley brewery operates twenty-four hours a day and employs over 700 persons. The plant's general manager is James McEvoy.

The Stroh Brewery Company is headed by Peter W. Stroh, the sixth generation of his family to run the corporation. As an active participant in the restoration of the Statue of Liberty, Peter Stroh has joined Lee Iacocca in his strong support of the restoration project. In the past two years Stroh has sponsored a five-mile "Run for Liberty," allowing all Americans to participate in the statue's restoration.

In its role as a responsible corporate citizen, The Stroh Brewery Company has supported national and community-based activities that contribute to various charitable, educational, and minority organizations. In the Lehigh Valley, Stroh has helped sponsor the Musikfest in Bethlehem, a nationally recognized music festival that is held for ten days during the month of August.

The Stroh Brewery Company, America's largest family-owned and -operated brewer, opened the Lehigh Valley facility in 1972. "The world's most modern brewery" is located at the intersection of routes 22 and 100.

CONNAUGHT LABORATORIES, INC.

Connaught Laboratories, Inc., in Swiftwater, Pennsylvania, is a component of the Life Sciences Division of the Canadian Development Corporation. The facility in Swiftwater is a wholly owned subsidiary of Connaught Laboratories, Ltd., based in Toronto, Canada. Connaught purchased the laboratories in 1978, and now offers the broadest range of vaccines available in the Western World.

The history of the Swiftwater facility dates back to 1896, when Dr. Richard Slee traveled to the Pocono Mountains for a period of convalescence following a bout with cholera. At the Swiftwater Inn he met and fell in love with the owner's daughter, Ella McGuinnis, and eventually married her. Following their marriage Dr. Slee purchased sixty acres of pastureland from his wife's family and constructed a small stone building to serve as a laboratory to produce a new type of smallpox vaccine. His laboratory went on to produce nearly all of the smallpox vaccine used by the military forces during the Spanish-American War.

In 1911 Dr. Slee began production of diphtheria and tetanus antitoxins. Fifteen years later management of the laboratory changed hands, yet expansion continued. Through the years the laboratory has remained an important biological facility and has shown continued growth and expansion under the direction of a series of owners.

The United States military has always represented a large part of the business at the Swiftwater laboratory. During World War I the facility expanded to manufacture antitoxins, and during World War II it produced half the supply of antitoxins and tetanus toxoids used by the military. Currently, the facilities at Swiftwater consist of twenty-four buildings including the original structure of 1896.

The Swiftwater laboratory has always played a significant role in the production of vaccines and the development of preventive medicines. Connaught Laboratories is the only biological-based company in North America, and it produces the broadest range of vaccines. The firm manufactures polio vaccines, including the inactive Salk vaccine and the oral Sabin vaccine. Connaught also produces the diphtheria-tetanus-pertussis (DTP) vaccine, as well as a yellow fever vaccine of which it is the sole

---

A mountain trout stream cuts across the beautiful estates of Connaught Laboratories. The quality-control building (pictured) is one of twenty-four structures at the Swiftwater facility.

manufacturer in North America. The facility is the largest producer of influenza vaccine in the world. Connaught Laboratories also produces the meningococcal and the cholera vaccines.

The Swiftwater facility has developed into a close-knit unit with a family and community orientation. There are several third-generation employees included in the company's work force of over 200, and many are drawn from the local community. The laboratories have a significant impact on the local economy and are involved in area charities, education, and sports. Currently, the Swiftwater facility is headed by David J. Williams, vice-president and general manager; Dr. Don P. Metzgar, vice-president of operations; and Patrick J. Sheridan, controller.

Connaught Laboratories, Inc., is involved in an active research program based in Toronto at the Connaught Research Institute. Part of the research group is housed at the Swiftwater laboratory. Genetic engineering is one of the areas being explored for the development of new and synthetic vaccines. Insulin was first produced commercially by Connaught Laboratories, and another area being studied is that of insulin research.

BUCKS COUNTY BANK & TRUST COMPANY

The decade of the 1950s was a time of incredible growth for Bucks County. U.S. Steel was building its mammoth Fairless Works, and residential communities such as Levittown were occupied by a steady influx of workers as soon as they were built. Nationwide, business was thriving as the post-World War II economy expanded. For the banking industry, it was a time of tremendous opportunity.

The local independent banks of Bucks County, with their heritage of community service and dedication to customers, had long recognized the potential in their backyards. "Fellow bankers of Bucks County, I entreat you to look more closely into the needs and opportunities of your own Bucks County," Jesse H. Harper beseeched the Bucks County Bankers Association in 1925, a year after its formation.

In 1953 Philadelphia National Bank merged with First National Bank of Conshohocken, among the first intercounty mergers in Eastern Pennsylvania. "The move reflects our mature judgment that banks should follow their customers," Philadelphia National president Frederic A. Potts reasoned. That reasoning made good business sense for the large metropolitan banks but was contrary to the community banking ideals espoused by the local independent banks of Bucks County.

On April 4, 1955, a handful of bankers, who had taken the initiative to preserve their banks, reopened their institutions as Bucks County Bank & Trust Company offices. Together the four banks had assets of about sixteen million dollars and the determination to persevere as community banks. Bucks County Bank was a combination of The First National Bank of Perkasie (founded in 1901), Quakertown Trust Company (1904), Perkasie Trust Company (1923), and Dublin National Bank (1927).

The First National Bank of Perkasie was formed about twenty-five years after the tiny borough of Perkasie was incorporated. Quakertown, al-

The headquarters of Bucks County Bank and Independence Bancorp, built in 1983, is located just outside Perkasie Borough in East Rockhill Township, Upper Bucks County.

though founded by Quakers in the 1730s, was populated primarily by the aggressive Pennsylvania Germans and was growing quickly when the Quakertown Trust Company was formed. The Perkasie Trust Company came along to service a growing population just before The First National Bank of Perkasie moved from its

original Victorian home office into a marble structure that some thirty years later became the first headquarters of Bucks County Bank. Dublin National opened for business in a community carved by Irish pioneers from neighboring Hilltown and Bed-

In 1924 this building replaced the Victorian home used by The First National Bank of Perkasie. The marble structure became the first headquarters of Bucks County Bank in 1955. Located at Seventh and Chestnut streets in Perkasie, it is now a branch office and houses several bank departments.

This Victorian home was the first office of The First National Bank of Perkasie, circa 1901.

minster townships. Its first office was a two-story brick house located not far from the current office on Main Street, constructed by the new Bucks

Morrisville Bank, founded in 1920, moved into these quarters in 1923. The stone building, known as the Hogeland House, was erected in 1802. Bucks County Bank's Morrisville main office is still located there.

County Bank in 1956.

These four institutions had been formed during times of rapid growth in Upper Bucks. In forming the larger Bucks County Bank, the founders positioned themselves in the mainstream of unprecedented countywide growth. Indeed, two more institutions were eventually added to the banking network.

In 1968 Chalfont National Bank (formed in 1925) joined Bucks County Bank, extending the institution's reach into the central portion of the county. And in 1982 Morrisville Bank (formed in 1920) joined Bucks County Bank, bringing with it a heritage of community banking in the lower reaches of the county, an area where Bucks County Bank had not previously operated. The Morrisville merger added four new offices in a region considered to be among the earliest settled lands in the state.

About the time a generation had grown up with Bucks County Bank, the industry was again in a period of opportunity and change. Federal deregulation was allowing banks to offer more products and services, opening up the industry to more competition. State governments were also loosening regulations, permitting intrastate and interstate expansion. Rules the banking industry had lived by since the Great Depression were changing rapidly.

In the face of a new challenge to community banking, Bucks County Bank formed a holding company called Independence Bancorp, Inc., in 1982. Independence Bancorp was a response to the new opportunities for similar community-oriented institutions to compete against metropolitan banks.

Bucks County Bank welcomed two more institutions under the Independence banner in 1983: Unionbank of the Lehigh Valley and Cheltenham Bank. Unionbank celebrated its fiftieth anniversary in 1985. Like Bucks County Bank, Unionbank is a strong, local institution with its focus on one region, the Lehigh Valley. Cheltenham Bank, sixty-one years old in 1985, was cited by the Bank Administration Institute in 1983 as "one of the nation's top banks in terms of financial performance."

By 1985 Bucks County Bank had 450 employees, assets of $700 million, and sixteen offices, with a seventeenth office receiving regulatory approval at mid-year. Independence Bancorp reported assets of $1.3 billion early in 1985, and plotted this strategy for the future: to stay close to what it knows best—basic banking business; to focus on selected market niches, such as the consumer market and small to medium-size businesses; and to differentiate itself on the basis of local identity, local decision making, and quality of service.

Together, the three institutions rank near the top in their peer group. Through their association with Independence Bancorp, they strive to carry out the goal that made them one: to retain their local identities while remaining responsive to their communities and customers.

UNION FIDELITY LIFE INSURANCE CO.

Union Fidelity Life Insurance Co. had one goal in sight in 1958 when it opened a small office in Center City, Philadelphia: to provide its customers with quality insurance plans. Today, from its corporate headquarters in historic Bucks County, Union Fidelity services more than one million customers nationwide. And it is recognized as one of the largest and most successful direct-to-the-consumer insurance specialists in the nation.

"Our success in the direct-response industry," says Ronald K. Holmberg, president and chairman of the board, "comes, I believe, from our philosophy of providing customers with top-quality service—first and foremost. That's the cornerstone around which our business was built."

In keeping with that philosophy, Union Fidelity's marketing efforts concentrate on offering a wide variety of quality life and health insurance plans to people of all ages. The firm is especially recognized for its services to senior citizens. In fact, since Medicare began in 1966, Union Fidelity's Medicare Supplement plans have protected over 2.2 million people aged sixty-five and over.

In addition to marketing and administering a variety of life and health plans, Union Fidelity is fast becoming a service and distribution channel for numerous other products and services. This expansion into new fields can be directly attributed to the June 1981 purchase of Union Fidelity by the Chicago-based Combined International Corporation.

At that time Union Fidelity joined Combined Insurance Company of America as one of the two major wholly owned subsidiaries in the Combined family. Since then, Ryan Insurance Group and Rollins Burdick Hunter, both Chicago-based firms, have been added. The Combined Group covers all areas of insurance sales and distribution, including direct sales, brokerage services, and direct response.

Union Fidelity Life Insurance Co. became a wholly owned subsidiary of the Combined International Corporation in 1981. The corporate headquarters is located in historic Bucks County.

To spread its message to the marketplace, Union Fidelity produces over 100 million direct-response advertising pieces each year. What's more, successful television and radio advertising—with such well-known endorsers as entertainers Danny Thomas and the late Arthur Godfrey and Pat O'Brien—has been used to market the firm's products and plans.

Union Fidelity employs nearly 1,000 highly trained professionals from the Philadelphia area to work in such fields as marketing, copywriting, graphic arts, printing services, market research, media, customer services, claims settlement, telemarketing, accounting, legal, actuarial, and computer services.

And for these employees, Union Fidelity Insurance Company provides many important services. There are behavior modification classes for those who wish to stop smoking or lose weight, and its Child Development Center, which opened in 1980, is well known in the Philadelphia area for providing an exceptional educational preschool environment.

BONNEY FORGE CORPORATION

The name "Bonney" has been synonymous with quality hand tools since 1876, the year a man by the name of C.S. Bonney started a small tool works company in Philadelphia.

Today that same name and reputation for quality products is the backbone of Bonney Forge Corporation, an international manufacturer of forged steel fittings and steel valves headquartered in Allentown.

The tool works plant that Bonney started in Philadelphia actually moved to Allentown in 1907, where a small drop-forging department was built for producing forged wrenches and tools. It wasn't long before trade shows featured displays of Bonney's new product—row after row of the well-known Bonney wrenches and hand tools, lined up side by side like marching soldiers.

The department increased rapidly and Bonney flourished. During World War I the firm supplied its regular line of tools to the U.S. government as well as a variety of war materials, including forged parts for gun carriages, mine-casting parts, motor truck bolts, and automatic pistol forgings.

In 1931 the firm added to its lineup two patented pipe-welding fittings—the Weldolet and Thredolet. During World War II Bonney worked

John A. Leone, president of Bonney Forge Corporation.

again for the Armed Forces, devoting 100 percent of its production to Army and Navy supplies.

After the war Bonney continued as a leader in the manufacturing and worldwide distribution of mechanics' hand tools. But major research and development focused on forged fitting products that would carry Bonney Forge into the future, among them the Bonney "O'Let" pipe fit-

In 1915 employees of Bonney Forge gathered for this company portrait.

tings, a branch connection for energy and industrial piping systems.

The Bonney Forge history includes several ownerships. In 1953 the business, which had long since been sold by the Bonney family, was sold to Miller Manufacturing Company in Detroit. Miller was then purchased by Gulf & Western Industries of Houston, Texas, in December 1964.

In 1982 Gulf & Western announced that it was going to divest of its holdings in Bonney Forge. Two years later a group of investors, headed by John A. Leone, then president of Bonney Forge Corporation, announced that it would purchase the firm from Gulf & Western.

Today the private corporation headed by Leone is a leading manufacturer of forged steel fittings and valves made from carbon steel, alloy steel, and stainless steel. Manufacturing facilities include three plants in the United States and three plants in Italy. About 40 percent of the Italian production is shipped as forgings to Bonney's U.S. operations for machining and assembling, while the remaining 60 percent is sold as finished products throughout Europe and other foreign countries, enhancing Bonney Forge Corporation's worldwide reputation for product integrity.

HIGH INDUSTRIES, INC.

A precast concrete project at One Logan Square, Philadelphia.

The company has grown into a multimillion-dollar giant. Yet it still receives phone calls from people asking for High Welding—who remember the old days when Sanford High, and his brother Ben, founded a small welding firm on West Lemon Street in Lancaster. The year was 1931.

Today High Steel Structures, Inc., is one of the largest and most respected fabricators and erectors of steel bridges east of the Mississippi, with involvement in bridge rehabilitation work as well as the construction of commercial and industrial buildings. And from its small downtown location, it has mushroomed into a sprawling complex that includes an ultramodern office, two production plants, a huge yard, and several auxiliary buildings in Lancaster, plus a third production plant in Williamsport.

One only has to look at the figures from the past decade to witness the company's phenomenal growth. During that time it has made the transition from a single-unit operation to nine operating companies that are backed by two centralized support groups to cover administrative and finance functions. And the employment roster has swelled from an average 500 in 1975 to over 1,500 today.

Every company has its turning point, sparked by a change in leadership, an improvement in technology, an expansion into new territories. For High, the leadership that spurred corporate growth can be credited to Sanford High's sons: Calvin, who came on board in the early 1950s, and Dale, who followed in 1963.

Another turning point, a move that clearly took the firm into the 1980s with tremendous growth opportunities, occurred in 1977 with the formation of High Industries, Inc.—parent company to all of the High interests.

Today High Industries, Inc., is made up of four groups of successful operations, some developed by the High family and others acquired as whollyowned subsidiaries. These include:

THE STEEL GROUP

High Steel Structures, Inc., still the kingpin of all the High companies, has the most employees and largest sales. Operating in twenty-three states, it has been involved in a long list of outstanding projects—including the longest curved steelplate girder bridge in Maryland, the I-95 Baltimore Harbor bridge, the steel superstructures of the Exton Shopping Mall in Chester County, and the Woolworth Distribution Center in northern Lancaster County. Many of the fabricated steel structures are actually assembled in the yard for reaming (bolt holes) to ensure the numerous components will fit properly when delivered to the job site.

The Steel Group also includes High Steel Service Center, Inc., a wholesale house for steel products and processing services started in 1978 in Lancaster.

THE CONCRETE GROUP

High Concrete Structures, Inc., of Denver R3, formed as Kurtz Precast Corporation and acquired in 1977 by High Industries, saw its customer base greatly enhanced with the 1982 acquisition of the Formigli Corporation of Williamstown Junction and Vineland, New Jersey. Together the two firms make up one of the largest and most important sources of precast and prestressed concrete east of the Mississippi, with start-to-finish capabilities in design assistance, manufacture, and erection of precast buildings, bridges, and parking garages.

High Concrete and Formigli have also worked on some outstanding projects, including the HUD Headquarters in Washington, D.C., One Logan Square in Philadelphia, Tannen Towers in Atlantic City (the tallest precast structure in the Western Hemisphere), and the Goldman Sachs building in New York City. And the group kicked off 1985 with its first joint venture—the Park Plaza Condo in Wilmington, Delaware. The project included two towers (nineteen stories each that house 240

Greenfield Corporate Center, in its country-like setting, is managed by High Associates, Ltd.

condominiums), a three-level parking garage, plus a five-level promenade consisting of apartments, exercise room, and swimming pool.

REAL ESTATE & CONSTRUCTION GROUP

The High name has been attached to or affiliated with a growing number of corporate centers, multihousing/apartment communities, and residential developments—in the areas of leasing, management, sales, construction, and development in Pennsylvania and New Jersey.

High Associates, Ltd., is a commercial/industrial brokerage operation formed in 1980 as a complement to High Realty Corporation, the group's residential real estate listing and sales office formed in 1976. In addition, there is a High Construction, Inc., acquired in 1978 as Lantz Builders, Inc., and renamed in 1986 to reflect its growth into a multistate contracting firm.

THE CABLE TV GROUP

The newest group in the High Industries operating companies list is comprised of three Cable TV systems, two in North Carolina (Univision) and one in Kentucky (Southern Cablevision). With a customer base of

A typical modern building constructed by High Construction, Inc.

12,000 subscribers, the group is currently enjoying rapid expansion with new construction, expanded program options, and intensified direct sales efforts.

The advantages of forming High Industries as a holding company have offered benefits to management and employees alike. Under the umbrella of a parent company, employees enjoy a high quality of life through benefit packages that were impossible to obtain when the individual companies operated independently. And since inventory controls, data processing, and accounting have been centralized on large-capacity comput-

ers, managers can make better operating decisions.

High customers have greatly benefited as well. Since each firm offers compatible services and products, they can be tied together to make a more competitive bid for a job.

On the Park Plaza Condo project, for example, Formigli is producing all of the hollowcore, balcony/beams, and interior core wall. High Concrete Structures is producing the columns, girders, beams, 24- and 32-inch tees, stairs, load-bearing wall panels, and exterior spandrels. And High Steel Structures is fabricating special steel shapes and tee sections, and providing the crane service necessary for erection.

One of the principal reasons for High Industries' success is its pride in quality and craftmanship, coupled with its understanding of customer needs.

As Sanford High used to tell his employees in the early 1930s: "Put down a good weld . . . and give good measure." A good weld meant quality work. A good measure meant extra effort, doing everything possible to stay on the leading edge.

High Industries, Inc., has never lost sight of Sanford High's way of doing business. Through tough, hard work, adherence to strategic principles, and responding to changes in the economic and competitive environment, the High management team looks to the 1990s with confidence.

I-95 in Baltimore, Maryland—a High Steel Structures, Inc., project.

531

KNOUSE FOODS COOPERATIVE, INC.

From a small beginning in April 1949, Knouse Foods Cooperative, Inc., has grown to become one of the largest apple-processing companies in the world. The firm was created when a group of prominent fruit growers in Pennsylvania, Virginia, West Virginia, and Maryland, feeling the need for more efficient marketing methods for their apples, joined forces to purchase the processing plants once owned by their leader, M.E. Knouse.

The new venture was not undertaken lightly. The Knouse Foods plants were valuable facilities. Purchasing them involved commitment of family savings and monies borrowed with mortgages on family farms. It was among the most costly initial cooperative capitalizations undertaken in the country, but the growers recognized the pressing need for a reliable processor as a purchaser for their fruit.

South-central Pennsylvania is apple country—the home of some of the finest orchards in the world. The slopes of the Blue Ridge mountains extend from Pennsylvania through Maryland and into Virginia, providing the rich soil and perfect drainage that each fall yields millions of bushels of outstanding fruit.

Knouse Foods Cooperative is owned by 158 apple growers throughout the Appalachian region. The cooperative provides them with a ready market for their crop while the growers provide Knouse Foods with a reliable source of fruit. Through their cooperative structure, the growers have benefited both as producers and as owners of the processing company.

LUCKY LEAF

Knouse Foods is best known to the buying public under its brand name, "Lucky Leaf," a label loved throughout the nation and found on more than 150 products including applesauce, apple slices, pie fillings, fruit juices, apple butter, and vinegar. Knouse also processes fruit for several top-selling private labels, and for commercial food service groups.

Lucky Leaf products have earned national recognition for many different reasons. Lucky Leaf whole baked apples, Dutch baked apples, and sparkling cider have won national awards for product and packaging innovation. The sparkling cider (a nonalcoholic champagne-like beverage) was developed for sale to nations that prohibit consumption of alcohol and won a Presidential "E" Award as an export product. It has gone on to extraordinary domestic popularity as well.

Lucky Leaf was the first processor to adopt sugar- and sodium-free natural applesauce and was also the first processor to convert its entire production facilities to wire-welded cans, eliminating lead solder from its food packaging. Lucky Leaf is continuing that tradition of industry leadership with its adoption of European-style aseptic packaging of its applesauce products.

MUSSELMAN'S

The Musselman family began canning apple products in Lancaster County early in the twentieth century. In 1907 they purchased a small

The old and the new are combined in these state-of-the-art packages (no refrigeration required) with the old line graphics of Lucky Leaf and Musselman's products.

cannery from the growers' cooperative of Biglersville, Adams County, and started the company that eventually became a world-class fruit processor.

The Musselman's brand gained early notice during World War I, when its plants at Biglersville and Gardners managed to maintain a steady flow of canned fruit despite labor, fuel, and transportation shortages. But the real key to Musselman's success was the innovative spirit of C.H. Musselman, its first president.

An imaginative grower, willing to take the long-range risks in planting orchards with an untested product, Musselman introduced Montmorency red tart cherry trees to Pennsylvania in the early 1920s. That decision led to outstanding success with Musselman's canned cherries.

An innovative processor as well, Musselman introduced canned applesauce in 1929. It became the flagship of the Musselman's product line. By the 1950s Musselman's was producing over fifteen million cases of applesauce each year and had more than 3,500 acres devoted to growing cherries, apples, and peaches.

The corporation was also early to recognize the marketing power of mass media; Musselman's celebrated its fiftieth anniversary in 1957 with saturation radio advertising and an elaborate television campaign led by Arlene Francis with her "Home" show, and Don McNeil's "Breakfast Club."

In 1960 Musselman's was acquired by the Pet Milk Company of St. Louis. The firm operated as a division of Pet Milk until 1981. It was purchased by Knouse Foods Cooperative in 1984.

Knouse Foods operates eight processing plants located at Peach Glen, Chambersburg, Orrtanna, Gardners, and Biglersville, Pennsylvania; Inwood, West Virginia; Newfane, New York; and Paw Paw, Michigan. With the capacity to store more than 3.6 million bushels of apples (including 652,000 in controlled-atmosphere storage), the company has been able to change a highly seasonal business into an efficient year-round commercial operation.

Continuing to meet challenges with innovative solutions, Knouse Foods has solved ecological difficulties with a cogeneration system that powers the Orrtanna plant with fuel derived from pomace, the pasty waste product of processed apples. Knouse also uses purified wastewater holding tanks to raise trout for the fish and game commission as a public service to area sportsmen.

Dean L. Carey succeeded M.E. Knouse as general manager of Knouse Foods in 1963, and as president of the cooperative in 1966. Carey says, "I'm proud that Knouse Foods Cooperative is recognized throughout the nation as an outstanding example of how growers and a processor willing to work together can produce success."

533

THE UNITED TELEPHONE COMPANY OF PENNSYLVANIA

The United Telephone Company of Pennsylvania is the third-largest telephone company in the Commonwealth. Its service area, principally South-central and Western Pennsylvania, includes about 6,015 square miles covering parts of twenty-six counties and more than ninety incorporated boroughs. Headquartered in Carlisle, the firm has operations in and around the towns of Bedford, Butler, Chambersburg, Columbia, Hanover, Martinsburg, Mifflintown, Mill Hall, and Waynesboro. United's 1,500 employees serve 256,000 access lines.

The company's service area has traditionally had a small-town and rural character, even though its operating territory extends to within fifteen miles of Harrisburg, York, and Lancaster, and within thirty miles of Pittsburgh. Many of these rural areas are developing a suburban character as industry and people realize the advantages offered by small-town locations.

Such highways as the Pennsylvania Turnpike and interstates 70, 79, 80, and 81 cross United's service area, providing easy access to major markets, outdoor recreational facilities,

and tourist attractions including the Gettysburg Battlefield and the Pennsylvania Dutch Country.

United offers corporate clients a complete range of communication services from single-line systems to sophisticated switching systems. The firm also provides telephone service to several prestigious colleges and universities in the area. Federal government facilities are also served by United.

United Telephone of Pennsylvania is part of the United Telephone System-Eastern Group, consisting of six telephone companies owned and operated by United Telecommunications, Inc., of Kansas City, Missouri. The six Eastern Group companies are Hillsborough and Montgomery Telephone Company, New Jersey Telephone Company, United-Sussex Telephone Company, Inc., United Telephone Company of Pennsylvania, United Telephone Company of New Jersey, and West Jersey Telephone Co. Together these companies serve 364,000 access lines with 1,983 employees.

United Telecommunications, Inc., is a diversified communications company with revenues of $3.7 billion and assets of $6 billion. It provides information transfer over voice, data, and video teleconferencing networks. It also offers other advanced telecom-

munication products and services that complement its network services.

United of Pennsylvania has consistently been a trend-setter in the telephone industry. The Cumberland Valley Telephone Company, a predecessor to United of Pennsylvania, offered customers dial service in the Harrisburg area as early as 1916. Most phone companies did not offer dial service until the mid-1950s.

Similarly, when digital switching came to the forefront in the 1970s, United of Pennsylvania became the first United phone company to install a digital office. (Digital switches send phone conversations as numeric codes rather than electrical signals.) The first digital office was installed in Emlenton, Pennsylvania, on September 23, 1978. By 1990 over 70 percent of the firm's offices will be digital.

Digital offices allow United Telephone to offer enhanced customer services such as call waiting tones and equal access. The Butler digital office was the First United Telephone System area to allow customers a choice of long-distance companies.

Digital technology goes hand in hand with the use of fiber optics, glass fibers used to transmit conversations. Fiber optics send voice signals using light pulses rather than

United Telephone Company's Pennsylvania operations and control center is located in Carlisle.

conventional electrical pulses. Fiber-optics technology offers greater capacity than copper cable and has a great weight and size advantage. In November 1978 the United Telephone Company of Pennsylvania became the first phone company in the Commonwealth to splice fiber-optic cable into service, using aerial, buried, and duct plant. There are currently eight fiber-optic routes in the state, totaling sixty-eight miles. United installed two more stretches of fiber-optic cable in 1985.

Most recently, United installed a new computerized service order entry and customer records billing system. This system has eliminated much paperwork and standardized service procedures by computerizing the service order, customer records, and billing procedures.

These and other new technological advances have increased United's efficiency by allowing for the consolidation of many functions. In its move to consolidate, United of Pennsylvania has established just one site for operator services in the state. It has also built an Operations Control Center in Carlisle to handle key service functions throughout the Commonwealth. Occupied in early 1985, the facility consolidates key customer service, network analysis, central office and line testing, and dispatch and repair functions previously handled in other offices. In 1981 United had thirteen offices to perform these functions. By the end of 1985 all were handled from the Operations Control Center in Carlisle.

By continuing the consolidation process, keeping abreast of the latest technology, and continuing to further develop the skills of its employees, United Telephone Company of Pennsylvania continues to fulfill its historic role of providing good service at reasonable cost throughout its Pennsylvania service area.

An early United crew took a break from stringing wire to pose for this photograph. The crew was working near Newville in 1907.

HARSCO CORPORATION

From its inception in 1853 as a manufacturer of railroad cars in Harrisburg to its current status as one of the nation's 300 largest industrial companies, Harsco Corporation's expansion and business philosophy have been steeped in the conservative traditions of the surrounding Pennsylvania Dutch heritage.

Harsco has over 290 manufacturing, distribution, reclamation, and service facilities in forty states and twelve foreign countries. The firm owns more than eight million square feet of production capacity and has assets exceeding $800 million.

The corporation's twenty-three products and services are spread among fifteen divisions, four of which are headquartered in Pennsylvania. About 3,500 residents of the Commonwealth are employees of Harsco, out of a total worldwide work force numbering approximately 12,000.

Harsco classifies its operations among four business segments: Defense, Primary Metals, Construction, and Fabricated Metals.

The Defense segment is situated in York County on a 130-acre complex with one million square feet of pro-

Jeffrey J. Burdge, Harsco's chairman and chief executive officer.

duction capacity and 2,700 employees. Harsco is the sole-source producer of mobile howitzers, ammunition supply vehicles, and battlefield recovery units for the United States government and over twenty-five free world nations.

The Primary Metals segment is led by metal reclamation and related spe-

cialty support services for steel producers and also includes the production of precision valves, high-pressure cylinders, and cryogenic storage containers.

The Construction segment includes scaffolding and shoring equipment, roofing granules, and industrial blasting materials as well as grating products, commercial doors, and plastic products.

The Fabricated Metals Division includes railway maintenance equipment, titanium and composite products, pipe fittings, process equipment, propane tanks, and structural panels.

Harsco traces its lineage to Central Pennsylvania in the early 1850s with the formation of the Harrisburg Car Manufacturing Company by eight entrepreneurs. After the Civil War its focus shifted to the production of oil tank cars and general machining activities. By the 1890s the firm, renamed Harrisburg Pipe and Pipe Bending Company, had become a leading producer of freezing cans and containers for ammonia gas refriger-

Harsco is the world's leading metal reclamation contractor and currently serves over sixty-five steel production sites worldwide.

ant. That began the corporation's long involvement with the storage and transportation of gases under pressure.

At the turn of the century the company began construction of an open-hearth and rolling mill close to the state capital, where it produced high-pressure seamless steel gas cylinders. Today Harsco is the oldest and leading domestic manufacturer of those cylinders, which are still produced at the same location. The company renamed itself Harrisburg Steel Corporation in 1935.

Harsco's involvement with defense activities also has a distinguished history. During World War I it manufactured shrapnel under contract to the U.S. Army. During World War II Harrisburg Steel produced 500-pound bombs for the U.S. government and the Allies.

Soon after the war president Joseph T. Simpson initiated an acquisition strategy to broaden the scope of products supplied to industrial markets. Simpson, who guided the evolution of the modern Harsco, led the company for thirty-six years. Since the early 1950s over seventy businesses have been acquired. The firm changed its name to Harsco Corporation in 1956, reflecting its expansion program and the international scope of the organization.

Harsco is the world's leading reclaimer or recycler of metallics from steel-making slag, and a major worldwide marketer of slag aggregates used in road base, rail ballast, and structural block. Other significant market positions include scaffolding and shoring products, industrial grating, plastic pipe products, maintenance equipment for the railroad industry, and air-cooled heat exchangers. The firm is also a leading producer of composite pressure vessels, cryogenic storage containers, and precision valves.

Currently the corporation is divesting product lines or divisions that no longer conform to its revised corporate strategies. Harsco continues to emphasize new product development. In accordance with this priority, engineers have developed several specialty plastic products including a square pipe for optical fiber installations, a compact heat exchanger for precise temperature control of areas such as computer environments, and a double-tube heat exchanger that prevents potable water contamination.

As it moves toward the twenty-first century, Harsco has made a broad commitment to upgrade technology throughout the corporation, applying new methods to such func-

Since 1960 Harsco has been the sole-source producer of the M88 battlefield recovery vehicle at its York County defense facility.

tions as engineering, marketing, distribution, and manufacturing. While the firm will continue to emphasize metalworking, its horizons have expanded into a wider range of metals, a higher level of technical specialty in both new products and markets served, and an entrance into some nonmetallic areas. This imaginative concept for Harsco's future reflects the leadership of Jeffrey J. Burdge, who has been chairman since 1983.

Harsco anticipates that growth will continue through both acquisition and internal development within a framework that balances the risks of diversification against the continued prudent management of current businesses, in keeping with the firm's conservative traditions. The tenets for growth contained in the company's strategic five-year plan include investment direction, cost reduction, technology advancement, international expansion, and product line management.

Technology, manufacturing, and computer advancement teams are in place throughout the corporation. The firm anticipates that its strong financial condition will afford an opportunity of deploying significant resources into both new and existing businesses, presenting Harsco Corporation with a window of opportunity for continued growth throughout the 1990s and beyond.

THE FIRST NATIONAL BANK OF PENNSYLVANIA

In 1852 a one-room banking firm named M. Sanford and Company first opened its doors to the public in Erie, Pennsylvania. Eleven years later, under the auspices of the newly created national banking system, Myron Sanford and his brother-in-law, Judah Colt Spencer, formed a partnership and received National Bank Charter Number 12 as The First National Bank of Erie.

Those were not easy times for the country or for Erie, a struggling young city with a population of 6,000. The bank had to contend not only with a chaotic national economy, but also with fires in 1863 and 1872 that drove it to temporary quarters. Faced with less adversity, earlier Erie banks had failed; First National persevered and prospered.

The stock market crashed in 1929, but prudent banking policies and secure accounts with healthy industries combined to keep First National healthy. In 1933 the federal government closed all banks in the nation to prevent panic and allow for thorough audits. First National would always find reason for pride in its performance during the crisis. The

The all-male staff of (at that time) The First National Bank of Erie manually posted items into leather-bound ledgers in the early years of this century. The bank hired the first female teller in the city of Erie in 1942.

Round-the-clock banking is offered to customers of The First National Bank of Pennsylvania today through the regional MAC network of banking machines and the national Plus System network.

bank reopened, without restriction, just one week later.

First National's initial experience with geographical expansion came in 1930. Faced with state prohibitions on branch banking and the logistical difficulties of handling a large cash payroll, First National's directors joined with a group of officials of General Electric and chartered the Lawrence Park National Bank.

New banking laws in 1945 allowed First National to absorb Lawrence Park as its first branch and to acquire the Bank of Wesleyville as its second branch office. First National acquired the Ensworth Bank in Waterford in 1949 as its third branch. The largest

merger occurred in 1969, when The First National Bank of Erie consolidated with The First National Bank of Meadville to become The First National Bank of Pennsylvania. The First National Pennsylvania Corporation, the holding company, was organized in 1981.

First National's branches are located to serve the public (at Erie International Airport, shopping centers, and other convenient locations throughout the region), industry (at the General Electric plant), and education (on the campus of Allegheny College). In 1985 the bank joined the regional Money Access Center® banking machine network and the national Plus System® network.

The First National Bank of Pennsylvania now has assets of more than $650 million. Lawrence F. Klima is the institution's president, and John C. Brugler is executive vice-president and chief financial officer. The bank's head office is in Meadville, with the corporate office located in downtown Erie, just a few feet away from one of First National's earliest locations.

JLG INDUSTRIES, INC.

In 1967 John L. Grove and his brother sold their Grove hydraulic crane manufacturing corporation to the Walter Kidde Company. In a little over twenty years they had built the business from nothing into an industry leader. John worked with Kidde for eight months but found the new life too restrictive—so he took an early retirement.

John was only forty-six at the time. Some say he was just too young to retire; others say his wife wanted him out of the house. The result is that he and a former colleague from his old corporation, Paul K. Shockey, joined forces. In 1969 they bought a struggling steel fabrication subcontractor then called Fulton Industries.

The partners observed that construction and maintenance operations expended massive quantities of time and money erecting and removing scaffolding. They reasoned that a mechanical device replacing elaborate scaffolds would save time and spare workers the fatigue of climbing up and down.

In eight months the two moved from concept to working prototype. Their aerial work platform featured the ability to reach over ground-level obstacles while working around overhead obstructions. It could move workers quickly and safely to the work area, and provide a stable platform.

Fulton Industries' twenty employees produced that first JLG machine in July 1970, in a 20,000-square-foot plant. The firm's dealer network loved it. The construction industry was quick to adopt the new machines, and industrial customers soon followed. From factories to shipyards to the Alaskan oil pipeline, JLG aerial work platforms became part of the American industrial landscape. Fulton Industries became JLG Industries on July 31, 1977.

JLG, headquartered in McConnellsburg, Pennsylvania, has become the world's largest manufacturer of self-propelled aerial work platforms incorporating both height and reach capabilities. In the process of growing

John L. Grove, president, chairman of the board, and founder of JLG Industries, with the first aerial work platform produced in 1970.

from a small specialized manufacturer to a larger industrial company, JLG expanded from telescopic boom platforms into scissor lifts, hydraulic cranes, and material-handling products.

Internationally, JLG has plants in Cumbernauld, Scotland, and Port

An early JLG aerial work platform at an application site.

Macquarie, Australia. Dealers are located throughout the world. Toyota of Japan manufactures JLG aerial work platforms under a license arrangement.

In only sixteen years JLG has grown phenomenally. Its first aerial platform had only a 27-foot reach. New JLG models extend up to 110 feet. Those twenty employees who produced the first prototype now number about 800. And today JLG aerial work platforms, boom truck cranes, and other industrial machines pace the industry.

GROVE MANUFACTURING COMPANY

You've seen the firm's products at a thousand construction sites—distinctive yellow mobile hydraulic cranes, the name "Grove" proudly displayed on their booms. Efficient, reliable, and powerful, Grove cranes are a symbol of industrial progress around the world.

Dwight L. Grove started his small business in the Pennsylvania community of Shady Grove in February 1946. The war was over, and the attention of the nation had turned from swords to plowshares. In a rented two-car garage, Grove went into business manufacturing wagons for area farmers.

Dwight's younger brother, John, joined the company two months later, and Wayne A. Nicarry joined the Grove brothers in May. The three took turns towing farm wagons behind their cars and selling them to farm equipment dealers. On January 1, 1947, they formed a partnership with Dwight Grove as the first president and chief executive officer.

Wayne Nicarry remained with the

J. Martin Benchoff, who joined the firm in 1954, is currently chairman and chief executive officer.

firm for thirty-nine years. He retired in March 1985, having served as president and chief operating officer of Grove since 1980.

Grove Manufacturing was an immediate success. By 1948 it had outgrown the garage and moved to the

western edge of the village. The firm gained design, production, and marketing expertise. Though not manufactured by Grove today, product lines came to include farm-related equipment, roll-back truck bodies, and fire ladders.

The owners encountered one frustrating difficulty. Manually shifting bulky steel materials and assemblies about the plant was difficult and time consuming. They realized that a small mobile crane would solve the problem, but a search revealed that nothing then on the market would suit their need. The answer, they decided, was to build it themselves.

By 1952 changes and added features had advanced their first crane design to the point that it was ready for the commercial market. It received immediate customer acceptance. By 1960 the firm had grown

Pioneering efforts by Grove over the years have resulted in a broad line of truck-mounted cranes with unparalleled performance and dependability.

The company's Shady Grove, Pennsylvania, complex is its center of global operations.

from a small handful of people to nearly 100 employees.

Then, one April day, it all seemed over. A spark ignited the paint in a dip tank. Within seconds, flames torched the tar roof and spread through the plant. Local firefighters joined employees in battling the blaze, but the entire manufacturing operation was lost. Much of the equipment and inventory was also gone, but the engineering records survived.

The story of the struggle to rebuild the plant is still told by company old-timers; a visitor is proudly shown the rebuilt facility where it all happened. With determination and pride, employees and neighbors worked around the clock and Grove was soon reborn and rededicated.

As the business advanced, it became clear that the firm's future lay with mobile hydraulic cranes. Through expansion and purchase, Grove acquired national and international operations. In addition to the Shady Grove complex, the company now has domestic facilities in Greencastle, Quincy, and Chambersburg, Pennsylvania; Falls City and Waverly, Nebraska; Taylorville, Illinois; Macon, Ohio; Coffeyville, Kansas; and Houston, Texas. Canadian plants are located in Burlington, Ontario; Edmonton, Alberta; and Montreal, Quebec. Other foreign facilities are in Recklinghausen, West Germany, and in Harefield and Sunderland, England.

Walter Kidde & Company, Inc. (now Kidde, Inc.), acquired Grove in 1967 and the pace of progress quickened. Crane production was aggressively expanded. Grove now has more than 1.5 million square feet under roof devoted to the production of cranes and aerial work platforms.

Since 1967 Grove has averaged four model introductions each year. It has expanded its product lines to include self-propelled manlift units

Representative of today's impressive line of rough-terrain mobile hydraulic cranes built by Grove. An RT is shown here working on the Statue of Liberty restoration project.

and lattice cranes, and its mobile hydraulic crane group to include the "all-terrain" class.

J. Martin Benchoff joined the Grove team in 1954. It was the beginning of a long, continuing relationship. Benchoff became president and general manager in 1969, and has led Grove into the modern era. He is currently chairman and chief executive officer.

The company's history has been marked by many product firsts, putting it at the leading edge of crane design technology. From those early Grove cranes that could pick up and carry two or three tons, Grove today has expanded to the broadest line of mobile hydraulic cranes with lifting capacities from two to 250 tons. Truck-mounted, rough-terrain, all-terrain, and industrial cranes, as well as a complete line of aerial work platforms, have made Grove a world-class corporation.

The firm's strong influence in world markets has even led to cooperative joint programs with the People's Republic of China. Grove's initial visits to China and the first sale of a Grove machine there occurred in 1979. Since that time an increasing number of Grove products, both in unassembled "kit" form and finished machines, have been shipped to China.

Grove products are also in wide use by the American armed forces. In 1982 Grove joined a select group of manufacturers that have received the Department of Defense Contractor Assessment Award recognizing "quality excellence" in its military products. Grove received the same recognition in 1983, a rare honor.

Grove no longer makes the farm wagons that comprised its first product line, but the cranes that it first designed to solve an in-house production problem have hoisted the business from rural wagon shop to world leadership in the manufacture of mobile hydraulic cranes, making Grove Manufacturing Company one of Pennsylvania's most successful international industrial corporations.

ALUMAX ALUMINUM CORPORATION

Each day hot rolled aluminum coil stands ready for further processing at a mill products plant in Lancaster. The plant is still remembered by many as "Howmet," a business that dates back to operations that began in an abandoned freight station some forty years ago.

However, when Howmet was acquired in 1983 by Alumax Inc., its mill products plant became a component of the country's fourth-largest aluminum producer. Alumax, headquartered in San Mateo, California, is a major U.S. integrated producer of aluminum and aluminum products. Alumax has 13,000 employees and operates 101 plants and fabricating warehouses, including eighty-nine in the United States and twelve in Canada, the United Kingdom, France, the Netherlands, and West Germany.

In Lancaster, the former Howmet mill products plant is part of the Alumax network, employing slightly more than 1,000 people who each week process millions of pounds of quality sheet and coil aluminum. The plant is large enough to perform the most demanding job, yet still concerned enough to make sure that

even the smallest order meets rigid and exacting metal tests. And throughout the Alumax complex there is an emphasis on pleasing the customer, being a good citizen in the community, and treating its employees like the valuable corporate assets they are.

The history of this Lancaster mill products plant began in 1946, when New Holland Metals Company was formed as a venture of what is now Sperry New Holland. Operations began in an abandoned freight station in Leola with five employees and one piece of equipment—a sheet corrugator. The initial product line consisted of aluminum roofing and siding for farm and industrial use.

The company outgrew the freight station, and by early 1948 the operation was moved to Mountville. With fifteen employees and more equipment, the product line was expanded to include rain-carrying systems.

New Holland Metals was divested from its parent company in early 1950. With the financial support of

This aerial view of the Lancaster plant shows both the production/maintenance and office facilities located on the 76-acre site.

Raymond Buckwalter, the firm was reorganized as Quaker State Metals Company. Three years later the firm and its 100 employees moved to a new plant on the Buckwalter farm, located along Manheim Pike in suburban Lancaster. A used rolling mill was purchased and installed, and is still in use today.

In 1958 Karl Leiberknect, a machinery manufacturer in Reading, acquired Quaker State and brought capital to the company that encouraged new development. A short time later, however, Haille Mines acquired Quaker State Metals and merged with Howe Sound Corporation to form a new enterprise known by the same name. By the conclusion of this series of transactions the company in Lancaster employed about 225 people. The infusion of capital enabled the Manheim Pike facilities to add casting, hot rolling, additional cold rolling, and finishing equipment to its aluminum production lines.

Yet another transaction occurred in 1962, when Pechiney Ugine Kuhlmann—a Paris-based metals, chemicals, and nuclear energy enterprise—bought controlling interest in the company. In 1966 the firm's name

was changed to Howmet Corporation, and two years later Howmet was separated into two divisions.

Mill Products still continues to produce and supply nonheat-treatable aluminum flat sheet, blank, and coil products—both bare and painted. The products are supplied to affiliate divisions and are also sold commercially to other manufacturers.

The Building Products Division (now called Home Products), housed first on the Manheim Pike, was moved to new headquarters in the Hempfield Industrial Park in 1972. This division is the direct continuation of the original New Holland Metals Company and continues to manufacture rain-carrying, soffit, and fascia systems; patio covers and skylights; foil insulation vapor barriers; shutters; and other building products.

Pechiney Ugine Kuhlmann gained complete control of Howmet Corporation in mid-1975. The company's name was changed once again, this time to Howmet Aluminum Corporation. And so it remained until 1983, when Howmet was acquired by Alumax.

Coils await shipment by truck in Mill Products' finished-goods warehouse.

This three-stand mill utilizes four rolls at each stand to reduce the aluminum from about .700 of an inch to approximately .090 of an inch. The three-stand mill runs up to 700 feet per minute.

The mill products plant, located on seventy-six acres at 1480 Manheim Pike, manufactures approximately 350 million pounds of semi-fabricated aluminum products per year. Aluminum sheet, coil, and blanks are sold to customers in the building and construction, automotive, utensil, and can stock industries. Some well-known customers include Carrier Air Conditioning Company, GTE Products Corporation, General Motors Corporation, Great Dane Trailers, ITT, Regal Ware, Inc.,

Wear-Ever Aluminum, Inc., and WestBend.

Alumax Aluminum Corporation looks forward to years of growth and the opportunity to continue its tradition of community service and providing a quality product to its customers that it has maintained for more than forty years—ever since a small operation, with five employees, got its start in an old freight station in Leola.

Alloyed rolling slabs, such as the one shown here, are manufactured at one of three 65,000-pound-capacity casting pits at Mill Products. These slabs will then be reduced to coil (reroll) form during the rolling operation.

CHESTER A. ASHER, INC.

Chester A. Asher, Inc., a fourth-generation candy family since 1892, is located in the heart of the historic Germantown section of Philadelphia.

Today the firm, which was started by the man who gave the business his own name, Chester A. Asher, produces over 200 different varieties of candy.

Asher founded his candy-making business in 1892 after coming to Philadelphia from Canada just two years earlier. The company began in Center City before moving to Germantown in the early 1900s. Eventually Asher's expertise was passed on to his four sons, who ran the business until 1966.

At that time the third generation of Ashers stepped into a firm marked primarily by deteriorating sales and inefficiency. But under the leadership of Robert B. Asher and John L. Asher, Jr., yearly production increased from 150,000 pounds of candy in 1966 to over three million pounds today.

That amounts to more than seven million dollars in sales, with 75 percent of sales in bulk chocolates and 25 percent in boxed candies. A fourth generation of Ashers has continued the Asher candy legacy; David B. Asher, John Asher's son, is now vice-president of Chester A. Asher, Inc.

Located about six miles northwest of Center City in the heart of historic Germantown, the Asher candy dynasty weaves back and forth in the downtown district. Its factories spread out over a series of buildings that includes one historical movie theater, a former Horn & Hardart cafeteria, a former junior department store, and an Asher plant building constructed in 1930. An intricate conveyor system runs throughout the buildings, providing a vital link between the different candy production areas.

Inside the buildings, generations of Ashers have created a reputation for making candy with the freshest and purest ingredients available. The chocolate used is the finest of Nestlé coatings. The selection of candies ranges from Asher's own Almond Butter Crunch to luscious chocolate-covered pretzels to assorted smooth and creamy fudge candies. And there is, of course, the traditional Philadelphia candy—the vanilla butter creams.

The candy factories are a candy lover's haven, filled with wonderful aromas and the bustling activity of modern-day candy production. In one area, chocolate is spread ever so thinly over a layer of creamy, smooth mint, the finishing touch for a tray of Hostess Mints. In another room, melted chocolate mixed with raisins is made into hundreds of Raisin Clusters. In another nook of the factory, an array of stainless steel kettles is filled with the makings of soft, creamy fudge.

The Asher candies are sold throughout the eastern half of the United States, and have just been offered west of the Mississippi River. The candy is sold in well-known department stores, candy stores, craft stores, and in Asher's own candy store in front of the firm's factory.

The Asher family is well known in Germantown, not only for its candy but for its active participation in civic affairs and historic preservation. Each year, on the first Saturday in October, Chester A. Asher, Inc., sponsors a vivid reenactment of the Battle of Germantown, a pivotal battle fought during the American Revolutionary War on October 4, 1777. Asher Tours Inc., a subsidiary of the candy business, offers year-round tours of numerous historic sites in Germantown.

And each historic adventure ends with a tour of one of Germantown's most recognized landmarks—the Chester A. Asher, Inc., candy factory.

SNYDER OF BERLIN

From this facility Snyder of Berlin, now a division of Curtice-Burns Corporation, distributes its products to Western Pennsylvania, Ohio, Kentucky, Maryland, West Virginia, Virginia, and Washington, D.C.

Start with newly harvested potatoes—more than sixty million pounds of them, more than half from the rich soil of the high-altitude farms surrounding Berlin, Pennsylvania. Keep them under precisely controlled storage conditions, and inspect them closely to maintain the highest possible standards of quality.

When you're ready, peel and slice them uniformly thin and smooth for frying. Wash the slices and rinse them to remove excess starch, then fry them to a crisp golden brown in a secret blend of vegetable oils. Then, after a light dusting with powdered salt and a quality-control screening, they're ready for cooling and packaging in the familiar and distinctive Snyder of Berlin foil bags.

The first "Snyder" chips were homemade by Eda Snyder in her old-fashion kitchen. Her husband, Edward, handled purchasing (buying potatoes) and helped with the packaging (putting the chips in bags). Their daughter, Edythe, handled distribution and marketing—she sold the potato chips to the neighbors. The company still owns as an honored heirloom the simple potato chipper that Eda Snyder used to found a modern business enterprise.

In 1947 a snack food plant was built in the town of Berlin and under the management and ownership of Edythe and her husband, "Barb" Sterner, the plant expanded its production of potato chips and added other snack foods to its product line. A modern packaging warehouse and an office building were added in 1964, and a second expansion was completed in 1968.

In 1972 Curtice-Burns Corporation of Rochester, New York, made Snyder of Berlin a division of its company, retaining the proud Snyder name and enabling it to create greater sales and accelerated growth.

Potato chips, rippled, plain, and in a variety of flavors, Cheese Curls, Cheese Pleezers, cheese popcorn, plain popcorn, pretzels, corn chips, tortilla chips, Puff-N-Corn, and a variety of other snack foods continue as Snyder of Berlin's leading products. The firm's distribution area primarily includes Western Pennsylvania, Ohio, Kentucky, Maryland, West Virginia, Virginia, and Washington, D.C.

From the family working together in the Snyder kitchen, the business has grown to a 205,000-square-foot plant and almost 285 employees. The company is still a community business. The methods have been adapted to changing times and growing demand, but Snyder of Berlin still remembers its origins and its dedication to good food and good people.

An array of snack food products manufactured and distributed by the firm from its Berlin headquarters.

MELLON BANK

Since 1869 Mellon Bank has been instrumental in financing Pittsburgh's commercial and industrial growth. The bank has been closely connected with the conception or development of Pittsburgh's major financial and industrial corporations. In a very real sense, American economic history is the history of Mellon Bank.

The founder, Thomas Mellon, was an attorney and judge of the Court of Common Pleas of Allegheny County. Mellon retired from the law at age fifty-six to open the private bank of T. Mellon & Sons. He had gained banking experience through board memberships and by aiding two sons in forming The East End Bank.

Mellon's bank occupied a two-story brick building. While the structure was modest, the firm's lending policy was ambitious. In 1871 the judge lent $10,000 to Henry Clay Frick, who was interested in building coke ovens for a growing Pittsburgh steel industry. A longstanding Mellon-Frick relationship developed. The rapid increase of business by 1871 required the firm to move to new quarters at 514 Smithfield Street. By 1874 deposits were nearly $600,000.

Mellon gave his son, Andrew, a one-fifth interest in the firm. The judge retired in 1880; Andrew became sole proprietor. In 1887 Richard B. Mellon, Thomas' youngest son, joined Andrew as an equal partner. R.B. had gained banking experience in North Dakota.

Displaying the optimism shown in the Frick loan and reinforced by its ability to weather the nation's financial panic of 1873, T. Mellon & Sons continued to facilitate capital growth for Pittsburgh industry. In 1889 the

Thomas Mellon founded Mellon Bank after retiring as an attorney and judge of the Court of Common Pleas of Allegheny County. Courtesy, Mellon Bank Archives

Mellons financed the Pittsburgh Reduction Company's aluminum production venture. Pittsburgh Reduction is known today as ALCOA.

Andrew Mellon and Henry Frick

joined a venture that formed the Union Transfer and Trust Company, an organization to specialize in corporate securities transfers. Mellon was elected president of the new entity. The securities business was disappointing; the firm was saved from dissolution through an expansion of services into the general trust business. The name was changed in 1892 to the Union Trust Company of Pittsburgh.

An era of sustained growth and innovative commercial lending began in 1895. Numerous businesses significant in the nation's modern industrial development were financed over a twenty-year period: the Carborundum Company, Crucible Steel, Pittsburgh Steel and Pittsburgh Railways, Gulf Oil, and the Koppers Company. Other Mellon-funded concerns included Union Steel, Pittsburgh Steel Car, and McClintic-Marshall Construction.

T. Mellon & Sons' evolution mirrored Pittsburgh's industrial vigor. In 1902 the bank incorporated and joined the national banking system. Mellon National Bank was chartered; the firm assumed T. Mellon & Sons'

R.B. Mellon (center, seated), son of the founder and president of the bank at the time of this 1922 photo, is flanked by W.S. Mitchell (left) and A.C. Knox (right), vice-presidents. Standing, left to right, are B.W. Lewis, cashier; A.W. McEldowney, vice-president; E.M. Foster, assistant cashier; and H.S. Zimmerman, cashier. Courtesy, Mellon Bank Archives

The Union Trust building, from an original artist's rendering, circa 1916. Courtesy, Mellon Bank Archives

assets and liabilities. In a further consolidation of Mellon interests, Union Trust acquired the shares of Mellon National. Operations were expanded in 1903 with the acquisition of Pittsburgh National Bank of Commerce and the establishment of a foreign bureau to promote international operations of Pittsburgh businesses.

Andrew Mellon served three U.S. Presidents as Secretary of the Treasury and later served as Ambassador to Great Britain. R.B. Mellon managed the family's interests. The 1920s were marked by important signs of Mellon's growth. Deposits reached $100 million. The bank constructed an impressive structure at 514 Smithfield Street to replace the assorted buildings into which Mellon operations had spread. The Mellbank Corporation, a bank holding company, was organized. Frank Denton, whom A.W. had met in Washington, was sent to Pittsburgh to administer Mellbank.

R.B. Mellon died in 1933; his son, Richard King, succeeded him. In the economically troubled 1930s Mellon acted to shore up the nation's finances. Mellon Indemnity Corporation was organized to issue bonds on Mellbank's member banks. Mellon Securities Corporation was established to underwrite and distribute general market stocks and bonds—

the Union Transfer and Trust spirit was alive.

In 1946 Mellon National Bank and Union Trust merged to form the Mellon National Bank and Trust Company. R.K. Mellon served as chairman, Denton as chief executive officer. In 1955 Mellon pioneered as an international leader in banking applications of computers and telecommunications. The bank continued expanding its horizons while focusing on a commitment to support Pittsburgh's growth. The Mellbank Regional Clearing House, a check-clearing service, was established for Mellon's correspondents, and the bank joined other Pittsburgh institutions to finance the Civic Arena's construction.

Continued growth led the firm in 1972 to establish Mellon National Corporation, a one-bank holding company. Mellon National Bank and Trust Company became Mellon Bank. Pennsylvania's legislature voted

The bank had occupied assorted locations until, in the 1920s, an impressive structure was erected at 514 Smithfield to consolidate operations. The lobby is shown here. Courtesy, Mellon Bank Archives

in 1982 to allow statewide banking, and in 1983 Mellon merged with the Girard Company. Philadelphia-based Girard was founded in 1835 and in 1981 had acquired Delaware's Farmers Bank, an early U.S. financial institution. Other banks were acquired in Northwest and Central Pennsylvania. All of these banks have long and proud histories of their own.

Mellon employs over 14,000 people in more than 500 locations worldwide. Major subsidiaries include Mellon Bank (Central), Mellon Bank (DE), Mellon Bank (East), Mellon Bank International, Mellon Bank, Mellon Bank (North), and Mellon Financial Services Corporation. Mellon has domestic offices in no fewer than twelve states and foreign locations in sixteen countries. Since 1869 Mellon's banking facilities have consistently symbolized quality and optimistic support for the nation's industry and people. T. Mellon & Sons' original building at 514 Smithfield Street could today fit in the lobby of One Mellon Bank Center, Mellon's newest headquarters building and a familiar landmark on Pittsburgh's skyline.

H.K. PORTER COMPANY, INC.

The terms used most often by financial journalists writing about Thomas Mellon Evans include "tycoon," "entrepreneur," and "an eye for bargains." He has been described by one business writer as a "financial genius" and "one of the most brilliant businessmen of the twentieth century." That reputation was hard earned and four decades in the making.

Evans' career as an investor, entrepreneur, and American industrialist started when he took over the failing H.K. Porter Company in 1939 and built it into one of the most profitable and productive industrial corporations in America.

Originally known as Smith & Porter, the company was founded in 1866 by Henry Kirke Porter. Reorganized in 1870 as Porter, Bell & Co., and incorporated in 1878 as H.K. Porter & Co., the Pittsburgh firm became America's leading manufacturer of light locomotives for narrow-gauge railroads, factories, industrial furnaces and mills, logging operations, mines,

street railroads, and all kinds of other specialized applications. From the Pittsburgh factories, Porter locomotives went out to help shape industrial development all over the world.

Porter was a New Hampshire native who came to Pennsylvania when he decided to manufacture locomotives. He and his wife, Annie de Camp Hegeman of New York City, had a significant impact on their adopted town. Mrs. Porter became a leader of the artistic and cultural life of turn-of-the-century Pittsburgh. In 1903 Porter was elected to Congress and moved to Washington. His family home, Oakland's Oak Manor, was later acquired by the University of Pittsburgh.

Porter died in 1921, leaving a company that produced 600 locomotives a year. It was the end of an era. Steam locomotives were yielding to electrics and diesels. The automobile was displacing streetcars, and trucks were beginning to take over the functions that had once been the domain of the narrow-gauge railroad.

Thomas Mellon Evans graduated from Yale University in 1931, in the midst of the Great Depression. His first job, as a clerk in the office of

William L. Mellon, head of Gulf Oil Corporation, paid $100 per month. Evans thrived under Mellon's tutelage. It was the start of a long and close relationship.

In 1935 Evans persuaded Mellon to "rent" him Gulf common stock as collateral for a loan used to purchase additional Gulf stock. The highly creative financial arrangement worked well, and Evans emerged with a significant profit, which he used to purchase H.K. Porter Company bonds, then selling at ten to fifteen cents on the dollar.

In 1939 the firm went into bankruptcy and the courts turned it over to its bondholders. To the surprise of much of the Pittsburgh financial community, T.M. Evans, only twenty-nine years of age and a newcomer in the Pittsburgh financial community, emerged as Porter's major shareholder and president. His rough manners and lack of concern with protocol and gentlemanly behavior caused some early friction with his board of directors, but his response was typi-

T.M. Evans, chairman, executive committee, H.K. Porter Company, Inc. Photo by Fabian Bachrach

K.R. Garrity, chairman and chief executive officer, H.K. Porter Company, Inc.

cally forceful and confident. With the help of friends in the Pittsburgh banking establishment, Evans acquired a controlling interest in the corporation.

Evans streamlined the administration of H.K. Porter, brought in his own managers, and initiated a series of creative financial activities leading to extensive acquisitions and resulting in corporate diversification. The technique would later gain widespread recognition as Evans' hallmark. To the conservative Pittsburgh financial community, young Evans seemed brash, unorthodox, and most certainly undiplomatic. Undeterred by its disapproval of his style, he continued to reshape H.K. Porter into an efficient profit center.

First Evans liquidated the unprofitable divisions of H.K. Porter; then he began a series of extraordinary acquisitions. Quaker Rubber of Phila-

delphia brought Porter into chemicals and related manufacturing. Delta-Star Electric of Chicago became part of H.K. Porter in 1950, along with Connors Steel of Birmingham, Alabama. Then Evans acquired the distinguished engineering and manufacturing firm of Watson-Stillman, followed by A. Leschen & Sons Rope Company (St. Louis), Alloy Metal Wire (Philadelphia), McLain Fire Brick (Pittsburgh), Pioneer Rubber Mills (California), Laclede-Christy Co. (St. Louis), and Riverside Metal Company (New Jersey).

These acquisitions did not all come easily. The managements of both Laclede-Christy and A. Leschen & Sons both fought the Porter bids. A generation before hostile takeovers became routine news stories, Evans made himself one of America's financial geniuses. The H.K. Porter Company that emerged was geographically and industrially diversified, a conglomerate created before the term itself, and a corporation

well protected from all but the most comprehensive of economic storms.

T.M. Evans is still active as the chairman of the executive committee of H.K. Porter. K.R. Garrity is chairman and chief executive officer. Corporate executive offices remain in Pittsburgh, but the contemporary, decentralized H.K. Porter also has plants and executive offices in Scotland, England, and the Netherlands, as well as domestic offices and plants in Virginia, Indiana, Ohio, Kansas, California, Michigan, New York, and Georgia.

The firm has not manufactured locomotives since 1950. Today's H.K. Porter Company, Inc., is a worldwide diversified manufacturer and supplier of high-quality products to business and industry. The corporation is primarily active in electrical and industrial products including automotives, rubber goods, and power transmission. Its gross sales are well over $200 million and it is still very much the business that T.M. Evans built.

Porter tank locomotive.

UGI CORPORATION

The second century. For most businesses, there is challenge enough in surviving the first 100 years, let alone venturing into the next. In fact, if a company knew at the start that the first 100 years would include incredible growth, legal battles waged and lost in the U.S. Supreme Court, and divestiture that included most of its assets, the odds for a long, continuous business history would be slim indeed.

And yet this scenario perfectly describes UGI Corporation, a diversified utility company based in Valley Forge. As it moves into its second century of continuous service, with an unbroken record of having paid cash dividends to shareholders for more than 100 years, UGI has focused on four major lines of business: utilities, propane, industrial gases, and oil and gas.

UGI's Gas Utility Division and Electric Utility Division represent the firm's largest segment, with 263,000 customers in fifteen Eastern Pennsylvania counties. Combined, the two utilities provide nearly $365 million in revenue for UGI. From the gas distribution utility, UGI's mainstay

Harrisburg, the state capital, is one of the cities in a thirteen-county Eastern Pennsylvania area served by UGI's Gas Utility Division.

business, 57 percent of the throughput goes to industrial firms, 22 percent to the residential market, and approximately 21 percent to the commercial market.

UGI conducts its nonutility business activities through wholly owned subsidiaries AmeriGas, Inc., which is organized as AmeriGas Propane and AmeriGas Industrial Gases, and UGI Development Company.

In the $7-billion propane industry,

AP Propane, Inc., distributes LP-gas to over 130,000 customers in Texas and fourteen eastern states. The firm is a joint venture of AmeriGas and The Prudential Insurance Company of America. AP Propane markets its products under the AmeriGas label. UGI ranks among the top ten distributors of LP-gas in the nation and is committed to significant expansion of its propane interests through acquisitions both within the joint venture and independently as AmeriGas Propane.

AmeriGas Industrial Gases operates nationwide and consists of four major businesses: production and sale of industrial gases and sale of welding supplies; production and sale of carbon dioxide; production and sale of specialty gases and equipment; and engineering, design, and construction of industrial gases plants. These businesses are conducted through the AmeriGas Industrial Gases and Carbon Dioxide divisions and through 50-percent joint ventures with Nippon Sanso K.K., the largest industrial gases company in the Far East. UGI is among the top ten companies in this $6-billion industry and has also targeted AmeriGas Industrial Gases for further growth through acquisitions and internal investment.

UGI Development Company's operating firms provide various oil field

Among the 207,000 UGI Gas Utility customers are hotels, motels, and restaurants that use gas for cooking, space heating, and water heating.

services in the Appalachian, Anadarko, Permian, and other basins. Activities include contract drilling, well completion and completion services, sale of oil field supplies, leasing of gas compression systems, oil and natural gas production, and, recently, the natural gas brokering business.

From those four bases UGI Corporation ventures into its second century with a commitment to excel. "Our mission at UGI Corporation in our second century," proclaims the firm's mission statement, "is to be a diversified operating company dedicated to achieving high profitability and solid growth through exceptional performance."

UGI traces its origins to June 1, 1882, when a group of enterprising Philadelphia businessmen formed the United Gas Improvement Company to take advantage of a promising new process for manufacturing gas to light homes, businesses, and streets. The new water-gas process had been developed by a renowned inventor named Thaddeus S.C. Lowe. Through the formation of UGI, his gas-making process, which he patented in 1872, was widely used throughout the United States and abroad. From its base in Philadelphia, UGI began building and operating water-gas plants nationwide; by its twentieth anniversary in 1902 the firm held interests in forty-five companies that were providing gas and electric services across the country.

In the early years of the twentieth century UGI continued to expand its utility interest through acquisitions in major operating territories. During the 1920s the corporation diversified into heavy construction, forming what was at that time the largest general engineering and construction firm in the country.

The firm was an important industrial power in the early 1930s when President Franklin D. Roosevelt launched his campaign to break up major public utility holding companies. UGI led the industry's fight against the enactment of the Public Utility Holding Company Act of

Residential heating is a major market for AmeriGas Propane which is among the nation's top ten distributors of LP-gas.

1935. The firm lost its fight, and the act became law. In 1938 UGI lost its legal battle against the act when the Supreme Court upheld the ruling. In 1941 the Securities and Exchange Commission began to implement the ruling.

At its financial peak at the end of 1940, UGI had assets of $846 million, was operating in eleven states, and held investments in four subholding companies, thirty-eight electric and gas utilities, and forty-eight non-utility companies. In 1943, under the government-imposed divestiture, the firm distributed to shareholders stock

Growth is planned for the Industrial Gases Division of AmeriGas, a producer of oxygen, nitrogen, acetylene, and argon, and distributor of these gases and welding supplies in Pennsylvania, the Midwest, the Southwest, and on the West Coast.

representing some two-thirds of its assets. UGI's status as a holding company ended in 1953 when it merged its small remaining gas and electric utility operations in Eastern Pennsylvania and became an operating company.

During the 1950s UGI regrouped, replacing manufactured gas with natural gas throughout its service areas and expanding its modest electric utility operations. Then, in 1959, it took the first step toward a larger role in the energy-distribution business by diversifying into the marketing and distribution of propane to areas not served by its natural gas utility.

Changes came even faster in the 1970s. In response to a shortage of natural gas from pipeline suppliers, a new management team led the company into gas exploration and development in Pennsylvania. This interest soon broadened into contract drilling and oil field supply and service operations.

Also in the 1970s UGI diversified its interests in compressed gases. Adding carbon dioxide and industrial gases businesses to its existing propane operations, UGI formed AmeriGas and used the new subsidiary as its vehicle for the acquisition of more than thirty additional propane and industrial gases firms within a five-year period.

And so the stage is set. UGI Corporation is ready for its second century of business.

GENERAL ELECTRIC

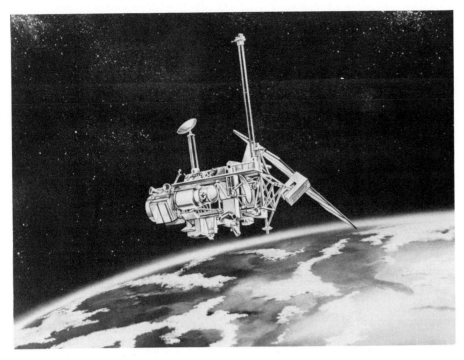

It is among the most familiar brand names in the world, appearing on products that are part of our daily lives. The "GE" symbol is part of America. To the consumer, GE means light bulbs, washing machines, dishwashers, and other heavy and light household appliances. To industry, General Electric means locomotives, oil well drilling equipment, motors, generators, and all the other electrical components that make things run.

General Electric employs 18,000 Pennsylvanians. Three major divisions are headquartered in the state. The Power Delivery Division is located in King of Prussia, Transportation Systems Business Operations in Erie, and Space Systems Division is in Valley Forge. General Electric also has plants in Bridgeville, making glass tubing; in Lebanon, manufacturing pollution-control devices; and in East Stroudsburg, manufacturing carbon products. In addition, GE operates five service shops in the state, with locations in Philadelphia, York,

An artist's concept of NASA's Upper Atmosphere Research Satellite, which is currently being developed by the General Electric Company Space Systems Division in Valley Forge. The spacecraft is thirty-five feet long and fifteen feet in diameter. It will carry ten scientific instruments to study the changing conditions in the stratosphere. Planned for a 1989 launch, UARS will be placed in orbit by the space shuttle.

Allentown, Johnstown, and Pittsburgh.

General Electric in Pennsylvania is a diversified operation, both geographically and in product lines. The company has major facilities in all four corners of the state, and General Electric products made in Pennsylvania range from giant locomotives

to space satellites.

General Electric locomotives for both domestic and foreign markets are made by the Transportation Systems Business Operations division, headquartered in Erie with a subsidiary plant in Grove City. General Electric/Erie was first planned in 1906; actual manufacturing operations began there in 1911. The first products were electric locomotives for use in mines and industrial plants.

With American involvement in World War I, General Electric's production in Erie shifted to artillery shells and ship turbines, but with the armistice, the plant returned happily to production of diesel-electric locomotives and refrigerator cabinets. In 1935 GE/Erie became the headquarters of the corporation's Transportation Department.

World War II again brought a shift to production of war materials. General Electric/Erie devoted all its facilities to the military. Instead of locomotives and refrigerators, gun mounts, turbines, howitzers, turrets, and searchlight power plants rolled off the assembly lines. With the return of peace in 1945, General Electric/Erie resumed its manufacture of civilian products.

Since then, the Erie plant has produced electric motors and generators, diesel-electric locomotives, and electric drives for rapid transit and commuter railroad cars. More than 7,000 people work at General Electric/Erie; its products are used all over the world. The division's most recent

General Electric's CALMA equipment is used to design very-large-scale integrated (VLSI) circuitry. Because the work is done in microns, it would be nearly impossible to do without the computer.

A General Electric technician demonstrates the production testing of a printed circuit card.

customer is the People's Republic of China, which has purchased 420 locomotives through 1985 worth $450 million.

The Power Delivery Division, headquartered in King of Prussia, serves the nation's electrical power transmission systems by manufacturing static relays, network protection devices, and numerous other components vital to the safe and reliable delivery of power from generating station to homes. In addition to the manufacturing facility in Malvern, the Power Delivery Division also operates GE's Elmwood Avenue facility in Philadelphia.

From transmission of power to transportation of people and products, GE in Pennsylvania is an essential part of life on earth. With the Space Systems Division, GE in Pennsylvania is also playing a central role in space.

General Electric has been part of America's space program since 1944, when the company was awarded a contract to develop long-range guided rocket vehicles. The division came to the Philadelphia area in 1956. Today Space Systems Division designs, develops, and produces satellite systems for earth observation and defense communications. It is actively involved in space communications, the space shuttle, development of a space station, and other space-related activities.

The GE Valley Forge Space Center dedicates more than 2.5 million square feet to facilities that include engineering, a solar vacuum test chamber, indoor and outdoor antenna ranges, and complete environmental testing facilities. Extensive facilities for research, development, system integration, assembly, and manufacturing are also part of the division's complex.

From this facility have come seven Nimbus weather satellites and five Landsat earth resources satellites—as well as satellites produced for the Defense Communications Agency, the Air Force, and the government of Japan. Other satellites and space probes are also powered by GE technology.

Space Systems Division employs about 8,000 people in the Philadelphia area, 6,400 at Valley Forge, and 1,600 at the Re-Entry Systems Operations facility. Other division employees work in Houston, San Jose, and the Washington, D.C., area.

A field application of General Electric's protective relays on power-vac switch gear.

MUHLENBERG HOSPITAL CENTER

Muhlenberg Hospital Center is a private, nonprofit hospital located in northwest Bethlehem. Today an acute care medical and surgical facility with 148 beds, the hospital was established by the Lutheran Church in 1956 to meet local needs. The movement to build the institution was started by the Board of Inner Missions, and in 1956 the articles of incorporation were signed by ninety-seven persons committed to building Muhlenberg Medical Center, as it was then named.

An important first step was the determination of the best location for the new facility. The search began for a tract of land large enough for extensive expansion and easily accessible to the surrounding communities. The final selection has proven to be a key element to the success of the hospital.

Located on 102 acres, which straddle Lehigh and Northampton counties, Muhlenberg Hospital Center is within easy reach of a seven-county area. A network of major highways converges upon this area of the Lehigh Valley, bringing many cities, towns, and rural areas within minutes of the institution. In addition, the Allentown-Bethlehem-Easton Airport is less than two miles from the facility.

The campaign to raise the funds needed to build the hospital was on a scale never before attempted in the Lehigh Valley area. In a short period of time over $1.5 million was raised through the hard work of over 3,000 volunteers and the generosity of the local communities. Additional funds were raised by the gifts given by area corporations and organized labor. Another source was the Lutheran Loyalty Program, in which more than 100 Lutheran churches in the Lehigh Valley area were involved.

Construction began in 1959, and two years later Muhlenberg Medical Center opened as a hospital for the chronically ill. Less than five years after incorporation, the plans were a reality. Upon opening, the hospital had a total inpatient capacity of 109.

Muhlenberg Hospital Center is a 148-bed acute care medical and surgical facility located in northwest Bethlehem.

During the 1960s Muhlenberg Medical Center became a center for Parkinson's Disease research. In 1969 the hospital added a 36-bed inpatient psychiatric care department and also developed an outpatient psychiatric care service. During that same period the institution was classified as a skilled nursing care hospital, and plans intensified to develop a full acute care hospital. In 1972 the east wing was added for medical and surgical departments, and most of the hospital's beds were classified as acute care.

A major expansion project began in 1979 and continued through 1984. A large ambulatory care wing was constructed on the east side of the building, and the ancillary services were relocated so that all emergency services were then located on one floor. The expansion project included the addition of thirty-two medical/surgical beds that were placed in the south wing. By 1981 the skilled care had been phased out.

It was during that period of expansion that the complete renovation of the original building took place. A great deal of careful planning went

The hospital's emergency room cares for patients of all ages.

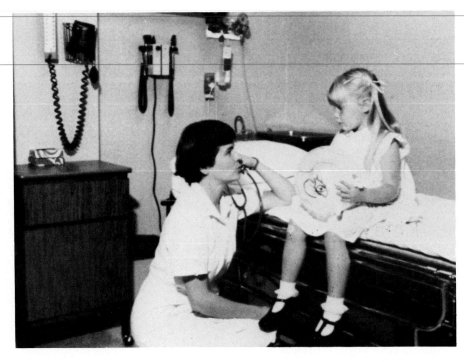

into the effort to create the most efficient layout for staff and patients. Today the pleasant decor, with its warm wall coverings and carpeted floors, helps to create a soothing atmosphere for the patients.

Presently, Muhlenberg Hospital Center has developed an extensive surgical program with increased work done in such areas as orthopedic surgery and eye surgery. The institution also offers excellent diagnostic services and nonsurgical care for coronary disease patients. The tradition of psychiatric care remains strong, and the psychiatric outpatient program is active.

Muhlenberg's emergency room is one of the largest in the area with over 24,000 visits annually. The design of the facility, which places the emergency room, the ancillary services, and the operating rooms on the same floor, allows for maximum efficiency. Three factors that have contributed to the emergency room's growth and success are its excellent staff, the quick turnaround time, and the location of the hospital.

Overall, the ambulatory care unit has shown the greatest growth. Muhlenberg is the area's leader in ambulatory, or one-day, surgery. Between the technology and new procedures used at the facility, patients are able to avoid hospital admissions for many surgical procedures.

Muhlenberg Hospital Center has a staff of 300 full-time and 200 part-time employees. The medical staff consists of 150 active staff physicians of a full complement of 295. In addition, there are 300 in-house volunteers who log 55,000 hours annually. The staff and volunteers present the personal touch that gives the hospital its warm and caring atmosphere.

During the initial fund-raising campaigns, two groups formed with the purpose of providing support for the new project. They have been active ever since those early days. The Auxiliary of Muhlenberg Hospital Center is a widespread network of female volunteers from Lehigh, Northampton, Monroe, and Carbon

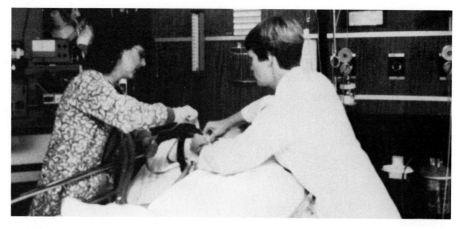

The intensive care/coronary care unit.

counties. The second group is the Men of Muhlenberg, which was granted a charter in 1960. This auxiliary of men is unique, as there are only four such organizations in the nation. Originally created to draw on the experience of retirees in the community, the Men of Muhlenberg grew quickly, and many younger men joined in the efforts to support the new hospital.

Two individuals, Dr. Clarence Reichard and attorney Jacob Kolb, have proven to be instrumental leaders in the success of Muhlenberg Hospital Center. Dr. Reichard served as its first president from 1956 to 1966. From 1966 until 1980 he was

Orthopedic surgery is performed in the Laminar air-flow surgical suite.

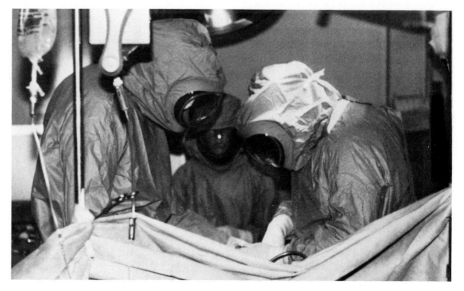

chairman of the board, and he is still an active board member. From the beginning Dr. Reichard was convinced of the need for the hospital and made a personal commitment to its success. Kolb served as vice-president from 1956 through 1966. He was president from 1966 until 1980, at which time he assumed the position of chairman of the board. Kolb has been a guiding force in the hospital's development.

Reichard and Kolb were two of the original ninety-seven incorporators in 1956. H. Scott Ashton, the Reverend Dr. Frank Flisser, Sara Fritch Henry, and the Reverend Walter A. Kuntzleman were also part of the original group committed to building the hospital. Their foresight and dedication has been rewarded as the Muhlenberg Hospital Center has served the Lehigh Valley community well during the past twenty-five years.

H.A. BERKHEIMER, INC.

From the modest beginning of a one-man office in a garage in Bangor in 1946, Harry A. Berkheimer's tax collecting service has grown into the largest independent tax service in Pennsylvania. The business started as a delinquent tax collection service, but Berkheimer's expertise in financial matters laid the foundation for a wider range of services. When Act 511 was passed in 1965, Pennsylvania became the only state to allow tax collection and processing to be contracted to the private sector. With the passing of this law, Berkheimer Associates became the cornerstone of a statewide tax service of which today there are twenty offices ranging across the state in such cities as Erie, Pittsburgh, Philadelphia, and Wilkes-Barre.

The home office of H.A. Berkheimer, Inc., remains in Bangor, but during the past four decades of growth the firm required several moves to increasingly larger buildings. Today the showcase Berkheimer Building houses 20,000 square feet of operating space. From a one-man business, Berkheimer Associates has grown to employ 170 people.

Currently, 911 school districts and municipalities call on H.A. Berkheimer, Inc., for financial assistance in earned income, occupational privilege, mercantile, business privilege, amusement, and other tax returns. Tax records and payments are processed with financial precision by the sophisticated data-processing center.

Harry A. Berkheimer began his tax collecting service in a garage in Bangor in 1946.

Berkheimer collects and disperses more than eighty million dollars annually. The finance department offers Berkheimer's customers total financial assistance in such matters as budget estimates, negotiations, and redevelopment or legal guidance. Berkheimer's experience in community planning and consulting, as well as the firm's vast resources, produce the results desired by its customers—

H.A. Berkheimer, Inc., grew from a one-man operation to twenty offices across the state. The Bangor headquarters is in this ultramodern facility at 50 North Seventh Street.

streamlined municipal operations and dollars saved.

A natural adjunct to the tax collection business is the Berkheimer Press. Housed in the Berkheimer Building, it has provided the key to successful processing of outgoing information. From design and layout to mechanical preparation and offset print production, the Berkheimer Press is equipped for rapid communication and has played an important part in the success of the company.

Harry Berkheimer retired in 1975 and his son, John D. Berkheimer, assumed the presidency of the firm. In this capacity he continues the tradition of excellent service established by his father.

H.A. Berkheimer, Inc., continues to grow and diversify. During the past two years the organization has been diversifying into collections and municipal fees other than taxes. Creditech, a branch of the parent corporation, deals with commercial and retail debt collection. Another division is Blackboard Resurfacing Company, which is a chalkboard and locker sales and refinishing business.

H.A. Berkheimer, Inc., is a unique business because Pennsylvania is the only state that permits the contracting of tax collection to private business. Berkheimer has proven the job can be done more efficiently and effectively. With its record of success as the leading tax service in the state, Berkheimer's future holds the promise of continued success and growth.

FRAZIER-SIMPLEX, INC.

Frazier-Simplex, Inc., was founded on July 29, 1918, as Simplex Engineering Company of Washington, Pennsylvania. Its founder, Chauncey E. Frazier, was a leading internal-combustion engineer. By the time he started Simplex Engineering, Frazier had an international reputation for his work in the electrification of soft coal mining and glass manufacture, power plant construction, and the design of more efficient methods of steel fabrication.

Frazier soon took his firm to the top of the engineering field with a series of innovative designs and installations. He was responsible for changes that modernized the American glass industry, dramatically improving both efficiency and quality. He directed the installation of the first Fourcault window-glass plant in the United States, designed the first electric-heated roller-type lehr for plate glass, and installed producer gas plants that completely eliminated burnout periods.

Simplex Engineering changed its name to Frazier-Simplex, Inc., in 1936 and moved to its current location at 436 East Beau Street in Washington. As Frazier expanded his activities, his company became America's foremost engineering consultant to the glass industry.

J. Earl Frazier, a son of Chauncey E. Frazier, joined the firm as a fuel engineer in 1928 and became president in 1945. He extended the concern's international activities, undertaking major projects in Latin America, Europe, and Asia.

Chauncey E. Frazier established a personal tone of individual leadership and faith in his staff that continues to set the tone at Frazier-Simplex. "I don't want to be bothered watching over you," he would tell new employees. "If you make a mistake, make it a damn big one so we can find it in a hurry."

There weren't many mistakes. Under J. Earl Frazier's leadership the firm designed and manufactured several innovative devices that are still in widespread use, including screw-

Chauncey E. Frazier, a leading internal-combustion engineer of his day, founded Simplex Engineering Company in 1918.

J. Earl Frazier, son of Chauncey Frazier, joined the firm in 1928 and served as president from 1945 to 1984.

batch and blanket-batch chargers for introducing raw materials into glass melt furnaces, fuel-conserving air-reversing valves, and suspended refractory wall systems. J. Earl Frazier was elected president of the American Ceramics Society in 1970.

Frazier-Simplex continues to lead the way in glass and steel engineering. Corporate clients include such giants as Brockway Glass, PPG, Bethlehem Steel, U.S. Steel, GTE, and Ford Motor Company. "Anyplace there's a flat glass plant," says

Clifford Crouse, "Frazier-Simplex has something in it."

Crouse, a Washington native who joined the enterprise in 1950, became president of Frazier-Simplex in 1984. Earl Frazier's son, Dr. John E. Frazier, M.D., is chairman of the board of Frazier-Simplex. Dr. Thomas G. Frazier, of Bryn Mawr, is vice-president of the corporation.

Frazier-Simplex, Inc., has been headquartered at 436 East Beau Street, in Washington, Pennsylvania, since 1936.

USAIR

USAir and Pennsylvania have shared a lot of history. USAir is the state's leading airline; more than 7,000 of its employees live and work in the Commonwealth. USAir first took to the skies flying the mail to small towns in the Allegheny Mountain region of Western Pennsylvania, and, while the airline's corporate headquarters is in Washington, D.C., its center of operations is Greater Pittsburgh International Airport.

It all started with Dr. Lytle S. Adams, a dentist from Chicago, who had an idea that had nothing to do with dentistry. An inventor in his spare time, he had developed a device that would enable an airplane to pick up and deliver mail sacks without having to land.

Adams demonstrated his system at the Chicago World's Fair when he met glider pilot and businessman Richard C. DuPont. DuPont was fascinated with the invention and began thinking about starting a business that would provide airmail pickup and delivery service to remote, isolated locations using Adams' device.

All American Airways' jaunty Stinson Reliants brought the first airmail service to many small Pennsylvania communities between 1939 and 1949, paving the way for what would become USAir, today one of the nation's largest and most successful airlines.

DuPont chartered All American Aviation, Inc., as a Delaware corporation. Then he filed bids on two experimental pickup routes advertised by the United States Post Office and won both of them without a contest. All American Aviation's bids established Air Mail Routes 1001 and 1002, connecting cities in Pennsylvania, West Virginia, Delaware, and Ohio.

The largest sections of both routes lay in the Allegheny Mountains and required flying over difficult terrain known for some of the worst possible weather and conditions. At a 1928 Air Transportation Association meeting it was even predicted that "the

day will never come when passengers will fly over the Alleghenies, because it is too dangerous."

More exacting conditions for testing airmail pickup would be hard to find, but All American Aviation went ahead. The first airmail pickup flight was on May 12, 1939. Norm Rintoul piloted the small plane that snatched a mail sack suspended between two steel masts in Latrobe, Pennsylvania. Flight mechanic Victor Yesulaites operated the winch that reeled in the bag.

All American Aviation carried the mail for ten years with a team of pilots, flight mechanics, and ground employees that returned romance and adventure to aviation. The stories of those who flew their scarlet Stinson Reliants may remind listeners of the barnstorming days of the 1920s, but the records show that it was also a serious business.

Ray Garcia, recently retired as USAir's assistant vice-president of customer services, began his airline career in 1942 as an airmail pickup flight mechanic. The flight mechanic operating the air-pickup gear was also an aircraft and engine mechanic and could make required repairs—in flight when necessary. Garcia still fondly remembers a farmer in Ohio who sent golden delicious apples in the mailbag.

Other farmers were not as happy to see the planes. Retired assistant vice-president of maintenance Calvin Martin remembers a different farmer who often fired his shotgun at the Stinsons because the planes disturbed his cows.

During the early years of airmail pickup flights, DuPont headed the company. Major Halsey R. Bazley joined All American in 1939 and headed the operations department. Bazley was named president in 1942, when DuPont left for military service.

With the introduction of the local-service airline era following World War II, All American Aviation decided the best route to continued survival and improved profitability was to carry passengers as well as the mail. It applied to become a local-service airline, part of the federally subsidized system of short-haul carriers.

All American Aviation received government approval to carry passengers early in 1949, moved its headquarters from Wilmington to Washington, D.C., and changed its name to All American Airways. On March 7 it started in the passenger transportation business with a fleet of eleven DC-3s.

Robert M. Love guided All American through the transition from airmail pickup to scheduled passenger service. Love remained active with the airline until 1975, when he was named director emeritus after serving as president, chairman, and as a member of the board of directors.

The first major cities on the All American system were Washington, D.C., Baltimore, Philadelphia, New York, Pittsburgh, Buffalo, and Cincinnati—with service to many of the smaller cities between. By 1953, when the company changed its name to Allegheny Airlines, Inc., the fleet consisted of thirteen DC-3s, and the route network had expanded to Erie, Cleveland, and to Parkersburg and Huntington, West Virginia.

That same year Leslie O. Barnes was named president, and Henry A. Satterwhite joined the board of directors. Satterwhite served as chairman of the board from 1956 to 1978. He and Barnes piloted Allegheny through the "feeder-line" era, off the federal subsidy, through two mergers, and into the jet age.

By 1963 the airline that had started with eleven DC-3s had a fleet of thirty-eight aircraft—twenty-three Convair 440 jetprops and fifteen Martin Executives. The growing fleet required increasingly specialized facilities, and, as a result, Allegheny moved its maintenance, engineering, flight operations, reservations, and flight-control personnel from Washington to a new, multimillion-dollar facility at Greater Pittsburgh International Airport.

In 1966 Allegheny introduced its first pure jet, the DC-9. The company's last piston-engine aircraft, a Convair, was phased out of service in September 1967.

The Allegheny Commuter System first took wing as a commuter airline assuming Allegheny's service between Hagerstown and Baltimore with four daily round-trip flights. This program enabled the firm to serve smaller markets without requiring federal subsidy payments. At the same time the communities gained by receiving more frequent service and the same benefits—joint fares, reservations, baggage checking—they had received from Allegheny itself.

The first Allegheny Commuter flight was on November 15, 1967. Today seven individual Allegheny Commuter airlines work with USAir to carry over two million passengers each year, servicing fifty-four local and connecting hub airports.

Allegheny was ready for more, but in the era of federal regulation of air transportation, airlines could only grow rapidly through acquisition. By merging with Indianapolis-based Lake Central Airlines (effective July 1, 1968), the Allegheny system expanded to seventy-seven airports, serving an area in which more than 50 percent of the nation's population lived. The airline stretched its regulated wings even farther in 1972 when it merged with Mohawk Airlines based in Utica, New York, making Allegheny the nation's sixth-largest passenger-carrying airline.

With its expanded system, the established Allegheny Commuter network, and a fleet of thirty-seven DC-9s, thirty-one BAC 1-11s, and forty Convair 580s, the airline was positioned for continued growth. In 1974 Allegheny became the first local-service airline to be removed from federal subsidy.

Barnes retired as president in 1975, and the board of directors elected Edwin I. Colodny to succeed him. Colodny had joined Allegheny in 1957 as assistant to the president; he held several other executive positions before being named chief executive officer in 1975.

The modern age of American aviation began in 1978 with the passage of the Airline Deregulation Act, a law that radically altered the nature of the industry. It brought with it a rapid growth in passenger volume on all the U.S. scheduled airlines, and Allegheny was no exception. Every month the airline broke records for numbers of passengers carried.

To meet new public demands, the airline modernized its equipment, phased out the last of the Convair 580s, and became an all-jet fleet. Company stock was listed on the New York Stock Exchange.

Responding to the new competitive atmosphere, Allegheny adopted innovative pricing practices, offering travelers a variety of discount-fare plans. It also began service to Houston followed by new service to Orlando, Tampa, and West Palm Beach. The following year Allegheny added flights to Birmingham, Phoenix, Tucson, New Orleans, and Raleigh-Durham.

Allegheny had become one of America's largest airlines, but market research revealed that it was still incorrectly perceived as a small, local-service carrier. Consultants suggested that Allegheny would not shake the "small" image without changing its name. Corporate executives sought a name that would reflect the airline's new size and scope. On October 28, 1979, Allegheny Airlines became USAir.

Taking advantage of newly won freedoms under deregulation, USAir has continued to expand. Its route network now stretches across the nation and includes seventy-four airports in twenty-eight states, the District of Columbia, and two Canadian provinces.

With its fleet of efficient aircraft, its flexible operations hub at Pittsburgh, and its strong balance sheet, USAir has performed well in the highly competitive modern era of aviation. In 1984 USAir Group reported net earnings of $121.6 million. The following year those earnings were $117.1 million, again a strong performance in a deregulated industry.

In 1984 USAir introduced America to the latest aviation technology with a new aircraft type—the Boeing

USAir's fleet of nearly 140 modern jets includes the popular Boeing 727-200.

737-300. This 138-seat, twin-engine jet, which USAir helped design, is the most advanced, fuel-efficient, and quiet jet of its size and range.

With nearly 600 daily arrivals and departures, USAir's Pittsburgh hub has become a model for the industry. It has made Pittsburgh an international gateway and one of the nation's most active and important air travel centers. USAir and Pennsylvania—they've flown a long way together.

ALPO PET FOODS, INC.

Joseph Sestak, president and chief executive officer of ALPO Petfoods, Inc., a wholly owned subsidiary company of GrandMet, USA, Inc., of Montvale, New Jersey.

The success and growth of ALPO premium canned dog food is a unique and, to some, puzzling study in sales and marketing. From a one-man, one-product enterprise begun in a basement in 1936, ALPO Petfoods, Inc., continues to expand from its one-product, one-brand franchise—ALPO—as the premium-brand dog food sales leader throughout the world.

Now a unit of Grand Metropolitan, PLC, London, England, ALPO Petfoods, Inc., has grown from its home base in Allentown, Pennsylvania, into a network of plants throughout the United States. And from its strong position as manufacturer of ALPO brand, the firm has expanded its product line to include dry dog foods, "jerky-type" pet treats, and ALPO TABBY label cat foods. For 1985 Joseph Sestak, president and chief executive officer, reported that

sales had reached $340 million with sales in 1986 expected to reach $380 million. The year 1985 was a record one for ALPO in both unit sales and profit dollars.

To initially open western markets in 1964 for the ALPO brand, the firm built a plant in Crete, Nebraska, that has been expanded over the years to meet market demand. In 1970 ALPO acquired Liv-a Snaps, Inc., Arden Hills, Minnesota, makers of Liv-a Snaps pet treats, now being marketed as ALPO SNAPS™.

Dry dog foods—with ALPO Beef Flavored Dinner as the flagship brand—were added to the premium pet food product line in 1975, followed by construction of a dry dog food manufacturing plant on the Allentown headquarters site.

Additional pet treat products were tested and introduced into national distribution. In 1983 ALPO Petfoods, Inc., acquired The Reward Company, Inc., of Chamberino, New Mexico, to manufacture pet treats under ALPO's quality assurance. That same year the firm acquired rights to the TABBY brand line of canned cat food, now being marketed under the ALPO TABBY label.

In January 1985, to better serve growing southern pet food markets, the firm acquired the pet food canning and processing facilities of Sun Coast Foods, Inc., Pascagoula, Mississippi.

Five decades earlier, Robert Hunsicker was confronting the Great Depression. A 1935 engineering graduate of Haverford College, Hunsicker temporarily took a reporter's job for the *Allentown Chronicle & News* while trying to decide how to launch his own business career.

In 1936, with $200 in capital, Hunsicker resigned from the newspaper and set up shop in a rented

basement at 717 Linden Street in downtown Allentown. There he installed a used meat grinder, a twenty-quart mixer, and a bake oven.

And history has it that on September 16, 1936, from his shop on Linden Street, Hunsicker sold his first package of "100% Meat Dog Food"—baked as a meat loaf and a very distinct improvement over the cereal and meat mixture being sold as dog food at the time. Hunsicker sold his product under a brand label called "All-Pro." And it was this product that started a company which today ranks as the number one manufacturer of premium canned dog food: ALPO Petfoods, Inc.

The history of ALPO and the legacy of Robert Hunsicker go hand in hand. Based on advice from kennel owners and veterinarians, Hunsicker set about to bake and pack the dog food himself, then sell the product door to door.

Gross sales for the first year were less than $7,000, but Hunsicker realized that there was a definite market for his all-meat dog food product. This prompted his first expansion in 1937 to develop a manufacturing line for his dog food. In a four-car garage, he set up a canning operation that switched production from baked meat loaves to canned dog food at the rate of six cans per minute, all done by hand.

Hunsicker then hired his first employee. Together they chopped horse meat, spooned it into cans, closed the cans, and placed them into the pressure cooker; the pair spent their evenings labeling the cans by hand. The "100% Meat Dog Food" busi-

The first building where ALPO was produced at the company's present location, South Whitehall Township, west of Allentown.

ness known as Allen Products Company was under way.

By 1941 distribution had spread to pet shops, veterinaries, and kennels in Pennsylvania and New Jersey. Gross sales for 1941 increased to $60,000. When World War II eliminated the availability of tinplate and glass for packing, Allen Products Company switched to packing horse meat chunks in two-pound cartons. Broth was added, and the product was quick frozen.

At the close of World War II in 1945, the garage-based all-meat dog food enterprise was fast becoming a dog food manufacturing plant. Gross sales had reached $200,000, and Bob Hunsicker moved the company into a 6,000-square-foot plant on Jerome Street, still in the city. Here he installed machinery: machinery to dice the meat, canning machinery, and two industrial retorts to pressure-cook the canned dog food.

Sales continued to increase. Hunsicker appointed his first sales manager, Daniel G. Pett, in 1948. Shortly thereafter he appointed a food brokerage firm, with offices in Philadelphia, to act as ALPO sales representatives to the growing supermarket grocery store chains. And supermarkets began accepting ALPO premium canned dog foods for distribution.

Hunsicker's expansion of Allen Products Company's dog food products into markets beyond his home base in Pennsylvania led him to seek registration of his All-Pro label with the U.S. Patent Office. His request was challenged by the Borden Company, which marketed a line of animal feeds, each bearing the suffix "Pro," across the many "Pro" brands sold by Borden.

The Patent Office upheld Borden's claim. There would be no objection, Borden's attorney said, if Hunsicker dropped the "R" in "Pro." Hunsicker went Borden one better, and also dropped an "L" in "All," combining the remaining letters into the now-familiar trademark: ALPO.

The first alleged use of the ALPO trademark was in August 1944. Formal request for registration with the U.S. Patent Office was begun in May 1963, with final approval of the ALPO trademark granted in January 1965.

Sales of ALPO continued to expand beyond the Pennsylvania market, mainly through the efforts of newly appointed food brokers. Advertising consisted solely of roadside signs, extolling the virtues of "100% meat—ALPO—Dog Food," and customer goodwill.

Hunsicker then decided to test the waters with Connecticut's largest supermarket chain. When he finished making his presentation to the pet food buyer, he was asked how much advertising ALPO was doing in Connecticut. "None," he responded. He did not get the account.

Almost at the same time, Hunsicker was approached by one Sid Tannenbaum to retain his firm as the ALPO advertising agency. Tannenbaum had just formed Weightman, Inc., so named since the firm had leased space in the Weightman Building in downtown Philadelphia. Tannenbaum needed the business; Hunsicker needed the advertising.

They agreed then, in 1949, on the first ALPO advertising budget. Sum total: $6,000. Campaign? Wherever ALPO was being distributed, Weightman bought one-inch newspaper advertisements, and if the price was right, the agency rented an outdoor advertising billboard sign. The copy line: "Your dog needs meat (not promises); ALPO is 100% meat."

Distribution now included the Eastern Seaboard. By 1952 sales for ALPO reached the million-dollar mark, and led to the incorporation of the firm in 1953 as Allen Products Company, Inc.

ALPO pet food commercial advertising "spots" were first televised in 1959, and Hunsicker, working with Weightman, decided that TV network advertising could open western markets, with or without product distribution. They gambled on the "Today" and "Tonight" shows and won the bet. Sales increased 40 per-

An aerial view of the ALPO complex includes the corporate headquarters building in the center of the picture, the dry pet food plant and warehouse at the top, and the premium canned pet food manufacturing facility and new product research and development pilot plant to the left.

cent, with one new market after another stocking ALPO. By 1961 about 80 percent of the company's advertising dollars was allocated to "spot" television. Television became the marketing tool of choice for ALPO and Weightman.

The year 1964 was a major turning point for Allen Products Company. Hunsicker felt that, in the long run, Allen Products Company could not compete with the large pet food companies and their substantial corporate financial backing. In November 1964 he finally accepted the offer made by the Liggett & Myers Tobacco Company to buy Allen Products as a wholly owned subsidiary company for a reputed twelve million dollars. Hunsicker remained chief executive officer until 1970, when he retired.

The Liggett Group, in turn, was acquired by Grand Metropolitan, PLC, London, England, in 1980; three years later Liggett Group assumed the corporate title of Grand-Met, USA, Inc., with headquarters in Montvale, New Jersey.

In 1983 Allen Products Company, Inc., began producing ALPO brand under the corporate name of ALPO Petfoods, Inc. The original corporate name, Allen Products Company, has been retained for expansion into dry grocery categories other than pet food.

As the firm marks its fiftieth-anniversary year in 1986, ALPO continues its commitment to research and pet food development. At the ALPO Pet Center alone, the firm will spend more than one million dollars to greatly expand nutrition study facilities for dogs and cats. The Pet Center's goal, shared by 1,000-plus employees: to produce a complete and balanced, nutritionally sound diet for dogs and cats.

PENN HILLS LODGE, INC.

The natural beauty of the Pocono Mountains has always drawn vacationers from nearby New York and New Jersey, and in 1944 Charles A. Poalillo, Sr., and his wife, Frances, came to the area from Berge County, New Jersey, in search of a small business they could run following their retirement. In Analomink, they discovered the overgrown and neglected property of the Penn Hills Tavern. The business, which had been closed for over three years, contained a gas station, a hotel built from a barn, and two small houses. However, the selling point of the property as far as the Poalillos were concerned was the beautiful Analomink Falls. Keeping the name Penn Hills, Poalillo opened a restaurant and bar that was run by the family. In fact, in the beginning the spot became a vacation site for his many aunts, uncles, and cousins from New Jersey.

At first Poalillo ran the hotel, but soon decided to build some individual cottages near the stream. As the business grew, the new cottages were enjoyed by honeymooners who preferred privacy over the hotel-style buildings of other resorts. With this innovation, Poalillo started a trend that has had a great impact on the resort business of the Pocono Mountains. He also made other improvements that included building a lake for swimming and boating.

In 1953 Charles Poalillo, Sr., passed away suddenly. His son, Charles, eighteen years old and recently graduated from high school, moved from his jobs of dishwashing, mowing lawns, and cooking to managing the resort with his mother. They made a great team, and Charles A. Poalillo III quickly adapted to his role. With his youthful, energetic direction, the resort continued to expand and grow. Unafraid of taking chances, Poalillo brought many innovations to both Penn Hills Resort and the Pocono Mountain resort industry.

In 1955 the Brodhead Creek flooded and caused terrible devastation in Monroe County. With one

Pocono Honeymoon Resorts Association (PHRA) was established in the early 1960s to promote the Poconos as "The Honeymoon Capital of the World." Shown are the original members (first row, left to right): Edward Strickland, Stricklands; Peter Rossi, Pocono Gardens; Harold Swenson, Pennsylvania Department of Commerce Travel Department; and James Moore, Honeymoon Haven. In the second row (left to right) are Walter Hoffman, Birchwood; Morris Wilkins, Cove Haven; Charles Poalillo, Penn Hills; and Paul Asure, Paradise Valley Lodge.

mile of the Brodhead Creek on the resort property, Penn Hills Resort was virtually destroyed. Of the thirty buildings on the property, only six were untouched. During that terrible night over 100 guests huddled with the staff and family on the third floor of the main building as the water rose relentlessly to over four feet above the second floor.

At the age of twenty-one, Charles Poalillo assumed the responsibility of rebuilding the family business. He and his mother applied for an SBA loan and began the project of rebuilding and repairing the resort. With the aid of local contractors and friends, Poalillo worked on the construction of new buildings and new roads. Within nine months Penn Hills Resort reopened its new facility complete with one of the Pocono's first air-conditioned dining room and cocktail lounge.

With the reopening of Penn Hills

Resort, Poalillo continued to expand the facility. In 1959 it had one of the first indoor pools in the area. During the mid-1950s a second lake was constructed. It was during that time that Poalillo realized the potential of the honeymoon business, and the resort began to shift from a family-oriented to a honeymoon resort. Gradually, the season lengthened and with the popularity of skiing in the early 1960s, the resort began year-round operations. Aware of the growing popularity of winter sports, in 1960 Poalillo opened Pocono Ice-A-Rama, an indoor ice-skating rink.

During the 1960s, after making the decision to develop and promote Penn Hills as a honeymoon resort, Poalillo designed and built the resort's famous Italian villas. Each of the thirty-five individual villas contained spacious accommodations that included a living room, bedroom, television, and fireplace. However, the most unique feature of the luxury suites was the Roman-style sunken tubs. The success of the round sunken tubs sparked the design of the red, heart-shaped tubs for which Penn Hills has become famous.

During the mid-1960s, construction of additional accommodations continued. Included in the development were the Riviera Towers, which offered three-tier balcony accommodations. Also, the outdoor pool in the shape of a wedding bell was built during that period.

It was during the mid-1960s that Penn Hills Resort introduced a modified American plan that immediately became popular. The plan differed from the three set meal times of the full American plan, and guests appreciated the flexibility of the new plan.

Today Penn Hills is a complete resort facility with an international reputation. Honeymooners have traveled to the resort from all fifty states as well as many foreign countries including England, Japan, Bermuda, Mexico, Germany, Canada, and Pakistan.

Penn Hills was the first Pocono resort to offer skibobbing, a popular winter sport in Sweden and Norway. Guests may also go snowmobiling, cross-country skiing, or down-hill skiing at the resort's new ski area at nearby Alpine Mountain. In the summer the nine-hole regulation golf course is a big attraction. The two lakes are used for swimming, boating, and canoeing, while the Brodhead Creek offers guests the opportunity to fish one of the state's best trout streams.

The ten-acre sports arena is the center of such activities as tennis, platform tennis, archery, rifle and skeet shooting, basketball, bocci, and ice skating. The Par Fitness Course offers Penn Hills' guests a unique

This aerial view of Penn Hills Resort shows the vast facilities available for couples to enjoy. Evergreen Park Golf Course, which adjoins the property, is a favorite of golfers from everywhere.

concept in physical fitness activities. The eighteen stations provide a complete program of physical fitness challenges.

As one of the most well-known resorts in the Pocono Mountains, Penn Hills Resort has been featured in magazines, radio, books, and newspapers. The resort has been spotlighted on

several television shows including the "Johnny Carson Show," "Good Morning America," "PM Magazine," and "NOW Magazine." Several international travel writers have published articles about the resort in newspapers in England and Germany.

When discussing the considerable success of his family business, Poalillo is quick to give credit to the cooperation of the resort owners of the local area. He believes that over the years he has learned much from his peers, and, by working together, the local resort owners have created the successful vacation haven that exists today.

The Pocono Mountain Vacation Bureau is an organization created to serve the needs of the Pocono Mountain resort industry, and Charles Poalillo has been closely involved with PMVB since its early years. As one of its first younger officers, Poalillo later became the bureau's youngest president and served in that position from 1969 until 1972. By that time PMVB had grown to such an extent that the full-time executive director expanded the office staff,

The newest addition to the resort is the Garden Terrace dining room overlooking the stream and golf course, a beautiful view year-round.

The newest addition for the Poalillo family is the Alpine Mountain ski area, which features 100-percent snowmaking and a new quad chairlift with a completely remodeled ski village.

The Penn Estates Resort Community features custom-built homes individually designed to suit each family's needs. Large windows and outdoor decks enable the family to enjoy the beautiful scenery of this spectacular mountain community.

and Robert Uguccioni, the current director, was hired.

Over the years PMVB has been instrumental in developing the area's tourist industry. During the 1960s the organization worked at having the state recognize tourism as a major industry. With the help of a state program of matching funds, PMVB has promoted tourism in Pennsylvania, and the industry has grown into a $7-billion business. The organization led the movement to reform the state liquor laws for the resort and restaurant businesses. The promotion of the Pocono International Raceway had been an important project of PMVB, and Poalillo is an active member of the board of directors of the facility.

In 1965 Poalillo helped launch the Pocono Honeymoon Resorts Association that has since become part of PMVB. The purpose of that organization is to promote honeymoons in the Pocono Mountains. The committee spearheaded an advertising campaign that has made the Poconos the national honeymoon capital, surpassing such previously traditional sites as Niagara Falls and Florida. Currently, Poalillo is active on PMVB's Ski Committee and the Winter

Sports Committee that launched the popular Winter Carnival.

Poalillo also has a wide range of professional and personal involvements. He is a member of several professional organizations including the Pennsylvania Hotel and Motel Association, the American Land Developers Association, and the Community Association Institute. He is also a member of the Pennsylvania Chamber of Commerce and the NEPA Regional Economic Council. Poalillo is one of the founders of the Monroe County General Authority and has been involved in numerous local charities such as the United Way, the Red Cross, and the Pocono Hospital of Monroe County.

Penn Hills Lodge, Inc., is the parent company that Poalillo heads. In addition to the resort, the firm has diversified into many facets of business, and current holdings stand at nineteen. One of the most successful is the Penn Estates Resort Community. Throughout the late 1960s Poalillo became aware of the lack of quality housing in the quickly growing Pocono region. With the construction of an improved network of highways and interstate roads, people from the metropolitan areas of Philadelphia and New York were interested in homes in the Poconos.

In 1974 Poalillo purchased a 1,200-acre tract that had been maintained by a hunting and fishing club. The forest tract, with its natural lake and

several streams, was an excellent location for the vacation and residential community that Poalillo envisioned. The initial plan was for Penn Estates to be a complete, self-contained community. Such a concept was ahead of its time, and the planning stage took more than two years. Employing experts in such areas as community planning and engineering, Poalillo researched and developed his concept of the Penn Estates Resort Community.

Using the most advanced technology and computerized designs, roads, sewer, and water systems were developed to suit the land contours of the property. Aerial topography was used to plan the community's water supplies and gravity sewer systems. Sales began in 1978, and by the mid-1980s over half of the 1,600 homesites had been sold. Poalillo planned a ten-year sell-out and a thirty-year build-out with the development of systems and sales following a master plan.

Penn Estates Resort Community is a residential, recreational community that offers active vacation enjoyment and secluded country living. Homesites have been laid out in relation to the natural environment. Poalillo's plan calls for more than 300 acres of open green space and wooded lots. Penn Estates has three spring-fed lakes and several natural streams as well as two heated outdoor pools. The million-dollar Penn Estates Resort Club area is the recreational and social complex for use by the residents and property owners.

The staff of Penn Estates runs an active year-round social program that helps to make the community unique. The Leisure Time Committee consists of property owners who assist with planning the social program. With such activities as outings, picnics, Meet Your Neighbor nights, and softball games, a real spirit of community has grown at Penn Estates.

The rental program at Penn Estates is a special service to the home owners. Currently, over 100 homes are included in the rental program. The property owner who uses his Penn Estates residence as a vacation home or a second home is able to rent it when it would otherwise be empty. The homes are rented to vacationing families, potential property owners, and new owners waiting for completion of their homes.

Future plans for Penn Estates in-

clude the introduction of the Community Association. This group would involve members in the running of the community. Poalillo credits a key part of the success of Penn Estates to his talented management and excellent staff.

Poalillo's most recent project has been the purchase of Alpine Mountain, formerly Timber Hill Ski Area.

Penn Hills Resort guests are greeted with this sign showing the featured entertainment each day. In the background is the Kissin' Bridge overlooking the lake and stream.

Lavish accommodations feature the world-famous sunken heart-shaped tubs at Penn Hills Resort, specially designed for the Pocono honeymoon resorts.

Poalillo placed his son, Charles R. Poalillo, in charge of the project. The ski area was completely renovated, and all the snowmaking equipment was replaced. All the runs and slopes have snowmaking capacity. The latest in design equipment including a quad lift, was added. The ski area can accommodate over 4,400 skiers per hour.

The ski base lodge was also renovated, and a new restaurant and lounge were built. An active program drawing on a talented staff was developed. Instruction and children's programs are part of what is offered at Alpine Mountain. Opening late in 1984, Alpine Mountain appealed to local skiers as well as out-of-state enthusiasts. Group rates and ski packages for local resorts have proven to be successful. Skiing at Alpine Mountain is available free of charge for the guests at Penn Hills and Penn Estates.

The Poalillo family's achievements in the resort industry have been remarkable. The family tradition continues as Charles R. Poalillo and his sister, Deborah A., join their father, along with Ernest Camlet, his nephew, in managing the expanding concerns of Penn Hills Resort, Penn Estates, and Alpine Mountain.

BLUE RIDGE PRESSURE CASTINGS, INC.

Blue Ridge Pressure Castings, Inc., of Lehighton, Pennsylvania, has always been a leader in the technology of die casting. The company was established in 1946, and production began in February of the following year. Two employees of the New Jersey Zinc Company, Thomas C. Wilson, an engineer, and Allen B. Behler, a metals investigator, were convinced that brass die casting would become a big business. Both men had extensive backgrounds and experience in the metal industry. In fact, while with the New Jersey Zinc Company, Behler was involved in the development of Zamak, a zinc die-casting alloy.

Behler and Wilson rented a 40- by 140-foot cattle barn located at the Lehighton Fairgrounds. Their original equipment consisted of one melting furnace, which held a 150-pound crucible; two holding furnaces, each holding 80-pound crucibles; two 150-ton-capacity die-casting machines; and a trim press. The machine shop contained a lathe, a milling machine, and a drill press, all of which were purchased from the government as war surplus equipment.

The original objective of Blue Ridge Pressure Castings was to become a manufacturer of high-quality brass die castings. Behler and Wilson were convinced that the brass die castings business had great potential because of several advantages offered by brass. Brass castings showed exceptional corrosion resistance and great strength.

By 1948 the business was well established, and the decision was made to expand into the manufacture of aluminum die castings. The following year Blue Ridge added the production of aluminum bronze permanent mold castings to its line. In 1951 the company entered the shell molding field to complement its other processes.

By 1953 the business had outgrown the cattle barn at the fairgrounds, and the following year it moved to its present location in the

A. Donald Behler, president and general manager.

Lehighton Industrial Park. At that point operations were divided between the two plant sites. Later that year a fire destroyed the original plant, which still housed the shell molding and the permanent molding operation. With the loss of that equipment Blue Ridge discontinued the molding operation and concentrated entirely on die casting. Shortly after the fire zinc die casting was added to the firm's operation. During

that same period a relatively complete production machining facility was added in order to completely serve the industry.

In 1959 the new plant was almost entirely destroyed by fire, with the greatest damage being to the production machining area and the machine shop. However, due to the persistence of both the owners and the employees, die-casting machines were in operation in less than one week. The secondary production and machine shop operations were performed in areas without a roof, and, in some cases, in shelters made of tarps. Repairs were made quickly, and the company continued to grow. Six additions were made between 1954 and 1985, and today the plant contains over 70,000 square feet of production space. In March 1966 both Behler and Wilson retired from the thriving business.

Today, led by Behler's son, A. Donald Behler, Blue Ridge Pressure Castings is the largest custom brass die caster in the country. As a leader

Andrew D. Behler, P.E., programs and monitors a fully automated, state-of-the-art, 600-ton die casting machine. A robot, on the right, removes a casting from machine.

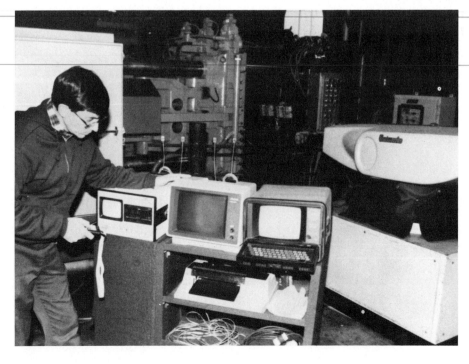

in the field, Blue Ridge was one of the first to use the vacuum process. The company has established a reputation for engineering and designing castings that other firms could not produce. Currently, Blue Ridge has eighteen die-casting machines and a complete machine shop facility that operates through three shifts. The machine capacity varies in size from 150 tons to 1,200 tons in locking capacity.

With such state-of-the-art equipment Blue Ridge manufactures parts that range in size from two ounces to twenty-five pounds. There is elaborate auxiliary equipment for surface finishing and machining of the castings. In addition to manufacturing facilities, the firm has a complete die

A portion of the modern casting bay equipped with machines to 1,200-ton locking capacity.

shop with both construction and maintenance capabilities.

The plant utilizes extensive automation systems including microprocessor-based control systems, robotics, and computerized monitoring systems. The company's application of SPC (Statistical Process Control) methods in the quality-control de-

partment aids in determining the process capability and monitoring the stability of the manufacturing process. Blue Ridge supplies metal parts to all types of industries, including leaders in the automobile, construction, electrical, tool, furniture, and computer fields. Some contract work is done for the government and the military.

As a major economic contributor to the local economy, Blue Ridge employs over 140 people including a complete engineering staff. The company produces and ships seven million pounds of casting annually. Blue Ridge has proven to be a strong business with regular sales spread throughout the eastern United States, Canada, the West Coast, and the Midwest. The firm has been active in the American Die Casting Institute, and president A. Donald Behler has served as national director of that organization for three years. Since 1978 Behler has also held the position of national director for the Delaware Valley Chapter of the Society of Die Casting Engineers.

Named after its beautiful location in the Blue Ridge Mountains, Blue Ridge Pressure Castings, Inc., is a strong testimony to the perceptiveness and hard work of its founders. As a leader in its field, the company holds the promise of continued success and growth.

An array of parts produced by Blue Ridge Pressure Castings serving the automotive, truck, hardware, appliance, electronic, and computer industries.

AIRWAY INDUSTRIES, INC.

From overnight and attaché cases to large pieces of luggage, Airway Industries of Ellwood City helps keep America properly packed for business and pleasure.

Samuel L. Weiner arrived in America in 1908, a thirteen-year-old immigrant from Snidrin, Russia. In 1909 he started work at the Grossman Trunk and Bag Company of Pittsburgh; after World War I he and a group of seven fellow veterans formed their own firm, Reliable Trunk and Bag, in a small storeroom on Pittsburgh's lower Fifth Avenue. At the time there were hundreds of small trunk and luggage manufacturers, but Reliable offered quality hand craftsmanship at a reasonable price and the fledgling enterprise thrived.

In 1950 Reliable moved to West Pittsburg (Lawrence County) and a 56,000-square-foot building (later expanded to 212,000 square feet). The company's more than 250 employees made three types of luggage—hard side or wood box, soft side or casual, and molded construction—in eight sizes and a variety of colors. Reliable had become a family business; employees included Jay, Leroy, and Dorothy Weiner, all children of the founder.

During the 1960s the firm purchased Airway of California (a small luggage manufacturer based in Los Angeles), along with two other companies, Boyle and Oshkosh. These acquisitions brought Reliable nationwide distribution and a full range of product lines. Reliable concentrated its focus on product and marketing while a newly formed subsidiary, Travel Products, Inc., continued manufacturing industrial and consumer products.

In 1969 Reliable changed its name to Airway Industries. By the end of the year Airway had expanded into foreign markets and had more than 350 employees. Leroy Weiner became president of Airway when his father died in 1970.

Airway took over the former Matthew Conveyer facility (328,000 square feet) in Ellwood City in 1976.

An example of Reliable Trunk and Bag's product line in 1926.

The firm had more than 750 employees by 1981, which proved to be the peak year for domestic production.

Leroy Weiner died in 1984. Jay Weiner is now president of Airway; his sister, Dorothy Girard, is corporate treasurer. Executive vice-president is Thomas Falloon; senior vice-president of sales and marketing is William Wilhoit; vice-president of operations is Anthony Mozzocio; vice-president of finance is Joseph Sergi.

Airway today is one of America's largest designers and distributors of fashion luggage, providing a wide range of high-quality travelware. The Airway Factory Outlet (formerly the Travel Products Factory Outlet of West Pittsburg), a giant warehouse-salesroom in Ellwood City, offers company products to the public. Airway luggage is distributed nationwide by over 10,000 retail outlets under the Airway and Atlantic brand names.

Airway Industries is a company born and raised in Pennsylvania. The community and its people have contributed greatly to the firm's success. From its founding in 1919 until today, sixty-seven years later, at Airway, people remain important.

Today Airway is one of the largest designers and distributors of fashion luggage in the United States.

SERVICE ELECTRIC CABLE TV, INC.

The large crowd that gathered in front of the Walsons' appliance store in June 1948 didn't realize that it was witnessing the start of a new industry. The citizens of Mahanoy City who blocked Main Street that day had gathered for their first look at television.

Until that time television reception in Mahanoy City had been impossible due to its location. The town sat in a bowl surrounded by the Appalachian Mountains some eighty-six air miles from Philadelphia. That was a problem that had to be solved if store owner John Walson and his wife, Margaret, were going to sell televisions. The solution created by Walson became the foundation for the nationwide cable television industry.

In 1945 Walson, a line serviceman for the Pennsylvania Power and Light Company, had obtained a General Electric franchise, and two years later he began selling televisions. Walson realized that people wouldn't buy sets unless they could receive good reception in their homes. After a series of experiments, he created a system that brought quality television reception to the community.

Walson erected a seventy-foot pole and antenna on the New Boston Mountain just outside of town. To prevent weakening of the signal, Walson designed modified boosters which he positioned every 500 feet. With permission from PP&L, he used its poles to bring the wire through the town to his store. With the possibility of good reception, the people of Mahanoy City bought televisions and became subscribers of Walson's new service—Community Antenna Television (CATV). During the first two years Walson ran cable to 1,200 homes.

From that beginning Service Electric Cable TV, Inc., has become the largest individually owned cable company in the nation. As the thirtieth-largest cable operator, the firm serves over 200,000 subscribers in 175 communities throughout Eastern Pennsylvania and New Jersey.

Walson's company has been a leader and innovator in the industry. He developed the technology for

---

John Walson, chief executive officer and chairman of the board, Service Electric Cable TV, Inc.

both the first three-channel and five-channel systems. Service Electric was the first to switch to the more effective coaxial cable and, in 1952, became the first cable television operator to receive television signals relayed by microwave technology.

With the home office located in Mahanoy City, Service Electric employs over 350 people and currently offers thirty-five channels to its subscribers. The company's television studios in Allentown are among the most elaborate color origination facilities in the cable industry and were the first in the nation to have local color television programming. In 1972 Service Electric and Home Box Office, a subsidiary of Time, Inc., succeeded in starting the first successful pay television venture in America.

In 1979, in recognition of his pioneering role in the cable television industry, entrepreneur John Walson received a Congressional Citation from the Ninety-sixth Congress of the United States and the National Cable Television Association. His ideas and innovations have laid the foundations for millions throughout America to enjoy better television.

DECISION DATA COMPUTER CORPORATION

A continent away from Silicon Valley—that California cradle generally regarded as the birthplace of high technology—one of America's most successful high-technology companies has grown up in the fertile soil of Penn's Woods to become the uncontested leader in its field. Decision Data Computer Corporation, headquartered in Horsham and now in its seventeenth year of operation, is the largest single independent supplier of IBM-compatible peripherals in the industry.

And though Decision Data may be a mere teenager in Pennsylvania's historic corporate family, the firm celebrated a "Sweet Sixteenth" birthday in 1984 as it witnessed its revenues and earnings increase by 40 percent, continuing a five-year uninterrupted growth trend that has defied the roller-coaster results of the high-tech industry nationwide.

Decision Data was founded in 1969 to manufacture computer peripheral equipment for processing the punched cards that were once the standard method for entering information into computers. Not long after the company had established itself as a leader in this field, the computer industry veered sharply away from the punched card. In 1977 Decision Data made a far-reaching strategic decision to concentrate its talents and effort on the design, manufacture, and marketing of computer printers—a decision that in time propelled the firm to the forefront of printer technology.

The transition was not easy, however. The costly shift in marketing directions produced several years of negative earnings. The company's stock, which had been actively traded on the over-the-counter market at prices as high as $54, fell to a dismal $1.50 per share. On Wall Street and elsewhere, there was a body of opinion suggesting that Decision Data had made a fatal mistake.

Into this gloomy scenario in 1980 stepped Richard J. Schineller, fresh from successful management stints with Management Assistance, Inc. (MAI), and Sorbus, Inc. Schineller

Decision Data Computer Corporation's 230,000-square-foot engineering and manufacturing facility in Horsham.

reorganized the company and engineered refinancing through additional stock offerings and the sale of common stock warrants to a corporation in the United Kingdom. The effort dramatically transformed Decision Data's balance sheet, and it enabled the firm to embark upon an intensive marketing effort, to develop a powerful service network, and to expand research and development efforts.

Richard J. Schineller, president of Decision Data Computer Corporation since 1980.

Decision Data's performance best reflects the effects of that reorganization. The company's annual revenues have surpassed the $150-million level, enabling it to buy back its outstanding stock warrants. More than 100,000 Decision Data products have been installed at over 15,000 customer locations, and its primary market—users of IBM Systems/34/36/38—is vigorous and growing.

The firm's principal products include high-speed line and serial printers, letter-quality printers, band printers, a variety of display terminal work stations (including a computing work station that doubles as a personal computer), and cluster controllers, all designed to be productive assets in the largest segments of the mainframe systems market. Decision Data employs more than 2,000 people in Pennsylvania, and in subsidiaries, sales offices, and service centers across the United States, Canada, and Europe.

Decision Data Service Inc., a wholly owned subsidiary also based in Horsham, provides across-the-board maintenance support for hundreds of companies using IBM Systems/34/36/38 host computers. This service embraces not just the central processors, but the full array of printers and work stations.

The service subsidiary also supports more than 450 users of Texas Instruments 990/10/12 minicomputers in large networks established by such organizations as Ramada Inns,

The versatile 6706 Dot Matrix Printer is ideal for applications requiring high-volume data processing, correspondence-quality printing, or a wide choice of graphic outputs.

Marriott, Hyatt, Blue Cross/Blue Shield, and AM International. The company also maintains a diverse mix of equipment for the Small Business Administration, and provides exclusive third-party service for equipment manufacturers who do not support their own products.

In 1983 Decision Data funded the establishment of a new subsidiary, International Computerized Telemarketing, Inc., based in Langhorne, to provide a wide range of computer-assisted direct-marketing services and software products. Due to its state-of-the-art systems and the deep marketing expertise of its management, ICT has been an immediate success, growing rapidly and profitably. More than 200 successful programs, including two million telephone calls, have been conducted for such clients as Bell Atlantic Mobile Systems, Sperry, and ITT.

Early in 1985 Decision Data pur-

The Decision Data Computer Corporation compatible peripherals allow more features, functions, and cost-efficiency out of IBM Systems/34/36/38.

chased POS Data Corporation, a California firm that specializes in the design, development, and marketing of integrated point-of-sale terminal systems for the restaurant industry. This subsidiary, renamed Decision Restaurant Systems, Inc., will expand the scope of Decision Data's operations into new and potentially lucrative markets.

By continuing its strategy of developing and marketing highly productive peripheral equipment for the IBM Systems/34/36/38 market, while

The Decision Data computing work station is both an on-line terminal (for an IBM Systems/34/36/38) and a stand-alone personal computer.

expanding into additional new and promising computer markets with its own computer-based systems and state-of-the-art peripherals, Decision Data Computer Corporation will no doubt sustain its current growth pattern, becoming one of Pennsylvania's most important businesses in the high-tech industry.

PENNSYLVANIA BLUE CROSS AND BLUE SHIELD PLANS

The Blue Cross and Blue Shield idea was a response to family financial problems without resorting to government intervention. Pennsylvania's Blue Cross and Blue Shield Plans originated as a form of nonprofit community self-help during the Great Depression of the 1930s, when unemployment and widespread poverty created extensive new problems for health care delivery.

Many people suffered inadequate medical care because they felt they could not afford it; at the same time hospitals were suffering the financial burdens of extensive charity care. First in Allentown and Pittsburgh, then in Philadelphia, Harrisburg, and Wilkes-Barre, community leaders recognized that the Blue Cross movement offered a solution. People would be assured hospital care through modest prepayment fees; hospitals would be assured payment for services—and financial survival.

Almost simultaneously, the Pennsylvania Medical Society gave approval to the prepaid medical care plan that became Pennsylvania Blue Shield. State legislation in 1937 and 1939 gave formal sanction first to the Commonwealth's spreading Blue Cross movement, then to the state's Blue Shield Plan.

The Plans created a new health care financing system. Early managers shared certain basic principles. The Plans would be nonprofit. They would make coverage available to the broadest possible population. The Plans would pay for needed services regardless of cost, rather than paying limited, fixed-dollar indemnities. Full benefits would be provided only through member hospitals and participating physicians, who would agree to certain conditions in order to control costs. All of these became distinctive marks of the Blue Cross and Blue Shield Plans.

At first only groups of employees were able to join, but as the Plans became stronger, they offered coverage to individual applicants. For many years now the Plans have accepted any Pennsylvanian who applies for coverage during open enrollment periods, regardless of the applicant's health or prior medical history.

From the early years a major concern was determining how to pay health care providers. Member hospitals were paid based on charges, on costs, on fixed per diem rates, and under individually negotiated agreements. Physicians were originally paid under a single-fee schedule, later under multiple-fee schedules related to patient income, and most recently through the "usual, customary, and reasonable" (UCR) method. Throughout those changes, the Plans worked continuously to balance the subscribers' interest in keeping costs

Early Blue Cross and Blue Shield offices were usually similar to the Capital Hospital Service (now Capital Blue Cross) office shown here.

down and the need to pay providers enough to assure the continued availability of services.

The Blue Cross success in meeting this complex challenge was evidenced by the rapid growth of the Plans. By the end of 1940 more than 600,000 Pennsylvanians were enrolled in Blue Cross Plans. Today nearly seven million people belong to the Plans.

The Blue Shield growth was slower, but by 1951 Pennsylvania Blue Shield had one million members, a number that doubled the following year and tripled by 1954. Today it is the largest such plan in the nation.

Following World War II the Plans realized that they needed a way to market their services nationally while preserving the benefits of local service and administration. E.A. van Steenwyk, executive director of both the Philadelphia and Allentown

Plans, and Abraham Oseroff of the Pittsburgh Plan were the national leaders in developing "syndication." American Viscose Corporation in Philadelphia became the first national account for the Blue Cross and Blue Shield organization (1948). Shortly thereafter, negotiations between the United Steelworkers and major steel companies resulted in the Pittsburgh Plan bringing thousands of steelworkers under the first industrywide agreement providing for uniform health care benefits.

By the early 1960s most Americans were covered under what had become a private system of national health insurance. Medicare and Medicaid were created in 1966 to protect the elderly and the poor—two groups largely unprotected by the existing system. But those programs, while accomplishing much, created heavy inflationary pressure in the health care system. The enormous flow of federal and state money, designed to create access for all, encouraged providers

Today Plan offices are located in a variety of urban and suburban settings. The modern, state-of-the-art operations of the Plans are typefied by this Pennsylvania Blue Shield headquarters in Camp Hill.

to expand facilities and services. Medical technology created miraculous but costly new forms of diagnosis and treatment.

The success of the original idea—prepayment for health care—had bred new commercial and public challenges. The burgeoning health care system, fed by third-party payment, recreated the very problem of escalating costs that had led to the founding of the Blue Cross and Blue Shield Plans.

The Plans had been working to contain costs since the early 1950s. Capital Blue Cross pioneered the adoption of utilization review (1958) as a way to ensure that hospital services to Blue Cross subscribers were medically necessary. The Pennsylva-

nia Plans have also led in expanding outpatient services through preadmission testing, ambulatory surgery, home health and skilled nursing care, and outpatient diagnostic testing.

Currently, health care financing and delivery are moving into a more competitive structure. To meet these challenges, Blue Cross and Blue Shield Plans in Pennsylvania continue to develop new cost-containing approaches including precertification of need, alternative delivery systems, and new provider payment schedules.

In a world far more complex than movement pioneers could have envisioned, the Plans retain their local orientation. Operating with the latest technology, they adhere to the early principles of nonprofit status, broad benefits, member providers, and their continued commitment to cover all segments of the population. Pennsylvania's Blue Cross and Blue Shield Plans remain what they have always been, a distinctively American blend of free enterprise and social concern.

575

WOOD-MODE CUSTOM CABINETRY

The company started as a small planing mill in 1942. Its founders—C.G. Wall, Sr., T.O. Gronlund, and R.E. Nellis—had eight employees, a $10,000 plant in Kreamer, Pennsylvania, and a million-dollar dream. They called their new enterprise Wood-Metal Industries and were planning to produce wood and steel cabinets. They never produced a single metal cabinet, but Wood-Mode, now with more than 800 employees and a million-square-foot manufacturing complex, has become America's largest manufacturer of custom-built cabinetry.

During World War II Wood-Metal secured government contracts to build shell cases, pigeon coops, ladders, and mess tables—all from wood. When the war ended company officials, foreseeing the future of wooden kitchen cabinetry, abandoned their planned line of metal cabinets and began manufacturing the products that would come to nationwide prominence as Wood-Mode Kitchens.

Even in the early years of corporate development, the founders adopted a willingness to adapt their products to the rapidly changing tastes and requirements of fashion. At first their main competition was the neighborhood carpenter who, working from scratch, could offer his clients a one-

The original home of Wood-Metal Industries in Kreamer.

of-a-kind kitchen. To meet this competition, Wood-Mode developed its systems approach, giving customers a choice not only of styles and finishes, but also of woods. The firm quickly gained a reputation for high-quality standards and control, and for innovative design, especially of its growing selection of special-purpose units.

As Wood-Mode expanded its product line, it also stretched its marketing area, which, by the late 1950s, reached west to the Mississippi. By the end of the decade Wood-Mode kitchens were being installed as far from Pennsylvania as Texas and Colorado. By the time of the company's silver anniversary, Wood-Mode had outgrown the kitchen and become Wood-Mode Custom Cabinetry,

manufacturing cabinets for the bath-room, bedroom, den, family room—cabinets for use throughout the home.

This new emphasis, combined with new styles, hand-rubbed grain-enhancing colors, innovative uses of new materials such as vinyl interiors (ending the need for shelf paper or other liners), more and better special-purpose units, its own patented under-drawer slides, and wide-scale use of such laminate finishes as the increasingly popular Formica, won Wood-Mode the dominant position among American cabinetmakers. By the end of the 1970s Wood-Mode's sales representatives were covering all of North America with installations in all fifty states and Canada as well as several other foreign countries.

During its evolution Wood-Mode has mastered a series of techniques and processes that are unique in the industry, starting with the finest raw materials. Almost 90 percent of the firm's lumber is grown in the forests of Central Pennsylvania. The lumber must be dried to precise moisture content before cutting begins, and in 1982 Wood-Mode found a new way to increase the efficiency of this time-consuming process. The company's new 800,000-board-foot pre-dryer reduces the first step of the drying process—preparing raw lumber for the drying kiln—from 120 days to 30 days.

From there, Wood-Mode maintains complete control over the product. The firm even makes all components for its cabinets, maintaining its own standards and quality controls. Its exclusive hand-rubbed finishing process has won widespread acclaim in the fine furniture industry as well as among cabinetmakers.

Since 1982 Wood-Mode has been totally energy efficient. Two wood chippers reduce the wood waste to proper size for burning. Two silos, each with a 34,580-cubic-foot capacity, hold a six-week supply of the fuel that is used to produce steam, the steam that not only provides heat but generates more than enough electric-

Today Wood-Mode cabinetry is custom manufactured at this modern complex on the site of the firm's original plant.

ity to meet all plant needs. In fact, Wood-Mode is now in the enviable position of selling its excess electrical power to the local electric utility.

In 1984, after nearly two years of planning and preparation, the company introduced its newest line of cabinetry, a European style that uses no front frame. To meet the manufacturing requirements of the European construction, Wood-Mode needed additional plant space and built a 25,000-square-foot addition as well as installing computer-aided design and manufacturing equipment. This new frameless line offers American consumers a combination of American raw materials and technology with the latest European look in cabinetry.

Together, Wood-Mode's traditional and European lines offer the consumer a choice of nearly twenty-five styles, thirty wood finishes, eighty different laminates, and five woods. To

help kitchen consultants and interior designers work with this extensive array of choices, Wood-Mode operates an elaborate training program with seminars both at its Kreamer plant and at regional locations throughout the nation.

Wood-Mode is still a closely held family corporation. All three senior corporate officials—C.G. Wall, Jr., chairman of the board; R.L. Gronlund, president and chief executive officer; and C.K. Battram, executive vice-president—are sons of corporate pioneers. That family concept is carried throughout the company. Parents, children, and cousins—occasionally three generations—work side by side. Nearly 40 percent of its staff have been with Wood-Mode for ten years or more.

By combining the traditional woodworking skills of such dedicated employees with the latest fashionable design and the most precise, sophisticated equipment available, Wood-Mode expects to maintain its position of leadership in the American custom cabinetry industry.

GS ELECTRIC

GS Electric, a manufacturing company on the southern edge of Carlisle, is a unit of General Signal Corporation. The corporation is a Connecticut-based company active in instrumentation and control technology for semiconductor production, telecommunications, industrial automation, energy management, and rail transportation. GS Electric, part of General Signal's Electrical Controls and Equipment Group, makes electric motors, primarily used in floor-care equipment.

GS Electric was established in 1968, when General Signal acquired the Motor Division of another Carlisle company that was discontinuing its motor production. General Signal built a new plant in Carlisle and provided the necessary capital. Much of the production equipment, inventory, and all of the trained employees had to be transferred to the new site.

The move was made over Labor Day weekend. On Friday, the production lines were shut down, and continuous shifts of employees worked through the next two days to move and install the lines at the new plant. On Tuesday, the sixty-eight employees reported to work at GS Electric. The new 20,000-square-foot plant was in full operation, and production and shipments resumed without interruption.

Originally the firm supplied motor components solely to the Regina Company, which was also a unit of General Signal. The parent concern has since divested itself of Regina, but GS Electric has remained Regina's supplier of motors for the electric broom and steamer carpet cleaners.

In 1972 GS Electric began marketing motors to Hoover, Eureka, and other manufacturers of floor-care, garden tool, and other consumer products such as weed trimmers, hot tub air pumps, and postage meters. To meet the increasing demands, GS Electric doubled both plant size and production. In 1978 the company expanded into power nozzle motor production, enlarged the facility to 64,000 square feet, and increased

GS Electric, part of General Signal's Electrical Controls and Equipment Group, is located at 1700 Ritner Highway, Carlisle.

production to 8,300 units per day.

In July 1979 General Signal acquired Voorlas Manufacturing Company of Racine, Wisconsin, and made it part of GS Electric. With the acquisition of Voorlas, GS Electric sharply increased both its motor-manufacturing capabilities and its customer base. A third facility, located in Hudson, Wisconsin, began producing motors in November 1981. GS Electric has 300 employees at the two Wisconsin plants. The Carlisle location houses headquarters activities. There is also a warehouse and distribution center in Glendale, California.

Under the leadership of former president Donald E. Miller and the current president, Samuel E. Park, rapid growth has continued. By 1986 the 300 employees at the Carlisle plant were producing 17,300 motors per day.

PENNSY SUPPLY INC.

A 1930s Pennsy Supply materials truck is strictly utilitarian. Note the hard-rubber tires and side curtains.

The streets of America may not be paved with gold, but paving those streets—along with providing asphalt, concrete, sand, gravel, stone, and other building materials and supplies—has proven to be the golden path to success for the Mumma family of Harrisburg, owners of Pennsy Supply Inc.

Pennsy Supply was founded in 1921 by Walter M. Mumma, a native of Steelton and descendant of a family that has lived in Central Pennsylvania since the early eighteenth century. Mumma was managing Harrisburg area sales for the Lehigh-Portland Cement Company of Allentown when he persuaded the firm to help him start his own organization, Pennsylvania Supply, as a general building materials company.

Walter Mumma's firm took a giant stride toward the future in 1928 when he started providing "transit-mixed concrete." Today Pennsy Supply (the original "Pennsylvania Supply" is now a holding company) owns four ready-mix concrete plants, four stone quarries, a sand and gravel plant, three asphalt facilities, and Elco Concrete Products Inc., a concrete block and ready-mix concrete plant in Meyerstown.

Bob Mumma, son of the founder, is the current president, chief executive officer, and chairman of the board. A 1936 graduate of Franklin and Marshall College with a bachelor of science degree in economics, he has been employed by Pennsy Supply since June 1936, with the exception of five years, 1941 to 1946, when he enlisted as a private in the U.S. Army and was honorably discharged as a lieutenant-colonel. He is a graduate of the Army Command and General Staff School.

In 1950 he became president and chief executive officer of Pennsy Supply when his father was elected U.S. congressman from the area.

Pennsylvania Supply's road construction operations became Kimbob Corporation in 1953 (named after Bob and his wife, Kim). In 1975 Bob's son, Robert Mumma II, purchased Kimbob. The former subsidiary has been extremely successful, contracting much of the highway construction within a fifty-mile radius of Harrisburg. "My son's one of my biggest customers," says Bob Mumma proudly.

The business philosophy that has led to Pennsy Supply's success is a total commitment to customer satisfaction. Throughout the Harrisburg headquarters complex hang signs reminding employees that the customer is the most important part of any business. The signs are almost as common a sight as the Pennsy Sup-

ply concrete mixers and delivery trucks that seem to be everywhere on Central Pennsylvania highways.

Bob Mumma's success record extends to his other activities as well. One of this nation's leading horsemen, he is best known as the breeder of Speedy Somolli and Burgomeister—both winners of the world's most prestigious trotting race, the Hambletonian.

He is also an outstanding civic leader who has worked consistently to improve the quality of life in the region. In 1961 he helped revive the tri-county United Way. At the end of the decade the city's leading columnist wrote that "the gloom, the defeatism, and the negativism of the early 1960s is gone from the Harrisburg area. There's a new spirit here." The community remembers and is grateful.

Pennsy Supply Inc. took a giant stride toward the future when it began to provide its clients with "transit-mixed concrete" in 1928. Photo circa 1930

ARTHUR ANDERSEN & CO.

The Arthur Andersen Worldwide Organization provides professional services in accounting, audit, tax, and management information consulting through more than 215 offices with more than 30,000 employees in 49 countries. The company opened its first office in Chicago in 1913.

All of its services relate in one way or another to an organization's overall financial operation. The firm's depth of practice stems from extensive expertise in accounting and auditing, in tax compliance and strategies, and from strength and experience in the planning, design, and installation of a wide variety of information systems.

In Pennsylvania, the firm has over 650 people in offices in Philadelphia and Pittsburgh. The Philadelphia office opened in 1946 with ten individuals. Today it has more than 450 employees. It is one of the largest of the "Big Eight" accounting firms in the city, and serves over 1,000 clients in all industries. The office, located at Five Penn Center Plaza, has grown by more than 80 percent in the past six years.

The Pittsburgh office opened in 1957 and has doubled its size in the past five years to more than 200 employees. Located in the downtown complex known as PPG Place, the office provides a wide range of services to its clients. The Pittsburgh office has a broad client base of over 500 clients, including both privately held and public companies as well as personal tax clients. It is committed not only to the needs of its clients but also to the continued growth of the city.

Arthur Andersen employees in Pennsylvania are actively involved in the communities where they live and work, holding leadership positions in nearly 200 civic and community organizations.

Arthur Andersen & Co. believes that its relationship with clients works best when it is based on professional respect and cooperation. This is only one of the traditional beliefs based on the culture instilled in the organization by its founder.

Arthur Andersen, 1885-1947.

These are the key elements of that culture: *Think straight/talk straight.* This credo is at the heart of the auditor's responsibility to clients and, equally, to the public that relies on the financial statements. *One-firm philosophy.* Arthur Andersen & Co. thinks and acts as one firm in serving clients throughout the world. *Growth from within.* Growth has come primarily by hiring, training, and developing personnel "from scratch." *Entrepreneurship.* It is a firm of entrepreneurs who share the responsibility of managing service to clients and managing the business of the firm. *Client focus.* The client, whether large or small, is at the center of all that's done. *Commitment to excellence.* Superiority is the measure of success, striving continuously for excellence in all that's undertaken. *One firm/one voice.* Although there's debate over accounting, regulatory, and other issues, once a conclusion is reached, all partners support it.

Arthur Andersen himself believed strongly in the value of this strong organizational culture.

Today's partners in Pennsylvania and around the world agree that adhering to "fundamental principles"—the firm's organizational culture—will be an equally important factor in the growth and success that will occur in the future.

THINK STRAIGHT/TALK STRAIGHT
ONE-FIRM PHILOSOPHY
GROWTH FROM WITHIN
ENTREPRENEURSHIP
CLIENT FOCUS
EXCELLENCE
ONE FIRM/ONE VOICE
THINK STRAIGHT/TALK STRAIGHT
ONE-FIRM PHILOSOPHY
GROWTH FROM WITHIN

MOTTER PRINTING PRESS CO.

"The future of printing newspapers," says John Motter of Motter Printing Press Co., "is flexographic." Once used primarily in the printing of cartons and other packaging materials, the firm's leaders believe that flexo is the printing technology of the future, destined to replace the presses traditionally used to print newspapers.

Motter Printing Press Co. should know. For more than thirty years some of the presses that print America's most popular publications have been manufactured at its York, Pennsylvania, plant. Few people outside of the printing industry may know about Motter Printing Press Co., but everyone knows the finished product. *Reader's Digest, National Geographic, Parade,* and *Ladies' Home Journal* are among the magazines that rely on Motter printing presses to produce the high-quality publications that their readers expect.

Motter Printing Press Co. was founded in 1953 by John C. Motter, but the roots of the business go back to 1838, when George F. Motter first opened a small machine shop in York. The company was passed down through several generations. In the early 1900s John C. Motter became an apprentice in the family business, and it was there that he first became interested in rotogravure printing machinery. The machine shop began manufacturing parts for printing presses during the Great Depression. Its first sale came in 1935, a press used to run a two-color shoe ad for a Sears, Roebuck and Co. catalog.

In 1953 John C. Motter and his sons, John Jr. and Frank, opened their own rotogravure printing press manufacturing company. Gradually they expanded, adding webfed letterpresses and offset presses to the Motter line. In November 1966 they consolidated all engineering, sales, and manufacturing operations at their current location, 3900 East Market Street. In 1973 the firm purchased the Kidder Press line and the Stacy Machine Company of Agawam, Massachusetts, and then in 1976 the

corporation acquired Rotographic Machinery Company of Owings Mills, Maryland. These acquisitions paved the way for the corporation to get involved with the flexographic packaging field which led to the development of flexographic equipment for newspaper printing.

John C. Motter is now more than ninety years old, but the spirit that led him to start his own business when most men were retiring is still potent. He is still preparing for the future and moving to meet the challenges of evolving technology.

In 1984 Motter Printing Press Co. moved its flexographic newspaper manufacturing operations from Agawam to York in preparation for the accelerating demand for new technology. Newspapers are still testing the process, but John C. Motter knows where those tests must lead. For over a quarter-century his company dominated the rotogravure press manufacturing industry. He intends to continue providing the research, engineering, and top-quality manufacturing necessary to produce the finest printing machinery in the world.

Executive and engineering offices of Motter Printing Press Co., designer and manufacturer of high-speed, webfed printing presses and allied equipment, at 3900 East Market Street in York.

AT&T

Imagine being able to store the equivalent of 100 typewritten pages of information on a surface the size of an infant's fingernail. With the skill of renaissance craftsmen, AT&T scientists in Pennsylvania create such wonders from one of the earth's most plentiful elements—sand.

The birth of such information age technology is taking place less than 100 miles from the site in Philadelphia where, in 1876, Alexander Graham Bell first publicly exhibited his wondrous new invention, the telephone.

For more than a century AT&T has played an integral part in the evolution of industry in Pennsylvania, providing top-flight information movement and management services for business, industry, institutions, and the home, and linking the Commonwealth with the world.

The accomplishments of two AT&T manufacturing facilities in Eastern Pennsylvania have led many to refer to that area as "the Silicon Valley of the East." Certainly the history of these high-technology plants, located in Allentown and Reading, closely parallels the history of modern electronics.

AT&T operators at the International Operating Center in Pittsburgh help callers from all over the United States to place calls to more than 250 countries around the world.

During nearly forty years of operation, AT&T's Allentown Works has been involved in three major technologies: the electron tube, the transistor, and the integrated circuit. In fact, the world's first production line for the transistor was established in 1951 at the Allentown Works.

In 1984 the Allentown Works dedicated its Silicon Operations Facility. There, silicon crystals of the purest semiconductor material are grown and processed into wafers, then into microscopic integrated circuit chips. The plant's current product families include metal-oxide semiconductors, digital bipolar integrated circuits, thin film devices, and discrete devices.

Most of the products manufactured at the Allentown Works are shipped to other AT&T locations, where they are installed in various sophisticated electronic systems. Since 1982 AT&T in Allentown has been a major producer of the 256K Dynamic Random Access Memory (DRAM) chip. In 1985 AT&T announced that the Allentown Works would introduce the world's first manufacturable megabit chip, which holds one million bits of data.

AT&T's Reading Works was conceived as a leading-edge technology plant and has earned a reputation as a pioneer in the field. Reading's first mission was to manufacture semiconductor devices for the United States government, which needed a reliable source of high-quality devices for the military and the fledgling space program. The original plant, opened by AT&T in Laureldale in 1952, was housed in an old converted knitting mill. An increased demand for semiconductor devices led to the construction of the current facility in 1962.

Today the Reading plant works closely with AT&T Bell Laboratories to bring new devices through the development stage into full manufacture. Very often product lines are moved to other locations so that Reading employees can tackle new challenges.

In the 1960s the Reading Works continued to manufacture transistors as well as diodes and traveling wave tubes. By the 1970s linear integrated circuits had been introduced and were becoming an increasingly important product line. Adding to the diversity of its products, Reading employees began to manufacture optoelectronics, microwave devices, magnetic bubble memories, lightwave components, and the plasma panel. Nearly all of the diverse products offered by AT&T contain components manufactured at the Reading Works.

AT&T's commitment as the producer of the highest-quality telecommunications and data-processing products and services is supported by the research and development activities of AT&T Bell Laboratories.

Widely regarded as the world's foremost industrial laboratory, AT&T Bell Laboratories opened its facilities in Allentown in 1948 to provide research and development support as the Allentown Works geared up for the mass production of transistors.

All satellite operations for AT&T, including the tracking and controlling of AT&T's Telstar 3 satellites, are directed by personnel at this facility near Hawley.

Since then, scientists at the Allentown laboratories have focused their efforts on the development and design of silicon integrated circuits and lightwave systems.

AT&T Bell Laboratories established a second Pennsylvania facility at Reading in 1958 to provide support to the Reading Works on military projects. This facility has been a forerunner in the introduction of new devices such as components used in electronic switching systems and lasers for lightwave systems.

AT&T has announced plans for the construction of a Solid State Technology Center in Eastern Pennsylvania. The center will be used for the development of integrated circuits and specialized electronic devices for state-of-the-art telecommunications and data-processing systems, particularly in the field of lightwave transmission. This facility will enable AT&T's scientists and engineers to exercise their talents to the fullest and, by so doing, to operate at the forefront of advanced electronics and communications technology without major modifications in the years ahead.

Nestled high in the mountains of Northeastern Pennsylvania near Hawley, AT&T's Satellite Operations Management Facility is one of the world's most advanced telecommunications control stations.

AT&T's Skynet* family of satellite services is orchestrated at Hawley. These services allow businesses such as broadcasters, computer companies, and retailers to interconnect computers, distribute television programs, set up video teleconferences, and transmit quality sound for high-fidelity monaural and stereo radio programming throughout the United States.

Skynet* is but one of many of AT&T's long-distance telecommunications services. Offerings such as AT&T WATS, 800 services, and private lines are made possible by a sophisticated transmission network that employs a mix of coaxial cable, microwave, satellite, and lightwave systems.

The future has arrived in Philadelphia, where AT&T has installed the world's first "service node." This state-of-the-art central office acts as a customer gateway to the spectrum of AT&T network services. The all-digital facility brings to customers the ability to effectively manage and control their communication services.

The world's most sophisticated telecommunications network is enhanced by AT&T's communications-based information systems, from "smart" telephones for the home to integrated business systems linking tens of thousands of people and machines.

Over the past four decades AT&T has developed a wide array of computers, software, and communications devices. In the 1980s, placed squarely in the broad arena of information movement and management, the company is constantly adding new capabilities in information processing, office automation, and building and factory management.

A force of thousands of AT&T technical consultants, service technicians, and marketing specialists operate from the firm's state headquarters in Bala Cynwyd. These highly trained professionals assist companies in solving business problems and furnish, install, and service the latest telecommunications equipment, through a network of regional and local offices, AT&T Phone Centers, and service agencies.

AT&T's Pennsylvania work force of nearly 20,000 places the company among the largest private employers in the state. The company has always regarded its people as its greatest resource. Across the length and breadth of the Commonwealth, AT&T's team of dedicated professionals brings the highest-quality, advanced technology telecommunications and computer products, services, and information systems to the citizens of Pennsylvania.

*A service mark of AT&T

Technicians at AT&T's Allentown Works oversee the production of silicon wafers as they are prepared for photolithography under the most rigorous clean-room conditions.

TOWERS, PERRIN, FORSTER & CROSBY

Towers, Perrin, Forster & Crosby (TPF&C), a firm of international management consultants and reinsurance intermediaries, is sometimes described as a "sleeping giant." This highly successful organization maintains a low profile that belies its position as one of the oldest and largest consulting firms in the world. And it has two prominent locations in Pennsylvania: Philadelphia (the first TPF&C office and original corporate headquarters) and Pittsburgh.

TPF&C offers a broad range of specialized services relating to the management of people—services that embrace most aspects of personnel planning, development, appraisal, and monitoring, as well as the design of remuneration programs (both salary and incentive awards) and pension and other employee benefit plans.

TPF&C was founded in Philadelphia by John A. Towers, Charles C. Perrin, H. Walter Forster, and Arthur U. Crosby, who completed the country's first pension consulting assignment, for Union Carbide, in 1917. In the early years the firm's activities revolved around actuarial services, employee benefits, and communications. In response to client needs during the growth-oriented 1960s, TPF&C expanded to include compensation and other human resource-related services.

The organization continued to diversify into the 1970s, when it began to offer specialized general management services, culminating in a merger with Cresap, McCormick and Paget in 1983. And through TPF&C's Insurance Consulting Unit, all such services can be applied to property, casualty, and life insurance companies.

Paralleling the diversification of services was the expansion of TPF&C worldwide. The first office outside the United States was opened in Montreal in 1956. Over the next three decades more offices opened in the United States and Canada, as well as in Europe, Latin America, Australia, and the Far East. Today there are forty offices worldwide and more than 6,000 client organizations.

The firm's clients include 92 percent of the *Fortune* 100 leading U.S. industrial companies, 65 percent of the *Fortune* 500 industrials, 46 percent of the *Fortune* 500 service companies, and about 20 percent of the

Reviewing innovations in recent client proposals are (left to right) Rick Anthony, Jack Vivanco, Bob Gore, and Art Croasdale, manager of Towers, Perrin, Forster & Crosby's Philadelphia consulting office.

500 largest companies located outside the United States. Yet TPF&C officials note that some of their most challenging assignments come from hundreds of clients with fewer than 1,000 employees.

Both the Philadelphia and Pittsburgh offices have impressive client accounts. In Philadelphia, TPF&C provides services to twenty-six of the area's twenty-eight *Fortune* 500 companies. The Philadelphia office has also conducted assignments for the four *Fortune* 100 industrial companies in the area of Eastern Pennsylvania, Southern New Jersey, Delaware, and Upstate New York, namely, Eastman Kodak Company, E.I. du Pont de Nemours, Sun Company, Inc., and Bethlehem Steel. Representative Pittsburgh office clients include Allegheny International *(Fortune* 500), PPG Industries, Westinghouse Electric Corporation (both *Fortune* 100), and PNC Financial Corp.

Size alone, however, does not provide the measure of a consulting organization. To gauge excellence, TPF&C prefers that less tangible factors be examined. To that end, Towers, Perrin, Forster & Crosby attributes its success to an unwavering commitment to quality consulting services that address client needs on a pragmatic, cost-efficient basis.

NATIONAL GLASS AND METAL CO., INC.

Gerard Clabbers admits that he has a reputation in Philadelphia. As owner of the National Glass and Metal Co., Inc., which he founded sixteen years ago, Clabbers is well known for installing the glass and fixtures in some of the city's most unusual and architecturally challenging buildings. The firm's projects include the Hershey Hotel, the Philadelphia Visitors' Center, the Port of History Museum at Penn's Landing, 3,200 windows for Three Penn Center, custom-made doors for City Hall, and special one-inch, 4,500-pound slabs of glass for the glass pavilion that houses the famed Liberty Bell.

Clabbers is also widely known as someone who has no qualms about going into a building and taking out materials—if the owners refuse to pay him for his work. Clabbers and fourteen other workers were once arrested for taking doors out of a building, prompting a television feature called "The Case of the Missing Doors."

Clabbers laughs today when telling the story, allowing that he was released after a day in jail and that despite his best efforts he was never paid for the doors in question, which doesn't exactly bother him. Clabbers' high-quality workmanship and his keen business sense have enabled the entrepreneur to guide his family-owned and -operated venture into a $20-million business.

National Glass and Metal Co. of Pennsylvania began in Oakford in

Seated (left to right) are daughter-in-law, Laurie Clabbers; president Gerard Clabbers; and Ann Clabbers. Standing (left to right) are three of the four sons presently active in the business: Michael, Neil, and Joseph.

1970, in a former post office building with about 800 square feet of floor space. Clabbers, who had an extensive background in glass and metal systems, used to work with his father and his six children cutting glass and making metal frames, waking the children at 5 a.m. before school to come work in the shop. Once, while cutting a piece of glass on the glass-

Neil Clabbers reviewing drawings with shop employee, Frank Eberhart.

cutting table, the whole table fell through the old wooden floor.

Sales for the first year were around $400,000. And it wasn't long before National Glass and Metal Co. was ready to expand. A new warehouse and office were built, and in 1976 the Clabbers family founded National Glass and Metal Company of New Jersey. In 1982 a wholesale residential building products division called CDS Sales and Service, Inc., was formed by the Clabbers family and partner Steve Sherr. In 1983 the corporate headquarters was established in Bensalem, and in December 1983 Ann Clabbers founded Lupton Architectural Productions, Inc., a company that manufactures commercial glass and metal products in Pennsauken, New Jersey.

Today Ann and Gerard Clabbers, three of their six children, and one daughter-in-law work at National Glass and Metal Co., along with sixty-five other employees. The business, which includes engineering, testing, manufacturing, and installation of architectural metal and glass, does not advertise. Through satisfied customers in buildings ranging from commercial to schools, hotels, shopping centers, and high-rise office complexes, National Glass and Metal Co. of Pennsylvania has built a reputation as one of the leading suppliers of glass and metal products in the Delaware Valley.

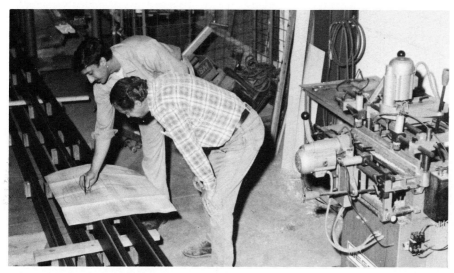

CHARLES JACQUIN ET CIE., INC.
JACQUIN PRESTIGE LIQUEURS

Its products include blackberry-flavored brandy, peach schnapps, ginger-flavored brandy, and creme de cacao. In total Jacquin makes sixty different cordials from extracts as pure as winter's first snow and, no doubt, much more delicious. Charles Jacquin Et Cie., Inc., was established in America in 1884 by a young Frenchman named Charles Jacquin, who had recently immigrated to the United States to produce cordials and liqueurs the way his family made them in France.

Today Charles Jacquin is the oldest cordial and liqueur company in the United States. A walk through the Jacquin corporate headquarters in Philadelphia reveals not only every imaginable flavor of cordials and liqueurs but also a burgeoning number of liqueur-enhanced items ranging from a luscious Devonshire brownie to strawberry preserves with Chambord Liqueur.

Norton Cooper, president of the company, recalls the background of the 100-year-old firm as smoothly as a Jacquin creme de menthe slides over ice cream.

History has it that upon his arrival in America, Charles Jacquin joined forces in New York with a Mr. Hochstater, who had a background in business. The firm prospered, but neither Jacquin or Hochstater had any heirs. When they died, their li-

The corporate headquarters of Charles Jacquin Et Cie., Inc., America's oldest cordial and liqueur producer, is at 2633 Trenton Avenue, Philadelphia.

The 102-year-old company produces every imaginable flavor of cordials and liqueurs.

queur business was left to Emanuel Osterman, who began working at Jacquin Liqueur when he was a young boy. During Prohibition Osterman continued to make cordials—though without alcohol.

When Prohibition ended in 1934, Osterman moved his operation from New York to Philadelphia, where he joined forces with Maurice J. Cooper, Norton Cooper's father. When Osterman retired in 1949, Maurice became the sole owner of the business. In 1979, several years after his father's death, Norton Cooper and several partners offered a leveraged buy out of the company to other family members and public shareholders and purchased all of the

company's stock.

Today Jacquin Liqueurs employs 400 people in five factories worldwide including a plant in Philadelphia where cordials and Jacquin Vodka (the most popular vodka in Pennsylvania) are bottled; a twenty-acre distillery in central Florida where Jacquin produces, among other things, its Florida Wine Cooler; a distribution plant in New Jersey; a liqueur operation in Chambord, France; and a liqueur plant in Plymouth, Devon, England, devoted entirely to the production of Devonshire Royal Cream Liqueur.

Together, the various plants account for $100 million in sales each year. Jacquin Prestige Liqueurs is the largest-selling line of liqueurs and cordials in Pennsylvania and along the Eastern Seaboard.

GREELEY AND HANSEN

In the spring of 1985, officials in Philadelphia literally pulled a switch to start the Water Department's first computer-controlled processing operation at the city's Southwest Water Pollution Control Plant. The computer system controls the level of water flowing into the plant and monitors the operation of pumping equipment at this oxygen-activated sludge plant, which pumps 210 million gallons of wastewater per day. Not only does the new computer system save money on energy costs for the city, it alerts operators to potential problems, such as flooding or equipment failure.

Working in tandem with the city's engineers to complete the project was an international engineering firm that for over seven decades has specialized in the fields of water, wastewater, and solid waste. That company is Greeley and Hansen.

Based in Chicago since 1914, Greeley and Hansen has provided service to more than 500 municipalities, states, federal agencies, and industries. The partnership, founded by Langdon Pearse and Samuel A. Greeley as Pearse and Greeley, has

The City of Philadelphia's Southwest Water Pollution Control Plant.

used the name of Greeley and Hansen since 1933.

The firm opened a branch office in Philadelphia in 1974, one of eight branch offices located throughout the United States and in Naples, Italy. The Philadelphia office provides expertise in process and design engineering in the environmental field, as well as all necessary support disciplines. Through its staff of about fifty

people, the Philadelphia office has been responsible for complete engineering services for over one billion dollars in water, wastewater, and solid-waste facilities throughout the area.

These projects include a complete water supply study for Allentown, the design of sewage-collection systems for housing developments in Abington, and operations assistance for the Delaware County Regional Water Quality Control Authority (DELCORA) in Chester. Also included are extensive facilities in Camden, New Jersey, and New York City, among others.

Since 1970 Greeley and Hansen has provided studies, design, and construction services to the City of Philadelphia's Water Department, engineering the substantial upgrade/expansion of the three existing wastewater treatment plants. The firm has also been authorized by the city to study alternatives for disposing of sludge from the plants.

For the future, the city is in good hands. The comprehensive wastewater-treatment and sludge-disposal studies conducted by Greeley and Hansen have encompassed costs, environmental effects, and numerous other factors. The actions being implemented as a result of these studies will accommodate the city's needs to the year 2020.

Little Lehigh Creek, Allentown's primary drinking water supply.

THE PHILADELPHIA STOCK EXCHANGE

In 1746 the mayor of Philadelphia, James Hamilton, appropriated $750 toward erecting an exchange. But it wasn't until 1754 that William Bradford, who later served under George Washington in the Revolutionary War, followed Hamilton's lead and opened the London Coffee House.

Its express purpose? "A licensed place to which to come and be centered the news from all parts of the world, an exchange upon which our merchants may walk and a place of resort where our chief citizens in every department of life can meet and convene upon subjects which concern the City and State."

And so it began, in the London Coffee House on the southeast corner of Market Street, an active market in bills of exchange, turnpike and bridge shares, and other early forms of negotiable capital. In 1790 the official Philadelphia Board of Brokers Exchange came into being, with the election of Matthew McConnell as its first president.

It would be two years before the rival exchange in New York was established. Therefore, the Stock Exchange in Philadelphia is the nation's oldest stock exchange, evolving in nearly 200 years from a regional to a national to an international exchange.

A glance through the voluminous history of this 200-year-old organization reveals a myriad of firsts—proof positive that the Philadelphia Stock Exchange has been launching revolutionary ideas since its inception.

The Philadelphia Stock Exchange (also known as the PHLX), became the nation's first stock clearinghouse in 1870. It also established the first associate membership arrangement with the Baltimore Stock Exchange in 1955, giving members of both exchanges access to each other's floors, thereby creating the forerunner of a national intermarket trading system. In 1973 the PHLX became the first exchange to offer an active odd-lot market in government securities, thus giving the small investor a liquid market in securities backed by the

This Grecian-style building housed the Philadelphia Stock Exchange from 1832 to 1876. Known as the Merchants Exchange Building, it was designed by William Strickland and is now part of the Independence Hall Historical Complex.

U.S. government. The following year the Exchange installed Centramart, the first fully automated internal computer system at a U.S. stock exchange.

In 1975 the Philadelphia Stock Ex-

change became the first regional exchange to trade in stock options. Two years later the Exchange installed PACE, the nation's first fully automated order delivery and execution system. In 1978 the PHLX provided the first linkage with another exchange, marking the beginning of

Nicholas A. Giordano and Martin L. Longstreth, Jr. (left to right), president and chairman of the board, respectively, of the Philadelphia Stock Exchange.

the Intermarket Trading System. In 1982 the organization became the first U.S. exchange to trade options in foreign currencies, and now trades options on seven currencies—the German mark, British pound, Canadian dollar, Japanese yen, Swiss franc, French franc, and the European Currency Unit. The following year it became the first exchange to trade put and call options on a gold/ silver index. PHLX now offers options on the Value Line Index, as well as an over-the-counter index— the XOC.

In the spring of 1985, the PHLX continued its role as an innovator when it established a fourth subsidiary to provide a futures exchange market known as the Philadelphia Board of Trade (PBOT). The PBOT, which began trading options on the Eurodollar, does not plan to duplicate products already traded on other commodity exchanges. Rather, it will be introducing products unique to the current financial futures industry.

Today the Philadelphia Stock Ex-

The Philadelphia Board of Brokers Exchange began in the London Coffee House in 1790 on Market Street. Nearly 200 years later the Philadelphia Stock Exchange occupies this modern building at 1900 Market Street.

change is the fastest-growing stock exchange in the country. The PHLX trades stocks in more than 1,200 of the largest and best-known companies. The vast majority of those stocks are traded on other exchanges,

but the PHLX also maintains a primary market in more than 100 stocks that are not listed on any other exchange.

Approximately 498 million shares were traded in 1985, a 10-percent increase over the 453 million shares traded the previous year. This increase in volume brought daily average volume up to approximately 2 million shares a day.

In addition to the PBOT, the Philadelphia Stock Exchange has three subsidiaries: Stock Clearing Corporation of Philadelphia; Philadelphia Depository Trust Company, which ensures the safekeeping of securities; and The Financial Automation Corporation of Philadelphia, which is the data-processing arm of the exchange.

On any given day the floor of the Philadelphia Stock Exchange is teaming with brokers carrying on the tradition first started by ten prominent Philadelphia businessmen who met at the London Coffee House and, later, the City Tavern. Today the PHLX is an international association of diverse member firms and individuals, including large and small brokerage houses, floor members, institutional investors, and large banks.

The Philadelphia Stock Exchange is proud of its 200-year-old history and looks forward to carrying on its tradition of service and innovation for investors.

The Foreign Currency Option Trading Floor.

PENNSYLVANIA LUMBERMEN'S MUTUAL INSURANCE COMPANY

It was a fact. The insurance companies believed that all lumber properties were potential fire hazards because wood, after all, burns. As a result, the insurance rates for lumber properties and businesses were higher than other enterprises—despite the fact that available records clearly showed that the fire loss ratio of the lumber industry was exceptionally low.

In 1895 a group of prominent eastern lumbermen decided they were fed up with the discriminatory practices of the insurance business and the high rates the firms imposed on lumber companies. For two years their many protests against the unjust rate structure had not only failed to change the position of the insurance

J. Frank Braceland, Jr., chairman of the board.

Cornelius A. Kane, president and chief executive officer.

The officers of Pennsylvania Lumbermen's Mutual Insurance Company are (seated, left to right) George M. Fleagle, treasurer; Cornelius A. Kane, president and chief executive officer; and Frank A. White, Jr., vice-president and secretary. Standing, left to right, are John E. Rice, vice-president; Fred R. Phillips, vice-president; and Richard J. Schmid, vice-president.

associations, they had backfired.

As an example, a young Philadelphia lumberman named Edward F. Henson had asked the Fire Underwriters' Association of Philadelphia for a lower rate, submitting facts and figures to substantiate his claim. Within days he received a reply: His

rate was increased!

With Henson leading the way, the lumbermen, all members of trade associations in the eastern United States, organized a mutual insurance company to write fire insurance on lumber operations only. Thus, the

Pennsylvania Lumbermen's Mutual Fire Insurance Company was born.

On March 1, 1895, the Pennsylvania Lumbermen's Mutual Fire Insurance Company began business. That Friday morning the following account appeared in a local newspaper:

"After many years of protest against rates which it is claimed have been excessive, the lumber and allied trades of this city and the state have secured a charter, under the style of the Pennsylvania Lumbermen's Mutual Fire Insurance Company, and will immediately commence the business of insuring their own stocks.

"The company has been organized with Edward F. Henson, of E.P. Burton & Co., president; Edwin H. Coane, of Henry C. Patterson & Co., treasurer; and William T. Bryan, secretary. The directors are Emil Guenther and Richard Torpin of this city; George F. Lance of Reading; S.H. Sturdevant of Wilkes-Barre; S.H. Keck of Allentown; and W.Z. Sener of Lancaster.

"Mr. Henson received the charter yesterday, and already from the trade there are applications for insurance amounting to over half a million dollars. . . . "

The year 1985 marked the ninetieth anniversary of the Pennsylvania Lumbermen's Mutual Insurance Company. (The word "Fire" was dropped in 1950.) And since its inception, PLM has never really deviated from its basic purpose of providing fair and knowledgeable insurance coverage to members of the lumber and woodworking industries.

From its headquarters in downtown Philadelphia, PLM provides insurance policies to close to 4,000 lumber businesses. Until recently the firm provided only property insurance. However, in 1981, casualty insurance was added to expand PLM's services to lumber businesses throughout New England, the Southeast, and the Midwest.

A page from the earliest book of the organization reveals that the first PLM office was set up in a rented room on the second floor of Henson's lumberyard office at 921 North Delaware Avenue, on the waterfront near Poplar Street. That proved to be an excellent location because most of the Philadelphia lumberyards were located on Delaware Avenue, and the proximity to the Delaware River allowed the lumber boats and barges to dock almost at the front door of most of the yards.

The first insurance policy was issued to Charles Betts for "$10,000 on lumber." It covered lumber stored on Pier 48, North Wharves, Philadelphia, which was close to the PLM offices.

The company grew larger and stronger as the years went by. And, although PLM was organized to insure only lumber property, in 1930 the decision was made to write what became known as general business insurance. That meant the creation of a new department, and it was almost the same as organizing a new company. However, each year more agents were added, more business written. The small lumber-writing insurance company was growing up.

The first office of PLM was on the second floor of E.F. Henson's lumber office at 921 North Delaware Avenue. From left to right are Miss Hughes, Miss Jefferis, E. Rushton, and H. Billeter.

Today lumber businesses still represent the overwhelming majority of policyholders at PLM. Although the firm's exclusive access to that market has over time been challenged by its competitors, PLM retains much of the original market that it has held for generations.

To continue to meet the needs of its clients, PLM has over the past few years broadened both its sales and marketing efforts, added a Loss Control Division, streamlined its processing, and upgraded its daily servicing capacity. Today the company employs 150 people and taps into a network of approximately 500 lumber insurance brokers to present and sell its policies.

The corporate offices have moved five times since 1895. And, according to president Cornelius A. Kane, the firm will move again in 1986 to new offices in downtown Philadelphia.

As it heads toward its 100th anniversary, Pennsylvania Lumbermen's Mutual Insurance Company likes to note that it is one of only five insurance companies nationwide that continues to specialize in the lumber business. And the company slogan fits the spirit of growth that has been the benchmark of this firm since 1895: "From a small acorn, a mighty oak."

THE PENNSYLVANIA STATE UNIVERSITY

Since its founding in 1855, The Pennsylvania State University has been a leader in providing research, education, and public service to the Commonwealth of Pennsylvania.

Dr. Evan Pugh, Penn State's first president, set the stage for many of the institution's accomplishments. He persuaded the state legislature to designate it Pennsylvania's land-grant institution in 1862, following President Abraham Lincoln's signing of the Morrill Land-Grant Act, thus legally obligating Penn State to offer a wide range of utilitarian and liberal studies. Despite its status as the Commonwealth's land-grant university, Penn State is not state-owned, but is state-related, with less than 25 percent of its total budget supplied by the Commonwealth.

Under its fourteenth president, Dr. Bryce Jordan (1983-   ), the university is taking steps to ensure that its academic excellence as a major, comprehensive, public research university will be extended to future generations of Pennsylvanians. These steps include measures to generate significant increases in funding from public and private sources and the strategic application of these funds.

Annually some 61,000 students and 3,800 faculty participate in the educational process at the University Park Campus in State College and at twenty-one other Penn State campuses throughout the state.

There are seventeen Commonwealth campuses: Allentown, Altoona, Beaver, Berks, Delaware County, DuBois, Fayette, Hazleton, McKeesport, Mont Alto, New Kensington, Ogontz, Schuylkill, Shenango Valley, Wilkes-Barre, Worthington Scranton, and York. They offer two-year associate degree pro-

grams and the first two years of programs for most majors, as well as continuing-education programs for their surrounding communities.

King of Prussia Center for Graduate Studies and Continuing Education and The Milton S. Hershey Medical Center in Hershey offer graduate degree programs, while Behrend College in Erie and Capital College at Harrisburg offer both baccalaureate and graduate degree programs.

President George W. Atherton (1882-1906) is considered the second founder of Penn State in recog-

nition of his ability to win widespread popular support for the institution. His administration increased enrollment, improved finances, and inaugurated strong programs in engineering and agriculture.

With the arrival of Milton S. Eisenhower, Penn State gained national attention. His tenure coincided with his brother Dwight D. Eisenhower's term as President of the United States. Milton Eisenhower worked to transform Penn State from a leading agricultural and engineering college to a university internationally recognized as well for its achieve-

When the first Old Main was completed in 1863 it was the entire university and served as dormitory, dining hall, classroom, laboratory, library, and administration building. In 1929-1930 the original building was razed and rebuilt on the same foundations with stone removed from the first Old Main. The new Old Main now houses the university's central administrative offices. Photo by Scott Johnson

ments in science and the liberal arts.

The presidency of Eric A. Walker (1956-1970) was marked by unprecedented expansion in enrollment, physical plant, curricular offerings, and research programs. Dr. Walker oversaw the development of Penn State's Milton S. Hershey Medical Center in 1963 (from a $50-million grant from the M.S. Hershey Foundation), the expansion of the Commonwealth Campus System, and the formation of a College of Arts and Architecture.

President John W. Oswald (1970-1983) successfully dealt with serious financial problems besetting the university and developed and implemented a long-range plan to guide it through the 1980s.

To date, more than 300,000 students have received Penn State degrees, some 150,000 of whom live and work in Pennsylvania.

Nearly 90 percent of Pennsylvania's population lives within thirty miles of a Penn State campus. More than 180,000 Pennsylvanians annually enroll in a variety of continuing-education programs offered under the auspices of Penn State's Commonwealth Educational System. This number will continue to increase as more adults take advantage of educational opportunities to advance their careers and enhance their lives.

In addition to educational programs, Penn State is noted for its research, which is funded by federal and state governments, business and industry, foundations, and individuals. In a National Science Foundation survey reported in 1985, Penn State ranked nineteenth nationally in research and development dollars received from federal agencies. Total research expenditures for 1985-1986 exceeded $145 million.

Through the quality of its research and teaching faculty, Penn State has attained international distinction in many of its agriculture and engineering programs, acoustics, meteorology, geography, English, psychology, speech communication, chemistry, astronomy, individual and family stud-

This aerial view of the central part of University Park Campus shows some of the 294 buildings and 4,767 acres that comprise Penn State's main campus.

ies, business administration, teacher education, art education, theatre arts, and health, physical education, and recreation.

Through a variety of cooperative public service programs, such as the Pennsylvania Technical Assistance Program (PENNTAP), the university makes its expertise available to assist business and industry in the application of advanced technologies to preserve and create jobs, and to solve economic, technical, and social prob-

lems in both private and public sectors of the economy. The Pennsylvania Cooperative Extension Service, operated by Penn State's College of Agriculture since 1907, reaches more than two million Pennsylvanians each year.

Throughout its history, Penn State has worked to meet the educational, research, and service needs of the Commonwealth and the nation. The university is dedicated to preserving its land-grant heritage of excellence and opportunity for all Pennsylvanians as it prepares to meet the challenges of the twenty-first century.

Evan Pugh, Penn State's first president, served from 1859 until his death in 1864.

George W. Atherton, Penn State's "second founder," was president of the university from 1882 to 1906.

METROPOLITAN EDISON COMPANY
PENNSYLVANIA ELECTRIC COMPANY

Metropolitan Edison Company and Pennsylvania Electric Company are proud to be numbered among the Commonwealth's industries that have made a significant contribution to the welfare and growth of Pennsylvania.

As Pennsylvania has developed over the years, so have Metropolitan Edison and Pennsylvania Electric. They stand for a system that serves the electric energy needs of more than 911,000 residential, commercial, and industrial customers. The firms' product, electricity, touches the lives of people in some way twenty-four hours a day, seven days a week, 365 days a year. Electricity from Metropolitan Edison's and Pennsylvania Electric's plants is sent over transmission and distribution lines to homes, schools, hospitals, businesses, indus-

tries, and fire and police departments around the clock. It travels throughout more than 20,889 square miles in Pennsylvania into over 1,020 communities and is there when it is needed.

The firms' combined payroll of about $218 million goes to employees who contribute significantly to the economic fabric of the broad Pennsylvania area they serve.

■ **Metropolitan Edison Co.**
▨ **Pennsylvania Electric Co.**

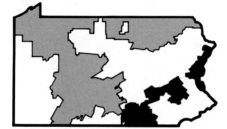

Recognizing a growing need for efficient energy usage and energy conservation, the parent company, General Public Utilities, developed a conservation and load management master plan that incorporates various strategies such as Time-of-Day incentive rates, residential energy home audits, weatherization programs, business and industry energy-management committees, and cogeneration programs to help customers get the most for their electric energy dollars.

Metropolitan Edison Company and Pennsylvania Electric Company are genuinely concerned with the energy needs and problems facing all of their customers and they are striving to find new and better ways to continue to contribute to the well-being of Pennsylvania and a brighter tomorrow.

GENERAL TELEPHONE COMPANY OF PENNSYLVANIA

The history of General Telephone in Pennsylvania stretches back to February 1897, when the Mutual Telephone Company was incorporated for "constructing, maintaining, and operating telephones in the City of Erie and adjoining Millcreek Township." The firm was capitalized at $25,000 and had ten employees. When Mutual issued its first telephone directory in 1899, it listed 160 subscribers.

Mutual was founded by local businessmen, led by the Erie Board of Trade, after attempts to persuade the Bell Company to lower its rates and improve service. At the time a business telephone cost seventy-five dollars a year, only slightly less than the annual rental on a typical six-room apartment. Telephone instruments provided by Bell to Erie subscribers were usually equipment discarded by growing systems in larger cities.

Mutual introduced a high-technology switchboard with 24-hour operator service, lower rates, and a rebate for stockholders. As a result, the company grew rapidly, both in capitalization and in subscribers. Mutual operators became friends of the entire community, a source of fire alarms and news, baseball scores, and election returns. By 1913 Mutual controlled over 60 percent of Erie's telephones and processed 48,000 calls per day.

Mutual operated in competition with the Bell Company until 1917, when the two groups entered into a qualified toll agreement. Mutual grew rapidly under the new arrangement, and in 1926 it acquired the local Bell operations in Erie, Corry, Union City, North East, Girard, and Fairview.

Mutual changed its name to Pennsylvania Telephone Corporation in 1930, when it acquired three other independent firms serving Johnstown, Oil City, and nearby counties. Pennsylvania Telephone itself became part of General Telephone Corporation in the same decade. The current name, General Telephone Company of Pennsylvania, was adopted in 1952.

Vandergrift Telephone Company

was acquired in 1954 and later was merged with General Telephone Company of Pennsylvania. In 1972 York Telephone and Telegraph Company and Princeton Telephone Company were both merged with General Telephone. Expansion continues, most recently with General Telephone's 1985 merger with Bethel and Mt. Aetna Telephone and Telegraph, which had been operated as an affiliated subsidiary since 1966.

Today the 2,277 employees of General Telephone Company of Pennsyl-

The sleek, modern console (top photo) replaced the traditional plug-in type of switchboard (bottom photo) when General Telephone cut over its Traffic Service Position System, a new computer-controlled system to handle operator-assisted long-distance telephone calls. With the new system, customers dial their own person-to-person, collect, credit card, third-number, and special billing calls.

vania serve approximately 375,000 customers in 126 communities. The firm is a subsidiary of GTE Corporation of Stamford, Connecticut.

AMP INCORPORATED

Opened in mid-1983, this headquarters facility for AMP Incorporated is located near the Eisenhower Interchange, overlooking the Harrisburg East Mall.

AMP Incorporated is part of your daily life. If you ride in a car, boat, train, or plane, watch television, or make a phone call, you are probably using AMP products. An international corporation based in Harrisburg, AMP is the world's leading producer of electrical and electronic connection devices. Whenever electrical wires, cables, printed circuit boards, or other components must be connected, AMP makes a device and related application tools and machines that will handle the job.

It all started with relatively simple uninsulated electrical wire terminals and hand crimping tools for use by aircraft and marine manufacturers—replacing slow and unreliable hand soldering. Increasingly complex connectors and sophisticated application machines have been added through the years.

The founder of AMP was Uncas A. Whitaker, a graduate of MIT (B.S.M.E.), Carnegie-Mellon (B.S.E.E.), and Cleveland Law School (L.L.B.).

His guiding principles were to find talented people and give them room to work, and to maintain leadership in an industry, take one product area and engineer it to perfection.

AMP was founded on September 15, 1941, in Elizabeth, New Jersey. Production facilities were moved to Glen Rock, Pennsylvania, in 1942. Since 1943 AMP has been headquartered in Harrisburg, with many of its

facilities concentrated in Central Pennsylvania.

Sales grew rapidly during the war years but the transition to a postwar economy proved stressful for the young company. Major cutbacks and economy measures were required as the firm changed its emphasis from military to commercial markets.

The way to renewed corporate prosperity was led by a new AMP product system—strip-formed terminals on reels applied with semi-automatic bench machines—and by policies for expansion still followed today: internal growth through new products, a strong engineering orientation, a full range of application tooling, direct sales and service, geographic dispersal of modestly sized facilities, and conservative financing.

In 1952 AMP created subsidiaries in Puerto Rico, France, and Canada, as well as the marketing subsidiary now known as AMP Special Indus-

The current leaders of AMP Incorporated are Walter F. Raab, chairman and chief executive officer (right), and Harold A. McInnes, president.

AMP supplies to its customers, directly or through AMP distributors and co-op cable assembly houses, a widening range of connectors and cable assemblies. These products include ribbon, coaxial, telephone, undercarpet, fiber-optic, and flexible flat cable and connector assemblies.

tries. As the decade progressed, AMP introduced new products such as pin and socket connectors, coaxial cable connectors, printed circuit board connectors, and more advanced application machines. Facilities were built throughout Central Pennsylvania, and foreign subsidiaries were opened in Australia, England, Holland, Italy, Japan, Mexico, and West Germany. In 1956 AMP Incorporated became publicly held.

When Whitaker died in 1975, Cleve J. Fredricksen was elected chairman. He was succeeded upon his retirement in 1981 by Joseph D. Brenner, who in turn retired in 1982.

Today AMP is led by chairman and chief executive officer Walter F. Raab and president Harold A. McInnes. Raab, a Wharton School graduate and CPA who joined AMP

in 1953, was elected treasurer in 1968 and vice-president in 1971. He became a director in 1975 and chairman in 1982. McInnes, a graduate of MIT, joined AMP as an engineer in 1965. He became president and a director in 1981.

Most of the customer systems that are expanding the market for AMP products today were not even conceived when the firm was created. The aircraft and marine manufacturers that were AMP's earliest clients are still valued customers. But now the company also supplies products to manufacturers of computers, instrumentation, telecommunication systems, home entertainment equipment, and such high-technology concepts as cellular radio, robotics, the 200-mile-per-hour French TGV railroad, and the space shuttle. Today more than 30,000 manufacturers use AMP's 160 product lines—over 300,000 part numbers.

Today's products include complex advanced connectors for coaxial cables, ribbon cables, fiber-optic cables, printed circuit boards, and flexible circuitry; cable assemblies; miniature electronic switches; and membrane switches and keyboards.

AMP is an unusual new-era, high-technology corporation—an

engineering-oriented company whose business is not labor, material, or capital intensive. It is geographically diverse, employing 22,000 people worldwide. Domestically, AMP employs 15,000 people (9,000 in Pennsylvania) in 150 facilities clustered around hubs in Central Pennsylvania, North and South Carolina, and the Shenandoah Valley area of Virginia—and in Arizona, Florida, and New Hampshire. Internationally, AMP's 25 wholly owned subsidiaries employ 7,000 people in over 50 facilities in Canada, Latin America, Europe, and the Far East.

AMP ranks 223 on the *Fortune* 500 list. Sales in 1985 exceeded $1.6 billion. The firm has consistently maintained a 15-percent compound annual growth rate since the early 1950s.

AMP's future is closely linked to the dramatic growth of the electronics industry. Micro-miniaturization of electronics, laser devices, and fiber optics all hold new challenges and opportunities.

As the leader in developing application equipment in the connector industry, AMP works closely with major customers to develop robotic systems for flexible, programmable automation to install or terminate many AMP products.

NATIONAL FUEL GAS COMPANY

Crews are laying a twenty-inch steel pipeline (Line K) to carry gas from producing areas in Pennsylvania to Buffalo.

The history of the use of natural gas in this country is, in fact, the history of National Fuel. Fredonia, New York, was the site of the nation's first gas well (1821) and the first gas-lighted streets. Western New York State, Northwestern Pennsylvania, and the Eastern Ohio region served by National Fuel today includes this historic location among its 500 service communities with a total population of 2,340,000. The Pennsylvania Division of National Fuel Gas Distribution Corporation, the public utility arm of the National Fuel system, is headquartered in Erie.

The path from its first well to contemporary corporation status has been marked by distinguished milestones. In 1868 National Fuel supplied the first industrial user, an Erie company. In 1886 it completed its first large pipeline, an 8-inch by 87-mile transmission line running from McKean County, Pennsylvania, to Buffalo, New York. It was the world's longest natural gas pipeline and a marvel of engineering and construction, built where there were no paved roads, no motor trucks, and no power tools.

The completed pipeline led the way to the consolidation of local independents into regional natural gas corporations. Continuing its tradition of innovative industrial leadership, National Fuel constructed a 1,000-horsepower, gas-driven compressor in its Halsey field. In 1916 National Fuel provided the nation's first underground gas storage facility at its Zoar field, near Buffalo.

The corporate life of National Fuel started on December 8, 1902, as a New Jersey firm with headquarters in New York. By February 1903 the new concern had purchased shares of capital stock of the following companies: United Natural Gas, Salamanca Gas, Buffalo Natural Gas, Provincial Gas, Pennsylvania Gas, Oil City Fuel Supply, Commercial Natural Gas, and Pennsylvania Oil Company. That initial action, followed by many other mergers, led to the consolidation of more than 160 originally independent firms.

National Fuel took its modern form in 1974, with the merger and restructuring of three separate companies: United Natural Gas Company, Pennsylvania Gas Company, and Iroquois Gas Corporation. Today's National Fuel Gas Company is a holding company for National Fuel Gas Supply Corporation, National Fuel Gas Distribution Corporation, Seneca Resources Corporation, Penn-York Energy Corporation, and Empire Exploration, Inc.

National Fuel's companies are engaged in all phases of the natural gas business—exploration, production, purchasing, gathering, transmission, storage, and distribution, together with by-product operations. In addition, Seneca Resources Corporation is also engaged in marketing timber and coal from its Pennsylvania land holdings.

The president and chief executive officer of National Fuel Gas Company is Louis R. Reif, who was elected chairman of the American Gas Association for 1984-1985. Bernard J. Kennedy is executive vice-president and general counsel. John M. Brown is executive vice-president.

Almost three-quarters of a century later, a section of the same line is being replaced. Some aspects of the natural gas business haven't changed very much.

CONTINENTAL BANK

From its executive offices in Philadelphia, Continental Bank serves the entire Delaware Valley, one of the largest markets in the nation.

Continental Bank is actually the result of more than eighteen mergers and acquisitions over the years. Primarily, the mergers reflect the parallel development of two regional banks: The Broad Street Trust Company of Philadelphia and Montgomery County Bank & Trust Company of Norristown.

The Broad Street Trust Company was incorporated in Philadelphia on October 21, 1921. Nearly forty-four years later, on August 2, 1965, the Broad Street Trust merged with the Montgomery County Bank to create Continental Bank and Trust Company. In June 1969 the name was shortened to Continental Bank.

During the early 1970s the executive management team at Continental, led by chairman of the board and chief executive officer Roy T. Peraino, developed a strategy to concentrate its banking efforts on lending to small and medium-sized Delaware

Continental Bank's executive offices are located at Centre Square in Philadelphia, across from City Hall.

Valley-based businesses.

It was a wise move. For one, the Delaware Valley has a rich and diverse economy, owing much of its diversity to the large number of small to mid-sized companies headquartered there. As Philadelphia's manufacturing base began to mature in the late 1960s and early 1970s, the region's economy began to rely more heavily upon service industries for growth. With this change in the economy there also was a shift in the size and borrowing needs of the firms within the market. Continental Bank, the Delaware Valley's premier small- to middle-market lender, was ideally positioned to respond to and profit from this opportunity.

Continental—the flagship of Continental Bancorp, a regional multibank holding company with assets of $4.8 billion—operates sixty branch offices in Bucks, Chester, Delaware, Montgomery, and Philadelphia counties, with 80 percent of its loans made to business.

The name "Continental" is synonymous with more than banking. In the Delaware Valley, Continental's officers and employees have established a tradition of serving the community—through leadership and active participation in numerous civic and community affairs. For example, each year since 1974, Continental has sponsored the largest one-day golf tournament in the country benefiting the Cystic Fibrosis Foundation. During the nation's bicentennial celebration, Continental Bank restored the Tomb of the Unknown Soldier of the American Revolution, located in Philadelphia's Washington Square, including the installation of a gas-fired eternal flame at the site.

Also, Continental sponsors a Merit Award dinner each year to raise money for the Cancer Research Center of The Children's Hospital of Philadelphia.

Continental Bank maintains its executive offices at 1500 Market Street, where its glass facade reflects the towers of City Hall. The bank's legal headquarters is in Norristown, Montgomery County, and its Operations Center is located in the Fort Washington Industrial Park, a key location for serving its customers throughout its five-county market area.

The Tomb of the Unknown Soldier of the American Revolution. Continental Bank refurbished the site in 1976 and installed the eternal flame. Each year the bank holds memorial services at the tomb to honor the memory of those who fought for our country's freedom.

CONRAIL

There are few corporations in the country that would qualify for the "Big Screen" if a screenplay were written about them. After all, such a coup would require drama, tragedy, confrontation, survival, and—in keeping with a society that keeps close tabs on its net worth—profit.

One such company, based in Philadelphia, has all these elements, and more. That company is Conrail, the Consolidated Rail Corporation, which runs a 13,400-mile system spanning fifteen states in the Northeast and Midwest.

Prior to April 1976 Conrail was six individual railroad companies in bankruptcy: The Penn Central Transportation Company, Central Railroad of New Jersey, Lehigh Valley Railroad Company, Reading Company, Lehigh and Hudson River Railway, and Erie Lackawanna Railway. Those railroads carried half of the rail freight of the most heavily industrialized region in the country. Their demise threatened not only the loss of regional services, but also a vital link in the closely integrated national rail system.

Congress responded to that pending tragedy and established Conrail as a for-profit corporation that combined most of the facilities of the six bankrupt systems. Conrail's principal goal was to create a financially self-sustaining freight rail service system in the region, which required a multibillion-dollar upgrading of its physical plant and facilities.

And statistics, pure and simple, tell this story's happy status. In 1978 Conrail reported a loss of more than

Conrail's 2,800 locomotives are the workhorses of a freight system that operates over 13,400 route miles in fifteen states. The SD-40-2 locomotives are shown here.

$400 million. In 1984 the firm reported what amounts to a remarkable $900-million turnaround, as net income rose to $500 million.

Conrail, with more than 4,000 miles of line in the Commonwealth, has a strong commitment to Pennsylvania. The railroad's corporate headquarters is in Philadelphia, and four of its seventeen operating divisions, two of its four operating regions, and three of its major freight car classification yards are located in the state.

Open-top hopper cars are loaded at a coal mine tipple for one of the many Conrail industrial and utility customers. Coal, which accounts for about 16 percent of Conrail's revenues, is delivered by Conrail for both domestic use by utilities and industry, and for export through ports at Toledo and Ashtabula, Ohio, and Philadelphia, Pennsylvania.

In addition, nearly 15,000 of the firm's 38,000 employees work in Pennsylvania (as of 1984).

Conrail's principal east-west route through Pennsylvania is the Pittsburgh Line between Harrisburg and Pittsburgh. From Pittsburgh, the line connects with other routes to Cleveland, Columbus, Cincinnati, Toledo, Detroit, Indianapolis, Chicago, and St. Louis. From Harrisburg, routes fan out to Philadelphia, Reading, Allentown, Washington, D.C., Baltimore, and the New York-New Jersey metropolitan area, connecting with other Conrail lines to New England and northward to Buffalo.

To keep these and other lines in Pennsylvania in top condition, Conrail has a continuing program of track maintenance and improvement. Since the corporation was created in 1976 it has invested more than $600 million in improvements to its Pennsylvania tracks alone.

Those improvements include the installation of continuous welded rail in place of traditional jointed rail over most of Conrail's principal routes. Throughout its system, the firm makes the necessary investments to ensure that its customers receive the service they need and demand. In 1985, for instance, Conrail carried out a $574-million system-wide capital investment program; a program of more than $500 million was undertaken in 1986.

Throughout its system, Conrail transported more than 181 million

These diesel locomotive traction motor wheel assemblies have been repaired and are awaiting shipment or installation at the Juniata Locomotive Repair Shop at Altoona, Pennsylvania.

tons of freight in 1985. This tonnage includes more than thirty-five major commodities, such as coal, coke, and ore; automobiles and automotive parts; farm and food products; chemicals; pulp and paper products; and general merchandise. To handle this freight, Conrail runs an average of 760 trains each day, drawing on an equipment fleet of about 90,000 freight cars and 2,800 locomotives.

The Northeast Rail Service Act of 1981 mandated a return to private-sector ownership (Conrail is 85-percent government owned) if Conrail achieved profitability. On February 8, 1985, Secretary of Transportation Elizabeth Dole announced that she was recommending to Congress that the Norfolk Southern Corporation be designated to acquire the federal government's interest in Con-

This TrailVan piggyback train carrying general merchandise is moving eastbound around Horseshoe Curve near Altoona, Pennsylvania. The curve is a well-known Pennsylvania landmark.

rail. Before Conrail is sold, however, many options are on the table to consider, including the possibility that Conrail should be sold to a group of investors and allowed to survive on its own and not be merged with another rail system.

Ultimately, the decision will be made in Congress, which must approve the sale and pass enabling legislation. And so the future of Conrail will be decided in exactly the same corridors of power where it was created in 1976.

Hollywood couldn't ask for a better script.

Conway Yard, located on the Pittsburgh-Chicago main line about twenty miles north of Pittsburgh, handles much of Conrail's east-west freight traffic. The yard is composed of two separate freight car classification areas where about forty through freight trains are processed each day.

601

PENNWOOD PRODUCTS/BEAU PRODUCTS

From their East Berlin, Pennsylvania, facilities, Pennwood Products and its sister company, Beau Products, provide the perfect finishing touches to thousands of homes throughout the world. Solid wood flooring products, high-quality cabinet pulls, solid wood sidings, and the finest precision-crafted moldings and trims have made Pennwood and Beau two of the most highly respected names in wood products.

If you want to see the firms' products, just look down. Pennwood has long been famous in the building industry as a producer of outstanding solid wood flooring. Its floors are found in executive offices from General Foods in New York to Arco Chemicals in California, and in commercial establishments from department stores such as the Bon Ton in Manchester Mall, York, to banks such as the Houston City Bank, Houston, Texas. Similarly, Beau Products' moldings and trims are found in better homes and commercial establishments throughout the nation.

Pennwood is now engaged primarily in the lumber business, purchasing raw hardwoods (primarily from Pennsylvania, New York and West Virginia mills), and drying, grading, and preparing the woods for use. Pennwood's largest single customer is Beau Products, which manufactures moldings, trim, flooring, handrails, picture frames, and other specialized wood products. Pennwood also supplies fencing and landscaping materials to the Central Pennsylvania market.

Pennwood was founded in 1942 by Newell E. Coxon, father of Newell E. "Skip" Coxon, Jr., and Jere M. Coxon, the current principals of the corporation. Newell Coxon, Sr., started his woodworks in a converted canning factory building. His first equipment consisted of a sawmill and two drying kilns. His first product: wooden heels for women's shoes.

Pennwood soon won respect for high-quality materials machined to fine tolerances, and the company expanded to the production of wooden

picture frame moldings in the 1950s. When Newell Coxon died in 1958, his wife, Ella I. Coxon, took over management of the firm.

Skip and Jere Coxon were still in school when their father died. Skip took over the presidency in 1961; Jere joined him as executive vice-president in 1966. The company expanded rapidly under their direction, fueled in part by the burgeoning popularity of bowling. Pennwood's hard maple alley floors proved popular both in the United States and in Japan.

The Coxons reorganized their firm in 1962, starting Beau Products as a separate operation. They expanded production of picture frame moldings and began manufacturing moldings for the kitchen cabinet industry. Other new products included plastic laminate vanity tops for the manufactured-housing industry, and shelving and furniture for schools and

Jere M. Coxon, executive vice-president (left), and Newell E. Coxon, Jr., president, at the National Kitchen and Bath Industry Show in Philadelphia in April 1986.

libraries.

Pennwood moved into flooring materials in 1972 when it started manufacturing its parquet flooring system under a contract with Arco Chemical Corporation. Gradually, this initial product evolved to become Pennwood's twelve-inch full-perimeter tongue and groove parquet flooring, a hardwood flooring system that became popular throughout the country.

In 1985 Pennwood sold its Parquet Division to Permagrain Products. Pennwood still supplies the lumber used to manufacture parquet floors, and Permagrain continues to produce the system under the Pennwood name. Unfinished hardwood flooring systems in strip, plank, and a variety of other patterns are manufactured through the Coxon family's Beau Products Company.

During the late 1970s Beau expanded into packaging products, working with Lok-Box, Inc. Lok Box contracted with Beau to produce white wooden packaging for the Mem Company's lime-scented colognes. The Franklin Mint turned to Beau to supply moldings and wood trim for its display cases of precious metal ingots and coins. To meet the demands of commercial packaging, picture framers, and interior designers, the Coxon brothers turned to exotic woods, including obeche from South Africa, koa from Hawaii, ramin from Malaysia, and mahogany from Brazil, Honduras, and Africa.

Most of the Coxons' products continue to rely on the traditional American favorite hardwoods: by far the most popular wood is oak, followed by cherry, ash, and maple. The leading products today are flooring and kitchen cabinet materials, wooden knobs and pulls, and prefinished wood moldings that can be attached to drawer edges, door fronts, and cabinet tops.

Beau's "Euroline" has led the nation in providing precision-milled, top-quality hardwood detailing designed especially to facilitate mass assembly operations. Similarly, the company's "Contura" and "Contempo" lines of interior hardwood moldings and trims are designed to add a unique custom touch to contemporary construction systems. Beau has attracted worldwide attention as a manufacturer of trim and moldings with the curved corners now in high demand by kitchen and cabinet designers everywhere. The firm's products are not only popular throughout America but are even exported to Germany and Belgium.

It's not all cosmetics, though, and Beau offers a lot more than just a pretty face. The company also manufactures hardwood plate rails, solid panels, and subassemblies that make cabinets and furniture durable and efficient as well as attractive.

Beau Products—from tree to trim.

In today's high-tech environment, Beau has developed ways of keeping the traditional beauty of wood in tune with the demands of the times. For high-stress commercial applications, the company uses an acrylic impregnation process that is coupled with artificial dyes and special hardening procedures. In use since the late 1970s, the process results in wood flooring and handrails that have not only unique physical qualities, but unprecedented durability.

Today Pennwood sits on a 17-acre site on Locust Street in East Berlin, Pennsylvania. The plant occupies 30,000 square feet, with a new 20,000-square-foot pre-drying facility scheduled for completion in late 1986. Beau occupies a separate 20,000-square-foot plant. They've come a long way since Newell Coxon, Sr., first began turning out high-quality wooden heels for ladies' shoes in his converted cannery back in 1942.

THE YORK BANK AND TRUST COMPANY

For more than 175 years The York Bank and Trust Company has contributed to the economic and community growth of York and York County. Originally organized as a banking association by eleven of York's leading citizens, The York Bank assumed the entire banking responsibility of the district on January 31, 1810. And, acting under the Omnibus Act of 1814, The York Bank was the only bank in York until 1845.

When The York Bank entered into the national banking system on November 26, 1864, the name of the institution was changed to The York National Bank. And so it remained until 1927, when the establishment of a trust department required that "and Trust Company" be added to its corporate name.

In November 1926 bank management recognized the need to assist

The main office of The York Bank and Trust Company is located at the corner of Market and Beaver streets in downtown York.

European immigrants in uniting their families. As a result, the institution organized the first travel agency in the area. The York Bank Travel Agency has continued to provide business and personal travel service for nearly sixty years.

The York Bank and Trust Company was created as a state-chartered financial institution in 1960 as the result of a consolidation with The York Trust Company. The emerging organization boasted ten branch offices located throughout the county.

In 1972 the bank provided the citizens of the area with access to the world of electronic banking by locating the area's first electronic cash dispensers in several of its branch offices. This initial entry into the emerging field of electronic funds transfer systems has evolved into the largest automatic teller machine network in York County, providing international accessibility through the CashStream and CIRRUS networks.

The dramatic changes in Pennsylvania's banking regulations in the early 1980s permitted The York Bank and Trust Company to join Continental Bancorp, Inc., a regional multibank holding company headquartered in Philadelphia, in March 1983.

The York Bank and Trust Company has long been the recognized market leader in direct lending to the business community. During the last decade it has further promoted local industrial growth by working closely with state and local industrial development authorities. Beyond these credit activities, the institution's range of business services has been expanded to include state-of-the-art information and money-management systems.

Operating twenty offices in one of the fastest-growing areas in Pennsylvania, The York Bank and Trust Company has achieved a preeminent position in its market by concentrating its resources and efforts on servicing the banking needs of individuals as well as small to mid-size businesses.

KRUSEN EVANS AND BYRNE

The law firm of Krusen Evans and Byrne has over forty attorneys engaged in a broad general practice with an emphasis on defense litigation. It is especially active in the important legal areas of asbestos and toxic waste liability. The firm's principal office is in the architecturally renowned Public Ledger Building overlooking Philadelphia's Independence National Historic Park. It has recently opened a satellite office in New Jersey.

The present organization is a far cry from the one formed more than fifty years ago. Leslie C. Krusen and Rowland C. Evans, Jr., had decided to start a firm while they were classmates at the University of Pennsylvania Law School. On June 2, 1930, Krusen organized the firm of Krusen Evans and Campbell with Evans and E. Perry Campbell, another Penn Law School graduate. The firm opened its doors for the general practice of law with a concentration in maritime litigation, probate, aviation law, and general business matters.

The firm was busy from its inception despite the effects of the Great Depression. Over the years additional attorneys came to the firm and added to its legal expertise. Thomas E. Byrne, Jr., joined the firm as an associate in 1942. He quickly became well known for his litigation abilities and on May 1, 1961, the firm adopted its current name of Krusen Evans and Byrne.

The firm's early litigation was clearly rooted in maritime matters. Its impact in that area of the law is well known. Krusen Evans and Byrne has been involved in numerous maritime cases that helped establish significant legal precedents. The firm's maritime practice over the years represented a commitment to Philadelphia as a shipping port and to the Commonwealth as an important partner in the country's merchant marine.

Today Krusen Evans and Byrne's practice is far more extensive. Despite its nautical heritage and its continued presence in maritime matters, locally, nationally, as well as interna-

The reception area for the offices of Krusen Evans and Byrne (above) in the Public Ledger Building overlooks historic Independence Hall (bottom), the nation's birthplace.

tionally, the changing commercial needs of the firm's national and international clientele during the past twenty years have necessarily broadened the scope of its services. Recently the firm began acting, together with three other firms, as counsel for the Asbestos Claims Facility in the city of Philadelphia and surrounding counties. The Claims Facility is the forerunner of alternative dispute resolution forums in the United States. The firm's defense litigation now

encompasses representation of corporations, manufacturers, shipping concerns, hospitals, physicians, and insurance companies. It maintains an active trial practice in the areas of products liability, insurance and commercial litigation, aviation matters, professional liability, civil rights, maritime personal injury, cargo and collision claims, and general casualty defense work. It is also active in structuring innovative lease financing arrangements. The firm represents clients in general corporate, commercial, estate and trust, family law, administrative, tax, labor, real estate, antitrust, bankruptcy, and pension matters on a national and international basis. At the same time it remains active in local civil and bar association community projects providing pro bono services.

When Leslie C. Krusen retired, he wrote a history of the firm he founded. He concluded, "On June 30, 1982, after sixty years at the bar and fifty-two with this firm, I retired knowing that Krusen Evans and Byrne is in good hands and can look to the future with confidence." The firm views the next fifty years with the same enthusiasm and commitment to quality legal services that Leslie C. Krusen set during his tenure.

LaBRUM AND DOAK

The year is 1905, and a young lawyer named William J. Conlen has just placed his shingle outside Philadelphia's Victory Building. His was a one-person law firm, specializing in admiralty and international law. At the time Conlen could not have known that the firm he founded would one day develop into the large, full-service law firm known today as LaBrum and Doak.

During the next fifty years Conlen's firm strengthened its insurance defense litigation business and broadened its legal practice to include bonding and surety matters, in addition to some corporate work.

General J. Harry LaBrum, one of Philadelphia's lawyer/activists with extensive contacts in business and government, was largely responsible for expanding the firm's client base during the period from 1930 to 1955. Indeed, the firm changed its name to LaBrum and Doak in 1955.

The period from 1955 to 1980 was characterized by steady growth, continued progress in its corporate practice, and national recognition as defense litigators for major insurance companies. Reflecting this growth, LaBrum and Doak grew from a seven-member firm in 1955 to one with fifty-five partners and associates in 1980. Moreover, LaBrum and Doak moved to larger quarters during this

General J. Harry LaBrum was largely responsible for expanding LaBrum and Doak's client base during the period from 1930 to 1955.

period, first to the IBM building in 1960 and, seventeen years later, to its current headquarters at 1700 Market Street where the firm occupies two floors in the IVB building.

Under the leadership of Daniel J. Ryan, chairman of its executive committee, LaBrum and Doak has

Under the leadership of managing partner Daniel J. Ryan, the firm has achieved planned and significant growth in many fields of practice since 1980.

achieved planned and significant growth in many fields of practice since 1980. It has grown from fifty-five to eighty-five lawyers, and has expanded its legal expertise to several new areas of specialization within its corporate and litigation departments. Its progressive recruitment program permits it to compete financially and otherwise with larger law firms for the best available legal talent drawn primarily from Philadelphia-area law schools.

Today LaBrum and Doak conducts a comprehensive full-service practice encompassing commercial litigation (including antitrust, securities, professional liability, toxic torts, and environmental pollution) as well as insurance defense cases and criminal matters. Its practice includes corporate, labor, tax, pension, real estate, decedent's estates, trust, and securities law. In addition to its Philadelphia headquarters, LaBrum and Doak also has offices in Norristown and Malvern, Pennsylvania; Woodbury, New Jersey; and New York City.

Recognizing their special responsibility as members of one of Philadelphia's larger law firms, a number of LaBrum and Doak's attorneys have played major roles in the growth and development of the greater Philadelphia area. Members have served as presidents of the chamber of commerce, the board of education,

United Way, and the Federation of Jewish Agencies. Member attorneys have also held a variety of other positions in the public and quasipublic sector.

Partners and associates have participated actively as members and officers of numerous professional associations and other organizations. Partners have served as presidents of the Defense Research Institute, the Association of Insurance Attorneys, the New Jersey Bar Association, and as chairmen of the insurance sections of the American Bar Association and the Pennsylvania Bar Association. Partners have also actively served on the boards of directors and committees of the Philadelphia Bar Association and as trustees of the Pennsylvania Supreme Court Disciplinary Boards, both as counsel and as hearing examiners.

The firm's litigators have been recognized by election to fellowship in the American College of Trial Lawyers, the International Academy of Trial Lawyers, the International Society of Barristers, and the American Board of Trial Advocates. Members have been named among the best lawyers in America and among the top litigators in Philadelphia in recent polls that surveyed the opinions of judges and lawyers.

LaBrum and Doak operates a 24-hour word-processing center and

Perry S. Bechtle (left) and Zachary R. Estrin, permanent members of LaBrum and Doak's executive committee, review a case with a client.

utilizes an extensive on-line data-processing network, including a computerized legal research department, to serve its clients effectively and efficiently. The use of such technology helps the firm control costs, improve the quality of its legal services, and

A 24-hour word-processing center is part of an extensive on-line data-processing network that enables the firm to serve its clients effectively and efficiently.

achieve its professional goals.

The concern is governed by members of the executive committee elected by the partners. In addition to Daniel J. Ryan, the other permanent members of the committee are Perry S. Bechtle and Zachary R. Estrin. Other partners rotate on the committee on an annual basis.

LaBrum and Doak, which started as a small firm, is now a full-service institution. It intends to continue to serve Philadelphia as a full-service firm committed to the delivery of quality legal services at an affordable cost, while broadening its base with branch offices wherever the need for its services exists.

SAUL, EWING, REMICK & SAUL

The law firm of Saul, Ewing, Remick & Saul, founded in 1921, has built its reputation on its skillful and innovative approach to legal problems. With over 100 attorneys, the firm has expanded beyond Philadelphia to offices in Malvern, Pennsylvania; New York City; Wilmington, Delaware; Marlton, New Jersey; and associated offices in Washington, D.C., Europe, and Scandinavia.

The firm conducts an aggressive and broadly based practice encompassing all aspects of civil and criminal law. Special emphasis is placed on corporate and banking law, tax-exempt and municipal financing, corporate securities work, real estate development and syndication, building construction law, dispute resolution and litigation, estate and trust planning and administration, taxation and financial planning, and labor relations.

Many of Saul, Ewing's attorneys deal in highly specialized areas of practice. For instance, the Health Group consists of a team of lawyers who concentrate on hospital and health care matters. Likewise, a number of litigation attorneys form the Government Contracts Group, which

The firm's offices are in Centre Square, located in the heart of Philadelphia's financial and business district. Photo by B&H Photographics

counsels companies who do business with the federal government. The firm also has a national reputation in the defense of persons accused of white collar crime, as one of its senior partners was a Watergate prosecutor.

To assist its clients in the international arena, Saul, Ewing became a charter member of the Interlex Group, a federation of seventeen law firms in eleven Western European countries, England, Ireland, and the United States that refers business among its members. The group meets annually to discuss its international practice. Saul, Ewing is one of only two law firms in the United States that is associated with Interlex.

Throughout the years Saul, Ewing has established an impressive client dossier that includes not only individuals regarding their personal and business matters, but also several of Philadelphia's largest banks and other area financial institutions; a major department store chain; a major supermarket chain; numerous real estate developers and syndicators; several major aerospace contractors; hospitals and life care communities; a major national railroad system; insurance companies; manufacturing, construction, and oil and gas exploration companies with national and international operations; numerous governmental bodies; and educational, cultural, and charitable institutions.

In addition to its representation of institutional clients, the firm has historically assisted entrepreneurs and emerging businesses to succeed financially in their respective arenas. Saul, Ewing strives not only to work closely with its clients and provide specialized services, but also to provide the modern, technological services that bring its work as close as possible to the cutting edge of progress. The firm's modern computer systems allow for the rapid synthesis of information in structuring commercial transactions and managing complex litigation. This technology allows its attorneys to fulfill their commitment to being both available and respon-

Computers help the firm's attorneys create a sound legal product with speed and precision. Photo by B&H Photographics

1975. That year it moved to the Centre Square complex, which is directly adjacent to City Hall in the heart of Philadelphia's financial and business district.

Saul, Ewing has been a respected Philadelphia law firm for over sixty-five years. The firm's sustained growth has paralleled its institutional clients' continuing development and the successful expansion of its clients' emerging companies. In preparing for its future growth, Saul, Ewing, Remick & Saul continues its commitment to meeting and anticipating its clients' needs for high-quality legal services rendered in a responsive, individualized, and personal manner.

sive to their clients while producing a sound legal product.

The firm's roots began with John G. Johnson, who in the late 1800s was the leader of the Philadelphia Bar and one of the most prominent lawyers in the country. Johnson is known to have argued more cases before the United States Supreme Court than any other lawyer in the court's history.

Following his death in 1917, Johnson's practice was carried on by a group of his associates who organized the firm of Pritchard, Saul, Bayard and Evans. In 1921 that firm was dissolved and some of its partners combined with other lawyers to form Saul, Ewing, Remick & Saul. For many years the dominant partners were Maurice Bower Saul, his brother, Walter Biddle Saul, Raymond Remick, and Joseph Neff Ewing, Sr.

In 1924 partners of the firm were principals in the construction and financing of the Packard Building at Fifteenth and Chestnut streets, where the firm maintained its offices until

Members of the firm meet their clients' needs for legal services in a responsive, individualized, and personal manner. Photo by B&H Photographics

UNITED PENN BANK

United Penn Bank as it appeared in the early years of its operation. The bank was located in a two-room office on the ground floor of the central building on Franklin Street in Wilkes-Barre. Photo circa 1912

At 9 a.m. on Thursday morning, July 9, 1868, the Miners Savings Bank opened its doors for business as the first such savings institution in Wilkes-Barre. There was one employee, who served as janitor, teller, bookkeeper, and cashier. The bank was located in a two-room office on the ground floor of a building on Franklin Street. Augustus C. Laning was the first president, serving from 1868 to 1875.

That was the beginning of the institution known today as United Penn Bank, which was acquired by Continental Bancorp, Inc., on August 17, 1984. At the time of the merger United Penn had total capital of $36 million—a striking contrast to the $75,000 in capital reported by Miners Savings Bank after its first year of operation.

In 1912 Miners Savings Bank merged with the Anthracite Savings Bank of Wilkes-Barre, a move referred to at the time as "the greatest among Pennsylvania financial institutions since the consolidation of the Continental and Equitable Trust Companies of Philadelphia." Miners Savings Bank became Miners Bank of Wilkes-Barre and moved into a new office building on the corner of Franklin and Market streets on May 31, 1913.

Two years later Miners Bank merged with Peoples Bank of Wilkes-Barre, becoming the largest financial institution in Luzerne County. On November 29, 1933, Miners Bank changed from a state-chartered institution to a nationally chartered bank, thus becoming Miners National Bank. Today UPB has thirty-four offices serving Luzerne, Lackawanna, Monroe, Wyoming, Columbia, and Pike counties in Northeastern Pennsylvania.

On July 1, 1969, Miners National Bank of Wilkes-Barre changed from a nationally chartered to a state-chartered institution. It then became United Penn Bank, a wholly owned subsidiary of United Penn Corporation, which was formed at the same time. By 1984 twenty-five branch offices in five Northeastern Pennsylvania counties operated under United Penn Bank.

On October 5, 1984, the board of directors of The Security Bank and Trust Company of Stroudsburg agreed that Security would merge into United Penn Bank. The merger, formally approved three months later, meant that Security's eleven branch offices would continue to serve Monroe and Pike counties, the fastest-growing portion of the Northeastern Pennsylvania market.

United Penn Bank as it appears today. In 1913 Miners Bank of Wilkes-Barre moved into a new office building on the corner of Franklin and Market streets. It has remained in these headquarters, with extensive remodeling of the structure completed in 1969.

CUTLER INDUSTRIES, INC.

Fifty years ago Robert T. Cutler never guessed that one day he would own the largest commercial sign business in the Northeast, a company that today literally lights the skyline with a canopy of colors as rich as those found on an artist's pallet.

Indeed, in 1936 Cutler had just organized a small sign shop called Cutler Sign Advertising Company in Chester, delighted and somewhat surprised that his background in retail sales enabled him to sell signs. Three years later, following a move to a small plant in Philadelphia, Cutler was not only selling signs but manufacturing them as well. In 1946 Cutler Sign Advertising Company produced its first bank sign for Broad Street Trust Company, now known as Continental Bank; at that time its bold neon red letters overlooked Market Street and West Penn Square. And the young entrepreneur was on his way to becoming one of the largest bank sign manufacturers in the country, as well as making his mark on the entire sign industry.

In the early 1940s Cutler was instrumental in the development of the use of plastic as a material for sign faces and letters. During that time his company also pioneered the use of cold cathode lighting for schools and other commercial applications. In 1954 the business was incorporated as Cutler Industries, Inc. In the late 1950s the firm developed a system of weather-forecasting sign dis-

Robert T. Cutler, founder and chairman.

plays that linked twenty Philadelphia National Bank locations through a telephone network, a technology considered highly innovative for its time.

Following the move in 1972 to its present headquarters in Bristol, Cutler Industries expanded its operations to include ATM (automatic teller machines) Environments and Turn-kiosks®, the patented, self-contained, drive-up ATM enclosure that provides top security and round-the-clock banking conveniences without costly service interruptions.

In the areas of creative design, manufacturing, and installation, Cutler Industries offers the latest in technology, service, and components, using only the highest-quality heavy-

This painting by Howard N. Watson depicts the Broad Street Trust Company sign, the first ever produced by Cutler Industries, Inc.

gauge aluminum, stainless steel, and brass. A Cutler innovation, a project management department tracks a project from beginning to finish for the customer. The new CADCAM system, a high-tech computer process, provides a method for substantial help in the design of each project and an economical method for cutting and manufacturing. With this new computer system, changes in design and manufacturing that used to take days to complete can now be accomplished within a very short period of time.

With new plants in Trenton, New Jersey, and New Kensington, Pennsylvania, Cutler Industries employs around 150 people. The company manufactures thousands of signs each year for many customers, including major banking institutions and a variety of other companies, ranging from Philadelphia's Veterans Stadium and the Indianapolis Motor Speedway to numerous casinos in Atlantic City and corridors throughout Philadelphia International Airport.

Cutler is now chairman of the company, and his son, Mark, serves as president. The only thing hanging on the wall of the chairman's office is a painting that Robert Cutler says has more nostalgic value to him than anything else. It is an artist's rendering of the first bank sign ever produced by Cutler Industries—a firm that celebrated its fiftieth anniversary in 1986.

SCHNADER, HARRISON, SEGAL & LEWIS

In January 1935 in Philadelphia, while the Great Depression was still deep, three lawyers ventured to open a new law office, borrowing $10,000 for the purpose. The new firm's entire gross receipts in its first year were a little over $60,000. Fifty years later the firm has 200 lawyers, with offices in New York City and Washington, D.C., operates on a national scale, and enjoys a prime reputation nationwide.

One of the founders died early. The others, in long lives, have left indelible imprints on the firm and on the profession. William A. Schnader, the senior co-founder, had served with great distinction as attorney general of Pennsylvania under two governors. Under his leadership, the firm soon developed a reputation for outstanding performance in litigation, and consistently expanded its expertise in other fields of practice.

In the commercial field, Schnader undertook a major initiative of national importance. In the late 1930s commercial law in the various states was archaic and extremely diverse, a situation that posed great difficulties in financing transactions that crossed state lines. In 1940, as president of the National Conference of Commissioners on Uniform State Laws, Schnader imaginatively proposed the preparation and adoption in every state of a new Uniform Commercial Code, to unify and simplify the law among the states on all commercial transactions. Having set this ambitious goal, Schnader personally raised the necessary funds, persuaded the American Law Institute to provide the drafting staff, and mustered state by state the banking, business, and legislative support to secure the code's eventual adoption nationwide. This enormous undertaking, which he conducted over more than a quarter of a century, has been described as the most massive single contribution ever made to American law.

Along the way Schnader drafted a new Philadelphia Home Rule City Charter, adopted in 1951, that still

continues unchanged today, and at the age of seventy-five, he led a successful drive to revise the Constitution of Pennsylvania. In 1960 he was awarded the Gold Medal of the American Bar Association, its highest honor.

As the firm's third co-founder, Schnader brought with him a young man of twenty-seven, Bernard G. Segal, who had been his right arm as deputy attorney general. Segal fully matched Schnader's intense devotion to clients and extended his regular day and night schedule to serve the profession in a multitude of areas. Supreme Court Justice Lewis F. Powell has written that he doubts "that any lawyer has ever held as many high offices in organizations of the legal profession as Bernie Segal."

Among many other functions, he has served brilliant terms as chancellor of the Philadelphia Bar Association and president of the American Bar Association. He has followed Schnader as first vice-president of the American Law Institute, and has been president of the American College of Trial Lawyers and of the American Bar Foundation. He has been a major force for civil rights

William A. Schnader, senior co-founder of Schnader, Harrison, Segal & Lewis, served under two governors as attorney general of the Commonwealth of Pennsylvania.

both before and after his tenure, by appointment of President John F. Kennedy, as co-chairman of the Lawyers' Committee for Civil Rights Under Law, an agency created by the President at Segal's suggestion.

Most particularly, for more than thirty years Segal has worked hard and productively to promote the high quality of the federal judiciary. Since 1953, when President Dwight D. Eisenhower appointed him chairman of a commission created by Congress after lobbying led by Segal, he has been a leader in the effort to raise inadequate levels of compensation that threatened to deprive the bench of outstanding judges and candidates. And during his long and intense service as chairman of the American Bar Association's Standing Committee on the Federal Judiciary, he conceived and effected a reform of immense significance.

Establishing a national network of knowledgeable lawyers, Segal developed the Standing Committee into an expert entity, competent to provide well-informed and politically impartial appraisals of the qualifications of any candidate for a federal judicial post. By persuading the Eisenhower Administration and its successors of both political parties, Segal led in establishing what has now become a settled rule under seven Presidents, that whatever political or ideological considerations may be involved, no candidate will be nominated to be a federal appellate or district judge whose professional and personal qualifications have not first been thoroughly investigated and appraised by the American Bar's Standing Committee. In view of the vast increase during these years in the number of federal judges and the great expansion of their jurisdiction, the importance of this achievement is hard to exaggerate.

Segal has presided on World Law Day, the opening event of biennial World Conferences of the World Peace Through Law Center held in various countries, the latest in 1985 in West Berlin. At the 1975 conference Segal was designated "World Lawyer," the only American to achieve that distinction. The next year he was awarded the Gold Medal of the American Bar Association, making the firm the only one to have two members who received this honor. Supreme Court Justice William J. Brennan has epitomized his view of Segal as "the symbol of our profession at its very best."

The tradition of service to the profession established by Schnader and Segal has been actively carried forward by younger partners. Irving Segal, Bernard's younger brother, has served for six years as regent or secretary of the American College of Trial Lawyers, and has been active for years on the ABA Committee on Federal Judicial Improvements. J. Pennington Straus originated the concept of a Uniform Probate Code and led in its preparation and adoption in thirty-seven states. Straus in 1970-1971, and George Nofer in 1983-1984, have served as president of the National College of Probate Counsel. Edward Mullinix has been co-chairman of the ABA's Special Committee on Complex and Multidistrict Litigation and active for five years on the Special Committee for the Study of Discovery Abuse. Jerome Shestack has served as a co-founder and chairman of the ABA Section on Individual Rights and Re-

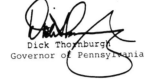

The law firm of Schnader, Harrison, Segal & Lewis has been an important part of a proud legal tradition, and the firm has played a significant role in preserving and continuing a distinguished system of justice and jurisprudence in Pennsylvania and throughout our country.

Dick Thornburgh
Governor of Pennsylvania

sponsibilities and its Standing Committee on Legal Aid, and as United States Representative to the United Nations Commission on Human Rights with the rank of ambassador. Paul Dembling has been successively general counsel of NASA and of the General Accounting Office, president of the Federal Bar Association, and president of the International Institute of Space Law. Donald Rivkin has served the Association of the Bar of the City of New York as chairman of its Committee on International Law. Ralph Snyder has been chairman of the Pennsylvania Bar's Committee on Taxation, Gordon Cooney

Bernard G. Segal (left) third co-founder, with Warren E. Burger, chief justice of the United States Supreme Court.

has served as a member of the Council of the ABA Section of Corporation, Banking and Business Law, and William Brown has been an innovative and highly successful chairman of the United States Equal Employment Opportunity Commission, and, more recently, chairman of the Special Commission investigating the MOVE tragedy in Philadelphia.

Although the practice of most Philadelphia firms has been local, the Schnader firm early acquired national reach, handling the countrywide business of large national clients headquartered outside Philadelphia, and lawyers from the Philadelphia office have personally conducted significant litigation and administrative proceedings in many other parts of the country. A conspicuous example is United Parcel Service, whose main offices have long been in the New York City area, but whose legal affairs are handled nationwide by the Schnader firm out of Philadelphia. Thus, when United Parcel decided to establish a countrywide package-delivery service, the essential task of securing local service rights against opposition in nearly every state, and before the Interstate Commerce Commission, was accomplished largely by Irving Segal, who, with the assistance of other lawyers from the Schnader firm, conducted the litigation in every part of the country. Similarly, lawyers from the Schnader firm have conducted litigation for New York-based RCA, NBC, and Hertz Corporation in California, Alaska, and elsewhere, and in Louisiana for New York-headquartered Ogden Corporation's local subsidiary, Avondale Shipyards.

In recent years the firm has expanded its locations with substantial offices in New York and Washington. The New York office has opened new fields in international law, and the office in Washington has brought new activity in the areas of government contracts, communications, and satellite and space law. As it enters its second half-century, the firm carries a high tradition toward new horizons.

WOLF, BLOCK, SCHORR AND SOLIS-COHEN

The firm that later became Wolf, Block, Schorr and Solis-Cohen was founded by Morris Wolf in 1903, shortly after his graduation from the University of Pennsylvania Law School. He and Horace Stern, his former professor, formed a law practice that has grown to be national in scope and comprises some 200 lawyers and a support staff of approximately 400. The firm's principal office is in Center City Philadelphia, and there is also a full-service office in West Palm Beach, Florida, and a small branch in the Great Valley Corporate Center in Malvern, Pennsylvania.

Wolf and Stern built the firm by taking on the most difficult cases

they could—cases holding little appeal to Philadelphia's old and established firms. Through their creativity and dogged thoroughness, the firm soon earned a reputation for successfully handling difficult assignments.

In the early days the firm focused on real estate matters, simple two-party commercial transactions, litigation, and the preparation of wills. Those were the typical matters that made up the business of most law firms of that period.

Today Wolf, Block is a firm that

ranks in size among the top 100 firms in the nation and has a practice that is national in scope. The firm's large and diversified business and financial practice is derived from a broad client base ranging from individual investors, developers, and proprietors to small and medium-size entrepreneurial organizations to large public corporations and financial institutions.

The firm's practice is rooted in the areas of commercial transactions, real estate, litigation, securities law, public finance, banking, taxation, labor law, and trusts and estates. Additionally, as commercial needs have changed, Wolf, Block has responded quickly to the modern legal climate and has ex-

From left to right are Charles G. Kopp, chairman of the firm's 1985 executive committee; David J. Kaufman, managing partner; and Robert M. Segal, chairman of the firm's 1986 executive committee.

panded its practice to include sports and entertainment law, environmental regulation and counseling, computer law, consumer law, toxic tort litigation, domestic relations, plaintiffs' and defendants' antitrust litigation, health care law, election law, government affairs, international transactions, white-collar criminal defense litigation, legal malpractice defense, and transportation law.

The need for legal representation has expanded so rapidly into new areas that various lawyers in the firm have formed separate practice groups that cross traditional departmental lines to meet client needs. Some examples are the Venture Development Group, Computer Group, Government Affairs Group, International Law Group, and the Professional Sports Management Group.

The groups are structured to handle all the legal aspects of clients who have special needs that frequently involve more than one of the areas of practice handled in the firm's eight departments: corporate, environmental, estates, health law, labor, litigation, real estate, and tax. For example, the Venture Development Group provides a single source for all of an emerging company's legal needs including the initial structuring and financing of an organization; real estate acquisitions; labor considerations; patent, copyright, and trademark applications; public offerings; and tax planning.

The special nature of Wolf, Block's practice has made its lawyers adept at creating practical solutions for the legal and business needs of all its clients. The firm's lawyers are frequently asked to take an active role as a source of business ideas and as a sounding board for business decisions. When called upon, they work closely with clients, and, through careful and intuitive probing, help the clients redefine their objectives and evolve fresh approaches to their business and legal needs and goals.

In these and many other ways, the lawyers of Wolf, Block have not only upheld the firm's long-standing repu-

tation for excellence and innovation, they have strengthened it. Many members of the business and legal community refer to Wolf, Block attorneys as "lawyers' lawyers." The reason is that in addition to working directly with individual clients, the firm is often brought into assignments on referrals from other lawyers who recognize its unique capabilities.

From its beginning Wolf, Block has been dedicated to creative excellence in its work and in service to the profession and community. This is reflected in the many contributions the firm's lawyers have made in these areas.

Horace Stern left Wolf, Block to become a judge. Later, after serving as chief justice of the Supreme Court of Pennsylvania, he rejoined the firm.

Wolf, Block has provided more chancellors of the Philadelphia Bar Association than any other law firm, with one partner serving as recently as 1983, and another who will serve in 1987. A partner also served as president of the Pennsylvania Bar Association and as a member of the board of governors of the American Bar Association. Another was the first chairman of the board of the Public Interest Law Center of Philadelphia. In 1984 yet another partner served as president of the Palm Beach County (Florida) Bar Association.

Wolf, Block attorneys are regular contributors to a variety of legal publications, and have spoken throughout the country in seminars and programs sponsored by bar associations, continuing legal education organizations, and other professional groups. Several lawyers serve on the advisory boards of publications and institutes, and others have taught regular curriculum courses at the four area law schools: Pennsylvania, Rutgers-Camden, Temple, and Villanova.

Present or former partners and associates have also served in a wide range of government posts. The list includes two members of the Supreme Court of Pennsylvania (one of

them becoming chief justice), two attorneys general of Pennsylvania, one U.S. District Court judge, one U.S. Court of Appeals judge, three solicitors of the City of Philadelphia, a tax legislative counsel to the U.S. Department of the Treasury, a commissioner of the Internal Revenue Service, a consultant to the Securities and Exchange Commission, and a general counsel to the Federal Housing Administration. Some lawyers have left the firm for such distinguished posts as mayor of Philadelphia, ambassador to Switzerland, and assistant to the President of the United States for Public Liaison.

One partner made the transition from a part-time teacher to a full-time professor and later became the dean of the University of Pennsylvania Law School. Over the years a number of other lawyers have left the firm for teaching careers at such law schools as American, George Washington, Harvard, Hebrew University, Hofstra, New York Law School, Ohio State University, Pennsylvania, Temple, and Wyoming.

The firm's lawyers have consistently provided leadership and counsel for civic, cultural, philanthropic, and religious activities in the Philadelphia area. Wolf, Block demands a willingness on the part of its lawyers, from first-year associates to senior partners, to take an active role in clients' affairs. At the same time the firm's lawyers value and maintain their individuality. They place a high premium on the quality of their lives and performance of community responsibilities as well as the excellence of their legal work.

The achievements of Wolf, Block, Schorr and Solis-Cohen lawyers demonstrate the firm's conviction that professional excellence does not end at the office door, that lawyers should not only serve the interests of clients in their practice, but should also serve the best interests of the community. These are the principles upon which the firm was founded, and to which its lawyers continue to subscribe.

ARCO CHEMICAL COMPANY

A merger in 1966 between two regional oil companies—The Atlantic Refining Company on the East Coast and Richfield Oil in the West—created a corporate entity that quickly made its mark in the energy business. Ultimately, Atlantic Richfield Company (ARCO) grew to become not only a major force in the oil industry, but one of the largest corporations in the nation.

The same year that Atlantic and Richfield merged, a decision was made in the company's Philadelphia headquarters to create a separate chemical division. While ARCO Chemical's contributions in those early years were modest, its long-term impact on the parent company and on the Pennsylvania economy has been considerable.

It was a breakthrough in the research laboratories—a way to oxidize propylene—that actually guaranteed the eventual success of the fledgling

chemical firm. Propylene oxide, the product that evolved, is used to make urethane foams and finds application in everything from clothing to home furnishings and insulation.

That technical innovation spawned a joint venture that saw the establishment of production facilities in the United States and abroad. The business, known as Oxirane, became one of the major success stories of the

With an increasing focus on technology and proprietary processes, ARCO Chemical's Newtown Square research and development facility will play a vital role in the company's future.

chemical industry in the early 1970s.

Today propylene oxide and the Oxirane business that was 100-percent acquired in 1980 are major contributors to an ARCO Chemical

ARCO Chemical's plant in Beaver Valley, which opened in 1943 to support the war effort, now manufactures polystyrenics that find application in hot and cold drink cups, insulation, and the automotive industry.

and the Beginnings of the Industrial Revolution in the United States." *Business History Review* 46 (Summer 1972): 141-181.

Davies, Edward J. II. "Elite Migration and Urban Growth: The Rise of Wilkes-Barre in the Northern Anthracite Region, 1820-1880." *Pennsylvania History* 45 (1978): 291-314.

Deasy, G.F. and P.R. Griess. "Effects of a Declining Mining Economy on the Pennsylvania Anthracite Region." *Association of American Geographers Annals* 55 (June 1965): 239-259.

Fetherling, Dale. *Mother Jones: The Miners' Angel; A Portrait.* Carbondale, IL: Southern Illinois University Press, 1974, 263 pp.

Miller, E. Willard. "The Southern Anthracite Regions: A Problem Area." *Economic Geography* 31 (1955): 331-350.

Murphy, Raymond E. and Marion Murphy. "Anthracite Region of Pennsylvania." *Economic Geography* 14 (October 1938): 338-348.

Powell, H. Benjamin. "The Pennsylvania Anthracite Industry, 1769-1976." *Pennsylvania History* 47 (1980): 3-28.

Roberts, Peter. *The Anthracite Coal Industry: A Study of the Economic Conditions and Relations of the Cooperative Forces in the Development of the Anthracite Coal Industry of Pennsylvania.* New York: Macmillan, 1901, 261 pp.

Petroleum

Asbury, Herbert. *The Golden Flood—An Informal History of America's First Oil Field.* New York: Alfred A. Knopf, 1941, 324 pp.

Botsford, Harry. *The Valley of Oil.* New York: Hastings House, 1946, 278 pp.

Cone, Andrew and Walter R. Johns. *Petrolia: A Brief History of the Pennsylvania Petroleum Region, the Development, Growth, Resources, etc. from 1859 to 1869.* New York: D. Appleton, 1870, 652 pp.

Conn, Francis and Shirley Rosenberg. *The First Oil Rush.* New York: Meredith Press, 1967, 141 pp.

Darrah, William C. *Pithole: The Vanished City: A Story of the Early Days of the Petroleum Industry.* Gettysburg: 1972, 252 pp.

Eaton, S.J.M. *Petroleum: A History of the Oil Region of Venango County, Pennsylvania.* Philadelphia: J.P. Skelly & Co., 1866, 299 pp.

Giddens, Paul H. *The Birth of the Oil Industry.* New York: Macmillan, 1938, 216 pp.

Henry, J.T. *The Early and Later History of Petroleum with Authentic Facts in Regard to Its Development in Western Pennsylvania.* Philadelphia: James B. Rodgers Co., 1873, 607 pp.

Miller, E. Willard. "Economic Geography of the Bradford Oil Region." *Economic Geography* 19 (April 1943): 177-187.

Forest Resources

Friedman, Jesse J., et al. *Forest Resources of Pennsylvania.* Harrisburg: Pennsylvania Department of Commerce, Bureau of Industrial Development, 1958, 98 pp.

King, Samuel A. "A Log Drive to Williamsport in 1868." *Pennsylvania History* 29 (1962): 151-174.

Theiss, Lewis E. "Lumbering in Penn's Woods." *Pennsylvania History* 19 (1952): 397-412.

Tonkin, R. Dudley. *My Partner, the River: The White Pine Story of the Susquehanna.* Pittsburgh: University of Pittsburgh Press, 1958, 276 pp.

AGRICULTURE

Alger, Hugh W. "Crops and Chores: Pennsylvania Farm Life in the 1890's." *Pennsylvania Magazine of History and Biography* 85 (1961): 367-410.

Ball, Duane and Gary M. Walton. "Agricultural Productivity Change in Eighteenth-Century Pennsylvania." *Journal of Economic History* 36 (March 1976): 102-117.

Bressler, Leo A. "Agriculture Among the Germans in Pennsylvania During the Eighteenth Century." *Pennsylvania History* 22 (1955): 103-133.

Dahlberg, Richard E. "The Concord Grape Industry of the Chautauqua-Erie Area." *Economic Geography* 37 (April 1961): 150-169.

Dunn, S.A., W.F. Johnstone, and B.J. Smith. *Pennsylvania's Food and Agricultural Industry through the 1980s: Dairy Industry.* University Park, PA: College of Agriculture, Pennsylvania State University, 1980, 19 pp.

Fletcher, Stevenson W. *Pennsylvania Agriculture and Country Life, 1640-1840.* Vol. 1. Harrisburg: Historical and Museum Commission, 1949, 587 pp.

_____. *Pennsylvania Agriculture and Country Life, 1840-1940.* Vol. 2. Harrisburg: Historical and Museum Commission, 1955, 619 pp.

_____. "The Subsistence Farming Period in Pennsylvania Agriculture, 1640-1840." *Pennsylvania History* 14 (1947): 185-195.

_____. *Leaders in Pennsylvania Agriculture.* State College, PA: 1957, 299 pp.

Gagliardo, John G. "Germans and Agriculture in Colonial Pennsylvania." *Pennsylvania Magazine of History and Biography* 83 (1959): 192-218.

Gasteiger, E.L. and D.O. Boster. *Pennsylvania Agricultural Statistics, 1866-1950.* Harrisburg: Pennsylvania Federal State Crop Reporting Service, 1954, 80 pp.

Hayward, W.J. "Early Western Pennsylvania Agriculture." *Western Pennsylvania Historical Magazine* 6 (1923): 177-189.

James, Henry F. *The Agricultural Industry of Southeastern Pennsylvania.* Philadelphia: University of Pennsylvania, 1928, 166 pp.

Miller, Frederick K. "The Farmer at Work in Colonial Pennsylvania." *Pennsylvania History* 3 (1936): 115-123.

Partenheimer, E.J. *Pennsylvania's Food and Agricultural Industry through the 1980s: Field Crops.* University Park, PA: College of Agriculture, The Pennsylvania State University, 1980, 27 pp.

Rizza, Paul and Susan Haylett. "An Overview of Pennsylvania's Changing Rural Land Use Patterns." *Pennsylvania Geographer* 15 (December 1977): 1-33.

Ross, Earl D. "Benjamin Franklin As an Eighteenth Century Agricultural Leader." *Journal of Political Economy* 37 (1929): 52-72.

Watts, Ralph L. *Rural Pennsylvania.* New York: Macmillan, 1925, 331 pp.

MANUFACTURING

General

Epps, Richard W. "Strategy for Industrial Development." *Federal Reserve Bank of Philadelphia Business Review* (November 1966): 3-17.

Miller, E. Willard. "Trends in the Localization of Manufacturing in Pennsylvania 1947-1964." *Pennsylvania Geographer* 5 (March 1967): 1-3.

Miller, E. Willard and Ruby M. Miller. *Pennsylvania—Natural Resources and Economic Development: A Bibliography.* Monticello, IL: Vance Bibliographies, 1985, 66 pp.

_____. *Pennsylvania—Transportation: A Bibliography.* Monticello, IL: Vance Bibliographies, 1985, 25 pp.

Pennsylvania Trends in Industry and Employment, 1916-1955. Harrisburg: Pennsylvania State Planning Board, 1957, 91 pp.

Robson, Charles, ed. *Manufactories and Manufacturers of Pennsylvania in the Nineteenth Century.* Philadelphia: Galaxy Publishing Co., 1875, 533 pp.

Stevens, Sylvester K. "A Century of Industry in Pennsylvania." *Pennsylvania History* 22 (1955): 49-68.

Swank, J.M. *Progressive Pennsylvania: A Record of the Remarkable Industrial Development of the Keystone State.* Philadelphia: J.B. Lippincott, 1908, 360 pp.

Pioneer Crafts and Industries

Bridenbaugh, Carl. *The Colonial Crafts-man.* New York: New York University Press, 1966, 214 pp.

Carey, A. Mervin. *American Firearms Makers: When, Where and What They Made from the Colonial Period to the End of the Nineteenth Century.* New York: Thomas Y. Crowell, 1953, 146 pp.

Daniel, Dorothy. "The First Glasshouse West of the Alleghenies." *Western Pennsylvania Historical Magazine* 32 (1949): 97-113.

Eckhardt, George H. *Pennsylvania Clocks and Clockmakers: An Epic of Early American Science Industry and Crafts-manship.* New York: Devin-Adair Company, 1955, 230 pp.

Gillingham, Harrold E. "Pottery, China, and Glass Making in Philadelphia." *Pennsylvania Magazine of History and Biography* 54 (1930): 97-129.

_____. "Some Early Brickmakers of Philadelphia." *Pennsylvania Magazine of History and Biography* 53 (1929): 1-27.

Heiges, George L. *Henry William Stiegel and His Associates: A Story of Early American Industry.* Manheim, PA: 1948, 227 pp.

Hunter, Dard. *Papermaking in Pioneer America.* Philadelphia: University of Pennsylvania Press, 1952, 178 pp.

Hunter, F.W. *Stiegel Glass.* New York: Houghton Mifflin Co., 1914, 272 pp.

Kauffman, Henry J. *The Pennsylvania-Kentucky Rifle.* Harrisburg: Stackpole Co., 1960, 376 pp.

_____. *Early American Gun-smiths, 1650-1850.* Harrisburg: Stackpole, 1952, 94 pp.

Kindig, Joseph K. III. *The Philadelphia Chair, 1685-1785.* York, PA: Historical Society of York County, 1978, 108 pp.

Parker, Peter J. "The Philadelphia Printer: A Study of an Eighteenth-Century Businessman." *Business History Review* 40 (1966): 24-46.

Salay, David L. "The Production of Gun-powder in Pennsylvania During the American Revolution." *Pennsylvania Magazine of History and Biography* 99 (1975): 422-442.

Wallace, John William. "Early Printing in Philadelphia." *Pennsylvania Magazine of History and Biography* 4 (1880): 432-446.

Wittlinger, Carlton O. "The Small Arms Industry of Lancaster County, 1710-1840." *Pennsylvania History* 24 (1957): 121-136.

Regional

Cochran, Thomas C. "Philadelphia: The American Industrial Center, 1750-1850." *Pennsylvania Magazine of History and Biography* 106 (1982): 323-340.

_____. "Early Industrializa-tion of the Delaware and Susquehanna River Areas: A Regional Analysis." *Social Science History* 1 (Spring 1977): 283-306.

Elder, Margaret. "Pittsburgh Industries that Used to Be." *Western Pennsylvania Historical Magazine* 12 (1929): 211-225.

Harper, Frank C. *Pittsburgh: Forge of the Universe.* New York: Comet Press Books, 1957, 320 pp.

Macfarlane, John J. *Manufacturing in Philadelphia, 1683-1912.* Philadelphia: Philadelphia Commercial Museum, 1912, 101 pp.

Miller, E. Willard. "The Industrial Devel-opment of the Allegheny Valley of Western Pennsylvania." *Economic Geography* 19 (October 1943): 388-404.

Patton, Spiro G. "Comparative Advan-tage and Urban Industrialization: Reading, Allentown and Lancaster in the 19th Century." *Pennsylvania History* 50 (1983): 148-169.

Thurston, George H. *Pittsburgh's Prog-ress, Industries and Resources.* Pitts-burgh: A.A. Anderson, 1886, 240 pp.

Wallace, Anthony F.C. *Rockdale: The Growth of an American Village in the Early Industrial Revolution.* New York: Knopf, 1978, 553 pp.

Zierer, Clifford M. "Scranton's Industrial Integrity." *Economic Geography* 5 (January 1929): 70-86.

Iron and Steel

Bartholomew, Craig. "Anthracite Iron Making and Industrial Growth in the Lehigh Valley." *Proceedings of Lehigh County Historical Society* 32 (1978): 129-183.

Benhart, John E. and Alfred W. Stuart. "Jones and Laughlin Steel Corpora-tion: An Analysis of Plant Locations." *Pennsylvania Geographer* 7 (May 1969): 1-8.

Bining, Arthur Cecil. *Pennsylvania Iron Manufacture in the Eighteenth Cen-tury.* 2d ed. Harrisburg: Pennsylvania Historical and Museum Commission, 1973, 215 pp.

_____. "Early Ironmasters of Pennsylvania." *Pennsylvania History* 18 (1951): 93-103.

_____. "The Rise of Iron Manufacture in Western Pennsylva-nia." *Western Pennsylvania Historical Magazine* 16 (1933): 235-256.

_____. "The Iron Plantation of Early Pennsylvania." *Pennsylvania Magazine of History and Biography* 57 (1933): 117-137.

Hughes, George W. "The Pioneer Iron Industry in Western Pennsylvania." *Western Pennsylvania Historical Maga-zine* 14 (1931): 207-224.

Hunter, Louis C. *Factors in the Early Pittsburgh Iron Industry.* Cambridge: Harvard University Press, 1932.

Moore, E.E. "Pittsburgh and the Steel In-dustry." *Pennsylvania History* 26 (1959): 54-68.

Oblinger, Carl. *Cornwall: The People and Culture of an Industrial Camelot, 1890-1980.* Harrisburg: Pennsylvania Historical and Museum Commission, 1984, 123 pp.

Paskoff, Paul F. *Industrial Evolution: Or-ganization, Structure and Growth of the Pennsylvania Iron Industry, 1750-1860.* Baltimore: Johns Hopkins Uni-versity Press, 1983, 182 pp.

Rodgers, Allan. "The Iron and Steel In-dustry of the Mahoning and Shenango Valleys." *Economic Geography* 28 (October 1952): 331-342.

Sharp, Myron B. and William H. Thomas. "A Guide to the Old Stone Blast Furnaces in Western Pennsylvania." *Western Pennsylvania Historical Maga-zine* 48 (1965): 77-100, 185-203, 271-295, 365-388.

Walker, Joseph E. *Hopewell Village: A Social and Economic History of an Ironmaking Community.* Philadelphia: University of Pennsylvania Press, 1966, 526 pp.

White, Langdon. "The Iron and Steel In-dustry of the Pittsburgh District." *Eco-nomic Geography* 4 (April 1928): 115-139.

Other Industries

Batchelder, Samuel. *Introduction and Early Progress of the Cotton Manufac-ture in the United States.* Boston: Lit-tle, Brown and Company, 1863, 108 pp.

Billinger, Robert D. "Early Pennsylvania Paper Making (1690-1865)." *Journal of Chemical Education* 17 (1940): 407-413.

Bining, William. "The Glass Industry of Western Pennsylvania, 1797-1857." *Western Pennsylvania Historical Maga-zine* 19 (1936): 255-268.

Clark, Malcolm. "The Birth of an Enter-prise: Baldwin Locomotives, 1831-1842." *Pennsylvania Magazine of His-tory and Biography* 90 (1966): 423-444.

Cole, Arthur H. and Harold F. Williamson. *The American Carpet Manufac-ture, a History and an Analysis.* Cambridge: Harvard University Press, 1941, 281 pp.

Dewhurst, Paul C. *The Norris Locomo-tives.* Boston: Railway and Locomotive Historical Society, 1950, 80 pp.

Francis, Devon E. *Mr. Piper and His Cubs.* Ames, IA: Iowa State University Press, 1973, 256 pp.

Gillingham, Harrold E. "Pottery, China,

and Glass Making in Philadelphia." *Pennsylvania Magazine of History and Biography* 54 (1930): 97-129.

Roscoe, Edwin S. *The Textile Industry in Pennsylvania: Report of a Survey on Status of the Industry.* University Park, PA: Pennsylvania State University, College of Engineering and Architecture, 1958, 213 pp.

Scoville, Warren C. "Growth of the American Glass Industry to 1880." *Journal of Political Economy* 52 (1944): 193-216, 340-355.

Tyler, David B. *The American Clyde—A History of Iron and Steel Shipbuilding on the Delaware from 1840 to World War I.* New York: Associated College Presses, 1958, 132 pp.

LABOR AND UNION ORGANIZATIONS

Bodnar, John E. *Immigration and Industrialization: Ethnicity in an American Mill Town, 1870-1940.* Pittsburgh: University of Pittsburgh Press, 1977, 213 pp.

Ehrlich, Leon. "Labor Arbitration in Pennsylvania, 1705-1950." *Temple Law Quarterly* 24 (1950): 107-136.

Filippelli, Ronald L. "Diary of a Strike: George Medrick and the Coal Strike of 1927 in Western Pennsylvania." *Pennsylvania History* 43 (1976): 253-266.

George, Henry. "Labor in Pennsylvania." *North American Review* 143 (1886): 165-182, 268-277, 360-370.

_____. "Labor in Pennsylvania." *North American Review* 144 (1887): 86-95.

Gluck, Elsie. *John Mitchell, Miner: Labor's Bargain with the Gilded Age.* New York: John Day Company, 1929, 270 pp.

Hogg, J. Bernard. "Public Reaction to Pinkertonism and the Labor Question." *Pennsylvania History* 11 (1944): 171-199.

James, Alfred P. "The First Convention of the American Federation of Labor, Pittsburgh, Pennsylvania, November 15th-18th, 1881." *Western Pennsylvania Historical Magazine* 6 (1923): 201-233.

_____. "The First Convention of the American Federation of Labor, Pittsburgh, Pennsylvania, November 15th-18th, 1881." *Western Pennsylvania Historical Magazine* 7 (1924): 29-56.

Johnson, James P. "Reorganizing the United Mine Workers of America in Pennsylvania During the New Deal." *Pennsylvania History* 37 (1970): 117-132.

Kuritz, Hyman. "The Labor Injunction in Pennsylvania, 1891-1931." *Pennsylvania History* 29 (1962): 306-321.

Sullivan, William A. *The Industrial Worker in Pennsylvania, 1800-1840.* Harrisburg: Pennsylvania Historical and Museum Commission, 1955, 253 pp.

Swetnam, George. "Labor-Management Relations in Pennsylvania's Steel Industry, 1800-1959." *Western Pennsylvania Historical Magazine* 62 (1979): 321-332.

Wolff, Leon. *Lockout, the Story of the Homestead Strike of 1892: A Study of Violence, Unionism, and the Carnegie Steel Empire.* New York: Harper & Row, 1965, 297 pp.

TRANSPORTATION

General

Swetnam, George. *Pennsylvania Transportation.* Gettysburg: Pennsylvania Historical Association, 1964, 81 pp.

Trails and Early Roads

Bell, Whitfield J., Jr. "Carlisle to Pittsburgh: A Gateway to the West, 1750-1815." *Western Pennsylvania Historical Magazine* 35 (1952): 157-166.

Coulson, Thomas. "The Conestoga Wagon." *Journal of the Franklin Institute* 246 (1948): 215-222.

Faris, John T. *Old Trails and Roads in Penn's Land.* Philadelphia: Lippincott, 1927, 259 pp.

Hanna, Charles A. *The Wilderness Trail.* 2 vols. New York: G.P. Putnam's Sons, 1911.

Herrick, Michael J. "The Conestoga Wagon of Pennsylvania." *Western Pennsylvania Historical Magazine* 51 (1968): 155-163.

Hunt, John C. "Over the Alleghenies into History." *American History Illustrated* 5 (August 1970): 24-33.

Jordan, Philip D. *The National Road.* Indianapolis: Bobbs-Merrill, 1948, 442 pp.

Landis, Charles I. "History of the Philadelphia and Lancaster Turnpike: The First Long Turnpike in the United States." *Pennsylvania Magazine of History and Biography* 42 (1918): 1-28, 127-140, 235-258, 358-360.

_____. "History of the Philadelphia and Lancaster Turnpike: The First Long Turnpike in the United States." *Pennsylvania Magazine of History and Biography* 43 (1919): 84-90, 182-190.

Miller, Carroll. "The Romance of the National Pike." *Western Pennsylvania Historical Magazine* 10 (1927): 1-37.

Rouse, Parke, Jr. *The Great Wagon Road—From Philadelphia to the South.* New York: McGraw-Hill, 1973, 292 pp.

Searight, Thomas B. *The Old Pike: A History of the National Road.* Union-

town, PA: 1894, 384 pp.

Shumway, George and Howard C. Frey. *Conestoga Wagon, 1750-1850: Freight Carrier for 100 years of America's Westward Expansion.* 3d ed. York, PA: G. Shumway, 1968, 281 pp.

Wallace, Paul A.W. *Indian Paths of Pennsylvania.* Harrisburg: Pennsylvania Historical and Museum Commission, 1965, 227 pp.

Wilkinson, Norman B. "The Conestoga Wagon." *American Heritage* 2 (1951): 2-6.

Wood, Jerome H., Jr. *Conestoga Crossroads: Lancaster, Pennsylvania, 1730-1790.* Harrisburg: Pennsylvania Historical and Museum Commission, 1979, 305 pp.

Canals

McCullough, Robert and Walter Leulea. *The Pennsylvania Main Line Canal.* York, PA: The American Canal and Transportation Center, 1973, 181 pp.

Macfarlane, James. "The Pennsylvania Canals." *Western Pennsylvania Historical Magazine* 2 (1919): 38-51.

Rhoads, Willard R. "The Pennsylvania Canal." *Western Pennsylvania Historical Magazine* 43 (1960): 203-238.

Shank, W. H. *The Amazing Pennsylvania Canal.* York, PA: American Canal and Transportation Center, 1973, 80 pp.

Railroads

Alexander, Edwin P. *On the Main Line: The Pennsylvania Railroad in the 19th Century.* New York: Clarkson N. Potter, 1971, 310 pp.

Archer, Robert F. *A History of the Lehigh Valley Railroad: "The Route of the Black Diamond."* Berkeley, CA: Howell-North Books, 1977, 351 pp.

Bogen, Jules T. *The Anthracite Railroads: A Study in American Enterprise.* New York: The Ronald Press Company, 1927, 281 pp.

Burgess, George H. and Miles C. Kennedy. *Centennial History of the Pennsylvania Railroad, 1846-1946.* Philadelphia: Pennsylvania Railroad Company, 1949, 835 pp.

Daughen, Joseph R. and Peter Binzen. *The Wreck of the Penn Central.* Boston: Little, Brown and Co., 1971, 365 pp.

Davis, Patricia T. *End of the Line: Alexander J. Cassatt and the Pennsylvania Railroad.* New York: Neale Watson Academic Publications, 1978, 208 pp.

Hilton, George W. *Amtrak, the National Railroad Passenger Corporation.* Washington, D.C.: American Enterprise Institute for Public Policy Research, 1980, 80 pp.

Hungerford, Edward. *The Story of the*

Baltimore and Ohio Railroad, 1827-1927. 2 vols. New York: G.P. Putnam's Sons, 1928.

Itzkoff, Donald M. *Off the Track: The Decline of the Intercity Passenger Train in the United States.* Westport: Greenwood Press, 1982, 161 pp.

MacAvoy, Paul W. and John W. Snow, eds. *Railroad Revitalization and Regulatory Reform.* Washington, D.C.: American Enterprise Institute for Public Policy Research, 1977, 246 pp.

McCarrell, David K. "The Coming of the Railroad to Western Pennsylvania." *Western Pennsylvania Historical Magazine* 16 (1933): 1-12.

McLean, Harold H. *Pittsburgh and Lake Erie Railroad.* San Marino, CA: Golden West Books, 1980, 236 pp.

Mott, Edward H. *Between the Ocean and the Lakes: The Story of the Erie.* New York: Ticker Publishing Co., 1908, 524 pp.

Rosenberger, Homer Tope. *The Philadelphia and Erie Railroad, Its Place in American Economic History.* Potomac: Fox Hills Press, 1975, 748 pp.

_____. "How Pittsburgh Gained an Additional Rail Outlet to Seaboard in the Twentieth Century." *Pennsylvania History* 35 (1968): 109-146.

Saunders, Richard. *The Railroad Mergers and the Coming of Conrail.* Westport: Greenwood Press, 1978, 389 pp.

Saylor, Roger B. *The Railroads of Pennsylvania.* University Park, PA: Bureau of Business Research, College of Business Administration, Pennsylvania State University, 1964, 332 pp.

Schotter, H.W. *The Growth and Development of the Pennsylvania Railroad Company, 1846 to 1926.* 2d ed. Philadelphia: Press of Allen, Lane & Scott, 1927, 518 pp.

Schusler, William K. "The Railroad Comes to Pittsburgh." *Western Pennsylvania Historical Magazine* 43 (1960): 251-266.

Sobel, Robert. *The Fallen Colossus [Penn Central R.R.].* New York: Weybright and Talley, 1977, 257 pp.

Wilson, William B. *History of the Pennsylvania Railroad Company.* 2 vols. Philadelphia: H.T. Coates Company, 1899.

Logging Railroads

Casler, Walter C. *Logging Railroad Era of Lumbering in Pennsylvania: Tionesta Valley.* Williamsport, PA: Lycoming Printing Co., no. 8, 1973, 112 pp.

_____. *Logging Railroad Era of Lumbering in Pennsylvania: Teddy Collins Empire—a Century of Lumbering in Forest County.* Williamsport, PA: Lycoming Printing Co., no. 9,

1976, 112 pp.

Kline, Benjamin F.G., Jr. *Logging Railroad Era of Lumbering in Pennsylvania: Pitch Pine and Prop Timber—the Logging Railroads of South-Central Pennsylvania.* Williamsport, PA: Lycoming Printing Co., no. 1, 1971, 96 pp.

_____. *Logging Railroad Era of Lumbering in Pennsylvania: "Wild Cutting" on the Mountain.* Williamsport, PA: Lycoming Printing Co., no. 2, 1970, 60 pp.

Taber, Thomas T. III and Harold M. Soars. "Logging Railroads and Logging Locomotives in Eastern Pennsylvania." *Now and Then* 12 (1957/1960): 225-236.

_____. *Logging Railroad Era of Lumbering in Pennsylvania: Ghost Towns of Central Pennsylvania.* Williamsport, PA: Lycoming Printing Co., no. 3, 1970, 76 pp.

_____. *Logging Railroad Era of Lumbering in Pennsylvania: Sunset along Susquehanna Waters.* Williamsport, PA: Lycoming Printing Co., no. 4, 1972, 96 pp.

_____. *Logging Railroad Era of Lumbering in Pennsylvania: The Goodyears, an Empire in the Hemlocks.* Williamsport, PA: Lycoming Printing Co., no. 5, 1971, 84 pp.

_____. *Logging Railroad Era of Lumbering in Pennsylvania: Whining Saws and Squealing Flanges.* Williamsport, PA: Lycoming Printing Co., no. 6, 1972, 96 pp.

_____. *Logging Railroad Era of Lumbering in Pennsylvania: Sawmills among the Derricks.* Williamsport, PA: Lycoming Printing Co., no. 7, 1975, 116 pp.

_____. *Logging Railroad Era of Lumbering in Pennsylvania: Tanbark, Alcohol, and Lumber.* Williamsport, PA: Lycoming Printing Co., no. 10, 1974, 116 pp.

Highways

Beyer, George R. *Pennsylvania Roads Before the Automobile.* Historic Pennsylvania Leaflet No. 33, Harrisburg: Pennsylvania Historical and Museum Commission, 1972.

Jones, Penelope Redd. *The Story of the Pennsylvania Turnpike.* Mechanicsburg, PA: P.R. Jones and E.N. Jones, 1950, 47 pp.

Stuehldreher, Mary. "Automobiliousness." *Western Pennsylvania Historical Magazine* 57 (1974): 275-288.

The Story of the Keystone Shortway. Williamsport, PA: Keystone Shortway Association, 1970, 96 pp.

Airlines

Smith, Frank Kingston and James P. Harrington. *Aviation and Pennsylvania.* Philadelphia: Franklin Institute Press, 1981, 186 pp.

Public Transit

Cheape, Charles W. "The Evolution of Urban Public Transit, 1880-1912: A Study of Boston, New York and Philadelphia." *Journal of Economic History* 36 (March 1976): 259-262.

DeGraw, Ronald. *The Red Arrow: A History of One of the Most Successful Suburban Transit Companies in the World.* Haverford, PA: Haverford Press, 1972, 398 pp.

Larson, Thomas D. and Peter M. Lima. "Rural Public Transportation." *Traffic Quarterly* 29 (July 1975): 369-384.

Samuels, Abram. "Reflections on Area Trolley Lines of Fifty Years Ago." *Proceedings of Lehigh County Historical Society* 32 (1978): 33-45.

Wainwright, Nicholas B. *History of the Philadelphia Electric Company, 1881-1961.* Philadelphia: Philadelphia Electric Company, 1961, 416 pp.

FINANCIAL AND COMMERCIAL

Daniels, Belden L. *Pennsylvania, Birthplace of Banking in America.* Harrisburg: Pennsylvania Bankers Association, 1976, 365 pp.

Holdsworth, John T. *Financing an Empire: History of Banking in Pennsylvania.* 4 vols. Philadelphia: S.J. Clarke Publishing Co., 1928.

Miller, William. "A Note on the History of Business Corporations in Pennsylvania, 1800-1860." *Quarterly Journal of Economics* 55 (1940): 150-160.

Nead, B.M. *Brief Review of the Financial History of Pennsylvania and the Methods of Auditing Public Accounts, 1682-1881.* Harrisburg: L.S. Hart State Printer, 1881, 56 pp.

Reiser, Catherine E. "Pittsburgh, The Hub of Western Commerce, 1800-1850." *Western Pennsylvania Historical Magazine* 25 (1942): 121-134.

Stradley, Leighton P. *Early Financial and Economic History of Pennsylvania.* New York: Commerce Clearing House, 1942.

Thompson, James H. "The Financial History of Pittsburgh: The Early Period, 1816-1865." *Western Pennsylvania Historical Magazine* 33 (1950): 43-64.

White, Edward. *A Century of Banking in Pittsburgh.* Pittsburgh: The Index Company, 1903, 81 pp.

INDEX

GENERAL INDEX

Italicized numbers indicate illustrations.

THIS BOOK WAS SET IN
GOUDY AND AURIGA TYPES,
PRINTED ON 70-LB. MEAD ENAMEL OFFSET
AND BOUND BY
WALSWORTH PUBLISHING COMPANY

M/89